A Companion to the Literature and Culture of the American South

Blackwell Companions to Literature and Culture

This series offers comprehensive, newly written surveys of key periods and movements and certain major authors, in literary culture and history. Extensive volumes provide new perspectives and positions on contexts and on canonical and post-canonical texts, orientating the beginning student in new fields of study and providing the experienced undergraduate and new graduate with current and new directions, as pioneered and developed by leading scholars in the field.

Published

—🏠

A Companion to Shakespeare's Works

—🏠

A COMPANION TO

THE LITERATURE AND CULTURE OF THE AMERICAN SOUTH

Edited by
Richard Gray and Owen Robinson

Blackwell
Publishing

350 Main Street, Malden, MA 02148-5020, USA
108 Cowley Road, Oxford OX4 1JF, UK
550 Swanston Street, Carlton, Victoria 3053, Australia

First published 2004 by Blackwell Publishing Ltd

Library of Congress Cataloging-in-Publication Data

A companion to the literature and culture of the American south / edited by Richard Gray and Owen
Robinson.
    p. cm. – (Blackwell companions to literature and culture; 23)
    Includes bibliographical references and index.
    ISBN 0-631-22404-1 (alk. paper)
  1. American literature–Southern States–History and criticism–Handbooks, manuals, etc. 2. Authors,
    American–Homes and haunts–Southern States–Handbooks, manuals, etc. 3. Southern
States–Intellectual life–Handbooks, manuals, etc. 4. Southern States–In literature–Handbooks, manuals,
etc. 5. Southern States–Civilization–Handbooks, manuals, etc. I. Gray, Richard J. II. Robinson, Owen.
                                III. Series.

                        PS261.C555 2004
                        810.9'975–dc22
                          2003020737

A catalogue record for this title is available from the British Library.

Set in 11/13pt Garamond 3
by Kolam Information Services Pvt. Ltd, Pondicherry, India

For further information on
Blackwell Publishing, visit our website:
http://www.blackwellpublishing.com

Contents

Acknowledgments

The debts I have accumulated in preparing this book are numerous. I owe a particular debt, of course, to my co-editor, Owen Robinson, who has been tireless in his preparation of the manuscript and organizing the collection into coherent shape. An equal debt is owed to all the contributors, who have taken time off from enormously busy schedules to produce what I believe is a series of outstanding essays. I would also like to thank my friends and colleagues in the Southern Studies Forum, the British Academy, and the British Association for American Studies – many of whom have also contributed to this volume – for their advice and expert opinions. Thanks are due also to my friends and students in the Department of Literature and to friends and colleagues at Blackwell, especially Andrew McNeillie and Karen Wilson, for their help and encouragement. Finally, my thanks are due to my family: my sons Ben and Jack, my daughters Catharine and Jessica, my son-in-law Ricky, and my grandsons Sam and Izzy – and, above all, to my wife Sheona. They have helped me to keep going when at times the task of working on this collection seemed endless. I am, as always, deeply grateful.

R.G.

My co-editor, Richard Gray, as well as being an inspiring scholar and colleague, is a good friend whose encouragement, advice, and support I gratefully acknowledge. I would also like to thank Karen Wilson and the editorial team at Blackwell, and the many fine scholars whose work comprises this book, for making its production such a cooperative and illuminating endeavor. Here in the Department of Literature, Film, and Theatre Studies at the University of Essex, colleagues, friends, and students – and in particular Joe Allard, Emily Barker, Herbie Butterfield, John Cant, Becky Degler, Maria Cristina Fumagalli, Mike Gray, Peter Hulme, Kim Lasky, David Musselwhite, Jim Philip, Kay Stevenson, Erna Von Der Walde, and Luke Whiting – have continually helped to shape my understanding of the South, the Americas, and literature, variously through discussion, collaboration, criticism, and fine East Anglian ale. Most of all, Esther Kober's understanding, kindness, patience, and wit are a constant marvel to me, her companionship a constant blessing.

O.R.

The editors and publisher also wish to thank the following for permission to use copyright material: Extract from "The South" by Langston Hughes, from *The Collected Poems of Langston Hughes*, 1994. Reprinted by permission of David Higham Associates.

Notes on Contributors

Will Brantley is a Professor of English at Middle Tennessee State University. He is the author of *Feminine Sense in Southern Memoir: Smith, Glasgow, Welty, Hellman, Porter, and Hurston* (1993) and articles on Evelyn Scott's nonfiction and Lillian Smith's FBI file. He is editor of *Conversations with Pauline Kael* (1996), and is currently editing the 50th anniversary reissue of Lillian Smith's *Now Is the Time*.

Robert H. Brinkmeyer, Jr. is Professor and Chair of English at the University of Arkansas. He has published widely in modern Southern literature and culture, including his book *Remapping Southern Literature: Contemporary Southern Writers and the West*. He received a Guggenheim Fellowship to complete a book on European totalitarianism and the white Southern imagination, 1930–50.

Susan Castillo is Head of English Literature and John Nichol Professor of American Literature at Glasgow University. She has published on early American writing, Native-American fiction, and Southern literature. She is also a writer of poetry and fiction; her book of verse, *The Candlewoman's Trade*, was published in 2003. Although she has lived abroad most of her adult life, she was born and grew up in the American South, and defines herself as a Southerner.

Barbara Ching is an Associate Professor of English at the University of Memphis and the author of *Wrong's What I Do Best: Hard Country Music and Contemporary Culture* (2001). With ethnographer Gerald W. Creed, she co-edited *Knowing Your Place: Rural Identity and Cultural Hierarchy* (1996).

Henry Claridge lectures in American Literature and American Studies at the University of Kent. He has previously taught at the universities of Warwick, Massachusetts, and Indiana. He is the editor of *F. Scott Fitzgerald: Critical Assessments* and *William Faulkner: Critical Assessments*; an edition of *Ernest Hemingway: Critical Assessments*, co-edited with Graham Clarke, is forthcoming. He has edited Hawthorne's *The*

Scarlet Letter and Tolstoy's *War and Peace*. He has also written on E. L. Doctorow, F. Scott Fitzgerald, and the literary history of Chicago.

James C. Cobb is Spalding Distinguished Professor of History at the University of Georgia. He has written widely on the economic, political, and cultural history of the American South. He is currently completing *Old South, New South, No South: A History of Southern Identity*.

Amy Cuomo is an Assistant Professor of Theatre at the State University of West Georgia, where she teaches and directs. Her research interests include Southern drama, gender, film, and popular culture. Her recent work, "How to Break into Film and Television," was published in *Southern Theatre*.

R. J. Ellis is Professor of English at Nottingham Trent University. He currently edits *Comparative American Studies*. His recent books include an edited collection of essays on *Faulkner and Modernism* (2000) and a study of Harriet Wilson (2003). He has published widely on African-American and Beat writing, including the monograph *Liar! Liar! – Jack Kerouac, Novelist* (1999).

Kate Fullbrook was Professor of Literary Studies and Associate Dean in the Faculty of Humanities, Languages, and Social Sciences at the University of the West of England. She is the author of *Katherine Mansfield* (1986), *Free Women: Ethics and Aesthetics in Twentieth-Century Women's Fiction* (1990), and, with Edward Fullbrook, *Simone de Beauvoir and Jean-Paul Sartre: The Remaking of a Twentieth-Century Legend* (1993) and *Simone de Beauvoir: A Critical Introduction* (1998). In addition, she published many articles and reviews and worked extensively as an editor. Kate Fullbrook died in 2003.

Mary C. Fuller is Associate Professor of Literature at the Massachusetts Institute of Technology. Her publications on early modern travel include *Voyages in Print: English Travel to America, 1576–1624*.

Ben Gidley is a Research Fellow at the Centre for Urban and Community Research at Goldsmiths College, University of London. His research has focused on the politics of race, identity, and belonging. His publications include *The Proletarian Other: Charles Booth and the Politics of Representation* (2000), "Ghetto Radicalism: The Jewish East End" in *New Voices in Jewish Thought, Volume 2* (1999), and *Reflecting Realities: Participants' Perspectives on Integrated Communities and Sustainable Development* (with Jean Anastacio et al., 2000).

Mick Gidley is Professor of American Literature at the University of Leeds. He has published essays on a wide range of topics in American literature and culture, including Faulkner, Cummings, and Bambara. His books include several on Indian themes, such as *Edward S. Curtis and the North American Indian, Incorporated* (2000) and *Edward S. Curtis and the North American Indian Project in the Field* (2003). Among the collections of essays he has edited or co-edited are *Views of American Landscapes* (1989),

Representing Others (1992), *Modern American Culture* (1993), and *American Photographers in Europe* (1994). He is currently writing a study of the photographer Emil Otto Hoppe.

Richard Godden teaches American literature and history at the University of Sussex. He is the author of *Fictions of Capital: The American Novel from James to Mailer* (1990) and *Fictions of Labor: William Faulkner and the South's Long Revolution* (1997). He is currently completing a study of Faulkner's later fiction, provisionally entitled, *Faulkner's Residues: The Poetics of an Economy*.

Allison Graham is Professor of Media and Communication Studies at the University of Memphis. She is the author of *Framing the South: Hollywood, Television, and Race During the Civil Rights Struggle* (2001), co-producer/director of the documentary film *At the River I Stand* (1993), and associate producer of the documentary film *Hoxie: The First Stand* (2003).

John Grammer is Associate Professor of English at the University of the South, in Sewanee, Tennessee, and author of *Pastoral and Politics in the Old South*. His essays and reviews have appeared in *American Literary History, Mississippi Quarterly, Southern Literary Journal*, and other publications.

Susan-Mary Grant is Reader in American History at the University of Newcastle-upon-Tyne. She is the author of *North Over South: Northern Nationalism and American Identity in the Antebellum Era* (2000), co-editor (with Brian Holden Reid) of *The American Civil War: Explorations and Reconsiderations* (2000) and (with Peter J. Parish) of *Legacy of Disunion: The Enduring Significance of the American Civil War* (2003). She is currently working on the development of American nationalism between the Civil War and World War I.

Richard Gray is Professor in the Department of Literature at the University of Essex. His books include *The Literature of Memory: Modern Writers of the American South, Writing the South: Ideas of an American Region* (which won the C. Hugh Holman Award from the Society for the Study of Southern Literature), *American Poetry of the Twentieth Century, The Life of William Faulkner: A Critical Biography, Southern Aberrations: Writers of the American South and the Problems of Regionalism* and *A History of American Literature*. He is also editor of a number of collections and anthologies, and a regular reviewer for various newspapers and journals, including the *Times Literary Supplement* and the *Literary Review*. He is the first specialist in American literature to be elected a Fellow of the British Academy.

Jan Nordby Gretlund is a Senior Lecturer in American Literature at the University of Southern Denmark. He has held ACLS or Fulbright fellowships at Vanderbilt, Southern Mississippi, and South Carolina's universities. He is the author of *Eudora Welty's Aesthetics of Place* and *Frames of Southern Mind: Reflections on the Stoic, Bi-Racial and Existential South*. He has co-edited four books: *Realist of Distances: Flannery O'Connor Revisited; Walker Percy: Novelist and Philosopher; Southern Landscapes*; and *The*

Late Novels of Eudora Welty; and has edited *The Southern State of Mind* (2000). He edited a special Southern issue of *American Studies in Scandinavia* (spring 2001). He is a member of the editorial board for the *South Carolina Encyclopedia* and a contributor to that volume; and he is literary editor of the European *Southern Studies Forum Newsletter*. He is writing a book on Madison Jones and editing a collection on Flannery O'Connor, plus a collection on "the South as another place."

Matthew Guinn is an Assistant Professor of English at the University of Alabama at Birmingham. He completed his PhD in 1998 at the University of South Carolina, where he studied under the late James Dickey. He is the author of *After Southern Modernism: Fiction of the Contemporary South* (2000).

Andrew Hook, Emeritus Bradley Professor of English Literature at the University of Glasgow, is a Fellow of both the British Academy and the Royal Society of Edinburgh. He has published widely on English, Scottish, and American literature. His seminal work *Scotland and America: A Study of Cultural Relations 1750–1835* is about to be reissued. The Andrew Hook Centre for American Studies at Glasgow is named in his honor.

Stuart Kidd lectures in American History at the University of Reading. He is co-editor of *The Roosevelt Years* and the author of a number of articles and essays on the cultural history of the United States during the 1930s. His monograph on FSA photography and the South, *The South Faces the Shutter: Roy Stryker, FSA Photography, and the South, 1935–1943*, will be published shortly.

Richard H. King teaches in the School of American and Canadian Studies at Nottingham University. He is the author of *A Southern Renaissance* and *Civil Rights and the Idea of Freedom* and has co-edited *Dixie Debates* with Helen Taylor.

A. Robert Lee, formerly of the University of Kent at Canterbury, is Professor of American Literature at Nihon University, Tokyo. His recent books include *Multicultural American Literature: Comparative Black, Native, Latino/a and Asian American Fictions* (2003), *Postindian Conversations*, with Gerald Vizenor (2000), *Designs of Blackness: Mappings in the Literature and Culture of Afro-America* (1998), and the essay collections *Herman Melville: Critical Assessments*, 4 vols. (2001), *Loosening the Seams: Interpretations of Gerald Vizenor* (2000), and *The Beat Generation Writers* (1996). Since 1998 he has been Annual Visiting Professor at Sunderland University.

Sharon Monteith is Reader in American Studies at the University of Nottingham. She is the author of *Advancing Sisterhood: Interracial Friendships in Contemporary Southern Literature* (2000) and co-editor of *Gender in the Civil Rights Movement* (1999) and *South To a New Place: Region, Literature, Culture* (2002). She is currently writing a book on representations of the civil rights movement in popular cinema.

Jerry Phillips is an Associate Professor of English at the University of Connecticut, where he also directs the program in American Studies. He has published essays on

Herman Melville, Matthew Arnold, Thorstein Veblen, Richard Price, and Octavia Butler. His essay on Edmund White is forthcoming in *The Oxford Encyclopedia of American Literature*.

Julius Rowan Raper is Professor Emeritus of English from the University of North Carolina, Chapel Hill. He has published three books on Ellen Glasgow, including *From the Sunken Garden: The Fiction of Ellen Glasgow, 1916–1945*. He is also the author of *Narcissus from Rubble: Competing Models of Character in Contemporary British and American Fiction* and an editor of *Lawrence Durrell: Comprehending the Whole*. In addition, he has published essays on a variety of Southern and contemporary novelists, as well as stories and poems.

Diane Roberts is Professor of English at the University of Alabama. Currently, she is the author of two books, *Faulkner and Southern Womanhood* (1993) and *The Myth of Aunt Jemima* (1994), as well as articles on *Southern Living* magazine, Eudora Welty, and the Neo-Confederate Movement. She is an essayist for National Public Radio in the United States and a writer and presenter of programs for BBC Radio 4 and the World Service, and she contributes columns to *The Times*, *The New York Times*, and *The St. Petersburg Times*. Her book about Florida, *Dream State*, was published in 2004.

Peter Stoneley is a Lecturer in the School of English at Queen's University, Belfast. He works for the most part on nineteenth-century American writing, and his most recent book is *Consumerism and American Girls' Literature, 1860–1940* (2003).

Linda Tate is an Associate Professor of English at Shepherd College in Shepherdstown, West Virginia. She is the author of *A Southern Weave of Women: Fiction of the Contemporary South* (1994) and editor of *Conversations with Lee Smith* (2001). Her book *Power in the Blood: A Family Memoir*, supported in part by a Rockefeller Humanities Foundation Fellowship at Marshall University's Center for the Study of Ethnicity and Gender in Appalachia, is forthcoming.

Helen Taylor is Professor and Head of the School of English, University of Exeter. She has published widely on Southern literature and culture, as well as women's writing. Her books include *Circling Dixie: Contemporary Southern Culture Through a Transatlantic Lens* (2001), *Dixie Debates* (co-edited with Richard King, 1996), *Scarlett's Women: Gone with the Wind and its Female Fans* (1989), and *Gender, Race, and Region in the Writings of Grace King, Ruth McEnery Stuart, and Kate Chopin* (1989). She is currently working on representations of Storyville, New Orleans, through the late nineteenth and twentieth centuries.

Jill Terry completed her doctoral research on orality in fiction by contemporary Southern women writers at the University of Exeter. She is Curriculum Leader for English at the University College Worcester, where she teaches a number of courses in American literatures. She has published on Alice Walker (*Critical Survey*, 2000) and has a chapter forthcoming in an edited book on Gayl Jones.

John White is Reader Emeritus in American History at the University of Hull. His publications include *Billie Holiday: Her Life and Times* (1987), and *Black Leadership in America: From Booker T. Washington to Jesse Jackson* (1990). He is co-editor (with Brian Reid) of *Americana: Essays in Memory of Marcus Cunliffe* (1998), and (with Richard Palmer) *Larkin's Jazz Essays and Reviews, 1940–84* (2001). His book *The Best of Intentions: Artie Shaw, His Life and Music* is due to appear in 2004.

Charles Reagan Wilson is Director of the Center for the Study of Southern Culture and Professor of History and Southern Studies at the University of Mississippi. He is the author of *Baptized in Blood: The Religion of the Lost Cause, 1865–1920* (1980), and *Judgement and Grace in Dixie: Southern Faiths from Faulkner to Elvis* (1995). He co-edited the *Encyclopedia of Southern Culture* (1989), and he is supervising production of a second edition of the *Encyclopedia* and publication of the *Mississippi Encyclopedia*.

Mark Zelinsky, Assistant Professor of English at Saint Joseph College in West Hartford, Connecticut, teaches a variety of theatre courses, including literature, history, and acting, as well as directing two productions annually. He specializes in American Drama with a particular interest in Tennessee Williams. Forthcoming publications include an essay in the *Tennessee Williams Literary Journal* and articles on Williams, Truman Capote, and Gore Vidal in *Notable Gays and Lesbians in American Theater History*. His most recent publication focused on the film and television adaptations of *A Streetcar Named Desire* and appeared in *Humanities in the South*.

Plates

Part I
Introduction

1

Writing Southern Cultures

Richard Gray

In 1931 John Peale Bishop wrote from France to his friend Allen Tate about the deepening economic crisis in the West. "Personally I feel there is no hope for us," he confided to Tate,

> unless we are willing to go back, examining our mistakes and admit them. To go on the way of machinization and progress to their ultimate destination, some American form of communism, is simply to applaud and hasten death. For death it will be, and no mistake. The Russians may well survive, for they are the beginning of something non-European; we are the end of all that is European. With us Western civilization ends.[1]

Bishop's remarks hit a responsive chord with Tate, who only two years prior to this, in his biography of Jefferson Davis, had identified the decline of the West with the defeat of the South, a region he called "the last stronghold of European civilization in the western hemisphere." For both men, in fact, what they agreed to call "the South" was the last great moment in culture. All that was left was to capture the moment of its passing and to commemorate its glory. More brutally, all that was left was the reality of loss and the realization of failure. As Tate put it to Bishop:

> The older I get the more I realize that I set out about ten years ago to live a life of failure, to imitate, in my own life, the history of my people . . . The significance of the Southern way of life, in my time, is failure . . . What else is there for me but a complete acceptance of failure? There is no other "culture" that I can enter into, even if I had the desire.[2]

True, Tate admitted, the contemporary crisis might very well bring about something devoutly to be wished: "the destruction of the middle-class capitalist hegemony." But, instead of millennial beginnings or cultural redemption, all that would result from this, he believed, was a rough beast slouching from Russia to be born. What was heaving into view, in short, was not a possible beginning but the end.

The imagination of disaster that Tate and Bishop shared in their correspondence and elsewhere – sometimes with a rather unseemly, lipsmacking relish – is surely one of the constants of Southern self-fashioning. So is their sense of aberration and anomaly. Whatever else Southerners may have in common (and it is sometimes very little), they have habitually defined themselves, as Tate and Bishop did, against a national or international "other." A familiar set of oppositions performs important cultural work here: "Southern" *vs.* "American"/"Northern"/"Western" (the slippage between these three terms is, in itself, a measure of the Southern sense of deviation from a "norm") = place *vs.* placelessness = past *vs.* pastlessness = realism *vs.* idealism = mournful, deeply felt endings *vs.* millennial, vaguely fancied beginnings. In this context, "South" and "North" end up functioning rather like a photograph and its negative, in a mutually determining, reciprocally defining relationship: the South *is*, in these circumstances, whatever the North *is not* and vice versa. It may be that all cultures do this, in order to define themselves. The difference with the Southern strategy is that it customarily begins from a consciousness of its own marginality and even "failure," its position on the edge of the narrative. The constitutive otherness of the North or the American is considered central; the South, in whatever terms it is understood, is placed on the boundary, posed as a (albeit probably preferable) deviation. This is a poignant reversal of the usual strategies of cultural self-position-ing. It would never have occurred to those who constructed the idea of the Orient, for example, to see their object of study as anything other than inferior to the enlightened West and on the dangerous borders of Western culture. The lesser breed was famously without the law. The idea of Southerness may or may not carry a moral burden. It may project on to the typology of itself, and its opposite, a sense of its own superiority and a claim to historical centrality of the kind Tate and Bishop both ventured – or of the sort the South Carolina politician William Lowndes Yancey was imagining when he declared:

> The Creator has beautified the face of the Union with sectional features. Absorbing all minor subdivisions, he has made the North and the South; the one the region of frost ... the other baring its generous bosom to the sun ... Those who occupy the one are cool, calculating, enterprising, selfish, and grasping; the inhabitants of the other are ardent, brave, and magnanimous, more disposed to give than to accumulate, to enjoy ease rather than to labor.[3]

Nevertheless, the claim cannot be made effortlessly, without a powerful sense of past exclusion, present discontent, and future peril; Yancey was, after all, speaking as the sectional crisis deepened towards war. Southerners start by seeing others with a more than usually astringent sense of how others see them; their arguments begin, as it were, *within* an argument already made that has shifted them on to the historical edge – an edge from which, quite possibly, they are about to fall off.

A word of caution is perhaps useful. These acts of regional self-definition made in the face of crisis are not, of course, simply fake. It is not that the South and the North or the American nation – even in the crudely simplistic terms imagined by Yancey – are merely falsehoods, fables, no more in touch with historical contingencies than, say, stories of the lost city of Atlantis. They are, however, *fictive* – and in a double sense. They are fictive, first, because they involve a reading of existence as essence. What Anwar Abdel Malek has to say about Orientalism is relevant here. Orientalists, he points out, "adopt an essentialist conception of the countries, nations, and peoples of the Orient under study, a conception which expresses itself through a characterized ethnist typology."[4] In short, they form a notion of a cultural "type" based on a real specificity but divorced from history. Similarly, the cultural work that has devised ideas of the South and Southerners, and their opposites, occurs in history, and is a result of the forces working in the field of historical evolution. But its end result is to transfix the beings, the objects of study and leave them stamped with an inalienable, non-evolutive character – to sever them from the living tissue of their moment in time. These constructions of regional types are also fictional in the sense that perhaps Yancey had at the back of his mind when he conveniently skipped over what he called "all minor subdivisions." The South has never *not* been made up of a number of castes, classes, and smaller communities that at best live in uneasy coexistence with each other and at worst are in active conflict – and some of which, at least, choose to claim that *their* South is *the* South, their story the master narrative of the region. Readings of the South are just that, readings; for better or worse, they involve selection and abstraction, a figuring and, in the purest sense of that word, a *simplifying* of history.

"Communities are to be distinguished," argues the historian Benedict Anderson, "not by their falsity/genuineness, but the style in which they are imagined."[5] And that "style," the terms in which an imagined community *is* imagined, has met with a peculiar series of challenges in the recent South – as the familiar sense of being peripheral and in peril has been exacerbated, for contemporary Southerners, by radical changes to both the material substance and the moral shape of their lives. As far as the economic imperatives are concerned, Southerners are now exposed to the demands of the marketplace – for good or (as Tate and Bishop would surely have seen it) for ill. With the collapse of the plantation system, the dispersal of the mill villages, and the breakdown of other places of settled employment, white males in particular have felt this exposure – but white women and African Americans have felt it too, as they have become more visible elements in the economy. The women's movement, together with the crumbling of traditional structures, has opened up female access to the marketplace. And the civil rights movement, together with subsequent federal legislation, has allowed blacks to become a more active and fluid, if still significantly disadvantaged, part of the labor force. The result is that the Southern workforce is now just over one-third white female, just under 10 percent black male, and just under 10 percent black female. In the words of one historian, Numan Bartley, summing up the changes of the recent past, in 1995:

A dynamic free-flowing workforce unburdened by labor union membership, unity, or much in the way of state protection or social legislation complemented the drive for economic growth while it undermined family, community, and the spiritual aspects of religion.[6]

Another historian described this transfer to the market economy, and commodification, of most of the adult population of the South much more succinctly; the South, he said, was now "a conservative capitalist's dream come true."

"Southerners feel," the social scientist Charles Lerche observed in 1964, "that they are struggling against an open conspiracy and a totally hostile environment." A similar point was made by another commentator, Sheldon Hackney, five years later: "the Southern identity," he observed, "has been linked from the first to a siege mentality" – and continued to be. Comments like these, made usually but not always about *white* Southerners, suggest that forms of Southern self-fashioning founded on resistance, aberration, and deliberate anachronism continue to flourish, even in a world of surfeit. This was a point made, in more detail, by the sociologist John Shelton Reed, when he came to write a concluding note to a new edition of his survey of Southern attitudes, *The Enduring South*. Reed found, he said, powerful feelings of being marginalized and even threatened still at work among the – mostly white – Southerners surveyed. More to the point, the data accumulated for this new edition only confirmed what he had claimed when *The Enduring South* had first appeared fourteen years earlier. "Cultural differences that were largely due to Southerners' lower incomes and educational levels," Reed declared, "to their predominantly rural and small-town residence" and "to their concentration in agricultural and low-level industrial occupations": all these, he said, "were smaller in the 1960s than they had been in the past, and they are smaller still in the 1980s." "A few" of these differences "have vanished altogether," he pointed out; and, as a result, "there are important respects in which Southerners look more like other Americans, culturally, than they have at any time for decades, if ever."[7] On the other hand, those differences that Reed labeled "quasi-ethnic," because of their putative origins in the different histories of the American regions, had, many of them, persisted. On the matters of localism, attitudes towards violence, gun ownership, and religion, white Southerners still revealed themselves to be distinctive, different.

In fact, if there appeared to be any significant change in mental maps between the 1960s and the 1980s, Reed commented, it was among non-Southerners. "Non-Southerners are becoming more like Southerners," Reed concluded, "in their tendency to find heroes and heroines in their local community, or even in the family... the conviction that individuals should have the right to arm themselves" and in their tendency "to have had the sort of religious experience that is theoretically central to Southern Protestantism." What has been called "the Southernization of America," by the historian John Egerton among others, suggests that one response to commodification, and the globalization of the material life, is resistance and even a kind of cultural reversion. Americans, and not just Southerners, seem to have reacted to the blanding of America, over the last two or three decades, by subscribing to cultural values that simultaneously register their anxiety about change and measure their difference from the corporate ethos. "The 'primitive' attitudes that east-coast liberals used to sneer at," a 1994 article in *The Economist* proclaimed, "are now those of America." That is surely too sweeping, but it underlines the point that surrender to the laws of the global village is not the only available option. On the contrary, Southerners have always shown how one viable response to feelings of being marginalized is to *build* on the margins, to root one's thinking precisely in the sense of being disempowered and different; and some non-Southerners, at least, appear to be imitating them. John Shelton Reed put it more wryly. "I do not want to suggest that Americans are becoming privatistic, born-again gun-slingers," he declared, "or that Southerners are." Nevertheless, he added, "perhaps there is a pattern here":[8] a pattern of convergence, that is, quite different from the one that anticipated an economically resurgent South simply becoming more like the rest of America.

Even a phrase like "the Southernization of America" is too simple, however, and, in the end, no more satisfactory than "the Americanization of the South." In its own way, it prescribes a model for understanding recent social change in the region that is just as monolithic and disablingly unitary as other terms that have become part of the currency of this debate: terms or phrases like, say, "the lasting South," "the everlasting South," "why the South will survive" – or, alternatively, "this changing South," "an epitaph for Dixie," "look away from Dixie." Non-Southerners have certainly gravitated towards Southern thinking in many respects. They range from the anonymous people surveyed in *The Enduring South* or the millions of non-Southern voters involved in what political scientists have called "an issue-driven switch" to the Republican Party, to a distinguished historian from the political left, Eugene Genovese, who then turned to the tradition of Southern conservatism as the only serious challenge – with the collapse of communism – to what he called "market-oriented bourgeois ideologies."[9] But several further twists are given to an already tangled situation by two other factors: the selling of the South, as a kind of giant theme park or American version of the heritage industry, and our greatly enlarged sense of the pluralism of *any* culture, including the Southern one. As for the selling of the region: in *Oral History* (1983) by Lee Smith, the old family homeplace still stands, but it has become an appropriately decaying part of a successful theme park called Ghostland. In the state of Mississippi, observes the central character in *Hey Jack!* (1987) by Barry Hannah, "I find there are exactly five subjects: money, Negroes, women, religion, and Elvis Presley. The rest are nothing."[10] And, as if to prove the truth of this observation, it is possible to go to Memphis, not far from where Hannah lives, and find "Negroes, women, religion, and Elvis Presley" all being turned into "money." Jostling close to each other are such signs of the times, and the new Southern tourism, as Presley's Graceland with its nine gift shops – or Beale Street reconstituted as a heritage site with the W. C. Handy statue, restaurants and shops selling African-American memorabilia, and the Center for Southern Folklore.

"This is America, where money's more serious than death."[11] Harry Crews's sardonic comment alerts us to a problem. There are no doubt noble motives at work in the construction of Southern tourist sites, among them the desire to make the past more accessible. But a tourist site is, pretty obviously, a way of making money and generating trade for the area; it belongs as much to the culture of consumerism as, say, a shopping mall. This is a very particular kind of commodification that turns the South itself – or, to be more exact, an idea or image of the South – into a product, a function of the marketplace. Like all good products, it has a clear identity. As movies such as *Driving Miss Daisy, Doc Hollywood,* and *O Brother, Where Art Thou?,* or advertisements for Jack Daniel's whiskey, tell us, the South is registered in popular perception and marketed as a desirable other, one potential, purchasable release from the pressures of living and working in a world governed by the new technologies and international capital. History is thereby displaced into aesthetic style. Via cultural work that Adorno called "receding concreteness," any possibility of a lived encounter with the past slips away, and we are left with a marketable artifact, a copy. What appears to be a process of remembering turns out, in the end, to be one of forgetting, since the realities of economic change, structural transformation, are masked, for the purposes of making a sale, by an image of cultural continuity. The ironies of Southern history have always run deep, and surely one of the deepest in recent times is this curious case of change within continuity within change. Some aspects of the South retain their grip on the imagination despite the economic metamorphosis of the region, but then that drift towards the past, the undertow of resistance itself becomes a saleable asset. The legends of the South are not necessarily dying, in other words, nor being fiercely protected or even resurrected; in some cases, they are merely being turned into cash.

The responses of Southerners themselves to this particular irony are perhaps worth measuring. After all, they are consumers too, and can be included among those to whom the South is being sold. One measurable reaction is resistance. "I wasn't into jazz as a kid" in New Orleans, the jazz musician Wynton Marsalis told the British Broadcasting Corporation in 1993, "I thought it was just shakin' your butt for the white tourists in the French Quarter." And, given that the director of the New Orleans tourist board once boasted, "Music is integral to our marketing plan,"[12] Marsalis's initial reluctance to become involved in a music to which he was so obviously suited seems understandable. Another reaction, its opposite, is to buy into the Southern performance of the good life. That buying ranges from the huge commercial growth of country music or what has become known as "Southern rock," in the United States generally but especially in the South, to a publishing phenomenon like *Southern Living.* Initiated as a magazine in 1966, out of a column that had run for many years in *Progressive Farmer, Southern Living* reinforces and defends an image of the region as a place of downhome securities, safe harbor for all those for whom, in the words of one commentator, "the South *is* distinct, *is* special, perhaps even chosen." With its articles on such traditionally Southern obsessions as hunting and fishing, entertaining and etiquette, tasteful decorating and dining, it offers a fantasy conduct manual – a guide to behaving well in a blessed, glossy landscape of gracious homes, immaculate furniture, and manicured lawns. The president of the company that began *Southern Living* said in 1985 that his company's mission was "to give people in the South a sense of pride in being Southern." This the magazine does by offering to its readers' gaze the promissory image of a place free of social anxiety or economic insecurity, in which the greatest problem becomes how to choose the right pattern for the silverware. The elusive object of desire here, to be claimed at the point of purchase, is the image of "Southern living" itself: what one analyst of the journal has called its construction of

> a South without memory of pellagra or racial unrest, a South where none of the parents are divorced, where burglary and street crime are unknown, where few have Hatteras yachts but one and all play golf and tennis at the club – and in the right outfits.[13]

Issues of class and race appear only in subtly coded, disguised form – in, say, articles about black college football players; the project is to reassure the mainly white, middle-class, Southern consumer by offering him (or, more often in this case, her) a familiar regional version of the culturally counterfeit – a copy of a world of easy but mannerly living for which, it turns out, there has never been an original. That project has been remarkably successful. By the middle of the 1990s, *Southern Living* could boast nearly two-and-a-half million subscribers; of these, over 80 percent had well-above average incomes and, more to the point, over 80 percent of them also lived in the South.

Another, more complicated reaction to the selling of the South is described in *The Revolution of Little Girls* (1991) by Blanche McCrary Boyd. The novel charts the growth of a young girl called Ellen Burns out of South Carolina and into womanhood, feminism, and a discovery of her own lesbianism. What is of special interest here, however, is one moment in her youth when, thanks to her workaholic father, the Burns family move out of a modest house on the outskirts of Charleston into "an old plantation out in the country" known as Blacklock. "I had never seen a house like the one at Blacklock, except in the movies," Ellen explains. "Each time *Gone With the Wind* was rereleased, our family, minus my father, went dutifully to see this tribute to what we had lost" – although the notion of loss is cultural rather than familial since, as Ellen points out, "my father had grown up poor." "We were minus my father," Ellen adds, "because he was tied up making money…so we could do things like move to Blacklock." "When 'Dixie' played," in the movie, she remembers, "I cried every time." "And when Scarlett O'Hara said, 'As God is my witness, I'll never be hungry again,'" she adds, "I'd think, *yeah, me [n]either*." Come the day the family move to Blacklock, Ellen is struck by the fact that, although "it didn't look like Tara," it has all the crucial paraphernalia of that Old South sold to an eager public in popular films and fiction, including slave cabins, huge oak trees, "a set of white columns" at the entrance to the estate, and "a white oyster-shell road that circled in front of the house on top of the hill." "I've seen this movie before," Ellen shouts out as they approach the house; and, although her father tells her to "Hush, Ellen," she cries out again, "I've seen this movie before!"[14]

Ellen Burns comes across in Boyd's novel as an edgy, sophisticated, often subversive person; and her immediate response to the plantation heritage that her family has, in effect, bought is characteristically subtle and self-conscious. With one, particularly ironic eye she can see how she and her family have been sold a product, through movies like *Gone With the Wind*. They have, she can appreciate, been taught what they have "lost," shown a gap in their lives that can supposedly be filled by the purchase of Blacklock and other gracious appendages of "Southern living." She can even perhaps perceive the irony of gazing at a relic of the past in terms of mediated images of that past, as if it were an imitation of an imitation, since in this world the authentic and the replica become interchangeable as products, transferable commodities. Nevertheless, Ellen also looks at this site of desire with genuine excitement, even elation; the fact that, as she sees it, she is moving close to a familiar movie set is an occasion for delight as well as wry humor. She is, in short, not only amused but also pleased. She soon comes to think of Blacklock as "cursed"[15] and is relieved when eventually, due to a downturn in the family fortunes, the estate is sold – to a group that want to replicate another image of traditional Southern living, by hunting wild duck in the rice paddies. But that is only a further element in what Fredric Jameson would call the logic of late capitalism: the climax is a matter of exchange, not of use. And it is a climax that Ellen enjoys, for all her irony: she looks at Blacklock, when she arrives there, with the gaze of the knowing consumer who desires no less because she understands the crude mechanisms of consumerism – that her desires have been generated by the marketplace. This self-aware, self-reflexive form of consumption is arguably the norm now. When we watch films like *Gone With the Wind* or, say, *Fried Green Tomatoes*, we are probably aware that we are looking at a counterfeit, a projection of our own culturally formed desires on to a particular location in Southern space and time. Still, we receive momentary satisfaction from it; we accept the counterfeit *as if* it were true currency. It is in these curiously hybrid terms that many non-Southerners currently buy the image of the South – just as Ellen Burns does when she arrives at "this movie" she has seen, she says, many times before. And that perhaps is what most contemporary Southerners do as well, including many of those subscribers to *Southern Living*.

All this, of course, begs the question of just what *kind* of South any of us may be trying to renew, transform, preserve, or purchase. Is it the South, for instance, of Wynton Marsalis or Blanche McCrary Boyd that is in the process of being sold? Or, perhaps, the South enshrined in *Southern Living*? Is it the South of those predominantly white Southerners for whom the Confederate flag is a proud emblem of regional heritage? Or of those, both black and white, for whom that same flag is a symbol of racial hatred? Questions like these have always hovered behind any attempt to chart Southern thinking, but the drawing of the mental maps of the region has become peculiarly challenging in the past few years with the growth of cultural pluralism. Makers of the South and things Southern whose work previously tended to be ignored or minimized, often for reasons of caste or gender or both, now come much more into debate and play.[16] They range from popular novelists like Margaret Mitchell, through blues singers and jazz musicians, film directors and country songwriters, to those numerous and frequently anonymous women and men who have resurrected and reshaped the traditions of African art in the region. Just as much at issue here is our vastly expanded sense now of precisely what "making" a culture involves: the recognition that a culture identifies and in fact creates itself by a variety of means – means that include the individual book or essay, of course, but go far beyond this to incorporate the artifacts of everyday life and the potentially endless products of mass culture, the voice heard perhaps in passing on the radio or images flickering on a screen. What emerges with particular power from all this is the possibility that even the process of commodification, the turning of an image of the South or regional icon into a marketable asset, could be regarded as playing an integral part in the making of a culture. After all, whether anyone likes it or not, Southerners are "known" to themselves and others through the mass media, among many other forms of communication. And what emerges with even more power is the fact that our perception of the South must now, more than ever before, acknowledge the various and often antagonistic influences and energies that go to make it up: we are faced, not so much with Southern culture really, as with Southern *cultures*.

Even within the relatively limited playing field of the novel, the variety – and, in some cases, mutual antagonism – of the influences that go to make up Southern culture(s) now is clear. "We need to talk, to tell," William Faulkner observed of Southerners once, "since oratory is our heritage." Old tales and talking have, in fact, long served as both a local art and a preservative tool – a customary, carefully cultivated skill and a vital medium for the transference of custom. Southerners talk; in doing so, they continue a tradition of storytelling and they sustain the substance of that tradition, its memories and legends – they speak, in short, both *out of* the past and *of* it. But exactly what past do they speak from and about? The answer to this, if we look at fiction of the last thirty years or so, turns out to be intriguingly mixed: once, that is, we go beyond certain obvious boundaries, points staked out by the major crises in Southern history. Take two books that have as their narrative pivots a heroic act of storytelling: *The Autobiography of Miss Jane Pittman* (1971) by Ernest Gaines and *Oldest Living Confederate Widow Tells All* (1989) by Allan Gurganus. Both revolve around an old woman recollecting and reshaping the past. Both could be described in the terms Gaines used for his novel, as "folk autobiography" or, equally, in those Gurganus chose for his, as the revelation of a secret history "truer than fact." For that matter, both draw some of their energy and inspiration from the same sources – interviews conducted in the 1930s by the Federal Writers Project. The fact remains, though, that the two women have a fundamentally different story to tell. Jane Pittman, whose recollections just about begin with the whipping she received for refusing to acknowledge the name "the master and the rest of them"[17] had given her, talks of a past that is another country, not only from the present, but from the relatively, racially more privileged past of Gurganus's Lucy Marsden, the wife and then widow of a Confederate captain. Jane Pittman may see connections across the racial divide – and, in particular, the common interests poor black and poor white have in the face of "the rich people" – but connection never becomes coincidence of interest. A simple, seminal choice of pronoun says it all: her fellow blacks she includes in "we," all others are "they."

"Granny... would lean back in her chair and start reeling out story and memory," recalls the protagonist, Ruth Anne Boatwright (known as "Bone") of *Bastard Out of Carolina* (1992) by Dorothy Allison,

> making no distinction between what she knew to be true and what she had only heard told. The tales she told me in her rough, drawling whisper were lilting songs, ballads of family, love and disappointment. Everything seemed to come back to grief and blood, and everybody seemed legendary.[18]

The older generation hand down stories of the past and, in the process, hand on its burden and inspiration: that is a common motif of Southern books, including recent ones, even when there is not one dominant voice. In *For the Love of Robert E. Lee* (1992) by M. A. Harper, the heroine Garnet Laney talks of a "genetic memory" that seems somehow activated by *her* grandmother, who tells her stories of the Civil War and the Lee family; while in *A Childhood: The Biography of a Place* (1978), Harry Crews recalls his upbringing "in a society of storytelling people" where, he tells us, "nothing is allowed to die... It is all... carted up and brought along from one generation to the next." There are the several people in *The Crossing* (1994) by Cormac McCarthy (a book that secretes a story of the South in a story of the Southwest) who dramatize and reveal what they, and surely the author, see as the fundamental fact of human life: that "things separate from their stories have no meaning" because "all is telling" and "therefore we can never be done with the telling." And then there is the character called William Wallace in *1959* (1992) by the African-American novelist Thulani Davis who, the narrator remembers, was so old that he "had more recollections of slavery than of freedom" and would repeat stories and speeches from the old times that everyone ended up learning, "like a blues song passed down the hands on the levee." The common threads running between oral histories like these are clear, but so are the differences. The past that is spoken into the present here is of a variable, plural kind. For Garnet Laney, for instance, the memories are spellbinding and romantic. They seduce her into the belief that she is actually playing a part in the Old Southern family romance, and in love with General Robert E. Lee. For Ruth Anne Boatwright, on the other hand, as for the young Harry Crews, the old tales are of dispossession, wanting and wandering, the plight of the landless and intermittently workless. There is no dear particular place as such that is recalled, only a general locality, as the Boatwrights and their kind "moved and then moved again" – "sometimes before we'd even gotten properly unpacked," Ruth Anne remembers – in search of a means to live.

"It's strange what you don't forget," begins *Machine Dreams* (1984) by Jayne Anne Phillips, before moving into an account of the indelible nature of memory, and how memory charges that elaborate network of feeling and faith we call the family. Similarly, early on in *The Annunciation* (1983) by Ellen Gilchrist, we learn of the memories the young central character "must carry with her always" because they are her "cargo," as she sees it, part of her that she carries *inside* her. This is a past of the bloodstream, kin, and instinct rather more than storytelling, but it carries with it the same burden of communality and difference – the same feeling that now, more than ever, the South needs to be read in plural terms. Most obviously, there are differences of racial memory. Jane Pittman tells of another country from the one mapped out by Lucy Marsden, peopled by what Gaines himself has called the "Black 'peasantry,'" "the blacks of the fields" whom "white writers" can only present as "caricatures." William Walker, in *1959*, tells stories of how he and his family were quite literally bought and sold, their bodies along with their labor made the subject of exchange. "He went to the white man's court to get his wife and children out after buying their freedom," Walker tells the several generations of his audience, "and the white man told him point-blank, 'You may say they are wife and children to you, but they are property still. Possession is nine-tenths of the law.'"[19] These are recollections inscribed in race, whose main cultural work is to identify what it means to be a *black* Southerner. As such, they are determinately other, outside and apart from the remembrances of whites – even the white dispossessed. And, in the same way, the instinctual past, the secret memories of African Americans, tend towards difference. Even a relatively privileged African-American character, like the main figure in *Meridian* (1976) by Alice Walker, is haunted by ghostly voices and presences that mark her off from the young white female protagonists of *Machine Dreams* and *The Annunciation*. "But what none of them seemed to understand," Walker says of her character,

> was that she felt herself to be, not holding something from the past, but *held* by something in the past: by the memory of old black men in the South who, caught by surprise in the eye of the camera, never shifted their position but looked directly back, by the sight of young girls singing in a country choir, their hair shining with brushings and grease, their voices the voices of angels.[20]

Walker, like Gaines or Davis, is speaking of the South, certainly, but of a South that has disentangled itself from many of the threads of white culture(s). It has its own projects and pieties, issuing from its own store of memories. So, much of the time, it writes its own separate history.

"The world is here," Ishmael Reed, the African-American writer born in Tennessee, ends one of his essays: "here" being, as the title of that essay makes clear, "America: The Multinational Society." That remark brings us right back to the problem, and the promise, of cultural pluralism. Even talking about the past, that old Southern pastime, suddenly becomes tricky when that talking takes place as Reed's does, in the mobile marketplace of modern culture, with its mix and occasional collisions of race and class. And gender: the shifting patterns of work practice among Southern females are clear. By 1970, women made up 39 percent of the workforce in the South, and by 1980 it was 43 percent. Affirmative action increased work opportunities, particularly for educated women, to the extent that one historian, writing at the end of the 1980s, could describe the change in the work and family patterns of Southern women as "a revolution." "The economic, demographic, and social changes that have occurred since World War II," she declared, "have diminished the differences between women in the urban South and women in other American cities."[21] Or, as one of Bobbie Ann Mason's characters snappily puts it, "Times are different now, Papa. We're just as good as the men." Not all women live in the urban South, however, even now. And even those that do find, like many of their country counterparts, that changes in labor practice do not necessarily equal changes in belief and behavior. "Men could do anything," the narrator of *Bastard Out of Carolina* recalls of her upbringing, well after World War II, "and everything they did, no matter how violent or mistaken, was viewed with humor and understanding." "What men did was just what men did," she adds. "Some days I would grind my teeth, wishing I had been a boy." The same wish, to become a member of an exclusive club of male privilege, prompts the more middle-class heroine of *The Revolution of Little Girls* to insist on playing the boy's parts in all her childhood games. "After the Tarzan serial at the movies every Saturday afternoon," she remembers, she insisted on playing Tarzan because "Tarzan had more fun." Unfortunately for her, though, "the real world was suspicious of girls who did not want to play Jane."[22]

And in the real world of the South many women continue to "play Jane." They remain wedded to a particular regional mystique, roles that slyly or more obviously are forms of subjection. "The past – not the one validated in schoolbooks but another kind, unanalyzed and undefined – hangs upon Southern women as if they were dispossessed royalty," Shirley Abbott has observed in *Womenfolks: Growing Up Down South*. "I never learned," she adds ruefully, "to construe the female sex as downtrodden and disadvantaged."[23] Abbott is talking, in particular, of her own conflicted role as an educated Southern white woman. The situation is all the trickier, however, and the conflicts even more conflicted, because many of the old divisions between women of different classes, and in particular between black and white women, remain. A measure of the grip traditional female roles still have on the Southern imagination is that ten of the fifteen states that never ratified the Equal Rights Amendment in the 1970s were in the South. And a measure, in turn, of the degree of tension *between* and *within* Southern women is that many of those Southerners opposed to the Amendment – maybe seeing it, as one of them put it, as a piece of "country club feminism" – were female. "Most working-class women . . . will never fall prey to the media-created fads which advertise themselves as 'women's liberation,'" a female labor activist from the South declared shortly after the Stop ERA campaign began in 1972. "Middle-class women's lib is a trend," a working woman in the region commented during the same period, "working women's liberation is a necessity." An African-American woman put it even more baldly and, besides, registered some of the resentment that strict demarcation between traditional white and traditional black female roles in the South has tended to produce. The women's movement, she insisted, "is just a bunch of bored white women with nothing to do – they're just trying to attract attention away from the black liberation movement."[24]

"It is going to take time," one social observer of Southern white women has argued, "for them to catch up to women in other parts of the country": catch up, that is, in terms of customary assumptions and social roles. Even professional women in the region, the evidence suggests, are less directed towards personal achievement and career goals than they are elsewhere in the United States; and for many other Southern women the pull towards the past is doubly powerful because there has been less of a significant *economic* advance. "I was raised in southern Georgia where any female past puberty was referred to as a lady," Harry Crews confesses in one of his essays. "You may by now have recognized in what I've written thus far," he goes on,

> that I've referred to the other half of the human race alternately as woman, lady, and girl. There is great confusion on the part of some men – and certainly I am one of them – about just what the hell we should call females.[25]

The confusion that Crews admits to, about the right names and roles for women, is something shared by many other Southerners, male *and* female. And it can be crippling. It has led some critics to suggest, for instance, that Crews himself is incapable of creating plausible women characters in his fiction. It can also be frustrating, especially for those many women in the South who experience division actively within them, in their understanding of themselves as well as in everyday social exchange. But sometimes it can be useful, even fruitful, provoking imaginative analysis of just what has caused the confusion; it may encourage those caught in the slippage between old beliefs and new behavior to think carefully about their plight.

What all this comes down to, really, is that Southerners are living *between* cultures. Some are living there more openly than others, and with more sensitivity to the problems that come with the territory; among these are Southern writers. All of them are living there, too, in a double sense. In local terms, Southerners are caught between the conflicting interests and voices that constitute the region and the regional debate. Similarly, on the national and even international stage, they betray intense uncertainty about whether to assimilate or to resist. Southern books, in particular, very often become a site of struggle between, on the one hand, the culture(s) of the South and, on the other, the culture of the global marketplace. As a matter of general practice, or even regional history, this is not quite as unusual, as extraordinary, as it may sound. The South as a term of self-identification was, after all, born out of crisis; and the area known as Southern has remained almost continually in a critical state. All that has happened recently is that change – and, especially, the information and consumer revolutions of the past few decades – has made things even more acutely critical than usual; there is a difference of degree, fundamentally, rather than of kind. Besides, no society anywhere is immune from crisis or exempt from the conflicting practices and interests that promote it. The South now is not a monolith but, then, no historical epoch is. On the contrary, as Fredric Jameson has argued, *any* social formation is a complex overlay of different methods of production which serve as the bases of different social groups and, consequently, of their worldviews. And in any given epoch a variety of kinds of antagonism can be discerned, conflict between different groups and interests. One culture may well be dominant: but there will also be – to borrow Raymond Williams's useful terms – a residual culture, formed in the past but still active in the cultural process, and an emergent culture, prescribing new meanings and practices. Southerners, in effect, like any other members of a society, are not the victims of some totalizing structure, since – to quote Williams – "no dominant culture ever in reality includes all human practice, human energy and human intention." Nor are Southern writers: they have the chance, maybe even the obligation, to insert themselves in the space between conflicting interests and practices and then dramatize the contradictions the conflict engenders. Through their work, by means of a mixture of voices, a free play of languages and even genres, they can represent the reality of their culture as multiple, complex, and internally antagonistic. They can achieve a realization of both synchrony and diachrony: a demonstration, on the one hand, of structural continuities between past and present and, on the other, of the processes by which those continuities are challenged, dissolved, and reconstituted. So they have a better opportunity than many other members of their society have of realizing what Hayden White has called "the human capacity to endow lived contradictions with intimations of their possible transcendence."[26] They have the chance, in short, of getting "into" history, to participate in its processes, and, in a perspectival sense at least, getting "out" of it too – and so enable us, the readers, to begin to understand just how those processes work.

About midway through *Edisto* (1983) by Padget Powell, the narrator of the novel, Simons Everson Manigault, describes how his mother, known locally as the Duchess, refuses to have a faulty air conditioning unit in their rundown "Southern barony" replaced. "Honey, when I was little, we didn't have all this," she tells her son. "Just consider we're going back through Margaret Mitchell's wind." The men who remove the unit refuse at first to believe that she will not order a new one. "They didn't know she was one of those readers of Southern literature who talk about progressive light changes at dusk," says Simons by way of explanation, "and how the air in the country is different than in the city, and how country crickets sing a different, more authentic tune than city crickets." The sort of "Southern literature" the Duchess favors is clearly not the sort in which she appears. *Edisto* begins on an old estate, "reduced . . . to a track of clay roads cut in a feathery herbaceous jungle of deerfly for stock and scrub oak for crop." And it ends in the suburbs, with Simons and his "vestigial baroness" of a mother moving into a place where, he says, "the oaks are all pruned . . . so they look like perfect trees in cement zoo cages." "It's somehow pleasant enough here," Simons comments, " . . . Condominia are all over, roads deliberately curve everywhere when they could go straight, the tinkling postcard marina, lobbies, lounges, links, limousines." "All the Negroes are in green landscape clothes," he observes, "or white service jackets, or Volvos with their kids in tennis togs." "It's the modern world," he concludes, "I have to accept it."[27] It is this kind of registering of pluralism and alteration in the contemporary South – "new Negroes in Volvos," others less privileged in mass-produced service outfits – that marks out much of the best recent Southern writing. And, in distinct contrast to Simons Everson Manigault, acceptance is not the right word for what writers like Padget Powell do. They do not "accept" the contemporary South; they take the measure of it by being a part of it and apart from it, and working at the consequent tensions. Writing both in and about their culture(s) and the changes, people like the author of *Edisto* – and there are many of them – dramatize what it means to be a Southerner now. In the process, they tell us what it means to live in history, Southern or otherwise, and potentially out of it; they offer the possibility of experience with understanding.

Of course, there is no single model of Southern writing now, any more than there is a singular frame for present or recent Southern culture(s). There are any number of strategies for dramatizing the slippage between old and new and the edgy, protean character of the contemporary South. Notably in fiction, where even traditional themes and familiar writing practices are given fresh and often unexpected twists. The small town social comedy that was a particular skill of earlier novelists like Ellen Glasgow, for instance, is still alive – in books like *Raney* (1985), *Walking Across Egypt* (1987), and *Killer Diller* (1991) by Clyde Edgerton; *A Short History of a Small Place* (1985), *The Last of How It Was* (1987), and *Call and Response* (1989) by T. R. Pearson; *North Gladiola* (1985) and *Modern Baptists* (1989) by James Wilcox; and even *Family Linen* (1985) by Lee Smith, *July 7th* (1992) by Jill McCorkle, and *A Good Scent from a Strange Mountain* (1993) by Robert Olen Butler. Only now the small town is a place like Listre, North Carolina, in Edgerton's fiction, Neely, North Carolina in Pearson's work, or the eponymous North Gladiola, Louisiana: a place, not too far from the Interstate highway, "jacketed with golf links and shopping centers,"[28] where the young eat Big Macs crouched in front of the television, while the well-healed older folk are rich enough, not only to join the country club, but also to travel regularly to Europe. Or it is a place like Lake Charles, Louisiana, in Butler's stories – or, for that matter, Galveston, Texas in *Boat People* (1995) by Mary Gardner or Falls Church, Virginia in *Monkey Bridge* (1997) by Lan Cao: the site of a new community, in this case Vietnamese Americans, adding a fresh ingredient to the rich cultural mix of the region. Sometimes, every other Southern novelist seems to be commemorating another regional fictional tradition – that of, say, Thomas Wolfe – by producing something that might be subtitled "growing up in the provincial South." Examples here, among many, are *Ride With the Horseman* (1982) by Ferrol Sams; *The Cheer Leader* (1984) by Jill McCorkle; *Edisto* by Padget Powell; *A World Made of Fire* (1985) by Mark Childress; *Ellen Foster* (1987) by Kaye Gibbons; *1959* by Thulani Davis; and *Father and Son* (1997) by Larry Brown. To mention *Edisto* and *1959* together, however, is to measure the difference between these novels: one the story of an exceptionally sophisticated, fatherless white son of a college professor, the other the tale of a motherless young African-American woman, growing up in a place where "there really wasn't anyplace a boy could take a girl"[29] – that is, if the boy and girl in question are black.

It is worth, perhaps, saying just a little more about the issue alluded to just now: that influx of new people into the South from other parts of the world, such as Vietnam, which has served still further to subvert, not just a monolithic reading of the region but any tendency to adopt a simply bipolar, biracial model. The impact of the hispanic presence was always to be felt in some parts of the supposedly solid South, for instance; and that presence has been enlarged by the several waves of immigration from places like Cuba. The literature written by and about Cubans in the South, particularly Southern Florida, includes *Raining Backwards* (1988) by Roberto Fernandez, a surreal tale of exile in Miami, *Dreaming in Cuban* (1992) by Christine Garcia and *The Perez Family* (1990) by Christine Bell. "I need a map," admits one Cuban immigrant in *The Perez Family*: a book which tells the story of a "family" that is not, strictly speaking, a family at all, but a makeshift group of refugees put together to gain priority for sponsorship. Needing a map to chart their way through the strange land of southern Florida, these characters offer a different angle of vision on their Southern surroundings, turning them sometimes into dream-scapes. Here, for instance, is Miami as seen by one of the members of the Perez family, the self-appointed leader and matriarch called Dottie:

> Miami in the afternoon sun is crayola and bright. Like a child's drawing, the city is imaginatively colored and unimaginatively out of proportion. Slender palms stand in disbelief against giant lego constructions. Soft clouds float by garish concrete. Rows of aqua and pink houses insult the shimmering sea and the sky they frame. The streets themselves parallel and intersect with the simple logic of a child's board game. Miami fit Dottie's idea of freedom perfectly – it was simple, gaudy, and close at hand.[30]

"The alienated city is above all the space in which people are unable to map (in their minds) either their own positions or the urban totality in which they find them-selves," argues Fredric Jameson. That may be true of these characters to begin with. But, as this passage intimates, many of them find a means of locating themselves in their new Southern space by relocating the emotional and metaphorical baggage they carry with them – together with a familiar cluster of tropes gathered around the notions of a lost childhood and a dreamlike paradise. Needing a map, they make one for themselves: one that recharts their new home, using fresh but somehow familiar coordinates. In the process, they offer altered geographies, another perspec-tive on the mixed, plural medium that the South and Southerners now more than ever inhabit.

"The day of regional Southern writing is all gone," a writer of an earlier generation, Walker Percy, claimed in 1971. "I think that people who try to write in that style are usually repeating a phased-out genre or doing Faulkner badly."[31] That claim, how-ever, rests on a familiar and surely tendentious premise – the one ingrained in that claim made by John Peale Bishop to Allen Tate to the effect that "With us Western civilization ends." The South is perceived as a cultural monolith, under threat and perhaps faced with imminent collapse. It follows from this premise that the Southern writer, if he or she exists, is defined as someone writing from within that monolithic structure; if nobody exists like that, then there can be no such thing any more as Southern writing. But the culture that, as a matter of self-identification, has defined itself as regional and Southern, has always been more mixed and fluid than this argument allows. The South has always represented itself historically as different, deviant, and (usually) in danger; and it has been marked, for good or ill, by its own sense, at any given time, of what it was different and deviating *from* and what it was in danger *of*. Southern writing, in particular, has consistently been produced by writers who resisted the monolith – not least because they worked from both inside and outside of their culture. That situation, of historical contingency and writerly resistance, has been exacerbated by the mix of recent social changes, but it has always been there. To assume otherwise is simply to accept a reading of Southern literature that equates it, more or less, with the Agrarian project. What we have now, in short, is an extension of what we have always had: different, developing social formations that those writers who are experiencing them choose to identify in regional terms – or, at least, choose to mark out using "South" and "region" as part of their fictional vocabulary. "With us Western civilization ends": Southerners, some of them and Southern writers especially, may be haunted by the imagination of disaster and the sense of an ending, but what the story Southern self-fashioning tells us, if it tells us anything, is that endings are also beginnings and that it is possible to survive and even triumph over disaster. Or, as the greatest of all Southern writers had the most autobiographical of his characters put it: "Maybe nothing ever happens once and is finished."

NOTES

1 To Allen Tate, August 25, 1931, in *The Republic of Letters in America: The Correspondence of John Peale Bishop and Allen Tate*, edited by Thomas D. Young and John J. Hindle (Lexington, KY, 1981), p. 48. See also, Allen Tate, *Jefferson Davis: His Rise and Fall* (New York, 1929), p. 301.

2 To John Peale Bishop, early June, 1931, in *Republic of Letters*, edited by Young and Hindle, p. 34. See also, to John Peale Bishop, April 7, 1933, p. 77.

3 John W. Du Bose, *The Life and Times of William Lowndes Yancey*, 2 vols. (New York, 1942), I, p. 301.

4 Anwar Abdel Malek, "Orientalism in Crisis," *Diogenes*, XLIV (1963), 107–8.

5 Benedict Anderson, *Imagined Communities: Reflections on the Origin and Spread of Nationalism* (London, 1991), p. 6.

6 Numan V. Bartley, *The New South, 1845–1980*, Vol. XI (1995) in *The History of the South*, edited by Wendell Holmes Stephenson and E. Merton Coulter, 11 vols. (Baton Rouge, LA, 1947–95), p. 468. See also, Ernest J. Gaines, *Catherine Carmier* (New York, 1993), p. 174; David R. Goldfield, "The City as Southern History: The Past and the Promise of Tomorrow," in *The Future South: A Historical Perspective for the Twenty-First Century*, edited by Joe P. Dunn and Howard L. Preston (Urbana, IL, 1991), p. 34; James C. Cobb, "The Sunbelt South: Industrialization in Regional, National, and International Perspective," in *Searching for the Sunbelt: Historical Perspectives on a Region*, edited by Raymond A. Mohl (Knoxville, TN, 1990), p. 39. Along with works already cited, useful recent discussions of the developments described here include Jacqueline Jones, *Labor of Love, Labor of Sorrow: Black Women, Work, and the Family from Slavery to the Present* (New York, 1985); Pete Daniel, *Standing at the Crossroads: Southern Life Since 1900* (New York, 1986); *The Evolution of Southern Culture*, edited by Numan V. Bartley (Athens, GA, 1988); *Southern Women*, edited by Caroline M. Dillman (New York, 1988); Priscilla C. Little and Robert C. Vaughan, *A New Perspective: Southern Women's Cultural History from the Civil War to Civil Rights* (Charlottesville, VA, 1989); Robert Weisbrot, *Freedom Bound: A History of America's Civil Rights Movement* (New York, 1990).

7   John Shelton Reed, *The Enduring South: Subcultural Persistence in Mass Society* (Chapel Hill, NC, 1986), pp. 91–2. See also, Charles O. Lerche, *The Uncertain South: Its Changing Patterns of Politics in Foreign Policy* (Chicago, 1964), p. 243; Sheldon Hackney, "Southern Violence," *American Historical Review*, LXXIV (1969), 925.

8   Reed, *Enduring South*, p. 100. See also, John Peet, "A Survey of the South," *The Economist*, December 10, 1994, p. 14. Also, John Egerton, *The Americanization of Dixie: The Southernization of America* (New York, 1974).

9   Eugene D. Genovese, *The Southern Tradition: Achievement and Limitations of an American Conservatism* (Cambridge, MA, 1994), p. 8. See also, Marjorie R. Hershey, "The Congressional Elections," in *The Election of 1996: Reports and Interpretations*, edited by Gerald R. Pomper (Chatham, NJ, 1997), p. 229. Also, *The Lasting South: Fourteen Southerners Look at their Home*, edited by Louis D. Rubin, Jr., and James K. Kilpatrick (Chicago, 1957); Francis B. Simkins, *The Everlasting South* (Baton Rouge, LA, 1963); "Fifteen Southerners," *Why the South Will Survive* (Athens, GA, 1981); John H. Maclachlan and Joe S. Floyd, Jr., *This Changing South* (Gainesville, FL, 1956); Frank E. Smith, *Look Away from Dixie* (Baton Rouge, LA, 1965); Harry S. Ashmore, *An Epitaph for Dixie* (New York, 1957). In 1983 the critic Fred Hobson observed "if pondering and examining the mind and soul of Dixie had seemed a Southern affliction before 1945," since then it had "assumed epidemic proportions": *Tell About the South: The Southern Rage to Explain* (Baton Rouge, LA, 1983), p. 297; and these, among many books, appear to prove that.

10 Barry Hannah, *Hey Jack!* (New York, 1988), p. 13. See also, Lee Smith, *Oral History* (New York, 1983), p. 292.

11 Harry Crews, *Florida Frenzy* (Gainesville, FL, 1993), p. 55. See also, Theodor Adorno, *Minima Moralia* (London, 1974), p. 235.

12 Connie Z. Atkinson, "'Shakin' Your Butt for the Tourist': Music's Role in the Identification and Selling of New Orleans," in *Dixie Debates: Perspectives on Southern Cultures*, edited by Richard H. King and Helen Taylor (London, 1996), p. 154. See also, p. 155.

13 Sam G. Riley, *Magazines of the American South* (New York, 1986), p. 240. See also, Diane Roberts, "Living Southern in *Southern Living*," in *Dixie Debates*, edited by King and Taylor, pp. 87, 90. On *Southern Living* see also, Peirce Lewis, "The Making of Vernacular Taste: The Case of *Sunset* and *Southern Living*," in *Dumbarton Oaks Colloquium on the History of Landscape Architecture: XIV*, edited by John Dixon Hunt and Joachim Welsschke-Bulmahn (Washington, DC, 1993), pp. 107–18. On Southern "performance," see Eric Sundquist, *To Wake the Nations: Race in the Making of American Literature* (Cambridge, MA, 1993), p. 273. On the popularity of country music, see Bill C. Malone, *Southern Music, American Music* (Lexington, KY, 1979); James C. Cobb, "From Muskogee to Luckenbach: Country Music and the 'Southernization' of America," *Journal of Popular Culture*, XVI (1982), esp. 82, 88. On "Southern rock," see Paul Wells, "The Last Rebel: Southern Rock and Nostalgic Certainties," in *Dixie Debates*, edited by King and Taylor, pp. 115–29.

14 Blanche McCrary Boyd, *The Revolution of Little Girls* (New York, 1992), pp. 77–80.

15 Boyd, *Revolution of Little Girls*, p. 120. See also, Fredric Jameson, *Postmodernism; or, The Cultural Logic of Late Capitalism* (London, 1991), p. 19. In this context, Jean Baudrillard's analysis of "the liquidation of all referentials" and the process of "substituting signs of the real for the real itself" is also relevant: *Simulations* (New York, 1983), p. 4.

16 One clear illustration of this is the range of material covered in *Encyclopedia of Southern Culture*, edited by Charles R. Wilson and William Ferris (Chapel Hill, NC, 1989).

17 Ernest Gaines, *The Autobiography of Miss Jane Pittman* (New York, 1972), p. 9; see also, p. 151; William Faulkner, "An Introduction to *The Sound and the Fury*," *Mississippi Quarterly*, XXVI (1973), 412; *Conversations with Ernest Gaines*, edited by John Lowe (Jackson, MS, 1995), p. 61; Allan Gurganus, *Oldest Living Confederate Widow Tells All* (New York, 1989), p. xix.

18 Dorothy Allison, *Bastard Out of Carolina* (London, 1993), p. 26; see also, p. 64; M. A. Harper, *For the Love of Robert E. Lee* (New York, 1992), p. 37; Harry Crews, *A Childhood: The Biography of a Place*

(1978), in *Classic Crews: A Harry Crews Reader* (London, 1993), p. 21; Cormac McCarthy, *The Crossing* (London, 1994), pp. 143, 155; Thulani Davis, *1959* (London, 1993), pp. 35–6.

19 Davis, *1959*, p. 35. See also, Jayne Anne Phillips, *Machine Dreams* (London, 1984), p. 3; Ellen Gilchrist, *The Annunciation* (London, 1984), p. 15; *Conversations with Gaines*, edited by Lowe, pp. 7, 17.

20 Alice Walker, *Meridian* (London, 1983), p. 14.

21 Julie K. Blackwelder, "Race, Ethnicity and Women's Lives in the Urban South," in *Shades of the Sunbelt*, edited by Miller and Pozetta, pp. 78, 88. See also, Ishmael Reed, "America: The Multi-national Society," in *Writin' is Fightin': Thirty-Seven Years of Boxing on Paper* (New York, 1988), p. 12.

22 Boyd, *Revolution of Little Girls*, p. 3. See also, Bobbie Ann Mason, *Shiloh and Other Stories* (London, 1988), p. 110; Allison, *Bastard Out of Carolina*, p. 23.

23 Shirley Abbott, *Womenfolks: Growing Up Down South* (New Haven, CT, 1983), p. 31. See also, for accounts of themselves by Southern women, *Speaking for Ourselves: Women of the South*, edited by Maxine Alexander (New York, 1977).

24 Helen H. King, "Black Women and Women's Lib," *Ebony*, March, 1971, p. 70. See also, Donald G. Mathews and Jane Sherron De Hart, *Sex, Gender, and the Politics of ERA: A State and the Nation (New York, 1990), p. 145; Hillbilly Women, edited by Kathy Kahn (New York, 1973), pp. 19, 183; Dolores Janiewski, Sisterhood Denied: Race, Gender and Class in a New South Community (Philadelphia, PA, 1985), pp. 152–78*.

25 Crews, *Florida Frenzy*, pp. 33–4. See also, Caroline M. Dillman, "Southern Women: In Continuity or Change?" in *Women in the South: An Anthropological Perspective*, edited by Holly F. Mathews (Athens, GA, 1989), p. 17. On the problem of the relationship between material change and changes in perception, see also Susan Middleton-Deirn and Jackie Howsden-Eller, "Reconstructing Femininity: The Woman Professional in the South," in *Women in the South*, edited by Mathews, pp. 59–70. On the particular problems faced by black women, see Jones, *Labor of Love, Labor of Sorrow*. For a critique of Harry Crews's fictional representations of women, see Patricia V. Beatty, "Crews's Women," in *A Grit's Triumph: Essays on the Work of Harry Crews*, edited by David K. Jeffrey (Port Washington, NY, 1983), pp. 112–23.

26 Hayden White, "Getting Out of History," in *Tropics of Discourse: Essays in Cultural Criticism* (Baltimore, MD, 1978), p. 17. See also Raymond Williams, *Marxism and Literature* (New York, 1977), p. 120. Also, Fredric Jameson, *The Political Unconscious: Narrative as a Socially Symbolic Act* (Ithaca, NY, 1981).

27 Padget Powell, *Edisto* (New York, 1985), p. 182; see also pp. 9–10, 104–5, 177–8.

28 Fred Chappell, *The Gaudy Place* (Baton Rouge, LA, 1994), p. 6. Clyde Edgerton, *Raney* (Chapel Hill, NC, 1985), *Walking Across Eygpt* (Chapel Hill, NC, 1987), and *Killer Diller* (Chapel Hill, NC, 1991); T. R. Pearson, *A Short History of a Small Place* (New York, 1985), *The Last of How It Was* (New York, 1987), and *Call and Response* (New York, 1989); James Wilcox, *North Gladiola* (New York, 1985) and *Modern Baptists* (New York, 1989); Lee Smith, *Family Linen* (New York, 1985); Jill McCorkle, *July 7th* (Chapel Hill, NC, 1992); Robert Olen Butler, *A Good Scent from a Strange Mountain* (New York, 1993); Mary Gardner, *Boat People* (New York, 1995); Lan Cao, *Monkey Bridge* (New York, 1997). On those elements, old and new, in the cultural mosaic of the South that make it much more than a bipolar, biracial society, see George Brown Tindall, *Natives and Newcomers: Ethnic Southerners and Southern Ethnics* (Athens, Georgia, 1995); Eric Gary Anderson, "Native American Literature, Ecocriticism, and the South," in *South to a New Place: Region, Literature, Culture*, edited by Suzanne W. Jones and Sharon Monteith (Baton Rouge, LA, 2002), pp. 165–183; Maureen Ryan, "Outsiders with Inside Information," in *South to a New Place*, pp. 235–252.

29 Davis, *1959*, p. 17. Ferrol Sams, *Run With the Horseman* (New York, 1984); Jill McCorkle, *The Cheer Leader* (Chapel Hill, NC, 1984); Mark Childress, *A World Made of Fire* (London, 1985); Kaye Gibbons, *Ellen Foster* (Chapel Hill, NC, 1987); Larry Brown, *Father and Son* (London, 1997).

30   Christine Bell, *The Perez Family* (New York, 1990), p. 40; see also p. 57; Fredric Jameson, *Postmodernism, or, the Cultural Logic of Late Capitalism* (Durham, NC, 1991), p. 90; Roberto Fernandez, *Raining Backwards* (Houston, TX, 1988); Christina Garcia, *Dreaming in Cuban* (New York, 1992).

31   Interview with Walker Percy, in *Conversations with Walker Percy*, edited by Lewis A. Lawson and Victor A. Kramer (Jackson, MS, 1985), p. 69. See also William Faulkner, *Absalom, Absalom!* (New York, 1936), p. 261. It is, of course, Quentin Compson who observes: "Maybe nothing ever happens once and is finished"; and while it would be wrong to identify character and author, the points of coincidence – and the relevance of this observation to Faulkner's narrative habits of repetition and revision – should not be overlooked.

REFERENCES AND FURTHER READING

Aaron, Daniel (1973) *The Unwritten War: American Writers and the Civil War.* New York.

Abbott, Shirley (1983) *Womenfolks: Growing Up Down South.* New Haven, CT.

Applebone, Peter (1996) *Dixie Rising: How the South is Shaping American Values, Politics, and Culture.* New York.

Alexander, Maxine (ed.) (1977) *Speaking for Ourselves: Women of the South.* New York.

Andrews, William L. (1988) *To Tell a Free Story: The First Century of Afro-American Autobiography, 1760–1865.* Urbana, IL.

Ashmore, Harry S. (1957) *An Epitaph for Dixie.* New York.

Ayers, Edward L. (1992) *The Promise of the New South: Life After Reconstruction.* New York.

Baker, Houston A. (1984) *Blues, Ideology, and Afro-American Literature.* Chicago.

Bartley, Numan V. (ed.) (1988) *The Evolution of Southern Culture.* Athens, GA.

Bassett, John E. (ed.) (1997) *Defining Southern Literature: Perspectives and Assessments, 1831–1952.* Cranbury, NJ.

Batteau, Allen W. (1990) *The Invention of Appalachia.* Tucson, AZ.

Berlin, Ira (1998) *Many Thousands Gone: The First Two Centuries of Slavery in North America.* Cambridge, MA.

Black, Earle and Black, Merle (1987) *Politics and Society in the South.* Cambridge, MA.

Black, Merle and Reed, John Shelton (eds.) (1981–4) *Perspectives on the American South: An Annual Review of Society, Politics, and Culture, Vols. I and II.* New York.

Blassingame, John W. (1972) *The Slave Community: Plantation Life in the Antebellum South.* New York.

Boles, John B. (1982) *Black Southerners, 1619–1869.* Lexington, KY.

Boles, John B. (1999) *The South Through Time*, 2 vols. Upper Saddle River, NJ.

Boles, John B. (ed.) (2002) *A Companion to the American South.* Oxford.

Bradbury, John M. (1963) *Renaissance in the South: A Critical History of the Literature, 1920–1960.* Chapel Hill, NC.

Bridenbaugh, Carl (1952) *Myths and Realities: Societies of the Colonial South.* Baton Rouge, LA.

Brinkmeyer, Jr., Robert J. (2000) *Remapping Southern Literature.* Athens, GA.

Bruce, Dickson D. (2001) *The Origins of African-American Literature, 1680–1865.* New York.

Bryant, Jr., J. A. (1997) *Twentieth-Century Southern Literature.* Lexington, KY.

Campbell, Jr., Edward D. C. (1981) *The Celluloid South: Hollywood and the Southern Myth.* Knoxville, TN.

Cash, Wilbur J. (1941) *The Mind of the South.* New York.

Cobb, James C. (1984) *Industrialization and Southern Society, 1877–1984.* Lexington, KY.

Cobb, James C. (1992) *The Most Southern Place on Earth: The Mississippi Delta and the Roots of Regional Identity.* New York.

Cobb, James C. (1999) *Redefining Southern Culture: Mind and Identity in the Modern South.* Athens, GA.

Cobb, James C. and Wilson, Charles R. (eds.) (1985–7) *Perspectives on the American South: An Annual Review of Society, Politics, and Culture, Vols. 3 and 4.* New York.

Cook, Sylvia Jenkins (1976) *From Tobacco Road to Route 66: The Southern Poor White in Fiction.* Chapel Hill, NC.

Cooper, Jr., William and Terrill, Thomas E. (1996) *The American South: A History.* New York.

Dameron, J. Lesley (1986) *No Fairer Land: Studies in Southern Literature Before 1900.* Baton Rouge, LA.

Daniel, Pete (1986) *Standing at the Crossroads: Southern Life Since 1900.* New York.

Davis, Richard B. (1978) *Intellectual Life in the Colonial South,* 3 vols. Baton Rouge, LA.

Degler, Carl (1974) *The Other South: Southern Dissenters in the Nineteenth Century.* New York.

Dunn, Joe and Preston, Howard L. (eds.) (1991) *The Future South: Historical Perspectives for the Twenty-First Century.* Urbana, IL.

Egerton, John (1974) *The Americanization of Dixie: The Southernization of America.* New York.

Fahr, Alice (2001) *The Imagined Civil War: Popular Literature of the North and South, 1861–1865.* Chapel Hill, NC.

Farnham, Christie Anne (ed.) (1997) *Women of the American South: A Multicultural Reader.* New York.

Faust, Drew Gilpin (1977) *A Sacred Circle: The Dilemma of the Intellectual in the Old South.* Baton Rouge, LA.

"Fifteen Southerners" (1981) *Why the South Will Survive.* Athens, GA.

Flint, J. Wayne (1980) *Dixie's Forgotten People: The South's Poor Whites.* Bloomington, IN.

Folks, J. and Perkins, John A. (1997) *Southern Writers at Century's End.* Lexington, KY.

Foner, Eric (1983) *Nothing But Freedom: Emancipation and Its Legacy.* Baton Rouge, LA.

Foote, Shelby (1958–74) *The Civil War: A Narrative,* 3 vols. New York.

Foster, Frances Smith (1993) *Written by Herself: Literary Production by African-American Women, 1746–1892.* Bloomington, IN.

Foster, Frances Smith (1994) *Witnessing Slavery: The Development of Ante-Bellum Slave Narratives.* Bloomington, IN.

Fox-Genovese, Elizabeth (1988) *Within the Plantation Household: Black and White Women of the Old South.* Chapel Hill, NC.

Franklin, John Hope (1994) [1947] *From Slavery to Freedom: A History of African Americans.* New York.

Fraser, Jr., Walter J. and Moon, Winifred B. (eds.) (1981) *From the Old South to the New: Essays on the Transitional South.* Westport, CT.

French, Warren (ed.) (1981) *The South and Film.* Jackson, MS.

Gaines, Francis Pendleton (1924) *The Southern Plantation: A Study in the Development and Accuracy of a Tradition.* New York.

Gallagher, Gary (1992) *The Confederate War.* Cambridge, MA.

Gayle, Addison (1975) *The Way of the New World: The Black Novel in America.* Garden City, NJ.

Genovese, Eugene D. (1969) *The World the Slaveholders Made.* New York.

Genovese, Eugene D. (1974) *Roll, Jordan, Roll: The World the Slaves Made.* New York.

Genovese, Eugene D. (1994) *The Southern Tradition: Achievement and Limitations of an American Conservatism.* Cambridge, MA.

Gilman, Jr., Owen (1992) *Vietnam and the Southern Imagination.* Jackson, MS.

Gilroy, Paul (1993) *The Black Atlantic: Modernity and Double Consciousness.* London.

Goldfield, David R. (1982) *Cotton Fields and Skyscrapers: Southern City and Region, 1670–1980.* Lexington, KY.

Goldfield, David R. (1987) *Promised Land: The South Since 1945.* Arlington Heights, IL.

Goldfield, David R. (1990) *Black, White, and Southern: Race Relations and Southern Culture.* Baton Rouge, LA.

Grammer, John (1996) *Pastoral and Politics in the Old South.* Baton Rouge, LA.

Grantham, Dewey D. (1994) *The South in Modern America: A Region at Odds.* New York.

Gray, Richard (1977) *The Literature of Memory: Modern Writers of the American South.* Baltimore, MD.

Gray, Richard (1997) *Writing the South: Ideas of an American Region.* Baton Rouge, LA.

Gray, Richard (2000) *Southern Aberrations: Writers of the American South and the Problems of Regionalism.* Baton Rouge, LA.

Gretlund, J. Nordby (ed.) (1999) *The Southern State of Mind.* Columbia, SC.

Griffin, Larry J. and Doyle, Don H. (eds.) (1995) *The South as an American Problem.* Athens, GA.

Guinn, Matthew (2000) *After Southern Modernism: Fiction of the Contemporary South.* Jackson, MS.

Gwin, Minrose (1985) *Black and White Women of the Old South: The Peculiar Sisterhood in American Literature.* Knoxville, TN.

Hale, Grace Elizabeth (1998) *Making Whiteness: The Culture of Segregation in the South, 1890–1940.* New York.

Harrison, Elizabeth Jane (1991) *Female Pastoral: Women Writers Re-Visioning the American South.* Knoxville, TN.

Hobson, Fred (1983) *Tell About the South: The Southern Rage to Explain.* Baton Rouge, LA.

Hobson, Fred (1991) *The Southern Writer and the Postmodern World.* Athens, GA.

Holman, C. Hugh (1972) *The Roots of Southern Writing.* Baton Rouge, LA.

Hubbell, Jay B. (1954) *The South in American Literature, 1607–1900.* Durham, NC.

Hudson, Charles and Tesser, Carmen C. (eds.) (1994) *The Forgotten Centuries: Indians and Europeans in the American South, 1521–1704.* Athens, GA.

Humphries, Jefferson and Lowe, John (eds.) (1996) *The Future of Southern Letters.* New York.

Janiewski, Dolores (1985) *Sisterhood Denied: Race, Gender, and Class in a New South Community.* Philadelphia, PA.

Jones, Anne Goodwyn (1971) *Tomorrow is Another Day: The Woman Writer in the South, 1859–1936.* Baton Rouge, LA.

Jones, Anne Goodwyn and Donaldson, Susan V. (eds.) (1997) *Haunted Bodies: Gender and Southern Texts.* Charlottesville, VA.

Jones, Gayl (1991) *Liberating Voices: Oral Traditions in African-American Literature.* Cambridge, MA.

Jones, Jacqueline (1985) *Labor of Love, Labor of Sorrow: Black Women, Work, and the Family from Slavery to the Present.* New York.

Jones, Suzanne and Monteith, Sharon (eds.) (2002) *South to a New Place: Region, Literature, Culture.* Baton Rouge, LA.

Kahn, Kathy (ed.) (1973) *Hillbilly Women.* New York.

King, Richard H. (1980) *A Southern Renaissance: The Cultural Awakening of the American South, 1930–1955.* New York.

King, Richard H. and Taylor, Helen (eds.) (1996) *Dixie Debates: Perspectives on Southern Culture.* London.

Kirby, Jack Temple (1978) *Media-Made Dixie: The South in the American Imagination.* Baton Rouge, LA.

Kirby, Jack Temple (1987) *Rural Worlds Lost: The American South, 1920–1960.* Baton Rouge, LA.

Kirby, Jack Temple (1995) *The Countercultural South.* Athens, GA.

Lamis, Alexander P. (ed.) (1999) *Southern Politics in the 1990s.* Baton Rouge, LA.

Lee, A. Robert (1998) *Designs of Blackness: Mappings in the Literature and Culture of Afro-America.* London.

Lerda, Valeria Gennaro and Westendorp, Tjebbe (eds.) (1991) *The United States South: Regionalism and Identity.* Rome.

Levine, Lawrence (1977) *Black Culture and Black Consciousness: Afro-American Folk Thought from Slavery to Freedom.* New York.

Lively, Robert C. (1957) *Fiction Fights the Civil War.* Chapel Hill, NC.

McKethan, Lucinda H. (1980) *The Dream of Arcady: Place and Time in Southern Literature.* Baton Rouge, LA.

McKethan, Lucinda H. (ed.) (1990) *Daughters of Time: Creating Woman's Voice in Southern Story.* Athens, GA.

Maclachlan, John H. and Floyd, Jr., Joe S. (1956) *This Changing South.* Gainesville, FL.

McMillen, Sally G. (1992) *Southern Women: Black and White in the Old South.* Arlington Heights, IL.

McPherson, James M. and Cooper, Jr., William J. (1998) *Writing the Civil War: The Quest to Understand*. Columbia, SC.

McWhiney, Grady (1988) *Cracker Culture: Celtic Ways in the Old South*. Tuscaloosa, AL.

Manning, Carol S. (1993) *The Female Tradition in Southern Literature*. Urbana, IL.

Mathews, Holly F. (ed.) (1989) *Women in the South: An Anthropological Perspective*. Athens, GA.

MDC 1996 (1996) *The State of the South: A Report to the Region and its Leadership*. Chapel Hill, NC.

Miller, Randall M. and Smith, John David (eds.) (1988) *Dictionary of Afro-American Slavery*. New York.

Mohl, Raymond A. (1990) *Searching for the Sunbelt: Historical Perspectives on a Region*. Knoxville, TN.

Monteith, Sharon (2000) *Advancing Sisterhood? Interracial Friendships in Contemporary Southern Fiction*. Athens, GA.

Moore, Jr., Winifred B. et al. (eds.) (1988) *Developing Dixie: Modernization in a Traditional Society*. Westport, CT.

Murray, Albert (1972) *South to a Very Old Place*. New York.

O'Brien, Michael (1977) *The Idea of the American South, 1920–1941*. Baltimore, MD.

O'Brien, Michael (1980) *Rethinking the South: Essays in Intellectual History*. Baltimore, MD.

Ownby, Ted (ed.) (1991) *Black and White Cultural Interaction in the South*. Jackson, MS.

Painter, Nell Irvin (2002) *Southern History Across the Color Line*. Chapel Hill, NC.

Palmie, Stephan (ed.) (1995) *Slave Cultures and the Cultures of Slavery*. Knoxville, TN.

Payne, L. (1981) *Black Writers in the Southern Renaissance*. London.

Perdue, Theda (1998) "Indians in Southern History," in *Indians in American History: An Introduction* edited by Frederick C. Hoxie and Peter Iverson. Wheeling, IL.

Petty, Carolyn and Weeks, Mary Louise (2002) *The History of Southern Women's Literature*. Baton Rouge, LA.

Prenshaw, Peggy (ed.) (1984) *Women Writers of the Contemporary South*. Jackson, MS.

Pudup, Mary Beth et al. (eds.) (1997) *Appalachia in the Making: The Mountain South in the Nineteenth Century*. Knoxville, TN.

Reed, John Shelton (1986) *The Enduring South: Subcultural Persistence in Mass Society*. Chapel Hill, NC.

Reed, John Shelton (1986) *Southern Folk Plain and Fancy: Native White Social Types*. Athens, GA.

Ridgely, J. V. (1980) *Nineteenth-Century Southern Literature*. Lexington, KY.

Roller, David and Twyman, Robert W. (eds.) (1979) *The Encyclopedia of Southern History*. Baton Rouge, LA.

Rubin, Jr., Louis D. (1963) *The Faraway Country: Writers of the Modern South*. Seattle, WA.

Rubin, Jr., Louis D. (1975) *William Elliott Shoots a Bear: Essays on the Southern Literary Imagination*. Baton Rouge, LA.

Rubin, Jr., Louis D. (1989) *The Edge of the Swamp: A Study in the Literature and Society of the Old South*. Baton Rouge, LA.

Rubin, Jr., Louis D. and Kilpatrick, James K. (eds.) (1957) *The Lasting South: Fourteen Southerners Look at their Home*. Chicago.

Rubin, Jr., Louis D. et al. (eds.) (1985) *The History of Southern Literature*. Baton Rouge, LA.

Sale, Kirkpatrick (1975) *Power Shift: The Rise of the Southern Rim and Its Challenge to the Eastern Establishment*. New York.

Schulman, Bruce J. (1991) *From Cotton Belt to Sunbelt: Federal Policy, Economic Development, and the Transformation of the South, 1938–1988*. New York.

Scott, Anne Firor (1970) *The Southern Lady: From Pedestal to Politics, 1830–1930*. Chicago.

Shapiro, Henry D. (1991) *Appalachia on Our Mind: The Southern Mountains and Mountaineers in the American Consciousness, 1880–1960*. Knoxville, TN.

Shields, David (1997) *Civil Tongues and Polite Letters in British America*. London.

Simkins, Francis B. (1963) *The Everlasting South*. Baton Rouge, LA.

Simpson, Lewis P. (1975) *The Dispossessed Garden: Pastoral and History in Southern Literature*. Baton Rouge, LA.

Simpson, Lewis P. (1989) *Mind and the American Civil War: Meditations on a Lost Cause*. Baton Rouge, LA.

Simpson, Lewis P. (1994) *The Fable of the Southern Writer*. Baton Rouge, LA.

Singal, Daniel J. (1982) *The War Within: From Victorian to Modernist Thought in the South*. Chapel Hill, NC.

Smith, Frank E. (1965) *Look Away from Dixie*. Baton Rouge, LA.

Stantling, Marion Wilson (1988) *The Slave Narrative: Its Place in History*. Washington, DC.

Stephenson, Wendell H. and Coulter, E. Merton (eds.) (1947–95) *The History of the South*, 11 vols. Baton Rouge, LA.

Tate, Linda (1994) *A Southern Weave of Women: Fiction of the Contemporary South*. Athens, GA.

Taylor, Helen (2001) *Circling Dixie: Contemporary Southern Culture through a Transatlantic Lens*. New Brunswick, NJ.

Taylor, William R. (1961) *Cavalier and Yankee: The Old South and American National Character*. New York.

Tindall, George B. (1995) *Natives and Newcomers: Ethnic Southerners and Southern Ethnics*. Athens, GA.

Vaughan, Robert C. (1989) *A New Perspective on Southern Women's Cultural History from the Civil War to the Present*. Charlottesville, VA.

Watson, Charles W. (1997) *The History of Southern Drama*. Lexington, KY.

Weisbrot, Robert (1990) *Freedom Bound: A History of America's Civil Rights Movement*. New York.

Whisnant, David E. (1994) *Modernizing the Mountaineer: People, Power, and Planning in Appalachia*. Knoxville, TN.

Williams, J. W. (1995) *Hillbillyland: What the Movies Did to the Mountains and What the Mountains Did to the Movies*. Chapel Hill, NC.

Wilson, Charles R. (1980) *Baptized in Blood: The Religion of the Lost Cause, 1865–1920*. Athens, GA.

Wilson, Charles R. (ed.) (1985) *Religion in the South*. Jackson, MS.

Wilson, Charles R. (1995) *Judgment and Grace in Dixie: Southern Faiths from Faulkner to Elvis*. Athens, GA.

Wilson, Charles R. and Ferris, William (eds.) (1989) *Encyclopedia of Southern Culture*. Chapel Hill, NC.

Woodward, C. Vann (1993) *The Burden of Southern History*. Baton Rouge, LA.

Wright, Gavin (1986) *Old South, New South: Revolutions in the Southern Economy Since the Civil War*. New York.

Wyatt-Brown, Bertram (1982) *Southern Honor: Ethics and Behavior in the Old South*. New York.

Part II
Themes and Issues

2

The First Southerners: Jamestown's Colonists as Exemplary Figures

Mary C. Fuller

As Wesley Frank Craven wrote on the first page of his *History of the South*, "to write of the South when there was no South is a task not without difficulties."[1] To argue for Jamestown as an origin for Southern history or culture presents one of those difficulties – if by doing so, one must make the case that something about those hundred or so Englishmen gathered behind a palisade on the Potomac in 1607 would exercise a defining influence on what became of Virginia, of America, and of the South hundreds of years later. Yet if such an argument about the early colonists is difficult to make, another one is easier: eventually, their real and symbolic descendants became many and prosperous enough that they cared about naming a beginning, and in that looking back, Jamestown assumed a new being – not just as a small settlement, but as the first colony of America and of the South. It is in the light of that looking back that I will consider it, in terms of our desire to know the past and make it our own.[2] The argument of this essay will be that however much or little the Jamestown settlers mattered to subsequent history, the way they are remembered matters a good deal. I will begin with one of the more recent acts of remembering.

Disney's 1995 animated movie, *Pocahontas*, offers two versions of how a colonist might have looked in Jamestown in 1607. The colony's governor – John Ratcliffe in the film, Edward Maria Wingfield in history[3] – is a hugely fat, dark-haired man. Under a crimson cloak, he wears a purple suit with breeches and lavender stockings; lavender cuffs and collar decorate his suit; he wears pumps with low heels, a beaver hat with a feather, and a large gold medal. He has the thin mustache of a villain and a small goatee; his hair is pulled into loose pigtails with a ribbonned bow on each side. Ratcliffe is attended by an etiolated manservant – Wiggins – and a pampered toy bulldog named Percy. His expressed intention in the film is to approach colonizing on the Spanish model, with the aim primarily of extracting precious metals. He unrolls for the colonists a map of the Spanish conquests in Mexico, and in case the point is not clear, exhorts them: "gold, boys, gold!"

The governor's opposite number is, of course, John Smith. Disney's Smith is a strapping young blond in a pale blue cloth shirt and vest, loose trousers and boots, the better to perform his role of getting out into the woods and courting a Pocahontas who is virtually the spirit of the land. Of course, the historical Smith represented himself somewhat differently. In the frontispiece to *The Description of New England* (1616), he enjoyed a full beard, bristling mustache, and receding hairline, and stood dressed in a closefitting jerkin, full Elizabethan trunks, and a metal gorget topped with a small ruff. Certainly, to depict him in this way would have muddied the visually expressed opposition of good guy and bad guy in the film.

The colonial setting of *Pocahontas* gives these depictions an added resonance, however, and even suggests a kind of argument – an argument in which Smith and the governor respectively stand for the new (American) man and the old (European) man. European man delights in extravagant display: he favors impractically luxurious clothing, and maintains dependents who serve primarily to mark his status. He flaunts his right to consume. His size, retinue, and dress put him at odds with the realities and exigencies of the colonial scene. American man, by contrast, shows himself to be physically equal to the challenge of the new land: muscular, frugal, dressed for action, his abilities pose an implicit challenge to a social superior's right to command. To be sure, these are caricatures; but they bear at least a distant resemblance to real arguments, and like many details of the movie, they are invented not from whole cloth but from a creative reading of the sources.[4] How, and in what terms, do the primary sources on Jamestown represent differences between the governor and Smith?

Once we turn to the sources, there are of course many more players. First-hand accounts of the colony's early days offer a cacophony of voices, documenting conflicts which began before the expedition ever set foot in Virginia. By the time the *Susan Constant* and *Godspeed* left the Canary Islands en route to America, Smith was already in chains, under suspicion of raising a mutiny.[5] Only upon arrival in Virginia, when the colony's instructions were opened, was he found to be appointed to the governing council, an appointment ratified by the remaining councilors after some delay. The colonists had arrived in April; in early June, a "murmur and grudg against certain preposterous proceedings" led to a petition for reform ("the Gentlemans Petityon") being submitted to the council.[6]

The original governing council of Jamestown comprised Edward Maria Wingfield, Smith, John Martin, Bartholomew Gosnold, John Ratcliffe, George Kendall, and Christopher Newport. Of these, Gosnold died in late August; after his death, "the Councell could hardly agree by the dissention of Captaine Kendall";[7] shortly after, Kendall was deposed and confined in the colony's pinnace. A few weeks later, Wingfield was deposed as president by the remaining three councilors (Newport had returned to England), and likewise imprisoned in the pinnace;[8] he was succeeded by Ratcliffe. In late November, the blacksmith James Read got into an argument with

Ratcliffe, and on being charged with misconduct, threatened to strike Ratcliffe with his tools; at the point of being executed, Read revealed a conspiracy headed by Kendall, who was then condemned and shot.[9] While Smith was absent (on the voyage up the Chickahominy which led to his capture by Opechancanough), Gabriel Archer was illegally sworn in as a councilor by Ratcliffe; when Smith returned in early January of 1608, Archer and his associates plotted to depose him if not to try and hang him, and were forestalled only by Newport's arrival. According to Wingfield, Archer himself scarcely escaped hanging.[10] Archer and Wingfield were sent back to England with Newport in April of 1608; Ratcliffe was deposed from the presidency in July, after "riotously consuming the store" and seeking to have the colonists build him "an unnecessarie pallace."[11] Smith succeeded to the office, but appointed a substitute while he was himself away exploring. When he returned in early September, Ratcliffe was in prison for mutiny.[12]

Smith took office as president in September, 1608. In May of 1609, another group of colonists arrived, among them Ratcliffe, Martin, and Archer (Ratcliffe and Martin presumably had returned to England with Newport in December). While they found Smith still serving as the elected president, the rest of the originally appointed council was dead; it was known that the Virginia Company had intended to set in place a new government, but both orders and governors had been shipwrecked and failed to arrive with the new colonists. In the interim between their landfall and the long-delayed arrival of the colony's newly appointed governors, Archer complained that Smith "gave not any due respect to many worthy Gentlemen, that came in our Ships,"and sought to replace him with a young man of better birth, "Master West, my Lord de la wars brother."[13]

Obviously, the colonists had their differences. In those differences, which elements resemble the lines drawn between Disney's Wingfield and Disney's Smith? Two of Smith's antagonists in 1609, Archer and Ratcliffe, described that conflict as clearly operating along class lines, setting "all the respected Gentlemen of worth in Virginia" in opposition to "this man," Smith, who they saw as allied with the sailors.[14] Yet there had been at least one other early focus for an animosity which was *not* so defined: Wingfield, the colony's first elected president, who came of a distinguished family and was the only one of eight signatories to Jamestown's charter actually to settle there. Smith's *True Relation* accused Wingfield of "hard dealing" and asserted that his ordering of the colony's affairs made him "generally hated of all."[15] We know of other men's accusations chiefly because Wingfield cites them defensively in his "Discourse": after Wingfield was deposed, Ratcliffe charged that he had denied him a knife, a chicken, and beer; Smith, that he had been insulted and given the lie; Martin, that Wingfield neglected governance to tend his meals, and had withheld provisions from Martin and his son. Chiefly, according to Wingfield, he was charged with "starving the colony" while he banqueted; other accusations included slander, atheism, conspiracy with Spain, and ambition to rule as king.[16]

Smith's most specific, repeated accusation was that Wingfield used his position to take a disproportionate share of the food, especially of the scarcer foods either perishable (beef and eggs) or non-renewable (oil and various alcoholic beverages). It was not just that Wingfield got more to eat: the accusation concerned not only what Wingfield ate but also with whom, consumption *and* distribution. Smith and others claimed Wingfield shared these reserved provisions with a small group variously described as servants, associates, or (more ambiguously) "his private": in other words, he fed his favorites. These charges were made against at least a perception of desperate shortage.[17] Smith attributed the colony's mortality to "want of victuall";[18] the colonists who complained against Wingfield remembered every spoonful of beer and penny knife denied them. (Knives were a useful medium of exchange with the Indians, who frequently did have food.) The provisions in question were not only familiar, valued sources of calories and nutritional variety, but also "Sack, Aquauitie, and other preseruatives for our health."[19] According to Wingfield's accusers, what were seen as medicinal provisions were being jealously kept from those who needed them; and further assertions that Wingfield "feasted," "banqueted," and "rioted" suggest he not only monopolized these medicinal liquors but also converted them to serve the ends of conspicuous consumption.

Yet unlike the returning colonists of 1609, who simply defended class privilege, Wingfield turned accusations of favoritism against the accusers, complaining that while "I neuer carryed any fauorite over with me, or intertayned any thear," the other councilors pestered him constantly to increase the food allowance for themselves "and for some sick *their* fauorites" (my italics).[20] The same was true for conspicuous consumption. While "the Master Presidentes and the Councellors spittes haue night & daie bene endaungered to break their backes so laden with swanns, geese, duckes, &c," Wingfield claimed, he himself "neuer had but one Squirrell roasted, whereof I gaue part to Master Ratcliff then sick; yet was that Squirell given me; I did never heate a flesh pott, but when the Comon pot was so vsed." Not only consuming frugally, he had also labored to increase the colony's food stores, and "mended the Common pott; hee had laid vp besides prouision for 3. weekes, wheate beforehand."[21]

It is also not the case that Wingfield simply opposed Smith. There was evidently animosity between them: Wingfield charged Smith with slanderously spreading the rumor "that I did feast myself and my servauntes, out of the Comon stoare," and reports that he was himself charged with slandering Smith, by saying that Smith concealed a planned mutiny, that he lied, and (in various versions) that although they might be equal in Virginia, Smith would be beneath his contempt at home.[22] Smith, as we have seen, made a number of allegations about Wingfield. Yet in Wingfield's text, Smith attracted nothing like the unalloyed animosity displayed towards Gabriel Archer, for instance; he notes that Smith was especially active in trading for corn, "which releued the Collony well," and that Archer and Gosnold were the only colonists capable of challenging his authority ("[Gosnold] could if he would; and the other...would if he could").[23] And when Wingfield defended his efforts to make men work, enhance the "common pot," and lay up stores of provisions, he adopted (at least rhetorically) some of the same strategies Smith would claim as his own in print.

If Smith himself "rioted," or kept favorites, the sources do not record it. We do know, however, of his friendship with someone whose behavior led to similar objections about food use and favoritism: the navigator Henry Hudson. Emanuel van Meteren speculates that Hudson was diverted from the northern passage search for which the Dutch had hired him in 1609, by "letters and maps which one Captain Smith had sent him from Virginia"; in these, Smith evidently indicated belief that a sea passage to Asia could be found in the latitude of Jamestown.[24] On Hudson's 1610 voyage, intended to search for a northwest passage to Asia, his crew mutinied, and left Hudson along with several other men adrift in an open boat in Hudson's Bay; all died. On examination, the surviving crew testified under oath that after a winter spent iced-in far to the south in Hudson's Bay, Hudson had been put out of the ship by the consent of its remaining healthy men, because he had "wasted victells by a scuttle made owte of his Cabin into the hold, and . . . Fedd his Favorites . . . which made those that weare not favored to give the Attempt and to performe it so violently."[25] We have only the testimony of the surviving mutineers to this specific allegation about Hudson's private access to food supplies, and the unequal rations given to his favorites. The records of the voyage, however, suggest Hudson had a tendency to exercise favoritism in ways that crossed the regular lines of rank and experience on shipboard, and this tendency had a powerful and disturbing effect on the ship's company.

One man – Henry Greene – had originally joined the expedition precisely as a recipient of Hudson's patronage. A young man of good birth whose bad habits had alienated his family and left him without means, he had been living in Hudson's house and was promised future employment by his means. Greene, described as unskilled at sea but "very inward with the master," came on board late, without the knowledge of the adventurers, and after an experienced Arctic navigator (Master Coleburne or Colbert) had been sent home. Greene's wages were to be paid (or not paid) out of Hudson's own pocket; some months into the voyage the two men came into conflict over a warm coat which Hudson initially agreed to let Greene have on credit, but subsequently gave to another man. Greene became one of the mutiny's two ringleaders. The man to whom Hudson gave the coat, Robert Bylot, had also been promoted by him in the course of the voyage to master's mate, replacing another experienced man who had fallen out with Hudson. This was only one of several times Hudson shifted the positions of master's mate and bosun, the most important positions on the ship after his own.[26] Bylot himself was subsequently replaced as mate with the ship's carpenter, because (according to survivors) "the master loved him"; the new mate's illiteracy left Hudson alone in possession of information about the ship's course, victualling accounts, and agreements, another source of grievance. The second of the mutiny's ringleaders (William Wilson) was among those promoted by Hudson in the course of the voyage.[27]

The men most bent against Hudson had both been touched by this shifting of favor. Hudson took and gave away positions which carried with them increased authority and higher wages; as things became more desperate, however, the power that really mattered was not the power of office, but the master's control over food and information, and the favor that mattered was measured in the extra rations rumored to be given to his favorites. The last days before the mutiny were filled with rumor over hidden provisions, inaccurate accounts, and the threat of violence in search of food. As starvation threatened, Hudson moved to assert a more absolute power, and those outside the inner circle rebelled in part for their own survival.[28]

The multiplying suspicions of the Hudson voyage about who had food, how much, and where, look not unlike what happened in Jamestown. There are two things we can take from these resemblances: first, practical men in positions of power might practice and be accused of practicing favoritism, and of "wasting" the common supply in ways not possible to the rest of the group; these were not vices specific to gentlemen. Second, what happened in Hudson's case had everything to do with the micro-politics of an under-provisioned ship iced-in far from home, and possibly very little to do with any other kinds of politics. If the conflicts in Jamestown remind us of social and political conflicts in England, in relation to which an American identity might trace its origins, we should remind ourselves to consider not only the context of home, but also an immediate colonial context of exigence and scarcity (real or perceived). In such a context, existing hierarchies might be remapped. Wasting provisions and feeding favorites wasn't only an assertion of hereditary class privilege, in its imitation of courtly behavior, but also a declaration that you were strong enough to survive, and to help your proponents to survive also – if necessary, at the expense of others. At least, that would be one way to think about Wingfield's accusations of hysterical over-consumption among the governing council, an appetite which he resisted for its potential actually to starve the colony. In parallel circumstances, Hudson gave way and simply apportioned all the ship's (official) remaining provisions among the men; some of the mutineers ate two weeks' rations in a day.

For more about Smith, we have to look beyond Jamestown, and to a part of his life which he described as preparation for the role he was to play there. Smith's autobio-graphical *True Travels* appeared in 1630, some sixteen years after he had returned to England from America for good; it begins with an account of Smith's adventures in Europe, Asia, and Africa during the years 1596–1605. The book matters here because Smith describes the events of *True Travels* as shaping what he did as a colonist, asserting that "the Warres in Europe, Asia, and Affrica, taught me how to subdue the wilde Salvages in Virginia and New-England, in America."[29] *True Travels* was Smith's own chosen account of self-formation.

Smith, a yeoman's son, left his apprenticeship at 16 or 17 to serve in the Netherlands and France. After peace was concluded in France, Smith returned home and found means to attach himself as a traveling companion to Peregrine Bertie, the younger son of Lord Willoughby, Baron Eresby – his family's landlord.[30] Soon after their arrival in France, the family dispensed with his services, providing passage money home; Smith went instead to Paris, where an acquaintance offered him letters of introduction to friends at the Scottish court of James VI. Smith delivered the letters, finding "kinde usage" but no means "to make him a Courtier"; he returned to Lincolnshire for an interval, and then to Europe again around 1600, with the twin aims to "see more of the world, and trie his fortune against the Turkes."[31]

The early parts of the account are confused, but the gist of it is that Smith's early years combined military service and more or less successful attempts at gaining aristocratic patronage. At least in the text's first chapter, the latter takes up more space (if less time) than the former. Smith's rambling journey towards the Turkish frontier – thick with tourism and adventurous incident – is repeatedly concerned with naming the "honourable persons" who were happy "to supply his wants": "the Lady Collumber, the Baron Larshan, the Lord Shasghe ... the Earle of Ployer ... Captaine la Roche."[32] Smith's autobiography suggests, to say the least, he did not look down on aristocratic patronage or on the position of being a client; in describing these contacts, he uses the naturalizing language of friendship and nurture. In Jamestown, he opposed a group who identified themselves as gentlemen; in his earlier life (and later autobiography), he aspired to connection precisely with that group.

Smith eventually arrived in Rome, where he called on Father Parsons, the famous English Jesuit, and wended his way eventually to Graz, where, perhaps through Parsons's intervention, another English or Irish Jesuit preferred him to a lord who in turn recommended him to Hans Khissl, Baron of Kaltenbrunn and general of the artillery under Arch-Duke Ferdinand. Smith soon found himself engaged along the Hungarian frontier. Here occurs one of the episodes in *True Travels* which (along with the narrator's enslavement to an enamored young Turkish woman) has occasioned the most comment from scholars: the challenge in which Smith claimed to have defeated three Turkish soldiers in single combat. As the Christian army prepared to besiege a town held by the Turks, a Turkish champion,

> to delight the Ladies, who did long to see some court-like pastime ... did defie any Captaine, that had the command of a Company, who durst combate with him for his head.

Smith was chosen by lot and, modestly clothed, met an opponent from the pages of romance:

> on his shoulders were fixed a paire of great wings, compacted of Eagles feathers within a ridge of silver, richly garnished with gold and precious stones, a Janizary before him, bearing his Lance, on each side another leading his horse.[33]

Smith defeated, killed, and decapitated not only the first but also two subsequent Turkish challengers. He won rich rewards: first, "a faire Horse richly furnished, a Semitere and belt worth three hundred ducats," and a promotion to regimental major; then, on the arrival of the Transylvanian prince, Zsigmond Báthory, Smith was granted a patent under Zsigmond's seal for "three Turkes heads in a shield for his Armes," the prince's picture in gold, and an annual pension of three hundred ducats.

This incident could not have happened in England. The Turks still fought with the lance, as travelers' accounts record, and single combat was practiced on the Transylvanian frontier; further to the west, mounted combat with the lance was an archaism, living on in the fictionalized form of the Accession Day tilts, in which richly accoutred courtiers took on personae out of medieval chivalric romance and jousted before audiences to honor Queen Elizabeth's accession to the throne. No longer a viable military technique, jousting in England was restricted to those whose social position gave them access to courtly pastime and whose means permitted them to engage in its costly display. Smith would have thus been doubly debarred. Yet he had in fact practiced riding with a lance, alone in the Lincolnshire woods, as the first chapter of *True Travels* records; a contemporary riding manual gave detailed instructions to those like Smith who wished to practice the skills of tilting by riding at the ring, a practice detached from the public and courtly venue of the tournament to become a form of popular as well as aristocratic recreation.[34]

It is as if by going east, Smith had remobilized not only the forms of chivalry (weaponry, ritual, individual prowess) but also its subtext, that arms and ennoblement go together: he returned home with money, rank, and a coat of arms. Smith's exploits were not absolutely *unlikely*, as some have charged; they were, however, unusual both socially and chronologically. Critics who talk about Smith's chivalry often see it as disturbingly out of place – temporally, socially, generically, culturally. It has been read as anachronistic, parodic, mendacious and self-glorifying, deviant, un-English and un-American. Smith's contemporaries themselves were richly aware of the dissonances inherent in Smith's chivalric practice.

True Travels appeared hard on the heels of an anonymously published poem titled *The Legend of Captain Jones*, which it was perhaps intended to preempt as a public account of Smith's life. (The prefatory material to *True Travels* strongly suggests Smith's life was also the subject of a stage play at one of the more lowbrow theaters.) The poem narrates the adventures of a titular hero who, like Smith in publishing his own life story, "At once both made and writ all Chivalrie." Jones performs a variety of Herculean or merely Gargantuan feats, turning lions inside out and farting into a ship's sail to get it moving; in between, he has his cabin boy read him medieval romances of English worthies and their deeds. No wonder he goes willingly to battle with the Spaniards: "better fate in this designe he wisht not, Then to cope single with their great *Don Quixot*." When he visits the court of Prester John, that prince worries that "Jones might so far on his owne strength presume, as / To seize his throne, as Cortez Montezuma's / Had done before."[35] The *Legend* neatly captures several linked properties of Smith's persona in *True Travels*: his self-promotion; the outsize scale of his adventures; the romance influences on his narrative; the vulgarity or class transgression which led him to imitate a feudal aristocracy he had encountered only in books; and the appeal for Smith of a Spanish chivalry exemplified by the two examples of Hernán Cortés and Don Quixote. (The conquistadors, like Smith and Quixote himself, were avid readers of romance.)[36]

Recall that the governor of Disney's Jamestown advocated imitating the Spanish. Spain had a particular resonance for Englishmen in the early seventeenth century. Though James I made peace with Spain in 1605 (and again in 1631), the Spanish were economic, religious, and political competitors, who had been poised to invade England only a few decades earlier; popular literature reviled the Spanish ambassador as a Machiavellian corrupter of the English court. The historical Wingfield was in fact accused of Spanish sympathies, an accusation he denied: "It is noised that I Combyned with the Spanniards to the distruccion of the Collony."[37] Both Smith and Wingfield associated Spain with the quest for American gold, prosecuted so successfully in the Americas. In a letter both signed, they begged the Virginia Council in London to send reinforcements lest "that all devouringe Spaniard lay his ravenous hands upon theas gold-showing mountaines."[38] Smith repeatedly mocked the colonists' search for gold in Jamestown, even when it had been mandated by the Virginia Company. He suggests in the *Proceedings* that some readers may be disappointed, because the colonists have neither massacred the natives "as did the Spaniards," nor filled their reports with

> relations of heaps, and mines of gold and silver, nor such rare commodities as the Portugals and Spanish found in the East and west Indies. The want whereof hath begot us . . . no less scorne and contempt, then their noble conquests and valiant adventures (beautified with it) praise and honor. Too much I confesse the world cannot attribute to their ever memorable merit.[39]

Here, the Spanish are first cruel, and then successful; those who criticize English colonists for not following the Spanish example are misinformed – yet that example deserves the highest praise. Smith's ambivalence here is resolved elsewhere: he admired some Spaniards a good deal. In a passage which Smith's habit of repetition caused to see print three separate times, he praises the "memorable attempts" of Hernán Cortés, Francisco Pizarro, and Ferdinand de Soto, and asks rhetorically what keeps his readers from "imitating the worthinesse of their brave spirits that advanced themselves from poore Souldiers to great Captaines, their posterity to great Lords, their King to be one of the greatest Potentates on earth."[40] Insofar as being a "Spanish" colonist meant looking for gold above all else, Smith was evidently against it. Insofar as imitating the Spanish meant that a soldier might achieve incredible upward mobility by winning a colonial empire, however, Smith was a proponent, and he suggests that reading the Spanish relations carefully should instruct those who expected immediate wealth.

True Travels shows us a Smith whose models and influences were extremely diverse, more so than can be adequately represented here. As a sample, I have singled out Smith's chivalry, as a nostalgic, neo-medieval imitation of a feudal aristocracy; his related admiration for conquistadors like Cortés, whose colonial practice was imbued with a complicated set of ideas about chivalry, romance, and horsemanship; and his (literally) catholic search for patronage, to the extent of seeking out the most famous and feared of English Jesuit priests. If we were simply interested in Smith, these elements in his autobiographical writing would certainly recalibrate understandings of his character. But they also bear more than a passing resemblance to larger facts about the colonial scene.

Spanish Jesuits had preceded English colonists in the Chesapeake; if they were no longer there in 1607, they would have been within the experience of many living Algonquians who were Jamestown's neighbors, a presence in the matrix of colonial encounter.[41] Moreover, Virginia would soon have an English Catholic and quasi-feudal neighbor to the north; George Calvert had invested in the Virginia Company as early as 1609, and by the 1620s was financing settlements on the east coast of Newfoundland, finally going there himself before concluding that Newfoundland's winters were too harsh for the settlement he had intended. Calvert's plan for a quasi-feudal plantation had a genealogy reaching back several decades, to Sir Thomas Gerard's proposals for an Irish plantation in 1569, and Sir Humphrey Gilbert's projects of the early 1580s – both of these projectors also imagined creating a place to which English Catholics might emigrate.[42] (Calvert had converted to Catholicism in the 1620s, and resigned as secretary of state in 1625, when he was created Baron Baltimore.) Avalon, Calvert's colony in Newfoundland, was chartered in 1623, and Calvert settled there with his family and at least one Catholic priest in 1628. After many colonists died of scurvy the first winter, Calvert returned by way of Virginia, where (although as a Catholic he was not permitted to land) he saw the possibilities offered by a more congenial setting. His son Cecilius succeeded after his father's death in having their rights transferred to what is now Maryland, and Maryland – like Avalon, the earlier Calvert colony in Newfoundland – was chartered virtually as an independent principality under Calvert as hereditary lord proprietor. Two Jesuit priests were among the first colonists in 1633.[43] Smith's autobiography, while not connected either to the Spanish priests who preceded him, or to the Maryland colonists who came after, might serve to remind us of both.

I began with the image of two early Southern colonists in symbolic opposition, and have attempted through a survey of sources to suggest that the terms of that opposition leave a good deal out. The importance of that omitted material can be suggested by the history of other readers' responses. Later detractors criticized Smith for precisely the qualities identified in this essay, a reception which may trace its pedigree to the Civil War; in 1867, Henry Adams went after Smith as a way of attacking "the Virginia Aristocracy."[44] In nineteenth-century America, the Smith of *True Travels* may have been unacceptable on more than the grounds of his own mendacity or the evil deeds of later Virginians. Walt Whitman's *Democratic Vistas* (1871) called for a general purging of chivalric romance from the national imaginary, in order to inaugurate a truly American literature. The figure I have described posed a threat to national identity, either by exemplifying a cultural dependence on England and on the past, which might disrupt the development of American cultural forms (Whitman); or by exemplifying the characteristics of a region which had broken with national norms (Adams). This Hispanic or chivalric character has been identified more generally as what distinguished the deviant, regressive Southern colonies as distinct from the Northern, Puritan ones taken to form the core of an American identity.[45]

If Smith was tainted with neo-medieval chivalry, with vulgar social climbing, with Catholic associations and Spanish longings, what then becomes of that proto-American identity which emerged so readily from a scene where such characteristics were projected onto his antagonist? Disney's history goes some way towards shaping Southern colonial history in the mold of Northern colonial history, as involving a reaction against the corruption or impurity of English values. Peter Hulme writes: "New England has a complex history but it has always been possible in retrospect to see it as having a coherence denied to Virginia": a coherence organized by Puritanism and by an opposition between "civilization and savagery."[46] But perhaps that incoherence presents us with an opportunity to remember, not only that the Spanish came first, but also that English implantation itself in the future United States *was* Catholic, or Anglican, or feudal, or all of these, as well as Protestant and covenanted.

In a sense, to look back at the Spanish presence in the Chesapeake, the feudal organization of Maryland, or the idea of making America a refuge for English Catholics, is to focus on national, political, and religious factors which did not become central parts of a colonial American identity. But America is no longer (if it ever was) a Puritan commonwealth. Smith can remind us of the heterogeneity of our colonial origins, through an apparent incoherence which is not a deviation so much as the model for another kind of national memory, acknowledging the shaping role of other times, other places, other politics, and other peoples. Perhaps the exemplary history of early Jamestown, in this way, can offer this present America something of use.

In closing, I would like to offer an anecdote about Southern origins, which is also an anecdote about historical memory. Early in 2001, you might have found yourself stuck in rush-hour traffic in what until fairly recently was a sleepy country town in Georgia. At the intersection I have in mind, you might have noticed a newly posted sign pointing south towards the historical downtown. Yet if you took the other direction, after a mile or so you would have seen — not an uncommon sight — a brick chimney rising out of a field.

This chimney belonged to a house built some hundred years ago by the family that lived in it, first as a two-room log cabin, growing to include a back kitchen, outbuildings, a second floor, and eventually the pillared facade which movies have taught us should decorate a Southern house. The oldest rooms had ceilings decorated with lamp-blacking, and hand-hewn mantlepieces. Thirteen children were born there. Some of them remembered their childhood as unending work, others as work they were glad to do. Most of their own children grew up visiting their grandparents' house and remembered it; so that even years later, after it had been sold, rented, finally left vacant and vandalized, and after the land had been divided by a highway, by inheritance and sale and development, you could see along with them where businesses had replaced pine trees, growing where there had been grapes, which had taken over from cotton — just as, in the house, you could brush aside bushes and walk in, through the front windows, into vacant rooms which kept the visible and invisible traces of one country family's life over the better part of a century.

This house burned down when the historical marker went up. The coincidence cautions anyone who would want to write (or read) about the past. It might suggest, for instance, that the prosperity and population growth which lead to the creation of marked historical districts also ensure that abandoned farmhouses will be burned down. More broadly, it might also remind a writer, or a reader, that historical narratives (including this one) come into being partly by displacing other possible narratives. The long-ago sale of that land went towards a great-grandchild's tuition fees at universities in the North, licensing – directly and indirectly – this essay. But the local informant I know best saw things differently, watching her parents' house decay from a suburban bungalow across the street. Born into the lingering memories of Reconstruction, she saw little but good in the concrete and symbolic value which the expansion of the late nineties brought to her corner of the South. This is not the way she would have told this story – but I tell it *as* I can, because I can, for her.

For R. B. F., 1902–1999

Notes

Much of the research for this essay was conducted at the John Carter Brown Library and the Folger Library, with support from the National Endowment for the Humanities – gratefully acknowledged here. For contributing to my understanding of history, I would also like to thank Ellen Coleman, Julia Crawford, Tommy Joyce Davis, and Billie Crenshaw.

1   Wesley Frank Craven, *The Southern Colonies in the Seventeenth Century, 1607–1689* (Baton Rouge: Louisiana State University Press, 1949), p. xiii.

2   Several distinguished scholars of colonial history have made important arguments on Jamestown and Roanoke as defining influences on later developments in the region; see, for instance, the early chapters of R. B. Davis, *Intellectual Life in the Colonial South* (Knoxville: University of Tennessee Press, 1978) and (for a more negative perspective) Sacvan Bercovitch, *The Puritan Origins of the American Self* (New Haven, CT: Yale University Press, 1975), pp. 136–43. Craven, while noting that Jamestown itself proved not to be "anything more than an unfortunate choice of the first planters," writes: "when we of the South return today to the site of old Jamestown, there to stand in the tower of the brick church . . . or to walk over the foundations of the first Statehouse . . . it is to think of some of the first men and influences to give shape to a Southern way of life" (*Southern Colonies*, pp. 132, 182). At a more local level, although most of the earliest Virginia colonists either died or left, my own workplace boasts direct or collateral descendants of both Thomas Savage and John Rolfe.

3   Ratcliffe took office after Wingfield was deposed; details can be found below.

4   Philip Barbour, Smith's editor and biographer, describes Wingfield as "the stubborn maintainer of social levels" on the expedition, who had Smith arrested "because he lacked 'proper respect' for Wingfield." He characterizes the heart of their quarrel as the opposed beliefs (on Smith's part) that their shared office and "the forest and the Indians that surrounded them made them . . . equal" and (on Wingfield's part) that "nothing could make them equal, since God and English social structure had ordained it otherwise." See Philip Barbour, *The Three Worlds of Captain John Smith* (London: Macmillan, 1964), pp. 114, 148. As an example of *Pocahontas'* quasi-historical details: Percy,

Ratcliffe's pet, was named for a prominent colonist: George Percy, the Duke of Northumberland's brother. (One of his accounts of the colony is cited below.) Numerous similar examples could be given.

5   See Smith, *The Proceedings of the English Colony in Virginia* (London, 1612), reprinted in Philip Barbour (ed.), *The Complete Works of Captain John Smith*, 3 vols. (Chapel Hill: University of North Carolina Press for the Institute of Early American History, 1986), I, pp. 206–7 (subsequent references to *Works*); and George Percy, "Observations gathered out of a Discourse of the Plantation of the Southerne Colonie in Virginia by the English," in Samuel Purchas, *Hakluytus Posthumus or Purchas his Pilgrimes* (London, 1625; reprinted Glasgow, 1906), XVIII, p. 404 (subsequent references to *Pilgrimes*).

6   "A relatyon of the Discovery of our River," Document 13, Philip Barbour (ed.), *The Jamestown Voyages Under the First Charter 1606–1609*, 2 vols., Works published for the Hakluyt Society, 2nd series 136–7 (Cambridge: Cambridge University Press, 1969), I, pp. 96–7. Barbour attributes this text to Gabriel Archer.

7   Percy, "Observations," p. 418.

8   Percy, "Observations," p. 145; Edward Maria Wingfield, "Discourse," Document 34, *Jamestown Voyages* I, p. 222.

9   Smith, *True Relation, Works* I, p. 41; Wingfield, "Discourse," p. 224.

10 "Discourse," p. 228.

11 Smith, *Proceedings, Works* I, p. 229.

12 Ibid, p. 233.

13 Gabriel Archer, letter dated August 31, 1609, Document 53, *Jamestown Voyages* II, p. 282.

14 Ibid, pp. 282–3; John Ratcliffe to Lord Salisbury, letter dated October 4, 1609, Document 54, *Jamestown Voyages* II, p. 284.

15 Smith, *True Relation, Works* I, p. 35.

16 Wingfield, "Discourse," pp. 219–20, 223.

17 Carville V. Earle, "Environment, Disease, and Mortality in Early Virginia," in *The Cheseapeake in the Seventeenth Century: Essays on Anglo-American Society*, ed. Thad W. Tate and David L. Ammerman (New York: Norton, 1979), pp. 96–125, has persuasively argued that mortality at Jamestown was due more to bad water than to nutritional deficiency. As early a colonist as George Percy understood the effects on health of drinking water "at a floud very salt, at a low tide full of slime and filth" ("Observations," p. 144).

18 *True Relation, Works* I, p. 33.

19 Ibid.

20 Wingfield, "Discourse," pp. 221, 216.

21 Ibid, pp. 223, 218.

22 Ibid, pp. 220, 223, 231.

23 Ibid, p. 223. See p. 228 for more comments about Archer.

24 *Commentarien Ofte Memorien*, excerpted as Document 52, *Jamestown Voyages* II, p. 274.

25 "Examination of the survivors of the *Discovery* on behalf of Trinity House," in *New American World: A Documentary History of North America to 1612*, ed. David B. Quinn, 5 vols. (New York: Arno Press and Hector Bye, 1979), IV, p. 294.

26 The master's mate was the first officer of the ship after the master (or captain); the bosun has charge of the ship's sails, rigging, anchors, and cables – the propulsion system of a sailing ship – and of daily work on deck.

27 Accounts of the voyage can be found in *Pilgrimes*, XIII; depositions by survivors are printed in Quinn, *New American World*, IV.

28 It should be noted that any knowledge of the voyage is necessarily based almost exclusively on survivors' accounts, with the exception of Hudson's log (which survives in incomplete form), and a note left by Thomas Woodhouse; both are printed in Purchas, *Pilgrimes*.

29   Smith, *Advertisements for the unexperienced Planters of New England, Works* III, p. 269.

30   Barbour (*Three Worlds*, pp. 86–7) speculates about a network of marriage and cousinage linking the Bertie, Wingfield, and Gosnold families; he proposes these connections as a way Smith might have become associated with Gosnold, and hence with the Jamestown venture.

31   *True Travels, Works* III, pp. 155, 157.

32   Ibid, pp. 158–9.

33   Ibid, p. 172.

34   Gervase Markham, *Caualerice, or The English Horseman* (London, 1607). On the obsolescence of the lance, see Geoffrey Parker, *The Military Revolution: Military Innovation and the Rise of the West, 1500–1800* (Cambridge: Cambridge University Press, 1988).

35   [David Lloyd], *The Legend of Captain Jones* (London, 1659), A5r, pp. 10, 57. *Legend* first appeared in 1631. For the argument that it targets Smith, see Alden T. Vaughan, "John Smith Satirized: *The Legend of Captain Jones*," *William and Mary Quarterly* 45 (1988).

36   On the reading habits of the conquistadors, see Irving Leonard, *Books of the Brave: Being an Account of Books and of Men in the Spanish Conquest and Settlement of the Sixteenth-Century New World* (Cambridge, MA: Harvard University Press, 1949).

37   Wingfield, "Discourse," p. 229.

38   Letter dated June 22, 1607, Document 12, *Jamestown Voyages* I, pp. 79–80.

39   *Proceedings, Works* I, p. 257.

40   Smith, *Description of New England, Works* I, pp. 328–9.

41   See Carl Bridenbaugh, "Opechancanough: A Native American Patriot," *Early Americans* (New York: Oxford University Press, 1981), pp. 5–49.

42   For a concise discussion which traces the intertwined history of feudal land grants in the English colonies (in Ireland, Newfoundland, Norumbega, and Maryland) and emigration schemes involving the English Catholic gentry, see David B. Quinn, "Introduction: Prelude to Maryland," in *Early Maryland in a Wider World*, ed. David Quinn (Detroit, MI: Wayne State University Press, 1988), pp. 11–29.

43   For further information, see Russell R. Menard and Lois Greene Carr, "The Lords Baltimore and the Colonization of Maryland," *Early Maryland*, ed. David Quinn, pp. 167–215; and Luca Codignola, *The Coldest Harbor in the Land* (Kingston and Montreal: McGill/Queen's University Press, 1988).

44   See Henry Adams, "Captain John Smith," *North American Review* 104 (1867). Adams's letter to John Gorham Palfrey, March 30, 1862, is cited in J. Leo Lemay, *The American Dream of Captain John Smith* (Charlottesville: University Press of Virginia), p. 8.

45   Bercovitch, *Puritan Origins*, pp. 137–9, esp. p. 139.

46   Peter Hulme, *Colonial Encounters: Europe and the Native Caribbean 1492–1797* (New York: Methuen, 1986), p. 139.

3

Slave Narratives

Jerry Phillips

Reader, be assured this narrative is no fiction. I am aware that some of my adventures may seem incredible; but they are, nevertheless, true.

(Jacobs 1999: 540)

A negro's word was not taken against a white man's in the days of slavery.

(Stroyer 1968: 74)

In *Life and Labor in the Old South*, Ulrich Bonnell Phillips (1963: 219) concluded: "ex-slave narratives in general . . . were issued with so much abolitionist editing that as a class their authenticity is doubtful." According to Phillips, the propagandistic qualities of the slave narratives make them dubious historical sources; they are best viewed as partisan fictions. That slave narratives were abolitionist propaganda, that they often made use of literary devices, is not to be denied. However, in the antebellum period, when the slave narrative came into its own as a distinct literary genre, the narratives were typically written and read as discourses of truth, even as that truth was stranger than fiction. The best of the slave narratives were regarded, by some readers, as not only faithful depictions of the antebellum South, but also as powerful commentaries on certain aspects of the human condition.

For example, in his introduction to the *Narrative of the Life and Adventures of Henry Bibb* (1849), Lucius Matlack reflected that although American slavery is "Naturally and necessarily, the enemy of literature, it has become the prolific theme of much that is profound in argument, sublime in poetry, and thrilling in narrative" (Osofsky: 1969: 5). In a review essay from 1849, Ephraim Peabody pronounced the narratives "among the most remarkable productions of the age, – remarkable as being pictures of slavery by the slave, remarkable as disclosing under a new light the mixed elements of American civilization, and not less remarkable as a vivid exhibition of the force and working of the native love of freedom in the individual mind" (1985: 19). As these evaluations suggest, slave narratives were conceived and received as political propaganda and literary art, social history and moral philosophy. To be sure, individual narratives vary in their emphases: some are self-consciously literary in their structure and style, others are sub-literary in the flatness of their narrative voice; some stay close to the task of factually describing plantation society, others are more philosophical, as the ex-slave ponders what is peculiarly human about human beings in the light of her former status as chattel property. But all the narratives share a rhetoric of truth, a rhetoric of witness testimony; and all claim the moral authority to correct "the pictures of slavery" given in proslavery arguments. One can account for the mixed character of the slave narrative, its blending of art and propaganda, fact and value, by attending to the cultural matrix in which the narratives were written and read.

The term "slave narrative" covers both dictated and self-authored testimonies of the African-American experience of human bondage. Slave narratives were published from the early eighteenth century until the mid-twentieth century, when former slaves provided a wealth of historical information to interviewers employed by the Federal Writers Project. However, "the golden age of the slave narrative," as Frances Foster (1979: 61) terms it, was clearly the period between 1830 and 1865, from the rise of immediate abolitionism to the close of the Civil War. The analysis of slave narratives offered in this essay mostly applies to "golden age" works, because it was during this period that the slave narrative reached its zenith as a literary form.

Slave narratives were deeply implicated in the strife between the sections, to the degree that they challenged the normative status of chattel slavery within American society. As Peabody wrote, "These biographies of fugitive slaves are calculated to exert a very wide influence on public opinion" (1985: 20). An anonymous reviewer in 1849 stated the matter very clearly: "This fugitive slave literature is destined to be a powerful lever...We see in it the easy and infallible means of abolitionizing the Free States" (1985: 28). Many of the narratives were published under the auspices of antislavery societies; these societies also played a key role in disseminating the narratives at antislavery meetings and lectures, at bookstalls, churches and by subscription. "The everyday life of a slave on one of our southern plantations...is generally little known at the North," observed Josiah Henson (1999: 727) in 1849. Fugitive slaves at the North were regarded by abolitionists as authorities on the slave system; indeed, as Dickson Bruce points out, they made these figures "the most visible symbols of the abolitionist cause" (2001: 213). In short, the fugitive slave became the literal embodiment of what Austin Steward called "antislavery truth" (1969: 190).

Abolitionists assumed that the audience for the slave narratives was Northern, white, reform-minded and religious, but potentially susceptible to proslavery values, especially racism. The abolitionists conceived of the audience as a latent moral force, because, in their view, it was the only remaining constituency in the United States that was really able to move on the slavery question. Hence Wendell Phillips's claim that "Northern opinion...is the real slaveholder in America" (1891: 21). Phillips was adamant "it is in the power of Northern opinion to say to slavery, cease – and it ceases"

(22). This faith in the communicative and transformative power of antislavery speech informs the texture of the slave narrative.

The ideal scenario wherein the communicative power of personal testimony moves the reader inexorably in the direction of antislavery truth, thereby revolutionizing public opinion, is described by William Lloyd Garrison in his preface to the *Narrative of the Life of Frederick Douglass* (1845). Garrison writes of hearing Douglass lecture at an antislavery convention: "I shall never forget his first speech . . . – the extraordinary emotion it excited in my own mind – the powerful impression it created upon a crowded auditory . . . I think I never hated slavery as intensely as at that moment" (Douglass 1999: 530). Garrison immediately understood that Douglass's rhetorical skills would lend a "powerful impetus" to both "the anti-slavery enterprise" and attempts to counteract "northern prejudice against a colored complexion" (531). As Marion Starling notes, "The abolitionists were ever alert to discover potential speakers among newly arrived slaves fleeing from the South to hoped-for freedom in the North. Those who showed capability for public speaking were encouraged to try out their skills in a slave narrative, usually following a definite form" (1988: xxvi).

Garrison's response to Douglass's voice points to the major concern of the slave narrative as a form of testimonial literature: the desire of the writer or the amanuensis to make the narrative voice the means by which the reader identifies with the slave. The key value here is the power of sympathy, the capacity to imagine another's pain as one's own. "He who can peruse [Douglass's *Narrative*] without a tearful eye," exclaimed Garrison, "must have a flinty heart and be qualified to act the part of a trafficker 'in slaves and the souls of men'" (532). Garrison's moral absolutism must be understood in the context of what John Beverley calls the "truth-effect" of the testimonial, for testimonials produce "if not the real then certainly a sensation of experiencing the real" (1993: 83). The reader's vicarious experience of the whips, chains, and thumbscrews of slavery will, in Garrison's view, suffice to show him or her that systems of human bondage are inherently cruel and sinful.

The testimonial structure of the slave narrative, with its sentimental rhetoric of bearing witness, was formed in direct opposition to proslavery canons of thought. Slave narratives ideologically engaged four kinds of proslavery apologia: plantation romances like John Pendleton Kennedy's *Swallow Barn* (1832), which celebrated the South in pastoral terms; conservative and reactionary philosophies like John Calhoun's "positive good" theory of slavery, which defended the plantation regime as the ideal solution to the class struggle between capital and labor; theological dissertations like Thornton Stringfellow's *A Brief Examination of Scripture Testimony on the Institution of Slavery* (1841), which argued slavery was God's plan for the uplift of heathen Africans; and finally, ethnological treatises, such as Samuel Cartwright's work on negro physiology, which asserted blacks were adapted by nature to serve the superior white race. As regards proslavery literary works, the ex-slave Solomon Northup mused: "Men may write fictions portraying lowly-life as it is, or as it is not . . . [But let] them know the heart of the poor slave . . . and they will find [that slaves] cherish in their bosoms the love of freedom, as passionately as themselves" (1999: 254–5). As regards reactionary political philosophy, Charles Ball opined: "such is the natural relation of master and slave . . . that no cordiality of feeling can ever exist between them" (1999: 424). In response to proslavery theology, Milton Clarke averred: "God has given every man the title-deed to himself, written upon his face" (Clarke and Clarke 1999: 645). And with respect to proslavery ethnology, Austin Steward reflected that "both the time and the talents of eminent men have been wasted in unsuccessful research for the line of demarkation between the African and the highest order of animals – such for instance as the monkey or Orang-Outang" (1969: 107). The sheer range of proslavery writings, their defense of King Cotton on all possible grounds, made the slave narrative something more, and less, than autobiography: more, in the sense that the experiences of the individual slave are allegedly representative of an oppressed race; less, in the sense that we learn more about the sociology of the slave system than we do about the inner life of a unique individual.

As the slavery controversy deepened, the secessionist ideal of a Southern nation, built on the edifice of slavery, began to take hold in certain strata of white Southern society. Concomitant with the development of Southern nationalism was the call for a distinctively Southern literature. If the South would prevail in the court of "public opinion," then "It is all important that we should write our own books," advised George Fitzhugh (1981: 279), the proslavery theorist from Virginia. The South had no choice but to defend itself with a literature of its own because, as one writer noted in *De Bow's Review*, "The pure stream of literature has been corrupted by the turbid waters of Abolition" (cited in Hubbell 1940: 194). Slave narratives were the corner-stone of abolitionist literature, and their widespread popularity incited Southern writers to make the case anew for the South. Indeed, so effective was the slave narrative in presenting "pictures of slavery by the slave" that apologists for the peculiar institution felt it necessary, on at least one occasion, to publish and promote a proslavery slave narrative, *Slavery and Abolition as Viewed by a Georgia Slave* (1861). The title page describes the author, Harrison Berry, as "The property of S. W. Price, Covington, Georgia." Berry testifies to the beneficent aspects of his enslavement, his freedom from the want, misery, and cruelty that allegedly characterize the lot of the free laborer, and particularly the lot of the free negro. Berry's sole concern throughout his narrative is to berate "the fanatical Abolitionists" whose agitations disrupt the harmonious relationship between master and slave, to the real detriment of the latter. The very existence of Berry's narrative proves that Southern nationalists felt that the claims of the slave narrative, at the bar of public opinion, could not go unanswered. To the extent that the nationalists criticized the genre from within, they implicitly conceded that slave narratives had real cultural force.

When the former slave John Thompson criticized Nehemiah Adams's *South-Side View of Slavery* (1854) for painting slavery in "glowingly beautiful colors" (1999: 441), he pointed to the overlap between antislavery and proslavery discourses. The slave narrative and the proslavery apology were antagonistically bound together in what M. M. Bakhtin calls a "social dialogue" (1981: 276). According to Bakhtin, "any concrete discourse (utterance) finds the object at which it is directed already as it were overlain with qualifications, open to dispute, charged with value" (276). To speak of an object is to contest or confirm the meanings it has already been given; moreover, it is also to anticipate what might be said of that object in the future, for, as Bakhtin puts it, "All rhetorical forms . . . are oriented toward the listener and his answer" (280). A complex of voices and value judgments attends the use of any word (what Bakhtin calls "heteroglossia") and this has the effect of making the objects of words highly volatile in their meaning. Bakhtin's theory provides useful insights into the stylistics of the slave narrative, the degree to which its formal qualities are determined by dialogic pressures.

The war of words between antislavery and proslavery writers took place as a war over the practical meaning of certain keywords like master, slave, black, white, happiness, kindness, cruelty, freedom, Christian, and American. Slave narratives were written on the assumption that their audience might have accepted the proslavery meanings assigned these words. Hence the lament of the ex-slave John Brown: "I do not think people know what slavery means." In order to clarify the real meaning of slavery, the ex-slaves attempted to negate the heteroglossia surrounding keywords, and, in the same gesture, establish the authentic moral power and truth-value of the black narrative voice. For example, consider the social dialogue surrounding the word "master" in the antebellum period. In proslavery discourse, the master is one who occupies towards the slave "the place of parent or guardian" (Fitzhugh 1960a: 89). However, in the slave narratives the word "master" carries very different connotations. In Douglass's *Narrative* it signifies one who is a "demon," a "robber," a "pirate," a man-stealer, a woman-whipper, and cradle-plunderer. In short, master essentially translates as sinner – and this singular meaning Douglass intends as a refutation of any attempt to assign saintly qualities to the planters. On occasion, the narratives will invert the usual meaning of master, so that the word connotes submission to sin rather than control of oneself and others. As Douglass puts it in *My Bondage and My Freedom* (1855): "The slave is a subject, subjected by others; the slaveholder is a subject, but he is the author of his own subjection" (1969: 105).

If the word "master" had no clear object, then the word "slave" was equally controversial. Proslavery writers attempted to link the meaning of the word "slave" to the values of happiness and contentment, as when James Hammond wrote, "I believe our slaves are the happiest three millions of human beings on whom the sun shines." Fitzhugh went a step further than Hammond when he argued: "The negro slaves of the South are the happiest, and, in some sense, the freest people in the world" (1960b: 18). In contrast to such utopian projections, the slave narratives associate the word "slave" with oppression, emasculation, suffering, unhappiness, despair, drudgery, dishonor, sexual exploitation, and enforced ignorance. For Frederick Douglass, the word "slave" conveyed to his mind "a sense of my entire dependence on the will of [another]" (1969: 45). For Lewis Clarke, it signified one who is "not permitted to open his mouth," but who must remain dumb like "a sheep before her shearers" (Clarke and Clarke 1999: 615). A vital keyword in the social dialogue between slave narratives and proslavery discourse was the term "family."

Proslavery writers contended that the slaveholder was the symbolic patriarch of an extended plantation family of both blacks and whites. However, the slave narratives made no greater charge against the plantation system than the claim that it habitually destroyed slave families, and thus violated God-given ties of sentimental attachment. What Mary P. Ryan calls "the convergence of domesticity and politics" (1982: 137) in the antebellum period was nowhere more evident than in the slavery debate. In language drawn from the sentimental novel, slave narratives capitalized on the moral force of the cult of domesticity by invariably describing painful scenes of slave family separation. (This convention was adopted by Harriet Beecher Stowe in *Uncle Tom's Cabin*.)

The phenomenological tendency of the slave narratives, as meditations on the nature of experience, is always to move from the meaning of slavery to the meaning of freedom. "It is a mistaken opinion," wrote Solomon Northup, "that the slave does not understand the term – does not comprehend the idea of freedom" (1969: 278). Frederick Douglass developed his understanding of "the idea of freedom" through active inquiry into the meaning of the word "abolition." Douglass relates: "the dictionary afforded me little or no help. I found it 'the act of abolishing': but then I did not know what was to be abolished" (1969: 555). The uselessness of the dictionary confirms Bakhtin's thesis that "A passive understanding of linguistic meaning is no understanding at all, it is only the abstract aspect of meaning" (1981: 281). Douglass learns that slavery is the object of abolition only after he has grasped the manner in which the words abolition and abolitionist are employed in actual utterances by Southern whites. He discerns that the words carry negative associations in the minds of white Southerners, and this is because (he deduces) they have something to do with the social status of blacks. Douglass eventually recognizes that the concept of abolition holds positive value in relation to his own situation: he restores to the word what Bakhtin calls its "dialogic orientation" (1991: 275), the sense in which its meaning in a given community is a matter for dispute.

In the composition of their narratives, all the ex-slaves are essentially involved in the project described by J. W. Pennington: to free their minds from ideological captivity by extinguishing proslavery values in their language. "It cost me two years' hard labor, after I fled," wrote Pennington, "to unshackle my mind; it was three years before I had purged my language of slavery's idioms" (1999: 141). The rhetoric of freedom which replaces "slavery's idioms" gives rise to the lyrical aspect of the slave narratives. Consider this passage from William Parker's "The Freedman's Story" (1866):

> How shall I describe my first experience of free life? Nothing can be greater than the contrast it affords to a plantation experience, under the suspicious and vigilant eye of a mercenary overseer or a watchful master. Day and night are not more alike. The mandates of Slavery are like leaden sounds, sinking with a dead weight into the very soul, only to deaden and destroy. The impulse of freedom lends wings to the feet, buoys up the spirit within, and the fugitive catches glorious glimpses of light through rifts and seams in the accumulated ignorance of his years of oppression. (Parker 1999: 753)

Parker's use of hyperbole ("nothing can be greater"), simile ("like leaden sounds"), alliteration ("deaden and destroy"), internal rhyme ("leaden/deaden") and metaphor ("freedom lends wings to the feet") clearly shows the literary aspirations of the black narrative voice. By playing off light against darkness and dead weight against airiness, Parker conveys the transcendent quality of the fugitive's journey from South to North: he makes the horizontal movement through quotidian space the symbolic equivalent of a vertical journey from earth to heaven. And by linking enlightenment to self-possession, he alludes to the Transcendentalist canard that autonomous selfhood leads to the experience of the divine within.

The slave narrative's message that freedom is a transcendent value can be viewed as incontrovertible evidence of the human drive towards independence. However, this existential motive is always historically situated in a given political world, and thus "the problem of freedom," as Orlando Patterson (1982: 341) terms it, the question of what it consists in and how one approaches and secures it, is always a problem of the appropriate social identity, the degree to which it can be readily attained. The slave narratives typically explore the dialectic between freedom and slavery through their treatment of the social meaning of race.

The political ideal of the narratives is to create identity between the words American, Christian, and Negro. So much antebellum law and custom made the phrases "African-American citizen" or "African-American Christian" something like logical fallacies: for it was commonly assumed among white Americans that blacks were without God, and, as inferior beings, they were not to be counted within the constitutional compact of American society. Such reasoning reached its apogee in the infamous Dred Scott decision of 1857, which held that blacks had no rights that a white man was bound to respect. "The inferiority of the negro," writes William Sumner, "was almost universally accepted in the South by all groups of proslavery theorists as a great primary truth. It led to the belief that slavery was the condition prepared for him by nature, and that it was the only condition he could occupy for the time being." The slave narratives criticize "the great primary truth" of black inferiority from two angles: often they deny the capacity of blackness to denote a natural slave; and they point out that the Rights of Man are authentic moral measures of the human condition only insofar as they are universally applied, that is, they cannot be rights of all men if they are enjoyed by only some men. If American society restricts the Rights of Man to the so-called "white race," then such a society has less to do with truth and natural justice than with hypocrisy and barbarism.

The narratives assert the complex relationship between racial identity and slave status. For example, William and Ellen Craft remind their readers "that slavery in America is not at all confined to persons of any particular complexion" (1999: 487). In fact, there have been cases of white children "kidnapped and sold into or reduced to slavery" (487) on the specious grounds that such children have African slave ancestry on their mother's side (in antebellum slavery, the child followed the condition of the mother). Then again, in the nineteenth-century South, the status of so-called mulattos, quadroons, and octoroons was always controversial, in the sense that they fell outside the simple black/white dichotomy that was codified into law as the relation-ship between the inferior and superior race. "Who can measure the amount of Anglo-Saxon blood coursing in the veins of American slaves?" asked Harriet Jacobs (1999: 571). The fact that some people were both black and white, that some black people were easily able to pass for white, were devastating rejoinders to the notion that black social identity necessarily implied slave status. Indeed, when a light-skinned slave like Ellen Craft succeeds in passing herself off as a white slaveholder; when the light-skinned fugitive William Wells Brown credibly acts the part of a slave trader, then the whole edifice of racial representation is brought into disrepute, as race is revealed to be less a natural reality than an arbitrary social value which falls short of reason.

The slave narratives contend that even if the ex-slave has no legal claim upon American citizenship, he or she is morally entitled to this status and the freedoms concomitant with it. In his introduction to Douglass's *My Bondage and My Freedom*, Dr. James M'Cune Smith assures the reader that Douglass is "a representative American man – a type of his countrymen" (Douglass 1969: xxv). A striking example of the ex-slave's claim upon American citizenship appears in William Grimes's *Life of William Grimes, The Runaway Slave* (1825):

> I am now entirely destitute of property; where and how I shall live I don't know; where and how I shall die I don't know, but I hope I may be prepared. If it were not for the stripes on my back which were made while I was a slave, I would in my will, leave my skin a legacy to the government, desiring that it might be taken off and made into parchment, and then bind the constitution of glorious, happy and free America. Let the skin of an American slave, bind the charter of American liberty. (Grimes 1999: 232)

The image of the United States Constitution bound in the whip-scarred skin of a former slave powerfully conveys the political claim of the slave narratives: that black personhood can be linked positively to republican freedom. Grimes's celebration of "the charter of American liberty," even in the face of dire circumstances created by the problem of freedom, hints at a belief shared by many of the ex-slaves: that if American identity equates with natural freedom, then who is more American, who has a greater appreciation of the meaning of freedom, than a fugitive slave, who has struggled, against all odds, for possession of herself? Slave narratives argue that slaves rather than masters are the true inheritors of the revolutionary republican tradition, with its grounding in divine and natural law.

William Grimes makes his beaten body the measure of his text and vice versa. In the slave narratives, the written word stands as a surrogate of bodily experience, that is to say, the language of the text putatively embodies the presence of a sincere individual who has known slavery as a slave. The hallmark of this will to embodiment is the narrative's rendition of the individual's speaking voice. The abolitionist use of the testimonial presupposed the performative qualities of voice and its linkage to a concept of truth as embodied in an individual's corporeal presence. Thus, when Angelina Grimkè characterized herself before the Massachusetts Legislature in 1838, "as a Southerner, exiled from the land of my birth, by the sound of the lash, and the piteous cry of the slave. I stand before you as a repentant slaveholder. I stand before you as a moral being . . . [who resolves] . . . to do all I can to overturn a system of complicated crimes" (1998: 279), one sees how voice and bodily presence are combined to produce a rhetoric of truth.

Grimkè impresses herself on her audience by using the rhetorical figure of anaphora, the repetition of a phrase in successive clauses ("I stand before you as a southerner. . . I stand before you as a moral being"). However, considered as a dialogic statement, her repeated utterance of the words "I stand before you" is not only the saying of something but also the doing of something. Specifically, it is the performance of the act of witnessing, the act of testifying. Then again, Grimkè's utterances also, implicitly, perform the act of converting the audience from a state of indifference or commitment to proslavery values to a state of moral consciousness wherein antislavery beliefs become natural. Because public lectures and church meetings were important venues for the dissemination of antislavery propaganda, abolitionist ideology and practice were steeped in the ethics of speech acts. As slave narratives developed into a distinct literary genre, they inherited the performative voice of the antislavery lecture.

That slave narratives enact a transition from orality to textuality, while seeking to preserve the moral force of the speech act, the sense that utterances are in themselves concrete ethical actions, is most evident in the prefaces and testimonials that white editors and patrons appended to the narrative proper, to establish its veracity. These formal attestations presented the black narrative voice to the imagined audience, with the background understanding that white supremacy has encouraged readers to think of blacks as naturally devoid of literary talents. Hence the ritualistic assurance by the editor that the narrative was indeed penned by the ex-slave. In his preface to *The Narrative of Moses Roper* (1838), Thomas Price verifies that the book is Roper's "own production" (Roper 1999: 491). Similarly, in his preface, Garrison states that "Mr. Douglass has very properly chosen to write his own narrative . . . rather than to employ someone else" (Douglass 1999: 532). In cases where the narrative has been dictated by the former slave to an amanuensis, the verification of the black voice cannot proceed on the grounds of authorship. Instead, the patron will claim that the narrative voice, if not identical, is a credible approximation of the ex-slave's speaking voice.

L. A. Chamerovzow, the writer and editor of John Brown's *Slave Life in Georgia* (1855), avers that the narrative is "a plain unvarnished tale of real slave-life, conveyed as nearly as possible in the language of the subject, written under his dictation." This emphasis on the textual as based in orality is also seen in J. C. Lovejoy's preface to the *Narrative of Lewis Clarke* (1846). Lovejoy observes: "Many persons who have heard him [Clarke] lecture, have expressed a strong desire that his story might be recorded in connected form. He has, therefore, concluded to have it printed" (Clarke and Clarke 1999: 607). The editor's concern with the truth effect of the black speaking voice can be understood in the context of the abolitionist desire to prevail, in the struggle against slavery, on rational, as well as sentimental, grounds. For abolitionists held that the slavery controversy was not a matter of relative truths: if the slave was honest in his or her account of what bondage meant, then the master had no real answer, and was obliged to concede the antislavery argument. However, at another level, the editor's verification of the black voice was related to the moral prestige associated with public speaking, particularly in the evangelical cultures of Quakerism and Methodism that were the backbone of immediate abolitionism. Like Grimkè's speech before the Massachusetts Legislature, the slave narrative, as performative utterance, presupposes the moral capacity of the audience to recognize truth when they hear and see it; and it also presupposes a latent willingness on the part of the audience to act on the truth, to become members of the abolitionist movement.

The textual evocation of orality as moral power can be analyzed in the terms of speech act theory. Mary Louise Pratt has summarized the value of speech act theory for literary study:

> Speech act theory provides a way of talking about utterances . . . in terms of the context in which they are made, the intentions, attitudes, and expectations of the participants, the relationships existing between the participants, and generally, the unspoken rules and conventions that are understood to be in play when an utterance is made and received.
>
> There are enormous advantages to talking about literature in this way, too, for literary works, like all our communicative activities, are context dependent. Literature itself is a speech context. And as with any utterance, the way people produce and understand literary works depends enormously on unspoken, culturally shared knowledge of the rules, conventions, and expectations that are in play when language is used in that context. (Pratt 1979: 86)

As we have seen, the slave narrative is bound to its context in a manner that shapes the narrative voice into a distinct kind of moral speech. Jürgen Habermas has devised a model of the ethics of performative utterance which might be usefully applied to slave narratives. Like Bakhtin, Habermas contends that language is inherently dialogic, that "every utterance must, at least implicitly, establish and bring to expression a certain relation between the speaker and his counterpart" (1979: 34). For Habermas, speech acts, ideally, are aimed at achieving mutual understanding of, and agreement on, "validity claims of comprehensibility, truth, truthfulness, and rightness" (3). In other words, an utterance must be grammatically sensible, consistently rational, fundamentally sincere, and functionally appropriate, with regard to "a recognized normative background" (3), in order to be grasped as valid truth.

Habermas's model helps to clarify the moral and political significance of the performative voice conventionally employed in slave narratives. Slave narratives achieve comprehensibility by leave of the plain style – a rhetoric which conceives of itself as a neutral medium, a simple mirroring of events which, in the last analysis, speak for themselves. Truth and truthfulness in the narratives are respectively matters of the ex-slave's personal experiences of bondage and his or her sincere attempts to enlighten the audience, by testifying in person as to what it felt like to be a species of property. The rightfulness of the slave narratives as abolitionist discourse, as attempts to present African-American speech in the (nominally) white public sphere, rests on the "normative background" of Christian and liberal republican values, which allegedly deny the right of one person to hold property in another. In short, by making validity claims the slave narratives obliged their readers to accept them as truthful statements rather than fanciful fictions.

Even in the North, black public speech was radical political action because blacks were routinely denied a voice in political affairs. The slave narratives repeatedly mention the fact that blacks were not permitted to speak to whites as social equals, that is, if they were permitted to speak at all. "It is not safe to contradict a master," wrote Solomon Northup, "even by the assertion of truth" (1969: 264). Charles Ball observed: "Silence is a great virtue when it is dangerous to speak; and I had long since determined never to advance opinions, uncalled for, in controversies between white people and the slaves" (1999: 422). And Frederick Douglass noted that the typical overseer "never allowed himself to be answered back, by a slave" (1969: 121). Slave codes made it illegal for blacks to testify against whites in courts of law. In both antebellum custom and law, black public speech was considered politically inappropriate, a violation of the norms of white supremacy. However, the success of the slave narratives as popular literature undermined the white supremacist model of the public sphere, and made it possible for African Americans to advance their claims upon American citizenship.

The denial of linguistic freedom for blacks, in both spoken and written discourse, was key to the planter's contention that slaves were essentially mindless brutes. Douglass noted that, try as she might, his former mistress could not deny "I was more than [chattel], and she felt me to be more than that. I could talk and sing;... I was human, and she... knew and felt me to be so" (1969: 153). Thus, one measure of the human in slave narratives is the given capacity of all human beings to express their uniqueness as individuals in comprehensible terms. As a lecturer on the antislavery circuit, Douglass was often introduced as "a 'chattel,' – a 'thing' – a piece of Southern 'property' – the chairman assuring the audience that it could speak" (1969: 360). The ironies here make plain the significance of a literature that presents the black voice as the index of black humanity.

For the individual former slave, the composition of an autobiographical narrative was a major step in the process of achieving self-possession. The narrative affirmed the humanity of the individual in singularly potent terms: I speak or write, therefore I am. "I could not possibly regard myself as a piece of property," wrote Harriet Jacobs (1999: 665). Jacobs desires recognition from others as a human being; this desire is shared by all the ex-slaves. John Brown reflects: "A slave is not a human being in the eye of the law, and the slaveholder looks upon him just as what the law makes him; nothing more, and perhaps even something less" (1969: 392). For the ex-slave, the act of writing or dictating a narrative (like the act of speaking in a lecture hall) accomplishes the ideological transition from thinghood to personhood, from non-being to being, from slavery to freedom. Thus, when Frederick Douglass writes at the close of his Narrative, "I subscribe myself, FREDERICK DOUGLASS" (1987: 595), he makes clear the psychological motive that impels the ex-slave to tell his or her story: to will oneself an authentic social identity, so that freedom can be viewed as a true symbolic rebirth.

Slave narratives were in one sense a Northern literature about the South produced by exiled Southerners. Yet, if one would grasp their character as literary-political discourse, then one must read them against proslavery writings in the context of what Jay Hubbell calls "the South's struggle for cultural independence" (1940: 183). As propaganda, the slave narratives did much to secure and circulate a credible image of African-American humanity. As social history, they are invaluable records of the daily life of the plantation system. As moral philosophy, they illuminate the complexities of the problem of slavery and the problem of freedom. And finally, as literary art, they are frequently memorable in voice, style, and imagery. Moreover, slave narratives have influenced modern writers like William Styron, Margaret Walker, Charles Johnson, and Toni Morrison. Such writers have understood that the narratives contain immutable truths about what it means to be human.

References and further reading

Anon. (1851) "Management of Negroes," *De Bow's Review* (March) vol. 10, 325–8.

Aptheker, Herbert (1989) *Abolitionism: A Revolutionary Movement.* Boston, MA: Twayne.

Bakhtin, M. M. (1981) *The Dialogic Imagination: Four Essays*, ed. Michael Holquist, trans. Caryl Emerson and Michael Holquist. Austin: University of Texas Press.

Ball, Charles (1999) [1836] *Slavery in the United States.* In Yuval Taylor (ed.) *I was Born: An Anthology of Classic Slave Narratives, Vol. 1.* Chicago: Lawrence Hill.

Beverley, John (1993) *Against Literature.* Minneapolis: University of Minnesota Press.

Bibb, Henry (1969) [1849] *Narrative of the Life and Adventures of Henry Bibb, an American Slave.* In *Puttin' On Ole Massa: The Slave Narratives of Henry Bibb, William Wells Brown and Solomon Northup*, ed. Gilbert Osofsky. New York: Harper and Row.

Brown, William Wells (1969) [1848] *Narrative of William Wells Brown, a Fugitive Slave.* In *Puttin' On Ole Massa: The Slave Narratives of Henry Bibb, William Wells Brown and Solomon Northup*, ed. Gilbert Osofsky. New York: Harper and Row.

Bruce, Dickson D. (2001) *The Origins of African-American Literature: 1680–1865.* Charlottesville: University of Virginia Press.

Carlyle, Thomas (1899) [1849] "The Nigger Question." In *Thomas Carlyle: Critical and Miscellaneous Essays Vol. 4.* London: Chapman and Hall.

Cartwright, Samuel (1969a) [1860] "Slavery in the Light of Ethnology." In *Cotton is King*, ed. E. N. Elliot. New York: Negro Universities Press, 691–706.

Cartwright, Samuel (1969b) [1860] "The Natural History of the Prognathous Species of Mankind." In *Cotton is King*, ed. E. N. Elliot. New York: Negro Universities Press, 707–16.

Cartwright, Samuel (1969c) [1860] "On the Caucasians and the Africans." In *Cotton is King*, ed. E. N. Elliot. New York: Negro Universities Press, 717–28.

Clarke, Lewis and Clarke, Milton (1999) [1846] *Narratives of the Sufferings of Lewis and Milton Clarke.* In Yuval Taylor (ed.) *I was Born: An Anthology of Classic Slave Narratives, Vol. 1.* Chicago: Lawrence Hill.

Craft, William and Craft, Ellen (1999) [1860] *Running A Thousand Miles For Freedom.* In Yuval Taylor (ed.) *I was Born: An Anthology of Classic Slave Narratives, Vol. 2.* Chicago: Lawrence Hill.

Davis, David Brion (1966) *The Problem of Slavery in Western Culture.* Ithaca, NY: Cornell University Press.

DeBow, James (1963) [1860] "The Interest in Slavery of the Southern Non-Slaveholder." In *Slavery Defended: The Views of the Old South*, ed. Eric L. McKitrick. Englewood Cliffs, NJ: Prentice-Hall, 169–77.

Douglass, Frederick (1969) [1855] *My Bondage and My Freedom.* New York: Dover.

Douglass, Frederick (1987) [1845] *Narrative of the Life of Frederick Douglass, an American Slave.* In *The Classic Slave Narratives*, ed. Henry Louis Gates. New York: New American Library.

Douglass, Frederick (1999) [1845] *Narrative of the Life of Frederick Douglass, An American Slave.* In Yuval Taylor (ed.) *I was Born: An Anthology of Classic Slave Narratives, Vol. 1.* Chicago: Lawrence Hill.

Engels, Friedrich (1972) [1884] *The Origin of the Family, Private Property and the State.* Harmondsworth: Penguin Books.

Fields, Barbara (1982) "Ideology and Race in American History." In *Region, Race and Reconstruction: Essays in Honor of C. Vann Woodward*, ed. J. Morgan Kousser and James McPherson. New York: Oxford University Press, 143–77.

Fields, Barbara (1990) "Slavery, Race and Ideology in the United States of America." *New Left Review* 181, 95–118.

Fitzhugh, George (1960a) [1854] *Sociology for the South.* In Harvey Wish (ed.) *Ante-Bellum: Writings of George Fitzhugh and Hinton Rowan Helper On Slavery.* New York: Capricorn.

Fitzhugh, George (1960b) [1857] *Cannibals All! Or, Slaves Without Masters.* Cambridge, MA: Harvard University Press.

Fitzhugh, George (1981) [1857] "Southern Thought." In Drew Gilpin Faust (ed.) *The Ideology of Slavery: Proslavery Thought in the Antebellum South, 1830–1860.* Baton Rouge: Louisiana University Press, 272–99.

Foster, Frances Smith (1979) *Witnessing Slavery: The Development of Ante-Bellum Slave Narratives.* Madison: University of Wisconsin Press.

Grimes, Willam (1999) [1825] *Life of William Grimes: The Runaway Slave.* In Yuval Taylor (ed.) *I was Born: An Anthology of Classic Slave Narratives, Vol. 1.* Chicago: Lawrence Hill.

Grimkè, Angelina (1998) [1838] "Speech Before the Legislative Committee of the Massachusetts Legislature, Feb. 21, 1838." In Gerda Lerner, *The Grimkè Sisters From South Carolina: Pioneers For Women's Rights and Abolition.* New York: Oxford University Press, 277–9.

Habermas, Jürgen (1979) *Communication and the Evolution of Society*, trans. Thomas Mccarthy. Boston, MA: Beacon Press.

Harris, Cheryl (1993) "Whiteness as Property." *Harvard Law Review* vol. 106, no. 8, 1709–91.

Helper, Hinton Rowan (1960) [1857] *The Impending Crisis.* In *Antebellum: Writings of George Fitzhugh and Hinton Rowan Helper on Slavery*, ed. Harvey Wish. New York: Capricorn.

Henson, Josiah (1962) [1858] *Father Henson's Story of His Own Life.* New York: Corinth.

Henson, Josiah (1999) [1849] *The Life of Josiah Henson, Formerly a Slave.* In Yuval Taylor (ed.) *I was Born: An Anthology of Classic Slave Narratives, Vol. 1.* Chicago: Lawrence Hill.

Hubbell, Jay (1940) "Literary Nationalism in the Old South." In David Kelly Jackson (ed.) *American Studies in Honor of William Kenneth Boyd.* Durham, NC: Duke University Press, 173–220.

Hughes, Henry (1963) [1854] *A Treatise on Sociology.* In *Slavery Defended: The Views of the Old South*, ed. Eric L. McKitrick. Englewood Cliffs, NJ: Prentice-Hall, 51–6.

Ignatiev, Noel (1995) *How the Irish Became White.* New York: Routledge.

Jacobs, Harriet (1999) [1861] *Incidents in the Life of a Slave-Girl.* In Yuval Taylor (ed.) *I was Born: An Anthology of Classic Slave Narratives, Vol. 2.* Chicago: Lawrence Hill.

Jefferson, Thomas (1964) [1785] *Notes on the State of Virginia.* New York: Harper and Row.

Kemble, Frances (1863) *Journal of a Residence on a Georgia Plantation in 1838–1839*. New York: Harper and Brothers.

Mann, Horace (1848) *Speech of Hon. Horace Mann on the Right of Congress to Legislate for the Territories of the United States and its Duty to Exclude Slavery Therefrom*. Boston, MA: J. Howe.

Murray, Charles and Hernstein, Richard (1994) *The Bell Curve: Intelligence and Class Structure in American Life*. New York: Free Press.

Northup, Solomon (1969) [1853] *Twelve Years a Slave: Narrative of Solomon Northup*. In *Puttin' On Ole Massa: The Slave Narratives of Henry Bibb, William Wells Brown and Solomon Northup*, ed. Gilbert Osofsky. New York: Harper and Row.

Northup, Solomon (1999) [1853] *Twelve Years A Slave*. In Yuval Taylor (ed.) *I was Born: An Anthology of Classic Slave Narratives, Vol. 2*. Chicago: Lawrence Hill.

Nott, Josiah (1963) [1854] *Types of Mankind*. In *Slavery Defended: The Views of the Old South*, ed. Eric L. McKitrick. Englewood Cliffs, NJ: Prentice-Hall, 126–38.

Olmsted, Frederick Law (1969) [1861] *The Cotton Kingdom: A Traveller's Observations on Cotton and Slavery in the American Slave States*. New York: Modern Library.

Parker, Theodore (1848) *A Letter to the People of the United States Touching the Matter of Slavery*. Boston: James Monroe.

Parker, William (1999) [1866] "The Freedman's Story." In Yuval Taylor (ed.) *I was Born: An Anthology of Classic Slave Narratives, Vol. 2*. Chicago: Lawrence Hill.

Patterson, Orlando (1982) *Slavery and Social Death: A Comparative Study*. Cambridge, MA: Harvard University Press.

Peabody, Ephraim (1985) [1849] "Narratives of Fugitive Slaves." In Charles T. Davis and Henry Louis Gates, Jr. (eds.) *The Slave's Narrative*. New York: Oxford University Press, 19–28.

Pennington, James W. (1999) [1849] *The Fugitive Blacksmith*. In Yuval Taylor (ed.) *I was Born: An Anthology of Classic Slave Narratives, Vol. 2*. Chicago: Lawrence Hill.

Phillips, Ulrich B. (1963) [1929] *Life and Labor in the Old South*. Boston, MA: Little Brown.

Phillips, Wendell (1891) [1842] "Irish Sympathy With the Abolition Movement." In *Speeches, Lectures, and Letters*. Boston, MA: Lothrop, Lee, and Shepard, 19–23.

Pratt, Mary Louise (1979) *Toward a Speech Act Theory of Literary Discourse*. Bloomington: Indiana University Press.

Roediger, David (1991) *The Wages of Whiteness: Race and the Making of the American Working Class*. New York: Verso.

Roper, Moses (1999) [1838] *A Narrative of the Adventures and Escape of Moses Roper From American Slavery*. In Yuval Taylor (ed.) *I was Born: An Anthology of Classic Slave Narratives, Vol. 1*. Chicago: Lawrence Hill.

Ryan, Mary P. (1982) *The Empire of the Mother: American Writing About Domesticity, 1830–1860*. New York: Haworth Press.

Starling, Marion Wilson (1988) *The Slave Narrative: Its Place in American History*. Washington, DC: Howard University Press.

Steward, Austin (1969) [1857] *Twenty-Two Years A Slave and Forty Years A Freeman*. In Robin W. Winks et al. (eds.) *Four Fugitive Slave Narratives*. Reading, MA: Addison-Wesley.

Stroyer, Jacob (1968) [1898] *My Life in the South*. In *Five Slave Narratives: A Compendium*. New York: Arno Press.

Takaki, Ronald (1990) *Iron Cages: Race and Culture in 19th Century America*. New York: Oxford University Press.

Thompson, John (1999) [1856] *The Life of John Thompson, A Fugitive Slave*. In Yuval Taylor (ed.) *I was Born: An Anthology of Classic Slave Narratives, Vol. 2*. Chicago: Lawrence Hill.

Tocqueville, Alexis de (1969) [1835] *Democracy in America*. New York: Harper.

Veblen, Thorstein (1947) [1906] "The Place of Science in Modern Civilization." In *Veblen on Marx, Race, Science and Economics*. New York: Capricorn, 1–31.

Veblen, Thorstein (1953) [1899] *The Theory of the Leisure Class*. New York: New American Library.

Vidich, Arthur and Lyman, Stanford (1985) *American Sociology: Worldly Rejections of Religion and Their Directions*. New Haven, CT: Yale University Press.

Weld, Theodore (1972) [1839] *Slavery in America: Theodore Weld's American Slavery As It Is*, ed Richard O. Curry and Joanna Dulap Cowden. Itasca, IL: Peacock.

4

Plantation Fiction

John M. Grammer

I

Most people even passingly familiar with American popular culture can call to mind the images that constitute plantation fiction: the hills and fields, the columned mansion, the courtly master and his family taking their ease on the veranda, their contented black retainers filling the evening air with song. These images, conjured by the lyrics of Stephen Foster, evoked in *Gone With the Wind* and the many novels and films that tried to duplicate its popularity, pressed into commercial service by the tourism bureaus of Southern states, constitute some of the best-known regional clichés in US culture. Put to the uses of fiction, the plantation image helped inform two of the most popular novels in US history, *Uncle Tom's Cabin* and *Gone With the Wind*, as well as the one often identified as the greatest, William Faulkner's *Absalom, Absalom!*

Plantation fiction's vocabulary of images and characters might have generated, and sometimes did generate, mere local color, picturesque representations of a quaint and archaic world, exotically appealing to readers from elsewhere. But usually this writing has tried to do more; it carries, more or less consciously, an ideological burden. Plantation fiction is a version of the literary pastoral, a mode, as Raymond Williams and others have shown, which can seldom avoid saying something about politics. Williams argued that pastoral literature usually turns on a tension between "the pleasures of rural settlement and the threat of loss and eviction" (1973: 17). It posits a world innocent of politics – because innocent of the conflicts that generate politics – but continually endangered by a surrounding world of political and economic corruption. Like other pastoral narratives since the day of Virgil's *Eclogues*, plantation novels are about the ownership of land and about some threat to the proprietor's quiet enjoyment of it. Literary plantations are often in danger of failing agriculturally and economically, which threatens their owners with debt and dishonor. Even in the most celebratory plantation fictions, *history* – the threat of change and loss – nibbles at the edges of the great estate. It is personified by the creditor, the sheriff, the grasping and litigious neighbor, and eventually by the carpetbagger, a real-life historical figure who might almost have been called into being by the Southern pastoral imagination. Pastoral is one of the literary modes, like epic and romance, that brings with it certain assumptions about human experience and thus, so to speak, does part of the author's thinking for him. Built into the deep structure of pastoral is a narrative of historical declension, an assumption that rural life and its attendant virtues and pleasures are archaic, part of the past and thus inevitably threatened by the future. So it is with plantation fiction, where one can almost always detect, on the horizon if not directly overhead, a cloud of historical doom.

But even the land itself is ultimately only one term within a symbolic vocabulary for addressing a deeper issue, that of social order. From the beginning the literary plantation has been the symbol of a social ideal, whose legitimacy is tested, and either affirmed or denied, by the trial of plot. The pastoral setting offers the writer a way of conferring the prestige of *nature* on some particular set of social arrangements; if he can make it stick, he will have conducted those arrangements safely out of the range of argument and criticism, since social contrivances might be changed and are thus worth discussing, while nature must simply be accepted. What social arrangements, if any, are natural? Plantation novels nearly always ask this question; by answering it they articulate a side — sometimes both sides — of an unfinished dialectic.

For the most part, plantation writing is a phenomenon of the nineteenth century, but in a sense its clarifying moment came later, in 1936. It was the year of *Gone With the Wind*, the most popular of all the literary celebrations of the Southern landed aristocracy, in some ways the apotheosis of the form. This was not what Margaret Mitchell intended; she believed she was writing, and in some ways she did write, a critique of the plantation legend. But its millions of readers — including David O. Selznick, who made the wildly popular film version of Mitchell's epic — have tended to miss the critique and see only what Malcolm Cowley called "an encyclopedia of the plantation legend" (quoted in Pyron 1991: 372).

Neither Cowley nor anyone else made that mistake about the other plantation novel of 1936, *Absalom, Absalom!*, which might be thought of as the ultimate deconstruction of the plantation novel. A brief look at two of its memorable scenes may clarify much about the tradition to which it responds. The first has Thomas Sutpen, born of the poor whites but on his way to being a planter, standing in a wilderness clearing, naked and muddy, surrounded by and scarcely distinguishable from his naked and muddy slaves, laying the foundations of his grand home. The other, more striking, shows the same man, bloody and stripped to the waist, standing over the fallen body of a slave, whom he has just beaten in a fight. A crowd of men surrounding the scene cheer what has evidently been a pugilistic exhibition. Then Sutpen's young son Henry "plunge[s] out from among the negroes who had been holding him, screaming and vomiting" (Faulkner 1990: 21). Henry's reaction is the clue: his shock, from which he may be said never to recover, is that of a child observing what Freud called "the primal scene," the spectacle of his parents making love. We might think of it, in the term coined by theorist Ned Lukacher, as a "cultural primal scene": Henry sees reenacted the creation of not his physical but his social being. Sutpen, determined to be a planter and knowing that this means slaveholding, has felt obliged to reenact what might be called the primal scene of slavery, the violent subjugation of a black person by a white one. His need to do so is evidently an aspect of what his friend General Compson calls his "innocence," his incapacity for the genteel deceptions by which other planters manage to conceal from themselves the nature of the institution that supports them.

Few plantation novels display the same "innocence," or could afford it, for obvious reasons. "Slavery, as an original question, is wholly without justification or defense," says a character in *Swallow Barn*, perhaps the first specimen of the genre (Kennedy 1986: 455). Therefore, in plantation fiction, it is almost never represented as an original question. Neither, for that matter, is the plantation itself: thus the Faulknerian scene in which the plantation house is being raised, by men not-yet clearly distinguishable by race and class, is equally subversive. The founding of the plantation, and the creation of slavery, its enabling institution, are normally "repressed" in plantation fiction, as troubling events may be in personal memory. A literary plantation house is usually represented, like the eponymous setting of *Swallow Barn*, as an "aristocratical old edifice," and the slaves have been in the family forever (Kennedy 1986: 27). Both have the immemorial status of nature itself. Though plantation writing frequently – indeed obsessively – contemplates the ending of the plantation and its institutions, it usually makes a specialty of obscuring their origins. Thus its most interesting moments are usually the ones when the mask slips a bit, when the fiction blurts out a little more than it meant to about its subject.

Today, plantation writing gets little critical respect, though it was once thought of as the South's principal contribution to American literature; in most modern anthologies or college courses devoted to Southern writing, it is represented by a single text, Thomas Nelson Page's "Marse Chan" (in which an aged former slave nostalgically recalls the "good ole times" of his enslavement), followed immediately by its antidote, a Charles Chesnutt "conjure" tale which satirizes such stories. This presentation of the material – making plantation writing a straw man, a defense of indefensible institutions, and offering enlightened readers the virtuous fun of knocking it over – can be useful as a way of providing context for the rich tradition of "anti-plantation" writing, from Harriet Beecher Stowe to Toni Morrison. But it obscures the complexity plantation writing sometimes achieved. There are plantation novels which show little interest in defending slavery, and others whose defenses of it concede so much that they seem like part of the attack. Plantation novels were in effect narrative mechanisms for thinking about social problems, and like most such generic mechanisms, they brought certain problems into sharp focus and obscured others entirely. In truth, the form was more intellectually resourceful, and generated more unexpected conclusions, than is generally supposed.

II

Literary representations of the plantation date almost from the beginning of English life in the Southern colonies. From the beginning they were informed by the idea of the pastoral, attributing to Virginia (and later other colonies) the virtues and pleasures which Europeans had immemorially associated with rural life. By the eighteenth century this tradition had found what would remain its conventional Southern form. Consider a well-known letter, dated 1726, from the Virginia planter William Byrd II to his English friend Charles Boyle, the Earl of Orrery:

> Besides the advantage of a pure Air, we abound in all kinds of Provisions without expence (I mean we who have Plantations). I have a large Family of my own, and my Doors are open to Every Body, yet I have no Bills to pay, and half-a-Crown will rest undisturbed in my Pocket for many Moons together. Like one of the Patriarchs, I have my Flocks and my Herds, my Bond-Men and Bond-Women, and every Soart of Trade amongst my own Servants, so that I live in a kind of Independence on ever yone, but Providence...Another thing, My Lord, that recommends this Country very much – we sit securely under our Vines and our Fig Trees without any Danger to our Property. We have neither publick Robbers nor private, which your Ldsp will think very strange when we have often needy Governours, and pilfering Convicts sent amongst us...Thus, My Lord, we are very happy in our Canaans if we could but forget the Onions and Fleshpots of Egypt. (Byrd 1726: 30)

The letter contains what would become the standard elements of the Southern pastoral. Byrd describes his plantation ("Westover," still standing on the banks of the James River) as a refuge – and a secure one, thanks to its self-sufficiency – from modernity. It is ultimately threatened only by whatever internal vices – a lingering taste for "Onions and Fleshpots" – may remain there. For Byrd, the plantation was not yet an ideologically disputed site; his letter defends plantation life only against an implied charge of dullness and provincialism, not moral turpitude or political injustice. And though Byrd conceives of his plantation as the home of specifically archaic virtues, which he implicitly contrasts with the restless modernity of Boyle's cosmopolitan world, he does not seem to have worried that these virtues were about to pass away; like many American writers before and after him, he seems to have conceived of his country as the place where pastoral virtue might escape the tragic history in which it usually figured and endure forever.

However, the circumstances which would eventually draw the plantation into the realm of ideological strife, as well as those which would seem to threaten it with extinction, are mentioned in Byrd's letter as well. When he boasts of the *security* of his property, its safety from both public and private robbers, he is claiming for Virginia landowners a special exemption from the fear that has always haunted the pastoral imagination, that of dispossession. By the early nineteenth century the literary plantation – like many actual ones, particularly in Virginia where the form had its origin – would become radically insecure financially, subject to the predations of "Robbers" of many sorts. Poor agricultural practices would rob the land of its fertility, while protective tariffs designed to help Northern manufacturers would push farmers ever nearer those nightmares of the pastoral imagination, debt and forfeiture of the land. From the nineteenth century onward these specters haunt nearly all plantation fiction.

And so, of course, do the "Bond-men and Bond-women" to whom Byrd also alludes. The allusion seems untroubled, and though his "Secret Diary" shows Byrd thinking a good deal about his slaves – alternately fretting over their welfare and punishing them for minor or non-existent infractions – he does not seem to have regarded slavery as a particular problem for himself or his region. But most later writers about plantations, whether they favored slavery or opposed it, have felt compelled to put the institution near the center of their regional pictures. Francis P. Gaines, in the first sustained study of plantation writing, argued in 1924 that the prominent presence of African-American characters is a defining feature of the genre (1924: 16–17). More recently, William Andrews (1991) has argued that, after the publication in 1831 of Nat Turner's *Confessions*, which made of its murderous protagonist the first fully realized black character in Southern writing, it became impossible for white Southern writers to avoid including individualized slave characters, complete with histories and inner lives, in their narratives. Vividly drawn African-American characters, placed prominently in the story, were in effect needed to testify against Nat Turner: to affirm, as literary slaves have frequently done in plantation fiction ever since, the essential benevolence of Southern institutions.

And yet there is an inescapable paradox in this necessity: a fiction that would convince us that African Americans are the natural dependents of whites must itself depend on the voices of its black characters. In plantation stories, unlike plantation life, the slave must *not* be silent. This circumstance always forces a small opening in what sometimes tries to be an ideologically sealed system, requiring it to raise at least one question whose answer must remain beyond the fiction's control: what else might this voice, so eloquent in praising the plantation, be able to say? Particularly in a republican culture where personal and political agency depended so strongly on eloquence, proslavery fiction took a necessary but significant risk in granting that virtue to slaves.

In fact the mere presence of those slaves, even if they had remained silent, created an almost insoluble problem for plantation writers. As practitioners of the literary pastoral, they were generically committed to an essentially elegiac view of their subject; their project was to describe a virtuous but vanishing world. As loyal Southerners, however, trying to speak for their region, they eventually came to feel politically committed to a very different project: that of defending, not mourning, the plantation and its institutions. Elegy and polemic were often yoked together in plantation fiction, a pairing that gave the authors some notably bumpy rides, but also generated most of the interest their work has for us now.

Some of these developments were anticipated in a novel sometimes thought of as a precursor of the plantation form, *The Valley of Shenandoah*, published by the Virginian George Tucker in 1824. It prominently includes several slave characters, who seem to be as real and three-dimensional as Tucker's limited novelistic powers could make them. But these slaves do not endorse their enslavement, nor does Tucker. His attitude seems to be that of his protagonist Edward Grayson, who calls slavery a "disease," albeit one that "admits of no cure" (Tucker 1971, I: 62). The novel italicizes that mild condemnation by showing us an auction in which slaves are painfully sold away from their homes and families. Later plantation writers would learn to place such images safely on or beyond the margins of their regional portraits. But Tucker was writing in 1824, before the Nat Turner revolt, before William Lloyd Garrison, in *The Liberator*, dramatically turned up the volume of abolitionist criticism of the South. Slavery was only one of Tucker's subjects, and in any case his purposes were not defensive but elegiac: *Valley* plots the decline of the Grayson family from the forfeiture of their Tidewater lands to a final apocalypse in which their daughter, Louisa, is seduced and abandoned by a visiting Yankee, and her brother Edward, confronting the scoundrel, is murdered on the streets of New York City. His fate is that of his family and, apparently, their institutions: as early as 1824 the plantation had been placed on the endangered species list, where most subsequent plantation fiction, antebellum and postbellum, firmly kept it.

The next major example of the form, published just eight years later, does little to relieve that gloomy picture. *Swallow Barn*, first appearing in 1832 (a revised version appeared in 1851), was a more professional specimen of prose fiction, composed by a writer of genuine talent, John Pendleton Kennedy. It displays the wit and good cheer one associates with Kennedy's literary model, Washington Irving, so that its essential pessimism may be harder to recognize. But it is unmistakably there. *Swallow Barn* is in form a travel narrative, an account by a Northerner of his sojourn in Virginia. This format, wherein some local scene is described by a sympathetic outsider, licensed many local color writers to paint their subjects in favorable tones, since the presumably objective outsider will not be suspected of sentimentality or ax-grinding. But here the blade cuts both ways, since Mark Littleton's accounts of life on the James River plantation where he spends a season are both affectionate and mocking, revealing an institution and a culture full of charm, but whose prospects are not necessarily much brighter than those foreseen in Tucker's apocalyptic novel.

Students who take up *Swallow Barn* are sometimes mystified by it: a long novel, full of reasonably interesting characters and situations, in which virtually nothing happens. These students are not, like inexperienced readers of Henry James, simply failing to notice the quiet calamities of the drawing room: *Swallow Barn* really comes about as close as fiction can to being plotless. Mark Littleton, the traveler from the North, comes to visit his Virginia relatives at Swallow Barn, "an aristocratical old edifice that sits, like a brooding hen, on the banks of the James River" (Kennedy 1986: 27). The people he meets there seem to have the seeds of plot in them. Mark's cousin Ned Hazard is in love with Bel Tracy, heiress of the plantation next door, and ardently pursues her hand. His quest is complicated by the efforts of a rival, Singleton Swansdown, and also by a longstanding property dispute between Bel's father Isaac Tracy and Frank Meriwether, master of Swallow Barn. And the plot thus promised is duly transmitted: Ned does his best to impress Bel by measuring up to the ideal of chivalry which she has imbibed from the romances she reads insatiably. He rides, hunts, and thrashes a local bully. Meanwhile, the lawsuit over the disputed land grinds onward.

But it transpires that, though a disputed title is serious business in most pastoral narrative, here the land in question is worthless swamp and the dispute over it is simply the chief diversion of bored Isaac Tracy. His affectionate neighbor Frank Meriwether thus does his best to assure that the dispute, after it has run its entertaining course, will be settled in Tracy's favor. Ned's courtship of Bel has a similarly foregone quality about it: his success is inevitable, but neither of them would want it to come too soon, without a certain number of complications. If plot requires surprise, then there really is none present in this odd romance. It is as though the main characters have all *read* plantation novels and are doing their best to reenact one: the book usually identified as the first true example of the form is also, already, a parody of it. What we see are a collection of stereotypical characters trapped, for the most part happily, in a world of amusing but pointless repetitions. Unlike Tucker's Virginia plantation, where the depredations of time are all too obvious, Swallow Barn, in its stasis, seems timeless. This spares Kennedy's characters the tragic status of Tucker's, making them instead just faintly ridiculous. And yet the result is the same: the social order represented by the plantation is marked as irrelevant to the bustling American world taking shape around it, a fact that – as Kennedy noted in his preface to the second edition of *Swallow Barn* – was already giving the Southern plantation "the tints of a relic of the past," one which "may, in another generation, become archaeological, and sink into the chapter of antiquities" (10). Another death sentence, along with an affectionate elegy, had been pronounced upon the Southern plantation.

It was not until somewhat later, in response to the increased volume and bulk of abolitionist criticism issuing from the North, that Southern writers roused themselves to resist these fated developments and began to think of the literary plantation as a weapon to be wielded in defense of Southern institutions. *The Partisan Leader* (1836), by the professor and polemicist Nathaniel Beverley Tucker, helped inaugurate this movement away from the elegiac. For one thing, it is actually set in the future, and a glorious future at that: a moment when the slaveholding states of the South have finally decided to secede from the American union and claim the prosperity and power to which their virtues entitle them. The novel concerns a Virginia plantation family, the Trevors, who become leaders in their state's belated effort to leave the union and join the other Southern states. The ensuing conflict between Northern regular soldiers and Southern partisans gives Tucker the chance to write some scenes of wilderness scouting and warfare reminiscent of James Fenimore Cooper, but his serious purposes are most evident in scenes that occur in the plantation house of Bernard Trevor, a planter, politician, and intellectual who guides Virginia's efforts to leave the union. Tucker shows us almost nothing of the plantation as a scene of pleasant rural life or agricultural production – fertile fields, scenic woods, tranquil streams – but only the interiors of the house itself, where the essence of Southern character and destiny is distilled in intense conversations among the principal characters. Tucker's polemical purposes tug considerably harder than his pastoral ones, and his plantation becomes the home not so much of conventional rural virtue as of a political ideology for which the novel tries to claim a glorious destiny.

This ideology asserts, prominently, the essential rightness of slavery as a system of labor and a morally appropriate condition for Africans. The slaves in *The Partisan Leader* do much more than testify about the virtue of Southern social arrangements; in a remarkable turn of plot, Tucker has them suit action to words, actually taking up arms against the Northern invaders. This episode confirms William Andrews's assertion about the effect of Nat Turner's *Confessions* on Southern narrative; the Trevor slaves, like the murderous Turner, are intelligent and militant, willing and able to pursue their aims violently. But in Tucker's fantasy those aims converge with those of their masters; the slaves take up arms, so to speak, in defense of their own enslavement. The plantation is thus revealed, alone among institutions in democratic, individualistic America, as the locus of a perfectly unified political will, a solidarity between superiors and subordinates which makes it, in the plot of the novel and in the literary world to which the novel was addressed, a formidable bludgeon for ideological combat. This plantation is no longer a pastoral retreat but a military headquarters, mobilized for war against all opposing institutions.

This is the polemical form of plantation writing to which "anti-plantation" novels reply. The most effective such reply, one whose influence on plantation fiction can hardly be overstated, was *Uncle Tom's Cabin* (1852). It is well known that Harriet Beecher Stowe's novel, which includes detailed portraits of two very different Southern plantations, borrowed much of that detail from the tradition we have been examining; Stowe herself had seen little of the South and had nothing much to draw upon except the conflicting traditions of plantation romance and abolitionist polemic. Her ability to bring the two together is perhaps not as surprising as it might seem; as we have seen, the plantation tradition itself, in its early phases, made room for critique as well as appreciation. But Stowe shifted the balance between these two, thus radically changing the meaning of the whole. Books like *The Valley of Shenandoah* and *Swallow Barn*, shaking their heads over the insoluble problems of the plantation South – diseases that "admit of no cure" – require nothing from their readers but a vague regret: in W. H. Auden's famous phrase, they "make nothing happen." Stowe's novel, by contrast, aimed to make several things happen: the reader is to cry, to be outraged, and finally to take political action in order to eliminate the evils Stowe imagined in the plantation South.

What made Stowe's critique so potent, as white Southerners saw it, was that it seemed to grant so many of the claims they had been accustomed to make for their region. Most of Stowe's Southern aristocrats are well-intentioned, essentially decent, and lack only the virtue that Southerners were usually willing to concede to the

Yankees anyway, that of energy. Many of them are kindly disposed toward their slaves, who often respond with love and loyalty. These planters are less villains than victims – of their love of leisure, of their high-minded indifference to matters of finance, of the unscrupulous tactics of avaricious outsiders. The results, foreseeable to anybody acquainted with the tradition of the pastoral, are debt and the loss of property – including slaves, who in Stowe's novel are in constant danger of being sold to satisfy an improvident master's creditors. The major slave characters are equally conventional: Tom's piety and fidelity link him with many literary slaves of both genders, and George Harris's masculine heroism makes him a cousin of Abe, the slave-turned-sailor whose brave death at sea is recounted in *Swallow Barn*. Little here would have surprised George Tucker or John Pendleton Kennedy. Yet somehow Stowe had turned these images against the people they were meant to flatter.

How were Southern writers to rebut a regional portrait they had largely drawn themselves? Dozens of them tried, producing novels whose very titles – *Aunt Phillis's Cabin*, by Mary H. Eastman, for example, or *Uncle Robin in his Cabin in Virginia, and Tom without One in Boston*, by John W. Page – declare their merely parodic and derivative nature; most are memorable only for their connection with Stowe's *tour de force*. A notable exception, though, is *Woodcraft*, first published in 1852 by the prolific South Carolina writer William Gilmore Simms. The novel was not, primarily, a rebuttal to Stowe. It featured characters Simms had used in previous books and formed the concluding chapter in a series of related novels about the Revolutionary War, and it appeared (under the title *The Sword and the Distaff*) at nearly the same time as Stowe's book. Even the most notable black character, a slave provocatively named Tom, had appeared in previous novels and cannot be counted among the literary offspring of Stowe's Uncle Tom. And yet this Tom does reprimand a fellow slave, who has addressed him as "uncle Tom," with "Don't you uncle me, you chucklehead!" (Simms 1983: 204), notifying us that Stowe's work is not absent from Simms's thoughts. The author himself remarked, after his book was published, that it was "probably as good an answer to Mrs. Stowe as has yet been published" (III, 222–3). It answers *Uncle Tom* not only by showing contented slaves and kindly masters but also by trying to reveal a virtuous social order, symbolized by the plantation, of which slavery is a part.

Woodcraft is the story of Captain Porgy, a Revolutionary soldier trying to resume civilian life at the war's end. The South Carolina countryside, having been occupied by the enemy for most of the war, is naturally in social chaos, as is Porgy's own home, "Glen-Eberley." Returning home with a group of his army comrades, he finds his once-grand plantation in ruins, its slaves absent, having hidden themselves in the swamp to escape the retreating British, and its mortgage now held by an unscrupulous parvenu, M'Kewn. The world has turned upside-down: lowborn scoundrels sit atop the social hierarchy, whose rightful leaders must solicit help from women and slaves to regain their positions. The novel follows Porgy's effort to restore not only his solvency but also what he and his author believe are the correct gender, class, and racial hierarchies, the components of the social order broken by war. This plot allows

Simms to display, piece by piece, the parts of his ideal social order and then let us watch as they are reassembled.

And yet this process also surrenders at least one claim made implicitly by many plantation novels before *Woodcraft*. For when Porgy returns home from war, finding Glen-Eberley reduced to a mere wilderness (the title refers to the Fenimore Cooper-style scouting and guerilla warfare by which the heroes must reclaim the land and resist their enemies), he is entering something like the state of nature. His slaves, hiding in the swamps, have likewise recovered something like an original condition of natural liberty, as have most people, white and black, in the surrounding countryside. Thus Porgy's project must be in effect a reenactment of some long-ago ancestor's establishment of the plantation and its social order. Simms gives us, that is, a (considerably tamer) version of the primal scenes Faulkner renders in *Absalom, Absalom!*, making us consider the plantation hierarchy "as an original question." He takes a significant risk by staging this reenactment, in which the wilderness gives way to cultivation and a chaotic postbellum democracy is transformed into a firm hierarchy in which planters, plain folk, and slaves are told where they belong and instructed to take their places.

Some of them, significantly, decline to do so, like the admirable Widow Eveleigh, who enjoys her independence too much to accept Porgy's marriage proposal at the end of the novel. And the squatter Bostwick, murderous and proud, goes to his grave cursing the landowners he has defied all his life. Such unassimilable characters inevitably call into question the social order established at the novel's end. But even harder questions are raised by some of the characters who are assimilated, like Tom, who at the book's conclusion declines Porgy's offer of emancipation. Physically and verbally resourceful, forceful and likable, Tom is far from the humble subordinate postulated by proslavery polemics. Though he declares his love for his master and his unwillingness to leave him, and though his protestations convince Porgy and presumably Simms, they are not likely to convince us. Tom's continued enslavement cannot seem natural; rather, like the proposed subordination of women like Widow Eveleigh and dispossessed whites like Bostwick, it seems a crude contrivance. None of those characters is small enough, or simple enough, to fit comfortably into the "place" which political doctrine and novelistic closure try to assign them at the book's end.

Even if we accept the inevitability of such contrivances and whatever discomfort they create, we will have a hard time thinking of them as providential. Thus *Woodcraft* risks the literary plantation's chief asset, the claim its institutions make to the status of nature. Is Simms's best novel mainly pastoral elegy, painfully conceding the plantation's role in a historical narrative that might end in its demise? Or is it mainly polemical, trying to silence critics and establish, by sheer forensic exertion, a bright and happy future for the South and its chief institution? To a remarkable degree it seems to be both; those unhappily yoked imperatives here generate a tension that makes *Woodcraft* both a strong example of plantation fiction and a serious questioning of some of the genre's cherished premises. It is important not primarily for the debate it seems to be having with *Uncle Tom's Cabin*, that is, but because of the livelier one it has with itself. *Woodcraft* is the most interesting of the antebellum plantation romances, the one most likely to repay serious reading today.

III

Of the important antebellum plantation writers, only Kennedy and Simms survived the Civil War, and only Simms continued to write. He had seen his hopes for the slave-and-planter South destroyed by the war's outcome and his own plantation home, "Woodlands," burned by stragglers from General Sherman's army. But he lived only five more years and for the most part left the future of plantation fiction, if any, to other minds. It was by no means clear that the form would have a future, since the circumstances that had produced it were now profoundly altered. In one sense postbellum Southern writers were much freer than their predecessors had been. Slavery, the political live wire that no antebellum plantation writer could avoid handling, had been abolished; there was no more need to reply to every abolitionist charge or to defend the permanent viability of the institution. But the defeat of the Confederacy brought new pressures. The lost war and its enormous costs made many white Southerners fiercely defensive of the cause for which so much had been sacrificed. Though they often disagreed about the ideological meaning of the Confederate war – had it been a defense of slavery or of the Constitutional rights of the states? – they clung tenaciously to the belief that their civilization had been worth all the sacrifices made in its defense. "No nation rose so white and fair, / None fell so free of crime," proclaimed a typical Confederate monument, one of the hundreds raised in courthouse squares all over the South in the years after Reconstruction. For a writer to suggest otherwise would have seemed literary treason and a deliberate insult to the two groups who had borne the heaviest costs of the war, "the Old Soldiers" and "the Ladies." Those designations were coined by Walter Hines Page, one of the few postbellum white Southerners capable of criticizing his region, in *The Southerner*, his nearly forgotten plantation novel of 1909, but all his contemporaries would have known who he meant and understood the pressure that the invocation of their names could exert. Yet at the same time Southern writers felt compelled, by imperatives of conscience and profit alike, to produce fiction that could appeal to Northern readers as well as Southern ones and thus aid in the necessary project of reconciliation. They hoped to reveal the South as a region which Northerners could again trust as a full partner in the union. What kind of fiction would gratify both wary Yankees and "Old Soldiers"? In answering that question, those writers turned again to that potent and protean symbol bequeathed them by their predecessors, the Southern plantation.

The pure form of postbellum plantation fiction was distilled by Thomas Nelson Page. Raised on a Virginia plantation during the Civil War, Page emerged as a significant literary voice with the oft-anthologized story "Marse Chan," which appeared in 1884. It was included in Page's first book, the story collection *In Ole Virginia* (1887), and its tone of nostalgic reverence for the antebellum plantation world characterized his many subsequent works of fiction and nonfiction. The story is introduced by a visitor to Virginia who, passing a decaying plantation house, meets Sam, a former slave. Sam is easily induced to tell the story of the house and its former occupants, and so we learn of the noble, courageous, kindly "Chan," who before the Civil War was Sam's master and inseparable companion. Though in all other respects an exemplary member of the planter class, Chan was a unionist (a commitment that ended his romance with the heiress next door, daughter of a fierce secessionist) and an uncomfortable slaveholder who had made plans to emancipate Sam. A loyal Virginian though, he rose to the defense of his state once it seceded and served heroically in – what else? – the cavalry. He died in battle, shortly before the war's end and just hours after receiving word from Anne Chamberlain that she would marry him after all. Sam, who had accompanied Chan to war, carried the body home and helped bury it himself in the plantation graveyard. Now his purpose in life is to care for Chan's bird dog, to lament the sorry state of the modern world, and to recall to any who will listen the ideal past personified by his dead master: "Dem wuz good ole times, master – de bes' Sam ever see!" (Page 1969: 10).

"Marse Chan" is anthologized so often because of the remarkable economy with which it manages to incorporate virtually every established cliché of plantation writing: the high-hearted cavalier, the beautiful, spirited belle he loves, the archaic virtue of the plantation world and the historical doom which hovers palpably over it, all attested to and certified, in picturesque dialect, by a loyal slave. What distinguishes it from the antebellum specimens that clearly inspired it is the efficiency with which it has expelled, certainly beyond the borders of the Channing plantation and almost beyond those of the story itself, the kinds of troubling details, suggestive of ideological conflict, that occasionally rear their heads in earlier plantation fictions. The Channing plantation, for instance, apparently faced no economic difficulties; indeed it was not, so far as Sam lets on, an economic institution at all, but a playground for black and white children and the scenic backdrop for unequal but deep friendships among their parents. Slaves were occasionally bought, to save them from a bad fate in other hands, but never sold – nor, for all we can tell, was anything else. Economics and politics exist in the story, but elsewhere: on Colonel Chamberlain's plantation next door, for example, where debt forces the sale of slaves and where political fanaticism frustrates the ordained love of Chan and Anne. But the Channing place is free from such troubles; though "historical" in the sense of belonging to the past, it is in a deeper sense the kind of idealized pastoral setting from which history has been banished; it is menaced only by destructive outsiders.

The plantation's freedom from ideological division is symbolized most perfectly by the voice that tells us the story, that of Sam, issuing from the bottom of the plantation hierarchy but identifying itself fully with the exemplary men at the top. As many plantation writers before the war had discovered, the testimony of the contented slave was nearly indispensable for plantation writing. The most famous specimen of this literary type, though, was not Page's Sam but another freedman who had first appeared in print eight years before "Marse Chan," Joel Chandler Harris's Uncle

Remus. Harris, who like Page had spent the Civil War as a small boy living on a great plantation, was a Georgia newspaperman who created one of the most lasting images of plantation life when he published *Uncle Remus: His Songs and Sayings*, in 1880. This work and its several sequels, for most of their careers, have been books for children, who were probably more interested in the doings of Br'er Rabbit and his enemies than in the presentation of the title character or his plantation milieu. Harris probably shared this disposition, being most interested in setting down, with what is now recognized as considerable accuracy, the animal tales he had heard recounted by the slaves on Turnwold plantation in middle Georgia. The opposite of much plantation writing, the Remus stories feature a very narrow cast of human characters: usually just Remus, an aging former slave, the little boy – called only that – who listens to his tales, his mother Miss Sally Huntingdon, and her husband John, a transplanted Yankee. These characters exist, furthermore, only in the slender frame narratives which introduce the animal stories. This gives Harris little chance to suggest, in the kind of elaborate detail favored by the antebellum writers, the full social spectrum of the plantation world. But we are given to understand, as we witness Remus's gruff affection for the child and the family's love for him, that this plantation, like its antebellum ancestors, is a pastoral setting devoid of conflict, where the racial hierarchy is unquestioned and benevolent. During the Civil War, we are told, Remus actually took up arms for the Confederacy, defending not slavery but his master, who was in the sights of a Union sniper when Remus brought his own rifle to bear on the invader. In the original newspaper version of this sketch, the Yankee dies, perhaps of surprise at being attacked by the man he is emancipating. In the version that appeared in the first Remus book, the victim turns out to be none other than John Huntingdon, who is nursed back to health by Miss Sally, marries her at war's end, and becomes Remus's postbellum employer. Harris's plantation world is the setting where all is forgiven and where ideological breaches – between master and slave, Yankee and Confederate – are painlessly healed: exactly the sort of South readers of both sections wanted to read about.

This should not be surprising, for Harris's memories of his own plantation boyhood were mostly pleasant. He recorded those memories in *On the Plantation* (1892), a novelized memoir of his experiences as the boy hired to be "printer's devil" on *The Countryman*, a newspaper published by Turnwold's owner, Joseph Addison Turner. The book was dedicated to Turner, whom Harris recalled with great affection, and his treatment of the plantation betrays no wish to question those memories. But Harris, like his fictional alter ego Joe Maxwell, had nonetheless an unusual vantage point on plantation life. He was a town boy and an illegitimate child in whom the benevolent Turner had taken an interest; his role on the plantation made him neither planter, slave, nor poor white but *sui generis*. Perhaps for this reason he was able to observe a good deal that sometimes escapes the notice of plantation fiction. Thus his cast of characters in *On the Plantation* includes not only "Harbert," a Remus-type who regales Joe with animal tales, but also Mink, a fugitive slave whom the boy assists without guilt or apology (the contrast with *Huckleberry Finn*'s treatment of the same material is striking); not only standard-issue, fox-hunting Southern cavaliers but also a pair of Confederate deserters, whom Joe and the novel itself treat with full sympathy. To be sure, the ideological conflicts hinted at by runaway slaves and AWOL Confederates are eventually explained away, blamed on bad people rather than flawed institutions, and are easily resolved by novel's end. Harris's vision of the plantation was essentially conservative, but his penchant for sharp-eyed accuracy sometimes gave his work a subversive capacity for surprise that its author may not fully have intended.

In the work for which Harris is best known, these surprises come not in the presentation of the plantation household itself but in the framed narratives about the days when "creeturs had lots mo' sense dan dey got now," when indeed "dey had sense same like folks" (Harris 1981: 32). The animals of the forest whose antics Remus describes are indeed human in all but physical form, but the resemblance is no compliment to humanity. Br'er Rabbit, Br'er Fox, and their siblings Bear, Wolf, Possum, and the rest are human in all the worst senses: they are proud, competitive, selfish, treacherous, and indifferent to the suffering their tricks and schemes inflict on one another. And yet their world is not a Darwinian state of nature but a fully social one in which murder and dinner parties are planned with equal care (indeed, are often parts of the same plan), and in which every animal's goal is not mere survival but social preeminence. At the top of the unstable hierarchy is Br'er Rabbit, morally no better than his peers but nearly always cleverer than they. His successes are a matter of exploiting the weaknesses of his enemies, like the sadism that leads Br'er Fox to try to kill him in what his victim assures him would be the worst possible way, being tossed into the briar patch ("Bred en bawn in a brier patch," laughs the rabbit as he scampers away). In Remus's revision of the Aesopian fable of the tortoise and the hare, Br'er Terrapin wins a footrace with Br'er Rabbit not by admirable persistence but by blatant fraud, stationing his look-alike relatives at intervals along the race-course. "But Uncle Remus," the boy protests, "that was cheating." Remus replies with what might be taken as the anti-moral of all the fables: "Co'se, honey. De beastesses 'gun ter cheat, en den fokes tuck it up, en hit keep on spreadin'" (84). It is indeed a world, mirroring the human one, in which conflict is the rule of life and nice guys finish last.

It is the opposite, that is, of the harmonious plantation world in which the tales are told. The realm of violence and strife inhabited by Br'er Rabbit is distanced from the "real" one of Remus and his employers – these are animals, and they lived long ago – but this camouflage should fool nobody. Harris himself noted that the tales were "allegorical" and that "it needs no scientific investigation to show why [the African-American narrator] selects as his hero the weakest and most harmless of all animals, and brings him out victorious in contests with the bear, the wolf, and the fox" (9). Like "Marse Chan," the Remus stories displace conflict beyond the borders of the plantation, but unlike Page's, they place it at the very center of the fiction. The fierce, individualistic, predatory world of the animals is itself a refutation of the claims made by the loyal Remus and his affectionate white patrons, an antipastoral allegory placed at the heart of pastoral narrative.

The Remus stories were read to children all over nineteenth-century America, including, fascinatingly, the children of Charles W. Chesnutt, the African-American writer whose plantation stories began appearing in *The Atlantic Monthly* in 1887 and were gathered between hard covers in the 1899 collection *The Conjure Woman*. The considerable popularity of Chesnutt's early fiction owed something, no doubt, to the general appeal of plantation writing of the Thomas Nelson Page variety, but they are now recognized as artful satires of such writing. The stories carefully reproduce the situation of "Marse Chan" and *Uncle Remus*: a former slave, Uncle Julius McAdoo, tells tales of life before the war to the Northerners who now own the North Carolina plantation where he has spent his life. Unlike Page's, though, Julius's stories are anything but affectionate: his matter-of-fact narrations are full of cruelty and injustice and represent the plantation as simply a business setting that existed to extract wealth from land and the labor of slaves. The world of Chesnutt's conjure tales is as unsentimental as the animal world Uncle Remus describes. Everybody — not just antebellum masters — is driven by the profit motive: it governs the conjurors, black practitioners of folk-magic who assist the slaves, but also, when the price is right, the masters; it governs John, the new Northern plantation owner, confident though he is of his moral superiority to his Southern predecessor; and emphatically it governs Julius himself, who always derives an economic benefit from his storytelling. Chesnutt's satires simultaneously undermine the Old South myth of the benevolent slaveowner and the Reconstruction myth of the liberating Yankee. Most importantly, in their presentation of the shrewd and unsentimental Julius, they explode the myth which helped reunite the two sections, that of the simple-hearted, grateful black retainer whose properly subordinate status, at least, white Northerners and Southerners could agree upon.

Chesnutt's stories hint at the potential for complexity and thoughtful critique in the plantation genre. But this potential was exploited by only a few of his contemporaries and successors. A modern reader could profit from looking at Opie Read's *My Young Master* (1896), whose narrator Dan — once a slave, now a Congressman — stunningly revises plantation fiction's typical narrating freedman. Also interesting is *The Southerner* (1909), the only novel of Walter Hines Page, a book editor and progressive journalist (and perhaps a distant cousin of Thomas Nelson Page). Page took a typical plantation story, the growth to manhood of a young Southern aristocrat, and made it a parable of his own efforts at reforming education, agriculture, and (to a small degree) race relations in the South. Nor should we forget another politically loaded plantation novel, *The Clansman* (1905), by Page's fellow North Carolinian Thomas Dixon. A virulently racist fable of Reconstruction and Ku Klux Klan resistance, *The Clansman* followed what had become a standard pattern by making its Southern plantation the site of regional reconciliation, the place where former Yankees and Confederates could come together — here in the mutually agreeable cause of restoring white supremacy and subjugating the briefly empowered freedmen.

But by Dixon's time plantation fiction had largely run its course as a form for serious literature. The prescriptions of "realism" and "naturalism," important in

Continental fiction since the middle of the nineteenth century, had gained enough authority in the US to make the plantation romance, with its idealized settings, stereotyped characters, and sentimentality, seem old-fashioned. When Southern writers again claimed a national audience, in the 1920s, they were of a different stripe, conversant with literary modernism and inclined, as the "Fugitive" poets of Nashville said when introducing their magazine in 1922, to "[flee] from nothing faster than from the high-caste Brahmins of the Old South" (quoted in Pratt 1991: xxiv). This was the generation that produced William Faulkner, Thomas Wolfe, and Erskine Caldwell, who had little use for the old idealizations of Southern country life. The Fugitives, once they became Agrarians, usually held up the small farmer, not the great planter, as the Southern social ideal. Even *Gone With the Wind* tried to correct the older plantation image by pointing out that antebellum planters, far from being an ancient aristocracy, were often just small farmers who had prospered.

But of course the most forceful reminder of that fact, and the most powerful work to come out of the plantation tradition, was *Absalom, Absalom!* Faulkner's novel is of course one of the touchstones of literary modernism, a *tour de force* to be placed alongside James Joyce's *Ulysses*. But it is also a plantation novel – or rather, its form arises from the strange conversation it seems to be having with the plantation novel, rather like the one *Ulysses* has with the story of Odysseus. It is startling to notice how many of the standard elements are present: the novel concerns a great estate and its extended family, black and white, and the historical doom which overshadows them all. The plot has at its center the courtship of the plantation belle, Judith Sutpen, by her attractive suitor, the Confederate hero Charles Bon, who dies tragically at war's end. There is a loyal ex-slave (Clytie) who like Sam ends up the custodian of the plantation and its stories. We learn many of these things in the same way we learn what happened to Marse Chan – by listening as a local witness tells the story to a curious Northerner (Quentin Compson and his Harvard roommate Shreve).

Adding up such details yields, I think, not a perverse misreading of Faulkner's novel but a recognition of Faulkner's own perverse, and quite deliberate, misreading of a tradition which for a long time dictated the terms of Southern narrative. Thus he gives us the testimony of a black witness of antebellum life – but it is Charles Bon writing (with captured Yankee stove polish) an elegantly ironic letter to his fiance, Judith. He shows us a young cavalier going off to war with his black companion – but Henry Sutpen does not know that Charles Bon is black, or that Charles is his brother. There is even a reenactment of Sam's sad return to the plantation at war's end, bearing the body of Chan – but here the white veteran, Henry, carries the body of the black one, whom he has just murdered. He has done so because Charles, of whose ancestry he has now been told, intends to marry Henry's sister Judith and thus make literal the metaphoric claim made by many plantation novels, that on the plantation blacks and whites belonged to one big, extended family.

Faulkner's work is not precisely a parody of plantation fiction, like Chesnutt's conjuring stories. Yet it obviously does demolish several of the clichés of plantation writing, on its way to an even more thorough annihilation of perhaps the most important premise of this fiction and the ideology that informed it: the idea that the hierarchies enshrined by the plantation system had been ordained by nature. Thomas Sutpen is not a born aristocrat but a poor white successfully impersonating one; Charles Bon is not a white gentleman but (by the racial conventions of his time) a black man "passing" for white. We see their identities contrived just as, in the two scenes I began by mentioning, we see the plantation itself constructed and its hierarchy violently established. And though Sutpen's plantation inevitably fails, in *Absalom, Absalom!* the tragedy is caused by disastrous flaws within the plantation world, not by wicked outsiders. The dead Confederate hero around whom the whole story revolves was killed, after all, not by the Yankees but by his own brother and comrade in arms.

And yet Sutpen's Hundred does fail, as literary plantations have been doing since *The Valley of Shenandoah* in 1824. This is to say that Faulkner's novel, though mercilessly exposing many of the conventions of plantation writing, spares the most essential of them. *Absalom, Absalom!* is the tragedy of people hoping, in their pastoral "innocence," to escape from history, but in the end finding history crashing down upon them. Sutpen has imagined his hundred square miles of fertile land precisely as a secure refuge from his own past and that of his family and class; Quentin Compson, in a notable revision of this Southern trope, hopes Harvard College will prove a similar refuge for him. But any reader of plantation fiction could tell them that it is no use: such refuges never last, and history will find you out in the end. That is the chief insight of the form, and the one that survives Faulkner's otherwise merciless deconstruction to become, obviously, the central idea of the novel. I began by suggesting that in even the most celebratory plantation romances, history may be found nibbling at the edges of the great estate. In what must surely be the least celebratory of them, history crashes through the gates of Sutpen's Hundred, wreaking havoc on its master's grand design; it follows Quentin Compson all the way to Harvard, reducing him to shivering misery as he lies in the New England dark, denying that he hates the South.

REFERENCES AND FURTHER READING

Andrews, William L. (1991) "Inter(racial) textuality in Nineteenth-Century Southern Narrative." In Jay Clayton and Eric Rothstein (eds.) *Influence and Intertextuality in Literary History* (pp. 298–317). Madison: University of Wisconsin Press.

Bakker, Jan (1989) *Pastoral in Antebellum Southern Romance*. Baton Rouge: Louisiana State University Press.

Byrd, William (1998) [1726] "Letter to Charles Boyle, Lord of Orrery." In William L. Andrews (ed.) *The Literature of the American South* (pp. 29–31). New York: Norton.

Chesnutt, Charles (2002) [1899] *The Conjure Woman*. In *Charles W. Chesnutt: Stories, Novels & Essays*. New York: Literary Classics of the United States.

Dixon, Thomas (1970) [1905] *The Clansman: An Historical Romance of the Ku Klux Klan*. Lexington: University Press of Kentucky.

Faulkner, William (1990) [1936] *Absalom, Absalom!* Corrected Text. New York: Vintage International.

Gaines, Francis Pendleton (1924). *The Southern Plantation: A Study in the Development and the Accuracy of a Tradition*. New York: Columbia University Press.

Grammer, John M. (1996) *Pastoral and Politics in the Old South*. Baton Rouge: Louisiana State University Press.

Gray, Richard (1986) *Writing the South: Ideas of an American Region*. Cambridge: Cambridge University Press.

Harris, Joel Chandler (1981) [1892] *On the Plantation: A Story of a Georgia Boy's Adventures During the War*. Athens, GA: University of Georgia Press.

Harris, Joel Chandler (1981) [1880] *Uncle Remus: His Songs and Sayings*. Atlanta: Cherokee Publishing.

Kennedy, John Pendleton (1986) [1832] *Swallow Barn; or, A Sojourn in the Old Dominion*. Baton Rouge: Louisiana State University Press.

Lukacher, Ned (1986) *Primal Scenes: Literature, Philosophy, Psychoanalysis*. Ithaca, NY: Cornell University Press.

MacKethan, Lucinda Hardwick (1980) *The Dream of Arcady: Place and Time in Southern Literature*. Baton Rouge: Louisiana State University Press.

Mitchell, Margaret (1936) *Gone With the Wind*. New York: Macmillan.

Page, Thomas Nelson (1969) [1887] *In Ole Virginia; or, Marse Chan and Other Stories*. Chapel Hill: University of North Carolina Press.

Page, Walter Hines (1909). *The Southerner: A Novel; Being the Autobiography of Nicholas Worth*. New York: Doubleday, Page.

Pratt, William (ed.) (1991) *The Fugitives: Modern Southern Poetry in Perspective*. Nashville, TN: J. S. Sanders.

Pyron, Darden Asbury (1991) *Southern Daughter: The Life of Margaret Mitchell*. New York: Oxford University Press.

Romine, Scott (1999) *The Narrative Forms of Southern Community*. Baton Rouge: Louisiana State University Press.

Simms, William Gilmore (1954) [1852] Letter to James Henry Hammond, December 15, 1852. In *The Letters of William Gilmore Simms, Vol. 3*. Columbia: University of South Carolina Press.

Simms, William Gilmore (1983) [1852] *Woodcraft; or, Hawks About the Dovecote; A Story of the South at the Close of the Revolution*. Albany: New College and University Press.

Simpson, Lewis P. (1975) *The Dispossessed Garden: Pastoral and History in Southern Literature*. Athens, GA: University of Georgia Press.

Stowe, Harriet Beecher (1982) [1852] *Uncle Tom's Cabin; Or, Life Among the Lowly*. In *Harriet Beecher Stowe: Three Novels*. New York: Literary Classics of the United States.

Taylor, William R (1961) *Cavalier and Yankee: The Old South and American National Character*. New York: George Braziller.

Tucker, George (1970) [1824] *The Valley of Shenandoah; or, Memoirs of the Graysons*. Chapel Hill: University of North Carolina Press.

Tucker, Nathaniel Beverley (1971) [1836] *The Partisan Leader: A Tale of the Future*. Chapel Hill: University of North Carolina Press.

Williams, Raymond (1973) *The Country and the City*. New York: Oxford University Press.

5

The Slavery Debate

Susan-Mary Grant

It was in Savannah in February of 1861, barely two months before the fall of Fort Sumter signaled the start of the American Civil War, that the newly formed Confederacy's vice-president, Alexander Stephens, delivered his famous "Cornerstone" speech. The main subject of his speech was the Confederate Constitution, which, Stephens declared, "has put to rest forever all the agitating questions relating to our peculiar institution, African slavery as it exists amongst us, the proper status of the negro in our form of civilization." The national Constitution, Stephens argued, "rested upon the assumption of the equality of races," but it was a compact built on sand. By contrast, he asserted, the Confederacy's "new government is founded upon exactly the opposite idea; its foundations are laid, its cornerstone rests, upon the great truth that the negro is not equal to the white man, that slavery – subordination to the superior race – is his natural and normal condition." By that time Stephens was, of course, largely preaching to the converted, but he acknowledged that this "truth has been slow in the process of its development . . . The errors of the past generation still clung to many as late as twenty years ago."

In fact, twenty years before Stephens spoke, many Southern proslavery leaders and intellectuals had recognized the problem, and were already busy constructing the foundations upon which the Confederate cornerstone would eventually come to rest. In a closely argued article written for the *Southern Literary Messenger* in 1839, the notable conservative Virginian Abel P. Upshur explored the political and social dimensions of "Domestic Slavery," and the growing need both to define and defend these. "Our peculiar systems have seldom been subjected to that analytic and philosophical examination, which is necessary to a proper understanding of their true character," Upshur noted. "Satisfied that the machine was working well, we have, hitherto, evinced but little curiosity as to the principles upon which it was constructed, and little inclination to inquire by what springs it was put in motion, or how it produced its results." However, he continued, "circumstances have forced upon us a more minute and careful examination of the various questions which arise from the institution of domestic slavery…the great distinguishing characteristic of the Southern states." Even among Southerners, Upshur observed, there had been no "concurrence of opinion upon the subject. We have been in the habit of contemplating it rather as a domestic than as a political institution," he argued, "and of course our judgments have not been altogether free from the influences of our private habits, our passions and our peculiar tastes." Attempting to make a virtue out of a necessity, he concluded it "is fortunate for us that we are no longer permitted to view it in so imperfect a light" (Upshur 1839: 677).

The "circumstances" that Upshur referred to were many and varied. A confluence of both national and international events prompted Southerners to give greater attention to their "peculiar institution" in the 1830s, not least of which was the abolition of slavery in the British West Indies in July of 1834. Before that, however, and much closer to home, was the publication of David Walker's famous *Appeal* (1829). Its full title, *Walker's Appeal, in Four Articles, together with a Preamble to the Colored Citizens of the World, but in Particular, and Very Expressly to Those of the United States of America*, made it clear that Walker, a free-born black from North Carolina, had Southern slaveholders in his sights. His advice to blacks – "If you commence, make sure work – do not trifle, for they will not trifle with you – they want us for their slaves, and think nothing of murdering us in order to subject us to that wretched condition – therefore, if there is an *attempt* made by us, kill or be killed" (quoted in Sydnor 1968: 223) – was hardly guaranteed to help white Southerners sleep easily in their beds. The discovery of copies of Walker's *Appeal* in Virginia, South Carolina, North Carolina, and Georgia prompted several state legislatures to pass ever more stringent laws in an attempt to prevent slaves from seeing the pamphlet.

Even while the state legislatures were attempting to deal with the threat posed by Walker's pamphlet, the pressure on the South was stepped up. In part this derived from the widespread newspaper coverage accorded the debate in the British parliament over the abolition of slavery in the colonies, which continued until the bill to abolish slavery was passed in 1833. In part, too, it came from the North. At the start of 1831 William Lloyd Garrison published the first issue of his abolitionist newspaper, *The Liberator*, in which he famously announced his intention to be "as harsh as truth and as uncompromising as justice" on the subject of slavery. Garrison did not advocate violence as such, but in the late July issue of *The Liberator* he did urge slaves to "strike for God and vengeance now" (quoted in Sydnor 1968: 225). In the following month one of the most dramatic slave insurrections that the South had witnessed occurred; the Nat Turner uprising in Southampton County, Virginia, during which some fifty-seven whites were killed.

Although the Turner insurrection was a localized affair, and the last significant slave revolt that the South experienced, Southerners were not to know that, and it caused widespread unease both at the time and for many years afterwards. In an article which appeared in the *Atlantic Monthly* barely a few months after the outbreak of the Civil War, Thomas Wentworth Higginson, the New England reformer and later colonel of one of the first black regiments, observed that the Turner uprising continued to represent "a memory of terror, a symbol of wild retribution" not just for Southerners, but for the nation as a whole. A direct link between Turner's actions and the sentiments of either Walker's *Appeal* or Garrison's abolitionist paper was never established, but was strongly suspected. In any case, Southerners regarded themselves – and not without good reason – to be under attack, and from several directions. The atmosphere of fear and suspicion that this engendered prompted one state, Virginia, to consider more fully the implications both of domestic slavery and the status of free blacks in the South. To this end, when its legislature met in December of 1831, it established a select committee in the House of Delegates to explore the issues. The ensuing debate, described by Joseph Robert as the "final and most brilliant of the Southern attempts to abolish slavery" (quoted in Sydnor 1968: 227), began in January of 1832 and lasted for two weeks.

Historians have generally concurred with Robert, and frequently cite 1832 as a crucial turning point as far as the slavery debate was concerned. In that year, the centennial of George Washington's birth, not only did the Virginia House of Delegates address the subject of slavery, but, within weeks of each other, two major publications on the subject appeared: William Lloyd Garrison's *Thoughts on African Colonization* and Thomas Roderick Dew's *Review of the Debate in the Virginia Legislature of 1831–1832*. In many ways, therefore, 1832 was a turning point, but not quite in the way that it has sometimes been portrayed. The debate of that year represented little more than a development of the Southern emancipationist and proslavery arguments that had already been aired in the state's Constitutional Convention of 1829, at which point, according to Hezekiah Niles, Virginians faced the stark choice between "the perpetual duration of slavery or the increase of a generous and free white population." No decision was reached then, nor would it be two years later, despite the fact that the Turner uprising did lend a certain urgency to proceedings. It was also the case, as Carl Degler reminds us, that "at no time did the House have before it a resolution calling for the ending of slavery or even a plan of gradual emancipation. The debate was over whether a committee's report ought to recommend the ending of slavery or not." Nevertheless, Degler notes, this in no way hampered "those who thought slavery wrong or inexpedient from voicing some of the harshest judgments on slavery ever to be heard in a public forum in North America" (Degler 1975: 16).

Among those who seized the opportunity to attack slavery was James McDowell, the future governor of Virginia. Although a slaveholder himself, he argued that the Turner insurrection was the writing on the wall. In response to the suggestion that it had been no more than a trivial affair, McDowell asked, rhetorically, "was that a petty affair which startled the feelings of your whole population . . . which wrung out from an affrighted people the thrilling cry . . . We are in peril of our lives; send us an army for defense?" No, he concluded, "it was the suspicion eternally attached to the slave himself, the suspicion that a Nat Turner might be in every family, that the same bloody deed might be acted over at any time and in any place, that the materials for it were spread through the land, and were always ready for a like explosion." McDowell had hit the nail on the head. As William Freehling notes, Turner's "anti-familial assault killed something more vulnerable" than its human victims; "Nat Turner murdered slaveholders' domestic illusion" (Freehling 1990: 180).

From the outset, however, the odds were stacked against slavery's opponents. In part, they were hampered by the fact they had no immediate solution to offer. In part, too, the Virginia debate – when one reads between the lines – was less about slavery *per se* and more about the power struggle then taking place between the dominant eastern aristocracy of the state and its western yeoman farmers, with the bulk of proslavery opinion coming from the Piedmont and Tidewater regions, the bulk of opposition from west of the Blue Ridge Mountains (Stampp 1942: 380; Sydnor 1986: 228; Freehling 1990: 178). As would still be the case two decades later, much of the argument on the side of abolition was couched in terms of what this would achieve for the white population rather than the black. In particular, it was agreed that, were the slaves to be freed, they should be encouraged to leave the state. Understandable concern was also expressed as to the general economic impact that abolition – gradual or immediate – would have. Defenders of slavery argued – as they would continue to do until the outbreak of the Civil War – that the institution accounted both for "the prosperity and superior manners of Virginians as well as of the good treatment and contentment of the slaves," supporting such rather vague assertions with rather more hard-headed denunciations of the right of any legislature to interfere with private property (Sydnor 1968: 227–8).

To a degree, however, the arguments on both sides were moot. In the end, rather than raising Southern awareness of the inherent dangers of the "peculiar institution," what the debate actually achieved was to bring home to the eastern slaveholders just how "precarious was their hold on the lower elements of Virginia society" (Stampp 1942: 381). The debate effectively "exposed a regime in need of new vocabulary, new thought, new action to consolidate slavery. Upper-class rulers who called slavery dishonorable almost invited renewed efforts to cure dishonor. Procrastinating Virginians needed at least a rationale for further procrastination" (Freehling 1990: 190). "Subsequent developments in Virginian public opinion were not in the direction of abolishing slavery," Sydnor notes. "In legislative elections in the spring of 1832, several of the antislavery delegates were defeated in eastern Virginia" (Sydnor 1968: 228–9). Such an outcome might have been anticipated, but it was not quite what the opponents of slavery had in mind. Another outcome of the Virginia debate – and a further nail in the coffin of Southern antislavery forces – was the appearance of Dew's famous *Review* of the issues involved. Its publication, according to Stampp, shows clearly that the "real challenge to the security of the slaveholders arose . . . within their own section and forced them to take a positive stand in the defense of slavery" (Stampp 1942: 381–2).

Again, Dew's work has often been identified as a turning point in the proslavery argument, despite the fact that its thesis was hardly new and its immediate impact relatively limited compared to the broader appeal it gained in the 1850s. Tise, in particular, takes issue with the fact that "historians continue to assert that Dew's *Review* set the pace for all proslavery literature that would later appear in the Old

South. Although Dew's *Review* would indeed be frequently cited," he argues, "it was a unique perspective on slavery in America that would not be repeated and would not need replication." At the same time, it neither appeared nor argued in a vacuum. The coincidence of its publication alongside Garrison's *Thoughts on African Colonization* was, as Tise notes, not without a certain irony. Although traditionally seen "as the most significant early voices of abolition and proslavery respectively," Garrison and Dew, Tise points out, "unknowingly joined forces in 1832 to kill America's favorite solution to slavery...colonization... Although Garrison spoke for radical emancipators and Dew for slaveholders, their criticisms largely overlapped to constitute a stirring refutation of a generation of American social thought." America's "interests must inevitably suffer by the removal of our colored population," Garrison argued. "Their labor is indispensably necessary and extremely valuable. By whom shall the plantations at the South be cultivated but by them?" (Tise 1987: 70–1). Dew concurred. Although the one thing that many of the Virginia delegates had agreed on was that colonization was the *sine qua non* of any emancipation plan, Dew devoted a large part of his *Review* to proving how impractical – economically, socially and, up to a point, morally – this would be. "It is in truth," he argued, "the slave labor in Virginia which gives value to her soil and her habitations; take away this and you pull down the Atlas that upholds the whole system."

In making his case, Dew aimed much of his ire at the free black population, drawing on several stock arguments concerning black labor in America that future proslavery spokesmen would develop and refine. "Much was said in the legislature of Virginia about superiority of free labor over slave," Dew noted, "and perhaps, under certain circumstances, this might be true; but in the present instance the question is between the relative amounts of labor which may be obtained from slaves before and after their emancipation." Slave labor, he asserted, was "vastly more efficient and productive than the labor of free blacks...In the free black, the principle of idleness and dissipation triumphs over that of accumulation and the desire to better our condition...the experiment has been sufficiently tried to prove most conclusively that the free black will work nowhere except by compulsion." Ultimately, Dew argued, whether free or slave, the "blacks have now all the habits and feelings of slaves, the whites have those of masters; the prejudices are formed, and mere legislation cannot remove them...It is better," he concluded, "that each one should remain in society in the condition in which he has been born and trained, and not to mount too fast without preparation."

Dew was convinced Southern slaves were happier and more contented than Northern blacks, and took issue with Thomas Jefferson's observation that the slave was more likely to hate than love or respect his master. "Mr. Jefferson," Dew argued, "is not borne out by the fact. We are well convinced that there is nothing but the mere relations of husband and wife, parent and child, brother and sister, which produce a closer tie than the relation of master and servant." This was a fairly direct contradiction of McDowell's observation regarding the lessons to be learned from Nat Turner's insurrection, but Dew seemed persuaded that, in his famous phrase, a "merrier being does not exist on the face of the globe than the negro slave of the United States." Further, what Dew saw as a wholly positive relationship between master and slave accounted, in his view, for the unique understanding of, and commitment to, the idea of liberty in the South. Slavery, Dew argued, effectively removed "the greatest cause of distinction and separation of the ranks of society. The man to the North will not shake hands familiarly with his servant, and converse, and laugh, and dine with him, no matter how honest and respectable he may be. But go to the South, and you will find that no white man feels such inferiority of rank as to be unworthy of association with those around him . . . it is this spirit of equality," Dew deduced, "which is both the generator and preserver of the genuine spirit of liberty."

Throughout his *Review*, Dew alternated between the attack and the defense, with perhaps rather more emphasis on the latter than he realized. As he saw it, Southern slaveholders were not dealing with "an evil of yesterday's origin" but with "an evil which is the growth of centuries and of tens of centuries; which is almost coeval with the deluge; which has existed, under different modifications, since man was man . . . the original sin of introduction," he repeated, "rests not on our heads." There was, clearly, an element of what Freehling terms "Virginia apologetics" in Dew's argument, and his *Review* was in no sense a watershed tract between the acceptance of slavery as a necessary evil and its later promotion as a positive good. When Dew composed his *Review*, Tise argues, he "seemed totally unaware of the rising storm and contented himself with criticizing the errors of the past" (Freehling 1990: 190–1; Tise 1987: 71). This is hardly surprising. Hindsight alone tells historians what the decade of the 1830s would bring. Even if Dew had been aware – and he most likely was – that a storm was brewing over this particular topic, he could not have foreseen the extent of it, nor the outcome.

If Dew's *Review* "did not lead a school of his Virginia contemporaries halfway towards the 1850s," it nevertheless included many of the proslavery arguments that had been developed prior to 1830 and several that would come to dominate the debate in the 1850s and even beyond (Freehling 1990: 193). Dew's critique of free black labor, for example, was reiterated even after the Civil War had settled the slavery debate once and for all, and became a stock element in the Reconstruction debate; his reliance on the Bible as justification for slavery had always been and would remain a constant and favorite theme of proslavery spokesmen; and even his throwaway observation that Northerners, unused to slavery, made the harshest masters of all would find its echo in the character of Legree, the evil overseer from Vermont in *Uncle Tom's Cabin*. All this, however, lay in the future. As many historians have argued, what Dew was doing in his *Review* was, in effect, reiterating and challenging the opinions of the past and, in the American case, that past stretched all the way back to the colonial period, to the very first recorded arrival of blacks in Virginia in 1619. As Dew had stressed, by the time he came to compose his *Review*, he was certainly not addressing an issue "of yesterday's origin."

Both Dew's pamphlet and the debate that prompted it followed what had, by 1830, become something of an American tradition in the slavery debate. The first blacks to arrive in the colonies hardly entered an uncharted wilderness as far as the issues of slavery and race were concerned. By the seventeenth century, Europeans were already in possession of a variety of – mostly negative – stereotypes relating to peoples of any culture different to their own, while slavery – and indeed other examples of unfree labor – as an institution was hardly unfamiliar to them. As an institution, Davis notes, slavery "has always given rise to conflict, fear, and accommodation," but at the same time "the grandiose visions of New World wealth . . . seemed always to require slave labor. The Negro slave thus became an intrinsic part of the American experience." In addition, "Anglo-American slavery was not unique in defining the bondsman as chattel property endowed with elements of human personality. Nor was Anglo-American society unusual in having to accommodate the underlying contradictions of the master–slave relationship" (Davis 1975: 41). What did set America apart from other slaveholding societies was, of course, its Revolution, and specifically the republican, natural rights philosophy that justified it, a philosophy that, at first glance, might be deemed wholly at odds with any support for unfree labor.

Prior to the Revolution, however, slavery was very much taken for granted in the colonies. Since the impulse to attack it was largely absent, so too was the need to defend it. At the start of the eighteenth century, two Massachusetts justices, Samuel Sewell and John Saffin, did cross swords over the issue, setting out their respective arguments in *The Selling of Joseph: A Memorial*, a pamphlet that Sewell, an opponent of slavery, produced in 1700, and in *A Brief and Candid Answer to a Late Printed Sheet, Entitled, The Selling of Joseph* that Saffin, a slaveholder, published in response the following year. What is revealing about this early debate is that Saffin's argument, in particular, utilized most of the elements that would become "typical" in proslavery literature up until the Civil War. Indeed, Tise argues that "almost four-fifths of the arguments used by nineteenth-century proslavery advocates were cited by" Saffin, including the historical and religious justification for slavery, the perennial fear of the free black population, the supposed cultural and civilizing benefits that the slave enjoyed, and the rather more obvious economic and social benefits accruing to the white population from slavery – all themes on which Dew and those who came after him relied (Tise 1987: 16–18).

The Revolution, of course, prompted at least some measure of reassessment of the issues. If it did "not solve the problem of slavery, it at least led to a *perception* of the problem" (Davis 1975: 285). It could hardly be otherwise. Having made the decision to break away from Great Britain and construct the resultant new nation on the basis of the self-evident truths "that all men are created equal, that they are endowed by their Creator with certain inalienable rights, that among these are life, liberty, and the pursuit of happiness," white Americans had created something of an impasse for themselves on the subject of slavery. The response, from the revolutionary era onwards, was, like Dew's in 1832, an awkward combination of defense and attack, charge and countercharge between antislavery and proslavery forces, most of whom, for most of the time, talked past rather than to each other. Much of the content of what would develop into the slavery debate was already in place by 1787, as the

Philadelphia Convention's discussion over the slave trade made clear. As James Madison noted, the argument that slavery "discourages arts and manufactures," prevents the immigration of a free white population "who really enrich and strengthen a Country," and produces "the most pernicious effect on manners" since every "master of slaves is born a petty tyrant," was counterbalanced by Charles Pinckney's blunt assertion that if "slavery be wrong, it is justified by the example of all the world." Although later opponents and defenders of slavery would refine such arguments, they rarely moved far beyond the framework established in these early debates.

Indeed, regarding the arguments adopted by the antislavery and proslavery elements as in any sense comprising a "debate" is in some ways inaccurate, since neither side maintained fixed positions; both antislavery and proslavery were flexible concepts, open to change and interpretation, by the participants themselves from the colonial era onwards and by historians since. Antislavery, as Davis argues, "has been used to describe an organized social force; political activity aimed at eradicating the slave trade or slavery itself; a set of moral and philosophic convictions that might be held with varying intensities; or simply the theoretical belief that Negro slavery is a wasteful, expensive, and dangerous system of labor which tends to corrupt the morals of white Christians" (Davis 1975: 164). Proslavery is equally impossible to pin down with any precision, and attempts to do so, according to Tise, have only resulted in a general misunderstanding of "crucial shifts and changes in proslavery thought" (Tise 1987: 12–14).

As alternate threads of social thought, neither antislavery nor proslavery was identifiable with any one section. Tise's exhaustive study of proslavery, in particular, has dispelled any remnants of the notion that the defense of slavery was a purely Southern concern. At the same time, it is necessary to draw some distinction between the more general role that proslavery thought played in the nation at large, and the rather more specific function it had for the South. The South, rather than the North, had of necessity to take a greater interest in the slavery debate, particularly once the institution had become "peculiar" to that section. Here, too, for many years historians argued that the revolutionary era saw little debate over the issue even in the South, even in Virginia, but this was not the case. Although hardly the all-consuming subject that it would become, the debate over slavery became more heated in the later eighteenth century, its defense apparently stimulated rather than restricted by revolutionary rhetoric. The proslavery petitions presented to the Virginia General Assembly only a couple of years prior to the Federal Convention, in 1784 and 1785, in response to the 1782 law permitting private manumissions, offered a glimpse of things to come. In part, these petitions were prompted by the activities of antislavery activists, especially religious groups such as Quakers, Methodists, and Baptists in the state in the 1780s. Two Methodist ministers, Thomas Coke and Francis Asbury, presented a petition in 1785 calling for the general emancipation of Virginia's slaves. This was thrown out, but not before, James Madison noted, "an avowed patronage of its principle by sundry respectable members." The proslavery petitions were rather better received, but they, too, were defeated. "While the actions of the Virginia legislature in 1785 indicated that there was some sympathy for the principle of emancipation," Schmidt and Wilhelm argue, "none of the delegates was willing to go beyond allowing private manumission and a sizable number agreed with the proslavery petitions presented to the House wishing to prohibit even private manumission" (Schmidt and Wilhelm 1973: 135).

If the activities of religious groups stimulated proslavery sentiment, the form this took owed much to revolutionary ideology. "The tone of the petitions is not one of guilt and defensiveness," Schmidt and Wilhelm observe.

> They contain a fierce assertion of property rights and liberty at the same time they deny the slaves' humanity and their right to enjoy freedom to participate in society. In the petitioners' eyes, religious justification gave added weight to the validity of their society, recently liberated from British oppression but based on a more profound form of oppression to which they were blind. (Schmidt and Wilhelm 1973: 136)

Harking back to the arguments proposed by Saffin some eighty years previously and looking forward to those of later antebellum defenders of slavery, the 1784 and 1785 proslavery petitions combined an absolute defense of property rights with the by-now standard dire warnings of the impact that free blacks would have on society. As the petition from Amelia County put it, emancipation is "exceedingly *impolitic*. For it involves in it, and is productive of Want, Poverty, Distress, and Ruin to the Free Citizen (quoted in Schmidt and Wilhelm 1973: 139).

Thomas Jefferson's famous excuse for the new nation's inability to square the ideal of liberty with the reality of slavery was, as he memorably put it in 1820, that Americans had "the wolf by the ears; and we can neither hold him, nor safely let him go. Justice is on one side, and self-preservation on the other." The Amelia County petitioners may not have put it so well or so succinctly, but they were making a similar point. They were not alone. In 1804 the American Convention for Promoting the Abolition of Slavery observed that public opinion in North Carolina "is exceedingly hostile to the abolition of slavery, that every attempt towards the emancipation of people of color is regarded with an indignant and jealous eye; that at present the inhabitants of that state, consider the preservation of their lives, and all they hold dear on earth, as depending on the continuance of slavery" (Finnie 1969: 327).

For many Southerners, clearly, as for Jefferson, "the scale tipped heavily towards self-preservation, which meant the preservation of a social order based on slavery" (Davis 1975: 183–4). Naturally, such views did not go unchallenged. Between the closing of the external slave trade in 1808 and the 1830s – Adams's "neglected period of anti-slavery" – the South experienced enough antislavery activity to keep slaveholders on the alert, even as the possibility of universal emancipation receded into the distance. The issue was debated, although not resolved, during the Kentucky constitutional elections of 1792 and 1799, and between 1808 and 1823 the Kentucky

Abolition Society welcomed over a hundred members. These activities led Allen to conclude that "two modes of antislavery activity prevailed in the South prior to 1830: the unorganized and halfhearted efforts of politicians like Jefferson and St. George Tucker, who concentrated on the evils slavery held for white society, and the more substantial efforts of clergymen, who emphasized the moral evil of holding men in chains" (Allen 1978: 171–2). Yet, far from posing a threat to slavery, this constant potential "for internal dissent ultimately became the South's major source of strength," producing, according to Davis, "a resolution . . . which committed the entire society to a moral defense of the slaveholder, a defense demanded by the major Protestant churches and by the political and military power of an immense and diversified white population (Davis 1975: 211–12).

Two years after Jefferson's famous – if not especially helpful – observation about the burden slavery conferred upon the nation, South Carolina experienced the Denmark Vesey insurrection, which only served to confirm Charlestonians' fears regarding their slave population. Several writers called for colonization efforts to be speeded up, as a means of freeing "the country of so unwelcome a burden" (Tise 1987: 59). The response from the South Carolina court that sentenced the conspirators, however, revealed how unlikely any radical solution actually was, and how entrenched both slavery and the defense of the slaveholder had become by 1822. Addressing the accused, the court noted that "in no age or country has the condition of slaves been milder or more humane than your own. You are, with few exceptions, treated with kindness, and enjoy every comfort compatible with your situation" (Davis 1975: 208).

A decade later, as Virginia tentatively probed the implications of the Nat Turner rebellion, little obvious headway had been made as far as the slavery debate was concerned. Few, if any, new elements had entered the debate, which continued to revolve around a combination of biblical, economic, and social issues relating to slavery. However, if neither the 1820s nor the 1830s can be isolated as "turning points" in any specific sense, those two decades nevertheless saw the slavery debate pick up speed, even if it failed to change direction. The reasons for this lay beyond the arguments themselves, specifically in the political arena. The Denmark Vesey plot occurred shortly after the debates over the Missouri Compromise; the Nat Turner insurrection and the response to it coincided with the Nullification Crisis of 1832–3. Both were to have serious repercussions as far as the South and the debate over slavery were concerned.

Jefferson, again, had a pithy observation to hand regarding the sectional implications of the Missouri Compromise: "this momentous question," he announced, "like a fire-bell in the night, awakened and filled me with terror." The debate over the tariff and the Nullification Crisis ten years later further developed the sectional theme which itself was, at base, about slavery and its future in America. While 1832 introduced little that was new to the slavery debate itself, after South Carolina's stand against federal legislation – albeit an abortive stand at that point – the whole issue of slavery and its defense became intrinsically linked to the development of Southern nationalism. "To support slavery," McCardell notes, did not alone make a man a Southern nationalist. But Southern nationalism, as a political movement, did require the exploitation of the proslavery argument. Exploitation, in turn, required ever more vivid methods of demonstrating the benefits of the peculiar institution. As a result, Southern nationalism eventually became associated with the most extreme and, at the same time, the most apparently convincing strain of the proslavery argument.

This development also coincided, he argues, with "the shift of Southern leadership from the divided and demoralized state of Virginia to the homogeneous, cotton growing state of South Carolina" (McCardell 1979: 49–50).

This shift did not happen overnight. There is perhaps too much store set on the notion that, following the Virginia debate and Dew's *Review*, the South's defenders of slavery abandoned the notion that slavery was a "necessary evil" and began to promote it as a "positive good." Again, elements of both viewpoints had been present from colonial times, and the 1830s did not mark an immediate and dramatic break from the traditions set by the earliest opponents and critics of slavery. As Freehling notes, historians tend to "label those who prefigure as transition figures. The trouble with seeing Dew as transitional is that no transition took place ... In his state, he worked largely alone ... the great Virginia proslavery writers – George Fitzhugh, William R. Smith, Thornton Stringfellow, and so on – were all luminaries of the 1850s. All were conscious they were attempting something fresh" (Freehling 1990: 193). Nevertheless, if not wholly reconfigured, the stakes were raised in the 1830s as far as the slavery debate was concerned. Perhaps nowhere was this made clearer than in the congressional battle over slavery petitions that began in 1835 and resulted, the following year, in the infamous "Gag Rule" (the 21st Rule), requiring all petitions relating to slavery to be automatically tabled without discussion. This held until John Quincy Adams managed to get it repealed in 1844. By effectively stifling debate over slavery petitions, Southern congressmen had ensured that in whatever form the slavery debate continued, it would not be at the federal level – not for nearly a decade, at least.

During the course of these congressional debates, James Henry Hammond, who was just embarking on a career that would in time see him become one of the great proslavery luminaries of the 1850s, set out his arguments against the abolition of slavery. Slavery to the South, Hammond argued, "is as natural as the climate itself." Further, slavery, according to Hammond, was "no evil. On the contrary," he continued, "I believe it to be the greatest of all the great blessings which a kind Providence bestowed upon our glorious region." For Hammond, slavery improved Southern wealth, manners, morality, religious life, and "genius." Ultimately, however, his defense of the institution rested on ancient prejudices: "The doom of Ham has been branded on the form and features of his African descendants," he argued, the "hand of fate has united his color and destiny. Man cannot separate what God hath joined" (Sydnor 1968: 336; Miller 1996: 138–9). There was nothing especially original in Hammond's argument. Jefferson had famously contemplated the question of whether black and white were equal in ability and intellect; by 1826, Thomas

Cooper, president of South Carolina College and leader of the Nullification campaign in the 1830s, had already concluded that blacks were "an inferior variety of the human species and not capable of the same improvement as the whites... the inferiority of natural intellect among the blacks cannot be denied," he asserted; they "are not capable of much mental improvement, or of literary or scientific acquirement'; and Dew had echoed this belief in his *Review* when he observed "the emancipated black carries a mark which no time can erase; he forever wears the indelible symbol of his inferior condition – the Ethiopian cannot change his skin, nor the leopard his spots." However, in the 1830s, such arguments became rather more common, as the base on which slavery's defense was constructed widened in conjunction with the growing sectional tensions between North and South.

The year after the Gag Rule was passed, the South's most famous spokesman, John C. Calhoun, rose in the Senate to pronounce on the recent debate over slavery petitions and attack the growing influence of abolitionists in the North. "We of the South will not, cannot, surrender our institutions," he argued. "I hold that in the present state of civilization," he continued, "where two races of different origin, and distinguished by color... are brought together, the relation now existing in the slaveholding States between the two is, instead of an evil, a good – a positive good."

Again, Calhoun's "positive good" thesis did not in and of itself mark 1837 as a turning point in the slavery debate, but it, like Dew's *Review*, provided a valuable snapshot of the current state of thinking as well as a useful framework on which other proslavery spokesmen could construct their arguments. Upshur's 1839 analysis of "Domestic Slavery" offers a case in point. Upshur threw pretty much all the ingredients of the slavery debate into the pot, although he was quite heavy-handed with the racial element, which he saw as synonymous with class. In the South, he noted,

> the slave is black, and the white man never is a slave. The distinction addresses itself to the eye, and is proclaimed wherever the two classes appear. It is certainly well calculated to inspire the humblest white man with a high sense of his own comparative dignity and importance, to see a whole class below him in the scale of society.

"Our safety," he argued, "is in the color of the slave; in an eternal, ineffaceable distinction of nature... His caste is everlasting, and whether bond or free, he is the negro still." With no obvious sense of irony, Upshur stressed the existence of slavery better prepared the white man for the enjoyment and full appreciation of freedom, and developed Calhoun's point about the contest between capital and labor. "In slaveholding countries this contest cannot easily arise," he declared: "In them, labor and capital unite in the same person... It is owing chiefly to this cause," he concluded, "that the condition of society at the south has always been more tranquil and less disturbed by factious outbreakings of the people, than it has been at the north."

Such arguments continued into the 1840s, as territorial expansion and the Mexican War (1846–8) further exacerbated the sectional debate over slavery. The *Southern*

Quarterly Review of 1845 repeated Calhoun's and Upshur's point by arguing that the Southern slave "is sure of employment, and therefore sure of subsistence. He never wanders about in pursuit of work. He has a fixed home, certain support, food, clothing, help when sick," supporting this assertion with the – by now – usual biblical and historical justifications for slavery. That "which is recognized, permitted, regulated, enjoined, by the divine law, cannot be sinful," it argued. "To assert that it may be, would be maintaining a proposition quite as extravagant, as that two and two make five. Slavery then being so recognized, permitted, regulated and enjoined, can by no possibility be a sin." In an echo of Hammond's argument, the *Quarterly Review* suggested that in "no country, have the arts or improvements of society flourished or advanced, but by the aid of slavery." It also suggested, somewhat disingenuously, that "the people of the Southern States have never formally vindicated, until lately, the rightfulness, advantages, and necessity of slavery, as established among us," and ascribed the upsurge of interest in the subject to the "perpetual din of the Northern and European press."

Although it has been argued that "it is doubtful whether the Abolitionists caused many Southern opponents of slavery to reconsider their position," the growth of abolitionism, and especially political abolitionism, did encourage them to state it more forcibly and with greater frequency (Stampp 1943: 13). At the same time, as Donald has pointed out, the "motives of these proslavery writers were less evident than their industry. It is by no means clear to whom their treatises were addressed or just what results they expected to produce through their circulation." They were not obviously writing for either a Northern audience nor, with the exception of James Dunwoody Brownson De Bow's tract on *The Interest in Slavery of the Southern Non-Slaveholder*, for a Southern yeoman one (Donald 1971: 5–6)

Donald's explanation for this early example of the Southern rage to explain was that many of the defenders of slavery from the 1840s onwards – among them George Fitzhugh, Edmund Ruffin, James De Bow, William Gilmore Simms, and James Henry Hammond – were all "unhappy men who had severe personal problems relating to their place in Southern society. Though ambitious and hardworking, all failed in the paths normally open to the enterprising in the South . . . Few of them had any large personal stake in the system which they defended" (Donald 1971: 12). In defending slavery, Donald argued, such men were, in part, attempting to write themselves into a society from which relative poverty had excluded them. Above all, however, they were "hopelessly nostalgic . . . defending not the social order which they knew . . . but an idealized paternalistic society which, as they believed, had formerly flourished in the South before it was undermined by the commercialization of urban life . . . and by the increasing democratization and decentralization on the frontier." Their defense of slavery, he concluded, was just one part of a more "general, though diverse, search for social stability in a rapidly changing world" (Donald 1971: 16, 18).

These proslavery voices, although becoming louder and more dominant in the 1840s and 1850s, did not yet have the floor entirely to themselves. There were many on the other side of the debate who considered the South's relative stability in the changing world of the nineteenth century to be a major part of its problem. The agricultural depression of the late 1830s and early 1840s, which reduced slave prices, produced renewed discontent with slavery in the Upper South. In this environment some Southerners, such as Samuel M. Janney, a Southern Quaker, and John Hampden Pleasants, the editor of the influential Richmond *Whig*, were still able to push an antislavery line without being drummed out of the region. Their vision for the South was the opposite of nostalgic. They looked to the future, and "envisioned an ideal society contradictory to the values of a slaveholding society... They held in high esteem such qualities as efficiency, prosperity, and progress," none of which slavery obviously promoted, as the 1840 census had made painfully clear (Hickin 1971: 166). Their focus on the relative decline of the South compared to the industry and growth of the free states was rather too close to Northern opinion even for their comfort, and they had to work hard to differentiate their views from those of what Pleasants described as "that incendiary brood" of Northern busybodies intent on telling the South how to manage its affairs. Nevertheless, like many Northerners, they identified slavery as the prime cause of Southern backwardness, and argued for its removal not, it must be stressed, on any moral grounds, but purely for the benefit of Southern whites. Pleasants was clear on that point: "In respect to *slavery*, I take no pious – no fanatical view," he asserted. "I am not opposed to it because I think it morally wrong, for I know the multitude of slaves to be better off than the whites. I am against it for the *sake of the whites*, my own race!" (Hickin 1971: 175, 179).

However, the differences between the views of antislavery supporters such as Janney and Pleasants and proslavery advocates such as De Bow, Fitzhugh, and Hammond were, by the late 1840s, less clear-cut than they seem at first glance. Several of the leading spokesmen for the proslavery cause, including Ruffin and Hammond, "followed the lead of James D. B. De Bow in urging the development of industrial and commercial enterprise to reduce dependence on the North" (Faust 1979: 65). The concerns of the proslavery spokesmen, according to Faust, arose less from their own personal circumstances and more from "the sorry state of intellectual endeavor in the region." The "issue on which all converged," she argues,

> was what they called the "philosophical" defense of slavery. Because of its combined moral and social import the problem of slavery seemed logically to belong to men of intellectual and moral superiority... Rather than the product of a social or economic elite, the proslavery argument was the creation of an intellectual class seeking to prove itself indispensable in defending the South's peculiar way of life.

Faust stresses the moral dimension of such endeavors, the emphasis on an ideal relationship between master and slave in which "duty and responsibility, not avarice," was key, and notes that later antebellum proslavery spokesmen were not above criticizing the institution as it was: their vision of moral stewardship, she argues, "reflected their hopes and fears more than reality. They sought ultimately not to describe the South, but to reform it." In an ironic parallel with the antislavery position, the proslavery argument, as Faust describes it, "was fundamentally a charter for reform" (Faust 1979: 67, 70–4).

By the 1850s, therefore, the "defense of slavery was no simplistic rationalization of a 'positive good,' not at least as written by the most sophisticated dialecticians," argues Freehling. "Rather, the best proslavery theorists, like most important American thinkers, devised fresh definitions and designs at a difficult level of abstraction" (Freehling 1991: 384). The titles of their deliberations make this clear. George Fitzhugh proposed a new *Sociology for the South* in 1854 and Henry Hughes, in that same year, published his *Treatise on Sociology; Theoretical and Practical*, in which he set out his arguments in favor of "warranteeism" as a means of ensuring the rights of both "warrantor" (slaveholder) and "warrantee" (slave). To what extent this new "scientific" approach really did bring fresh thinking to bear on the issues is, however, debatable. Certainly there was a greater emphasis on moral stewardship, itself predicated on the need to protect and improve an inferior race, on the proslavery side of the equation by the 1850s. At the same time, the traditional arguments did not disappear, but rather were placed in this new context. Fitzhugh's argument in *Sociology for the South* that the "negro slaves of the South are the happiest, and in some senses, the freest people in the world," was hardly a world away from Thomas Dew's argument in 1832; nor, indeed, was Hammond's "Mudsill" theory, presented four years later, obviously a radical departure from what had gone before. "In all social systems there must be a class to do the menial duties, to perform the drudgery of life," Hammond argued. "Such a class you must have or you would not have that other class which leads progress, civilization, and refinement. It constitutes the very mud-sill of society and of political government; and you might as well attempt to build a house in the air, as to build either the one or the other, except on this mud-sill."

Although the decade of the 1850s is regarded as the high point of the slavery debate, as a time when the "big guns" of Southern proslavery and nationalist ideology – Edmund Ruffin, James Henry Hammond, Henry Hughes, George Fitzhugh, William Lowndes Yancey, Robert Barnwell Rhett, and James De Bow – were at their most powerful, in fact their arguments were not, in any real sense, part of an identifiable dialogue, whether with antislavery elements in their own section or beyond it. By the time Hammond made his "Mudsill" speech in 1858, the "slavery debate" *qua* debate had, in effect, ceased to exist, replaced by an internal monologue whereby Southern intellectuals utilized history, the Bible, and the sciences in order not just to defend but to validate and, above all, understand the South's peculiar institution along with the way of life that it created. Their arguments cannot, by this time, be separated from the political context in which they were framed, nor from the broader scientific racism – a national, not a sectional, development – that informed and supported them. To an extent, the broader context had always influenced the debate: both anti- and proslavery arguments reflected and informed the wider social and racial issues that America as a whole, and not just the South, was struggling with in its search for order during the antebellum era (Tise 1987: 12–14; Faust 1979: 78).

By the 1850s, however, the political battle over slavery and its expansion, together with the growth of a distinctive Southern nationalist ideology predicated on the proslavery position, meant that the South had moved beyond debate to outright defense, at the federal level at least.

This is not to suggest that the struggle that Southern proslavery intellectuals undertook during this final decade before the Civil War made all their arguments moot was not genuine. In their increasingly desperate attempts to find not merely justification but guidance in the Bible, proslavery advocates – secular and divine – "doggedly refused to accept race alone as an adequate justification for the social order." Above all, they sought to transform slavery as it was into slavery as they believed it ought to be, not just for the sake of the slave, but also for their own salvation. "Prominent proslavery theorists," Genovese notes, "who normally relied on secular argumentation – George Frederick Holmes, William Gilmore Simms, Nathaniel Beverley Tucker – also cited the Bible to warn that a wrathful God would punish Southerners who failed to live up to their ideals" (Genovese 1998: 5, 9–10). Yet their efforts were, to a very great extent, in vain. Whether motivated by self-interest, moral or religious guilt, or a genuine belief that their peculiar institution really did offer the only realistic relationship between capital and labor in an unfair world, they were faced with the task of squaring an impossible circle, of providing a resolution for an evil that was neither theirs in the making nor, by the late 1850s, within their ability to resolve. For antebellum Southerners the slavery debate had, by the late 1850s, run its course. They would not address the issue head on again until close to the end of the Civil War, until, indeed, the writing was on the wall both for slavery and for the Confederacy. Even then, the debate over emancipation as a possible means of propping up the Confederate war effort was, at best, luke-warm. By that point, many Southerners might well have felt betrayed by the South's proslavery spokesmen, who for so long had assured them that theirs was the best of all possible worlds and worth defending with their lives. If any of them considered the slavery debate at all, they might, finally, have grasped the irony of Abel Upshur's confident assertion:

A people whose own soil supplies them with all the requisite means of defense, will rarely yield even to a superior power, so long as they shall continue to be animated with a due love of their independence and freedom. Such a people, whether they be owners of slaves or not, have much more to fear from themselves than from an invading enemy... it is not from the power of the conqueror that free nations have most to dread. Their own follies and vices are their worst enemy.

References and further reading

Adams, Alice Dana (1908) *The Neglected Period of Anti-slavery in America, 1808–1831*. Boston, MA: Ginn.
Allen, Jeffrey Brooke (1978) "Were Southern White Critics of Slavery Racists? Kentucky and the Upper South, 1791–1824." *Journal of Southern History*, 44: 169–90.

Davis, David Brion (1975) *The Problem of Slavery in the Age of Revolution, 1770–1823*. Ithaca, NY: Cornell University Press.

Degler, Carl N. (1975) *The Other South: Southern Dissenters in the Nineteenth Century*. New York: Harper and Row.

Donald, David (1971) "The Proslavery Argument Reconsidered." *Journal of Southern History*, 37: 3–18.

Faust, Drew Gilpin (1979) "A Southern Stewardship: The Intellectual and the Proslavery Argument." *American Quarterly*, 31: 63–80.

Finnie, Gordon E. (1969) "The Antislavery Movement in the Upper South Before 1840." *Journal of Southern History*, 35: 319–42.

Freehling, Alison Goodyear (1985) *Drift Toward Dissolution: The Virginia Slavery Debate of 1831–32*. Chapel Hill: University of North Carolina Press.

Freehling, William W (1972) "The Founding Fathers and Slavery." *American Historical Review*, 77: 81–93.

Freehling, William W. (1990) *The Road to Disunion: Secessionists at Bay, 1776–1854*. New York: Oxford University Press.

Freehling, William W. (1991) "James Henry Thornwell's Mysterious Antislavery Moment." *Journal of Southern History*, 57: 383–406.

Genovese, Eugene D. (1998) *A Consuming Fire: The Fall of the Confederacy in the Mind of the White Christian South*. Athens, GA: University of Georgia Press.

Hickin, Patricia (1971) "Gentle Agitator: Samuel M. Janney and the Antislavery Movement in Virginia, 1842–1851." *Journal of Southern History*, 37: 159–90.

Horsman, Reginald (1981) *Race and Manifest Destiny: The Origins of American Racial Anglo-Saxonism*. Cambridge, MA: Harvard University Press.

McCardell, John (1979) *The Idea of a Southern Nation: Southern Nationalists and Southern Nationalism, 1830–1860*. New York: W. W. Norton.

Miller, William Lee (1996) *Arguing About Slavery: The Great Battle in the United States Congress*. New York: Alfred A. Knopf.

Robert, Joseph C. (1941) *The Road from Monticello: A Study of the Virginia Slavery Debate of 1832*. Durham: University of North Carolina Press.

Robson, David W. (1980) "'An Important Question Answered': William Graham's Defense of Slavery in Post-Revolutionary Virginia." *William and Mary Quarterly*, 37: 644–52.

Schmidt, Fredrika Teute and Wilhelm, Barbara Ripel (1973) "Early Proslavery Petitions in Virginia." *William and Mary Quarterly*, 30: 133–46.

Stampp, Kenneth M. (1942) "An Analysis of T. R. Dew's Review of the Debates in the Virginia Legislature." *Journal of Negro History*, 27: 380–7.

Stampp, Kenneth M. (1943) "The Fate of the Southern Antislavery Movement." *Journal of Negro History*, 28: 10–22.

Stewart, James Brewer (1973) "Evangelicalism and the Radical Strain in Southern Antislavery Thought During the 1820s." *Journal of Southern History*, 39: 379–96.

Sydnor, Charles S. (1968) [1948]. *The Development of Southern Sectionalism, 1819–1848*. Baton Rouge: Louisiana State University Press.

Tise, Larry E. (1987) *Proslavery: A History of the Defense of Slavery in America, 1701–1840*. Athens, GA: University of Georgia Press.

Upshur, Abel P. (1839) "Domestic Slavery," *Southern Literary Journal*, October: 677–87.

6

Southern Writers and the Civil War

Susan-Mary Grant

One of the South's most prolific writers, Robert Penn Warren, famously began his "meditations" on the Civil War centennial with the observation that the war was, "for the American imagination, the great single event of our history. Without too much wrenching," he continued, "it may, in fact, be said to *be* American history. Before the Civil War we had no history in the deepest and most inward sense." One hundred years after the fall of Fort Sumter, Warren noted, the war still "grows in our consciousness . . . larger than life, massively symbolic in its inexhaustible and sibylline significance." However, for a long time, he argued, "custody of the War was for the most part relegated to Southerners" (Warren 1998: 3, 80). Warren believed the war's significance was truly national by 1961, yet his own interest in, interpretation of, and thoughts on the conflict highlighted the special place it held in the Southern imagination as the centennial celebrations got underway. In an article published the following year, Richard Harwell analyzed the continuing fascination that the Civil War held. He, like Warren, saw it as "the common heritage of all Americans – the defeated Rebel and, sometimes, still defiant Southerner, the Yankee yeoman of New England, the Midwesterner whose region has known only one war on American soil, and Americans of later immigration now established in a new world and seeking American roots." Moreover, he argued, the Civil War was "a convenient war for reading. It has a beginning and an end . . . It was a one-language war in its actions and in its records. Compared to later wars, it was a small war. It was a well-reported war. Most of all, it was a gallant, heroic, exciting war." Its participants, he concluded, still "seem real in 1962" (Harwell 1992: 4–5).

However, despite Warren and Harwell's assertions that the Civil War was of truly national import, in fact the centennial celebrations had a distinctly Southern slant to them. Indeed, it seemed to some that the centennial was designed purely to commemorate and celebrate the Confederacy. John Hope Franklin noted "the greater enthusiasm for the observance is in the former Confederacy rather than elsewhere," while the *New York Post* commented in February of 1961 that "if the next five years of commemorating proceed along the lines of the first few months, they'll be whistling 'Dixie' at the Appomattox Courthouse enacted in 1965, and General Grant will hand his sword to General Lee" (Franklin 1962: 105). A recently published book on the South by David Goldfield, entitled *Still Fighting the Civil War* (2002), reveals that, as the sesquicentennial approaches, the Civil War remains, in some respects, of greater significance to Southerners than to other Americans. The Civil War, writes Goldfield, "is like a ghost that has not yet made its peace and roams the land seeking solace, retribution, or vindication." Nowhere is this ghost more evident than in the work of Southern writers, many of whom transformed the literal events of America's most destructive conflict into the literature that, to a very great extent, continues both to reflect and define the South.

The importance of the Civil War to Southerners has long been recognized. "To the Southern writer who would deal with the past," Walter Sullivan argued, "the Civil War is the most significant image of all. For it is the pregnant moment in Southern history, that instant which contains within its limits a summation of all that has gone before, an adumbration of the future" (Sullivan 1953: 114). Similarly, in their study of Civil War fiction, David Madden and Peggy Bach note "it has often been argued that it was the War Between the States itself that shaped the consciousness of the Southerner," and suggest "in some sense every work of fiction by a Southerner is an expression of the long-developing cause, the bloody agony, and the lingering effect of the war" (Madden and Bach 1991: 8–9).

Although critics have long appreciated that the war was a formative event both for the South as a region and for Southern writers as a group, they have not especially appreciated the literature that resulted. Daniel Aaron was making a general critical point when he described the Civil War as "not so much unfelt as unfaced," but others have been more direct in their criticism of Southern literary output (Aaron 1973: xviii). Louis D. Rubin, for example, observed: "more than a thousand novels have been written about the war by Southerners alone," but concluded: "most of the South's Civil War fiction . . . is wretched stuff . . . There is no *War and Peace* about the South and its army . . . all we have is *Gone With the Wind*" (Rubin 1967: 184, 185, 186). Even Madden and Bach consider it "strange that although most Civil War novels are by Southerners, no Southern writer of major importance, except Evelyn Scott and William Faulkner, has produced as his or her best work a Civil War novel." Even the best Southern novels, they argue, "do not generally compare well on artistic grounds with Northern fiction about the war," and they cite, among others, John William De Forest's *Miss Ravenel's Conversion from Secession to Loyalty*, Ambrose Bierce's *Tales of Soldiers and Civilians*, and Stephen Crane's *The Red Badge of Courage* as examples of "classic" Civil War fiction, all of it originating from northern pens (Madden and Bach 1991: 14).

However, even William Faulkner rarely addressed the Civil War directly – only *The Unvanquished* (1938) deals with the war years themselves – but in his work the ghost of that conflict is everywhere evident. Faulkner's war, argued Aaron, "is multidimensional. He sees it as historical event, as a mirror reflecting personal and sectional character, and . . . as a buried experience that must be unearthed before it can be understood" (Aaron 1973: 315). Faulkner's most famous, and frequently quoted, invocation of the war perfectly captures both the sense of loss and the link between past and present in Southern culture:

> For every Southern boy fourteen years old, not once but whenever he wants it, there is the instant when it's still not yet two o'clock on that July afternoon in 1863 . . . and it's all in the balance, it hasn't happened yet, it hasn't even begun yet . . . and that moment doesn't need even a fourteen year old boy to think *This time. Maybe this time* with all this much to lose and all this much to gain. (Faulkner, *Intruder in the Dust*, 1948)

Faulkner was not the first author to identify the centrality of the Civil War to the South. In *Life on the Mississippi*, Mark Twain summed up the continuing significance of the war to Southerners some twenty years after Appomattox. "In the North," he observed, "one hears the war mentioned, in social conversation, once a month; sometimes as often as once a week; but as a distinct subject for talk, it has long ago been relieved of duty." However, he continued, "the case is very different in the South. There, every man you meet was in the war; and every lady you meet saw the war . . . In the South, the war is what AD is elsewhere: they date from it." "You notice, of course," a Southerner comments to Twain, "that we are nearly always talking about the war. It isn't because we haven't anything else to talk about, but because nothing else has so strong an interest for us." This frequent invocation of the war, Twain concluded, "shows how intimately every individual was visited, in his own person, by that tremendous episode. It gives the inexperienced stranger a better idea of what a vast and comprehensive calamity invasion is than he can ever get by reading books at the fireside" (Twain, *Life on the Mississippi*, 1883).

More than a generation separated Mark Twain from William Faulkner, yet the two were linked by their relationship to the South broadly, to the Civil War specifically, and in particular to the memory of that conflict in the South. As Lewis Simpson observes, Twain effectively "created the model of the crucial role Faulkner enacted: that of the Southern author as at once a participant in and ironic witness to a drama of memory and history that centered essentially in the never-ending remembrance of the great American civil conflict of 1861–1865." Both acknowledged the "obligation of the writer to serve as a witness, not to the actual historical event, but to the remembrance of it" (Simpson 1991: 152). Twain, like Faulkner, only indirectly addressed the war itself in his fiction. His satirical novel *A Connecticut Yankee at King Arthur's Court* (1889) may have been influenced by the Civil War, although Twain himself asserted it was "not written for America; it was written for England." However, elsewhere in his work, Twain made a direct connection between the feudal system that he satirized in *A Connecticut Yankee* and the Civil War.

In *Life on the Mississippi* Twain blamed Sir Walter Scott for setting "the world in love with dreams and phantoms; with decayed and swinish forms of religion; with decayed and degraded systems of government; with the sillinesses and emptinesses, sham grandeurs, sham gauds, and sham chivalries of a brainless and worthless long-vanished society." Scott's writings, Twain declared, did "measureless harm," especially in the South, where such ideas "flourish pretty forcefully still." In the South, Twain argued, "the genuine and wholesome civilization of the nineteenth century is curiously confused and commingled with the Walter Scott Middle-Age sham civilization; and so you have practical, common-sense, progressive ideas, and progressive works, mixed up with the duel, the inflated speech, and the jejune romanticism of an absurd past that is dead, and out of charity ought to be buried." Indeed, Twain went so far as to declare that Sir Walter Scott "had so large a hand in making Southern character, as it existed before the war, that he is in great measure responsible for the war."

Twain himself served, albeit very briefly, with the Confederate irregulars in Missouri during the war, so he was in the position of witness both to the conflict and to the memory of it. He turned the experience to literary use in a piece that appeared in *Century Magazine* in 1885, entitled "The Private History of a Campaign That Failed." At that time, *Century Magazine* was in the middle of publishing a series of Civil War articles written by former combatants and civilians on both sides. It proved to be immensely popular, and was published in an illustrated four-volume set, *Battles and Leaders of the Civil War*, in 1887. Twain's contribution, however, was rather different from the rest, and indeed from Southern writing about the war in general. Here, too, Twain took the opportunity to ridicule what he regarded as the "Walter Scott disease," in his description of one of his companions, "a fair sample of the kind of stuff we were made of," as "ignorant, good-natured, well-meaning, trivial, full of romance, and given to reading chivalric novels and singing forlorn love-ditties." Twain's description of the rapidity with which the reality of war dispelled their romantic illusions was, as he himself put it, "a not unfair picture of what went on in many and many a militia camp in the first months of the rebellion."

Twain's disillusionment was shared by a great many Confederate troops, but the majority of them never became well-known authors, so their perspective on the war has been largely overlooked. The recent surge of interest in how "Johnny Reb" and "Billy Yank" viewed their respective causes has brought some alternative perspectives to light. Sam Watkins, for example, recalled how war weariness took its toll on Confederate troops in his short story, "Co. Aytch," published in 1882. Following conscription, which the Confederacy introduced in 1862, Watkins recalled how his company's "pride and valor had gone, and we were sick of war and the Southern Confederacy." "The glory of the war, the glory of the South, the glory and the pride of our volunteers," he noted, "had no charms for the conscript." The exemption of men who owned twenty or more slaves simply rubbed salt into the wound, and Watkins, in common with many Southern troops, bitterly resented the fact that the rebel cause had become a rich man's war and a poor man's fight. The horrific reality of combat, combined with the devastation wrought by disease, led Watkins to conclude that he and his company "were tenfold worse than slaves." Morale, he wrote, "was a thing of the past." Yet despite Watkins's harsh assessment of his experience, or perhaps because of it, he believed the Confederate troops "died the death of heroes." "I sometimes think," he mused, "that surely our brave men have not died in vain. It is true, our cause is lost, but a people who loved those brave and noble heroes should ever cherish their memory as men who died for them" (quoted in Ayers and Mittendorf 1997: 126–35).

Sam Watkins had, doubtless in part through sharing his reminiscences, made his own peace with the past. He believed, when he wrote, that "the North and South have long ago 'shaken hands across the bloody chasm.' The flag of the Southern cause has been furled never to be again unfurled; gone like a dream of yesterday, and lives only in the memory of those who lived through those bloody days and times." For a great many Southerners, however, the past could not readily be laid to rest, and their memories proved to be long ones, becoming in time traditions to be passed on to succeeding generations. In the war's immediate aftermath, however, some could take comfort from the words of Henry Timrod, the "Laureate of the Confederacy," whose poems such as "Carolina" and "Charleston" offered Southerners the reassurance that theirs had been a glorious defeat at the hands of Northern barbarians. Timrod was writing during the war (he died just after in 1867) and his work therefore has an immediacy that later writers lack. However, already in his poetry one can see the beginnings of what would, in time, come to be dominant themes in Southern writing about the Civil War, at least for the remainder of the nineteenth century: the glorification of a cause lost, combined with the invocation of a mythical antebellum civilization gone but never to be forgotten. Timrod himself believed that history would acknowledge the heroism of the South, arguing that his generation would, in time, "assume the proportions of Paladins, and with ghostly hands thrust from our unforgotten graves, challenge future generations to prove themselves men by measuring their strength, their virtue and their heroism with our own" (quoted in Aaron 1973: 241–2). His poetry best expressed this belief. The opening lines of "Ode," written for a memorial service in Charleston, looked toward "the tardy years / Which keep in trust your storied tombs," while "Carolina" encouraged Southerners to "Hold up the glories of thy dead; / Say how thy elder children bled, / And point to Eutaw's battle bed, / Carolina!"

In the wake of defeat, Southerners needed little encouragement to heed Timrod's call. In the longer term, however, the blatantly sentimental images of such poems as "Maryland, My Maryland" by James Ryder Randall, "Little Giffen," inspired by the battle of Shiloh in 1862 and written by Francis Orrery Ticknor, or "Lee to the Rear," by John R. Thompson, editor of the *Southern Literary Messenger* before the war and a staunch advocate of the Lost Cause after it, proved more popular. "Lee to the Rear" recalled how "Fate, with his pitiless band, has furled / The flag that once challenged the gaze of the world." In a similar vein, but with even wider appeal, was "The Conquered Banner" by Father Abram Joseph Ryan, another notable supporter of the Lost Cause. To this day, "The Conquered Banner" features prominently on many Civil War websites, disproving by its popularity – and continuing relevance, given the heated debate over the Confederate flag – the pessimism of its final stanza: "Furl that banner, softly, slowly! / Treat it gently – it is holy – / For it droops above the dead. / Touch it not – unfold it never, / Let it droop there, furled forever, / For its people's hopes are dead!" Dead they might have been, but they were, in time, to enjoy a very long afterlife.

The poetry of Timrod, Thompson, and Ryan notwithstanding, the immediate postwar period saw little in the way of literary representations of the war, although there was a widespread desire on the part of many Southerners to tell their side of the story. "The Southern rage to explain," Hobson notes,

> took a decidedly different turn in the years after Appomattox . . . If many of the writers of the 1850s . . . had written in large part to convince Northerners of the justice of their position, virtually all the postbellum apologists wrote to reassure and persuade their fellow Southerners – and themselves. And they spoke not out of pride so much as pain and suffering.

One work hot off the press almost as soon as Lee had surrendered was Edward Pollard's *The Lost Cause* (1866), in which Pollard "tried to convince his readers, and himself, that the South had not yet been truly defeated. It had only lost the military phase of a much larger struggle." (Hobson 1983: 87–9). Following Pollard's lead, in 1869 a group of former Confederates founded the Southern Historical Association, with a view to promulgating the South's side of the tragic national story. In addition, several romantic novels inspired by the war, together with a few memoirs, did appear in the immediate postwar period. These included *Surry of Eagle's Nest* (1866), *Mohun* (1869), and *Wearing of the Gray: Being Personal Portraits, Scenes and Adventures of the War* (1867), by John Esten Cooke, *Tiger-Lilies* (1867), by Sidney Lanier, and *The Cavalier* (1901), by George Washington Cable, all authors who had served in the Confederate army.

However, a great number of the diaries, memoirs, and letters written by Southerners either during the conflict or shortly afterwards did not see publication until the twentieth century, which does not necessarily mean that the views contained in them remained unexpressed until then. One exception was the diary of General Richard Taylor, son of Zachary Taylor. Described by Edmund Wilson as "perhaps the masculine document that, from the point of view of realistic intelligence, is most nearly comparable to Mary Chesnut's diary" (Wilson 1987: 299), Taylor's *Destruction and Reconstruction: Personal Experiences of the Late War* appeared in 1879. Unlike the South's Civil War poets, diarists like Taylor at least addressed the main issue behind the war: slavery. The "extinction of slavery was expected by all and regretted by none," Taylor announced, perhaps rather optimistically, given the prevalent sentiments of much of the postwar South.

Mary Chesnut, of course, whose *Diary From Dixie* first appeared in 1905, was and remains the most famous diarist of the Civil War South. Well placed socially to provide readers with a full and varied account of the days of the Confederacy, Chesnut, in common with other women diarists such as Kate Stone and Sarah Morgan, offered, in places, a rather more critical assessment than many of the male writers did of the

Southern cause and its likelihood of success. At one point she commented on General Winfield Scott's appraisal of the South's capacity for extended conflict. "We will not take care of things, or husband our resources. Where we are, there is waste and destruction," she noted. "If it could all be done by one wild desperate dash, we would do it; but he [Scott] does not think we can stand the long blank months between the acts, the waiting. We can bear pain without a murmur, but we will not submit to being bored" (quoted in Wilson 1987: 282–3).

Chesnut is most famous, of course, for her "poor women, poor slaves" comparison. Her fellow female diarists, although less detailed – and indeed less opinionated – in their descriptions of the war in the South than Chesnut, also had something to say about the South's peculiar institution, its impact on the region, and its demise during the war. Kate Stone, whose diary, *Brokenburn: The Journal of Kate Stone, 1861–1868,* was eventually published in 1955, was born into the same social class as Chesnut. Brokenburn was the name of the Louisiana cotton plantation she lived on, and was forced to flee from in the face of Grant's push on Vicksburg. Wilson described Stone as "the typical Dixie heroine, as approved by the Southern traditions," and observed of her diary: "All the miseries of the war years are here. The Negroes threaten them and the Yankees molest them. The silver has to be buried in order that it may not be stolen. One of Kate's young brothers is killed in battle, and another dies of fever" (Wilson 1987: 261).

Stone also experienced what she described as the "moral guilt" of slavery. She felt, she wrote, "how impossible it must be for an owner of slaves to win his way into Heaven" (quoted in Wilson 1987: 261–3). Ultimately, in his assessment of the South's female diarists, Wilson concluded Stone's writings were slightly wooden, her reactions somewhat detached from the events that she experienced. He found Sarah Morgan to be a livelier character, in part because her circumstances were rather different from those of either Chesnut or Stone. *A Confederate Girl's Diary* was published in 1913, and it certainly offered a more complex, and more critical, picture of Southern attitudes during the war. In part this was because Morgan had close relatives fighting on the opposite side, and being officially at war with them did not alter her loyalties, a fact that met with local disapproval. As she wrote: "I have a brother-in-law in the Federal army that I love and respect as much as anyone in the world, and shall not readily agree that his being a Northerner would give him an irresistible desire to pick my pockets, and take from him all power of telling the truth." In attempting to steer a middle path between both Northern and Southern extremists, Morgan faced an impossible task, and given her terrible descriptions of the Union army's behavior it is quite remarkable that she retained her equanimity throughout the war. But Morgan had few illusions about the Southern cause. "It is a rope of sand, this Confederacy," she observed in 1862, "founded on the doctrine of Secession, and will not last many years – not five" (quoted in Ayers and Mittendorf 1997: 116).

It was not until the 1870s and 1880s that published works on the war began to appear in greater numbers. When they did so, in the form of the battlefield reminiscences such as *Century Magazine*'s "Battles and Leaders" series or the *Annals of the War* (1879), a compilation that began as a series of articles in the Philadelphia *Weekly Times*, their reception was mixed. Clearly, as David Blight has shown, there was an enormous market for soldiers' reminiscences, and they fulfilled an important function in helping former combatants come to terms with their war experiences. In an odd juxtaposition of the military and the mythical, the work of the Virginian Thomas Nelson Page, whose stories of life in "Ole Virginia" painted such a benign image of the antebellum South, began to appear alongside the soldiers' reminiscences in *Century Magazine* in 1884. Both functioned as a means of reconciliation between North and South. Page's stories, in particular, fed both the Northern and the Southern desire to regard the antebellum South as some kind of Golden Age of racial and social harmony, and the Civil War itself as a shared trial that, ultimately, welded both sides more firmly together. "It was hard to make the Civil War seem cozy," Wilson observed, "but Thomas Nelson Page did his best" (Wilson 1987: 614). Together, soldiers' memories and Page's stories began to nudge slavery and emancipation out of the picture of the war, and helped support the Southern belief that their cause had been noble and just.

Along with diaries such as Chesnut's and Morgan's, which have stood the test of time, or rather of literary quality, a tidal wave of diaries, letters, and novels relating to, recollecting, and revisiting the Civil War poured off the presses between the turn of the twentieth century and the end of World War I. A brief glance at the sheer amount that was published might lead to the conclusion that virtually every Southerner published something on the war in this period. A great many of these works, but by no means all, comprised women's reminiscences either of their own wartime experiences or those of their male relatives. This period saw the publication of, among others, *A Virginia Girl in the Civil War, 1861–1865: Being a Record of the Actual Experiences of the Wife of a Confederate Officer*, edited by Myrta Lockett Avary (1903), Laura Elizabeth Lee Battle's *Forget-Me-Nots of the Civil War: A Romance Containing Reminiscences and Original Letters of two Confederate Soldiers* (1909), and Dolly Sumner Lunt Burge's *A Woman's Wartime Journal: An Account of the Passage Over a Georgia Plantation of Sherman's Army on the March to the Sea* (1918). The children's' Civil War was also not forgotten, as Thomas Hughes's *A Boy's Experience in the Civil War, 1860–1865* (1904) showed, and a host of diaries and memoirs published by former Confederate soldiers and officers testified to "the impulse felt by many Southerners to retell the story of the war itself – to define the region in terms of the one, crucial moment in its history when it tried to defend its culture and its identity by simple force of arms" (Gray 1986: 76). In this period, too, the novelist Mary Johnston published *The Long Roll* (1911) and *Cease Firing* (1912), extremely popular books in their day, that expressed both "pathos and the endearing mutuality of sacrifice among soldiers" North and South (Blight 2001: 5). Most of these works have long since been forgotten, but at the time, the market for them was booming.

As Richard Gray has argued, "what emerged from all this activity... was not so much a recovery as a reinvention of the past and a reassertion of established regional codes. Translated into the Confederate officer and the humble trooper, both the patriarchal and the populist models reappeared, dressed for conflict now but trailing the familiar associations" (Gray 1986: 76–7). Through the literary representations of Confederate generals, Southerners expressed different aspects of the patriarchal, aristocratic ideal. In aggregate, the dashing, heroic, knightly qualities of J. E. B. Stuart, the rather more conservative approach of Wade Hampton, the courtesy of Beauregard, the wisdom of Joseph Johnston, and the culture of Leonidas Polk "formed a kind of tableau, a detailed and comprehensive portrait of 'the ancient chivalry' of the region and all its equally glamorous, uniformly flattering possibilities." The epitome of chivalry, the individual who was deemed to contain within himself all these various aspects of the Southern ideal, was, of course, Robert E. Lee, who was portrayed "as a combination of gallant knight and sober squire, romantic cavalier and Christian gentleman." "The virtual apotheosis of Lee in the years after the war," Gray notes, "had as its main aim the perpetuation and the development of the patriarchal image of the South." Lee was "a tangible reminder of the lost cause, all that the Confederacy had fought for" (Gray 1986: 77–82). He was seen as an ideal and, simultaneously, as a representative figure, standing both above and alongside the soldiers he led. As Carlton McCarthy put it in his reminiscences, *Detailed Minutiae of Soldier Life in the Army of Northern Virginia* (1882), the fame of individual leaders such as Lee and "Stonewall" Jackson "is an everlasting monument to the mighty deeds of the nameless host who followed them through so much toil and blood to glorious victories" (quoted in Gray 1986: 82).

The nameless host, of course, had their own version of the war to recount. Those works written by soldiers were rather different in tone and in approach from the celebratory volumes produced in praise of the Confederacy's leaders. In their portrayal of "Johnny Reb, the common soldier of the Confederacy," many of them, in common with Sam Watkins, highlighted, even if they did not dwell on, the hardships endured by the rank and file during the Civil War. Yet, like Sam Watkins, when these soldiers looked back on their experiences, it was the bravery of their comrades they recalled, and the impulse to commemorate both them and their cause that drove them to ensure that future generations had on record something other than the North's version of the Civil War.

Ultimately, where the patriarchal and the populist accounts of the war coalesced was in the emerging cult of the Lost Cause, which gathered momentum as the nineteenth century drew to a close and which found expression through both history and literature. As Blight observes, "just as reminiscence reflects the need to tell our own stories, so too crusades to control history demonstrate the desire to transmit to the next generation a protective and revitalizing story." He cites Douglass Southall Freeman, Lee's most famous biographer, for whom "the Lost Cause was Virginia's civil religion," and who, in a 1918 speech, proclaimed: "wind and water, and sky and ground alike, are vocal with the chords of our dead fathers. Oh! did a people ever live in the midst of such great traditions as ours?" (Blight 2001: 291). Freeman's reverence for the Confederacy, in common with much of the vast output that represented the

South's memorial industry at the turn of the twentieth century, reflected an "almost desperate need for sectional and racial justification," but not everyone concurred with Freeman's perspective.

One unusual example was John Singleton Mosby, of "Mosby's Rangers" fame, whose guerilla exploits against the Union army garnered him a large popular following both during and after the war. *Mosby's War Reminiscences and Stuart's Cavalry Campaigns* appeared in 1887, and *The Memoirs of Colonel John S. Mosby*, edited by his brother-in-law, appeared in 1917, the year after Mosby's death. Although Mosby's exploits became a staple of Lost Cause mythology, Mosby himself grew increasingly disenchanted with the mythmaking tendencies of the postwar South. "Men fight from sentiment," he argued, and after "the fight is over they invent some fanciful theory on which they imagine they fought." Like Taylor, Stone, and Chesnut, Mosby expressed no regret at the destruction of slavery, but nor did he apologize for its existence in the first place. "I am not ashamed that my family were slaveholders," he wrote: "It was our inheritance . . . I am not as honored for having fought on the side of slavery – a soldier fights for his country – right or wrong – he is not responsible for the political merits of the course he fights in. The South was my country" (quoted in Blight 2001: 298–9).

Walter Hines Page was another who had little time for Lost Cause mythmaking. Page was 10 years old when the war ended, and was therefore exposed from childhood onwards to the full impact of the Civil War memorial industry that developed in the South. He was not impressed. I "sometimes thought," he wrote,

> that many of the men who survived that unnatural war unwittingly did us a greater hurt than the war itself. It gave every one of them the intensest experience of his life and ever afterwards he referred every other experience to this . . . their loyalties were loyalties, not to living ideas or duties, but to old commanders and to distorted traditions. They were dead men . . . moving among the living as ghosts; and yet, as ghosts in a play, they held the stage. (Quoted in Rubin 1956: 149–50)

He made the point forcibly in his work *The Southerner: A Novel, Being the Autobiography of Nicholas Worth*, first serialized in the *Atlantic Monthly* in 1906 and then published in 1909. In this, he explored the impact of three very different "ghosts" that haunted the South: slavery, religious orthodoxy, and the Confederate dead. Reverence for the latter, he argued, "held back the country almost in the same economic and social state in which slavery had left it." Concern for the economic and social state of the early twentieth-century South was not all that irritated Page. He was, in effect, reacting against an atmosphere infused with the past and with the war. However, even as the Civil War memorial industry peaked in the early years of the new century, the generation whose experiences fueled it was passing away. As Paul Buck phrased it, after 1900 "the greater portion of the generation which had listened with awe while the guns boomed in Virginia and the ships of war steamed on the Mississippi slept in silent graves in which the issues for which they had contended were buried with them. The old had given way to the new" (quoted in Rubin 1956:

151). Of course, the handover did not occur overnight. Although change came, in some respects it came slowly, particularly as far as the South's relationship with the Civil War was concerned.

Writing on the cusp of this change was Ellen Glasgow, whose main Civil War novel, *The Battle-Ground*, appeared in 1902. Although her intention was to expose the "deadly illusion of power and order, and especially of the effects of the illusion and its loss on a varied group of people who had always lived in its grip," Glasgow acknowledged the continuing impact of this illusion on the South. "If I have dealt with the spirit of romance," she wrote, "it is because one cannot approach the Confederacy without touching the very heart of romantic tradition" (Dillard 1991: 66–7). The romantic theme was one she emphasized in her novel. The hero of *The Battle-Ground*, Dan Montjoy, approaches the conflict from an essentially romantic perspective, viewing it as "a great fox hunt . . . a page turn from the eternal Romance; a page upon which he and his comrades should play heroic parts." Years later, following the devastation of the First World War, Glasgow recalled "the worst of such hostilities was not the thought of death in battle; it was not even the thought of the young and the best who were sacrificed . . . the worst part of war is that so many people enjoy it" (Dillard 1991: 71). She was later, in a famous phrase, to accuse the South of a serious deficiency of "blood and irony," and certainly when *The Battle-Ground* first appeared the Southern literary landscape looked guilty as charged.

Yet, as the nineteenth gave way to the twentieth century, the writings of those who had lived through the Civil War were about to be supplanted by the work of a new generation who had no first-hand experience of the conflict but whose inheritance comprised – and whose literary creations suffered – the full burden of Southern history. In the same year, 1905, that Mary Chesnut's *Diary From Dixie* first appeared, Robert Penn Warren was born. He, together with other writers of the Southern literary renaissance, including William Faulkner, Allen Tate, and Thomas Wolfe, represented a new start, and in time a new way of approaching the South, its literature, and its Civil War heritage. It was a heritage that many of them rebelled against, but that none of them could avoid. They had to reckon with the dominance of Lost Cause mythmaking, with the all-pervasive sense of loss that the region's Civil War survivors exuded, and with the fixation on the past almost to the exclusion of the present. They also had to come to terms with the changes brought about by World War I, and especially with the loss of idealism that followed that conflict.

The Civil War and World War I were very different conflicts, but the overlap between the semicentennial of the Civil War and the outbreak of conflict in Europe brought them, in some ways, together. In purely practical terms, as both Northerners and Southerners joined up to fight, sectional differences – already blurred by the Spanish–American War of 1898 – further diminished. Living in an environment shaped in so many crucial ways by the Civil War, Southern writers were well placed to consider the parallels, as Allen Tate explained. After World War I, he wrote, "the South again knew the world, but it had a memory of another war; with us, entering the world once more meant not the obliteration of the past but a heightened consciousness of it." A few years later he described the "backward glance" that the South gave as it became, once more, fully part of the American nation. It was that backward glance, he argued, that "gave us the Southern renascence, a literature conscious of the past in the present" (quoted in Rubin 1956: 154). Tate himself expressed this sense of the past in the present most famously in his poem "Ode to the Confederate Dead" (1926), in which the narrator contemplates the gravestones, the "seasonal eternity of death," and the "thousand acres where these memories grow."

Another writer who highlighted the link between the Civil War and World War I was Thomas Wolfe. In *The Web and the Rock* (1939) Wolfe's hero, George Webber, visits Richmond with some friends for a football game. The year is 1916. Wolfe describes their reactions to the former capital of the Confederacy:

> They felt in touch with wonder and with life, they felt in touch with magic and with history. They saw the state house and they heard the guns. They knew that Grant was pounding at the gates of Richmond. They knew that Lee was digging in some twenty miles away at Petersburg. They knew that Lincoln had come down from Washington and was waiting for the news at City Point. They knew that Jubal Early was swinging in his saddle at the suburbs of Washington. (Wolfe, *The Web and the Rock*)

Past and present merge in this passage, but the present was soon to dominate in devastating ways. "Next year," wrote Wolfe, "the nation went to war." The hero of the football match that day in Richmond, Jim Randolph, is wounded in France. On his return, his friends perceive a change: "they knew that there was something lacking, something had gone by," wrote Wolfe, "they had lost something, something priceless, precious, irrecoverable." The parallels with the Civil War generation in what follows are not overtly stated, but nor are they difficult to draw:

> The truth is that the war formed a spiritual frontier in the lives of all the students at Pine Rock in Webber's day. It cut straight across the face of time and history, a dividing line that was as clear and certain as a wall ... The America that they knew before the war, the vision of America that they had before the war, was so different from the America and the vision of America they had after the war. It was all so strange, so sad, and so confusing. (Wolfe, *The Web and the Rock*)

In the sequel to *The Web and the Rock*, *You Can't Go Home Again* (1940), Webber again considers the impact of warfare on the nation, but this time it is the Civil War he recalls, although in a very similar way. "Sometimes it seems to me," he mused, "that America went off the track somewhere – back around the time of the Civil War, or pretty soon afterwards. Instead of going ahead and developing along the line in which the country started out, it got shunted off in another direction – and now we look around and see we've gone places we didn't mean to go." Wolfe's confluence of past and present, of the Civil War with World War I, was typical. The writers of the Southern literary renaissance, Rubin argues, were of "the new South, and yet not of it, seeing the life of the 1920s against the image of an earlier period." They consciously rejected "the mint julep South of Thomas Nelson Page" and thought of themselves "as representatives on the literary plane of the idea of the new, modern, progressive South." They were not, Rubin concluded, "going to stand for any nonsense from ladies' clubs and poetesses laureate of the United Daughters of the Confederacy" (Rubin 1956: 156–7). And yet, in their focus on the decline of the South in the 1920s – on the power shift that took place from the Compsons to the Snopeses – writers such as Tate, Wolfe, and Faulkner evoked an earlier, heroic age, one that members of groups such as the United Daughters of the Confederacy would have had no difficulty recognizing. Where they differed was in their focus on "the burden of the guilt of the South . . . the impossible load of the past" (Rubin 1956: 159).

However, with the exception of Evelyn Scott's sweeping Civil War novel *The Wave* (1929) and Faulkner's *The Unvanquished* (1938) – both somewhat neglected novels now – the writers of the Southern literary renaissance did not set their work in the Civil War era, but rather approached it obliquely. They were not oblivious to the fact that the Civil War had been a national event, that it had had an impact on the North, too. Wolfe, for example, describes a Union army veteran living in Brooklyn, whose "room was filled with books, records, papers, and old clippings bearing on the war and on the part his regiment had played in it." The Civil War, he wrote, "had been the great and central event in old man Wakefield's life. Like so many of the men of his generation, both North and South, it had never occurred to him that the war was not the central event in everyone's life" (*You Can't Go Home Again*). Yet they understood that, for the South, the war had cast longer shadows. It was those shadows that interested them, its long-term impact, its particular legacy for Southerners. They all, like Wolfe, sought to uncover and convey what it was that was "twisted, dark and full of pain" in their heritage. They understood, as Faulkner has Gavin Stevens say in *Requiem for a Nun*, that "the past is never dead, it's not even past."

It was via the character of Quentin Compson that Faulkner most forcibly expressed both the sense of the past in the present in the South and the oppressive weight of that past. In *Absalom, Absalom!* (1936), Quentin tries to describe his sense of the South to his Canadian roommate, Shreve, at Harvard. His story meets with amazement. "What is it?" Shreve asks,

> something you live and breathe in like air? a kind of vacuum filled with wraithlike and indomitable anger and pride and glory at and in happenings that occurred and ceased fifty years ago? . . . so that forevermore as long as your children's' children produce children you won't be anything but a descendant of a long line of colonels killed in Pickett's charge at Manassas?

Quentin corrects him: "Gettysburg," he says. "You can't understand it. You would have to be born there." In *Absalom, Absalom!* Quentin represents what Simpson describes as "a highly self-conscious, romantic, doomed embodiment of the lost

Confederacy" (Simpson 1991: 162). Like the fall of the House of David – which is what Faulkner was referring to in his title – "the fall of the South," argues Sundquist, "seemed more and more to Faulkner, in myth and in fact, an extended fulfillment of prophecy or, more exactly, a lasting curse for original sin" (Sundquist 1983: 130).

The same year that saw the publication of *Absalom, Absalom!* also saw the appearance of a very different novel, one that has come to dominate and to a great extent define the popular perception of the Civil War, Margaret Mitchell's *Gone With the Wind* (1936). Critics may dismiss Mitchell's work as little more than a historical romance, and disparage it for not reaching the literary standards of *War and Peace*, but *Gone With the Wind*, as book and film, has probably been read and seen by a bigger audience. On its publication it was hailed by the *Washington Post* as "the best novel that has ever come out of the South," and by the *New York Sun* as having "the strongest claim of any novel on the American scene to be bracketed with the work of the great from abroad." *Gone With the Wind* undoubtedly owed some of its popularity to the fact that it appeared in the midst of the Depression. The determination of its heroine, Scarlett O'Hara, in the face of adversity both during and after the Civil War, would certainly have struck a chord with many readers at the time. Its lasting appeal reveals that it strikes a chord still, whatever its literary merits. This is due in part, argues Kathleen Diffley, to the fact that *Gone With the Wind* follows the traditional "organizing rhetoric of home and family," and its central scene "is an image of domestic conflagration, in which the cannons and torches of invading soldiers are turned against women alone and about to give birth" (Diffley 1984: 371). Indeed, the focus on domestic travails as a means of exploring the Civil War and its impact was a feature of several Southern novels of the 1930s, including Faulkner's *The Unvanquished*, Allen Tate's *The Fathers* (1938), Caroline Gordon's *None Shall Look Back* (1937), and T. S. Stribling's *The Forge* (1931).

With the outbreak once more of war in Europe, the 1940s saw a temporary decline of interest in the Civil War, up to a point. Wilbur Cash's *The Mind of the South* appeared in 1941, and although it did not dwell on the Civil War it did explore the growth of the sentimental theme in the South. Men "have everywhere and eternally sentimentalized the causes of their wars, and particularly the causes that were lost," he noted, but "I doubt that the process has ever elsewhere been carried to the length to which it was carried in the South." The following year saw the publication of a little-known novel that reaffirmed the presence of the past in the present for many Southern writers, *Red Hills and Cotton: An Upcountry Memory*, by Ben Robertson. Robertson was a journalist who divided his time in Europe during the war between reporting on the conflict and writing about his youth in South Carolina, in particular his grandfather's and his great uncle's stories about the Civil War: they talked "on and on," he wrote, the "Seven Days' Battle, the Wilderness. General Jackson in the valley of the Shenandoah. General Lee. The sound of the Yankees' pickaxes, digging under Petersburg. And Richmond, always Richmond." And when they had finished talking, Robertson recalled, "we would sit on for a while, alone on the piazza in the great motionless night, and our hearts would nearly break within us. We had lost, we had lost." Robertson's memories of loss, however, were of a different kind from those of some Southerners. Secession, he wrote, "smote us to the depths of our conscience. We loved the United States, the Union was like the Ark of the Covenant, it was holy. Our leaving the Union still troubles us in the true Biblical manner – into the third and fourth generations" (quoted in Ayers and Mittendorf 1997: 141–7).

World War II had only just ended when Robert Penn Warren's Pulitzer Prize-winning novel, *All The King's Men*, appeared, with its juxtaposition of the lives of Louisiana Governor Willie Stark, his aide and the novel's narrator Jack Burden, and Burden's great-uncle Cass Mastern, who sought in the Civil War the death he felt he deserved for the sin of adultery. A decade later, Warren published *Band of Angels* (1955), one of the very few novels on the Civil War and its aftermath not to approach the subject from a predominantly white, male perspective. Margaret Walker's *Jubilee* (1966), similarly, was unusual in telling the story from the slaves' perspective, but it hardly started a trend. Recent writings, while continuing the theme of the past in the present in the South, are more balanced in their approach. The most notable, perhaps, is Allan Gurganus's sweeping novel, *Oldest Living Confederate Widow Tells All* (1984). In describing how he came to write the story of Lucy Marsden, the eponymous heroine of his book, Gurganus observed: "the fact is I really grew up in the nineteenth century, because North Carolina in the 1950s, the early years of my childhood, was exactly synchronous with North Carolina in the 1850s."

North Carolina also provided the inspiration for one of the most recent Civil War novels – soon to be a film – Charles Frazier's bestselling *Cold Mountain* (1997). In an interview he gave on the writing of his novel, Frazier revealed that its central male character, Inman, was in fact his great great uncle, who fought in the Civil War, although the character was also partly based on his grandfather. Frazier also observed that "there are two kinds of books about a war: there's an *Iliad*, about fighting the war, and about the battles and generals, and there's an *Odyssey*, about a warrior who has decided that home and peace are the things he wants." To some degree, the shift in Southern writing about the Civil War over the years parallels this distinction. The historian Charles Roland may have described the Civil War as *An American Iliad* (1991), but in Southern writing about the war since its conclusion we can see that it is, in fact, very clearly an *Odyssey*, for Southerners above all.

From the period of the Civil War onwards, Southern writing on the Civil War has been, to a very great extent, structured around the issue of loss: loss in the most obvious sense of military defeat, the mythical loss of an antebellum Golden Age invoked by the Lost Cause, and the loss of innocence after World War I that Wolfe so eloquently described. Faulkner summed it up in his response to Malcolm Cowley's question of why Southerners had devoted so much of their literature to the Civil War whereas Northerners had not. The "Northerner had nothing to write about," replied Faulkner. "He won it." There has been much criticism of the Southern fascination with the Civil War, of the literary merit – or lack thereof – of much of the writing that has resulted, of the uses to which the Civil War past has been put and, above all, of the negative racial implications of this fascination, which remain unresolved to this day. Robert Penn Warren believed the war had given the South, in his famous phrase, "the Great Alibi." "By the Great Alibi," he argued, "the Southerner makes his Big Medicine. He turns defeat into victory, defects into virtues" (Warren 1998: 55). Yet Southern writers did and do more than this. By returning to the Civil War past, Southern writers continue very much in the tradition set by Faulkner who, as Gray argues, understood that the past was not dead, but was rather "a living presence capable of growth." (Gray 1986: 181). In the changing uses to which Southern writers have put, and continue to put, the Civil War, it is clear that the South's past, and its present, is infinitely open to both growth and change.

References and Further Reading

Aaron, Daniel (1973) *The Unwritten War: American Writers and the Civil War*. New York: Oxford University Press.

Ayers, Edward L. and Mittendorf, Bradley C. (eds.) (1997) *The Oxford Book of the American South: Testimony, Memory, and Fiction*. New York: Oxford University Press.

Bach, Peggy (1991) "On Evelyn Scott's *The Wave*." In David Madden and Peggy Bach (eds.) *Classics of Civil War Fiction* (pp. 96–109). Jackson: University of Mississippi Press.

Blight, David (2001) *Race and Reunion: The Civil War in American Memory*. Cambridge, MA: Belknap Press of Harvard University Press.

Diffley, Kathleen (1984) "The Roots of Tara: Making War Civil." *American Quarterly*, 36: 359–72.

Diffley, Kathleen (1992) *Where My Heart is Turning Ever: Civil War Stories and Constitutional Reform*. Athens, GA: University of Georgia Press.

Dillard, R. H. W. (1991) "On Ellen Glasgow's *The Battle-Ground*." In David Madden and Peggy Bach (eds.) *Classics of Civil War Fiction* (pp. 63–82). Jackson: University of Mississippi Press.

Dowdey, Clifford (1992) [1939] "Are We Still Fighting the Civil War?" *Southern Literary Messenger*, I: 12–15. Reprinted in Richard Harwell (ed.) *Gone With the Wind as Book and Film* (pp. 86–9). Columbia: University of South Carolina Press.

Fahs, Alice (2001) *The Imagined Civil War: Popular Literature of the North and South, 1861–1865*. Chapel Hill: University of North Carolina Press.

Franklin, John Hope (1962) "A Century of Civil War Observance." *Journal of Negro History*, 47: 97–107.

Garrett, George (1991) "On Mary Johnston's *The Long Roll*." In David Madden and Peggy Bach (eds.) *Classics of Civil War Fiction* (pp. 83–95). Jackson: University of Mississippi Press.

Goldfield, David (2002) *Still Fighting the Civil War: The American South and Southern History*. Baton Rouge: Louisiana State University Press.

Gray, Richard (1986) *Writing the South: Ideas of an American Region*. Cambridge: Cambridge University Press.

Harwell, Richard (1992) [1962] "Gone With Miss Ravenel's Courage; or Bugles Blow So Red: A Note on the Civil War Novel." *New England Quarterly*, 35: 253–61. Reprinted in Richard Harwell (ed.) *Gone With the Wind as Book and Film* (pp. 3–10). Columbia: University of South Carolina Press.

Hobson, Fred (1983) *Tell About the South: The Southern Rage to Explain*. Baton Rouge: Louisiana State University Press.

Lively, Robert (1957) *Fiction Fights the Civil War: An Unfinished Chapter in the Literary History of the American People*. Chapel Hill: University of North Carolina Press.

Madden, David and Bach, Peggy (eds.) *Classics of Civil War Fiction*. Jackson: University of Mississippi Press.

Rose, Willie Lee (1979) *Race and Region in American Historical Fiction*. New York: Oxford University Press.

Rubin, Jr., Louis D. (1956) "The Historical Image of Modern Southern Writing." *Journal of Southern History*, 22: 147–66.

Rubin, Jr., Louis D. (1967) *The Curious Death of the Novel: Essays in American Literature*. Baton Rouge: Louisiana State University Press.

Rubin, Jr., Louis D. et al. (eds.) (1990) *The History of Southern Literature*. Baton Rouge: Louisiana State University Press.

Simpson, Lewis P. (1991) "On William Faulkner's *Absalom, Absalom!*" In David Madden and Peggy Bach (eds.) *Classics of Civil War Fiction* (pp. 151–73). Jackson: University of Mississippi Press.

Sullivan, Walter (1953) "Southern Novelists and the Civil War." In Louis D. Rubin, Jr. and Robert Jacobs (eds.) *Southern Renascence: The Literature of the Modern South* (pp. 112–25). Baltimore, MD: Johns Hopkins University Press.

Sundquist, Eric (1983) *Faulkner: The House Divided*. Baltimore, MD: Johns Hopkins University Press.

Warren, Robert Penn (1998) [1961] *The Legacy of the Civil War: Meditations on the Centennial*. Lincoln: University of Nebraska Press.

Wilson, Charles Reagan and Ferris, William (eds.) (1989) *The Encyclopedia of Southern Culture*. Chapel Hill: University of North Carolina Press.

Wilson, Edmund (1987) [1962] *Patriotic Gore: Studies in the Literature of the American Civil War*. London: Chatto and Windus.

7

Visualizing the Poor White

Stuart Kidd

The Report of the President's Committee on Farm Tenancy in February 1937 established that tenancy had increased from 25 percent of all American farmers in 1880 to 42 percent in 1935. Two-thirds of the nation's tenants were in the South, of whom the majority – again, two-thirds – were white. The most disadvantageous form of tenancy arrangement, sharecropping, accounted for only 10 percent of the nation's tenant farms, but a higher proportion of Southern farms – 39 percent. In 1930, 1.1 million white families were tenants or sharecroppers in the South. The report expressed concern that insecurity of tenure, combined with the small size of landholdings and the farming of submarginal land, posed "a threat to the integrity of rural life." As the National Emergency Council's Report on Economic Conditions in the South of 1938 expressed it, "many thousands of them are living in poverty comparable to that of the poorest peasants in Europe."[1] The Resettlement Administration (RA), established in 1935, and its successor of 1937, the Farm Security Administration (FSA), were the New Deal's responses to the problems of Southern rural poverty in depression America. Through a range of programs, including rehabilitation and farm purchase loans, and resettlement, the agencies sought to ameliorate the conditions for the South's rural underclass.

The recuperation of the Southern tenant was not solely a matter of economic and social policy. Southern poor whites, who would be the beneficiaries of much of the government aid, had negative associations in American culture that stretched back to the colonial period and which these agencies were obliged to address to cultivate and retain public and political support for their expensive programs. This was the function of the Information Division and its Historical Section which, under the leadership of Roy E. Stryker, specialized in photography. They provided publicity material, both for circulation within the agency and to the national media. Between 1935 and 1943, 24 photographers attached to the Historical Section took over 16,000 photographs of the South and its people. The group included luminaries such as Walker Evans, Dorothea Lange, and Ben Shahn and, also, photographers who made a more substantial, quantitative contribution to the Southern Series of Stryker's file, such as Arthur Rothstein, Russell Lee, Marion Post Wolcott, and Jack Delano. None of them had been born or raised in the South and, except for Dorothea Lange, who worked out of California, most were based in the industrial centers of the Northeast and Midwest. In 1936 Stryker spurned the opportunity to employ a Mississippi resident when he rejected the application of Eudora Welty, who had done photographic work for the Works Progress Administration.[2] The photographic project's engagement with the South and its poor white population would be negotiated by non-Southerners fueled with a sense of New Deal purpose and inspired by a region and a people with whom they were unfamiliar.

The photographers testified to the idealism and commitment of the era, which gave point and purpose to their work. Arthur Rothstein recalled the "great excitement" and the "missionary sense of dedication" which prevailed in the Historical Section and a determination to make "the United States a better place to live in." Jack Delano echoed Rothstein's sentiments, for he recalled "there were many wrongs in our country that needed righting, and I for one believed that my photographs would help to right them." The abstract concept of "the people" provided a focus for this idealism. Even photographers like Carl Mydans, not overtly motivated by political considerations, recalled an intense concern for "people." "If you go through the files," Mydans advised, "you will know that of all things these photographers felt strongly about the people around them." Delano defined the overriding aim of the Historical Section's project as its "search for the heart of the American people" and he believed the sentiment that united an otherwise diverse group of professionals was a concern to register "the pulse of the nation through its people."[3]

As creative intellectuals, the photographers were intrigued by the cultural image of the "common man." Bernarda Shahn recalled her husband's "glee that these people are so real and are so ordinary, and that each one, in his ordinariness, is so markedly unique."[4] This cult of the transcendent commoner was based on a double contradiction: that the poor in substance were rich in spirit, and, reviving Alexis de Tocqueville's paradoxical formulation of the national character, that "the people" were the last true individuals left in America. Marion Post Wolcott was impressed that deplorable living conditions had not left the people absolutely demoralized. "Many of them seemed to have some hope left, which surprised me," she recalled. Fundamentally, the aesthetic interest in the poor was grounded in a relationship between poverty and character whose significance for the photographers was not that character existed despite poverty, but that it was a product of it. As Jack Delano reflected, "The toil and drudgery and the constant battle for survival do bestow a kind of beauty on the human face and figure to which artists have always been sensitive."[5] Suffering became the *sine qua non* of character. Furthermore, their subjects' literal and metaphorical distance from modern society allowed them to serve as yardsticks for America in the metropolitan age. Atomized as sharecroppers, tenants, and day laborers, they were "people"; congregating in the courthouse square, in church, at fish fries, or at memorials, they were a "folk." Only a scattering of images of the comfortable classes exists in the Southern Series and privately owned, prosperous farms and housing for the affluent form a small portion of the file. There are not ten images which identify landlords or plantation owners and managers, so few that Stryker mistakenly claimed the file contained none at all when responding to a request for material in 1940.[6] Writing to Stryker from Kentucky in 1940, Marion Post Wolcott reflected on the quality of subjects and their social standing. She claimed the "extremely poverty stricken people" were more cooperative and more authentic as subjects. "But these more prosperous farmers, and middle 'classes' — they will have none of it," she said, "unless they look right, well dressed, powdered, and unless they know who you are and what it's for."[7]

The plight of "the people" was the more poignant for the distress which the photographers observed and recorded in their work. When Russell Lee was detailed to cover rural poverty in the Mississippi valley, he considered that "the best time of the year" for the project would be after Christmas when sharecroppers and day laborers would be short of money. "I know that Arkansas and Mississippi . . . are expecting a hard winter," he wrote, "with probably some near starvation if not actual starvation."[8] One of Marion Post Wolcott's first assignments was to photograph migratory labor in Florida. Appalled at the discovery of children confined in slovenly hovels and toddlers with their faces covered in the black mud which caused "muck rash," she wrote angrily to Stryker, "Jesus, what a country this is . . . I continue to be startled and shocked and amazed, no matter what I've expected."[9] However, intrigue and indignation were often in tension in the photographers' responses to the region. Jack Delano conveyed his ambivalence in a letter to headquarters during 1941, while he was working intensively in the South accompanied by his wife:

> What a place this "South" is — it's got us ga-ga but we like it . . . Both Irene and I are finding it pretty easy to get along with people down here and to get accustomed to Southern ways . . . This sure seems like the most tortured, primitive, poverty stricken (economically and socially) and wasted area I've ever seen. Yet the potentialities are so great that one doesn't become disgusted with it but feels rather that the South must come out of it even tho' it has so many strikes against it.[10]

Alongside an outrage about the extent of Southern poverty, the photographers identified another South, which was as much the product of their imaginations as their experiences. In scale and sentiment the rural and small town South was the antithesis of the metropolitan milieu in which they lived and worked. The same decadent culture which bred poverty and oppression had also preserved individualism, community, character, and self-sufficiency, characteristics of urban life outside the South which were being progressively eroded. Such impressions were reinforced by their encounters with the South's people, whose apparent helplessness in the face of economic hardship ennobled their stoicism and indifference. The cultural historians Richard H. Pells and David P. Peeler have suggested how an alienated, progressive intelligentsia searched for community and belonging during the depression decade, and Peeler claims a trenchant "social criticism" and a search for "social solace" informed their work in equal measure. The binary is particularly apposite to the photographers' responses to the South.[11]

Some of the photographers' work is suffused with sentiment and nostalgia for a bygone era. Main street and the courthouse square provided the principal locations for the photographers' representations of the small town as a community and they invest the country town of the RA/FSA photographic file with a pronounced masculine character. In the wake of the Nineteenth Amendment of 1920, which granted the vote to women and which inaugurated a decade of change in women's status, the Southern small town harkened back to an earlier and more conservative sexual politics. The courthouse square tended to be an exclusively male preserve and while main street served as the focal point of the whole community, it was the men who leaned or squatted against walls, loafed on street corners, and sat on sidewalk kerbs who provided the most engaging subjects. Their unselfconscious and relaxed manner invited comparison with the mass anonymity and bustle of the populations of America's cities. Mark Adams, the Information Division's staff writer, noted how Russell Lee portrayed the residents of San Augustine, a small town of just over one thousand inhabitants in eastern Texas, as "leisured, hospitable and obliging." Adams accepted Lee's interpretation of small towners' characteristics uncritically. He attributed them to the space taken for granted by rural communities but unavailable to "city people" and to a shared culture denied to urbanites "swallowed up in the turbulence of the megalopolis." "The thing which makes a small town different from a three-hundred family development in the Bronx," Adams wrote, "the thing that makes it distinctive, and interesting, and whole, is its tradition."[12]

The appeal of small town society to the photographer accounts for their indignation about Southerners who were denied a sense of place and were made rootless by cancelled tenancy contracts, mechanization, and soil erosion. The caption was a significant adjunct to the photographers' craft, for it not only clarified or dramatized the point of view of the visual imagery, but it also enhanced the photographs' marketability for newspaper and magazine outlets. Covering migratory white berry pickers in southeastern Louisiana in 1939, Russell Lee photographed squalid day laborers' cabins, and of one near Iberia, he recorded: "The flies were swarming in their unscreened shack which contained little furniture. The children all had noticeably bad teeth and their legs were covered in sores, probably impetigo."[13] Sometimes first-person testimony added drama to a caption and shaped the viewer's response to the image. In the captions to her photographs of migratory labor in Florida, Marion Post Wolcott allowed her subjects to outline the seriousness of their circumstances. One woman from Missouri revealed how her family paid $5 per month for uncleared camp land at Canal Point without water, electricity, or sanitary facilities. "We ain't never lived like hogs before," she declared, "but we sure does now – it's no different from 'hog livvin'." Packers at Belle Glade suffered similar conditions. Two families from Tennessee, each with four children, lived in a tin and burlap shack on a rat-infested site next to a canal. "We didn't know it was like this here," claimed one of them. "If we had, we'd never a come."[14]

It is widely understood, following the work of William Stott, that the photographic project invested its unprivileged subjects, and the Southern rural underclass in particular, with a "voice."[15] Equally, it is plausible to argue that Southern poor whites bestowed upon the Historical Section a future. In 1937 not only did the Bankhead-Jones Farm Tenant Act establish the Farm Security Administration which guaranteed the survival of the Historical Section, but also public interest in farm tenancy gave the Section greater prominence and shifted the emphasis of its role from servicing the agency to providing visual copy to the media. "We will be able to use everything we can get," Stryker wrote to Russell Lee. "The *New York Times, Des Moines Register*, and various other papers are hollering now for anything we can get hold of on farm tenancy."[16] The national press was hungry for sensational copy that exposed the suffering of the South. In November and December 1936, while planning the pilot editions of their new magazine, the editors of *Look* asked Stryker for "intimate pictures of typical families of the type to be reached by the Resettlement Administration." They were to illustrate an article whose working title was "Can such conditions exist in the United States?" The subsequent photo-essay was heralded by a double banner headline, "Children of the Forgotten Man!" and "Humanity Hits Bottom in the Deep South," and the featured photographs of squalid poverty reflected the rubrics' drama. Arthur Rothstein's image of a distraught, small child from North Carolina, clumsily wielding a stick and dressed in a torn smock of sackcloth, loomed out of the page devoid of any context because the picture editors had cropped out the background. With more imaginative flair than respect for factual accuracy, *Look* claimed the child was "Alone and Hungry" while his sharecropper-parents worked all day in the fields of the "Sunny South." Other images of children, either alone or in the company of sorrowful mothers, conveyed the poignancy of the cotton South's desperate poverty. *Look*'s muckraking initiative was widely imitated in 1937. In January, a picture story syndicated by the Register and Tribune Photoservice, entitled "Poverty's Pioneers," appeared in the *Des Moines Register* and the *Indianapolis Star*. Under the strapline, "Beaten by Thin Soil, Gnawing Hunger, They are 'Moving On'," five photographs, mostly taken in the South, illustrated inadequate housing and transience. The *Boston Sunday Post* conjured even more drama in its pictorial essay of February 14, "Uncensored Views of Share-Croppers' Misery." In each case the outlets relied upon Stryker's file for their illustrations.[17]

Stryker not only approved of this reportorial tendency, he also encouraged it. He was delighted with *Look*'s treatment and wrote to the editor, Gardner Cowles, with wry satisfaction: "I am getting a little worried for fear that the South will send a delegation up to your office after that double-page spread of sharecropper pictures." The photographers realized the value to Stryker of, what Dorothea Lange termed, "hard boiled publicity negatives." Lange was especially aware of Stryker's voracious appetite for marketable images, and in 1937 feared that her chief would make an exclusive presentation of a set of her negatives to *Life*, rather than reserve them to illustrate a forthcoming Senate report. Lange's comments not only cast light upon Stryker's priorities, but also indicate that the photographers were well attuned to the requirements of the mass-circulation media. She proposed a different set of prints for *Life* which would produce "a different effect" and entail "a different story – more dramatic, more moving, much more human."[18] The media would ensure that the half-formed clichés in the photographers' responses to, and constructions of, the South – the "blight," "transcendence," and "sense of place" – would be firmly related to popular genres of cultural representation, often with an emphasis that the photographers had never intended.

The popular press which Stryker cultivated drew upon and perpetuated well-established conventions in the representation of the Southern poor. Indeed, the cultural image of poor whites was amenable to manifold and contradictory construction. Poor whites were presented as alien people, confined outside the mainstream of a modernizing America. This was the tone of the media's response to one of the earliest photographic assignments undertaken by the Historical Section.[19] During the autumn of 1935 Arthur Rothstein photographed the people of the Hollows of Virginia's Blue Ridge Mountains who were about to be resettled to make way for the establishment of the Shenandoah National Park. According to a reporter from the *Washington Star*, "they were almost entirely cut off from civilization," and the *Washington Post* headlined an article with "Blue Ridge Families Get a Transfer – From 19th to 20th Century." Journalists summoned powerful myths about lost civilizations in their claims that the families' isolation had been so complete that within the Hollows a dialect or "archaic tongue" had been preserved which was thought to resemble "the language of the English peasantry in the time of Elizabeth." However, anthropological wonder was coupled with indignation that such pockets of serious poverty could exist and journalists used the example of the Hollows to debunk the rural myth. The *Washington Star* featured Rothstein's study of Blanche Nicholson and her son standing in the doorway of their "cabin in the brush," which had stood for over a century but "was not the kind the song writers talk about." *The Nation's Agriculture* used the same photograph to illustrate "'rural slum' conditions and low living standards" and reflected: "there may be happiness here but we doubt it." On occasion, isolation and need shaded into aberration. By drawing upon Erskine Caldwell's *Tobacco Road* (1932) for headlines, the mountain poor were related to a range of values that provoked disapproval. *Mayflower's Log* alerted its Washington readers about "nearby Tobacco Roads," as if the source of some moral contagion was unacceptably close. Ben Shahn's well-known study of Sam Nichols, a pensive tenant farmer in late middle age who lived in the Ozarks of Arkansas, elicited a similar response. The *Boston Sunday Post* referred to him as "An Arkansas Jeeter Lester," while the *Buffalo Times* regarded him as irredeemable, almost too old and hopeless to benefit from government help.[20] Later in the decade another popular novel would inspire the headlines that accompanied the Historical Section's images of migratory labor in the South. However, the wave of sympathy produced by John Steinbeck's *The Grapes of Wrath* (1939) could be transformed into anxiety by press headlines such as "American Nomads" and "'Okies' at Our Door."[21]

Rothstein's work with the folk of the Hollows inspired one further variation of archetypal representation by the national press which emphasized the charming and quaint aspects of the lives of Southern poor whites. As they appeared in the *Houston Chronicle*'s Sunday pictorial feature in 1936, entitled "Out in the Country," the folk of the Hollows in Rothstein's photographs served as picturesque examples of "American types and the American scene." Studies of Mrs. Tenie Nicholson, in particular, served to exemplify local color. The *St. Louis Globe-Democrat* referred to her as "a sunbonnet mother of Virginia," while the *Washington Post* reproduced her portrait alongside a caption which transformed her into an anonymous symbol of the "Good Wife." In such contexts the poverty of the Hollows residents was ignored or evaded and Rothstein's portraits became examples of the American Scene. The *Washington Post* even used some of Rothstein's studies to promote a "See America First" attitude to tourism: "Millions of Americans go abroad every year to see the 'quaint sights and people,' little realizing, apparently, that right in their own back yard the sights and people are 100 percent quaint as well as 100 percent American." As the decade progressed, and as the images were recycled in the press, they served as powerful visual statements of American values in an era of global crisis. On January 28, 1940, the *New York Times* included an article on "Old-Fashioned Winter" in its magazine section which featured a series of photographs, illustrating the picturesque aspects of seasonal rural life. One image featured Russ Nicholson peeling apples, an example of how "farm folk still 'settle down' for the winter, living the old ways and the good ways handed down from generation to generation." When the editors of the WPA Guide to Virginia chose the illustrations for their volume of 1940 they turned to images of the Hollows residents to represent the "Old Dominion" charms "along the highway."[22]

The abuse involved in dramatizing the circumstances of these displaced people was compounded by the inaccuracies involved in many of the reports that accompanied Rothstein's photographs. Inaccuracies in wire service reporting deprived the Hollows people of their specific identities. Fennel Corbin was identified as "Femmel Carbin" in both the *Houston Chronicle* and the *Washington Star*, while editorial exactness was sacrificed for a succinct caption in the *Washington Star* which had him transferred *to* Virginia to be resettled. The *Seattle Star* moved Blanche Nicholson and her son a greater distance. They were used to illustrate conditions in Benton County, Washington: "The women grown old before their time, standing hopelessly looking into the future . . . Benton County resettlement planning has eliminated much of this." Rothstein's photographs of the mountaineers were also adopted by the press to serve as generic representations of Southern poverty, and they failed to distinguish between the upland and lowland poor. When the *New York Times* used Fennel Corbin's portrait to illustrate an article on farm tenancy legislation in 1937 it identified him as a "Share-Cropper," while the Dodson family and their home served for the editors of *Look* to exemplify the desperate circumstances of the South's cotton sharecroppers.[23]

The Historical Section became party to the media's misrepresentation of Southern poor whites in 1939 when Alvis and Gladys Reed of Winslow Township, Arkansas, sued the *Saturday Evening Post* which had featured a photograph and caption by Arthur Rothstein that described them as "sharecroppers," rather than their accurate status as "tenants." It was not the Historical Section's practice to require its photographers to secure releases on their pictures and subjects' written permission was not sought to authorize the developing, retention, and circulation of images. "Our experience shows inoffensive use of pictures raises no objections," Stryker claimed in 1941. However, incidents of resentment and even resistance remind us that the photographers' subjects considered themselves to be persons rather than "people," and individuals rather than American archetypes. Sometimes photographers received a hostile reception and strict boundaries were established by their subjects. When Dorothea Lange worked near Gordonton in Person County, North Carolina, she found that the "gay and folksy" farmers who joked and posed before her camera and appeared "much interested in the photographing" were reluctant to allow her to take photographs inside Wheeley's Church. The pastor was obliged to intervene to prevent Lange from shooting images of the monthly preaching Sunday, when the primitive Baptist church was full to capacity. The circumstances of the making of the image which so offended the Reeds remind us of the gulfs of class, geography, and power which so often produced images loaded with tension and ambiguity. A pregnant Mrs. Reed and a group of her children were photographed by Rothstein on the porch of their cabin while being interviewed by an officer from the RA, from whom the Reeds had negotiated a loan. Confronted by a New York photographer and a government official, with her husband working in the fields, it is little wonder that Mrs. Reed's expression is so startled and confused. In search of a summarizing image of Southern white poverty, Rothstein may have felt that the precise details of the Reeds' identity were incidental, but for the Reeds themselves they were crucial to their status within the community.[24]

The Reeds' discomfort raises the question of an appropriate visual documentary strategy to represent the unprivileged people of the South. From the outset, Stryker was aware of the nature and responsibilities of documentary photography and struggled to have his photographers adopt appropriate strategies. A trained economist and social historian, Stryker was an advocate of a social scientific documentary practice. He regarded his photographers as "historians of the present" and encouraged them to adopt an empirical approach to their work, which would invest it with "credibility," "the dignity of fact," and "the integrity of truth." "The job is to know enough about the subject matter, to find its significance in itself, and in relation to its surroundings, its time, and its function," he believed. Stryker distinguished the work of his photographers from that of "pictorialists" and "photo-journalists." The former evaded reality by embellishing it; the latter distorted actuality by dramatizing it. In contrast, he described his own team as "photo-reporters" or "investigators who use the camera as a record mechanism."[25] Their work was informed by a discipline akin to visual anthropology and, as Stryker defined them, his photographers' portfolio of skills included an extensive subject knowledge and contextual sensitivity; rigorous captioning practice; the production of extended and in-depth photographic series; and

Plate 1   Arthur Rothstein: Wife and child of a sharecropper, Washington County, Arkansas, August 1935.

the ability to undertake collaborative assignments with academia. His intention was to achieve legitimacy for the photographic project through the authoritative nature of its work.

Stryker's ideas were not always shared or appreciated by his photographic team. Often, their creative impulses were at variance with their head of Section's rigorous procedures. Frequently, Stryker expressed irritation that the negatives submitted by his photographers of soil erosion lacked an explanatory cultural context. He complained they were either preoccupied by the aesthetics of the eroded land or employed strategies that used the human figure, in the manner of nineteenth-century landscape painters, to alert the viewer to the scale of a natural wonder. Arthur Rothstein supplied one of the few satisfactory images. It featured an Alabama boy of Walker County, wearing torn dungarees, leaning against a rickety cabin, and listlessly viewing a nearby eroded hillside. For Rothstein, the image contained a "cause and effect relationship," while for the photographic critic Arthur Ellis, it illustrated the capacity of the single frame to generate both narrative and drama – "to make a picture tell a story." The Historical Section was so impressed with Rothstein's visual relation of ecological devastation to its economic and social consequences that it was used to illustrate how "special qualifications" were required for the Section's photographers in an application to convert them to civil service status.[26]

While Stryker sought to place the Southern poor white into an appropriate visual context, he was also adamant his photographic file should feature their subjects "doing" as well as "being." A memorandum of 1937 claimed the photographic file's primary significance was its "unfailing emphasis on people" and it continued, "no one was ever asked by a . . . photographer to get in front of his camera or to pose merely to achieve a specious kind of 'human interest' in an otherwise dull picture. People in . . . photographs are there because they belong there: they are at work, they are amusing themselves, they are going about their business." This stipulation brought Stryker into conflict with his photographers for producing too many iconic studies. On one occasion he admonished Russell Lee, "You have done many pictures of the families standing in front of their house or shack. They appear a bit stiff taken in this manner. These would be all right, provided we could show members of the same family in the house and doing various things." Neither did Stryker believe Walker Evans represented the Section's work at its best, despite its critical acclaim. When the Cleveland Museum sought to organize an exhibition of RA/FSA material in 1939, Stryker reflected, "The Director wants sweet and lovely 'art' from us; the nicest of Walker Evans, for example. He will have to use some of our more brutal stuff or we won't play ball." Significantly, of the 80 prints selected for Cleveland, only one was by Evans.[27]

The development of in-depth picture stories, like rigorous captioning, was intended to expedite the Historical Section's service to the media, facilitate the work of the Information Division, and legitimize the medium of documentary photography. It also accorded with Stryker's own respect for the depth and thoroughness of empirical social scientific enquiry. The requirements of the press were especially influential in persuading Stryker to develop in-depth photo-series. Corresponding with Russell Lee in 1937, he listed various leading newspapers and news agencies that were interested in picture stories. "One of them made a very interesting suggestion regarding [the] tenant problem," Stryker wrote. "They would like a story which could be labeled 'The Tenant's Day' or 'A Day In a Tenant's Life.'" During

1938 the photo-story was officially recognized by the Information Division as the preferred working method for the agency's photographers. It was decreed that "a sequence of pictures...is far more effective than single, isolated shots" and was preferred by the "best picture editors." During the next year, in his own statement on the Section's work, Stryker recognized the contributions of photo-magazines such as *Life* and *Look* to new working methods. By 1940 he was no longer riding the bandwagon, but attempting to organize it by encouraging picture editors to publish the Historical Section's photographs as sets.[28]

From the photographer's viewpoint, depth often nullified the drama so evident in the spontaneity or the dramatic orchestration of photographers' fleeting encounters with the South's downtrodden. Stryker's new sociological emphasis required that subjects' lives be recorded rather than symbolized and reportage was substituted for the patient craft that had made many of Walker Evans and Dorothea Lange's photographs so powerful. Even the human interest photo-stories appear mundane and restrained. The Evan Wilkins family of Stem, North Carolina, whom Marion Post Wolcott photographed in November 1939, were neither rural innocents nor blighted poor whites. They represented a new type of farmer who was both entrepreneurial and versatile. The Wilkins are shown attending a tobacco auction in Durham, using the services of a bank, and Post Wolcott recorded a besuited husband, Evan, in the Durham suburbs peddling butter which had been made by his wife in their farmhouse kitchen. By adopting a middle-distance perspective, for the most part, Post Wolcott declined to invest her subjects with charisma and focuses the viewer's attention on action rather than character. However, there is no heroism in the gathering of grass and leaves for pig bedding or in a shopping expedition for apples and candy in Durham. The very notion of Walker Evans photographing the Wilkins debating whether to buy linoleum in a Durham store is preposterous, but it registers developments within the Historical Section and the growth of Stryker's influence in the later stages of the project.[29]

Nevertheless, as late as 1941 the Information Division expressed concern about the iconographical nature of the Historical Section's photographic file and the ways in which it had contributed to the media's stereotyping of the FSA's own clients as "wards of government," "problem children," or "sterling examples of American manhood." Stryker responded to this unease by issuing a shooting script to his photographers, "Suggestions for Community Photographs," which prescribed clear guidelines for their work with clients. "Keep in mind that the purpose is to show that the residents are leading normal, settled lives," Stryker wrote. This involved not only depicting them as working clients or members involved in their community, but also as people who ate, slept, laughed, raised children, gossiped, read books, and washed clothes.[30]

There were, of course, distinct political limits to the ways in which Southern poor whites could be represented. Despite the occasional reference to the Southern Tenant Farmers' Union, the Historical Section generally avoided overt expressions of class conflict. Stryker's concern to distance his unit from political partisanship and his

Plate 2   Marion Post Walcott: Farmers eat a lot of ice cream and drink lots of beer while waiting for tobacco to be sold at auction sales outside warehouse, Durham, North Carolina, November 1939.

strict distinction between the proper sphere of the documentary reporter and the photo-journalist both restricted his photographers' subject matter. Industrial labor was regarded as an appropriate subject, especially in the South where agricultural and industrial roles were interchangeable. However, Marion Post Wolcott's coverage of a strike by the International Union of Mine, Mill and Smelter Workers (CIO) in Ducktown, Tennessee, during September 1939, was restrained. The strikers she depicted appear as exhausted as the environment they inhabit. They sit around the front of the Ducktown Hotel, waiting for strikebreakers, surrounded by handmade signs which urge their counterparts not to "scab." Significantly, Post Wolcott did not wait to record the confrontation of striker and strikebreaker. Only the crude placards indicate that these are workers on strike and some of them were photographed next to road signs and the unlikely nameplate of the Ducktown Hotel. The placards take on the appearance of rustic and innocent curios, rather than instruments of industrial challenge. Their disassociation from political agency is almost as acute as that of the lugubrious figures who fashioned them.[31]

However, in May 1941 Jack Delano photographed a textile mill workers' strike for union recognition in Greensboro, Georgia, and he recorded a range of emotions rare in the Historical Section's coverage of Southern poor whites. Unlike Post Wolcott,

Delano openly addressed the nature of labor disputes. The union is identified not only in the placards proclaiming the CIO, but also in the captions. Shots of the inactivity of the pickets are supplemented by the strikers marching through the community, singing selections from the union songbook and confronting the chief of police. In one telling image, a picket confronts the police chief with his placard and its message: "Judas Betrayed His Lord For 30 PCS Silver – What's Your Price?" The most dramatic images are of women pickets hectoring strikebreakers, recruited from the neighboring countryside, with mock applause and derisory sneers. Although these images lack the intensity of press photographs of labor conflict in the industrial Midwest, their characteristics are uncommon in the Southern Series. They have both movement and moment. They are concerned with a contemporaneous aspect of social conflict; they emphasize workers as an organized and active collectivity; and they express the emotions generated by industrial conflict. Delano invested the textile workers of Greensboro with agency.[32] The brief series reminds us that the lived experience of Southern poor whites encompassed a wider range than is suggested by the passive, naturalized characters who inhabit the file and whose potential for action is registered only in stringing fences, driving mules, preserving fruit, and other prosaic activities. Bitterness and determination were not qualities considered suitable to project to the American public or to cultivate support for the RA and FSA's programs. However, occasionally they are registered in the photographers' captions, such as that accompanying Carl Mydans's image of a man and woman carrying their belongings in bags and sacks on a highway in Crittenden County, Arkansas. The caption indicates that for them movement is a form of resistance, for they advised the photographer, "Damn'd if we'll work for what they pay folks hereabouts."[33]

Stryker considered that accurate and relevant captions were a vital adjunct of documentary professionalism as well as a political necessity. Full captions had an operational function in that they identified particular rehabilitation subjects to whom the photographers might return for either "progress" or "before and after" shots. "If you take pictures of clients," Stryker instructed Marion Post Wolcott in 1939, "be sure you get their names ... if we have pictures of prospective clients we may want to rephotograph them in another year." More troubling for Stryker was the prospect of inexact or imprecise information being supplied to the media. Indeed, during 1936 there were at least three cases where the veracity of the Section's material was questioned. As Stryker explained to Allen William Grobin, a Resettlement Administration official, "If I gave A.P. a picture on something in Oklahoma and because my factual data was slim, I faked some of the dope and built it up that way, it might pass muster until it hit some Oklahoma paper where they would know better. I can see them complaining to the A.P. about it and naturally, the A.P. would complain to me or you. It would be bad for our reputation." Stryker also came to regard the caption as an important defense against accusations that the Historical Section was manufacturing "propaganda." This was the light in which the Texas newspaper the *Amarillo Globe* interpreted a photograph taken by Carl Mydans in March 1936 of a bedraggled mother and child outside their makeshift home on Route 70 in Tennessee. "As

Plate 3 Jack Delano: CIO pickets jeering at a few workers who were entering a mill in Greensboro, Greene County, Georgia, May 1941

propaganda," the *Globe* explained, "pictures are particularly effective because they appeal to the emotions."[34] In an age when the very term was associated with totalitarian European states and when "revisionist" opinion about the causes of American intervention in the Great War stressed the contributory role of allied "propaganda," government publicity was inherently suspect.

However, there were distinct limits to Stryker's ability to influence his photographers to adopt "good practice" and during 1941 Stryker was criticized by his superiors about casual captioning and the anonymity of subjects.[35] The preponderance of anonymous subjects in the file has led some cultural historians to speculate that the construction of a universalized "common man" stereotype was intentional. It is argued that the prevailing cultural trend of iconic, democratic humanism, combined with the contradictory, sociological conviction that economic problems subsumed the individual, encouraged the Historical Section to generalize rather than specify both its images and captions.[36] While a scan of the Southern Series coverage of tenant farmers indicates that the anonymous caption predominates by a ratio of about 3 : 1, it is notable that the majority of occasions when subjects are identified are clustered in the period 1939–41, when Stryker's photographers were accompanied by academics associated with Howard Odum's Sub-Regional Laboratory project at the University of North Carolina, or the sociologist Arthur Raper in Georgia. Knowledgeable about local families and sometimes acting as notetakers, the influence of academics was more decisive than that of Stryker in countering any tendency to cloak the South's rural poor in the anonymity of the "common man."

Captioning, contextualization, and depth of coverage were central aspects of the documentary working method which Stryker sought to cultivate once the Historical Section was securely established. They were intended to enhance the unit's service, but Stryker also regarded them as ingredients of documentary professionalism. The degree of success he achieved is debatable. Ironically, as Stryker and the FSA began to grapple with the complexities of the construction and reception of the tenant farmer's cultural image, the press was beginning to lose interest in the agency's current visual publicity, as Stryker discovered when *Look* refused a number of offers of material in 1939. Although the Historical Section continued to provide the press with "More Views of Rural Wreckage," there was a discernible shift in the usage of FSA photographs towards the end of the decade. Essentially, this involved a recycling and reevaluation of the Section's earlier work. Instead of the anxiety and defensiveness which Ben Shahn captured in a rehabilitation client's wife of Boone County, Arkansas, during 1935, three years later, the *Washington Daily News* claimed: "The Camera Sees: Strong Faith." No one photographer's work contributed more to this trend than that of Walker Evans. The publication of *American Photographs* and the prestigious exhibition of his work at the Museum of Modern Art in 1938, its first one-man show for an American photographer, established the reputation of Evans and, by association, enhanced that of the Historical Section. In a review of the book, headlined "This Our Native Land: America, the Beautiful," the *Washington Daily News* found Evans's work reassuring about America and its people. "Mr. Evans no more attempts to point up the awfulness of it all than he does to fiddle around with arty, soft-focus effects," the reviewer claimed.[37]

The aesthetics of tragedy which Evans had most powerfully summoned in his work in Hale County also found favor with the Left, still captivated by popular front Americanism well after its passing. Reviewing an exhibition of FSA photographs at the Photo League in New York City during 1940, Robert Disraeli wrote of the "haggard" faces of "harried people" which contained a beauty and strength despite the ravages of the depression. He continued:

> One cannot leave them without a feeling of optimism that here, expertly and beautifully done, we have the grim record of a passing phase in the life of our country; and that in the future our descendants will say when looking at these pictures: "those were the faces of our ancestors who overcame their difficulties with heroic determination and forced themselves upward into the sun and into the golden air so that we might live in a world of beauty and justice.

For Elizabeth McCausland, a member of the editorial advisory board of the Photo League and reviewer for the *Springfield Union and Republican*, aesthetics and politics were interdependent in the Historical Section's images, for she wrote: "the photographers have produced work which is beautiful because it is meaningful."[38] Institutional and cultural forces more powerful than Roy Stryker determined the nature and significance of his photographic project and its images of Southern poor whites.

Global war and American preparedness also had an impact upon the Historical Section's representation of the South's small farmers. The intention was to justify the continuing relevance of the FSA's agricultural programs during wartime, which required an integration of the South's poor whites into the war effort and into the mainstream of American culture. After the fall of France in the summer of 1941, the South's small farmers became a national asset rather than a national problem, since they were shown to contribute to "Food for Defense" and diversified their output to meet defense requirements. When Jack Delano visited Hale County, Alabama, in 1941, the site of Walker Evans's assignment with James Agee five years earlier, he photographed a cattle ranch. "The barn in the background was formerly the cabin of a sharecropper," reads one of his captions.[39] In June 1942 the Historical Section concluded its work with the South's small farmers under the auspices of the Department of Agriculture. John Collier visited the FSA's project at Escambia Farms in northwestern Florida, and celebrated the rebirth of a community. Escambia Farms was a 13,000-acre tract in Okaloosa County containing over 80 families, each installed in a 4- or 5-room house on a plot of about 95 acres of farmland. Collier's report described how a "desolate" community had achieved salvation through cooperation and government assistance after the RA's intervention in 1936. The collapse of the local lumber industry during the 1920s had serious consequences for the environment as well as the economy, for its legacy was a topography of scrub pine, burnt stump, and swamp. Human resources were equally wanting. The majority of Escambia Farms' clients were farmers "who had failed, sharecroppers whose life had always hung in the immediate future, meal following meal, day following day, year following year, with no link, no purpose." However, Collier marveled at the rejuvenation of the community since the establishment of Escambia Farms. "Where the door yards were bare earth, there is now grass, and bright trumpet vines climb up the trellised porches," he wrote. "Planted trees have grown to cast their shade on the hot sandy soil." The family of George McLelland served to illustrate the project's benefits to small farmers. Collier portrayed the McLellands as responsible, modern farmers who terraced their land, grew a marketable and soil-conserving crop mix, and cultivated a Victory Garden which provided for their own needs. Collier's photo-narrative clearly attributes the McLellands' stability and sufficiency to FSA assistance. George McLelland is shown consulting with his FSA supervisor and taking his bean crop to the local cooperative for sale. Also, Collier's captions note how his mule was bought with an FSA loan and was insured by the cooperative.[40]

Once the United States had entered the war, the South's white working class was no longer represented by Stryker's photographers as attached to low wage and low value industries in need of reform. The Southern industrial worker became a bulwark of the war effort in the Historical Section's images, and Stryker encouraged his photographers to compose photo-stories about individual workers. John Collier composed a photo-series about Albert F. and Fay Saunders Smith, a young couple at the Cousa

Court Housing project in Childersburg, Alabama. The Smiths were indistinguishable from affluent young Americans anywhere, a rendering which Collier sought to reinforce in a proposed outline for a bio-pic feature. His draft story centered on a girl of seventeen winning a prize of $50 in an essay competition on government housing and investing it in a business course which enabled her to become a secretary and to acquire "the class" to win her sweetheart, a physical education instructor at a local school. Obtaining jobs at the Powder Plant and government, they were able to marry in style and "live happily ever after." Collier's images of the Smiths showed how they had made Huey P. Long's fantasies of the early 1930s come true for themselves. Through a combination of personal initiative and support from the state, they were

Plate 4 John Vachon: A farmer plowing, Roanoke County, Virginia, March 1941.

the owners of a house, a radio, and an automobile.[41] As the RA/FSA photographic project had contributed to the myth of the "common man" through its coverage of the Southern tenant during the 1930s, so it helped an alternative myth emerge during wartime – that of the "Sunbelt South."

The Southern tenant came to assume a central place in the iconography of the depression years and a cultural nationalism which celebrated and often sentimentalized the "common man," whose character was the stronger for the circumstances in which it was wrought. The photographers, the critical elites searching for new paradigms for a society convulsed by change and economic depression, and a media hungry for exotic actuality were primarily responsible for the transformation of the tenant into a cultural symbol. Stryker's own documentary ambitions and the working methods he introduced to achieve them were eclipsed in the process. Ultimately, he would be remembered best for the work he organized while aggressively courting publicity rather than for his efforts on behalf of social research. Stryker would have placed "the people" neither on a crucifix nor a pedestal; however, he was no idealistic champion of them. Stryker was something of a contradiction in terms: an inner-directed administrator with ambitions to establish photography as a respectable tool of social research.[42] He became a captive of his own contradictions, required by administrative necessity to make compromises with his photographers and obliged to pander to the expectations of the media and the arts establishment in order to maintain the Historical Section's high profile. Such bureaucratic considerations determined Stryker's actions rather than any recognition that his own documentary vision would have consigned the lower orders to the peripheries of the public attention, in documentary books and journals of social criticism. Arguably, "the people" might have been accorded more respect, but they would have had less prominence.

NOTES

1 United States, *Farm Tenancy: Report of the President's Committee, February 1937* (Washington, DC: Government Printing Office, 1937), pp. 3–5; United States National Emergency Council, *Report on Economic Conditions of the South* (Washington, DC: Government Printing Office, 1938), pp. 21–2.

2 Stuart Kidd, "Eudora Welty's Unsuccessful Application to Become a Resettlement Administration Photographer," *Eudora Welty Newsletter*, XVI (1992): 6–8.

3 Interview of Arthur Rothstein conducted by Richard K. Doud, May 25, 1964, microfilm, 831, 835, *Oral History Collections*, Archives of American Art; Delano quoted in Greg Day (ed.) "Folklife and Photography: Bringing the FSA Home. Recollections of the FSA by Jack Delano," *Southern Exposure* 5 (nos. 2–3, 1977): 126; Mydans and Delano quoted in Hank O'Neal, *A Vision Shared: A Classic Portrait of America and its People, 1935–1943* (New York: St. Martin's Press, 1976), pp. 94, 240.

4 Shahn quoted in Bernarda Bryson Shahn, *Ben Shahn* (New York: Harry N. Abrams, n.d.), p. 135.

5 Interview with Marion Post Wolcott conducted by Richard K. Doud, January 18, 1965, microfilm, 1150, *Oral History Collections*, AAA; Delano quoted in Day, "Folklife and Photography," p. 126.

6 Stryker to Edward R. Trapnell, May 29, 1940, Records of the Farmers Home Administration, Box 127, *Record Group 96, Series 2*, National Archives.

7   Post to Stryker, July 28 and 29, 1940, microfilm NDA 30, 323–4, *Stryker Papers,* AAA.

8   Lee to Stryker, November 1938; January 18, March 17, 1939, microfilm NDA 31, 401; 434, 485, *Stryker Papers*, AAA.

9   Post to Stryker, January 1939, microfilm, NDA 30, 74, *Stryker Papers*, AAA.

10 Delano to "Toots" (Clara D. Wakeham), March 28, 1941, microfilm NDA 25, 1086–7, *Stryker Papers*, AAA.

11 Richard H. Pells, *Radical Visions and American Dreams: Culture and Social Thought in the Depression Years* (New York: Harper and Row, 1973); David P. Peeler, *Hope Among Us Yet: Social Criticism and Social Solace in Depression America* (Athens, GA: University of Georgia Press, 1987), pp. 108–9.

12 Memorandum from Adams to Stryker, n.d., Notes on San Augustine submitted to *Travel Magazine*, microfilm Reel 15, 536, 538, *FSA-OWI Textual Records*, Library of Congress.

13 General Caption # 15, Jean Lee report, microfilm Reel 19, 85–7, *FSA-OWI Textual Records*, LC.

14 Captions, microfilm Reel 9, 343, 347, *FSA-OWI Textual Records*, LC.

15 William Stott, *Documentary Expression and Thirties America* (New York: Oxford University Press, 1973).

16 Stryker to Lee, December 1 and 9, 1936, microfilm NDA 31, 7, 20, *Stryker Papers*, AAA.

17 Gardner Cowles, Jr., to Stryker, November 23, 1936, microfilm NDA 24, 260, *Stryker Papers*, AAA; *Look* 1 (March 1937), 18–19; *Des Moines Register*, January 10, 1937; *Indianapolis Sunday Star*, January 10, 1937; *Boston Sunday Post*, February 14, 1937.

18 Stryker to Cowles, January 13, 1937, microfilm NDA 24, 262; Lange to Stryker, February 12, 1936, April 2, 1937, microfilm NDA 30, 517, 644, *Stryker Papers*, AAA.

19 Stuart Kidd, "The Farm Security Administration Photographic Project's Reinvention of the Southern Poor White in the 1930s," in Lothar Honnighausen and Valeria Gennaro Lerda (eds.) *Rewriting the South: History and Fiction* (Tübingen: Francke Verlag, 1993), pp. 219–30.

20 *Washington Evening Star*, March 8, March 17, 1936; *Washington Post*, November 3, 1935; *The Nation's Agriculture*, February 1936, 7; *Mayflower's Log*, May 1936; *Boston Sunday Post*, February 13, 1937; *Buffalo Times*, February 14, 1937.

21 *Washington Daily News*, March 1, 1940; *Washington Post*, March 31, 1940.

22 *Houston Chronicle*, March 8, 1936; *St. Louis Globe Democrat*, ca. May 1940, clippings file, microfilm Reel 22, *FSA-OWI Textual Records,* LC; *Washington Post*, March 1 and 4, 1936; *New York Times*, January 28, 1940; Federal Writers Project of the Federal Works Agency, Works Projects Administration, American Guide Series, *North Carolina: A Guide to the Old North State* (Chapel Hill: University of North Carolina Press, 1939), pp. 562–3.

23 *Seattle Star*, July 29, 1936; *New York Times*, February 14, 1937; *Look* 1 (March 1937), 18.

24 The photograph appeared in Samuel Lubell and Walter Everett, "Rehearsal for State Medicine," *Saturday Evening Post* 211 (no. 25, December 17, 1938), 23; Gilfond to Mr. V. G. Brown, February 23, 1937, microfilm Reel 2, 930; General Captions No. 23 and 24, microfilm Reel 18, 55, 61, *FSA-OWI Textual Records*, LC.

25 Roy E. Stryker, "Documentary Photography," in *The Complete Photographer* 4 (no. 21, April 10, 1942), 1364–74, and "The FSA Collection of Photographs," in Roy Emerson Stryker and Nancy Wood, *In This Proud Land: America 1935–1943 as Seen in the FSA Photographs* (London: Secker and Warburg, 1974), p. 8; Memorandum for Donald P. Stephens from Stryker, November 4, 1939, microfilm FSA/WDC 1, 90, *Stryker Papers*, AAA.

26 Stuart Kidd, "Art, Politics and Erosion: Farm Security Administration Photographs of the Southern Land," *Revue Française d'Études Américaines: "La Terre Américaine,"* 48/49, 291–7; Arthur Rothstein, "Direction in the Picture Story," *The Complete Photographer* 4 (no. 21, April 10, 1942), 1358–9; *Washington Post*, August 21, 1938.

27 "Still Photography," memorandum prepared for budget purposes, RA, n.d., ca. 1937, microfilm, NDA 8, 13; Stryker to Lee, January 13 and 19, 1937, microfilm, NDA 31, 40, 46; Stryker to Post, December 27, 1938, microfilm NDA 30, 33, *Stryker Papers*, AAA; Stryker to Van Fisher, December

21, 1938; "Excerpts from letter to Mr. Stryker from Mr. Van Fisher," December 13, 1938; Stryker to William M. Milliken, January 20, 1939; Stryker to Fisher, March 21, 1939, microfilm Reel 3, 108, 109, 150, 155, *FSA-OWI Textual Records*, LC.

28 Stryker to Lee, January 13 and 19, 1937, microfilm NDA 31, 40, 46, *Stryker Papers*, AAA; Fischer to All Regional Information Advisers, "Special Memo on Photography," May 4, 1938, microfilm Reel 1, 728, *FSA-OWI Textual Records*, LC; "The FSA Photographer": draft document with reference to photographers' civil service status, microfilm FSA/WDC 1, 232, *Stryker Papers*, AAA; Stryker to Bernard Deis, January 20, 1940, Box 130; Stryker to Jean Boudin, April 23, 1940, Box 131, *RG 96, Series 2*, NA.

29 See the following prints: LC-USF 33-30723-M3/ -30732-M5/ -30731-M5; LC-USF 34-52799-D/-52878-D/ -52884-D/ -52889-D/ -52901-D/ -52904-D/ -52905-D.

30 John Fischer to George Wolf, January 18, 1941 and attachment, "Suggestions for Public Relations Committee, New Orleans Conference," Box 26, *RG 96, Series 2*, NA; "Suggestions for Community Photographs," n.d., microfilm NDAS 8, 944–5, *Stryker Papers*, AAA.

31 "Copperhill, Ducktown, and Isabella," microfilm Reel 18, 26, *FSA-OWI Textual Records*, LC. For a selection of Post Wolcott's studies of the strikers at Ducktown, see, LC-USF 33-30522-M2/-30523-M1/M2/M5/ -30524-M1/ LC-USF 34-52142-D/ -52159-D/ -52160-D/ -52172-D.

32 Representative images of labor militancy during the Greensboro strike are LC-USF 33-20923-M2/ -20924-M3/ -20926-M4/ -20928-M1/ -20936-M2 & M4/ -20937-M3.

33 LC-USF 34-6322-D.

34 Stryker to Post, April 1, 1939, microfilm NDA 30, 129, *Stryker Papers*, AAA; Stryker to Grobin, February 26, 1936, microfilm Reel 2, 861, Press clipping, *Amarillo Globe*, ca. 1936, microfilm Reel 22, Clippings File, *FSA-OWI Textual Records*, LC.

35 Memorandum for Stryker from Fischer, January 16, 1941, Box 146, *RG 96, Series 2*, NA; "Gossip Sheet," May 2, 1942, microfilm NDA 21, 98, *Stryker Papers*, AAA.

36 For statements of this claim, see James C. Curtis, "Dorothea Lange, Migrant Mother, and the Culture of the Great Depression," *Winterthur Portfolio* 21 (spring 1986), 4; Lawrence W. Levine, "The Historian and the Icon: Photography and the History of the American People in the 1930s and 1940s," in Carl Fleischhauer and Beverly W. Brannan (eds.) *Documenting America, 1935–1943* (Berkeley: University of California Press, 1988), pp. 25–7.

37 Stryker to O. B. Dryden, March 23, 1939, microfilm Reel 2, 799, *FSA-OWI Textual Records*, LC; *Washington Daily News*, October 1, December 1, 1938.

38 *Photo Notes*, May 1940, 3; *Springfield Sunday Union and Republican*, September 11, 1938.

39 See *Lots 1627–1629* Reel 94, Prints & Photographs, LC; James C. Derieux, "Big Discovery in the South," Collier's, August 1, 1942, 55; Delano's caption is to LC-USF 34-44431-D.

40 "The Story of Escambia Farms," microfilm Reel 13, 489–91, *FSA-OWI Textual Records*, LC; *Lot 64*, Reel 11, Prints & Photographs, LC.

41 Collier to Stryker, May 31, 1942, microfilm NDA 25, 871, *Stryker Papers*, AAA; Collier's photo-story on the Smiths is *Lot 177* Reel 13, Prints & Photographs, LC.

42 Stryker's role as a bureaucrat is evaluated in Stuart Kidd, "Bureaucratic Dynamics and Control of the New Deal's Publicity: Struggles between Core and Periphery in the FSA's Information Division," in Robert A. Garson and Stuart S. Kidd (eds.) *The Roosevelt Years: New Perspectives on American History, 1933–1945* (Cambridge: Edinburgh University Press, 1999), pp. 105–21.

8

Southern Appalachia

Linda Tate

In 1965, fledgling novelist Lee Smith pulled James Still's 1940 novel *River of Earth* off the Hollins College library shelf. Born and raised in the mountain community of Grundy, Virginia, Smith was studying writing at Hollins with her mentor Louis Rubin, who had shared with her the work of great Southern writers such as Eudora Welty.

But then Smith came across Still's novel. "At the end of the novel," she recalls,

> I was astonished to read that the family was heading for – of all places! – Grundy!...I read [the] passage over and over. I simply could not believe that Grundy was in a novel!...*River of Earth* was as real to me as the chair I sat on, as the hollers I'd grown up among. (Quoted in Guralnick 2001: 146)

Until she read the ending of this landmark Appalachian novel, Smith had imagined far-flung places and outrageous scenarios in her early efforts at writing. But when she read Still's work, Smith began to understand that she might have something to say about her home.

Literary scholar Joyce Dyer tells a similar story of discovering Appalachian literature, not through her doctoral studies (when she focused on Southern literature) but through a book given to her by a relative. "At college and then graduate school," she writes,

> I was deeply attracted...to Southern literature. But I never once had the courage to raise my hand and ask my teachers why there were no mountains in the stories they assigned. The stories my family told all had mountains in them, and the visits to my cousins in West Virginia had been beautiful, hilly rides. The tacit lesson I so wrongly absorbed was that the mountains *had* no literature. (Dyer 1998: 13)

When she finally did encounter Appalachian literature, Dyer responded with the same keen sense of recognition Smith had felt: "Here were mountain roads, strong women like my grandmother Coyne, storytellers like my father, histories of other outmigrants, stories about coal, words and sayings that fit my mouth" (13).

As any review of personal essays by or interviews with Appalachian writers will reveal and as any scan of Appalachian studies scholarship makes clear, Appalachia has often held a stepchild relationship to the larger South and the accompanying field of Southern studies. "Always part of the mythical South," historian Ronald D. Eller writes in his foreword to *Confronting Appalachian Stereotypes: Back Talk from an American Region*,

> Appalachia continues to languish backstage in the American drama, still dressed, in the popular mind at least, in the garments of backwardness, violence, poverty, and hopelessness once associated with the South as a whole. No other region of the United States today plays the role of the "other America" quite so persistently as Appalachia. (Eller 1999: ix)

Similarly, Rodger Cunningham (1996) argues that while the South may be labeled "Other" by the North, Appalachia becomes the "Other's Other" – "a region marked by a double otherness that complicates its very sense of its own being" (42). As Robert J. Higgs and Ambrose N. Manning, the editors of *Voices from the Hills*, the first substantial anthology of Appalachian literature, state in their introduction,

> For the most part, Appalachia has been regarded as a poor but eccentric relation of the rest of the South and in anthologies passed off with a tall tale or two and a story illustrative of local color... [T]he effect is a rather facile dismissal of one of the most complex and fascinating regions of America. The impression... is one of hurried patronage and academic condescension. (Higgs and Manning 1975: xix–xx)

Satirical descriptions addressing the same issue appear in *The Future of Southern Letters*, in pieces written by fiction writer Fred Chappell and poet Jim Wayne Miller. Writing for the 1996 volume, Chappell imagines a 2001 interview with Wil Hickson, a fictional figure whom Chappell depicts as an emerging young Appalachian writer who speaks to the future of the region's literature. The fictional Hickson looks back at the decades-long development of Appalachian literature. In reflecting on the ways in which Appalachian literature has been received by Southern studies scholars, Hickson says:

> Appalachian Literature was just a little tiny bit of a thing, with only Thomas Wolfe and Harriette Arnow as nationally ranked reputations, and here it was nestled like a toadstool beside a rotting log against Southern literature, which may still be the proudest literary tradition in the United States. (Chappell 1996: 58)

Miller takes an equally creative approach in his piece, "... And Ladies of the Club," in which he imagines a conversation between himself and Sut Lovingood, the fictional character from George Washington Harris's nineteenth-century Appalachian tall tales. Throughout his conversation with Sut, Miller critiques the 1985 reference work, *The History of Southern Literature*, detailing its limitations, particularly from the perspective of Appalachian studies. Miller tells Sut about a 1986 *Chronicle of Higher Education* interview with Louis Rubin, one of the volume's general editors. "Southern literature," Miller quotes Rubin as saying in the *Chronicle* interview, "is very much the product and image of something which is geographically and historically and culturally a kind of homogeneous unit" (Miller 1996: 89). And this, Miller tells Sut, is precisely the problem with *The History of Southern Literature* – and Southern studies in general. "This assumption of a homogeneous South," Miller states, "rather than recognition of the South's diversity, is the reason why the Appalachian South (and other subregions) fail to come into sharp focus" (89). It is as if, Miller says, Southern studies scholars are trying "to banish poor cousins to the outhouse and put out the best uncracked china for company" (88).

Attempting to define the geographical and cultural boundaries of Appalachia further complicates the task of providing a history of Appalachian literature. Though the map edges for the region are fuzzy, Southern Appalachia can loosely be understood as the mountainous areas of the South – the highland regions of eastern Kentucky, eastern Tennessee, northern Alabama, northern Georgia, western North Carolina, western Virginia, western Maryland, all of West Virginia, and even southeastern Ohio and parts of western South Carolina. The more difficult question becomes one of establishing boundaries around Appalachian *culture*. "Just as we cannot define precisely where Appalachia begins and ends geographically," write the editors in volume two of *Appalachia Inside Out*, "neither can we say exactly where the culture and customs of the region begin and end" (Higgs, Manning, and Miller 1995: xi). "It is a complex place in every sense," notes Joyce Dyer, editor of *Bloodroot*. "Geologically, historically, culturally, and genealogically we are only beginning to understand it" (Dyer 1998: 7). Perhaps Appalachian short story writer and novelist Gurney Norman expressed it best in an interview with Dyer. "The concept of Appalachia," Norman told Dyer, "is no longer considered confined to a geographical region, to a neighborhood, to a decade. . . . It is . . . best understood as a spirit, 'a spirit that has leapt out of strict Appalachian ground'" (5).

But the question of Appalachian literature involves more than its stepchild relationship to the South, its marginalization in the larger American consciousness, the vexing question of geographic boundaries, and the rather vague definition of "Appalachian culture." For the literary historian, the very notion of when Appalachian literature *begins* is perhaps the most essential – and most frequently misanswered – question. Traditionally, scholars have seen Appalachian literature as beginning with the local color writers of the late nineteenth century. Even those scholars who have critiqued these early contributions by urban, middle-class writers who visited the mountains and wrote their impressions for national magazines have nevertheless seen this as a kind of starting point. The prominence of Mary Noailles Murfree, for example, has been so profound that even "native" writers have found it difficult to step out from beneath her shadow. Where Southern writers have written with the anxiety of the William Faulkner influence, Appalachian writers have had, not one of their own as the major figure setting the tone for the region's writing, but instead an outsider who misunderstood and misrepresented mountain people. Writers from the Deep South may have to find ways to stake out their own turf, to distinguish themselves from Faulkner and his legacy, but Appalachian writers have had to reclaim their regional literature from a faulty start, working carefully — and in some ways unsuccessfully — to establish a more accurate vision of their world.

Scholars such as Henry Shapiro are precisely on target when they talk about the ways in which Appalachia was "invented" in the late nineteenth century by local color writers, missionaries, teachers, and industrialists — outsiders who "discovered" the mountaineers. But even this careful approach shifts our attention to the *outside* forces that shaped Appalachian culture and literature rather than the cultural and creative traditions that have been with Appalachian people all along. In looking for a more accurate starting point for discussing Appalachian literature, one could go back much further in time to a consideration of the oral tradition — the ballads and folktales the Scots-Irish, Cherokee, African, German, British, and other mountain people brought with them. Alternatively, one could go much further ahead in time, leaping to the 1930s and the outpouring of work by "native" Appalachians who claimed their region as the source of their literary endeavors.

Taking the traditional approach — that is, starting with written accounts about mountain people written by outsiders who visited the region — one might begin with a consideration of writers who contributed accounts before the rise of the local color movement. In editing *Voices from the Hills*, Higgs and Manning choose early travel accounts as a beginning point for their landmark anthology of Appalachian literature. Similarly, Cratis Williams, the major scholar in the early development of Appalachian literary studies, notes in "The Southern Mountaineer in Fact and Fiction":

> Forerunners of Murfree in the field of fiction began to catch fleeting glimpses of the highlander as early as 1824. That he was not defined and brought into focus until after the Civil War, however, is not surprising, for he had not crystallized as a regional type distinguishable from the old hunter, the frontiersman, the ruffian on the border, or the poor white until he had been subjected to a generation of debilitating poverty and cultural despair that turned him backward in time. (Williams 1975–6: 42–3)

According to Williams, some of the early works that contain at least limited descriptions of mountain people include novels and short story collections by William Gilmore Simms, Augustus B. Longstreet, John Esten Cooke, Harden E. Taliaferro, and George Washington Harris. Anticipating the local color fiction movement, Rebecca Harding Davis's *Life in the Iron Mills*, set in the industrialized city of Wheeling, [West] Virginia, appeared anonymously in the *Atlantic Monthly* in 1861 and was read by Emily Dickinson, Louisa May Alcott, Nathaniel Hawthorne, Ralph Waldo Emerson, Herman Melville, and others.

But it is with the actual advent of the local color movement – and its famed arrival in Southern Appalachia – that scholars such as Williams mark the beginning of Appalachian literature. Thus, says Williams, 1884 – the year in which Houghton Mifflin published *In the Tennessee Mountains*, a collection of Murfree's stories that had previously appeared in the *Atlantic Monthly* – stands as a kind of "*annus mirabilis* in the history of the mountain people in fiction . . ., the time at which the Southern mountain people had become generally recognized as a people possessing their own idiosyncrasies, not to be confused with other Southern types" (Williams 1975–6: 134). While Murfree was clearly the predominant figure in this movement, Shapiro (1978) notes "some 90 sketches and more than 125 short stories [were] published between 1870 and 1890" (18) in such national magazines as the *Atlantic Monthly, Harper's,* and *Lippincott's.* "The mountaineer who stood on his heights and watched the industrial revolution creep nigh was no stranger to the American reading public," explains literary historian Charlotte Ross (1995). "He had been duly noted by travelers as early as 1784 . . ., christened 'mountaineer' by 1824 . . ., and thrust into prominence by Mary Noailles Murfree and John Fox, Jr., by the end of the nineteenth century" (203).

While some of the writers who emerged during or just after this movement had transplanted themselves and thus were partly "of" the mountains (one thinks, for example, of Emma Bell Miles and her 1905 book, *The Spirit of the Mountains*), most of this early literature about Appalachia was written by non-Appalachians. Some outside observers, such as William Goodell Frost, president of Berea College, and Lucy Furman, a teacher and house-mother at Hindman Settlement School in Knott County, Kentucky, were clearly well intentioned, but even these outsiders with "missionary" agendas were wont to see mountain people as separate from and different than "mainstream," "national" Americans. Mountaineers were throwbacks to older times, they believed, holdouts from modern progress. In a famous phrase, Frost titled an 1899 *Atlantic Monthly* article: "Our Contemporary Ancestors in the Southern Appalachians." Other writers were apparently not so well intentioned but instead jumped on the local color bandwagon to advance their own careers. Shapiro (1978), for example, describes the writing of this period as the "literary exploitation of the Southern mountains" (20), while Helen Lewis and Rich Kirby liken this cultural exploitation to the industrial devastation beginning at the same historical moment. "Outsiders," write Lewis and Kirby (1995), "mined the vivid and unique culture of the mountains, as the 'local color school' of writers . . . cranked out novels and pulp fiction filled with picturesque and rather savage hillbillies" (651). Regardless of the intention, these local colorists and missionaries nevertheless promoted a "vision of Appalachia as a strange land inhabited by a peculiar people," as Will Wallace Harney described the region in an 1873 issue of *Lippincott's Magazine* (quoted in Shapiro 1978: 3). Thus, as Shapiro argues, these writers "established Appalachia in the public consciousness as a discrete region, in but not of America" (18).

As noted earlier, particularly influential in this regard was Mary Noailles Murfree, a Murfree of Murfreesboro, Tennessee. Writing under the pseudonym Charles Egbert Craddock, Murfree originally wrote "pale stories of sophisticated life" for *Lippincott's*

Magazine (Williams 1975–6: 134) but then began writing stories about the Tennessee mountains which were enthusiastically received by *Atlantic Monthly* editor, William Dean Howells. Murfree's first story to appear in *Atlantic Monthly* was "The Dancin' Party," which was published in the May 1878 magazine. This was followed by seven other stories in the magazine, and in 1884, all eight stories were published as *In the Tennessee Mountains,* a landmark work in the history of non-native Appalachian literature. Subsequently, Murfree wrote *The Prophet of the Great Smoky Mountains* (1885), the first novel in American fiction concerned primarily with mountain people and their problems (Williams 1975–6: 124). Despite her impact on the local color movement and the portrayal of Appalachia to the wider American reading public, Murfree actually "knew very little about Appalachia" (Shapiro 1978: 19). Williams (1975–6) cites her "failure to become intimately acquainted with more mountaineers and with their social history" (135), and Shapiro notes: "her own observations of the region and its people were limited to girlhood summers spent at Beersheba Springs, a favorite watering place of the Tennessee gentry, and to a brief journey in search of local color during the summer of 1886, *after* the publication of *In the Tennessee Mountains*" (Shapiro 1978: 19; my emphasis).[1]

Following in Murfree's footsteps was John Fox, Jr., a native of Kentucky who left the region to attend Harvard University and Columbia Law School and then returned due to poor health. The author of *The Little Shepherd of Kingdom Come* (1903) and *The Trail of the Lonesome Pine* (1908), Fox joined his father and his brother "in their business operations" in the mountains of Kentucky "during the boom, sparked by English capital, that led to the development of the mineral resources in the tri-state area surrounding Cumberland Gap" (Williams 1975–6: 211). Eventually settling in Big Stone Gap, Virginia, Fox was an enthusiastic explorer of the area. As Williams notes, "his tramps, horseback rides, and fishing and hunting trips through the mountains enabled him to become well acquainted with the manners and customs of the people" (211). Though Williams describes Fox's *Little Shepherd* as "the first really widely read romance of the mountains" (216) and *The Trail of the Lonesome Pine* as perhaps "the best fictional interpretation of mountain life ever achieved" (219), most scholars today view Fox's contributions to Appalachian literature as limited and as advancing, rather than correcting, stereotypes of the region.[2]

While Fox's contributions were significant – and are still felt in the outdoor drama of *The Trail of the Lonesome Pine* produced each summer in Big Stone Gap – it is Murfree who set the tone for subsequent literature about Appalachia. "Murfree," Williams argues,

> bequeathed a legacy to her literary descendants. The reader who turns from a representative sampling of her fiction to that of almost any other writer of mountain fiction can readily trace her influence, for her creation of a literary mountaineer from a narrowly limited real mountaineer was so successfully done that writers who have attempted to present a literary mountaineer based on any type of real mountaineer other than the one she selected have met with an indifferent popular success. (Williams 1975–6: 152)

But the persistent influence Murfree has exerted comes not from "the validity of her private experience" but, rather, "on her ability to establish the otherness of Appalachia...to offer an insider's view which validated the impressions of outsiders" (Shapiro 1978: 20). With ready stereotypes in hand – and, perhaps more importantly, with permission to use them freely in their fiction – numerous writers joined Murfree in writing local color sketches and sensational tales about mountain people. "By providing her generation with a clear conception of Appalachia as an essentially alien land," Shapiro notes in his discussion of this "discovery" of Appalachia, Murfree's "work facilitated the emergence of Appalachia as a viable field for fiction, and her own success encouraged other authors to take the region as their subject" (20).

With Murfree's work as a blueprint, non-native Appalachian writers began to look for the recognizable mountain type. What emerged was "genre" fiction clearly written and published solely for the purpose of profit. Williams (1975–6) says these "sensational opportunists...simply picked up well-defined stereotypes and, *without even so much as paying the mountains a visit*, set their mystery novels, their lurid romances, and their sentimental effusions in mountain settings" (187; my emphasis). Finally, Charlotte Ross summarizes the devastating effect of these early literary "miners." "The reading public," says Ross,

> knew the mountaineer as a tall, rangy Anglo-Saxon who was by blood and inclination an undiluted pioneer...with an eighteenth-century mind and an ever-ready rifle....The dime novels of the 1890s, the moralistic fiction of the 1900s, and the many years of local color sketches, popular thrillers, and boisterous frontier humor had severely damaged his image. As a fictional stereotype, he fell just short of the ridiculous. (Ross 1995: 204)

While local color writers were engaged in their hit-and-run observations (echoed later by photographers and writers such as James Agee and Walker Evans in the 1941 volume *Let Us Now Praise Famous Men*), cultural expression – particularly a vibrant storytelling tradition – was alive and whole in the mountains. Part of the "discovery" of the mountains was the early twentieth-century collection of mountain ballads by such folklorists as Cecil Sharp, Olive Dame Campbell, and Maud Karpeles.[3] While the work of these folklorists could certainly be (and has been) subjected to the same scrutiny brought to bear on the work of the local color writers, these folklorists nevertheless had stumbled across native narrative expression. Seen from this perspective, it would be possible to say that Appalachian literature actually has its roots in Europe and Africa, as well as in the Native American communities of the Cherokee and Shawnee. Numerous examples abound: ballads brought over from the British Isles, lively storytelling traditions from white settlers in Appalachia as well as from slaves and free African Americans in the region, and a rich mythology tradition from the Cherokee, Shawnee, and other Native American communities who had resided in the mountains for centuries. Jack tales, trickster figures, and cautionary tales are pervasive throughout the region; the telling of tales and the singing of story are part and parcel of traditional Appalachian expression. "There has always been and continues to be," says Jim Wayne Miller (1977), "a reciprocal relationship between oral and written literature. And so oral literature is a legitimate concern of Appalachian literary scholarship" (86). For this reason, Appalachian literary history, says Miller, should include "folktales, ballads, hymns, riddles, saws, and epitaphs" (84).

Seeing Appalachian culture and literature from this "native" perspective allows us to recover an entirely different – and richer – cultural story than the one we see when we begin with Murfree and the other local color writers. Old ballads, such as "Barbry Allen," have been part of the mountains' rich oral tradition since Scots-Irish settlers arrived. Jack tales – as collected by folklorist Richard Chase and told in recent years by veteran storytellers such as Ray Hicks – came with the Scots-Irish as well. The rare early written volume, such as Emma Bell Miles's 1905 book, *Spirit of the Mountains*, makes clear that some were able to hear and recognize the importance of these songs and stories. And later volumes, such as Jean Ritchie's 1955 book, *Singing Family of the Cumberlands*, show the endurance of this oral tradition, the way story and song are woven seamlessly into everyday family life, thus shaping the expression of modern artists in the mountains. Many of the contemporary Appalachian women writers featured in *Bloodroot* also "frequently talk about the importance of the stories they heard growing up, of the oral history of their region, stories that spilled freely from the mouths of neighbors and relatives and friends. They breathed in those stories, the oxygen of their future work" (Dyer 1998: 8).

Seen – or perhaps heard – in this way, with mountain voices at the center, the emergence of literature by "native" Appalachians in the 1930s is not at all surprising. Framed by two classic American novels – James Still's *River of Earth* (1940) and Harriette Arnow's *The Dollmaker* (1954) – this outpouring of writers from the region marks a significant shift from literature written *about* Appalachians to literature written *by* Appalachians. "What's significant about the modern literary movement in this region in the last fifty years," noted Gurney Norman in 1984,

> is that we have native people who have become the writers, who know where to shine the light and who know the experience from the inside. Up until about 1930, the books and stories about these mountains were written by people from the outside looking in, and it's only in the last half-century that we've had our own native literature. (Quoted in Williamson 1994: 308–9)

With the shift to native writers, explains Williams (1975–6), "the writers who gave direction to mountain fiction...were those whose voices spoke for him [the mountaineer] rather than of him" (358). It is important to note that, not only did these writers speak with greater authenticity and sensitivity about the region, but they also drew from the rich oral tradition of the mountains. Moving away from the biased and limited viewpoints of Murfree, Fox, and their followers, these writers had a wellspring of native expression from which to draw. On the surface, this is most readily seen in the more careful and judicious use of dialect (which local color writers had abused to a great degree), used now not to distance the writer and reader from the peculiar mountaineer but to bring the mountaineer and his experience to vivid life. A key figure in this emergence of an indigenous literary movement is the prolific Jesse Stuart. The author of more than sixty volumes (novels, stories, essays, poems, and autobiography), Stuart counts among his better-known novels *Taps for Private Tussie* (1943) and *Daughter of the Legend* (1965). Stuart's volume of "sonnets" in *Man with a Bull-tongue Plow* (1934) tells the story of one farmer's life. Similarly, Louise McNeill, of Pocahontas County, West Virginia, brought her poetic skills to bear in *Gauley Mountain* (1939), an epic portrayal of the settling of the fictional mountain and the rise of industrialism in the area. Her later work – both her volume of poetry, *Elderberry Flood* (1977), and her autobiography, *Milkweed Ladies* (1988) – speak to her impressive, but overlooked, contributions to heartfelt regional understanding. Other important work of this period was contributed by writers who might in some ways be considered non-native writers but whose impulse in writing about the region came from a marked decision to speak "with" mountain people rather than for them. Elizabeth Madox Roberts's 1926 novel, *The Time of Man,* still deserves more than the sporadic attention it has received over the years since its early strong reception. Grace Lumpkin's proletariat novel, *To Make My Bread* (1932), also merits continued study.

The clear culmination of the 1930s came in Still's seminal 1940 novel, *River of Earth*. Still – who had grown up in Alabama, attended graduate school at Vanderbilt, and then settled in Knott County, Kentucky, when he joined the staff at the Hindman Settlement School – had begun publishing his short stories during the 1930s in the *Atlantic Monthly* and the *Saturday Evening Post*. Pieces of *River of Earth* initially appeared in these magazines, and *On Troublesome Creek*, a collection of Still's short stories, was published in 1941. Still's vision of mountain people flows out of his own rootedness to Troublesome Creek. Still, says Williams (1975–6), "has visited the people and learned their language, their traditions, their habits of thought and action." As a result, he "interprets their life with tenderness and compassion" (367). Up until his death in 2001, Still served as a lively mentor to a number of emerging Appalachian writers and was a key part of the Hindman Settlement School Writers Workshop. *Wolfpen Notebooks*, published late in Still's life, was culled from years of journal keeping, reflecting the close observation of nature and place which defined Still's years on Troublesome Creek.

Increasingly, women's voices were heard in the emerging literature by native Appalachians. Of particular note is the work of Mildred Haun and Wilma Dykeman. Haun's 1941 composite novel, *The Hawk's Done Gone*, tells the story of Dorthula White and her experiences from young girlhood through old age. Written in first-person narrative, the related stories weave in and out, creating a kind of narrative quilt that mirrors the actual quilt Dorthula makes as a young woman and carries with her throughout her life. Dykeman's contributions to Appalachian literature have been considerable, both in terms of her nonfiction – through her study of the French Broad River – and in terms of her substantial body of fiction, including *The Tall Woman*

(1962), *The Far Family* (1966), and *Return the Innocent Earth* (1973). Dykeman has been especially notable as an articulate spokesperson for the development and appreciation of Appalachian literature and culture.

While Roberts, Lumpkin, McNeill, Haun, and Dykeman all made substantive contributions to the emergence of native Appalachian literature, without a doubt Harriette Simpson Arnow stands as the most important Appalachian woman writer before 1970. Like Dykeman, Arnow wrote both fiction (including novels such as *Mountain Path*, 1936, and *Hunter's Horn*, 1949) and nonfiction (including two classic histories of the region, *Seedtime on the Cumberland*, 1960, and *The Flowering of the Cumberland*, 1963). From this impressive canon, the most remarkable of these works is her 1954 novel, *The Dollmaker*. This novel tells the story of Gertie Nevels and her family as they leave their home in eastern Kentucky to look for work in Detroit factories. Her extraordinarily thorough and careful research into the history of the region has enriched not only her fiction but also her nonfiction studies.

When Cratis Williams wrote his seminal work *The Southern Mountaineer in Fact and Fiction* in 1961, he believed that the mountaineer as the focal point of fiction was rapidly dying out and that, as a result, Appalachian literature was nearing its end. Nothing could have been further from the truth, for the true "Appalachian Renaissance" was still to come in the 1970s. During this decade, a number of crucial developments occurred in literature, culture, and scholarship. Appalachian studies programs began to spring up at a number of regional colleges and universities, including Appalachian State University, the University of Kentucky, and East Tennessee State University, just to name a few. *Appalachian Journal* had its debut in 1972, and the Appalachian Studies Association was formed in 1977. University presses, as well as a tiny group of independent and community-based presses, began to see the value of publishing works by and about Appalachian authors. Community-based organizations, such as the Appalachian Consortium, Appalshop, and the Highlander Center, either came into existence or energetically increased their efforts to support the creative work of Appalachian people. Guy and Candy Carrawan's collection of oral history pieces and songs of the region, *Voices from the Mountains* (1975), is a prime example of the work that staff members at organizations such as Highlander were undertaking. Appalshop's Roadside Theater, under the direction of Ron Short, and playwright Jo Carson made significant strides in using the region's rich oral tradition as the main source material for new drama. Festivals – highlighting Appalachian music, storytelling, craft, and other elements of the oral tradition – emerged throughout the region, and the *Foxfire* project emerged as a linkage between the Appalachian community and the educational system.

Writers native to the mountains were particularly active during the 1970s, with fiction writer Gurney Norman and poets Jim Wayne Miller, Jeff Daniel Marion, and Bob Snyder at the forefront of this work. Norman, a native of eastern Kentucky, had left the region for California, where he became one of the editors of the *Whole Earth Catalog*. Eventually, like many other displaced Appalachians, Norman returned to eastern Kentucky and began creating fiction based both on his tie to the mountains and his experiences in California. His 1972 novel, *Divine Right's Trip*, is a blending of these concerns, while his collection of related short stories, *Kinfolks*, focuses more specifically on a community in eastern Kentucky. Like Norman, who became and continues to be centrally important as a commentator on Appalachian culture and a mentor for emerging writers in the region, Jim Wayne Miller not only contributed substantially to the development of Appalachian poetry but also wrote many critical essays and was a beloved teacher and mentor for many before his death in 1996. Particularly important in his creative work were Miller's "Brier" poems, in which a fictional "brier" (mountain man) experiences shifts and changes in his life in the Appalachian mountains. Filled with humor and good sense, Miller's poems still serve as a touchstone for many younger writers in the region. Along with Norman and Miller, other Appalachian Renaissance poets, such as Jeff Daniel Marion and Bob Snyder, helped to form writers' collectives and workshops throughout the region. In 1971, the Southern Appalachia Writers' Cooperative was formed in Beckley, West Virginia. Part of "Antioch Appalachia," a satellite program sponsored by Antioch College, the group included Norman, Miller, Snyder, Don Askins, Peggy Hall, and Jim Webb. As the "Soupbean Collective," this group produced *Soupbean: An Anthology of Contemporary Appalachian Literature*.

In the last two decades, the Renaissance has taken root and flourished. In his piece for *The Future of Southern Letters*, Chappell imagines his fictional young writer, Wil Hickson, describing the mantle that was passed from the older generation of Appalachian writers to the generation currently emerging. Hickson says, "That's what sets my generation apart from our predecessors. To paraphrase the old poem by Ezra Pound, 'They broke the wood, Now is a time for carving.' I think we'll be able to do some carving to be proud of" (Chappell 1996: 60). With the wood broken by earlier native writers such as James Still, Harriette Arnow, Gurney Norman, and Jim Wayne Miller, writers in the 1980s and 1990s have been whittling literature that would have been unthinkable to the local color writers at the end of the previous century. Writers such as Robert Morgan, Wendell Berry, and Fred Chappell emerged in more recent years, not only as fiction writers but also as scholars and essayists. More recently, young men such as Chris Offutt, Pinckney Benedict, and Silas House have expanded the possibilities for fiction by Appalachian men.

Increasingly, scholars, readers, writers, and presses have begun to understand that Appalachia is not a monolithic region, not the popular backwater populated only by descendants of the "original" Anglo-Saxons. Instead, more and more attention has been given to the multicultural dynamics of the region. Historians have concluded that, while the Scots-Irish are indeed the largest ethnic group in the mountains, "many other ethnic groups settled in the mountains" (Blethen 1995: 2). As H. Tyler Blethen notes, the earliest of these settlers were Native Americans. "European immigrants," he writes, "included significant numbers of English, Germans, French, Welsh, and Italians, and people of African descent also settled through the region" (2–3). More recently, scholars such as Brent Kennedy and Darlene Wilson have explored the rich and fascinating history of the Melungeons in Appalachia. In short, says Blethen, "Southern Appalachia, since the Revolution, has been shaped by ethnic and cultural diversity" (3). Marilou Awiakta has enthusiastically and energetically written and spoken about her Cherokee Appalachian heritage, and in her landmark volume, *Selu: Seeking the Corn-Mother's Wisdom* (1994), she draws links between Cherokee rootedness, Scots-Irish cultural traditions, and the rising encroachment and power of the atomic age, particularly as she felt it in her childhood in Oak Ridge, Tennessee, where the atom bomb was first created.

Writers who have reminded us of the African-American contribution to the mountains include scholar Henry Louis Gates, Jr., who describes his childhood in Piedmont, West Virginia, in his memoir *Colored People* (1994); Nikki Giovanni, whose poetry celebrates, in part, her upbringing in Knoxville, Tennessee; and Ed Cabbell, whose poems, scholarship, and efforts to preserve African-American and oral traditions in southern West Virginia have been ongoing and unflagging. The most significant work in this regard, however, has undoubtedly come from the "Affrilachian" poets, a group of African-American poets from the Appalachian region who discovered each other at the University of Kentucky at Lexington. Led unofficially by poet Frank X. Walker, the group has been supported and encouraged by Gurney Norman and includes such figures as Kelly Ellis and Nikky Finney. The Affrilachian poets seek to make African-American cultural life and experience in Appalachia more visible, not only to the world outside Appalachia but also, perhaps more significantly, to white communities in the region.

While work from all of these writers has been significant and in itself would constitute a continuation of the Renaissance, a sizable piece of the emerging literature has been written by Appalachian women. Writers such as Mary Lee Settle, Lee Smith, and Denise Giardina are "driven by the important and compelling and passionate mission to define Appalachia for the first time, to see it distinct from the cotton South, to understand its place in women's lives, to write its story, and to bring it up to date" (Dyer 1998: 9). Underscoring the importance of women writers to the continuing Appalachian Renaissance is a radio series produced by WMMT, the Appalshop station. Entitled *Tell It on the Mountain*, the series features the work of Nikki Giovanni, Marilou Awiakta, Lee Smith, Mary Lee Settle, Barbara Kingsolver, George Ella Lyon, Michelle Y. Green, Jo Carson, Bobbie Ann Mason, Sharyn McCrumb, Wilma Dykeman, Lou Crabtree, Rita Quillen, Anne Shelby, and Denise Giardina.

Mary Lee Settle stands as one of the veteran novelists of this generation. A prolific writer of more than ten book-length works, Settle is particularly important for a series of five novels known as *The Beulah Quintet*. Novels in the series include (listed in the chronological order of the time periods in which they are set): *Prisons* (1973), *O Beulah Land* (1956), *Know Nothing* (1960), *The Scapegoat* (1980), and *The Killing Ground* (1982). Taken together, these five novels tell the story of West Virginia, from the earliest backgrounds in Cromwell's England through immigration to the New World and the settling of what would become West Virginia. More recently, her memoir, *Addie* (1998), has contributed to a deeper understanding of family, generations, and stories in the region.

Turning her attention to what might be termed "folk history," Lee Smith concentrates in her novels of Appalachia on the development of mountain communities. In novels such as *Oral History* (1983) and *Fair and Tender Ladies* (1988), Smith gives voice to multiple generations of mountain families, strong-voiced storytellers such as Granny Younger and Ivy Rowe. Nearly all of Smith's prolific work has focused on Appalachia, both the Appalachia of the past — illuminating the world that existed for itself even as outside missionaries were "discovering" it – as well as the Appalachia of current times, teasing out the tensions felt in the region as it is splintered and torn in the face of modern pressures. Other significant works about Appalachia by Lee Smith include *Black Mountain Breakdown* (1980), *The Devil's Dream* (1992), *Saving Grace* (1995), as well as a number of the stories in her collections, *Cakewalk* (1981), *Me and My Baby View the Eclipse* (1990), and *News of the Spirit* (1997). Smith's magical storytelling is captured as well in a 1996 Kentucky Educational Television documentary on her work and in *Conversations with Lee Smith*, a collection of interviews conducted with Smith since 1983.

Denise Giardina, at once an Episcopal lay priest, a Mountain Party candidate for governor of West Virginia, and a successful novelist, provides perhaps the most accessible – and progressive – historical fiction about the region. Her twin novels, *Storming Heaven* (1987) and *The Unquiet Earth* (1992), tell the story of the West Virginia and Kentucky coalfields, from the early mine wars to the more recent effects of the federal War on Poverty on people of the region. *Saints and Villains* (1998) reveals Giardina's interest in the larger world, focusing as it does on the life of Dietrich Bonhoeffer, a Nazi resistor. This latest historical novel also represents Giardina's coming of age as a substantial novelist, one of the best of her generation, and many readers look forward to her bringing her considerable gifts to bear again on Appalachian issues and themes.

Rounding out the lively field of Appalachian letters at the turn of the millennium is the popularity and success of a number of the region's writers. Like Giardina, Sharyn McCrumb has evolved throughout her career, moving from the writing of pure genre fiction and, in doing so, winning every crime fiction award in the United States. In addition to writing her Elizabeth MacPherson detective novels, McCrumb has begun in recent years to focus her attention on what she terms her "ballad novels," which beautifully weave together mountain legends, historical crimes, and contemporary regional issues.

Appalachian children's literature has been popular as well, with Cynthia Rylant winning the Newberry, Caldecott, and American Book Awards. Originally from West Virginia, Rylant focused most of her early books on stories of the mountains – both in picture books for the very young and in young adult novels for the adolescent reader. More recently, Rylant has created books that move further afield from place but continue to be powerful and evocative nevertheless. George Ella Lyon has also developed a strong following, not only as a children's book author but also as a poet, novelist, and essayist. Lyon has been especially generous in her encouragement of other writers and accessible in her work with the community. Frequently a workshop leader at Hindman Settlement School Writers Workshop, Lyon speaks strongly to the need to record one's voice, one's stories, one's connection to the place and to the land. The author of several children's books, Lyon has also written an adult novel, *With a Hammer for My Heart* (1997).

Other Appalachian writers who have enjoyed popular success include Cormac McCarthy, Gwyn Hyman Rubio, and Charles Frazier. McCarthy has been, throughout his career, sporadically considered an Appalachian writer, focusing as he does on his native Knoxville, Tennessee, and the surrounding area in his early novels. More recently, McCarthy has turned his attention to the Southwest, particularly in his "Border Trilogy." Rubio's first and only novel to date, *Icy Sparks* (2001), was selected for Oprah Winfrey's Book Club. Frazier's hugely successful first novel – and again, only novel to date – *Cold Mountain* (1997), has much to do with the region, but perhaps since it does not deal in the patterns and plot lines that Murfree set so early with *In the Tennessee Mountains*, most critics have not yet situated the work in the context of Appalachian fiction.

Bobbie Ann Mason and Barbara Kingsolver – both consistently appearing on the *New York Times* bestseller list – are also often grouped with other writers of the region. Though Mason writes about western Kentucky – hundreds of miles from the Appalachian end of the state – she nevertheless writes about a South that is too often not captured in a discussion of the Deep South. Like other Appalachian writers, Mason writes of working-class and lower-middle-class Kentuckians, and for this reason her work is sometimes linked with the mountain region. Her memoir, *Clear Springs* (1999), perhaps makes the case most persuasively for considering Mason a distant cousin of the region, with its attention to place and rhythm and the tension between a rural upbringing and an increasingly suburban, even urban, adulthood. While Kingsolver initially focused her creative attention on her adopted home of Arizona, then turning to her childhood experience in Africa with her bestseller *The Poisonwood Bible* (1998), in recent years she has more frequently "come home" to Southern Appalachia in her fiction. Her novel, *Prodigal Summer* (2000), is set completely in the region and reveals Kingsolver's concern with ongoing issues of the environment and culture in the mountains. Kingsolver is also a prolific essayist and comments not infrequently on both her Kentucky and Cherokee roots.

At the heart of this outpouring of creativity from Appalachian writers is a lively community, a kind of ongoing oral tradition delivered via the written word. As Gurney Norman points out, all of the current outpouring of the written word in Appalachia calls the reader back to mountain folklore, ballads, Jack tales, and simple storytelling on the front porch. "The storyteller," says Norman,

> opens the old channels of memory, so that he has a renewing function – to remind, or *re-mind*, to renew the mind of, the listener or the audience, to make sure that the audience remains in continuity and in a continuous *feeling* association with what has gone before. (Quoted in Williamson 1994: 308; original emphasis)

Readers who bring themselves to the words of these mountains find Lee Smith's stories – whether she is telling them herself at one of her many public appearances or workshops or whether she's conjuring the voice of a midwife in the mountain; Jo Carson's, Angela Debord's, and Rema Keen's playwrighting, storytelling, and dramatic monologues that bring grandmothers and mountain activists to life; and Sheila Kay Adams's and Betty Smith's ancient ballads and old tales, as they craft them in the written word and share them as well in old-fashioned tellings and singings. From mountain to mountain, poets such as Barbara Smith and Kirk Judd, Rita Quillen and Sherrell Wigal, Kathryn Stripling Byer and Llewellyn McKernan speak and listen to one another – on the phone, on paper, via email, in public performances, at workshops, conferences, and festivals. A visitor to a music festival such as the Clifftop Appalachian String Band Festival might be just as likely to hear a poem as an old fiddle tune ringing out across the campsite, a student at a cultural workshop such as West Virginia's Augusta Heritage Festival might sit with old-time music vocalist Ginny Hawker before heading to a class with poet and fiddler Doug Van Gundy, and after a day watching Lee Smith nurture emerging writers, just as she did Lou Crabtree and Silas House, at the Hindman Writers Workshop, a participant could likely end up singing ballads with Betty Smith till the wee hours of the morning.

"It's a family-feeling situation," says Gurney Norman:

It's amazing to be a writer in a community that has this kind of definition, where you assume that the people who are reading your stories are in some sense your neighbors. . . . To be a writer in a *neighborhood* is a rich experience. . . . That is about cultural *health*. We have a sense of community here that links the older generation of thinkers and writers with a middle generation, and both of them speaking to a younger generation. (Quoted in Williamson 1994: 301; original emphasis)

Founded in 1977, Hindman Settlement School Writers Workshop – which has had among its many teachers Gurney Norman, James Still, Jim Wayne Miller, George Ella Lyon, Kathyrn Stripling Byer, Hal Crowther, Chris Offutt, Lee Smith, Betty Smith, Sharyn McCrumb, and many others – has been especially important in the nurturing and continued liveliness of this unique community. According to Joyce Dyer, Hindman

has been a profoundly significant experience for many of these authors, and they remember it. There is no question that it has had a direct and dynamic influence on emerging Appalachian writers and is in some part responsible for the literary quickening of the region. (Dyer 1998: 11)

Despite all of this wonderful work – both written and oral, literary and cultural – stereotypes about Appalachia die hard. The outside world, it would appear, still feels compelled to comment on this "different" and "other" place and, unfortunately, still often misunderstands it. Any number of instances of continuing prejudices about Appalachians could be listed, but perhaps the most disturbing of recent years has been Robert Schenkkan's dramatic project *The Kentucky Cycle*, which won the Pulitzer Prize for drama in 1992. Hailing from California, Schenkkan visited Kentucky for a weekend in 1981, read Harry Caudill's frequently critiqued – but nonetheless famous – *Night Comes to the Cumberlands* (1963), and without conducting much further research, proceeded to write an epic musical Broadway show about the region. In outrage, a number of Appalachian writers and scholars protested by writing essays and editorials and ultimately by publishing *Confronting Appalachian Stereotypes: Back Talk from an American Region*. George Ella Lyon, quiet in her carriage but strong in her voice and moral stance, says, "anyone familiar with the history of outsiders' views of the region will see in *The Kentucky Cycle* the same weary plod through outraged pity, preconceived notions, self-righteous reductionism and psychosocial projection that has been the mark of literary tourism for so long" (quoted in Billings 1999: 10). Particularly frustrating is the timing of *The Kentucky Cycle*, coming as it did after two decades of such a lively creative period in the region. "What about the long-term effects," asks Lyon, "of Appalachian community leaders, writers and artists, teachers, historians and sociologists to battle the very reductive picture Schenkkan reaffirms?" (Billings 1999: 10).

Despite these problems, the literature survives, the native voices of the mountains continue sounding across the region. Gurney Norman, on a characteristically optimistic note, says, "Things work out. Good work gets done. The talented writer who perseveres will find her way" (quoted in Williamson 1994: 309). The perceptive reader and observer will find, as Norman says, "there is an intensity and power in the creative ferment in this new generation that's incredible and beautiful to see."

Near the end of his imagined interview with the "fictional" writer Wil Hickson, Fred Chappell asks Hickson about his literary influences. Listening to Hickson's rhythmic voice and easy storytelling, Chappell – and his readers – might understandably trace Hickson's imagined work to the ballads passed down by Jane Hicks Gentry or to the Jack tales passed down by storytellers such as her distant cousin Ray Hicks. And if, like Chappell, the reader knows that Murfree and Fox and their contemporaries missed a thing or two about life in the real mountains, they will know that Hickson will not cite those local colorists as his literary forebears. But thinking back to Lee Smith's oft-told story of finding James Still's work in the library at Hollins College, Chappell – and his readers – might easily anticipate that Hickson would mark the start of Appalachian literature with that classic 1940 novel, *River of Earth*.

But, no, Hickson traces his influence to a later time – but what is for him a true beginning time. "When I read [Lee Smith's] novel *Oral History*," he says, echoing her own story of discovering her literary inspiration James Still, "it was a real revelation to me. It's easy to see now that this one novel is probably the seminal work for current Appalachian fiction. It's where we all come from now, whether we know it or not. She's the mother of us all" (Chappell 1996: 56).

Ultimately, for all true Appalachian writers, the task has been to claim the literature for themselves, to make the magic of the written word give voice to the power of the voice on the wind, the song in the holler. Jim Wayne Miller, such a powerful figure in this lively community full of powerful folks, said: "Writing that allows us to 'live with' people rather than 'look at' them is preferable" (Miller 1977: 87) and again, "the most vigorous literature of the Appalachian region [is] the writing which is an expression *of* the region and not a report *on* it" (Miller 2001). Poet, novelist, essayist, and environmentalist Wendell Berry says simply, in a famous phrase, Appalachian literature is "local life aware of itself." And Wilma Dykeman succinctly sums things up when she says Appalachian literature is "as unique as churning butter and as universal as getting born" (quoted in Miller 1977: 90).

Eschewing Mary Noailles Murfree as the creator who gave them to themselves, who "discovered" them into existence, the powerful mountain writers of the last eighty years have found that the story of who they were was inside them all along. "Finding out about yourself," says Jim Wayne Miller,

> can be a political act in itself.... Believing a new thing about yourself may involve assimilating something that is very old, something out of the past. And the new thing will not make you someone else, but will make you realize who you have been all along. (Quoted in Williamson 1979: 274)

Notes

1   For a different perspective on Murfree's work as a local color/regionalist writer, see Marjorie Pryse, "Exploring Contact: Regionalism and the 'Outsider' Standpoint in Mary Noailles Murfree's Appalachia," *Legacy* 17, 2 (2000): 199–212. It might be noted that Marjorie Pryse is a women's studies and American literature scholar, rather than a scholar of Appalachian literature as a whole.

2   For insightful discussion of Fox and his legacy to the literature and culture of the region, see Darlene Wilson's essay, "A Judicious Combination of Incident and Psychology: John Fox Jr. and the Southern Mountaineer Motif," in *Confronting Appalachian Stereotypes: Back Talk from an American Region*, ed. Dwight B. Billings, Gurney Norman, and Katherine Ledford (Lexington: University of Kentucky Press, 1999), pp. 98–118.

3   For a helpful discussion of the "songcatchers," see Shapiro (1978), especially chapter 10: "The Folksong Revival and the Integration of the Mountaineers into Modern American Civilization: The Triumph of Pluralism."

References and Further Reading

Billings, Dwight B. (1999) "Introduction." In Dwight B. Billings, Gurney Norman, and Katherine Ledford (eds.) *Confronting Appalachian Stereotypes: Back Talk from an American Region* (pp. 3–20). Lexington: University of Kentucky Press.

Blethen, H. Tyler (1995) "The Scotch-Irish Heritage of Southern Appalachia." In Robert J. Higgs, Ambrose N. Manning, and Jim Wayne Miller (eds.) *Appalachia Inside Out: A Sequel to Voices from the Hills, Vol. 1: Conflict and Change* (pp. 2–8). Knoxville: University of Tennessee Press.

Chappell, Fred (1996) "The Shape of Appalachian Literature to Come: An Interview with Wil Hickson." In Jefferson Humphries and John Lowe (eds.) *The Future of Southern Letters* (pp. 54–60). Oxford: Oxford University Press.

Cunningham, Rodger (1996) "Writing on the Cusp: Double Alterity and Minority Discourse in Appalachia." In Jefferson Humphries and John Lowe (eds.) *The Future of Southern Letters* (pp. 41–53). Oxford: Oxford University Press.

Dyer, Joyce (1998) "Introduction." In Joyce Dyer (ed.) *Bloodroot: Reflections on Place by Appalachian Women Writers* (pp. 1–15). Lexington: University of Kentucky Press.

Eller, Ronald D. (1999) "Foreword." In Dwight B. Billings, Gurney Norman, and Katherine Ledford (eds.) *Confronting Appalachian Stereotypes: Back Talk from an American Region* (pp. ix–xi). Lexington: University of Kentucky Press.

Gray, Richard (2000) *Southern Aberrations: Writers of the American South and the Problems of Regionalism*. Baton Rouge: Louisiana State University Press.

Guralnick, Peter (2001) "The Storyteller's Tale." In Linda Tate (ed.) *Conversations with Lee Smith* (pp. 140–52). Jackson: University of Mississippi Press.

Higgs, Robert J. and Manning, Ambrose N. (eds.) (1975) *Voices from the Hills: Selected Readings of Southern Appalachia*. New York: Frederick Ungar.

Higgs, Robert J., Manning, Ambrose N., and Miller, Jim Wayne (eds.) (1995) *Appalachia Inside Out: A Sequel to Voices from the Hills, Vol. 2: Culture and Custom*. Knoxville: University of Tennessee Press.

Lewis, Helen, and Kirby, Rich (1995) "All That Is Native and Still Undefined: A Response to David Whisnant." In Robert J. Higgs, Ambrose N. Manning, and Jim Wayne Miller (eds.) *Appalachia Inside Out: A Sequel to Voices from the Hills, Vol. 2: Culture and Custom* (pp. 651–4). Knoxville: University of Tennessee Press.

Miller, Jim Wayne (1977) "Appalachian Literature." *Appalachian Journal*, 5, 82–91.

Miller, Jim Wayne (1996) " . . . And Ladies of the Club." In Jefferson Humphries and John Lowe (eds.) *The Future of Southern Letters* (pp. 87–92). Oxford: Oxford University Press.

Miller, Jim Wayne (2001). "Appalachian Literature: At Home in this World." In Sandy Hudock (ed.) James Still Homepage. http://faculty.uscolo.edu/hudock/jshome.html.

Ross, Charlotte (1995) "Industrialization and the Attrition of Mountain Characteristics: A Fictional Study." In Robert J. Higgs, Ambrose N. Manning, and Jim Wayne Miller (eds.) *Appalachia Inside Out: A Sequel to Voices from the Hills, Vol. 1: Conflict and Change* (pp. 203–13). Knoxville: University of Tennessee Press.

Shapiro, Henry D. (1978) *Appalachia On Our Mind: The Southern Mountains and Mountaineers in the American Consciousness, 1870–1920*. Chapel Hill: University of North Carolina Press.

Williams, Cratis (1975–6). "The Southern Mountaineer in Fact and Fiction," abridged version. *Appalachian Journal*, 3.

Williamson, J. W. (1979) "Interview with Jim Wayne Miller." In J. W. Williamson and Edwin T. Arnold (eds.) *Interviewing Appalachia: The Appalachian Journal Interviews, 1978–1992* (pp. 260–76). Knoxville: University of Tennessee Press.

Williamson, J. W. (1994). "Interview with Gurney Norman." In J. W. Williamson and Edwin T. Arnold (eds.) *Interviewing Appalachia: The Appalachian Journal Interviews, 1978–1992* (pp. 292–309). Knoxville: University of Tennessee Press.

9

The Southern Literary Renaissance

Robert H. Brinkmeyer, Jr.

With all the revisionary work in Southern literary study in the last twenty-five years, the once well-nigh universally accepted designation of the Southern literary renaissance – the period of literature spanning roughly from 1920 until the late 1940s – has come under serious interrogation and reconfiguration. The renaissance canon, for instance, now looks quite different than it once did, when Allen Tate and his followers firmly controlled the critical debate; it is much enlarged and more diverse, with many more women, African-American, and reformist writers standing alongside the likes of William Faulkner, Thomas Wolfe, and Robert Penn Warren. For some revisionists, this opening up of the canon has not gone far enough: some have set out to erase the Southern literary renaissance altogether, arguing that the designated period was all along merely a figment of Allen Tate's imagination, an idea created by Tate and endorsed by his colleagues merely to promote themselves and their ideas in the literary and cultural debates of their day. Look closely, this thinking goes, and the renaissance disappears; what is left is merely more Southern literature, pretty much as it has always been and continues to be.

Now seems like a good time to reassess the reassessment: that is, to examine the idea of the Southern literary renaissance now, many years and many rewritings later. Questions I hope to address along the way include: Should we dismiss outright the Agrarian/New Critical paradigm and substitute a new paradigm or paradigms? Or should we revise the old paradigm, accepting its basic validity but correcting its limitations? And if we dismiss outright the idea of the renaissance, then what idea should take its place? Finally, all these questions point to a broader one – what does Southern literature from 1920 to the late 1940s now look like and what, if anything, makes the literature from this period distinctive, worthy of the title of a renaissance? We may find out that Tate's paradigm ends up being a good bit more flexible than it was in his and his followers' hands; that though it was once used to exclude from discussion many writers outside mainstream white male writing, it now, oddly enough, gives us a way of understanding the more rich and diverse Southern canon that has replaced the one established by Tate and the New Critics.

Tate and the Beginnings

Few would have predicted the literary outburst that occurred in the American South from around 1920 through the late 1940s. Only a few years before, H. L. Mencken had savagely attacked the South's cultural sterility in his infamous essay "The Sahara of the Bozart" (1917), declaring the South "is almost as sterile, artistically, intellectually, culturally, as the Sahara Desert," adding: "it would be impossible in all history to match so complete a drying-up of a civilization."[1] By 1922, however, even Mencken was noting a developing critical spirit in the South, and in 1925 he would declare: "Just what has happened down there I don't know, but there has been an immense change of late. The old sentimental snuffling and gurgling seem to have gone out of fashion; the new southern writers are reexamining the civilization they live under, and striking out boldly."[2]

Mencken was not the only critic to note the emergence of Southern writing in the interwar period; indeed, by the late 1920s several critics were beginning to suggest the South was evolving into the literary center, rather than the backwater, of American writing. As significant as Mencken and other critics were in bringing attention to the Southern literary scene, however, it was Allen Tate, fresh from the Agrarian enterprise, who had the greatest influence in defining the literary period and giving it an identity – the Southern literary renaissance. Although Tate was not the first to suggest it, his forthright declaration of a Southern renaissance took hold immediately among critics and then held its place for several generations to follow; it was his configuration of the renaissance, both in terms of aesthetics and theme, that almost single-handedly established the canon and critical apparatus for interpreting it.

Tate did not announce a Southern literary renaissance (he spelled it "renascence") until 1945, but he laid the groundwork for his declaration in his 1935 essay, "The Profession of Letters in the South." Early on in his brief survey of the Southern literary tradition, Tate sounds a bit like Mencken from "The Sahara of the Bozart," arguing that for much of its history the South has been a cultural wasteland. Although deeply sympathetic to what he conceived of as the stable and traditional culture of the Old South, Tate suggests the conformity enforced by antebellum society (mainly because of the political crisis) had stifled critical thinking and expression, damaging creative expression not only during the pre-Civil War years but also for long after. So smothering and unrelenting have forces of Southern conformity remained, Tate says, that he reaches a stunning conclusion: "We lack a tradition in the arts; more to the point, we lack a literary tradition. We lack even a literature."[3]

The South, of course, did not lack a literature, but it did lack a literature to Tate's liking, one that merged cultural and artistic influences from the larger world of cultural modernism with traditional materials of the South. Preparing the way for his declaration of artistic flowering later in his essay, Tate declares: "the arts everywhere spring from a mysterious union of indigenous materials and foreign influences: there is no great art or literature that does not bear the marks of this fusion."[4] This is precisely the process that Tate saw happening in the best Southern writing of the 1920s and 1930s: Southern traditionalism fused — usually accomplished only through wrenching artistic and psychological violence — with literary and cultural modernism. Tate himself knew well the difficulty of successfully achieving such fusion and the temptation to settle comfortably into one mode of thinking — what in fact he saw many of the lesser Southern writers doing, abandoning traditionalist allegiances in order to embrace modernist expression (often configured in leftist politics) or ignoring modernist developments in order to embrace uncritically Southern sentiments. The best writers, on the other hand, and Tate of course included himself in this group, embraced rather than avoided the difficult demands and challenges arising from conflicting artistic and cultural allegiances. The charged tension between the modern and the traditional, for Tate, ignited the burst of literary expression in Southern writers of the 1920s and 1930s, a burst he believed couldn't be maintained because the irreversible forces of historical change were progressively destroying traditional society:

> The considerable achievement of Southerners in modern American letters must not beguile us into too much hope for the future. The Southern novelist has left his mark upon the age; but it is of the age. From the peculiarly historical consciousness of the Southern writer has come good work of a special order; but the focus of this consciousness is quite temporary. It has made possible the curious burst of intelligence that we get at a crossing of the ways, not unlike, on an infinitesimal scale, the outburst of poetic genius at the end of the sixteenth century when commercial England had already begun to crush feudal England.[5]

Ten years later in "The New Provincialism" (1945), Tate wrote that his comments from "The Profession of Letters in the South" were "written at the height of the Southern literary renascence" and that "that renascence is over; or at any rate that period is over; and I write, we all write, in the time of the greatest war."[6] "With the war of 1914–18," Tate adds, "the South reentered the world — but it gave a backward glance as it stepped over the border: that backward glance gave us the Southern renascence, a literature conscious of the past in the present."[7]

With these few sentences, Tate redirects the history of Southern literature, announcing both the Southern literary renaissance and its demise. By 1945, Tate says, the renaissance was over because of a dramatic change in cultural circumstance: the South was no longer looking backward but forward; unlike in 1918, when the South was reentering the modern world, in 1945 the South *was* the modern world. Writing during a time of extreme nationalism and burgeoning internationalism, Tate foresees a continuing widespread diminishment of regional culture and identity in the United States, with a resulting erosion of literature fueled by the modernist/traditionalist tension. "Will the new literature of the South, or of the United States as a whole, be different from anything that we knew before the war?" Tate asks early in the essay. "Will American literature be more alike all over the country? And more like the literature of the world?"[8] By the end of the essay Tate concludes that modern attitudes downplaying the significance of place, history, and tradition (which he oddly calls "provincialism"; the provincial person, he writes, "cuts himself off from the past, and without benefit of the fund of traditional wisdom approaches the simplest problems of life as if nobody had ever heard of them before")[9] have grown so powerful that even in the South regional attitudes no longer vitally shape cultural dialogue. "From now on we are committed to seeing *with*, not *through* the eye," Tate writes: "we, as provincials who do not live anywhere."[10]

Tate's groundbreaking declaration and discussion of a Southern renaissance, both in terms of the movement's origins and endings and in terms of the literature's theme and content, crucially shaped the idea of the renaissance in the minds of critics for decades to come. Tate, of course, was not working entirely alone: his reading of Southern literature between the wars was largely endorsed by most of his New Critical brethren, including former Agrarians John Crowe Ransom, Andrew Lytle, and Robert Penn Warren, along with several younger critics who just missed out on being Agrarians, including Cleanth Brooks and Richard Weaver; and then later by a whole host of like-minded critics, including among others, Louis Rubin, Walter Sullivan, Robert Jacobs, Robert Heilman, George Core, Hugh Holman, and (though his position is more complicated) Lewis Simpson. Although this latter group of critics were of course not all speaking with one voice, they shared a fundamental critical method and perspective – derived primarily from Tate – that dominated Southern literary studies until well into the 1970s, when serious reassessments began.

The perspective endorsed by Tate and his many followers – and the perspective used to define the Southern literary renaissance and its canon – was a complicated and not always consistent mix of formalism and social criticism. Despite their decidedly formalist aesthetics, which downplayed the significance of biography, history, and politics in critical analysis – in effect bracketing off artistic expression from social and historical reality – these critics nonetheless linked their aesthetics to cultural politics. They saw the great theme of the Southern literary renaissance as the clash between traditional and modern cultures, with the refined order of traditionalism giving way to the rapacious forces of cultural modernism. Their own sympathies and allegiances were decidedly traditionalist; and they argued, if not in so few words, that so, too, were those of the important Southern writers from the period. In declaring that the great literature of the Southern renaissance shared both a formalist aesthetics and a central subject, the New Critics and their followers created a well-defined critical template for establishing the canon and for interpreting individual works. Richard Gray appropriately entitles this template "literary traditionalism" – a template, that is, for canonizing works portraying cultural traditionalism in ways "literary" by New Critical standards.

Exemplars of the Southern renaissance by this model included William Faulkner, Stark Young, Katherine Anne Porter, Caroline Gordon, and of course the New Critics themselves, particularly Tate, Ransom, Lytle, and Warren, who were all distinguished writers. As poets and novelists themselves, many of the New Critics were of course not entirely disinterested in their analyses of Southern literature between the wars – as a number of critics have pointed out, Tate, Ransom, and Warren in particular were describing and endorsing a type of literature they themselves were writing. Speaking specifically of Tate's role as critic and writer, Michael O'Brien observes: "he was staking a claim for himself and his contemporaries," adding: "the logic was circular, made possible for Tate because he was both inside and outside the canon, both poet and critic, using the standing of the poet to justify the authority of the critic, the acumen of the critic to justify the strategy of the poet."[11]

Including writers in the canon of course meant excluding others, and the New Critical formula did just that, banishing to the margins of art and significance a number of writers whose work did not measure up either aesthetically or politically. Indeed, so strong was the connection in New Critical analysis between aesthetics and politics, that a writer's politics (particularly if those politics were reformist) in effect defined his or her aesthetics. "To write of the poor was to write of the political and to write of the political was not to write as a regionalist," Richard Gray observes, adding that the New Critical position might be best defined by one simple rule: "anything that strays from the true path of literary traditionalism wanders into the wilderness of dogma, social protest, propaganda, and 'message.'"[12] As Gray's comments suggest, the most damning charge that the New Critics could bring upon writers was that they had sacrificed the complexity of artistic expression for the simplicity of melodrama used to promote dogmatic political positions. Predictably, the primary targets of the New Critics were those writers who openly attacked Southern traditionalism and endorsed, implicitly if not explicitly, widespread social reform. These included most prominently women, African Americans, and leftists (particularly those who wrote about poor whites). With only a few noteworthy exceptions, these writers were typically casually dismissed, typed as treacly sentimentalists or misguided propagandists, either way aesthetic and political misfits. In effect, the New Critics (and the orthodox critics following them) attempted to represent the South and its literature as free from the turmoil of gender, race, and class dissent – or at least free from the turmoil that could not be eventually quelled and controlled, if not in reality then at least in the literature.

The Revised Canon

In the last several decades the canon established by the New Critics and their followers has undergone major revision and enlargement, the by-words of 1980s and 1990s literary and cultural criticism – race, class, and gender – succinctly identifying the primary perspectives at work in this revisionary enterprise. Feminist critics have been particularly productive and vocal in their efforts, typically by pointing to a tradition of women's writing in the South stretching back into the nineteenth century that they argue better contextualizes Southern women's writing of the 1920s and 1930s. All but ignored by the orthodox critics, this tradition encompasses not only writers of fiction and poetry but also those of diaries, journals, and letters, and brings to visibility, if not always prominence, numerous writers previously overlooked. A crucial text in the feminist remapping, Anne Goodwyn Jones's *Tomorrow Is Another Day: The Woman Writer in the South, 1859–1936* (1981) explores a line of white Southern women's writers who, through mask and deception, interrogated and critiqued Southern cultural practices, particularly the cult of Southern womanhood and its ideals of passivity and voicelessness. Jones goes so far as to call this line of writing a tradition, arguing that it "grew in the soil of the South's historical endorsement of southern women as writers and of the southern woman's own rejection of the tradition of patriarchy. Its hallmarks include the critique, implicit or direct, of racial and sexual oppression, of the hierarchical caste and class structures that pervade cultural institutions, and of the evasive idealism that pushes reality aside."[13] The writers Jones discusses include Augusta Jane Evans, Grace King, Kate Chopin, Mary Johnston, Ellen Glasgow, Frances Newman, and Margaret Mitchell.

Besides Jones, a number of other feminist critics, including, among many others, Louise Westling, Minrose Gwin, Lucinda MacKethan, Peggy Prenshaw, Carol Manning, Helen Taylor, and Patricia Yaeger, have explored the underlying patriarchal politics at work in the formation of the Southern canon and have brought serious critical attention to many women writers who previously had received only little, if any, attention as writers of the Southern renaissance. As a number of feminist critics have pointed out, Southern women writers of the renaissance have been dismissed, if not ignored, by the orthodox Southern critics because they characteristically do not work on the grand historical scale – what Richard King, drawing upon Nietzsche, identifies as monumental[14] – that Southern men do, instead focusing more on the domestic, quotidian aspects of Southern life. While the orthodox critics have thus seen women writers as avoiding the large, complicated history of the South, feminists have argued it is actually in everyday affairs that people most directly confront and negotiate (and suffer from) what Patricia Yaeger calls "the hardest facts of southern life."[15] "We need not look to 'monumental' historical consciousness – not to fathers or grandfathers or even large women – to understand the complexities that the weight of tradition brings to bear on the diurnal round of Southern life," Yaeger writes. "Thus short stories, cookbooks, girlish fantasies, and personal vignettes can become sites for measuring a political crisis in the making. These private narrative forms have public dimensions implicated in the appointment of power."[16]

If some feminist critics have argued for a line of women's writing distinct from the male-configured and male-dominated Southern renaissance, others have worked to include more women inside the renaissance as it is generally conceived. Of particular significance to this latter effort are the works of Kate Chopin and Ellen Glasgow. Characteristically deemed precursors to the renaissance, Chopin and Glasgow are now often seen by some feminist critics as active participants in that renaissance, writers whose work both stands up to the toughest critical standards and interrogates the same crucial themes and concerns of Southern culture and identity as do writers already canonized in the renaissance, such as William Faulkner, Thomas Wolfe, and Robert Penn Warren. Enfolding Chopin and Glasgow into the Southern literary renaissance of course pushes back the opening of the period, and that origin has continued to be pushed back further and further. Carol Manning, for instance, in a boldly entitled essay, "The Real Beginning of the Southern Renaissance," locates the renaissance's origins in the late nineteenth-century women's movement, when women writers from the South began going through – and writing about – the same sorts of cultural displacements and interrogations as writers from the 1920s and 1930s.[17] Besides Chopin and Glasgow, Manning sees a number of lesser-known writers as founding figures, including Anna Julia Cooper and Belle Kearney.[18]

Similar recovery work and canon reconfiguration have also been done by critics examining African-American writers. As with feminist reappraisals, much work has also been done to recover writers both before and during the time of the Southern renaissance, often by establishing a line of literary descent and influence that has little to do with white writers and thus with the Southern renaissance as traditionally configured. Much of this work has focused on the significance of African-American folk culture, particularly its oral and musical traditions (blues, jazz, and spirituals), in shaping a tradition of black Southern writing that runs counter to the dominant white canon as defined by the New Critics. Henry Louis Gates, in an analysis of Zora Neale Hurston, identifies an important element in much African-American writing, what he calls "the speakerly text" or "the voice of the black oral tradition."[19] Gates argues the speakerly text "is that text in which all other structural elements seem to be devalued, as important as they remain to the telling of the tale, because the narrative strategy signals attention to its own importance, an importance which would seem to be the privileging of oral speech and its inherent linguistic features."[20] And it is in the oral speech that shapes the speakerly text that one finds both "a repository of socially distinct, contrapuntal meanings and beliefs" and a narrative voice (seen most masterfully in Hurston's work) that

> echoes and aspires to the status of the impersonality, anonymity, and authority of the black vernacular tradition – a nameless, "self-less" tradition, at once collective and compelling, true, somehow, to the unwritten text of a common "blackness." For Hurston, the search for a "telling" form of language, indeed the search for a black literary language itself, defines the search for the self.[21]

Related to the work of Gates and others who have explored the significance of folk culture to African-American writing (including, among others, Houston Baker,

Robert Stepto, Michael Awkward, Barbara Johnson, and Keith Byerman), has been recent work exploring the connections between the New Negro Renaissance of the 1920s (as opposed to the Southern renaissance) to developments in writing by African Americans from the South. These studies have looked at both the significance of Southern writers within the movement and the significance of Southern culture to the art and identity of New Negro writers (even those not from the South). Led by such critics as Houston Baker, William Andrews, Trudier Harris, Thadious Davis, and Cary Wintz, this reappraisal has been particularly significant in contextualizing black literature from the South, not only regionally and nationally, but also internationally, particularly with regard to trends in literary modernism.

Although much African Americanist criticism examines Southern black writers essentially in isolation from white writers, other significant work has emphasized the interpenetration of white and black cultures – and thus the interpenetration of literary traditions – in the South. It is not merely, as Ladell Payne puts it, that "southern writers, black and white, utilize common sources and common values,"[22] but that black and white cultures have, despite the rigid boundaries historically enforced by segregation, fundamentally influenced and shaped each other in ways that go to the heart of personal identity and cultural beliefs. W. J. Cash's observation in *The Mind of the South* (1941) – that the relationship between blacks and whites "was, by the second generation at least, nothing less than organic. Negro entered into white man as profoundly as white man entered into Negro – subtly influencing every gesture, every word, every emotion and idea, every attitude"[23] – has become a guiding principle in much recent critical work, even if Cash himself is rarely cited.

Related to the critical enterprise of remapping the Southern literary renaissance by dismantling the black/white cultural opposition is the similar work being done by critics of liberal and leftist Southern writers (both black and white, but particularly white writers of labor strife and the sufferings of poor whites) of the 1920s and 1930s. This work has typically focused on revising the art *vs.* politics opposition used so unquestioningly by the New Critics to dismiss writers of the poor and the working class, pigeonholing them as merely writers of social agitation who deliberately manipulate art for the sake of dogma. Critics leading the way include those doing work in the fields of popular culture, regionalist studies, New Historicism, and whiteness studies. No longer are poor whites "Dixie's Forgotten People";[24] and no longer forgotten are the writers who wrote about them, among others, T. S. Stribling, Erskine Caldwell, Lillian Smith, Grace Lumpkin, Harry Harrison Kroll, Myra Page, Elizabeth Madox Roberts, and Olive Tilford Dargan (aka Fielding Burke). With the possible exceptions of Caldwell (whose work from the 1930s has of late generated fiercely debated interest, particularly in its wild mixture of narrative modes and in its use of the grotesque) and Smith (whose nonfiction, particularly *Killers of the Dream*, is now seen as groundbreaking and crucial in Southern cultural and intellectual history), none of these writers has gained unqualified acceptance as a major author. But even if not of the first order, they are no longer simply typed as writers of simple and obvious melodrama, work fit for the dustbin rather than the library. Instead, their writing is now for the most part being seen as an important expression of the Southern renaissance, appreciated for its complexity and richness, and particularly for its redefining of cultural stereotypes enforced by the dominant Southern culture.

The Southern Renaissance Now

What now to make of the Southern literary renaissance? Revisionary work in Southern literary study has reconfigured literature of the 1920s, 1930s, and 1940s, not only vastly opening up the canon but also calling the very idea of the renaissance into question. Returning to the questions I posed early on: How should we now configure the renaissance, assuming we still accept there was one? With the expanded canon is there anything significant that links the writing – other than chronology and regional identity – that would warrant the designation not only of a literary period but also of a period of great worth? These are the matters I would like to address in this final section.

Surprisingly enough, in terms of the fundamental themes and concerns with which Southern writers worked, the Southern literary renaissance looks pretty much the same, even with the much enlarged canon. And perhaps even more surprisingly, Tate's paradigm of the clash of the traditional and the modern still seems significant, even for those writers whom that paradigm was once used to exclude. This is not to say that Tate and his colleagues did not stake out political positions in their analyses of the Southern renaissance – positions that were of immense importance personally, professionally, and culturally, particularly as the Agrarians evolved into the New Critics – but it is to suggest that Tate developed an idea for understanding Southern literature between the wars that was even more encompassing than even he realized (or would have wanted to accept), given his championing of traditionalism through literary and cultural analysis of the South. At the risk of sounding reductive and simplistic, then, I would like to suggest that rather than discarding Tate's paradigm we should extend and revise it, accepting its fundamental premise of cultural awakening while abandoning its pigeonholed perspective conflating politics (including race) with aesthetics.

Extending Tate's paradigm allows us to follow Richard King's lead in positing the defining impulse of Southern renaissance writing as the interrogation and ultimate demystification of Southern traditionalism, coming at a time of immense intellectual energy deriving from the perceived clash of traditional and modern cultures.[25] While certainly Southern writers from other periods explored and questioned cultural paradigms, that impulse appears decidedly intense and far-reaching in the interwar period, encompassing the work of a wide range of authors of all stripes: conservatives, liberals, modernists, traditionalists, African Americans, whites, men, women – just about everybody, in other words. That such a diverse group of writers were interrogating Southern culture and its traumatic history does not mean that they all worked from the same ideological and artistic positions, nor that they all explored the same areas of conflict and came to the same conclusions. Of course they did not. But they all (or at least, almost all) explored the dimensions of a Southern culture that, by the light of their own growing self-consciousness, were no longer immediately taken for granted, no longer experienced as entirely natural, no longer unreservedly accepted. Theirs was a literature, in the famous words of Ellen Glasgow, in which "irony is an indispensable ingredient of the critical vision,"[26] written during a time, quoting W. J. Cash, of "the growth of the modern mind" when "the new analysis and criticism was steadily going forward."[27]

Ironic critical vision, arising from troubled self- and cultural-consciousness, structures almost all of the best literature of the Southern literary renaissance, surfacing even in works where it is least expected, including the work of the traditionalists. It is one of the significant ironies of the period that while the Agrarians and their sympathizers typically pled in their essays for a traditional society founded on the pillars of family, community, and historical memory, they often with trenchant irony undercut in their literature (and even occasionally in their essays, particularly in Tate's case) that very traditionalist position. Even John Crowe Ransom, in some ways the most serious-minded of the Agrarians (he set out to study economics, for instance, when the group was criticized for knowing nothing of the nuts and bolts of business and farming), nonetheless at times critiqued the Agrarian stance in his poetry, most obviously in "Captain Carpenter," where the poem's withering irony points to the quixotic nature of the Agrarian warriors. Much of the fiction by writers usually identified with traditionalist sympathies similarly ends up either calling into question or severely critiquing the traditionalist positions the works ostensibly appear to endorse. While these works typically work from and with the clash between the traditional and the modern, on the surface siding with the former and savaging the latter, ironic undercurrents work to expose the flaws of traditionalism, usually by establishing similarities to, rather than differences from, the modernity that threatens it. Caroline Gordon, for instance, masterfully undercuts many of the cherished ideals of Southern traditionalism in her fiction. Her first novel, *Penhally* (1931), follows several generations of a family as they struggle to hold their plantation together amid the turmoil of change; they fail in large part because the family is finally as rapacious as the Yankees and businessmen they fear. The old staple of Southern apologists, the plantation romance, becomes in Gordon's hands something close to an anti-plantation novel, the downfall coming primarily from within rather than from without. Similar undercutting of Southern traditionalism appears in much of Gordon's other fiction, most notably in *None Shall Look Back* (1937), a savage indictment of misguided heroism during the Civil War. Gordon's ironic vision represents less the exception than the rule for other writers of the renaissance, traditionalist and non-traditionalist alike.

But as is so frequently the case, it is Tate who best illustrates the tortuous (and tortured) position of the traditionalist. Having rediscovered his Southern roots in the mid-1920s after he moved to New York City ("I think if I'd stayed in the South, I might have become anti-Southern, but I became a Southerner again by going East,"

Tate later observed),[28] Tate embarked on a Southernist crusade that culminated in his deep involvement with the Agrarians. In letters to Donald Davidson, he forthrightly declared, "I've attacked the South for the last time," and, in reference to his biography of Stonewall Jackson, "Since I'm convinced that the South would have won had Jackson not been killed, I'm doing a partisan account of the Revolution. The Stars & Bars forever!"[29] But Tate's allegiances were not so clear-cut in his essays and poetry. He intended "Remarks on the Southern Religion," which was included in the Agrarian symposium *I'll Take My Stand* (1930), to be a partisan defense of fundamentalism, but the essay ends up being instead an analysis of the failure of the Southern tradition to heal the damaging split in the modern consciousness, between what Tate called "a self-destroying naturalism and practicality" and "a self-destroying mysticism."[30] "How may the Southerner take hold of his Tradition?" Tate asks near the end of the essay, a question embodying the ironic self-consciousness (Southern tradition not unthinkingly accepted but deliberately chosen) that shapes and haunts Southern writing of the renaissance. His answer: "by violence," by which he means a psychological violence, explained in the paradox with which he closes his essay: "[The Southerner] must use an instrument, which is political, and so unrealistic and pretentious that he cannot believe in it, to reestablish a private, self-contained, and essentially spiritual life. I say that he must do this; but that remains to be seen."[31]

Psychological violence of the sort Tate identifies in "Remarks on the Southern Religion" underlies his poem "Ode to the Confederate Dead" (1927), one of the key texts of the renaissance. No typical ode celebrating the fallen Confederates, Tate's poem explores why the poet *cannot* write an ode to the Confederate dead. The poet's attempts to identify with and honor the dead fail because he cannot recapture their commitment and belief. All his efforts to connect with the Confederates fail because the connection is not unthinking; his efforts at meaningful connection repeatedly fail as his modern critical self time and again severs the bond, despite the poet's desire to honor the past, as he knows that as a good Southerner he should. The poem, as does "Remarks on Southern Religion," ends inconclusively; and it is not surprising that after first completing it in 1927, Tate returned to it several times over the next decade for revisions and reworkings. "Ode to the Confederate Dead" clearly expresses Tate's deepest dilemmas as Southern and modern poet – dilemmas, though expressed from different perspectives and with different emphases, he shared with many other Southern writers of the renaissance.

William Faulkner comes immediately to mind, and particularly his character Quentin Compson as developed in *The Sound and the Fury* (1929) and *Absalom, Absalom!* (1936). Quentin's agonizings about his Southern past and identity have become in Southern criticism almost the stuff of legend, for many the touchstone of the Southern experience and Southern literature. And while a demythologizing backlash has set in recently – Michael Kreyling attacks what he calls "the Quentin thesis," saying "Quentin is the major life-support system in southern cultural discourse"[32] – to ignore the centrality to Southern writing of Quentin and more generally of Faulkner in terms of the basic issues of race, identity, and history with which they struggle finally distorts more than it enlightens. While Quentin is a young, intelligent, comfortably-off, white male, his paralyzing psychological trauma need not be understood only in those terms. Quentin feels caught in the web of Southern culture and history, a fate shared by most fictional characters during the renaissance. Not many of these characters share Quentin's fate – suicide – but they almost all share in his struggles to achieve identity and a measure of psychological – and at times bodily – freedom in a complicated, if not suffocating, South.

Similar crises, though often more physically threatening to life and limb, surface in much of the writing by African Americans. Although characteristically marked by violent and dramatic confrontations with the South's rigid system of racial oppression, much African-American writing at the same time deftly interrogates issues of identity and culture in the South in ways similar to those found in much of the white writing. While many critics argue as if *The Sound and the Fury* and *Absalom, Absalom!* are the *ur*-texts of modern Southern literature, they might want to consider instead Jean Toomer's *Cane* (1923), which appeared years before both of those Faulkner novels. Toomer's *tour de force* of high modernism, mixing voices, styles, and genres, explores the rich dynamics of African-American life in both the South and the North, focusing most tellingly on the agonizing efforts of a young black intellectual, Ralph Kabnis, to come to terms with his Southern roots. Psychological struggles similar to Kabnis's – he is drawn to the sensuous details of the land and its folk, at the same time that he is repelled by the countryside's squalor, ignorance, and violence – echo throughout Southern literature of the period, white and black. Kabnis's intense love-hate feelings toward the South, fostered by the split between his head and heart which leaves him paralyzed (until the end), seem downright Faulknerian: "Kabnis, a promise of soil-soaked beauty; uprooted, thinning out. Suspended a few feet above the soil whose touch would resurrect him."[33] Or, perhaps more correctly, Quentin's agonizings seem downright Toomerian.

Central to Kabnis's psychological turmoil – and indeed to much of the tension in *Cane* – is the matter of the educated African-American's relationship to black folk culture. This complicated issue might be put this way: at a time when African Americans are struggling to improve themselves, becoming better off and frequently leaving the South, what should their relationship be with black folk culture? Should they put the Southern folk experience entirely behind them? What do they gain by that? What do they lose? Or can they go home again, literally and metaphorically, somehow incorporating the values and passions of the folk in their modern identities? These questions, echoed later from the white perspective by Tate in "Ode to the Confederate Dead" (what should one feel toward one's heritage? – "What shall we say who have knowledge / Carried to the heart?"),[34] remained unanswered in *Cane* (as they do in Tate's poem), suggestive of the immense emotional and intellectual complexity involved in the effort by Southerners – blacks and whites alike – to establish healthy relationships with their heritage.

This effort haunts much of the African-American fiction of the Southern renaissance, the range of responses typified at the extremes by the work of Richard Wright

and Zora Neale Hurston. Although Wright's relationship with the South was more
conflicted than generally accepted (seen most visibly in *Black Boy*'s lyric lists describing Wright's boyhood wonder with the South amid all the horror), he characteristically pounds home in his fiction and autobiographical work the oppressiveness of
Southern culture, both black and white. For Wright, black folk culture seemed more an
absence than a presence – its cultural emptiness (Wright working with the Victorian
understanding of culture as high culture) represented all that blacks were deprived of in
terms of Western civilization. "Whenever I thought of the essential bleakness of black
life in America," Wright comments in *Black Boy*, "I knew that Negroes had never been
allowed to catch the full spirit of Western civilization, that they lived somehow in it
but not of it. And when I brooded upon the cultural barrenness of black life, I wondered
if clean, positive tenderness, love, honor, loyalty, and the capacity to remember were
native with man."[35] While black folk culture was for Wright one more of the many
hurdles he had to overcome in his struggle for individuality, for Hurston the culture of
the folk was the source of inspiration and fulfillment. Trained as an anthropologist and
schooled by Franz Boas, Hurston understood culture not as the highest creative
expression of a people but as the complex system of social dynamics that knits
communities together. For Hurston, black folk culture, rich, complicated, and nurturing, was to be embraced rather than spurned; and throughout her fiction and nonfiction, Hurston draws from it, melding the orality of black folk life into her prose and
celebrating the empowering knowledge of its lore.

If on some basic psychological level Southern African-American writers explore the
complex negotiation of regional identity, they certainly present a quite different
portrayal of Southern society from most white writers, particularly the traditionalists.
In this they share much with white women writers (particularly those not canonized
by the traditionalists) and with writers of the rural poor, including those of the
mountain South. Writers from all three groups portray Southern culture's startling
inequalities of race, gender, and class – inequalities that make efforts at improvement,
both individual and social, not merely difficult but often dangerous. Patricia Yaeger
underscores this aspect of Southern writing when she observes: "Is southern literature
about family and community? Sometimes. But it is more likely to be about struggle,
crisis, cultural emergence and emergency."[36] Women writers, as we have already
noted, frequently use mask and deception in order simultaneously to invoke and
critique Southern traditionalism, particularly its gender relations. This dual motion,
fueled by penetrating irony, can be found throughout Southern women's writing,
from Ellen Glasgow to Katherine Anne Porter, from Caroline Gordon to Lillian
Smith, from Frances Newman to (yes) Margaret Mitchell. But the master of the
method is perhaps Eudora Welty, who begins her career late in the renaissance with *A
Curtain of Green* (1941). No one is more delicate in her dissection of the small-town
South, celebrating its virtues and its hilarious quirkiness while at the same time
uncovering its threatening dangers and cruelties.

Writers of the rural poor characteristically focus less on gender troubles than on
economic turmoil, often by portraying the efforts to navigate a fast-changing social

order, with farms failing and industries and urbanization transforming the landscape. Mobility is crucial: to be able to move means not being immobilized by the system; mobility represents an assertion of power and a step up, if not always the social ladder then usually the economic one. And it is precisely poor white mobility that the traditionalists rail against in their writing; poor whites, by traditionalist thinking, are tolerable in their place (on the fringes of society), intolerable when they are out of place (inside society). William Alexander Percy's *Lanterns on the Levee* (1941) perhaps best manifests this attitude, portraying the migration of poor whites into the Mississippi Delta as a terrifying flood every bit as destructive as the Mississippi River's overflowing in 1927. It is attitudes such as Percy's that writers of the rural poor seek to counter, often by placing a heavy emphasis in their fiction on the Southern system's efforts to keep people "in place" (the dark underside of the traditional Southern celebration of place). Frequently, their work is structured by the tension between the paralysis of staying in place and the dangers (and rewards) involved in moving, with perhaps the most compelling examples coming in the work of Erskine Caldwell, particularly *Tobacco Road* (1932) and *God's Little Acre* (1933). The Lester family in *Tobacco Road* is utterly ground down by rural poverty and their marginalization from the social order. Theirs is a world of starvation and inertia, one that could have been avoided, as the narrator comments of the plight of Jeeter and others like him: "Co-operative and corporate farming would have saved them all."[37] In what can only be read as a stinging rebuke to the Agrarian celebration of small farming, Jeeter's love of the land and his unwillingness to leave smack of Agrarian rhetoric and ideology – and it is that rootedness, in effect making Jeeter a powerless (and ridiculous) Agrarian hero, that condemns him to fall ever deeper into the abyss of poverty and despair.

That so much of the literature of the Southern renaissance manifests similar fundamental crises of identity and region is not to say that the renaissance did not have a trajectory of development. Indeed, it did have such a trajectory, one that roughly follows a classic bell curve of beginning, development, peak, and falling off. In the early years of the renaissance, many writers focused less on struggling with their Southernness than freeing themselves from it. The editors of three important literary magazines that began during this period, *The Double Dealer* in New Orleans, *The Reviewer* in Richmond, and *The Fugitive* in Nashville, declared literary independence and eschewed what they characterized as the South's rose-colored literary tradition. In *The Fugitive*'s first issue, the editors announced that the Fugitive writer "flees from nothing faster than from the high-caste Brahmins of the Old South;"[38] and the editors of *The Double Dealer* proclaimed (with a characteristic-for-its-time dismissal of a Southern women's literary tradition) their goal to forge a new literary path:

> It is high time, we believe, for some doughty, clear visioned penman to emerge from the sodden marshes of Southern literature. We are sick to death of the treacly sentiments with which our well-intentioned lady fictioneers regale us. The old traditions are no more. New peoples, customs prevail. The Confederacy has long since been dissolved.

A storied realm of dreams, lassitude, pleasure, chivalry and the Nigger no longer exists. We have our Main Streets here, as elsewhere.[39]

The obvious reference to Sinclair Lewis at the end of *The Double Dealer*'s announcement points to the trend toward literary realism that developed in Southern literature of the 1920s. Lewis Lawson points out that literature from this period, particularly with regard to the new and developing writers, exhibited increasingly realistic appraisals of Southern society, including clear-eyed looks at many pressing social problems, such as rural poverty and racial violence.[40] By the mid-1920s, many writers who had shown little interest in regional matters (their literary rebellion instead primarily one of aesthetics), including the Fugitive poets, began turning their eyes to the homeland, in part because of the controversy surrounding the Scopes trial, in part because of the growing interest in regionalism throughout America.

The connection with the regionalist impulse cannot be underestimated. Regionalism's rise and fall (regionalist thinking and politics become important forces in the United States in the 1920s, peak in the early 1930s, decline throughout the 1930s, and all but disappear by the end of World War II) closely parallels the path of the Southern renaissance, and no doubt the political and literary situations were integrally connected, both drawing from and shaping the cultural dialogue in the South. The connections between regionalist forces and the Agrarians are obvious, but the connections extend much further into the Southern literary environment. Regionalism's decline in the 1930s occurred in part because of the growing nationalism (and internationalism) in American political thinking resulting from the rise of totalitarianism in Europe. This reconfiguration of regionalist political ideology – regionalism now seen in an international context – has visible manifestations in Southern literature, particularly from the mid-1930s on, as Southern writers begin to reconfigure their understanding and representations of the South in light of European totalitarianism. This reconfiguration can be seen most explicitly in cultural criticism; Clarence Cason's *90° in the Shade* (1935), W. J. Cash's *The Mind of the South* (1941), William Alexander Percy's *Lanterns on the Levee* (1941), and Lillian Smith's *Killers of the Dream* (1949), for example, all explore issues related to and/or use metaphors drawn from European totalitarianism in their discussions of South culture.

While generally less explicit, similar explorations nonetheless fundamentally shape the imaginative literature. Some writers, such as Thomas Wolfe and Katherine Anne Porter, write works specifically about Nazi Germany (Wolfe's "I Have a Thing to Tell You," 1937; Porter's "The Leaning Tower," 1941), while others, such as Carson McCullers and Robert Penn Warren, configure the South's ideological struggles with modernity in terms that owe much to the political and racial issues foregrounded in Nazi Germany and other European dictatorships. McCullers's *The Heart Is a Lonely Hunter* (1940) and *The Member of the Wedding* (1946) portray characters haunted by the deteriorating world situation in Europe, and it is that situation – rather than Southern cultural disorder – that the protagonists use to interrogate and understand the confusions in their problematic personal lives. Warren's *All the King's Men* (1946), the work generally regarded as signaling the end of the Southern renaissance, depicts the rise and fall of a Southern demagogue who calls to mind not only Huey Long but also Hitler and Mussolini; if Willie Stark's life parallels Long's, Hitler's and Mussolini's careers provide Warren (and his readers) the larger context for representing and understanding Stark's control of Louisiana politics – even if Warren leaves those connections all but unstated in the novel.

McCullers's and Warren's novels point to the waning of regional consciousness and focus that was soon to become even more pronounced in postwar Southern literature. As regionalism died quietly as a vibrant political movement after World War II, overwhelmed by the new world order and the Cold War, so too did the Southern literary renaissance, its once compelling issues of Southern history and identity no longer so to the new set of emerging writers. Postwar Southern writers, as a number of critics have pointed out, typically focus less on regional than existential issues, less on the cultural stresses of Southern society than on the anxieties and psychoses of the self, less on Southern history than on personal history. By the early 1950s the Southern literary renaissance was over and done. Southern literature still thrived, but it was a different Southern literature, one in which regional issues and identity became less sites of struggle than casually invoked backdrops for atmosphere and parody. This literature from the later period has yet to be defined by any encompassing designation, in part because of the tremendous diversity of expression resulting from the waning of regional issues – Southern writers, for the most part unhampered by the matter of Southern traditionalism, now go off in myriad directions in their explorations of modernity and postmodernity.

Writing from this later period lacks what the literature of the Southern renaissance had: a fundamental narrative, worked and reworked from various angles and perspectives, that loosely but significantly bound together a wide range of writers across lines of race, class, and gender. Literature of the renaissance, for all its visible traditionalism, actually unites groups of writers who at first glance seem to have nothing to do with each other (and in their day, probably wanted to have nothing to do with each other). And it may be only now, after decades of revisionary work, that we can finally see the full scope of the integrated renaissance, using, ironically enough, a paradigm that for years was the primary tool for establishing a canon every bit as segregated as the culture from which its writers sprang.

Notes

1   H. L. Mencken, "The Sahara of the Bozart," in *Prejudices, Second Series* (New York: Knopf, 1920), pp. 136, 137.
2   H. L. Mencken, "Literature and Geography," *Chicago Tribune*, May 10, 1925; quoted in Fred Hobson, *Serpent in Eden: H. L. Mencken and the South* (Chapel Hill: University of North Carolina Press, 1974), p. 62.
3   Tate, "The Profession of Letters in the South," in *Essays of Four Decades* (Chicago: Swallow Press, 1968), p. 520.

4   Tate, "The Profession of Letters in the South," p. 531.

5   Tate, "The Profession of Letters in the South," p. 533.

6   Allen Tate, "The New Provincialism," in *Essays of Four Decades* (Chicago: Swallow Press, 1968), p. 535.

7   Tate, "The New Provincialism," p. 545.

8   Tate, "The New Provincialism," p. 535.

9   Tate, "The New Provincialism," p. 539.

10   Tate, "The New Provincialism," p. 546.

11   Michael O'Brien, "A Heterodox Note on the Southern Renaissance," in *Rethinking the South: Essays in Intellectual History* (Athens, GA: University of Georgia Press, 1993), p. 166.

12   Richard Gray, *Southern Aberrations: Writers of the American South and Problems of Regionalism* (Baton Rouge: Louisiana State University Press, 2000), pp. 162, 106.

13   Anne Goodwyn Jones, *Tomorrow Is Another Day: The Woman Writer in the South, 1859–1936* (Baton Rouge: Louisiana State University Press, 1981), p. 45.

14   Richard H. King, *A Southern Renaissance: The Cultural Awakening of the South, 1930–1955* (New York: Oxford University Press, 1980), p. 7.

15   Patricia Yaeger, *Dirt and Desire: Reconstructing Southern Women's Writing, 1930–1990* (Chicago: University of Chicago Press, 2000), p. 129.

16   Yaeger, *Dirt and Desire*, p. 131.

17   Carol S. Manning, "The Real Beginning of the Southern Renaissance," in *The Female Tradition in Southern Literature*, ed. Carol S. Manning (Urbana: University of Illinois Press, 1993), pp. 37–56.

18   No doubt critics could go back further if they wanted to locate writers who share issues with writers from the 1920s and 1930s, but besides recovering some early writers and contextualizing them in a larger frame, little actually seems to be gained in terms of understanding the literary renaissance, given the immense historical and cultural differences between the nineteenth- and twentieth-century South; and indeed, once we delve back into the nineteenth century, a number of male writers emerge who could easily fit into the renaissance paradigm, including George Washington Cable and Mark Twain, and going further back, Edgar Allan Poe. The danger here, of course, is that the Southern literary renaissance begins to become Southern literature as a whole, a move that few critics would want to argue; while there may be many overriding themes that connect most Southern writers from all periods, there's a danger in using those themes to overemphasize continuity, particularly given the South's traumatic history.

19   Henry Louis Gates, "Zora Neale Hurston and the Speakerly Text," in *Southern Literature and Literary Theory*, ed. Jefferson Humphries (Athens, GA: University of Georgia Press, 1990), pp. 142, 143.

20   Gates, "Zora Neale Hurston and the Speakerly Text," pp. 142–3.

21   Gates, "Zora Neale Hurston and the Speakerly Text," p. 144.

22   Ladell Payne, *Black Novelists and the Southern Literary Tradition* (Athens, GA: University of Georgia Press, 1981), p. 6.

23   W. J. Cash, *The Mind of the South* [1941] (New York: Vintage, 1989), pp. 49–50.

24   Wayne Flint, *Dixie's Forgotten People: The South's Poor Whites* (Bloomington: Indiana University Press, 1979).

25   King, *A Southern Renaissance*, p. 8. King has suffered mercilessly for his decision to exclude African Americans and women writers (save for Lillian Smith) in his analysis of Southern renaissance writers' interrogations of the family romance; whatever the validity of these criticisms, King's insights into the overall intellectual climate of the interwar period in the South are astute and informed.

26   Ellen Glasgow, *A Certain Measure: An Interpretation of Prose Fiction* (New York: Harcourt, Brace, 1943), p. 28.

27   Cash, *The Mind of the South*, p. 372.

28 Quoted in Irv Broughton, "An Interview with Allen Tate," *Western Humanities Review*, 32 (1978): 329.

29 Allen Tate, *The Literary Correspondence of Donald Davidson and Allen Tate*, ed. John Tyree Fain and Thomas Daniel Young (Athens, GA: University of Georgia Press, 1974), pp. 191, 198.

30 Allen Tate, "Remarks on the Southern Religion," in Twelve Southerners, *I'll Take My Stand: The South and the Agrarian Tradition* [1930] (Baton Rouge: Louisiana State University Press, 1977), p. 163.

31 Tate, "Remarks on the Southern Religion," pp. 174, 175.

32 Michael Kreyling, *Inventing Southern Literature* (Jackson: University of Mississippi Press, 1998), p. 105.

33 Jean Toomer, *Cane* [1923] (New York: Liveright, 1975), p. 96.

34 Allen Tate, "Ode to the Confederate Dead," in *Collected Poems, 1919–1976* (Baton Rouge: Louisiana State University Press, 1977), p. 22.

35 Richard Wright, *Black Boy: A Record of Childhood and Youth*, restored text [1945] (New York: Harper Perennial, 1993), p. 43.

36 Yaeger, *Dirt and Desire*, p. 44.

37 Erskine Caldwell, *Tobacco Road* [1932] (Athens, GA: University of Georgia Press, 1995), p. 63.

38 *The Fugitive*, 1 (April 1922): 1.

39 Quoted in Lewis Lawson, *Another Generation: Southern Fiction Since World War II* (Jackson: University of Mississippi Press, 1984), pp. 5–6.

40 Lawson, *Another Generation: Southern Fiction Since World War II*, pp. 7–8.

10

The Native-American South

Mick Gidley and Ben Gidley

The South was the South Before it Became *the* South

There is a sense in which long before twentieth-century thinkers began to codify the common experiences of those who inhabit a definable region of the modern United States, using such expressions as "the idea of the South" to do so, the South was already the South. There is a sense in which well before European explorers actually navigated their ships into harbors on what we now think of as the coasts of Florida or Virginia, certainly long before the existence of a political entity that wished to perpetuate its agrarian, slaveowning economy and way of life, creating the renowned "burden of Southern history," the South was already the South.

In Native, pre-Columbian times, roughly the terrain now thought of as the South constituted what anthropologists define as the Southeast culture area. The concept of the culture area involves an interaction of dominant environmental features with material means of survival, with patterns of behavior, and with systems of belief, to create a commonality of life-ways among groups of people who might otherwise be divided by language or ethnicity (in this case tribal group). The culture area, so conceived, is not rigid, biologically determined, or natural. Like the notion of "the South" itself, and as its name implies, it is *cultural* and, at least partly, a product of perception. That is why in some accounts the indigenous peoples of the greater Chesapeake bay region are excluded from the Southeast culture area (and categorized as Northeast in culture), whereas we would wish to include them – partly because their life-ways really were so similar, but also because in the era of early contact, as we will see, they gave rise to two of the deepest myths of the South: the stories of Roanoke and Pocahontas.

We know that in pre-Columbian times the indigenous peoples of the region – the Caddos, the Choctaws, the Chickasaws, and the Muskogees or Creeks, to name only some of the more numerous groups – inhabited a largely low-lying land rich in rivers and alluvial deposits, with vast swamps of cypress and cane. There was plentiful game, a wealth of fish, many varieties of wild plant food, and the ground could easily be cleared for the raising of corn, beans, and gourds. In the higher lands of the southern Appalachians and the Piedmont – inhabited by such groups as the Cherokees and the Catawbas – life was slightly harder, with greater differences between the seasons, but people's needs were still met with relative ease. It is not surprising that reverence for the land was a cardinal belief. Jimmie Durham, the Cherokee artist and activist, has written: "in the language of my people . . . there is a word for land: *eloheh*. This same word also means history, culture and religion. We cannot separate our place on Earth from our lives on the earth nor our vision nor our meaning as a people."

Despite the neatness of the geographical congruence between the Southeast culture area and the South, the destruction of Native peoples, especially during the early periods of encounter with Europeans, was so thorough that it would be absurd to claim too much in the way of cultural survival. When the first colonists of what is now South Carolina encountered the Yamassees, they thought them powerful and warlike, yet before the end of the eighteenth century the Yamassees had fled to Spanish Florida, there to vanish entirely. Europeanizations of some of the Indians' tribal names – Alabama, Apalachee, and Mobile, for example – have been affixed to particular locations and physical features, but the bulk of the actual people have disappeared or were forcibly removed out of the South. The Tuscaroras of North Carolina, for example, fled before the onslaught of settlers and joined the Iroquois Confederacy in the Northeast. The eradication of Indian tribes in the Southeast was probably more wholesale than in any other culture area. At best, these Indians are, in Robert Heizer's apt phrase, "almost ancestors."

Nevertheless, in the early twentieth century, with the rise of cultural nationalism in the United States, there were several attempts to see Indians – at least in general – more directly *as* antecedents. One was made by Mary Austin, the California novelist, dramatist and, significantly, environmentalist. During the 1920s, when her reputation was at its height, she campaigned for Indian religious freedom in opposition to the US Bureau of Indian Affairs, which was trying to suppress traditional ceremonies. What is most notable from our perspective is that she contributed a chapter on "Aboriginal" literature to the final volume of the four-volume *History of American Literature*, published in 1921 as a supplement to the *Cambridge History of English Literature*. This chapter, although not written by a professional scholar, constitutes the first academic attention to Indian literature in a national context. Her opening sentence reads: "Probably never before has a people risen to need a history of its national literature with so little conscious relation to its own aboriginal literature." In an anticipation of D. H. Lawrence's views on the "spirit of place," expounded in his *Studies in Classic American Literature* of 1923, Austin established a continuity between what she terms "the territory that is now the United States" and Indians. "Something more than . . . scholarly interest attaches to this unparalleled opportunity for the study of a single racial genius," she argues.

To the American, it is also a study of what the land he loves and lives in may do to the literature by which the American spirit is expressed. These early Amerinds had been subjected to the American environment for [up to] ten thousand years. This had given them time to develop certain characteristic Americanisms. They had become intensely democratic, deeply religious, idealistic, communistic in their control of public utilities, and with a strong bias towards representative government. The problem of the political ring, and the excessive accumulation of private property, had already made its appearance within the territory that is now the United States. And along with these things had developed all the varieties of literary expression natural to that temperament and that state of society – oratory, epigram, lyrics, ritual drama, folktale, and epic. (Austin 1921)

We have quoted Austin's description of pre-contact Indian America at some length to emphasize her geographical determinism (it is as if the New World space will *inevitably* produce democracy and the other institutions she mentions) and the high degree of continuity she saw between Indian America and modern America. From hindsight it is easy to discern that she overstated the case about *both* Indian America and the modern United States. While she claimed a universal "democracy" for Indians, certain of the traditional Indian societies in North America, including ones in the Southeast culture area, were definitely hierarchical, sometimes with quite rigid caste systems. In fact, Austin tended to collapse the notable diversity of aboriginal North America into one generic "Amerind." With respect to modern America, it is blindingly obvious that, even in 1921, very few of the states were "communistic in their control of public utilities," and none would have used such vocabulary.

Austin's interesting chapter constitutes a valiant effort to come to terms with American Indian expression. Two years later she published *The American Rhythm*, a collection of translations – what she called her "reexpressions" – of the poetry of various tribes, in which she took all of her ideas a little further. In particular, as a practicing advocate of the then-new free verse, Austin believed that poetry should not be poured – as it were – into preexisting (European?) forms, but should arise in natural rhythms from the subconscious, which responds organically to the environment. Furthermore, just as Walt Whitman had envisaged aboriginal names "syllabled from the air," so Austin spoke of rhythms arising from the very physicality of the individual poet's body. She asserted a poem emerges and is shaped by the bodily rhythms of the man or woman – from "the breath, the *lub*-dub, *lub*-dub of the heart," and from the barely perceptible rhythms of the central nervous system – where the psychic and emotional health of the individual is registered. Some readers will realize that this kind of organicism is not new in American culture (we are thinking of Emerson and Thoreau, as well as Whitman), and that it also anticipates later poetic manifestos by William Carlos Williams and Charles Olson (notably in his case during his period in the South at Asheville, North Carolina, while running Black Mountain College). They insisted that "the breath" rather than the sentence is the natural unit of measure and meaning for the American poet.

The contention of this essay, on the other hand, is that the persistent organic relationship to the landscapes of the South is always mediated by *culture* and changes through *history.*

Native Experience and Representation in the Post-Conquest South

If geographical determinism rules at the levels of the nation and the individual, so it does at the level of the region. Indeed, in coming to terms with the aboriginal South as a *region* we have necessarily invoked ideas of the *nation.* This is a reflection of the historical fact that the South has experienced both the mixture and separation of these categories to an extraordinary degree. Perhaps most strikingly, it could be claimed that the major thrust of *United States* Indian policy (removal, reservations, extinguishment of communal ownership of land and, later, the deliberate subordination of the tribal identity of Indian individuals through "assimilation") was originally a *Southern* policy. It was first "successfully" brought to bear by Andrew Jackson – who was both from the South and identified with the South – specifically against the Southern tribes, before being enacted against people after people across the continent as the nation expanded westwards. Thus, thirty years before Navajos were herded together in 1864 for their infamous "Long Walk" from the Canyon de Chelly region of Arizona to Bosque Redondo in New Mexico, 16,000 Cherokees were forced, in 1838, to take the "Trail of Tears" from their homelands east of the Mississippi to "Indian Territory," later to become Oklahoma. Nearly a quarter of them died on the way.

Nevertheless, Native American aspects of Southern history are still often disregarded – in a manner similar to the way in which most scholars would now acknowledge that African-American aspects of Southern history were too long neglected. In many standard works on Southern literature and culture you will find *no* mention of Indians. These days, though entries on the more numerous tribes may appear in such massive compilations as the *Encyclopaedia of Southern Culture* (1989), Indians are rarely envisaged as *constitutive* of Southern identity. Understandably, Charles Hudson, a leading present-day student of these peoples, has pointed out that "the Southeastern Indians are the victims of a virtual amnesia in our historical consciousness." In Leslie Fiedler's famous topological classification of American fiction, only "the Western" is characterized by the archetypal encounter between whites and Indians; "the Southern," for him, features exclusively, even claustrophobically, conflicts between whites and blacks. It is impossible easily to correct such "amnesia," or to escape such binary divisions, because – in the psychohistory of the South once settled by "Europeans" – they are inextricably tangled up in a veritable "complex" of race.

In the period of settlement, the topography of the South is defined by the interplay between two features. On the one hand, there are the vast tracts of plantation land, with monoculture farming of cash crops: tobacco, cotton, and rice. On the other hand, hedged around the margins of the plantations, are zones of mountains or wetlands, such as the Appalachians, the Great Dismal Swamp of North Carolina, and the bayous of Louisiana. Historically, as is well known, the South has also been defined by the color coding of peoples into black and white, the "one-drop" rule dictating that anyone not wholly white was to be considered black. This white supremacist episte-mology of race was backed up by Jim Crow segregation laws and a politics of terror. However, just as there have been marshlands, mountains, and piney woods outside the monoculture plantations, there have also been spaces to which people have removed themselves, imaginatively or in reality, to escape raciology's color codes. The Great Dismal Swamp, for example, is the setting for the events of Harriet Beecher Stowe's *Dred* (1856) and for part of Martin Delany's *Blake; or The Huts of America* (1859). In both antislavery texts, the Swamp is seen as a place of freedom, outside the racial terror of the plantation South.

Because Indians stand in part outside this color coding, images of the Indian have often been a way that Southern culture has imagined itself beyond what Frantz Fanon, speaking of a parallel situation, called, in a famous phrase, the "manichean delirium" of its racial economy. In *Blake*, for instance, the hero, Henry, encounters a group of Indians named the "United Nation." Their "intelligent old chief" teaches him the value of confederation, arguing that blacks in Africa, like Indians in America, need to confederate to get independence from whites. People have identified themselves *as* Indian in order to place themselves outside the plantation world's segregated space. Or they have identified *with* Indians, for example in literature or in music, to leap imaginatively beyond it. The romance of the Indian in the South, then, has been tied up with the brutal realities of racial terror and the plantation economy.

Native Southern – and National – Myths (1): Roanoke

In 1587 Sir Walter Raleigh attempted to establish an English colony on the island of Roanoke in North Carolina, leaving over a hundred settlers before departing. When he returned a year later with supplies, the colony was deserted, the word "Croatan" (the name of a nearby Indian tribe) carved on a tree. According to John White, due to be the colony's governor, the carvings were "to signifie the place, where I should find the planters seated, according to a secret token agreed upon betweene them and me at my last departure from them . . . for at my coming away, they were prepared to remove 50 miles into the maine." In the early seventeenth century, John Smith of the Jamestown colony found some evidence that descendants of the colonists were living among the Chesapeake Indians. John Lawson, an English explorer in the early eighteenth century, spent time among the Hatteras Indians, descendants of the Croatan, who, he said, had gray eyes and were literate, thus confirming, he thought, their relationship to the lost colonists. Over the years, many communities have identified themselves as descendants of the lost colonists, or have been identified as such by others. For example, the Pembroke Tribe of Robeson County, North Carolina (who apparently were light-skinned and spoke an archaic English and bore the names of many of the lost colonists) was "discovered" by Hamilton Macmillan in 1880; they are now known as the Lumbee.

The evocative myth of Roanoke's lost colony has passed into Southern folklore. It is learnt by American schoolchildren; it was the subject of North Carolina playwright Paul Green's *The Lost Colony* (1937), a pageant enacted on the island each year; it found its way into the vision of William Faulkner, who named his house Rowan Oak. Whichever version of the story is actually true, what is certain is that as long as they have been in the Americas, white people have been escaping the mapped and policed worlds of the European empires, "running to the hills," "going Indian." As long as there have been black people in the Americas, they have been doing the same, escaping the chattel slavery of the colonial plantations and the wage slavery of later plantations. As long as black and white people have been on their continent, Indians have been resisting and adapting. These three peoples have mixed with each other since their first meeting, escaping the mapped and policed categories of "black" and "white" and "Indian." They have created new communities, new cultures. At the same time, the dominant culture has not only resisted such mixing in life: it has also privileged other myths that serve ultimately to counter the Roanoke story and all it symbolizes.

Native Southern – and National – Myths (2): Pocahontas

In 1608, as every schoolchild knows, John Smith, the leader of the newly established first English colony in Virginia, when about to have his head chopped off by the powerful and "savage" Chief Powhatan, was saved by the chief's daughter, Pocahontas. She interposed herself between the ax and Smith; supposedly, she "got his head in her armes, and laid her owne upon his to save him from death." A few years later, after giving other aid to the white settlers, enabling them to survive in the New World, Pocahontas – who was, of course, beautiful – married another colonist, John Rolfe, who took her and their infant son to England. There, renamed Rebecca, she was feted and had her image engraved in European finery, but also became ill in the damp, unfamiliar climate, died, and was buried at Gravesend. The story of Pocahontas – despite being based on the scantiest of documentary evidence (Smith himself did not mention Pocahontas' role in his rescue until relating it for the third time, in 1624) – has been endlessly repeated and elaborated in verse, song, plays, operas, novels, and films. It animated other, similar if less palatable stories, such as the eighteenth-century one of the Indian girl Yarico who, out of love, rescued the Englishman Inkle, only to be sold into slavery by him, her monetary value increased by the fact that she was pregnant with his child.

Even supposedly "historical" accounts, such as that by the Southern poet John Gould Fletcher in *John Smith – Also Pocahontas* (1928), actually give us myth, and

John Barth's comic novel about an early tobacco planter, *The Sot-Weed Factor* (1960), with its bawdy spoof "secret historie" by John Smith, may be seen as a riotous debunking of it. Hart Crane, in his major poem *The Bridge* (1930), knew that he was offering myth, and overtly identified Pocahontas with the New World, indeed with the American earth itself. In 1962 Philip Young produced a brilliant essay, "The Mother of Us All: Pocahontas," in which he tried to identify the roots of the story's mythic power. It depends, he thought, on a half-acknowledgment of guilt over the ill-treatment of Indians: by "taking her to our national bosom we experience a partial absolution. In the lowering of her head we feel a benediction. We are so wonderful she loved us anyway." Yet, at the same time, despite the wedding-like rituality of Pocahontas' supposed act, she did not marry Smith, and in the constant retelling of the story there is, too, an acknowledgment that this lack of fulfillment is peculiarly appropriate. The Indian must be domesticated (renamed Rebecca, converted to the dominant Christian faith), but the white man or the American – so often, as here, gendered as male – cannot, so to speak, be Indianized. Clearly, like the Roanoke myth, this is a story of *both* the South and the nation.

Native Histories (1): The Earliest Southerners

Temple Mound culture – perhaps descended from the earlier Hopewell culture, which built mounds mainly for burial purposes – dominated the Mississippi valley, and beyond, for centuries, achieving its peak about AD 1300 to 1500. A remnant of it survived when Europeans first reached the Southeast, mainly in material form – huge, wide-based ceremonial earth mounds, up to a hundred feet high, upon which temples were built and around which stockaded villages clustered – but also in vestiges of systems of belief. For example, a Death Cult, involving the widespread deployment of the buzzard as a symbolic ornament, seems to have animated in common peoples as far apart as those to become Creeks in what is now Georgia and those to become Caddos in what is now Texas. These "predecessors," as Faulkner graphically called them (his term implying both that they pre-deceased later named Indian groups, such as those who populate his own Yoknapatawpha, and that subsequent groups will *also* pass away), produced a culture that sought extremities, especially of visionary experience, that seems to have sanctioned the ritual torture of enemies and the ingestion of powerful "purifying" emetics, and that enjoyed fast and furious games, with wagers for high stakes. Archeologists have retrieved some stunning Mound artifacts – pottery, delicately engraved conch shells, textiles, and Deer Dance masks, complete with horns and carved from single pieces of wood. The Temple Mound culture also established some life patterns that were to feature in later Indian – and, for that matter, non-Indian – settlements, most interestingly, hierarchical, even aristocratic, social structures.

Thomas Jefferson, who promulgated the agrarian values that have underlain so much Southern thought ever since, was also the first person, as far as we know, to excavate a mound systematically, and he described his efforts in the chapter of *Notes on the State of Virginia* (1785) titled "Aborigines." It is important to remember that this publication was written *for the use of a Foreigner of distinction, in answer to certain queries*, queries as to whether the New World environment was *naturally* inferior to that of the Old. Needless to say, Jefferson concluded it was not, and his excavation of the Indian past in the form of an eroding mound (a burial mound, as he discovered), joined to his defense elsewhere in the volume of the rhetorical skill and poetic power of the Indian oratory of his own time, together with other data, was offered as part of the evidence. However, as many commentators have shown, this did not mean that Jefferson was able to free himself from beliefs in a hierarchy based upon racial difference. Indeed, Richard Drinnon (1980), with reference to Jefferson's Indian views, has pointed up the statesman's "extraordinary capacity to sound like an enlightened reformer while upholding the interests of the planter class."

Interestingly, the few representations of Temple Mound culture in fiction, such as the Vicomte de Chateaubriand's *Les Natchez* (1827), take the story on to its aristocratic survivals in Natchez and parallel tribal histories during the early period of European contact and beyond. By the time we get to Faulkner's depiction of the world of the Chickasaws during the early years of white settlement in Yoknapatawpha, as told in such works as *Go Down, Moses* (1942), the culture the Indians exhibit is a confluence of Indian hierarchical social structures with, precisely, the interests of a "planter class"; Faulkner's chief, Ikkemotubbe, himself owns slaves. Although less well dressed, he is depicted like an animation of a telling 1869 photograph of the historical George W. Stidham, an aristocratic and slaveowning Creek, whose interests compelled him to support the Confederacy. The photograph, made by an unknown camera worker, shows an autocratic-looking man with "Indian" features in fine "citizen's dress"; his young uniformed son is on one side, his wife, a child in arms, and daughter, all generously clothed, on the other side: the image codifies familial power and possession — even though that power was to prove illusory.

Native Histories (2): Contact Episodes in the Southeast Culture Area

The Southeast culture area — despite, or really because of, the comparatively long contact with Europeans — has not been the site and occasion for markedly penetrating or evocative ethnographies. There is nothing for the Southeast like Washington Matthews's translation of Navajo ceremonies, John Neihardt's wondrous retelling of a Sioux personal history in *Black Elk Speaks* (1932), or the many graphic volumes Franz Boas devoted to the complex social organization of the Kwakiutls. Rather, in the Southeast, more than ordinarily painstaking, patient, and perceptive figures, such as James Mooney, Frank G. Speck, and John Reed Swanton, did their best to salvage a coherent view of cultures under an ever-imminent threat of eradication. Despite the fact that introduced infectious diseases carried off thousands of these people, that whole villages were deliberately slaughtered, and that many communities and individuals were pressed into slavery, the anthropologists we have named were also able to collect examples of beautiful quill and bead work, Cherokee Eagle Dance wands and Yuchi ball-sticks.

These anthropologists also scoured earlier records of "contact," such as William Bartram's *Travels in North and South Carolina, Georgia, East and West Florida* . . . (1791), with its vivid observations of the daily lives of such peoples as the Cherokees, Creeks, and Choctaws, or the various French accounts of the death and funeral, in 1725, of Tattooed Serpent, the last Great Sun chief of the Natchez, that Swanton translated and incorporated into his "Indian Tribes of the Lower Mississippi and Adjacent Coast of the Gulf of Mexico." They looked for examples of Indian *self*-representation – both in myth and in the genres identified by Austin: "oratory, epigram, lyrics, ritual drama, folktale, and epic." (Needless to say, this in itself constitutes a problematic claim, in that *all* such material has had to undergo a series of translations – from the oral to the written, between at least two languages, and from the past to the present.) Mooney, for example, translated from the written Cherokee alphabet famously devised by Sequoyah many of the beautiful shamanic formulae employed by the Cherokees – "for obtaining long life," "to frighten a storm," to neutralize a witch, or, even, "to destroy life," which goes, in part:

> Your soul I have put at rest under the earth.
> I have come to cover you over with black rock.
> I have come to cover you with black slabs, never to reappear.
> Toward the black coffin in the Darkening Land your path shall stretch out.
> So shall it be for you.
> (Mooney 1891)

Speck did similar work with Creek and Yuchi records. It would be inappropriate to attempt a potted summary here. We intend, instead, first, to comment on just one of the self-representations, an example of oratory; and, second, to mention the Indian "origins" of certain seemingly "Southern" features, while bringing to the fore aspects of corresponding Indian adaptations of "white" forms. This should, in turn, undermine *all* of these racially charged adjectives – a theme to be continued hereafter.

Most of the Indian oratory that survives in print has done so because the speech concerned was delivered in a council with whites and recorded in some form by a white clerk. In effect, this surviving oratory – if not, of course, the tradition of oratory as a means of emergence into leadership from which it derives – should be seen as a product of *interaction* between Indians and whites. The proposed enforced removal of the Creeks in 1829, for instance, was the occasion for Speckled Snake's great speech, in which he repeatedly played with the notion that the white man had grown at the expense of the Indian: "When the white man first came over the wide waters, he was but a little man... very little... But when [he] had warmed himself at the Indian's fire, and had filled himself with the Indian's hominy, he became very large... His hands grasped the eastern and western seas." And the white man, in this engorged state, hardly knew the dangers of his own bulk: "He loved his red children, but he said: 'You must move a little farther, lest by accident I tread on you.'" "Brothers!" Speckled Snake concluded, "I have listened to a great many talks from our Great Father. But they always began and ended with this: 'Get a little farther; you are too near me.'" The use of root metaphors – what Jefferson and other commentators rightly considered the "natural" eloquence of Indian oratory – gives the speech a sense of inevitability; everything it claims is, indeed, granted the authority of Nature itself.

In the mingling of peoples and cultures on the restless frontier, it was not only in words that new, hybrid genres came into being. For example, the Seminoles – themselves a tribal grouping that took in, as we shall see, many African Americans and others – developed the design and sewing of patchwork quilting in strip form, and used it to decorate ceremonial clothing. That is, they adopted a form commonly employed by white women in the making of coverlets and the like, and applied it to their dress. Interestingly, quilting was an activity that women of *different* European ethnicities came together to practice, which allowed them to merge their separate traditional patterns, creating new, "American" ones in the process; eventually, the strip designs pioneered by the Seminoles were themselves merged into the twentieth-century American quilt tradition. Perhaps the most spectacular – but also the most mundane – of all cultural crossovers occurred in what Alfred Crosby (1972) has dubbed "the Columbian exchange": when foods and other items of consumption that had been domesticated by Indians, such as tomatoes, maize, and potatoes, were made familiar to whites and, over time, became staples of European diets. In this connection, perhaps the most problematic "gift" was tobacco – not so much because of its deleterious effects on health, but because while just one of many crops for Indians, and largely grown for ceremonial smoking, it became, through much of the South, *the* cash crop suitable for exploitation on a plantation basis and, therefore, evermore closely associated with slavery. It set the pattern of a plantation economy that was to spread across the South, from tobacco and rice to "King Cotton."

Something similar happened in other, less material, ways. It could be argued, for example, that one of the more unusual aspects of Indian social organization in the Southeast was the frequency with which various tribal groupings were able to create confederacies around and in defense of their common interests. The Natchez and their neighbors formed a loose confederacy to defend themselves against the French. The Creeks, at the urging of Speckled Snake and others, created the Muskogee alliance. The Chickasaws and the Choctaws readily and frequently abstained from rivalry with one another to secure greater bargaining power in negotiations with whites: they were at first thus able to resist incursions and, when they had to yield, their joint strength enabled them at first, paradoxically, to gain separate reservations for each of them in "Indian Territory." Delaney's "intelligent" chief had a basis in fact. If, as several historians of political thought have argued, the US Constitution is influenced by the preceding League of the Iroquois, the Southern Confederacy – *the* defining moment of Southern identity as traditionally conceived – had its Indian precursors.

Native Histories (3): Creoles

The Americas in general have been a space of creolization, a "New World" in a very real sense: its cultures are new, not simply hybrids or survivals of previous African or European cultures. They are creole cultures: creative responses to new situations. In areas like the South, where contact between indigenous peoples and Europeans and Africans began so early, we can see *Indian* cultures as creolized too, as marked by the newness of American civilization. We cannot restrict our thinking – or this commentary – exclusively to aboriginal groupings that preceded European conquest.

The colonization of the Americas by the European powers was followed almost immediately by exploitation of its natural resources. Over the centuries, huge tracts of wilderness have been cleared and planted for monocrop cultivation for export. Until very recently, this business was extremely labor intensive. From the thirst for labor was born the institution of slavery. However, as anthropologist Sidney Mintz (1970, 1971) has pointed out, from this brutal regime there also emerged, in turn, new identities, as "the Afro-Americans – the Negro peoples of all the Americas – struggled against both the terms of their condition and the forces that sought to strip them of their past." This creative struggle for new identity is *creolization*. As Mintz continues, the word creole "signifies something of the Old World, born in the New... combining elements from African, American Indian, and European pasts," but reconfigured to forms that are *American*:

> American here means new, means of the New World ... And in this perspective, it is not the precise historical origins of a word, a phrase, a musical instrument or a rhythm that matters, so much as the creative genius of the users, molding older cultural substances into new and unfamiliar patterns, without regard for purity of pedigree ... The vision of cultural purity as a seamless past, only diluted and never enriched by change, misses the point about culture. Culture changes all the time, no matter what people might do to embed it in ideological amber. It is in fact the ways that a people employ their culture creatively, tactically, and responsively that distinguish the toughness and resiliency of the culture itself.

One family of peoples who epitomize the creole cultural creativity to which Mintz is referring here are the maroon communities of the plantation Americas. The term "maroon" comes from the Spanish term *cimarrón*, for wild or runaway livestock. Maroons are the members of communities formed by runaway slaves at the fringes of plantation life. Although the term is more commonly used in the Caribbean, the Southern historian Hugo Prosper Leaming has researched two maroon groups in the United States: those of the Carolinas and the nomadic maroon tribe the Ben Ishmaels. He defines them as "Fugitives from servitude who established a hidden settlement" (in Sakolsky and Koehnline 1993).

From the early eighteenth century, the Great Dismal Swamp in North Carolina – but also helpfully situated, like many other maroon habitations, as a political borderland, in this case between Virginia and North Carolina – has been a space of gathering together of Indians displaced by the spread of the plantations, Irish refugees, and runaway black slaves and white indentured servants. Among the peoples of the Swamp are the Nansemond Indians. Into the twentieth century, they maintained a distinct Indian identity, culture, religion, and crafts, despite having identical mixed genetic origins to some of their neighbors who called themselves "white" or "colored." Similarly, the maroons of the Southern Piedmont Hills of South Carolina were a coming together of disparate elements, their cultural creativity emerging in the plantation experience: "Fraternization between the three . . . peoples did not begin on the frontier," Leaming claims. "They labored together on the same plantations . . . 'bound together by a fellowship of toil'."

The Ben Ishmael or Ishmaelite tribe – unsympathetically represented as the family of Ishmael Bush in James Fenimore Cooper's *The Prairie* (1827) – emerged around the time of the American Revolution and was submerged again early in the twentieth century. "That the Ishmaelites were fugitives," says Leaming, "is shown by their double removal, first from the Southeast to frontier Kentucky, then [when Kentucky was incorporated into the plantation world] on to the unexplored Old Northwest; and by their ethnic components, the three subject peoples of the South's slavery society: chattel slaves or 'free' blacks, remnants of destroyed Native American nations, and European indentured servants or their landless, despised children." Despite the heterogeneity of their origins, they forged a distinct, new culture, to which they clung proudly, thinking of themselves as a *tribe* or family. "I reckon ours is the oldest family in the world," said George Ishmael, one of their leaders.

Similarly, the Seminoles, who continue to maintain an independent tribal identity, were a gathering together in the eighteenth century of Creek Indians regarded as renegades, members of African villages set up by the Spanish as a buffer zone against the expanding English (and later American) plantation world, older maroon communities displaced from their swamp and forest refuges by the expansion of that world, and *esteluti*, more recent runaway slaves. "*Seminole*, a Creek word meaning runaways or rebels," claims Doug Sivad (Sakolsky and Koehnline 1993), "identifies not a nation but rather a composite made up of many nations: Black and Red people who united in rebellion to preserve their cultures and maintain their freedom." The Ishmaelites ran away twice. Many Black Seminoles, however, never stopped running: first into the marshes of Florida, then some in long boats to the Andros Islands of the Bahamas and Guanabocoa in Cuba, others to "Indian Territory" – or "Los Pla'ns," as they called it – and then on through Texas to Mexico, where many live now. The repeated act of removal served to distribute or circulate traditions, ideas, and stories of struggle.

The intercultural nature of these groups made them anomalous in the plantation world, where the organization of labor was structured by the categories of race. As Mintz stated, "the 'reality' of race [was] . . . as much a social as a biological reality, the inheritance of racial traits serving as raw material for social sorting devices, by which both stigmata and privileges may be systematically allocated." A new color scheme came about: "savage red" for the Indians, "mottled gray" or tawny yellow for the European underclass, and of course black for the African slaves; "the ruling classes," wrote Cedric Robinson (1983), "stood in dramatic, white relief." But it was their intercultural heritage that also enabled them repeatedly to display great linguistic and diplomatic skills and a propensity for alliances. The Seminoles allied with the Spanish in Florida, other Indian and maroon groups, and the Mexicans, and Vincent Bakpetu Thompson (1987) notes that the Black Seminoles in particular were renowned for their ability to act as cultural brokers. The maroons of the Dismal Swamp allied themselves to the Indians, to the British Loyalist armies in the American Revolution, and to the North during the Civil War. This go-between role illustrates, too, the cultural creativity that is at the heart of creolization.

These maroon peoples of the South – who also include the North Carolina Croatans, the Tennessee Melungeons, the Delaware Moors, the Redbones of the old Texas border, and the "Issues" of Amherst County, Virginia – often claimed Indian status in order to find a place in the segregated school or court systems. Their claims to be Indian were generally denied by the authorities, who chose to call them "colored." In the late nineteenth century, raciologists came up with the term "tri-racial isolates" to name them. Peter Lamborn Wilson writes:

> "Tri-racial isolate communities" in America have good reason to avoid publicity. In the first place, even the term used to describe them carries a freight of sociological and even eugenical connotations. It has the cold ring of "scheduled caste" or "marginal group," pseudo-scientific vocabularizing as a mask for Control. One could even prefer the old-fashioned bluntness of a phrase like "mixed-blood tribe" to such techno-bureaucratese as "tri-racial isolate community." The ancestors of such groups might well have vanished into the woods precisely to escape a culture of terror which labeled them "prostitutes," "Hessian deserters," "slaves" – and then "mongrels," "racial degenerates," "the feebly-inherited" . . . this verbal terror culminated in the actual terror of "racial purity" laws and campaigns of extermination. (Sakolsky and Koehnline 1993)

In the period from the 1880s to the 1920s, tri-racial isolates found themselves the object of study of the new "science" of eugenics. Race scientists like Charles Davenport, Arthur Estabrook, and Henry Goddard examined these communities, and developed scientific rationales for their elimination.

Estabrook studied the tri-racial "Issues" of Amherst County, preserving their anonymity by naming them "Mongrel Virginians," and recommended genocidal practices against such groups. Similar conclusions were drawn in Estabrook's analysis of data collected on a small tri-racial community he named the Jukes and in his associate Goddard's study of the Kallikaks, a New Jersey tri-racial group. These peoples were described as "feeble-minded" or "morons," terms which gained popular currency at that time. The Melungeons were another victim of eugenics' attack on the "feebly-inherited"; even today, for many, "Melungeon" is synonymous with "moron" in the South, thanks to the propaganda of the movement. And, as Leaming has shown, the Ben Ishmaels were the objects of systematic eugenicist policies in the states in which they lived.

The purity or impurity of origins of these groups has also been an issue in another way. While many of them have claimed to be Indians, others saw that if it could be shown that they were not, their rights to *land*, as indigenous people, would be weakened. In Virginia in 1843, planters attempted to take land from the Pamunky Indians, legitimating their claim by arguing that the Pamunky were no longer "Indian," having interbred so much, mainly with African Americans. The Pamunky succeeded. Other Virginia mixed tribes, such as the Nottaway, Gingaskin, and Mattopony, were not so lucky; consequently, the Pamunky are the only Virginia Indian tribe still in possession of their lands today. More recently, the Lumbees have been denied their claim to Indian status by the Bureau of Indian Affairs because of the "impurity" of their origins, despite a very distinct tribal way of life.

Natives Represent the South

"The White Man's Indian," as Robert E. Berkhofer in 1978 termed the set of tropes invented to represent Native Americans in a huge variety of "white" texts, was predominantly the creation of writers from the North and the West — most prominently, of course, Cooper — and was largely based, if on *any* actual peoples, on tribes from the Northeast and, later, the Great Plains culture areas. (Some of the influential fictions produced by Chateaubriand in French at the beginning of the nineteenth century were set among peoples of the Southeast, but these settings exerted such influence precisely because of their highly romantic non-specificity.) But Southern writers were not totally absent. Most famously, in the nineteenth century, William Gilmore Simms, in such novels as *The Yemassee* (1835) and others of his "Border Romances," made melodrama out of the struggles between the Yamassees and the early settlers of his beloved South Carolina. Mark Twain, in his famous essay "The Literary Offenses of James Fenimore Cooper," chose to attack Cooper's indulgent imitation of Sir Walter Scott, but mainly he excoriated Cooper's characterization of Chingachgook. For Twain, Cooper's Indians were romanticized, with no relation to reality. Yet Twain too often failed to apply his standards of realism to his Indian characters, reducing them to demonic stereotypes, such as Injun Joe in *The Adventures of Tom Sawyer* (1876). Mary Murfree, late nineteenth-century author of numerous "local color" works set mainly in Tennessee, wrote about the Cherokees, and her contemporary Kirk Munroe produced *The Flamingo Feather* (1887), a much-read Seminole adventure for children. In the twentieth century, Robert Penn Warren composed a volume-length – indeed epic – poem on a heroic Indian topic, but it was one native to the Plateau culture area of the Northwest: *Chief Joseph of the Nez Percé* (1983). Southeastern aboriginal peoples were sometimes treated by significant twentieth-century Southern writers. Most obviously, Faulkner, in populating his "apocryphal county," not only included graphic coverage of earlier generations of Chickasaws and Choctaws but also created such "modern" survivors as Sam Fathers. Sam Fathers, it is important to realize, was a creole: he had more than one "father," and these men were of different races.

The musics of the South, especially country and blues during the twentieth century, have been spaces in which issues of race have been worked through in a more thoroughly *communal* manner than is possible in literature. But, as is the case with literature, the history of these musics is punctuated by moments when the South's racial order was stretched or transcended, and moments when this order was reaffirmed. Southern music has been a space for *both* trans-racial dialogue *and* brutal exclusion. Southern musicians and songwriters have routinely drawn on material from across the color bar in a way that is often occluded in standard accounts of racialized genres like "country and western" or "rhythm and blues" (or their predecessors, "hillbilly" and "sepia"). Indian blood and the figure of the Indian have played important roles in this vital hidden history of crossing and mixing.

Dan Penn, one of the architects of Southern soul, writer of songs like "Do Right Woman," was partly Indian, with Creek relatives on his mother's side and Cherokee on his father's. Yet when his racial identity is discussed, it is generally in terms of being a white musician working in a predominantly black genre. A very different example is Pappy Neal McCormack, also from Alabama, a pioneer of the steel guitar in whose band a young Hank Williams got his first breaks. McCormack was Indian, but in the 1930s and 1940s when he was performing, states like Alabama had legislative discrimination against Indians, and he passed himself off as a native of Hawaii.

In contrast, other Southern music artists have asserted both real and imaginary Indian blood. Blues musicians who have said they are part Cherokee, Choctaw, or Creek include Big Joe Williams, Jimi Hendrix, Big Chief Ellis, T-Bone Walker, Leadbelly, Charlie Musselwhite, Roy Brown, Lowell Fulson, Champion Jack Dupree, and Charlie Patton. Similarly, country musicians have made this claim, most notably Johnny Cash, born in Arkansas and often described as one-fourth Cherokee. In a recent radio interview with Tim Robbins, Cash revealed this was purely imaginary on his part:

Yeah, I guess I wanted to be part Indian so bad I said I was. I made a lot of Indian friends. Something about my music, the songs of incarceration, like on my first records, like "Folsom Prison Blues." There is a family of Ute Indians in Salt Lake City, named a son after me. He was a seventh son of a seventh son, and they named him Johnny Cash Tso. T-S-O. They welcomed me in their home and made me a part of their family circle, and I felt like I was one of them.

Cash's identification with Indians was demonstrated by his courageous 1964 recording of a powerful song exposing ongoing injustices to contemporary Indians, "The Ballad of Ira Hayes," written by Paul LaFarge, and a whole album that year, *Bitter Tears: Ballads of the American Indian*.

For some of these musicians, the claim to be Indian was a way of hiding other forms of mixed identities; for others, it was an imaginative means of escaping the binary racial order of the South; still others were forced to hide this aspect of their lives. A similar ambivalence can be found in the lyrics of Southern music. Many songs in the Southern music repertoire betray faint traces of an Indian presence. Bluegrass classic "Georgia Piney Woods" by the Osborne Brothers describes the narrator's home as "Ancient home of the Creek and the Cherokee – and me." In songs like this, Southerners' claims to an autochthonous or indigenous status are legitimated by reference to these "almost ancestors." Something similar occurs in Woody Guthrie's "Oklahoma Hills":

> 'Way down yonder in the Indian nation
> I rode my pony on the reservation
> In the Oklahoma Hills where I was born
> 'Way down yonder in the Indian nation

Many Southern songs echo the Pocahontas story. For example, "Way Down in Shawneetown," a river boatman's song recorded by Dillon Bustin, says:

> I've got a gal in Louisville, a wife in New Orleans
> When I get to Shawneetown I'll see my Indian Queen.

Likewise, "The Banks of the Pamanaw" tells the story of a white man's love for "this Indian maid," who had been abandoned on the riverbank by her parents and her (Indian) lover. Most famous of such songs is the enigmatic "Shenandoah." There are various versions of this, and the song has been linked to Old World sea shanties, but in most versions the white narrator is in love with an Indian maid – the daughter of an Indian chief – he has seen in a camp on the banks of the river. While the narrator is unable to win her love, another character, a "Yankee skipper," sells her father firewater and steals her away across the river. As in the Pocahontas myth, the song half-acknowledges white guilt in its treatment of the Indians, while in this case displacing that guilt onto the North, represented by the Yankee skipper.

Other Southern songs register the presence of natives in a more antagonistic way. For instance, in songs like "Tennessee Stud" by Arkansas' Jimmy Driftwood, Indians are simply savage attackers, trials for the hero to overcome:

One day I was riding in a beautiful land
I run smack into an Indian band
They jumped their nags with a whoop and a yell
And away we rode like a bat out of Hell
I circled their camp for a time or two
Just to show what a Tennessee horse can do
The redskin boys couldn't get my blood
'Cause I was a-riding on the Tennessee Stud.

These modern popular Southern songs, in different ways, work through the ambivalent position of Indians in the South, and the ambivalent relationship of whiteness to Indian identity.

During the same period, Indian writers from the South have not achieved the fame accorded certain Native figures from other regions, most especially Kiowa author N. Scott Momaday, but some have nevertheless done significant things. In recent times, Joy Harjo, of Creek descent, has gained a considerable reputation in *both* music and writing. She performs as a songster – appealing to Native and mixed audiences – and has produced poetry for publication in books and literary journals. Interestingly, while her work may have local references to Creek experience, it has definite resonance in generalized (pan-) Indian life, and "on the lower frequencies," as Ralph Ellison's *Invisible Man* so famously said, it speaks to anyone. Indeed, the protagonist of Harjo's most celebrated poem, "The Woman Hanging from the Thirteenth Floor Window" (1983), though living on "the Indian side of town" and thinking of the stigmatized "color of her skin," also faces – or succumbs to – the brutality of modern urban life, wherever lived.

We must close on a problematic note. Harjo's regional and ethnic affiliations *do* matter, but to what degree? Today, we see that Zora Neale Hurston and other African-American writers of the South, such as Ernest Gaines or, even, Alice Walker are, indeed, Southern. They treat – may we say? – archetypally Southern experience, and they do so in a manner that many would consider "Southern." As yet, in histories and literary histories, when such figures as Jimmie Durham or Joy Harjo appear, they do so as "Indians," not as Southerners. We would argue that – however fractious, embittered or, indeed, beautiful their work – they do also represent the South, but a metaphorically expanding South, a South becoming ever less defined by the binary oppositions and codings it has inherited.

References and further reading

Austin, Mary (1930) [1923] *The American Rhythm: Studies and Re-expressions of Amerindian Songs.* Boston, MA: Houghton Mifflin.
Austin, Mary (1921) "Non-English Writings II: Aboriginal," in William Peterfield Trent, et al. (eds.) *A History of American Literature*, Vol. 4. New York: G. P. Putnam's Sons, pp. 610–34.

Bold, Christine (1993) "Regions and Regionalism," in Mick Gidley (ed.) *Modern American Culture: An Introduction*. New York: Longman, pp. 94–119.

Bradkin, Cheryl Greider (1980) *The Seminole Patchwork Book*. Atlanta, GA: Yours Truly.

Ceram, C. W. (1971) *The First American: A Story of North American Archaeology*. London: Cape.

Cox, John Harrington (1925) *Folk-Songs of the South*. Cambridge, MA: Harvard University Press.

Crosby, Alfred W. (1972) *The Columbian Exchange: Biological and Cultural Consequences of 1492*. Westport, CT: Greenwood Press.

Drinnon, Richard (1980) *Facing West: The Metaphysics of Indian Hating and Empire Building*. Minneapolis: University of Minnesota Press.

Fiedler, Leslie A. (1972) *The Return of the Vanishing American*. London: Paladin.

Gidley, Mick (1990) "Sam Fathers's Fathers: Indians and the Idea of Inheritance," in Arthur F. Kinney (ed.) *Critical Essays on William Faulkner: The McCaslin Family*. Boston, MA: G. K. Hall, pp. 121–30.

Harris, Marvin (1968) *The Rise of Anthropological Theory*. New York: Thomas Y. Crowell.

Heizer, Robert and Kroeber, Theodora (1968) *Almost Ancestors*. San Francisco: Sierra Club.

Hudson, Charles (1976) *The Southeastern Tribes*. Knoxville: University of Tennessee Press.

Laws, G. Malcolm (1964) *Native American Balladry*. Washington, DC: American Folklore Society.

Lomax, John A. and Lomax, Alan (1994) [1934] *American Ballads and Folk Songs*. New York: Dover.

Mooney, James (1891) *The Sacred Formulas of the Cherokees*. Washington, DC: Bureau of American Ethnology, 7th Annual Report.

Mintz, Sidney (1970) "Creating Culture in the Americas." *Columbia University Forum*, 13: 3–13.

Mintz, Sidney (1971) "Toward an Afro-American History." *Cahiers d'Histoire Mondiale*, 13: 318–30.

O'Brien, Michael (1979) *The Idea of the American South, 1920–1941*. Baltimore, MD: Johns Hopkins University Press.

Paul, Diane B. (1995) *Controlling Human Heredity*. Atlantic Highlands, NJ: Humanities Press.

Perdue, Theda (1988) "Indians in Southern History," in Frederick E. Hoxie (ed.) *Indians in American History*. Arlington Heights, IL: Harlan Davidson, pp. 136–57.

Price, Edward T. (1951) "The Melungeons," *Geographical Review*, 41: 256ff.

Prucha, Francis Paul (1984) *The Great Father: The United States Government and the American Indians*, 2 vols. Lincoln: University of Nebraska Press.

Robinson, Cedric J. (1983) *Black Marxism*. London: Zed Books.

Rogin, Michael Paul (1975) *Fathers and Children: Andrew Jackson and the Subjugation of the American Indian*. New York: Alfred A. Knopf.

Sakolsky, Ron and Koehnline, James (eds.) (1993) *Gone to Croatan*. New York: Autonomedia. Contains essays by Koehnline, Leaming, Sivad, and Wilson.

Speck, Frank G., with J. D. Sapir (1911) "Ceremonial Songs of the Creek and Yuchi Indians," *University of Pennsylvania Museum Anthropological Publications*, Vol. 1, No. 2: 157–245.

Swanton, John Reed (1911) "Indian Tribes of the Lower Mississippi and Adjacent Coast of the Gulf of Mexico." *Bureau of American Ethnology Bulletin*, 43: 139–57.

Swanton, John Reed (1979) [1946] *The Indians of the Southeastern United States*. Washington, DC: Smithsonian Institution.

Taylor, Colin (ed.) (1991) *The Native Americans: The Indigenous People of North America*. London: Salamander.

Thompson, Vincent Bakpetu (1987) *The Making of the African Diaspora in the Americas*. New York: Longman.

Turner, Frederick W., III (ed.) (1977) *The Portable North American Indian Reader*. Harmondsworth: Penguin Books, pp. 249–50.

Ware, Vron and Back, Les (2001) *Outside the Whale*. Chicago: University of Chicago Press.

Wilson, Charles Reagan and Ferris, William (eds.) (1989) *Encyclopedia of Southern Culture*. Chapel Hill: University of North Carolina Press.

Woodward, C. Van (1960) *The Burden of Southern History*. Baton Rouge: Louisiana State University Press.

Young, Philip (1972) [1962] "The Mother of Us All: Pocahontas," in *Three Bags Full: Essays in American Fiction*. New York: Harcourt Brace Jovanovich, pp. 175–203.

11

Southern Music

John White

Music – instrumental and vocal – has been a creative, distinctive, and vibrant element of the South's culture from the Colonial period to the present. Reflecting the region's demographic structure, it was an amalgam or fusion of "black" and "white" creations and interactions. From the late nineteenth century and into the twentieth, what were originally Southern musical creations and genres became "nationalized" as commercial and technological innovations (records, radio, films, and television), and the massive population movements out of the South, disseminated "Southern music" to a national and international audience.

In the twentieth century, Southern-born performers and songwriters like Louis Armstrong, Jelly Roll Morton, Sidney Bechet, Bessie Smith, Jimmie Rodgers, Doll-1 Parton, Elvis Presley, Little Richard, Hoagy Carmichael, and Johnny Mercer became household names. As one historian has aptly commented: "Music was one of the South's great natural resources and one of its most valuable exports."[1] Again, Southern musicians and songwriters have created positive and negative images of their region as one of marked religiosity and misery, triumph and defeat, nostalgia and realism, harmony and discord. And, like Southerners themselves, Southern music has been rough and refined, dramatic and poignant, secular and sacred. Most importantly, it was a synthesis of British and African traditions and influences, with important contributions from European immigrant groups – like the French and the Germans – who settled in the Southern states.

Among the South's most fertile and enduring musical forms have been the spirituals and gospel music, minstrelsy, the blues, ragtime, and jazz. Considered singly or collectively, all of these forms were characterized by black/white interaction, adaptation, and "borrowing." The South's best-known song, "I Wish I Were in Dixie's Land" (1859) – subsequently loved or despised as "Dixie" – (the anthem of the Confederate States of America) contains the stanza:

> Oh, I wish I was in the land of cotton
> Old times there ain't ne'r forgotten
> Look away – look 'way, away Dixie land.

Ironically, "Dixie" – claimed by the black-faced minstrel Daniel Decatur Emmett (1815–1904) as his original composition – may well have been "taught" to him by two African-American musicians, Ben and Lew Snowdon. Emmett and the Snowdon brothers are buried in cemeteries only 2 miles apart in Ohio. The Snowdon family came from the South to Knox County in the early nineteenth century. Members of the African Methodist Episcopal Church, they were locally famous as composers, dancers, instrumentalists, and singers. As Howard and Judith Sacks have plausibly suggested, it is distinctly possible that the Snowdons "shared" the words of "Dixie" with Emmett (later a Union partisan) long before the song's sensational debut on Broadway. Deconstructions of the song suggest that it might, among other things, represent the African-American tradition of "protest by way of parody," an "expression of themes of diaspora in the North," and a nostalgic (and decidedly feminine) evocation of the Old South.[2] To later generations, "Dixie" conveyed conflicting resonances. Since the 1960s, African-American students at Southern state colleges and universities have protested against its performance at football games. Most Southern whites (blissfully unaware of its racially mixed and "Yankee" origins) continue to regard "Dixie" as *the* Song of the South.

Such conscious or unconscious interracial borrowings have not been uncommon. In the twentieth century, it was an African-American blues singer, Arthur "Big Boy" Crudup, who provided Memphis's favorite son, Elvis Presley, with his first hit in his "cover" of Crudup's "That's All Right, Mama." As Bill Malone has remarked, the young Presley "sang with a heavily black-tinged style" yet never appeared to question the region's racial values or etiquette: "His manners, with a profusion of 'sirs' and 'ma'ams,' epitomized Southern courtesy."[3] Southern music has reflected the essential bi-raciality of a society premised, until recently, on the assumption of white superiority and black inferiority. In his *Notes on the State of Virginia*, Thomas Jefferson (1743–1826), third president of the United States, and a slaveholder, acknowledged – and then questioned – the musical abilities of African Americans:

> In music they [blacks] are generally more gifted than whites with accurate ears for tune and time, and they have been found capable of imagining a small catch. Whether they will be equal to the composition of a more extensive run of melody, or of complicated harmony, is yet to be proved.[4]

Sacred Songs and Spirituals

From the Colonial period and into the early twentieth century, religiously inspired songs and rituals were the most widespread popular music forms in the South.

The religious music of black and white Southerners drew heavily on the Bible and the English tradition of hymnody. At the camp meetings of the Second Great Awakening in the early 1800s, blacks and whites learned and borrowed songs from each other.

The shape-note method – a distinctive form of musical notation in which four musical syllables (fa-sol-la-mi) were represented by shapes positioned on the musical staff to indicate their pitch – had been introduced into New England in the early 1800s. Itinerant singing-school teachers brought the method to the South, where it was incorporated into the sacred harp music of black and white Primitive Baptists and Methodists. In 1844 two Georgia Baptist singing-school teachers, Benjamin F. White and Elisha King, compiled *The Sacred Harp*, a compendium of 573 four-part folk hymns, which became (and remains) the bible of the Southern rural singing-school movement. Strongly Calvinist in their theology, the religious texts contained in *The Sacred Harp* were primarily those of eighteenth-century English hymn writers, most notably, Isaac Watts (1674–1748):

> Death, 'tis a melancholy day, to those who have no God,
> When the poor soul is forced away, to seek his last abode.

Sacred harp singing took place at informal gatherings and annual reunions, with a strong emphasis on the family and the recently deceased. The folklorist Alan Lomax, in the liner notes to his collection of sacred harp recordings, "White Spirituals from the Sacred Harp" (New World Records), observed: "The Sacred Harp folk feel [as if] they belong to a big family that will someday be singing its harmony with the angels." Lomax quotes an elderly white Alabamian sacred harp singer to good effect: "I believe that every living word in that there book [*The Sacred Harp*] is as true as the gospel." Down to the present, sacred harp singing, with its otherworldly religious outlook, sense of community, and musical conventions, continues to reflect traditional Southern culture and piety.

During slavery, the African origins of black music were most evident in religious songs or "spirituals," marked by polyrhythms, call-and-response patterns, improvisation, and vocal mannerisms. The African-American poet and novelist James Weldon Johnson, writing in 1925, believed the slaves' religious songs possessed "a striking rhythmic quality and a marked similarity to African songs in form and structure," but noted perceptively that they were also infused with "the spirit of Christianity" by a people in need of a "religion of compensation in the life to come for the ills suffered in the present existence." The spirituals, Johnson and subsequent commentators suggested, sustained the slaves of the Old South: the songs/stories of the passage of the Hebrews in the fiery furnace, the release of the Children of Israel from bondage in Egypt, the experiences of Daniel in the lion's den, were songs of deliverance. They were also, and significantly, communal expressions of religious belief.

Contemporary white observers were impressed – and sometimes affected by – the performances and imagery of the slave spirituals. Mary Boykin Chesnut, the wife of a

South Carolina slaveowner, described a service she attended at a black church on her husband's plantation in 1861:

> Jim Nelson, the driver, [a] full-blooded African, was asked to "lead in prayer." He became wildly excited. Though on his knees, facing us, with his eyes shut, he clapped his hands at the end of every sentence, and his voice rose to the pitch of a shrill shriek. Still, his voice was strangely clear and musical, occasionally in a plaintive minor key that went to your heart. Sometimes it rung out like a trumpet. I wept bitterly. It was all sound, however, and emotional pathos. It was the devotional passion of voice and manner that was so magnetic. The negroes sobbed and shouted and swayed backward and forward, clapping their hands and responding in shrill tones, "Yes, my God!" "Jesus!" "Aeih!" "Savior!" "Bless de Lord, amen – &c." Suddenly, as I sat wondering what next, they broke out into one of those soul-stirring negro camp-meeting hymns. To me this is the saddest of all earthly music – weird and depressing beyond my powers to describe.[5]

The slave spirituals drew without regard for biblical chronology – or even accuracy – on the whole Bible story, conflating the New Testament with the Old and the Old with the New. The Genesis story of Adam and Eve in the Garden of Eden, discovering their nakedness, is paralleled in the spirituals by the lines:

> Oh, Eve, where is Adam?
> Oh, Eve, Adam is in the garden
> Pinin' leaves

The story of Noah and the Flood is echoed in the injunction:

> Noah, Noah, build this ark
> Build this ark without hammer or nails.

James Mason Brown, Kentucky-born attorney and author, who joined the Union army and rose to the rank of colonel, contributed a vivid description of the spirituals to *Lippincott's Magazine* in 1868. "We have seen," Brown wrote, "negroes alternately agonized with fear and transported with a bliss almost frantic" as they sang a hymn, "The Book of the Seven Seals," which was "replete with the imagery of the Apocalypse, picturing the golden streets of the New Jerusalem and the horrible pit of destruction." Although some slave religious songs had been borrowed from those sung by white Protestant congregations, Brown observed that this was a highly selective borrowing: "the favorites were always such as abounded in bold imagery or striking expressions appealing to ardent hope or vivid fear." One spiritual in particular amazed Brown – "a hymn in which the Christian was likened to a traveler on a railway train":

> The conductor was the Lord Jesus, the brakemen were eminent servants of the Church, and the stoppages were made at Gospel depots to take up waiting converts or replenish

the engine with the waters of life or the fuel of holy zeal. The allegory was developed with as much accuracy and verisimilitude as though the author had carefully studied the *Pilgrim's Progress*; yet it was imagined and composed by Oscar Buckner, an illiterate and ignorant negro slave.

There had been under slavery, Brown concluded, a distinctively black musical tradition, but one already being distorted and caricatured by the antics of "burnt cork" negro minstrels, with "scarcely a feature of person, music, dialect or action that recalls, with any dramatic accuracy, the genuine negro slave of former years."[6]

The first comprehensive collection of slave spirituals was published in 1867: *Slave Songs of the United States*, edited by William Francis Allen, Charles Pickard Ware, and Lucy McKim Garrison. But the songs were transcribed in conventional musical notation, and inadequately conveyed the *manner* in which they had been performed. As Lawrence Levine and other commentators have observed, slave spirituals were essentially *improvised* songs; at no time did slaves create a "final" version of a spiritual. The product of what Levine terms "an improvisational communal consciousness," flexibility, spontaneity, and adaptation marked the spirituals – both in their creation and performance. "Singing the spirituals," Levine contends, "was both an intensely personal and vividly communal experience."[7] Alain Locke, in his essay on "The Negro Spirituals" (1925), noted:

> The Spirituals are spiritual. Conscious artistry and popular conception alike should never rob them of this heritage. It was to an alien atmosphere that the missionary campaigning of the Negro schools and colleges took these songs. And the concert stage has but taken them an inevitable step further from their original setting. We should always remember that they are essentially congregational, not theatrical, just as they are essentially a choral not a solo form.[8]

In his perceptive essay "Of the Sorrow Songs," the closing chapter of *The Souls of Black Folk* (1903), W. E. B. Du Bois viewed the spirituals as the "articulate message of the slave to the world," as songs of affirmation and religious faith.

It was the Fisk Jubilee Singers from Fisk University in Tennessee (founded in 1865 to educate the freedmen) who introduced African-American spirituals to a worldwide audience – and also revived the financial fortunes of their school. Founded in 1867 by George L. White, a music teacher and treasurer at Fisk, the Jubilee Singers performed before Henry Ward Beecher at the Plymouth Congregational Church in Brooklyn, at the World Peace Jubilee in Boston in 1872, and for William E. Gladstone and Queen Victoria in England. Although the Jubilee Singers – conscious of white disparagement of black culture – performed "sanitized" and "arranged" versions of the slave spirituals, they brought the form to appreciative audiences. Mark Twain said that he would "walk seven miles" to hear the Fisk Jubilee Singers, whose "music made all other vocal music cheap." The success of the Jubilee Singers prompted other Southern black colleges to form their own touring choirs.

Gospel Music

Black gospel music – rooted in shape-note singing, spirituals, the blues, and ragtime – emerged in the early twentieth century. Like the blues, "gospel" is a term elusive of precise definition, and is generally taken to include a form of musical expression which combines secular and sacred forms with religious texts and concerns. Thomas Andrew Dorsey (1899–1993), a Georgia-born pianist, arranger, and composer, is affectionately (if not entirely accurately) remembered as the "Father of Gospel Music." The composer of over a hundred songs, including "Precious Lord, Take my Hand," Dorsey was influenced by his exposure to shape-note singing, the rural blues, and the "vaudeville" blues of Gertrude "Ma" Rainey and Bessie Smith. At the 1921 National Baptist Convention, Dorsey became convinced that his mission was to evangelize through music, but had his first commercial success with King Oliver's Creole Jazz Band recording of "Riverside Blues" in 1923. For the remainder of his career, Dorsey composed and recorded both secular and sacred music, and worked with such stellar gospel singers as Mahalia Jackson and Sallie Martin – the "Mother of Gospel Music."

Part of black gospel's appeal was that in "live" performances it encouraged audience participation. By the mid-1930s, record companies and radio stations capitalized on and further promoted black gospel music. After 1945, African-American gospel quartets like the Soul Stirrers, the Dixie Hummingbirds, and the Five Blind Boys of Alabama enjoyed nationwide popularity. Within the South, the fundamentalist Pentecostal churches were particularly welcoming to gospel quartets. In the North, as Ray Allen, in his important study *Singing in the Spirit: African-American Sacred Quartets in New York City* (1991) observes, migrant black Southerners responded to the public appearances, recordings, or broadcasts of these performers (and *performances*) with their evocations of traditional life, family, and home. Allen suggests that despite the South's legacy of slavery, racial oppression, and economic exploitation, the popularity of Southern-derived gospel quartet singing "appears to be part of a larger movement to revive and sustain traditional Southern beliefs and practices in the contemporary urban North."[9]

Gospel music performed by Southern whites (usually vocal quartets or family groups, accompanied by a piano, guitar, or other stringed instruments) has been closely related to the rural secular music and folk traditions of the South. What became the thriving "gospel music business" reflected two aspects of the region's religious and nineteenth-century musical history: its evangelical revivals and shape-note singing schools. But "white gospel" music also drew much of its fervor and form from the Holiness-Pentecostal movement of the late-nineteenth and early-twentieth centuries. A Tennessean, James D. Vaughan (1864–1941), a member of the Church of the Nazarene, founded the Vaughan Publishing Company of Lawrenceburg, Tennessee, the most important of gospel music publishing houses, in the early 1900s. An astute entrepreneur, Vaughan not only marketed paperback gospel songbooks but also formed his own record company, and sent gospel quartets to churches and singing conventions to advertise his products. During the 1930s Vaughan claimed to have sold over 5 million songbooks. More rhythmical, sentimental, and optimistic than older hymns, such white gospel songs as "What a Friend We Have in Jesus" and "Bringing in the Sheaves" became part of the Southern folk tradition. It is often referred to as "traditional gospel" – to distinguish it from the "pop gospel" music of the 1950s and the "praise music" of the 1970s.

Minstrelsy

The most popular form of theatrical performance in America in the nineteenth century, blackface minstrelsy emerged during the 1820s and reached its peak during the years 1850–70. Minstrel performances presented stereotypical and demeaning caricatures of African Americans, romantic portrayals of life on the slave plantations of the South, and, in Mel Watkins's phrase, served to "codify the public image of blacks as the prototypical Fool or Sambo." The career of Thomas Dartmouth Rice – later known as "Daddy Rice, Father of American Minstrelsy" – is generally thought to have marked the beginnings of blackface minstrelsy. Starting in 1829, Rice began to feature a song and dance – "Jump Jim Crow" – in his stage act. He claimed it was based on observations of an old and deformed African-American stable hand he had seen in Louisville, Kentucky. For the original performance, Rice even borrowed the man's ragged clothing – a long blue coat and striped trousers. The chorus of Rice's song contained the lines:

> Wheel about an' turn about an' do jes so,
> An eb'ry time I wheel about, I jump Jim Crow.

Following Rice's overnight success, blackface minstrelsy quickly evolved into a highly stylized formula based on song, dance, music, and set routines.

After 1865, black performers also joined the ranks of minstrelsy, and came to dominate the genre. They were, however, owned and controlled by white entrepreneurs – the most famous of whom was Charles Callender, owner of the Georgia Minstrels. These African-American performers were required to conform to the (demeaning) conventions of the minstrel show, yet as many authorities suggest, whether performed by white men in blackface ("Ethiopian Delineators") or by blacks, minstrelsy exposed and introduced white Americans to African-American culture – if only in a caricatured form. More significantly, minstrelsy provided a nursery for Southern black composers, musicians, and comedians. W. C. Handy, who was to gain fame with his composition "St. Louis Blues," played the cornet with Mahara's Minstrels; blues singers Gertrude "Ma" Rainey and Bessie Smith were featured performers with the Rabbit's Foot Minstrels; and the comedian Bert Williams – the first African-American to perform in the Ziegfeld Follies – used blackface in his famous portrayal of an antebellum Southern rustic.

Whites usually wrote the music used in minstrel shows – popular songs with syncopated rhythms. Although he never lived in the South, Stephen Foster (1826–64) contributed to the myth of the Old South with such songs as "Old Folks at Home" and "My Old Kentucky Home." Florida and Kentucky have adopted these compositions (respectively) as their official state songs. Alain Locke wryly observed that Foster's ballads "did more to crystallize the romance of the plantation tradition than all the Southern colonels and novelists put together."

The Blues

After the Civil War the blues – a conflation of late nineteenth-century ballads, work shouts, field hollers, and spirituals – emerged in the American South, and later moved North. The use of the term "blues" to define an African-American song form dates from the early twentieth century. The seedbeds of the blues were the farms, plantations, and small towns of the Deep South. Many commentators cite the Mississippi Delta as the provenance of the blues and, in the first decades of the twentieth century, the blues tradition certainly developed most fully in that region.

Like the spirituals, the blues conveyed feelings of sadness and joy, resignation and protest. African characteristics of the blues included call-and-response patterns, 12-bar, 3-line *aab* stanzas, vocal mannerisms and inflections, and the use of stringed instruments – notably the guitar (which had African antecedents). Early blues songs were usually divided into three equal parts, each containing a single line of verse. The second line usually repeated the first and (as in the work song) the third line rounded off the first.

> If you see me comin', heist your window high;
> If you see me comin', heist your window high.
> If you see me goin', hang your head and cry.

A short instrumental response or "comment" on the singer's guitar or piano answered each line.

In the Deep South of the 1920s the African-American church and the blues represented both antithetical and complementary impulses. Blues lyrics and performances, in many respects, expressed a "secular religion." They shared some of the features of African-American oral sermons: the repetition of phrases, formal composition and extensive improvisation, explanations and directives. The black oral sermon and the blues performance had structural and improvisational similarities, and both were concerned with the Golden Rule. Jeff Todd Titon suggests that like the black preacher, who "voiced the ethic of the church community," the blues singer "expressed the aspirations of the blues culture" – the everyday concerns of men and women attempting to cope with the vicissitudes of life in a hostile world. Blues performers were also able to explore taboo subjects – particularly those relating to sexual matters – through the use of veiled metaphors and double entendres. They also evoked a sense of *place* in their listeners. While female blues singers – Ma Rainey, Bessie Smith, and Ida Cox – were professional vaudevillians, male blues singers were usually farmers or seasonal laborers, accompanying themselves on guitar, who entertained their neighbors with both "borrowed" and freshly minted lyrics.

Lawrence Levine maintains:

> The blues was the most highly personalized, indeed, the first almost completely personalized music that [African] Americans developed to lack the kind of antiphony that had marked other black musical forms. The call-and-response remained, but in blues it was the singer who responded to himself or herself either verbally or on an accompanying instrument [and] represented a major degree of acculturation to the individualized ethos of the larger society.[10]

The blues also came in regional guises. In Georgia and Virginia they were more melodic and showed more similarities to ragtime and folk ballads than they did in the Southwest – where they were often played on the piano as well as the guitar. But it was the Mississippi Delta blues, with their strong rhythmic drive, which achieved the widest dissemination, with the exodus of black migrants to Chicago and other Northern cities in the First and Second Great Migrations of the twentieth century.

Robert Johnson (1911–38), born in Hazelhurst, Mississippi, learned to play the blues on the harmonica and guitar as a child. His legendary series of recordings with their references to magic, the Devil, and unrequited love, poetically evoke black life in the Delta. "Me and the Devil Blues" contains the haunting lines:

> Early this mornin'
> When you knocked upon my door
> And I said, "Hello, Satan,
> I believe it's time to go."

Blind Lemon Jefferson (1897–1929) was born near Dallas, and became one of the most popular blues men in the South. The most commercially successful of rural blues musicians, Jefferson made a series of recordings in Chicago during the late 1920s which reflected the themes prevalent in the African-American oral tradition: sexual relationships, poverty, natural disasters, and life in prison. Other notable Southern blues performers who achieved international fame include Huddie Ledbetter ("Leadbelly"), Aaron "T-Bone" Walker, McKinley Morganfield ("Muddy Waters"), B. B. King, and John Lee Hooker.

The blues did not enjoy widespread popularity until the decade of the 1920s – largely as a consequence of the activities of two black Southerners. William

Christopher Handy (1873–1958), born in Florence, Alabama became known (misleadingly) as the "Father of the Blues." As a young man he studied the organ and music theory, and then played the cornet in Mahara's Minstrels (and was later its music director), before touring the South with his own orchestra. Minstrels, he later recalled, "were a disreputable lot in the eyes of a large section of upper-crust Negroes," but added that minstrel shows featured "the best [musical] talent of that generation." One of the first musicians to annotate a twelve-bar blues measure, Handy was the composer of the "Memphis Blues" (written in 1909 and published in 1912), and "St. Louis Blues" (published in 1914). Handy remembered that he had first heard the blues being sung "on a plantation in Mississippi," and, excited by the singer, had been "seized with a desire to play and sing, imitating his style." He also explained that his earliest pieces differed from the then-popular ragtime compositions that were sweeping the country:

> To have composed a number, however joyous, with sixteen bars to a strain, I would have been following in the steps of other writers of ragtime, but this composition ["Memphis Blues"] carries twelve measures to a strain – typical "blues" – which makes me somewhat proud to know that I have added another form to musical composition and to the world.[11]

Handy certainly exaggerated his role as the composer of a new "musical form," but he was one of the earliest composers to take a loosely structured folk idiom and formalize it into its most regular 12-bar format. Afflicted in the 1940s by blindness and a debilitating stroke, Handy lived to see his greatest compositions given their finest performances by Louis Armstrong and his All Stars in their celebrated 1954 album "Louis Armstrong Plays W. C. Handy."

Handy's great contemporary, Perry Bradford (1893–1970), was born in Montgomery, Alabama. Like Handy, he worked in minstrel shows (and also as a solo pianist) before concentrating on musical direction and song writing. In 1920 Bradford was responsible for the recording debut of Mamie Smith on the first recording session to feature an African-American blues singer. It was Smith's version of Bradford's composition "Crazy Blues" that initiated the craze for blues singing – Smith's record sold more than a million copies. Bradford had earlier observed the performances of Ma Rainey across the United States, and was convinced that African-American musicians deserved to be included in the catalogues of the major recording companies. Moving to New York, Bradford (nicknamed "Mule" for his stubbornness), remembered:

> I tramped the pavements of Broadway with the belief that the country was waiting for the sound of the voice of the Negro singing the blues with a Negro jazz combination playing for him or her.[12]

After rejections from Columbia and Victor, Bradford persuaded the manager of Okeh Records to record Mamie Smith. Okeh went on to include in its "Colored Catalog" such major African-American jazz musicians as King Oliver, Louis Armstrong, and Duke Ellington.

But it was Bessie Smith (1894–1937) who brought the blues to a national audience, and influenced every subsequent blues singer. Born in Chattanooga, Tennessee, Smith built up a devoted following among black Southerners as she toured the region in vaudeville troupes during the 1920s. In Atlanta, Georgia, Smith performed at the 81 Theatre, part of the nationwide Theatre Owners Booking Association (TOBA) circuit – known among poorly paid and exploited African-American performers as "Tough on Black Asses." Moving to Philadelphia, she quickly became a favorite performer for the African-American residents of Northern cities. Bill C. Malone, in his insightful survey *Southern Music, American Music* (1979), suggests "there had probably been no singer before Bessie Smith who so effectively communicated with the black masses, and none who achieved such an heroic stature among them." Smith's first record, "Downhearted Blues," sold 780,000 copies, and established her reputation. During the 1920s she recorded with Louis Armstrong and Sidney Bechet. It was her ability to use her vocal technique and resources to express the *meaning* of her songs that made "The Empress of the Blues" such a commanding performer and artist. The white saxophonist Bud Freeman recalled that Smith's phrasing was "exquisite . . . she had the most fantastic voice I was ever to hear." Her popularity in the North declined in the late 1920s, with the passing of the blues craze, but Smith remained popular in the South. Adopted (and patronized) by the white patrons of the Harlem Renaissance, Smith made a successful adaptation to the style of the Swing Era, and appeared to be on the verge of a comeback when she was killed in a road accident on the way to an appearance in Clarksdale, Mississippi, in 1937.

Only a few Southern-born white singers have been notable blues performers. The Texan-born and part Native American trombonist Jack Teagarden (1905–64), who joined the Louis Armstrong All Stars in 1946, was a consummate singer of the blues. But in the years before World War II other Southern whites began to perform blues-inflected material learned from black musicians, and by the 1920s, "hillbilly" performers from across the South were recording the blues. Jimmie Rodgers (1897–1933), born in Meridian, Mississippi, combined the backcountry blues of African-American artists with the tradition of German and Swiss yodeling, popularized on the vaudeville stage, to produce the "blue yodel" that became his musical signature. (In a 1930 recording, Louis Armstrong accompanied Rodgers on his hit recording "Blue Yodel No. 9.") Rodgers, in turn, influenced such later stars as Hank Williams, Gene Autry, and Willie Nelson, and was the first singer inducted into Nashville's Country Music Hall of Fame, in 1961.

Ragtime

By the 1890s various strands of Southern folk music – minstrel shows, string and brass band music – coalesced into "ragtime," which became an American craze. The ragtime boom also saw the entry of a (partly) Southern-born musical style and its exponents into the national culture. Condemned by conservatives and public moralists for its association with energetic dancing (the "cakewalk") and "primitive" rhythms (in fact, they were extremely complex), ragtime raised the curtain on what became known as the "Jazz Age." As the British author J. B. Priestley remarked: "Out of this ragtime came the fragmentary outlines of the menace to old Europe, the domination of America, the end of confidence and any feeling of security, the nervous excitement [and] the feeling of modern times." More accurately, after the spirituals, ragtime was the next original African-American musical style to emerge as a genre in its own right.

Originally a syncopated (or "ragged timed") and rhythmically lively style of solo piano performance, later applied to other forms of popular music, ragtime was characterized by the juxtaposition of a syncopated treble against a steady bass. Primarily a written music, ragtime performances were influential in shaping the solo and collective improvisation of early jazz, and formed the basis of the "stride" piano style associated with such performers as James P. Johnson and Thomas "Fats" Waller.

Ragtime's most celebrated exponent was Scott Joplin (1868–1917). Born near Texarkana, Texas, Joplin showed precocious musical skills, and after some formal tuition began to perform across the South as an itinerant pianist. His most famous composition, "Maple Leaf Rag" (1899), had sold more than 500,000 copies in sheet music by 1909 – a reflection of the growing numbers of pianos in American homes. In the early years of the twentieth century, Joplin published numerous rags – including "The Entertainer" (1902), featured in the 1973 movie *The Sting*. Toward the end of his life, an ailing Joplin (he had developed syphilis) produced his full-length rag opera, "Treemonisha," at the Lincoln Theatre in Harlem.

The ragtime vogue also pointed to future developments in the popular music industry: the proliferating sales of sheet music and piano rolls, the advent of phonographic recordings, and the rise of large orchestras. An Alabama-born composer, conductor, orchestra leader, and musical entrepreneur made a major contribution to ragtime and the "prehistory" of orchestrated jazz. James Reese Europe (1881–1919) was born in Mobile, the son of a former slave father and freeborn mother. James Reese (like his sister and brother) showed an early aptitude for music. When the family moved from Mobile to Washington, DC, he studied the violin under Joseph Douglass, grandson of the famous Frederick. In 1902 Europe moved to New York City, the Mecca for African-American entertainers and musicians, and quickly established a reputation as a songwriter and arranger. In 1912 Europe presented the first (and hugely successful) "Concert of Negro Music" to an integrated audience at Carnegie Hall, and the following year began to record for Victor Records. During World War I, Europe won respect for his excellent military band, the 369th Infantry – nicknamed the "Hell-fighters" – and for the concerts it performed in France. The 369th Infantry brought the sounds of American ragtime, blues, and the syncopated music that presaged big band jazz to European audiences. After the Armistice, Europe began a nationwide tour with the demobilized 369th Regimental Band and received the congratulations of his fellow Alabamian W. C. Handy for its rousing performance of "St. Louis Blues," and a commendation from the *Chicago Defender* that "Europe and his band are worth more to our Race than a thousand speeches from so-called Race orators and uplifters." At the time of his death – he was fatally stabbed by his drummer while appearing in Boston – Europe was the outstanding exemplar and exponent of an evolving African-American musical form that would in the 1920s and 1930s take America (and the world) by storm.

Jazz

A glittering jewel in the crown of Southern music, jazz – a melding of white and black folk musics, African, European, and American influences – has become one of the great musical cultures of the world. Some historians and musicologists contend jazz originated in New Orleans, and was then transmitted across the rest of the United States. In fact, by the 1920s, jazz was being played in Los Angeles, Chicago, Kansas City, and New York, and was another example of the cultural transmission and adaptation that marked the Northern migration of black (and white) Southerners in the twentieth century.

Yet jazz fully deserves its association with New Orleans, historically the most musical of all American cities. "Classical" music in the Old South flourished in New Orleans, where operatic performances were staged from the late eighteenth century. Visitors to the city remarked that slaves and free blacks hummed operatic arias as they walked through the streets. In the 1830s, African Americans in New Orleans formed a Negro Philharmonic Society with over a hundred members. Louis Moreau Gottschalk (1829–69), the most celebrated American composer of the early nineteenth century, mixed European romantic forms with the African rhythms and Creole melodies he had experienced as a child in New Orleans. Until the 1850s, Congo Square was the venue for African-derived drumming and dancing displays. The city had an established brass band tradition – which intensified during the Civil War with the presence of military bands. During the Reconstruction period, African Americans in New Orleans took advantage of the availability of both musical instruments and teachers to pursue their musical interests.

The presence in New Orleans of a Creole subculture added to the city's musical mixture. While the Creoles (who lived uptown) favored European musical traditions, and were able to read music, they also had a strong tradition of dancing, and may have brought a special rhythmic conception to jazz. By 1900 there were a large number of black and Creole bands playing many kinds of music – waltzes, ballads, and quadrilles – at a variety of functions and venues. Street bands in New Orleans played marches, popular songs, and hymns. In the area of Storyville, the vice district of the city, blues, ragtime, and popular tunes were performed by informal groups – including such future jazz luminaries as Louis Armstrong, Sidney Bechet and Jelly Roll Morton. But the principal model for the early New Orleans jazz bands were the city's dance bands, which played for funerals, picnics, and sporting events, and combined ragtime, the blues, and other popular music to produce the first jazz music, distinguished by its meter – 4/4 time – which players began to divide unevenly, a device that became a defining characteristic of the music.

Although it is a vexed issue, the genesis of jazz may be briefly summarized as follows. In the eighteenth and nineteenth centuries, an indigenous black folk music developed from African and Euro-American elements. From this syncretic mixture emerged plantation and minstrel songs, ragtime and the blues. Jazz itself developed from a merging of these forms with contemporary popular music. Creole and Cajun folksongs, Caribbean music, brass band marching music, and African rhythms were heard on the streets of the city in the last decade of the nineteenth century. As the spread of Jim Crow discrimination and segregation reduced the social distinctions and distance between uptown Creoles and downtown blacks, they began to perform together throughout the city. Early jazz compositions often identified these locations in their titles – "Basin Street Blues," "Canal Street Blues," "South Rampart Street Parade" – or had Southern references – "Atlanta Blues, "Memphis Blues, "Georgia Grind." Embryonic "New Orleans jazz" was initially polyphonic music, based on collective improvisation by "front-line" instruments: the cornet or trumpet, trombone, clarinet (or saxophone), and three "rhythm" instruments: the piano, banjo/bass, and drums. Again, the major African-American innovators of jazz – notably the cornetists Joe "King" Oliver and Louis Armstrong, the saxophonist/clarinetist Sidney Bechet, and the pianist/composer Ferdinand Jelly Roll Morton, were New Orleans-born musicians.

Ironically, the band that sparked a nationwide consciousness of and enthusiasm for this new popular music was the Original Dixieland Jazz Band, a group of five white New Orleans instrumentalists led by cornetist Nick LaRocca. After playing in Chicago in 1916, the band moved to New York City and met with sensational receptions during their residency at Reisenweber's Restaurant. In 1917 the ODJB (as it became known) was the first jazz band to make phonograph recordings: "Livery Stable Blues" and "Dixie Jazz Band One-Step" released by the Victor company. The barnyard noises and "comical" effects – including rooster calls and a braying donkey in "Livery Stable Blues" – caught the popular imagination, and catapulted the ODJB into national and international prominence. Detractors of the ODJB assert (with some justification) that none of its members were particularly skilled musicians, that the group's phrasing was rhythmically stilted, and that it merely simplified the music of African-American New Orleans groups. Yet the ODJB had an enormous impact, and to the (principally white) record-buying public provided exciting and exotic new sounds that stimulated the mind and body.

But it was two African-American musicians, both born in New Orleans – Louis Armstrong (1900–71) and his mentor, Joe "King" Oliver (1885–1938) – who were to transform jazz from its focus on the collective ensemble to that of the improvising soloist. As a child, Armstrong lived in the poorest quarter of the city, and received his formal musical instruction at the Colored Waif's Home. As a young cornet (later trumpet) player, Armstrong attracted the attention of Joe Oliver, a prominent New Orleans musician and bandleader. Oliver invited Armstrong to join him in Chicago (a prime destination for many black New Orleans musicians in the 1920s), and unwittingly changed the course of jazz history – and American popular music. It was in Chicago in the early 1920s that King Oliver's Creole Jazz Band made the first recordings of "authentic" New Orleans jazz. More importantly, a series of studio sessions by Armstrong – the famous "Hot Fives" and "Hot Sevens" – also recorded in Chicago in the 1920s, represented the first full flowering of the jazz art, and caused the music to be taken seriously. As Gunther Schuller in his study *Early Jazz* (1968) observes, the Hot Five recording of "West End Blues" on June 28, 1928, marked a decisive stage in the evolution of jazz:

> When Louis Armstrong unleashed the spectacular cascading phrases of the introduction to "West End Blues," he established the general stylistic direction of jazz for decades to come. Beyond that, this performance also made it quite clear that jazz would never again revert to being solely an entertainment or folk music. The clarion call of "West End Blues" served notice that jazz had the potential capacity to compete with the highest order of previously known musical expression.[13]

The greatest of all jazz performers, Armstrong brought his virtuoso trumpet playing, unique vocal style, and unforced geniality to millions of people throughout the world. Fittingly, his seminal contributions to jazz have been commemorated in his native city, and, in recent years, promulgated by another New Orleans-born trumpet player, the remarkable Wynton Marsalis.

The Musical South

During the twentieth century, through the mediums of radio and records, the spirituals, ragtime, the blues and jazz entered the American national consciousness. Yet from the 1920s, other Southern musical forms attracted attention. String bands and fiddlers were heard in radio broadcasts. The South's most famous radio show – the Grand Ole Opry – began as the WSM Barn Dance. Sponsored by the R. J. Reynolds Tobacco Company in 1939, the Grand Ole Opry became a national institution. Based in Nashville, Tennessee, WSM covered most of the United States by 1932; twenty years later, it had a coast-to-coast chain of 176 stations, reaching an estimated weekly audience of 10 million listeners.

Zydeco – the music of black Creoles in Southwest Louisiana – an amalgamation of French and African musical traditions – is a syncopated dance music, strongly featuring the button accordion, which became popular on records made during the late 1920s and early 1930s. Its most celebrated exponent was Louisiana-born Clifton Chenier (1925–88). "Tex-Mex music" (or *Musica Tejana*), commercially recorded in the 1920s, is the folk music of Texan Americans. It drew on the polka and accordion music of the German communities living in the state, and featured (Spanish) singing guitarists. Western Swing – an amalgam of ragtime, New Orleans jazz, and country/classic blues – also borrowed from the big band Swing of the 1930s. Bob Wills (1905–75), born in east Texas, combined blues and jazz idioms to traditional fiddle music (later adding brass, reeds, and drums to his orchestra) to produce a distinctive and essentially light-hearted sound. Charles R. Townsend suggests Wills's innovations in music provide another example of that "cross-fertilization" which "brought together two strains of culture in the American South, one white, one black."[14] In 1968 the Country Music Association promoted Wills to its Country Music Hall of Fame.

The South also contributed to the emergence of rock and roll, a melding of black and white popular dance music which emerged in the 1950s (and a white variant of the black Rhythm and Blues forms of the 1940s). Many Southern whites, already organizing to protest against the implications of the Supreme Court's 1954 landmark *Brown* decision, which ruled segregation in public schools to be unconstitutional, mobilized to attack the new music, with its interracial appeal, suggestive lyrics, and disturbing connotations of male sexuality. Although Bill Haley, a Michigan-born singer, is usually credited with the first major rock and roll hit ("Rock Around the Clock," 1955), he was soon eclipsed by Elvis Presley (1935–77). Born in Tupelo, Mississippi, and raised in Memphis, Tennessee, by impoverished but religious parents, Presley listened to country music on the radio and experienced the fervor of hymn singing as a member of the First Assembly of God Church. Presley's sultry good looks and expressive voice made him an icon of the new youth culture based on music. In 1954 Presley released "That's All Right Mama" on the Memphis-based Sun Records label. Although it was not a bestseller, the record defined the Southern roots of rock and roll – a "white" interpretation of a black song, which transmuted African-American emotion into a new synthesis of country music and the blues. In 1955 Colonel Tom Parker became Presley's manager, and secured his signing with RCA records. A string of "classic" rock and roll hits for Presley soon followed – "Heartbreak Hotel," "Blue Suede Shoes," and "Hound Dog." Television appearances and movies established Presley's place as a major figure in popular culture, and one who had achieved an international iconic status even before his death. By 1956, Presley was no longer identified as a *Southerner*. Since his death, however, his Memphis home, Graceland (opened to the public in 1982), has become one of the South's most popular (and revered) tourist attractions.

The South – despite continuing opposition to black and black-derived forms of music – also produced other (black and white) rock and roll innovators. A partial listing would include Roy Orbison, Conway Twitty, Carl Perkins, Buddy Holly, Fats Domino, Little Richard, and Jerry Lee Lewis. Out of this roster, Bill Malone concludes that Lewis, who "often acted as if he had walked out of the pages of Wilbur Cash's *The Mind of the South*," is perhaps "the prototypical [white] Southerner, embodying both puritanical and hedonistic traits."[15] Lewis scored his first major hit in 1957 with "Whole Lotta Shakin' Goin' On," received the avid attentions of the press when he married his 13-year-old second cousin, and was one of the wildest onstage rock and roll performers.

Lewis's African-American contemporary, Little Richard (Richard Penniman), born in Macon, Georgia, began singing at school and church functions. In 1955 he released "Tutti Frutti" – one of the first rock and roll hits, followed by "Long Tall Sally" and "Good Golly Miss Molly." Little Richard's diction and deportment were unequivocally "black." Brian Ward comments that when the unimpeachably Caucasian crooner Pat Boone produced a cover version of Little Richard's "Tutti Frutti," the results were unintentionally hilarious, and threatened "to deafen listeners with the whip-crack of perfectly articulated consonants."[16] In 1957 Little Richard revealed his Southern-bred religiosity by withdrawing from the music scene and entering a Bible school.

As even a brief (and selective) summary indicates, the South has made major contributions to a variety of musical forms. Some of these – particularly the blues, jazz, and rock and roll – have become part of an international musical lingua franca – and can no longer be considered uniquely Southern. Again, reflecting one of the major American demographic shifts of the twentieth century, Southerners (white and black) took their musical heritage with them as part of the cultural baggage carried by all migrants. Yet the South retains its identification with the popular music it has created from the Colonial era to the present. Many musicologists to the contrary, New Orleans is still widely regarded (and is pleased to advertise itself) as the birthplace of jazz; Memphis glories in (and profits from) its dual distinctions as a synonym for blues culture and the guardian of the Presley shrine; Nashville – "Music City, USA" – has come to embrace its worldwide identification with "hillbilly" and "country" music. In the mid-nineteenth century the South, acutely conscious of its culture and traditions, signally lost its bid for independence, when it failed to defeat the invading Northern forces. After 1865, "unreconstructed" white Southerners defiantly sang:

> O I'm a good old Rebel
> Now that's just what I am,
> For this "Fair Land of Freedom"
> I do not care AT ALL;
> I'm glad I fit against it,
> I only wish we'd won,
> And I don't want no pardon
> For anything I done.

In peace and in war, music was an integral part of the South's identity and distinctiveness. Unlike the Confederate States of America, it survived, prospered, and entered the fabric of the national culture. Not least, the South's music has brought comfort, inspiration, and joy to Southerners and non-Southerners alike.

Notes

1   Dewey W. Grantham, *The South in Modern America: A Region at Odds* (New York: Harper Collins, 1994), p. 322.

2   Howard L. Sacks and Judith Rose Sacks, *Way Up North in Dixie: A Black Family's Claim to the Confederate Anthem* (Washington: Smithsonian Institution, 1993).

3   Bill C. Malone, *Southern Music American Music* (Lexington: University of Kentucky Press, 1979), p. 105.

4   Adrienne Koch and William Peden (eds.) *The Life and Selected Writings of Thomas Jefferson* (New York: Random House, 1944), p. 258.

5   C. Vann Woodward (ed.) *Mary Chesnut's Civil War* (New Haven, CT: Yale University Press, 1981), pp. 213–14.

6   James Mason Brown, "Songs of the Slave," in Bernard Katz (ed.) *The Social Implications of Early Negro Music in the United States* (New York: Arno and the New York Times, 1969), pp. 25–6.

7   Lawrence W. Levine, *Black Culture and Black Consciousness: Afro-American Folk Thought From Slavery to Freedom* (New York: Oxford University Press, 1977), p. 246.

8   Alain Locke, "The Negro Spirituals," in *The New Negro: An Interpretation* (New York: Atheneum, 1980), pp. 201–2.

9   Ray Allen, *Singing in the Spirit: African-American Sacred Quartets in New York City* (Philadelphia: University of Pennsylvania Press, 1981), pp. 201–2.

10   Levine, *Black Culture and Black Consciousness*, p. 221.

11   Alyn Shipton, *A New History of Jazz* (New York: Continuum, 2001), p. 42.

12   Shipton, *A New History of Jazz*, p. 46.

13   Gunther Schuller, *Early Jazz: Its Roots and Musical Development* (New York: Oxford University Press, 1968), p. 89.

14   Charles R. Townsend, "Bob Wills," in Charles Reagan Wilson and William Ferris (eds.) *Encylopedia of Southern Culture* (Chapel Hill: University of North Carolina Press, 1989), p. 1090.

15   Malone, *Southern Music American Music*, p. 103.

16   Brian Ward, *Just My Soul Responding: Rhythm and Blues, Black Consciousness and Race Relations* (London: UCL Press, 1998), p. 49.

12

Country Music

Barbara Ching

A Southerner talks music.

Mark Twain, *Life on the Mississippi*, 1874

The vast region south of the Potomac is as large as Europe. You could lose France, Germany and Italy in it, with the British Isles for good measure. And yet it is as sterile, artistically, intellectually, culturally as the Sahara Desert. It would be difficult in all history to match so amazing a drying-up of civilization.

H. L. Mencken, "The Sahara of the Bozart," 1917

Lurking in the background of almost any statement about the South . . . is a comparison to the rest of the United States. If people say Southerners are lazy, or violent, or religious, they mean: compared to Northerners – not to Mexicans, to Martians, or to some absolute standard.

John Shelton Reed, *My Tears Spoiled My Aim and Other Reflections on Southern Culture*, 1993

My epigraphs only seem antithetical. Music, as we imagine Southerners speaking it, sounds simultaneously exotic and ordinary. In Twain's words, it does not even merit so abstract and formal a verb as "to speak"; Southerners use music for the much more colloquial and mundane task of talking. Music, down there, descends from a civilized art to the mere commerce of everyday life. While jazz and the blues, originally black forms of music, have gained respect through extensive study and urban(e) audiences, country music remains a degraded dialect of Southern-speak, beloved but scorned for its distinctively pathetic themes, its ostensibly untrained musicianship, and its association with lower-class whites, known variously as crackers, hillbillies, and white trash.

None of us has to believe a word of this. I would cross the Sahara of the Bozart to hear some of the music I will be talking about. My point, in this essay, is to explore the cultural logic of marking a certain kind of music as Southern, and to emphasize that politics (i.e., power relations) have shaped what we hear Southerners saying. For, as my third epigraph implies, the South is defined by the North, and, in both literal and psychic geographies, the North is above. Terms such as "the New South" or "the Sunbelt" telegraph an often-articulated sense that money and power, the sources of civilization, are moving south, but a righteous panic often accompanies these demographic observations. For example, Jimmy Carter and Bill Clinton, the Southerners who were elected president in the last quarter of the twentieth century, were regularly derided as hillbillies and "bubbas," as if their positions of power were anomalies rather than expressions of the public will. Humorist Roy Blount, Jr., in *Crackers* (1980), his book on the Carter presidency, summed up the situation by writing his own country lyric:

> I got the redneck White House blues.
> Even when we win one, we lose.
> The President's from Georgia,
>   but he's wearing shoes
> I got the redneck White House blues.

In fact, this Southern music does seem to speak continually of an "us" against "them" battle in which they, the North, continually emerge as more cultured, more successful, more virtuous, or, to put it more bluntly, richer, more fashionable, more progressive, and less racist. In this musical language the occasional Southern victory is countercultural: what Southern historian Jack Kirby Temple (1995) has described as "redneck discourse" in which the Confederacy stands not for "the enslavement of black folks but resistance to . . . national norms of work discipline and consumption" (72). In this case, anyone can speak Southern. As Jim Goad put it in his *Redneck Manifesto: How Hillbillies, Hicks, and White Trash Became America's Scapegoats*,

> the way I look at, anywhere more than fifty miles outside of New York and LA might as well be Texas. By class and attitudinal definitions, a redneck need not be from the South – the Nebraska cornhusker, the California desert rat, the Northwestern logger, and the Maine lobsterman all fit the type. But . . . mainstream America has designated the American South as the redneck homeland. (Goad 1997: 88–9)

The fact that this form of Southern can be so readily spoken and understood shows its importance. It is a metaphor that allows us not only to scapegoat but also to luxuriate in a pastoralism we think *we* (not the South) lost. In this lost country, we had time but no money; responsibility, but no power. It was a lot like childhood, but now we are the heads of households. Anything outside of this paradigm, no matter how recurrent or cataclysmic, strains the prevailing cultural logic: imagine, rednecks in the White House!

The reason that this logic prevails may be a simple tautology of power. It is because we said so. Statistics, though, can be marshaled to justify the situation, demonstrating that the South has lower per capita income or higher infant mortality rates. Nevertheless, the ideology has been in place longer than the numbers. For example, ever since the dawn of a distinctly American brand of popular music, songs presented a charmingly lost South to the nation. A short rhetorical exercise might easily convince you of the centrality of this imagery. Can you name a tradition of songs and artists associated with the Midwest? Why have we never heard songs like "Is it True What they Say About The Upper Midwest," "My Old Nebraska Home," or "That's What I Like about the Mid-Atlantic"? "The Charleston" thrilled the masses, but has anyone ever danced the "Rapid City"? Stephen Foster (1826–64) composed some of the most famous odes to the South, such as "Oh, Susanna," "My Old Kentucky Home," and "The Old Folks at Home" from a preexisting, antebellum set of bucolic images. Many were written before he ever ventured below the Mason Dixon line and before the first shot was fired in the Civil War. Likewise, Foster's contemporary, Daniel Emmett, a native of rural Ohio, wrote "Dixie" in 1859 while performing in a New York minstrel show. In these primordial examples of American popular song, the South was the land of cotton presided over by benevolent white folks back home. However softened by sentimentality, a backward and downward gaze characterized the singer's perspective. More importantly, the songs achieved their popularity before radio and the phonograph associated particular songs with particular singers. These bestsellers often sold best as sheet music for home performances. In order to hear the song, purchasers had to speak the music for themselves. In contrast, what commercial country music did was present Southerners to the mainstream; their music was then purchased as a record to be pondered, but not performed, by the purchaser. In other words, radio and records put Southerners on display. Whereas Yankees once may well have sung words such as "still longing for the old plantation, far from the old folks at home" in their own parlors, they now had progressed into the dream houses of modernity (never mind how segregated the suburbs). Now Southerners spoke music while others listened. In turn, the Southerners who retained the label "country" never completely submerged themselves in the mainstream. Instead, they seem to emerge eternally afresh from the swamps and mountains of the South. Thus, country music, whether on record, in a novel, or on the screen, is now firmly associated with the South, and it can be consistently used to freeze the sunny South in its old ways, keeping it down and out of the mainstream.

While Southern imagery in popular song predates the Civil War, the history of country music as Southern music can conveniently be started in 1927; how it came to be associated with the South is a story I will tell in the historically convenient (albeit extremely truncated) form of a hit parade. This format will underscore how country music speaks Southern, although I cannot begin to introduce every important speaker. Instead, I focus on songs, singers, and certain recurring connections that strongly articulate the Southern theme, especially bluegrass, but also rockabilly and Southern rock. Although the music has never been formally called "Southern Music," it easily could have been. In fact, the music industry first called it folk or "hillbilly" when *Billboard* began to publish sales charts in 1944; it adopted the term "country and western" in 1949. In 1962 it dropped the term "western" from its country hits listings. But, while it lasted, the West was where enterprising young men such as Ohioan Leonard Slye (aka Roy Rogers) and Gene Autry went while hillbillies stayed back home. Hollywood was the West in country and western; the country is Dixie. As Jimmie Rodgers sang in his "Blue Yodel No. 1," it's "T for Texas, T for Tennessee."

1925: The Grand Ole Opry

In the early 1920s many radio stations featured rural music, including WLS in Chicago's *National Barn Dance*. In 1925, Nashville's WSM hired George Hay, from WLS, as station director. At the end of the year, the station announced a Saturday night program devoted to "old familiar tunes." The program was not known as *The Grand Ole Opry* until 1927. From the start, though, Hay cultivated a hillbilly image for the show by creating backwoodsy names and nicknames for the performers (Dr. Bate and his Possum Hunters, for example) and encouraging them to dress in gingham and overalls instead of the Sunday best most originally chose to dignify their public appearances. In 1927 the station became an NBC affiliate and acquired enough airpower to broadcast over about half of the country. The Barn Dance program then aired immediately after one of the programs NBC provided – Dr. Walter Damrosch's *Musical Appreciation Hour*. One night Hay pointedly contrasted the two programs by speaking Southern, noting that "for the past hour we have been listening to music taken largely from grand opera, but from now on we will present 'The Grand Ole Opry'."

1927: The Bristol Sessions

While the Opry gets credit for putting country music on the radio, Midwest-born talent scout Ralph Peer put it on record when he paid a visit to Bristol, a town straddling the Tennessee and Virginia state lines. He hoped to find artists for Victor Talking Machine Company's "Old-Time Melodies of the Sunny South" division. Through previous experience, he knew that he could make money with this style of music. In Atlanta in 1923 he had recorded what many believe to be the first country record, Fiddlin' John Carson's twin sides, "The Little Old Log Cabin in the Lane" and "The Old Hen Cackled and the Rooster's Going to Crow." Although Peer thought Carson's singing was "pluperfect awful," the record sold well. He also pioneered blues recording, inventing the term "race records" to describe the music of his black artists; implicit in the "Sunny South" rubric was some notion of white music, even though the previous century's creation of old-time Southern melodies often implied a black, or blackface, performer. Likewise, many country musicians have readily acknowledged black mentors and role models, and music historians have thoroughly documented the interrelationship between the blues and country, the imaginary distinction saying as much about country music as the genealogical facts. Similarly, Peer's temporal adjectives created another significant paradox: popular music thrives on novelty, no matter how superficial; now Peer wanted to use familiarity as a novelty. The long lost could serve as well as the newly contrived – in fact, Peer preferred the latter since he could copyright it. Luckily, on this visit, he discovered both the "mother" of country music, Maybelle Carter (who formed a trio with A. P. Carter, her brother-in law, and his wife, Sara, who was also a cousin to Maybelle), and its "father," Jimmie Rodgers, a railroad worker from Meridian, Mississippi. Mother, as usual, represented long-lost home, family, tradition. Daddy, though, was a rambling man plunging into the modern world with its attendant pleasures and shocks.

As Curtis Ellison (1995: 34ff.) has noted, Rodgers made the mold for the country star: a wildly popular loser publicly suffering from all sorts of social ills and personal pain. His extensive touring put him in constant contact with his audience; in his interaction with them, he created the impression that he was a criminal constantly finding himself "In the Jailhouse" or a homesick drifter "Waiting for a Train." Although his stardom physically separated him from the South, he longed to return to "Daddy and Home," "My Little Old Home Down in New Orleans," or "The Dear Old Sunny South by the Sea" (the lyrics of this song specify that home was a "shack"). Rodgers died of tuberculosis in 1933, when he was only 36 years old, thereby giving the supreme demonstration of how intensely he suffered from the ills he sang about. In fact, the sound he cultivated – a strained falsetto known as his "blue yodel" and his pioneering use of the steel guitar – were deliberately fashioned to evoke misery.

Like Rodgers, the Carter family portrayed a world of Southern misery. But while Rodgers always played to his audience, the Carters seemed to be singing from the home rather than the stage. They never sang songs that were currently popular, but instead reworked old ones and created new ones that sounded old. A. P. "found" their songs as he rambled about the mountains, reworking traditional melodies or Victorian sheet music. Like Jefferson's ideally independent Virginia yeoman, the Carters seemed not to need the music industry. But in fact they could live off neither the land "In the Shadow of Clinch Mountain" (their Virginia home) nor their performing income. A. P. held factory jobs in Detroit; Maybelle and her husband moved about while he worked as a railroad clerk. Sara and A. P. quietly divorced in 1933. Nevertheless, they always presented themselves as a family peacefully settled in the mountains even as they regularly sing of lives disrupted by poverty and domestic strife. They praise "My Dixie Darling," or "The Green Fields of Virginia," or "My Home in Tennessee." Most often, though, their songs either impersonally describe catastrophe or admonish against succumbing to it. Rodgers bemoaned the loss of "Daddy and Home," while the Carters sang about the difficulty of holding on to these comforts. "Hold Fast to the Right" (1937), for example, imagines a young man, in need of employment, leaving home and facing whirling eddies of temptation; the values acquired from "mother at home" offer a life preserver to grasp, although the lyrics also imply that maintaining a grip on them will test the young man's strength. Their theme song, "Keep on the Sunny Side" (1927–8), with its imperative mode, encourages cheer precisely because truly experiencing it is rare. The first words of the song note "there's a dark and a troubled side of life" which listeners *will* encounter; the "sunny side" is offered only for viewing. For true optimism, compare the ease conveyed by the words of Broadway lyricist Dorothy Fields' nearly contemporaneous "On The Sunny Side of the Street" (1930): to abandon your troubles, "you just direct your feet" there. In the Carter's cosmology, the place with "No Depression" is heaven, not here.

Nevertheless, the Carters did not sing ecstatically about salvation. "Can the Circle Be Unbroken," yet another Carter signature song, describes children mourning their mother's death. It again notes that "there's a better home awaiting in the sky," although the questioning title seems to doubt even that. The song's most striking image, too, offers little comfort. Rather than seeking ritual closure, the singer begs the undertaker to move slowly. The bereaved family wants to keep the corpse. The unbroken circle amounts to keeping company with this deathly image. This desolation has proven the most enduring theme of the Carters. Although the Carter Family disbanded in 1943, Maybelle and her daughters performed as the Carter Sisters and Mother Maybelle for many years. After daughter June married Johnny Cash, the family tradition of enduring sorrow and loss gathered even more strength. The family appeared regularly on Cash's 1960s network television show and toured with him through the 1990s.

Compared to the glittering sophistication proposed by 1930s Hollywood or the gleaming abundance unfolding during the mid-century folk revival – the periods of the Carters' greatest popularity – the Carters offer little reinforcement for American dreams. Although they may have been innovators, their style bespeaks genteel impoverishment. Maybelle Carter introduced the twanging, percussive guitar to country music. To put it simply, she used her thumb to pick the melody on the bass strings while her fingers rang harmonic rhythm on the higher strings. Sara's vocal style reinforced this sedate and self-sufficient elegance. They unwaveringly announce surrender to constant sorrow. The sorrow, in fact, sounded like a force rather than a fate. It had nothing to do with their personalities or choices in life. In many of the songs, such as "Dixie Darling," Sara takes the role of a lovesick man; in others, such as "Single Girl, Married Girl," she bemoans the fate of women in general. Rodgers, the wandering "singing brakeman," suffered much more spectacularly and personally for his rambling. He demonstrates with every tuberculosis-strangled breath how disastrous the loosened grip could be. Rodgers, like many country singers after him, came to stardom by fleeing the embattled territory that the Carters portrayed. He left the South, but the flight took all he had. He could only dream of daddy and home; the Carters pretended to be living the dream – such as it was. Rodgers was the troubadour and star; the Carters were the bedrock. In both cases, though, the music made the South and sorrow into a resounding chord. In *The Devil's Dream* (1992), Lee Smith's novel loosely based on the Carter Family (and dedicated to "all the real country artists"), one of the artists at the Bristol sessions begins to cry. She senses that making her sorrow public will only intensify it: "it seems to her that they have just given up something precious by singing these songs here to these strangers, and she feels a sudden terrible sense of loss.". In other words, the singer of the songs of the sunny South paid the price of progress. Others looked back and down with pleasure, safely ensconced in the twentieth and twenty-first centuries.

1945: Bill Monroe Invents Bluegrass Music

Kentuckian Bill Monroe played on the Grand Ole Opry from 1939, but his distinctive sound dates from 1945, the year Earl Scruggs, an extraordinary banjoist, joined Monroe's string band, the Bluegrass Boys. Before Scruggs, the banjo, whether picked by an African-American minstrel or a hayseed like the Opry's Uncle Dave Macon, had signified comic minstrelsy. In Monroe's band, though, Scruggs's banjo energized what would have been otherwise simply old songs. Like Maybelle Carter, one of his idols, Scruggs created a rhythmic technique that allowed him to play both melody and harmony (Dawidoff 1997: 117). He also played stunningly fast, which made him perfect for the Bluegrass Boys. As Robert Cantwell notes in his brilliant and loving book on the subject, "bluegrass was the method which Bill Monroe designed to play old-time music in the modern world" (Cantwell 1984: 68). In particular, though, Monroe designed it to play on the Opry. The "breakdown," the musical structure which spotlights each instrument, works perfectly in the one-microphone format of a radio broadcast; likewise, the "high lonesome" sound of Monroe's keening voice, combined with the tightness and striking speed of his ensemble, sharply distinguished Monroe from the mid-century Opry cast. His ethos, too, set him apart. He performed with "an absolute seriousness," which, Cantwell observes, "defied the show's comic conventions" (76). The seriousness, though, was novelty in Ralph Peer's sense of the word; it masqueraded as the old, and it not only brought recognition to Monroe's great gifts, it also reinvigorated the solemnity of the Carters' Southern sadness.

1952: "Honky-tonk Blues," Hank Williams

The "Honky-tonk Blues" was on Hank Williams's mind from the start of his chart career (1947's "Move It on Over"). He recorded it several times before releasing the 1952 hit version. In this song, the honky-tonk, a bar where country music plays, becomes a compulsive enactment of failure. The singer says he left his "home down on the rural route" only to find life worse in the city. For solace, he goes into "*every* honky-tonk in town" – even though he knows this compulsion only makes him feel worse. To cure these blues (he says) he needs to go back to the farm, where, evidently, there would be no need for honky-tonk music. But the honky-tonk differs very little from the rustic home once country music and the sunny South become inseparable. For his return, he says, he'll "tuck my worries underneath my arm." He's doing a dance routine (he's going to "scat" back to the farm) and his troubles are a prop. He is like Jimmie Rodgers, a professional exile demonstrating how simultaneously impossible it is to leave the South *and* find a home outside of it. Like Jimmie Rodgers, Williams appeared to pay the ultimate price for this public suffering: he died, at the age of 29, en route to a performance.

1956: "Dixie Fried," Carl Perkins

The term "rockabilly" is a coinage blending rock and roll with "hillbilly," and Craig Morrison, in his definition of the term, lists "Southern origin" as an essential quality. He also notes that several of the key figures associated with the music considered the word a slur (Morrison 1996: 1–4). In fact, several rockabilly classics achieved high spots on the country charts, including Carl Perkins's celebrated "Blue Suede Shoes" and "Dixie Fried." That song, in particular, links the new sound to the South. But while the music sounds electrically energetic, like youth itself, the lyrics tell of joy becoming pain. The singer, the life of the party, gets drunk and violent, and the police, ever in the role of higher power in our depictions of the South, haul him off to jail. Incarceration, rather than jubilation, ultimately defines being dixie fried. The most hopeful sentiment expressed is a refusal to submit. While the narrator remains in prison, he urges his audience to "rave on." Just keep dancing to the music. Naturally, after the rockabilly rush, Perkins found a home touring with Johnny Cash and the remaining members of the Carter clan.

1962: "The Ballad of Jed Clampett," Lester Flatt and Earl Scruggs

The postwar boom years celebrated upward mobility. Success required leaving that home down on the rural route. In the 1960s, what American, whether ensconced in a Park Avenue apartment or huddled in a home on the prairie, had not heard the story of a man named Jed? Three weeks into its 1962 debut season, *The Beverly Hillbillies* topped the Nielsen ratings (Cox 1993: 15). In that era of three networks, often over 50 percent of the television sets in America were tuned to *The Beverly Hillbillies*. These poor mountaineers were not so much congratulated for their improbable Ozark oil strike as they were told that they ought to be in California, specifically, Beverly Hills. Like Jimmie Rodgers and Hank Williams, though, they never completely crossed over the Mason Dixon line. The South stayed with them, and the song that introduced this show can be continually rewritten to tell the story of Southern ne'er do wells; I have heard stories of men named Jim Baker or Bill Clinton. No matter that Flatt and Scruggs, who had left Bill Monroe's band in 1948, were masters of bluegrass, a twentieth-century innovation. The story told in sound and television screen said that hillbillies could not live in the modern world. (Occasionally, the story lines even implied that they were too good for that world.) In 1971 CBS, hoping to lose its rustic image, canceled the popular program along with several other Southern-themed comedies. The story of the man named Jed, though, still circulates daily in syndication.

1972: *Will the Circle Be Unbroken*, Nitty Gritty Dirt Band

The folk song revival of the late 1950s and early 1960s brought the Carter family back into the public ear. Although A. P. died in 1960, and Sara remained in retirement, Maybelle played on stages all over the United States – the 1963 Newport Folk Festival, for example. Needless to say, she remained a public Southerner. In 1966 Nashville's industry newspaper, the now-defunct *Music City News*, bestowed the title of "mother" of country music on Maybelle. Bill Monroe and Flatt and Scruggs, too, played before enthusiastic folk audiences, and Scruggs, in particular, was drawn to the new sounds of the day, such as Bob Dylan's brand of electrified folk. In fact, his desire to innovate forced Scruggs and Flatt to dissolve their partnership in 1969. Scruggs went on to form the Earl Scruggs Revue with his longhaired, rock-loving sons. After John McEuen, of the California-based Nitty Gritty Dirt Band, heard the Revue in concert, he impulsively asked Scruggs to record an album with the Dirt Band, whose music heretofore had been aimed at the pop charts. Scruggs immediately agreed and recruited many of his Nashville colleagues to join the project (Maybelle Carter, Roy Acuff, Vassar Clemens, Merle Travis, Doc Watson et al.). In the hands of the Dirt Band, the country legends were clearly marked as Southerners. A photograph of Robert E. Lee in a circular frame anchors the cover of the widely acclaimed album, with Confederate and Union (American) flags on either side of the frame. The Confederate side lists the country stars featured on the album, while the side with the victor's flag lists the individuals comprising the Nitty Gritty Dirt Band. (And the group's next album drove the point home by taking the title *Stars and Stripes Forever*). The caption goes on to answer the title's question in the negative: *Will the Circle Be Unbroken?* No, because "music forms a new circle." Even so, there was little new music – but the recreated classics did introduce many baby boomers to early country music. The opening cut – former Bluegrass Boy Jimmy Martin singing the "Grand Ol' Opry Song" – puts listeners firmly "*down* in Nashville," followed by a funereal "Keep on the Sunny Side," featuring a plodding demonstration of Mother Maybelle's picking technique. The interviews with Maybelle and the other stars further authenticate the enterprise, and reverential press coverage, like Chet Flippo's *Rolling Stone* feature, lent it importance. The rousing whole-cast version of the title song seems to demonstrate the unity of country and rock, but in the end, even the music reinforces the Civil War-themed cover photo. "Will the Circle Be Unbroken" is *not* the last song on the record. The closing statement, an instrumental version of Joni Mitchell's "Both Sides Now," emphasizes instead the duality of the enterprise.

Plate 5 *Will the Circle be Unbroken* album cover.

The *Circle* album made the Californian Dirt Band into serious artists and spokesmen for the country tradition, the Ralph Peers of the second half of the twentieth
century. In particular, they seem to have turned the Carter song "Will the Circle Be
Unbroken" into a hymn to country music tradition. They spent most of the 1980s on
the country charts; in 1989 they recorded a sequel, *Circle II*. Some of the country
guests from the first album, such as Roy Acuff, Jimmy Martin, and Earl Scruggs,
returned, but the reprise also included some of the biggest names in 1960s rock, such
as Chris Hillman and Roger McGuinn of the Byrds, Levon Helm of The Band, and
former Eagle Bernie Leadon. It was dedicated to Mother Maybelle, who died in 1978.
Her photograph replaces Robert E Lee in the circular frame featured on the cover art;
this time the caption expresses absolute certainty about the enterprise: "and the circle
will continue." Johnny Cash, reigning paterfamilias of the Carters, introduces the
album with yet another tune about the link between the living and the dead, "Life's
Railway to Heaven," a traditional number previously recorded by Roy Acuff, Patsy
Cline, and Bill Monroe. Maybelle's daughters sing harmony, and his daughter,

Roseanne Cash, appears later on the album. In some studio banter included on the album, Emmylou Harris (simultaneously a country traditionalist and country rock pioneer) praises the cast for returning "the living room" to the music, but they also further personify the deathly presence created by the Carters: in fact, they turn Maybelle into that lingering corpse. As in the first album, the penultimate cut is an all-cast version of the title song, but with a new verse further solidifying the Dirt Band as ringmasters in the circular relations between North and South:

> We sang the songs of childhood
> hymns of faith that made us strong
> ones that Mother Maybelle taught us
> and the angels sing along.

In a 2001 interview in *Country Music Magazine*, the Dirt Band says they are considering a *Circle III* album, but for now, Nashville's Country Music Hall of Fame most visibly keeps the circle rolling. Originally established in 1961, the museum had been in a music row building since 1967; in 2001 it moved to a new location in downtown Nashville, a veritable $37 million embodiment of the Carter tune and the persistence of the old Southern sound. A vast rotunda, lit by churchy clerestory windows, forms what the museum itself (on its website) calls the "Hall of Fame proper"; bronzed images of Hall of Fame members adorn the walls; a copy of WSM's broadcasting tower plunges from the dome of the ceiling to the center of the floor. A fresco serving as a vast circular windowsill is inscribed in plain upper case: Will the Circle be Unbroken. Once visitors leave the building, the museum's publicists claim, they "return to a new kind of town square, *now less a center of commerce and government* and more a seat of Southern culture. Looking back at the Country Music Hall of Fame's dramatically lighted rotunda . . . huge slabs of crab orchard stone adorning the circumference may be recognized as the notes to 'Will the Circle Be Unbroken'" (emphasis mine). They are still talking music down there, not doing business or exercising power (is that Northern culture?), and now they have written it in stone.

1974: "Sweet Home Alabama," Lynyrd Skynyrd

Rock and roll, like country music, was born in the South, but rock and roll quickly rose above its raising. It became "rock" without the fluidity of roll, firmly ensconced among the forms of popular culture taken seriously. We suddenly had rock critics, pronouncing on what was worth listening to, from such non-country and western locales as San Francisco's *Rolling Stone* and Manhattan's *The Village Voice*. While Southern music historian Bill Malone argues rock was a national phenomenon flattening out regional differences among youth (Malone 1979: 106–7), it may be more accurate to say that rock rendered all of its listeners Californian. California, after all, was the place you ought to be. By then, to be Southern, rock had to drape itself in a Confederate flag. When that happened, it was in response to Neil Young's slurs on a South that was banished with the emancipation proclamation but that had heretofore been romanticized in popular song: the steamy, swampy South of antebellum white privilege. "I heard screaming and bullwhips cracking," he sang in "Southern Man" (1970); his "Alabama" (1971) condescendingly dreamed of making friends with George Wallace's state. The north-Florida based Lynyrd Skynyrd, supposedly avid fans of Canadian-born, California-based Young, nevertheless defended Alabama with Southern chivalry and swagger. In particular, they seemed to separate racist politics from the place. "In Birmingham *they* love the governor (boo! boo! boo)"; the verse concludes that those who feel otherwise can love their home and claim their Southern identity with a clear conscience. "Sweet Home Alabama" has since been incorporated into the country repertoire; the Charlie Daniels Band covered it, and on *Skynyrd Friends* (2000), a tribute album featuring many country artists, Alabama, the bestselling country group of all time, included their version. Hank Williams, Jr. made his career loudly proclaiming the brotherhood of Southern rock and country, particularly in his "If the South Would Have Won" (1988), a fantasy in which he imagines himself becoming president and declaring the day Skynyrd leader Ronnie Van Zant died a national holiday of the Southern states. Even in the imperative mode, then, he would be speaking of defeat.

1990: *No Depression*, Uncle Tupelo

It took adolescents a surprisingly long time to capitalize on the countercultural potential of country music. Finally, the St. Louis-based yet obviously Southern-influenced Uncle Tupelo expressed their post-punk angst with a compelling combination of the sangfroid of the Carter Family and the bourgeois-shocking antics of Jimmie Rodgers and his descendants. The album's title cut remakes the Carter tune, although it does not change the theme; both versions depict the afterlife as an escape from the economic and psychological hardship of the Great Depression (whether it takes place in the 1930s or the late twentieth century). The song "Flatness," composed by band leaders Jeff Tweedy and Jay Farrar, about the miseries (and self-pity) of alcoholism, alludes to the Carter's theme song, "Keep on the Sunny Side": "there's darkness in this life, but the brighter side we also may view." While the album was released by Rockpile, an independent label, its influence was enormous. In September 1995 *No Depression*, a Seattle-based journal devoted to covering "Alternative Country," began publication. In the journal's website, editors Grant Alden and Peter Blackstock explain that their title "refers to the 1930s Carter Family song . . . the 1990s Uncle Tupelo album . . . and an internet discussion board called No Depression/Alternative Country." (While not so clearly an homage, *The Grindstone*, started in June of 1995, and devoted to covering music that's "too cool for radio," appears to get its name from "Grindstone," another Tweedy/Farrar song on Uncle Tupelo's 1992 album, *March*

16–22, 1992.) While Blackstock and Alden both eventually moved south, their Southernness, like that of Uncle Tupelo and many other alternative country musicians, seems entirely metaphorical. Alden moved to Nashville "to learn something about country's past, and maybe to figure out how its present got so screwed up" (Alden 1997: 2); Nashville, to him, represents modern America. He, the musicians featured in *No Depression*, and its readers "have all chosen paths away from the siren calls of mainstream society" (Alden 2001: 2). They seem to prefer the old times: the magazine's typeface, unglossy paper, and grainy black and white photography hark back to the depression, and a good portion of each issue is devoted to older (even dead) country musicians and reissued albums.

Journalist Nicholas Dawidoff's *In the Country of Country* (1997) provides another example of the *No Depression* South. Dawidoff visited many country artists in their hometowns; to his credit, he conducted wonderful interviews with most of them. Yet his literary perspective belongs to the tourist, looking back and down on a place where he would not want to live, and that he does not imagine can change. He claims that Ralph Stanley's Appalachian home "is *stuck* in the Depression" (89). He calls his prologue "The Spirit of Jimmie Rodgers" and his epilogue "No Depression." But the past and present look about the same: archival photos of a dusty drab South mix with contemporary ones in similarly grim black and white. From Rodgers to Uncle Tupelo, the essential nature of the music varies little. Dawidoff characterizes it as "songs... about common people everywhere, for common people everywhere" (13); as much as he admires it, he also notes that it "set me down among people who might be said to have nothing to do with my own existence" (6).

2000: *O Brother, Where Art Thou?*

The Coen brothers' film *O Brother, Where Art Thou?* (2000), set in 1937 rural Mississippi, seems to imagine the Sahara of the Bozart blooming. As a man-made flood washes over his homestead, Everett Ulysses McGill, the film's consistently wrongheaded hero, jubilantly proclaims "the South is gonna change... Yessir, a veritable age of reason – like the one they had in France." In other words, he envisions his defeated culture being washed into the mainstream, becoming indistinguishable from the North. Southerners, then, would speak reason, not music. The narrative itself, though, does not support such blissful thinking. The Coen brothers claimed to be retelling Homer's *Odyssey*, but their Ulysses is a small-time con man whose Penelope does not faithfully wait for him; indeed she divorces him, tells their daughters that he died in a railroad accident, and sets out to marry a "bona fide" suitor – Vernon Waldrip, campaign manager for Homer Stokes, the reform party gubernatorial candidate. The allusion to *Sullivan's Travels*, Preston Sturges's 1941 comedy about a Hollywood director who wants to redeem himself from the upbeat studio formulae that had made him rich, also indicates that Ulysses has it wrong. Sullivan sets out on his own odyssey in order to make a socially conscious film. The

"O Brother" part of the title, though, tells us to roll our eyes at such dreaming, and the Coens' borrowing reinforces that interpretation. Sullivan's travels through the South teach him that people, particularly Southern reprobates, prefer the easy fantasies of film. Sullivan ends up right back where he started – giving his audience something to laugh at. It follows, then, that these hopeful Southerners will remain culturally dry and dusty.

"Old-timey" music, Ralph Peer's grail, weaves the fantasies in the Coens' film. While Hollywood comedy made Sullivan rich, Everett and his fellows will be unwitting country music stars. In the meantime, Everett promises to lead his two chain-gang mates to $1.2 million from an armored car heist he had supposedly hidden at his home in Ithaca, Mississippi's Arktabutta Valley. He gives their quest urgency by noting that the TVA will soon flood the territory (he really just needs their help so he can see his wife before she marries). Their first adventure after their escape, though, suggests the scheming Everett has no control over his destiny. They meet a blind black man with the gift of prophecy: "you will find a fortune," he assures them, "though it will not be the fortune you seek." Their next encounter with an African-American leads them to that fortune. After stealing a car, they pick up Tommy Johnson as he hitches a ride "out in the middle of nowhere." He tells them that he came to that particular crossroads so he could sell his soul to the devil in exchange for supernatural guitar picking skills (an allusion to the legend of bluesman Robert Johnson). Most interestingly, the devil turns out to be a stereotypical Southern sheriff: "white . . . with mirrors for eyes . . . an' allus travels with a mean old hound." Indeed, a Sheriff Cooley, wearing mirrored sunglasses even at night, with a bloodhound by his side, pursues the men throughout the film. (Although he recalls No Eyes, the nemesis of Cool Hand Luke, in the 1967 film, the relentless chain-gang boss had nothing to do with the musical talent of the banjo-strumming, country singing small-time Georgia criminal.) Tommy plans next to visit a radio station in Tishamingo where he has heard the owner will "pay folks money to sing into a can." Sensing a quick buck, Everett seizes upon the scheme. At the station he introduces himself as Jordan Rivers with his group the Soggy Bottom Boys, promising "songs of salvation to salve the soul." Throughout the film, Everett mocks Southern religiosity, and the bathroom humor of the Soggy Bottom Boys singing into cans further expresses that scorn. Nevertheless, Everett is about to sell his soul; after that, he will be bogged into that particular soggy bottom from that moment on. The quartet easily and suddenly renders an excellent performance of "Man of Constant Sorrow" before they head back on the lam. Unbeknownst to them, the record becomes a huge hit. It appears that country music stardom, a gift from the devil (as it is in Lee Smith's *The Devil's Dream*), will make their treasure.

The encounter with the unnamed record producer introduces race as a theme of both the film and its music. He makes explicit the racial distinction that Ralph Peer only implied, at the same time that he confirms its imaginary nature. After Everett tells him that they are black with the exception of their guitarist, he tells the Soggy Bottom Boys that he wants "ol' timey material," *not* "Negro songs." Everett then reverses the group's racial composition, and since the producer is blind, he cannot verify the facts. Most interestingly, his ears cannot make the distinction, either, but the film continues to link the sound with whiteness. Just before the group's next performance, they rescue Tommy from a Ku Klux Klan lynching. Along with the expected robes and flaming cross, the screenplay characterizes the racists by specifying that they chant "in a high hillbilly wail." While the Grand Wizard, Homer Stokes, rants about protecting "our hallowed culture 'n' heritage," the three convicts disrupt the ceremony by ambushing the color guard, donning their robes, somehow acquiring blackface makeup, and parading the Confederate flag. With all stunned eyes upon them, they fling the flag into the crowd. When they lower the burning cross, the crowd flees. The chaos enables the quartet to rush to Homer Stokes's campaign banquet where they regale the crowd with their music. Stokes, recognizing them from the Klan meeting, denounces them as "miscegenated," but the crowd boos him. His rival, incumbent Governor O'Daniel, seizing on the opportunity to work the room, pardons the Soggy Bottom Boys and promises to use them as his "brain trust" once he is reelected. To further the theme of reconciliation, Everett's wife, who is in attendance, realizes that her ex will be able to support the family as a Soggy Bottom Boy, so she agrees to have him back — as long as he retrieves her wedding ring from the soon-to-be-flooded homestead.

But the movie does not end on this comedic note of reconciliation. Pappy O'Daniel's support for integration is clearly opportunistic, and his power to effect change seems limited. When the Soggy Bottom Boys visit Everett's cabin the next day, they encounter once more the devilish sheriff who has prepared nooses for them; since he considers himself a higher authority than the governor, he pays no heed to their pardon. Only the rushing waters save them, but the wedding ring ends up at the bottom of the new lake. The movie closes with Penelope again rejecting Everett, while his daughters and the blind prophet sing "Angel Band," a plea to be carried off to an "immortal home." The happy ending is postponed, and in any case will be reserved for the saved. Everett, as yet unsaved, has only the devil's music for the future. That circle, we have been repeatedly told, remains unbroken.

Like me, the Coens claim to love the music, and give it such a central place in the film that in the liner notes to the soundtrack, they claim to have "almost" made a musical. What is most remarkable, though, is the way that the wildly popular country music soundtrack to the film puts the South in its place: the backwater in which it started. The Soggy Bottom Boys' theme song, "Man of Constant Sorrow," reprises throughout the film, and this song truly characterizes McGill's life and his drowned homestead. In an ecstatic review of the film (printed in the soundtrack's liner notes), Robert K. Oerman praises the music, noting that

> it all works brilliantly, both within the context of the film and outside as a listening experience . . . It speaks as vividly to us today as it did to listeners generations ago.

In fact, the soundtrack skillfully blends performances specifically created for the film with archival recordings going as far back as 1928. The circle, such as it is, is a cycle more than a symbol of unity. It remains unbroken because the South, as represented in this strain of country music, remains the land of old times. The rest of us celebrate progress, whether it be working on the railroad or surfing the worldwide web, but no matter how torrential the mainstream, McGill's homeland cannot be cleansed of sorrow and defeat. One of the film's easiest ironies is our belief that the Enlightenment he hopes for never came. We get that message because what we call true country music, or pure country, or old-time country speaks it endlessly, and that, evidently, is why we cherish it.

The sales success of the soundtrack shows just how deeply we cherish it, and just how strongly the music reinforces our sense of the South. Without any significant radio airplay, typically a necessary condition for significant sales figures, the soundtrack topped *Billboard's* country sales charts for nine weeks in 2001. *Oxford American* columnist Hal Crowther's gushing reaction to this anomaly unabashedly announces the cultural psychology at work. The soundtrack, he says, "is not a mere anthology of vintage Southern music but a genuine piece of the rock: the bedrock, the Rock of Ages where we secretly long to cling." This retrogression becomes particularly clear in *Down from the Mountain*, the 2001 film *about* the soundtrack. In May 2000 the soundtrack musicians (including alternative country favorites Emmylou Harris and Gillian Welch) performed music from the yet to be released *O Brother* in a benefit concert for the new Country Music Hall of Fame; to further emphasize the connection to country music tradition, it took place at Ryman Auditorium, a former church, Confederate monument, and home of the Opry between 1943 and 1974. The Coens hired documentarian D. A. Pennebaker to film the rehearsals and performance. The title provides a fit answer to the first film's question: "O Brother, Where Art Thou?" The film's long opening, set to Ralph Stanley singing "Man of Constant Sorrow," shows the bluegrass legend's trip *down* from his Clinch Mountain home (filmed in black and white) into Nashville's limo-laden, skyscraper-filled streets (filmed in neon-drenched color). So insistent is the director on making this point that he also spells it out: the opening frame, black background with white lettering, reads "Ralph Stanley came down from the mountain to Nashville." The conceit of country meets city seems absurd, since Stanley had been making the trip since he began performing in the late 1940s, but the point is familiar: the descent from the mountain into the big city can happen over and over again. Those who undertake the journey, though, will suffer from the honky-tonk blues until they die. As in *O Brother, Where Art Thou?*, only death brings happiness; this film ends with two songs about heavenly bliss: "Angel Band" again and "I'll Fly Away."

My point in this essay has been neither to criticize country music nor Southerners (although I do hear racism, sexism, and mindless provinciality in some songs), but instead to show how the two have entered into a cultural dynamic that encourages us to hear the music as a homely monument to an eternally old South. The forces at play in this dynamic are as large as American history and geography itself, but journalist Tony Horwitz provides an excellent summary of them. After traveling through the 1990s South speaking to Civil War enthusiasts, he concludes:

The issues at stake in the Civil War – race in particular – remain raw and unresolved, as did the broad question the conflict posed: Would America remain one nation? . . . The whole notion of a common people united by common principles – even a common language – seemed more open to question than at any period in my lifetime. (Horwitz 1998: 386)

In this essay, I have described how country music speaks Southern as opposed to that ideal (but in reality, Northern) common language. Certainly, there are other things to hear; I have said very little about the compelling talent of nearly every musician mentioned here, but you can take it from me that these musicians deserve their fame. More persuasive still, put on a record and open your ears.

REFERENCES AND FURTHER READING

Alden, Grant (1997) "Hello Stranger," *No Depression* (May/June): 2.

Alden, Grant (2001) "Hello Stranger," *No Depression* (January/February): 2

Bargainnier, Earl F. (1977) "Tin Pan Alley and Dixie: The South in Popular Song," *Mississippi Quarterly*, 30, 4: 527–64.

Blount, Roy, Jr. (1980) *Crackers*. New York: Knopf.

Cantwell, Robert (1984) *Bluegrass Breakdown: The Making of the Old Southern Sound*. Urbana: University of Illinois Press.

Coen, Ethan and Coen, Joel (2000) *O Brother, Where Art Thou?* London: Faber and Faber.

Cox, Stephen (1993) *The Beverly Hillbillies*. New York: Harper Collins.

Crowther, Hal (2000) "The *O Brother*hood," *Oxford American*, 5th Annual Music Issue: 15–17.

Dawidoff, Nicholas (1997) *In the Country of Country: People and Places in American Music*. New York: Pantheon Books.

Ellison, Curtis (1995) *Country Music Culture: From Hard Times to Heaven*. Jackson: University of Mississippi Press.

Goad, Jim (1997) *Redneck Manifesto: How Hillbillies, Hicks, and White Trash Became America's Scapegoats*. New York: Simon and Schuster.

Horwitz, Tony (1998) *Confederates in the Attic: Dispatches from the Unfinished Civil War*. New York: Random House.

Keel, Beverly (2001) "Connecting the Circle: Landmark Nitty Gritty Dirt Band Sessions Celebrate a Special Anniversary," *Country Music* (August/September): 102.

Malone, Bill C. (1985) *Country Music USA*, revd. edn. Austin: University of Texas Press.

Malone, Bill C. (1979). *Southern Music/American Music*. Lexington: University of Kentucky Press.

Malone, Bill C. (1993). *Singing Cowboys and Musical Mountaineers: Southern Culture and the Roots of Country Music*. Athens, GA: University of Georgia Press.

Morrison, Craig (1996) *Go Cat Go! Rockabilly Music and Its Makers*. Urbana: University of Illinois Press.

Oermann, Robert K. (2000) "The Music of *O Brother, Where Art Thou?* Comes to Life." Liner notes: *O Brother, Where Art Thou?* soundtrack. Universal City, CA: Mercury Records.

Peterson, Richard (1997) *Creating Country Music: Fabricating Authenticity*. Chicago: University of Chicago Press.

Reed, John Shelton (1993) *My Tears Spoiled My Aim and Other Reflections on Southern Culture*. Columbia: University of Missouri Press.

Smith, Lee (1992) *The Devil's Dream*. New York: Ballantine.

Temple, Jack Kirby (1995) *The Countercultural South.* Athens, GA: University of Georgia Press.
Wolfe, Charles K. (1999) *A Good-Natured Riot: The Birth of the Grand Ole Opry.* Nashville: Country Music Foundation and Vanderbilt University Press.
http://www.countrymusichalloffame.com/museum/
http://www.grindstonemagazine.com/mainset.html
http://www.nodepression.net/

13

The Civil Rights Debate

Richard H. King

That the civil rights movement in the South changed the legal-constitutional, political, and social landscape of the South and the nation is incontrovertible. That it was also a catalyst for far-reaching changes in the cultural and intellectual history of the region and the nation is a matter to which much less attention has been paid. If Charles Eagles's (2000) comprehensive essay on the historiography of the civil rights movement is any indication, historians have dealt overwhelmingly with the legal, political, and social issues raised by the movement and have left cultural and intellectual matters to someone, anyone, else. But that clearly is unsatisfactory. If we are to understand the history of the civil rights movement (or of the 1960s or of the South in the 1960s), then shifts in modes of consciousness and representation in values and beliefs must be addressed. For that, historians of the civil rights movement must begin to think harder about the relationship between cultural creation and political and social change. To the objection that such matters are properly the province of the specialist in literary, art, and music criticism or history, one can only respond that the "full" history of the civil rights movement is not being confronted if what is produced is confined to conventional political and social history.

In what follows I want to take up three historiographical issues involving the civil rights movement in whole or in part. One concerns the relationship between the civil rights movement and mainstream Southern (and American) politics from roughly 1945 to 1972. The second bears on the international dimensions of, and emerging global perspective in, the movement and its aftermath in the late 1960s. My third focus will directly deal with the civil rights movement as an intellectual and cultural movement. In taking up these three issues, I am not suggesting that there are no other issues worth debating in considering the civil rights movement. For instance, over the last decade or so, much has been made of the question: "When did the civil rights movement begin?" Implicit in the question is the assumption that its origins were surely prior to 1956 (the Montgomery Bus Boycott) or 1954 (*Brown vs. Board of Education*), with start-up points located in biracial attempts at union organizing during World War II or even the New Deal of the 1930s.

But though this is an interesting issue, I do not see it as crucial, since it involves a convention of naming. One way to distinguish matters here would be to see the civil rights movement precisely as a "movement." Using the term "movement" implies that a large number of black (and white) people in the South sought in a fairly sustained fashion over a specific period of time to destroy the Jim Crow system of segregation and disfranchisement triggered off by the 1954 Supreme Court decision and the Southern reaction to that decision beginning a couple of years later (Klarman 1994). On this view, the era of the civil rights movement would be located roughly between 1954 and Martin Luther King's assassination in 1968. After that year, there was no major civil rights legislation passed; the man who had become the symbolic, even real, leader of the movement had been assassinated; and the action organizations such as the Southern Christian Leadership Conference (SCLC), Student Non-Violent Coordinating Committee (SNCC), and the Congress of Racial Equality (CORE) entered a period of decline and/or shifted their ideological orientation toward black power.

This is not to say that there were no protests against segregation or for the vote or for better pay and working conditions for workers of both races before 1956. The labor movement in the South sponsored protests, strikes, and actions during and after World War II, which often involved a significant amount of interracial cooperation. Moreover, court cases having to do with civil rights and voting rights were constant presences in the legal system from Reconstruction on. Protest organizations such as the Urban League and the NAACP emerged in the early part of the twentieth century. Moreover, Vincent Harding (1981) has identified what he names a "Great Tradition" of African-American protest that traces back at least to the Declaration of Independence and comes back up through the first and greatest slave revolt in San Domingo, the abortive slave revolts in North America in the first three decades of the nineteenth century, the abolitionist and antislavery movements, and on through Reconstruction. My point here is that we should distinguish the civil rights *movement* from the longer-lived civil rights *struggle* and both of these from the tradition of historical memory and moral and political thought informing the struggle for freedom, equality, and justice. Without that tradition and absent the legal and political struggles before the 1950s, the civil rights movement could scarcely have come into existence. But that does not mean that everything that bears on the struggle for black freedom, equality, and justice is properly seen as part of the civil rights movement (Kuryla 2001).

There is a substantive matter of considerable importance in considering the effects of the civil rights movement on Southern and national politics and vice versa. To focus on such a question is to refocus matters on predominantly white mainstream political ideologies, movements, organizations, and issues, though, one hopes, from a more complex perspective than was the case in the beginning of civil rights historiography. Such a "mainstream" focus is no more important than understanding what Charles Payne (1995) has called the "movement culture" at the grassroots level. But without some notion of what was happening in and to mainstream politics – the upshot is a relatively happy story of the emergence of a new form of Southern politics in which race as an explicit issue had faded in importance – the successes and failures of the movement culture are hard to understand.

Specifically, one issue that needs more thinking through concerns the fate of American and Southern liberalism and radicalism after 1945. Though American liberalism exited the war with union membership at its peak and with a powerful New Deal legacy at its back, by 1950 it had been rocked back on its heels with Southern liberalism mirroring the downward trajectory of its national counterpart (Sullivan 1996; Egerton 1994; Bartley 1995). In five short years, the "popular front" liberalism of the left wing New Deal had all but collapsed. Why? One explanation has been to identify the "Cold War" in the widest sense of that term as the culprit. In this view, the Cold War political ethos of ideological conformity, the bitter disputes within organized labor over communist influence, and the disastrous 1948 Henry Wallace campaign, combined with the creation of government loyalty programs, the depredations of HUAC, and the sudden appearance on the scene of Senator Joseph McCarthy himself in 1950, all worked to radically limit the range or depth of progressive politics in post-1945 America. What replaced it, so this story goes, was "vital center," Cold War liberalism, which downplayed a critique of corporate America, was lukewarm on grassroots politics, and made anti-communism a litmus test of political acceptability, particularly in union matters. In such a climate, civil rights measures which might have followed on from the recommendations of President Truman's Civil Rights Commission ("To Secure These Rights") were largely stillborn. Indeed, recent studies have further reinforced the importance of anti-communism as a factor stifling radical impulses and grassroots activism, along with mainstream liberalism, before and during the civil rights era (Polsgrove 2001; Lewis 2003).

The postwar history of the American working class also suggests reasons for the decline of working-class and liberal militancy. In *The Cultural Front* (1996), Michael Denning suggests that, though the Great Migration brought millions of white and black Southerners to Northern urban and industrial centers, particularly after 1945, the composition of that workforce militated against advances in grassroots radicalism and popular support for radical politics. In the short run, then, the political culture of Southern working-class people come north failed to perpetuate the prewar political culture of left wing, popular front radicalism. Black working-class men and women had little experience with politics in general, since they had been largely excluded from the political process in the South, not to mention the wide cultural gap separating white and black Southerners from the immigrant and urban based political culture among Northern workers. Indeed, that sector of the population was itself being drained of left wing support by McCarthyism, growing affluence, and upward social mobility. Whatever the political resources of Southern black culture – and they turned out to be considerable just a few years hence (here Payne's "movement culture" is relevant) – they did not revitalize a working-class political culture in the North.

Nor were white Southern working-class men inclined toward political radicalism or even participation in unions, except as an expedient, rather than as a way of life. Southern white working-class culture was too individualistic and too obsessed with racial issues to provide much impetus for a renewed interracial social and economic liberalism in the North.

This then is one sort of explanation for the moderation of postwar American liberalism and its failure to take the lead in pushing for racial change as part of a comprehensive package of economic and social reform and political militancy. Though President Truman acted decisively in certain areas (e.g., the desegregation of the armed forces) and was committed rhetorically to changes in race relations, and Hubert Humphrey, then mayor of Minneapolis, had fought for a strong civil rights plank in the 1948 Democratic Convention platform, there was little sense of urgency in the Executive Branch, the Congress, or the country at large on racial matters. Even at that, Truman was reelected in 1948, despite losing 39 electoral votes to the States Rights Party (Dixiecrats), in retrospect an augury of things to come in the next two decades. Enough conservative Southern Democrats, along with moderate and liberal Southern Democrats, remained loyal to prevent a full-scale Southern secession from the Democratic Party. And African Americans in the South, but more importantly in the North and West, where many could vote for the first time, helped the Democrats retain the White House and Congress in 1948, while Henry Wallace and the Progressive Party failed to drain away as many votes from the Democrats as had been feared.

When the Republican Party captured the presidency and Congress in 1952 (albeit for only two years), the Democratic Party, willingly or not, moved inexorably toward the center. With the Congress again in Democratic hands in 1954, its leadership was in the hands of two Southerners – with Texas's Lyndon Johnson as Senate Majority Leader and Sam Rayburn as Speaker of the House. Significantly, it was under Johnson's leadership that the first Civil Rights measure since Reconstruction was passed in 1957 (with another in 1960). But many Northern liberals felt that Johnson had all but gutted the bill in trying to insure its passage and to placate his erstwhile Southern allies, such as Georgia's Richard Russell. In response to Montgomery in 1955–6 and Little Rock in 1957, and with the emergence of Massive Resistance, the White Citizens Councils, and a revived Klan across much of the Deep South, North Carolina, and Virginia, Southern liberal and moderate politicians were pulled – or fled – toward the Right. In general, they were afraid to take a leadership role in speaking out for compliance with the "law of the land." For most Southern liberals, it was the better part of valor to look to regional economic development as an answer to the race question rather than directly confronting it in the political arena. Once the rising economic tide had lifted all the boats, it was reasoned, political and civil equality would follow closely behind. By the early 1960s, white Southern liberalism had lost most of the initiative in the racial struggle that it ever possessed, almost all of the Southern delegation in Congress having signed the Southern Manifesto in 1956 (Chappell 1994, 2003). (Ironically, Tennessee's Estes Kefauver was more "liberal" on race in his campaign for the 1956 Democratic presidential nomination than was the national Democratic standard bearer and darling of Northern liberals, Adlai Stevenson of Illinois.) The larger point here is that race and radicalism were the two issues that drove American and Southern politics rightward in the first decade and a half after the end of World War II.

In this context the terms "moderate" and "moderation" have an interesting history and not just among elected officials. In *Blessed are the Peacemakers* (2001), Jonathan Bass explores the role that white moderates played in the most volatile of the civil rights campaigns: Birmingham, spring 1963. Taking the eight white clergymen, the type of men whom Martin Luther King implied in his "Letter from Birmingham Jail" were the real obstacles to racial justice, Bass shows just how difficult it was for white moderates, with the best will in the world, to work effectively for racial change without severing their ties to the (white) communities and institutions.

Aside from the various ways the eight men responded to events in the spring of 1963, and then later, Bass's book offers a sustained exposure to the mind of the Southern moderate/liberal. Indeed, by the early 1960s, Southern liberalism was all but synonymous with the moderate ideology of middle-class, professional, and business men and women. The older populist-oriented liberalism of Huey Long, Hugo Black, or even Jim Folsom was a thing of the past; not it, but the racialized politics of George Wallace, seemed the wave of the future. But the moderate ideology, or "mind-set," assumed, against most evidence, that there were more moderates than extremists in the South; and also tended to create a moral-political equivalence between white extremists such as the Klan and the White Citizens Councils and black protest efforts by the NAACP, not to mention Dr. King and SCLC or SNCC. The ideology of moderation assumed that change was best when it came gradually and under the direction of local people, not outside agitators. This in turn implied that civility was *the* prime political virtue and that any issue could, and should be, compromised. Ultimately, the moderate assumption was that the leaders of both sides were better placed than the people (i.e., mob rule) to handle such political matters. Where possible, disputes should be settled in the courts, not in the streets. The overall impression from Bass's book is that white Southern moderates were figures of genuine decency and good will but were also deeply naive about the nature of politics. They assumed that their idea of morality – an individual, face-to-face ethic of civility and compromise – was an adequate response to all possible moral and political dilemmas. But this turned out to be a serious mistake in a situation where it was not just a matter of adjusting interests but also of confirming identities, establishing self-respect, and creating a sense of moral and political personhood on both sides of the racial line. In such a situation, moderation was often helpless or ended by siding with the existing "power structure" by default.

In recent years, Numan Bartley has challenged this account of the postwar shift in Southern and national politics, according to which liberal timidity in racial matters was part of liberalism's move to the center in the face of a conservative and anti-radical political mood (Bartley 1995). Bartley's counter-thesis is that, rather than hesitancy and moderation, postwar American (and Southern) liberalism identified itself too closely with racial issues and assumed that the solution to the region's racial problems lay in transforming racial attitudes, not in social and economic development. According to Bartley, the Myrdalian view that the American dilemma was a "white man's problem" led (mainly white, mainly Northern) liberals to identify *white* people in general, the white *working class* in particular, and the *Southern* white working class especially as the core of the problem. Where the union movement had once been the institutional grassroots anchor of liberalism in the region, by the late 1950s and early 1960s civil rights organizations such as SNCC and SCLC became, in effect, the institutional embodiment of liberalism's cause south of the Mason Dixon line. Unions were written off in the South – and often in the North – as part of the problem rather than as part of the solution, hopelessly compromised (and torn asunder) by anti-communist struggles in the late 1940s and themselves responsible for, or in agreement with, racially exclusionary policies. In this new racial liberalism, as portrayed by Bartley, black people became the main agency of historical change in the South and in the nation.

The results – a "progressivism shorn of any economic critique and absolutely unmarked by the radical protest of the past decade," which had "sharply narrowed the liberal agenda," claims Bartley – were entirely predictable (Bartley 1995: 72–3). Over time, the white Southern working-class and blue-collar vote deserted the Democratic Party; increasingly, something like this happened in the North, too. One of the great shocks of postwar liberal politics came when Alabama governor George C. Wallace entered the Democratic primaries in 1964 in Maryland, Wisconsin, and Indiana and garnered 43 percent, 34 percent, and 30 percent of the votes, respectively, against a sitting president, Lyndon Johnson. In the long run, Wallace failed to translate this protest against the civil rights movement and racial liberalism into a strong third party movement (Carter 1995). But by loosening the hold of the Democratic Party on the white blue-collar vote, North and South, it was easier for those voters to then move into the Republican column in presidential elections (for example, in 1972) and in elections at the congressional, state, and local level.

This then is Bartley's explanation for why the heart of the New Deal coalition, the white working class and lower middle class, fled the Democratic Party. It was a "white backlash" against the liberal decision to commit the Democratic Party to the cause of black Americans. Courted by a Republican Party, which was finding a populist voice, the "emerging Republic majority" was drawn not just from the newly prosperous country club Republicans (Easy Street), the traditional areas of Republican support (Main Street) and of financial control (Wall Street), but also from the white working-class base of the Democratic Party in the South (Phillips 1969). After Wallace's near assassination and the stabilization of Southern racial politics by moderate white Southern governors such as Jimmy Carter, Dale Bumpers, and Ruben Askew, the white flight from the Democratic Party became more like a slow hemorrhage, but it continued in fits and starts over the ensuing decades.

There are, of course, problems with Bartley's thesis. For one thing, there were many forms of Southern liberalism in the post-1945 period. It is difficult to believe that someone like Lillian Smith, whom Bartley sees as symptomatic of the moralization of racial politics in the postwar South, was really that representative. For another, Bartley implies more conscious awareness and more political choice on the part of his moralizing liberals than was probably the case. And, finally, he neglects the fact that popular front liberalism, for all its emphasis upon social and economic reform, was more, rather than less, forthright on racial issues than were the Cold War and moralizing liberals. But aside from whether Bartley's explanation for the shift in American and Southern liberalism is entirely convincing, it does at least offer a specific explanation why and how the Democratic Party became the party of African Americans and forfeited the loyalty of the white working class and lower middle class in the South after the mid-1960s. Whatever else, it challenges the view that the Democratic Party and liberalism generally were only reluctantly committed to racial reform.

From a broader perspective, it was the postwar dream of Southern liberal analysts such as political scientist V. O. Key that Southern politics would become more rational, that is, operate according to economic self-interest, if the "solid" Democratic South was replaced with a two-party system divided along clear economic and social fault lines. Once this happened, Key hoped that race would be de-emphasized, while economic issues would occupy the central place in the liberal ideology, thus paving the way for a white working-class–black coalition within the Democratic Party. What happened, however, was that realignment took place, but the interracial coalition did not emerge as a strong, emotionally compelling force in Southern politics. Race did fade in importance as an explicit issue once the 1965 Voting Rights Act began to have effect, but only to be replaced by code phrases and issues ("forced busing" and "law and order") and post-civil rights issues such as affirmative action. Interestingly, these were national as much as they were regional issues and thus one effect of the civil rights movement was to deracialize and to an extent deregionalize Southern politics.

All that said, one of Key's hopes was dashed, since the new post-1960s Southern politics both reflected and helped bring about a shift rightward in American and Southern politics on most other issues besides race and gender. This "Southernization" of American politics matched what John Egerton has named the "Americanization of Dixie." Though at the time the civil rights movement, a major part of the political and cultural insurgency in the 1960s, seemed to presage a progressive sea-change in American and Southern politics, in the long run, the civil rights movement, in conjunction with the antiwar movement and the New Left, were unable to stave off, and may have helped encourage, a shift in the political mainstream to the Right in the post-1960s period.

Still, there was a paradoxical side effect to the general rightward trend of politics in the post-1945 South, whether or not the straight "Cold War" thesis or Bartley's "moralization" variation is embraced. Specifically, it was only because the institutions, policies, and ideologies of the Old Left, New Deal liberalism and unionism grew so weak that a black-led civil rights movement was able to emerge in the late 1950s and early 1960s. Mainstream civil rights organizations such as the NAACP and the Urban League were outflanked by activist groups such as SNCC and SCLC, along with CORE. With white liberalism on the defensive, African Americans had a better chance to shape their own institutions, programs, and ideologies without being quite so directly under the thumb of the white-controlled organizations and institutions of liberalism. Of course, the white liberal "establishment" exerted considerable control over the shape and direction of the movement, but it did not control that movement in the way it might once have been able to. In this sense, the decline of liberalism made possible the rise of black political self-formation. This was the "fortunate fall" of the civil rights movement.

Cold War Internationalization – and Beyond

Nor, as we shall see, are paradox and ambiguity foreign to a consideration of the civil rights movement from an international perspective. Recent work in this area, undertaken primarily by legal scholars and political scientists, has focused new attention on a claim that has always been mentioned in perfunctory fashion – that the Cold War imperatives of American foreign policy helped open the way for the civil rights measures of the 1950s and 1960s (Dudziak 2000; Layton 2000; Skrentny 1998; Von Eschen 1997). One of the immediate implications of their work is that, crucial as the grassroots perspective on the civil rights movement may be, the emergence of the civil rights movement must also be seen as part of the same historical currents that produced the dissolution of the French, Dutch, and British empires in the post-1945 world. But the ambiguous effects of the Cold War are immediately evident. On the one hand, the shift rightward in American politics after 1945 tended to neutralize the anticolonial impulse central to mainstream American politics, much less to liberal left politics generally, and in African-American circles particularly. At the same time, however, American foreign policy makers increasingly realized that in order to gain the support of newly independent "Third World" governments in Asia and Africa, American racial practices had to be brought into line with America's ideals as embodied in what Myrdal called "the American Creed." Toward that end, for example, the Justice Department filed *amicus curiae* briefs in the various civil rights cases leading up to *Brown vs. Board of Education*, and these made clear the foreign policy considerations at stake in righting America's racial wrongs. Thus there was what Derrick Bell has called a "convergence of interests" between civil rights advocates and American national interest after 1945, while Mary Dudziak has usefully summed up the situation by observing: "The Cold War was simultaneously an agent of repression and an agent of change" (Dudziak 2000: 251).

This turn toward racial reform at home was accompanied, as already mentioned, by a growing conservatism in American policy on the colonialism issue. With the onset of the Cold War in earnest by 1947–8, American foreign policy viewed decolonization much more warily, since it seemed to offer an open invitation to Soviet expansion into the Third World. This fear of Soviet penetration was exemplified in the Congo crisis in the early 1960s and most clearly – and disastrously – in the decision to pick up the French colonial commitment, now dressed out as the containment of communism, in Indo-China. Mirroring this cooling of anticolonial ardor in American foreign policy was the Soviet Union's assumption of the role of global champion of decolonization (at least outside of Eastern Europe).

The result of all this was that, roughly, from 1948 on, pre-movement civil rights forces within the United States split into two camps (Von Eschen 1997). The Council on African Affairs (CAA), along with individuals such as W. E. B. Du Bois and Paul Robeson, took a militantly anticolonial and pro-Soviet line in matters of foreign policy having to do with decolonization. At the same time, organizations such as the NAACP began soft peddling their anticolonial rhetoric so as to maintain their alleged influence in the corridors of national power. Thus, the new Cold War racial liberalism justified its support for full black civil and political rights by pointing to the propaganda value of such measures in the Cold War competition with the Soviet Union. At best, it was a shrewd strategy, a piece of moral realism, to play Cold War politics for civil rights purposes; at worst, it transformed a moral issue into a matter of *realpolitik* calculation and grew tongue-tied on the larger issues of colonialism and Western capitalism. In all this, there were figures such as George Padmore and C. L. R. James, both of Trinidad, along with Richard Wright, then living in France, who maintained a critical position on Western colonialism while refusing to become apologists for the Stalinist Soviet Union. It was not, needless to say, a position that attracted much popular support from established quarters; nor is it a position that has received much attention in the current historiography on race and American foreign policy.

By the late 1950s a certain thaw began in the frozen Cold War postures and a renewed interest in the Third World manifested itself. At this point, however, much of the new work on civil rights in an international perspective seems to leave off. In fact, CORE had explicitly adopted Gandhian civil disobedience as a philosophy and a tactic in its American campaigns in the 1940s. Martin Luther King, Jr. made a pilgrimage to India in the late 1950s to consult with surviving Gandhians, while he, along with several other black leaders, attended the inauguration of Kwame Nkrumah as prime minister of Ghana in 1957, an event of signal importance in the decolonization of Africa. Earlier, in 1956, Richard Wright published his reactions to the Bandung Conference of non-aligned nations in 1955 and also offered a long and sometimes tortured account of his visit to the Gold Coast in *Black Power* (1955). In the early 1960s, several Northern black intellectuals, including LeRoi Jones and Harold Cruse, were profoundly influenced by their visit to Castro's new revolutionary Cuba. This reopening of links with anticolonial forces took another leap forward in 1964 when several SNCC members, fresh from the disillusioning experience of the Democratic Convention in Atlantic City, NJ, toured Africa and while there met with Malcolm X, himself on a journey toward establishing American–Third World connections and away from the racial exclusivity of the Nation of Islam.

But as the civil rights movement peaked and began to search for new areas of engagement by the mid-1960s, the more radical of the activists, particularly from among SNCC members, began to establish identifications rather than just connections with the Third World. Where the earlier anticolonialist ideology focused on colonialism as a system of capitalist domination and anticolonialism was defined by the Marxist-Leninist perspective, 1960s black radicals were coming to see African Americans as a colonized people and the "colonial analogy" as a useful analytical and political tool (Carmichael and Hamilton 1967). In this new perspective, the Third World, not Europe, became the site of revolutionary upheaval. Among the fragmenting civil rights cadres in the South and newly emerging radical black groups in northern and western cities, the work of the Martinique-born physician and freedom fighter in Algeria, Frantz Fanon, found an enthusiastic reception, even though Fanon's work explicitly rejected race as the basis of national liberation struggles. Sympathy with, even open support for, the Viet Cong and North Vietnamese cause became quite common after the mid-1960s. At the 1967 New Politics Conference in Chicago, former SNCC members and other veterans of the movement proposed expressions of sympathy with the Palestinian cause in the Middle East. All this betokened a return to the explicit anticolonial and pro-Third World orientation of the 1930s and 1940s, though at a different level of complexity, with race and politics looming larger and class analysis and economic issues taking something of a back seat. In general, the Soviet Union had lost much of its luster as a champion of decolonization and the proletariat of the First World had long since lost any resemblance to a revolutionary vanguard. Indeed, the lonely "third way" position staked out by Padmore, James, and Wright in the 1940s and 1950s now seemed much more compelling, since it had sought to sidestep conventional Cold War position-taking. Still, the new anticolonialism never subjected the Soviet Empire to the same sort of moral and political critique as it did the empires of the West. At best, in the spirit of Bandung, it tried to steer clear of the dead-end of Cold War polemics altogether.

The important historiographical point here is that, though the early Cold War period between 1945 and 1960 has received substantial treatment in recent years, considerable work needs to be done on the revival of anticolonialist sentiment among African Americans in the 1960s. One suspects that there was a rough correlation between those who saw the colonial analogy as relevant within the United States and those who were in the process of moving beyond the agenda of the civil rights movement itself. Indeed, this international "turn" in the movement was itself a symptom of the disintegration of the mainstream civil rights movement. To model one's political vision on the ideology of national liberation, politically and culturally, seemed incompatible with a commitment to non-violence and to a generally liberal or Western socialist vision of politics and society. Though Martin Luther King increasingly spoke out against the war in Vietnam and against American corporate power, he never made solidarity with Third World liberation movements central to his vision. As Penny von Eschen (1997) has rightly observed, "[Anti-] colonialism ... was not a programmatic part of the Civil Rights Movement"(186).

This in turn suggests that just how and why the movement dissolved after 1965 needs more explicit attention. Another somewhat contradictory aspect of the history of the movement also emerges at this juncture. Just as Pan-Africanism and Negritude as cultural and political ideologies were fading in Africa, their American counterparts emerged with full force in the Black Power/Black Consciousness/Black Arts movements of the late 1960s. And though there are distinct continuities between the mainstream civil rights movement and the later Black Power/Black Consciousness phase of the black struggle, the question as to how much continuity (black empowerment and self-respect) and how much new departure (racial essentialism and abandonment of non-violence) there were needs more careful empirical study and conceptual exploration.

Generally, then, historians of the civil rights movements need to raise their sights beyond the local and regional level. Indeed, something like Paul Gilroy's (1993) "Black Atlantic" thesis needs to be developed in its political, as well as cultural, aspects. To what extent, for instance, did the civil rights movement resemble or differ from Third World liberation movements? George Fredrickson has done pioneering work in comparing systems of racial oppression and political liberation movements in the United States and in South Africa, but there is much more to be done. In addition, examination of the civil rights movement in light of the various political revitalization movements hastening, and then following upon, the collapse of the Soviet Union and its Eastern bloc empire suggests that the civil rights movement was not just a liberal reform movement, but something different from either that or from a Third World revolutionary movement (King 1992).

The Civil Rights Movement as an Intellectual and Cultural Movement

If the historiography of the civil rights movement tends toward geographical provincialism, it also inclines, as already suggested, to slight the new forms of cultural and intellectual consciousness generated in and by that movement. Much of this derives from the fact that historians of the civil rights movement are generally political and social historians, with little interest or training in intellectual or cultural history. Not surprisingly, then, they have little awareness of cultural and intellectual factors; nor is it clear that they can recognize, much less understand, such work when confronted with it. Charles Eagles's claim that this author's (RHK) work in the intellectual history of the movement "got mired in theoretical and philosophical considerations only peripherally related to the rhetoric of the movement"(Eagles 2000: 834–5) seems less a criticism than a confession of unwillingness to think through the issues taken up in *Civil Rights and the Idea of Freedom*. Confronted with a text that attempts to chart one aspect of the intellectual history of the movement, Eagles proceeds to dismiss it as irrelevant without further explanation, a prime example of what might be called "hit-and-run" criticism. If that is not enough,

Eagles then proceeds to observe that the "rhetoric and its meanings" of the civil rights movement need examination, which was precisely the starting point of the book he has just summarily dismissed.

Beyond all that, Eagles also understates things considerably when he says that besides "various facets of Martin Luther King's thought, the intellectual history of the black freedom struggle has received scant attention" (834). Undoubtedly more work in the intellectual history of the movement is called for, but there is already more than he suggests. Both Keith Miller's *Voices of Deliverance*, a study of King's rhetoric, and Charles Marsh's *God's Long Summer*, two works that Eagles does praise, can very plausibly be called intellectual histories. Besides the several works on Martin Luther King's thought that Eagles footnotes, there is also Lewis Baldwin's investigation of the black religious roots of King's thought, while Anita H. Patterson has recently linked King to a tradition of American transcendentalist thinking, which includes Emerson and Du Bois. David Chappell's forthcoming study of the early movement's relation to American liberalism will stress the Niebuhrian roots of much of the best thinking emanating from the movement, especially from King himself. Yet, for all the movement's great influence, there has been, as far as I know, relatively little study of the effects of the movement on American religious and theological thinking in the 1960s or afterwards, once one leaves King and his circle.

Falling somewhere between institutional and intellectual history, the influence of the movement on the theory, practice, and content of American education has only barely begun. August Meier and Elliott Rudwick's *Black History and the Historical Profession, 1915–1980* (1986) provides a solid foundation for grasping the intellectual history of black American history, while Gabrielle Edgecomb's *From Swastika to Jim Crow* (1993) investigates the intellectual influence of the émigré academics who fled Nazi Germany on black college students from the 1940s on into the 1960s, some of whom became central figures in the movement. Moreover, though Peter J. Ling (1995) has made a valuable start, we need a comprehensive study of the various educational innovations within the movement, from citizenship schools in the Sea Islands of South Carolina to the freedom schools that sprang up during Freedom Summer. Overall, many of the initiatives in teaching black history came out of the civil rights movement's own efforts at grassroots education.

Another fruitful area for the intellectual historian seeking to understand the intellectual impact of the movement is the veritable explosion of African-American historiography since the 1960s. The notions of "history from the bottom up" and of intellectual history as the "history not of thought but of men thinking"(Levine 1977: ix) were powerful influences on, and were reflected in, the works of Lawrence Levine, John Blassingame, Sterling Stuckey, Eugene Genovese, and others. Their work on the origins and development of slave culture clearly grew out of a renewed interest in the potentially radical political role of religion that manifested itself so clearly in the movement. More recently, in his *Mercy, Mercy Me* (2001), a penetrating discussion of African-American art and culture in the 1960s, James C. Hall suggests the "anti-modernist" strain in African-American consciousness that emerged in that decade represented, first, "an internationalization of African-American consciousness"(13), and, second, expressed a distinctly religious or at least spiritual dimension. Everyone, from E. Franklin Frazier and Richard Wright to Gunnar Myrdal and Marxists in general, assumed the reactionary nature of religion in the 1930s and 1940s – Marx's dictum that religion was the "opiate of the masses" being the presiding assumption. But by the 1970s there had been a fundamental rehabilitation of religion among many black intellectuals and students of the black American experience. The new view was that the seminal role played by religion in the Southern movement did not betoken some intellectual and cultural atavism, "interesting" in a folkloric way but irrelevant to the main action of the 1960s on a national level. Rather, the movement stood at the cutting edge of a shift in African-American (and general American) consciousness which politicized grassroots religion and spiritualized African-American music and painting. The historiographical point here is an important but simple one: the history of slavery and slave culture had to be rewritten in the light of the civil rights movement's catalytic role in reconfiguring black consciousness.

In other areas of American intellectual history, the effects of the civil rights movement have yet to be factored in. Future historians of American political and constitutional thought seeking to understand the return of "rights talk" to a central position in legal and political thought since the 1960s, will need to take into account the role that the civil rights movement played in reviving notions of rights and freedom. These themes/ideas have kept liberal political thought in business in the decades since then. It is further testimony to the yeasty effects of the movement that many of the dominant motifs associated with recent communitarian thought, especially "citizenship" and "community," were central concerns not just of the movement leaders and intellectuals but also of the participants in the civil rights movement at the grassroots level. Indeed, the idea of participatory democracy, so central to the New Left conception of politics, was drawn in large part from the theory and practice of community organizing taught by civil rights activists.

It is of course neither possible nor desirable to distinguish too sharply between the cultural and intellectual impact of the civil rights movement and that of Black Power/ Black Consciousness/Black Arts movements. High artistic creation and crass commercial record sales, the composition of a novel and the decision to produce a film, do not fit neatly into eras and movements. Still, in general, the influence of the racial struggles of the 1960s on the fiction and the film of the post-1960s period has been considerable, particularly in the last decade or so. From the perspective offered by Allison Graham's *Framing the South* (2001), Bartley's insistence that white Southern liberalism found it easy to blame the so-called "rednecks" for the South's (and the nation's) racial problems finds ready confirmation in any number of films about racial themes, including, of course, Alan Parker's *Mississippi Burning* (1988). Nor have "regular" historians of the movement fully tapped into the rich psychological explorations and historical textures offered in even early fictional treatments of the movement, beginning with the work of Alice Walker (1976) and Rosellen Brown (1984).

A consideration of the dominant role played by music in the 1960s illustrates the difficulty in separating the civil rights phase (predominantly Southern) from the Black Power phase (mostly urban and Northern) and the political from the cultural dimensions of African-American insurgency. But the enormous impact that the movement had on popular music and, reciprocally, the crucial role that music played in the civil rights movement is clear. What linked the politics of the movement with the artistic expression of the black community was the central role of public perform-ance in both. Within the movement the tradition of spirituals and black church music in general was transformed into a new genre of music, the "freedom songs." At the same time, developments in secular music (rhythm and blues) and sacred music (gospel) combined to produce any number of black artists whose work anticipated or echoed the themes of the civil rights movement and black consciousness. Indeed, it is tempting to link the dominant theme of expressive "freedom" within jazz circles from the mid-1950s on with the civil rights movement's slogan of "freedom now" and to emphasize that "freedom" was never only narrowly political; rather, it referred more widely to the achievement of personal and group autonomy of expression and action (Hersch 1995–6).

Yet others link movements of the 1960s, such as "free jazz" or the "New Black Music," to the idea of a black, shared "spirituality" linking rhythm and blues, soul/Motown, and the avant-garde jazz. Indeed, this was LeRoi Jones's point in his widely influential "The Changing Same (R&B and the New Black Music)" essay of 1966. The "same" Jones refers to is just that shared sense of black spirituality, one that seems to take on trans-historical and transcultural characteristics. This ontologically based black spirituality in turn dictated exclusivist forms of black political organization and action. Jones's rejection of this "blank, any place 'universal' humbug" (198) was a long way from the civil rights movement's inclusive rhetoric of freedom and black and white together. A more general reflection of the shift in racial consciousness over the course of the 1960s can be seen in *Black Fire*, the pioneering collection of black writing offered by Amiri Baraka (aka Leroi Jones) and Larry Neal in 1968. In it, there was scarcely any mention of the Southern civil rights struggle, with violence not non-violence, black solidarity not interracial cooperation, and Malcolm X not Martin Luther King, as dominant preoccupations and themes of the essays, fiction, poetry, and plays collected there.

Finally, to understand the political and cultural debates within black America at the time (and since), the historiography of black America in the 1960s needs to think more about the continuities, as well as the discontinuities, between the Southern civil rights movement and the Northern Black Power/Black Consciousness/Black Arts movements and to engage more with the cultural as well as the political aspects of the freedom struggle in the broadest sense. A recent work such as Brian Ward's *Just My Soul Responding* (1998) repays close attention just because it offers a much more complex (and more interesting) picture of the relationship between the civil rights movement and the sphere of popular music. Ward notes, for instance, that popular R&B and soul artists often articulated "black" themes and concerns in general in their work (e.g., Sam Cooke's "Change is Going to Come," or James Brown's "Say it Loud, I'm Black and I'm Proud," or Aretha Franklin's "RESPECT") yet were reluctant to commit publicly to the civil rights movement. On the other hand, the avant-garde jazz community, which by the 1960s had lost much of its audience among African Americans, was politically and musically radical; and this was reflected quite explicitly in their music (e.g., Charles Mingus's quirky "Fables of Faubus" or John Coltrane's "Alabama," a brooding, haunting musical meditation on the death of the four young girls in the Birmingham bombing of September 1963, or Max Roach's "Freedom Now" Suite). The irony is that the jazz wing of what Jones referred to as the New Black Music, which Jones considered so expressive of black spirituality, found its most enthusiastic audiences among white people. Ward also acknowledges the role that white, as well as black, folk musicians played in making the civil rights movement known in song, not to mention the subtle, though significant, role that a kind of white "country-soul" sound played in much of the soul and R&B of the 1960s. The general point is a paradoxical but important one: what the Black Arts movement offered as the main evidence for racial uniqueness was a thoroughly hybrid form of music, combining sacred and secular, Northern and Southern, white and black, urban and country traditions. Overall, as Ward suggests, the hybrid nature of much black music of the 1960s was a "cultural cognate of what the freedom struggle...was primarily about" (224).

These are just some of the issues that future work on the civil rights movement might take up. In general, then, the central point of this essay has been that the historiography of the civil rights movement (taken broadly) must make even more of an effort to break down, not confirm, disciplinary, generic, and even ontological boundaries. Moreover, the politics of the civil rights movement can scarcely be cordoned off from mainstream national or Southern politics and political culture; the regional and national dimensions of the civil rights movement must increasingly be placed in the context of a post-World War II global struggle for political and cultural self-determination; and, finally, the boundaries between political and cultural action, movements, and ideologies must be made problematic, at least as objects for study, analysis, and explanation.

REFERENCES AND FURTHER READING

Baldwin, L. (1991) *There is a Balm in Gilead: The Cultural Roots of Martin Luther King Jr.* Minneapolis, MN: Fortress Press.
Bartley, N. (1995) *The New South, 1945–1980.* Baton Rouge: Louisiana State University Press.
Bass, S. J. (2001) *Blessed are the Peacemakers: Martin Luther King, Jr., Eight White Religious Leaders, and the 'Letter from Birmingham Jail'.* Baton Rouge: Louisiana State University Press.
Brown, R. (1984) *Civil Wars.* New York: Alfred A. Knopf.
Carter, D. (1995) *The Politics of Rage: George Wallace, the Origins of the New Conservatism, and the Transformation of American Politics.* New York: Simon and Schuster.

Chappell, D. (1994) *Inside Agitators: White Southerners in the Civil Rights Movement*. Baltimore, MD: Johns Hopkins University Press.

Chappell, D. (forthcoming) *A Stone of Hope: Prophetic Religion, Liberalism, and the Death of Jim Crow*. Chapel Hill: University of North Carolina Press.

Denning, M. (1996) *The Cultural Front: The Laboring of American Culture in the Twentieth Century*. London: Verso.

Dudziak, M. (2000) *Cold War Civil Rights: Race and the Image of American Democracy*. Princeton, NJ: Princeton University Press.

Eagles, C. (2000) "Toward New Histories of the Civil Rights Era," *Journal of Southern History*, 35: 815–48.

Edgecomb, G. (1993) *From Swastika to Jim Crow: Refugee Scholars at Black Colleges*. Malabar, FL: Krieger Publishing.

Egerton, J. (1994) *Speak Now Against the Day: The Generation Before the Civil Rights Movement in the South*. Chapel Hill: University of North Carolina Press.

Fredrickson, G. (1995). *Black Liberation: Comparative History of Black Ideologies in the United States and South Africa*. New York: Oxford University Press.

Gilroy, P. (1993) *The Black Atlantic: Modernity and Double Consciousness*. London: Verso.

Graham, A. (2001) *Framing the South*. Baltimore, MD: Johns Hopkins University Press.

Hall, J. C. (2001) *Mercy, Mercy Me: African-American Culture and the American Sixties*. New York: Oxford University Press.

Harding, V. (1981) *There is a River: The Black Struggle for Freedom in America*. New York: Harcourt Brace Jovanovich.

Hersch, C. (1995–6) " 'Let Freedom Ring!': Free Jazz and African-American politics," *Cultural Critique*: 97–123.

Jones, L. (1966) "The Changing Same (R&B and New Black Music)." In *Black Music* (pp. 180–211). New York: William Morrow.

King, R. (1992) *Civil Rights and the Idea of Freedom*. New York: Oxford University Press.

Klarman, M. (1994) "How *Brown* Changed Race Relations: The Backlash Thesis," *Journal of American History*, 81: 81–118.

Kuryla, P. (2001). " 'Mississippi in their Heads': Historians' Identity and the Linguistic Rules of the Civil Rights Movement." Unpublished paper, Vanderbilt University.

Layton, A. S. (2000) *International Politics and Civil Rights Policies in the United States, 1914–1960*. Cambridge: Cambridge University Press.

Levine, L. (1977) *Black Culture and Black Consciousness: Afro-American Folk Thought from Slavery to Freedom*. New York: Oxford University Press.

Lewis, George (forthcoming) *"With Baited Breath": Segregationists, Anti-Communism and Massive Resistance, 1945–1965*. Gainesville: University of Florida Press.

Ling, P. J. (1995) "Local Leadership in the Early Civil Rights Movement: The South Carolina Citizenship Education Program of the Highlander Folk School," *Journal of American History*, 29: 399–422.

Ownby, T. (2002) *The Role of Ideas in the Civil Rights South*. Jackson: University of Mississippi Press.

Patterson, A. (1997) *From Emerson to King: Democracy, Race, and the Politics of Protest*. New York: Oxford University Press.

Payne, C. (1995) *I've Got the Light of Freedom: The Organizing Tradition and the Mississippi Freedom Struggle*. Berkeley: University of California Press.

Phillips, K. (1969) *The Emerging Republican Majority*. New Rochelle, NY: Arlington House.

Polsgrove, C. (2001) *Divided Minds: Intellectuals and the Civil Rights Movement*. New York: W. W. Norton.

Skrentny, J. D. (1998) "The Effect of the Cold War on African-American Civil Rights: America and the World Audience, 1945–1968," *Theory and Society*, 27: 237–85.

Sullivan, Patricia (1996) *Days of Hope: Race and Democracy in the New Deal Era*. Chapel Hill: University of North Carolina Press.

Von Eschen, P. M. (1997) *Race Against Empire: Black America and Anticolonialism, 1937–1957*. Ithaca, NY: Cornell University Press.

Walker, A. (1976) *Meridian*. New York: Washington Square Press.

Ward, B. (1998) *Just My Soul Responding: Rhythm and Blues, Black Consciousness and Race Relations*. London: UCL Press.

Wright, R. (1956) *The Color Curtain: A Report on the Bandung Conference*. Cleveland, OH: World Publishing.

Wright, R. (1995) *Black Power*. New York: Harper Perennial.

14

Southern Religion(s)

Charles Reagan Wilson

William Faulkner said that he used religious images and characters in his fiction because they were a part of the north Mississippi where he grew up. "It's just there," he said, and indeed, religion has been "just there," a fundamental force in shaping the American South into a distinctive place (Gwynn and Blotner 1959: 41). Religion justified slavery and the Confederate crusade, but it also inspired slave rebellions and civil rights reforms. It comforted suffering people in war, defeat, poverty, and discrimination. Religion provided worldviews for Southerners that nurtured a sense of identity and mission. Along with rigid racial attitudes, an agricultural economy, and rural life, peculiar patterns of religion within American culture gave a distinctive twist to Southern culture. The image of the Bible Belt shaped perceptions of outsiders and still reflects an unusual authority for the scriptures, the word, that has been central to creativity in the region. Religion raised spiritual issues that creative people would explore in literature, music, and art, and today it is changing as Southern society changes.

Evangelicalism is the religious tradition that has long dominated the American South. It insists that religious experience is the essence of faith. With a Calvinist-inspired dim view of human nature, it is a religion of sin and salvation. The central theme is the search for conversion, which can then lead to a transformed life. Evangelical churches are not unique to the South at all, but the distinctiveness of religion in the South is that an interdenominational tradition, centered in Baptists, Methodists, Presbyterians at times, Pentecostals, and sectarians, has been the dominant one in the region for so long, profoundly shaping not just religion but also social, economic, and political life, as well as cultural expression. A civic religious tradition has shaped a regional identity, tying together the cultures of Christianity and self-conscious "Southernism," sometimes causing Southerners to blur the lines between the two. Interpretations of Southern religion have stressed the close ties between churches and the broader regional society, often suggesting that religion has been in "cultural captivity" (Eighmy 1972).

Samuel S. Hill is a seminal figure in pointing to Evangelicalism as the hegemonic religion that provided considerable religious unity in the South despite very real differences among believers and despite a range of smaller groups outside the evangelical mainstream. The central theme of Southern religion, Hill wrote over two decades ago, was the search for redemption, for conversion from sin to salvation. His use of the term "central theme" harked back to historian Ulrich B. Phillips's famous dictum that the central theme of Southern history was white supremacy, and Hill's work raised religion to the level of race relations as an interpretive framework for understanding the South. Hill also pointed out that, despite their denominational differences, evangelical Protestant groups shared so much theology, ritual, and outlook toward the world that it seemed "legitimate to speak of a transdenominational 'Southern church' embracing what may be called 'popular Southern Protestantism.'"

Religious geographers reinforce Hill's insight, emphasizing the religious homogeneity of the South, compared to national diversity. Even today, Protestantism dominates, and the region continues its traditionally high rates of church membership. While Baptists represent the largest religious group in most counties in the South, their greatest strength extends from southern Appalachia, into Georgia, Alabama, and Mississippi, into northern Louisiana and Texas, and into southern Arkansas and Oklahoma. Methodists have been the main competitors of Baptists in the South, a larger group than the latter until the growth of Baptists after the Civil War. Baptists succeeded in evangelism, using farmer-preachers to spread the word among the people with whom they lived, while Methodists grew on the work of circuit-riding preachers and regular camp meetings (Hill 1985).

Areas of geographical diversity exist throughout the South that are exceptions to this demographic pattern. Roman Catholics are a historic presence in south Louisiana, particularly shaping the landscape there, but also in parts of Texas, south Florida, and along the Gulf Coast. Jews do not have large population concentrations, although cities like Atlanta, Memphis, and Charleston have significant communities, and smaller concentrations of Jewish population are scattered in small towns throughout the region. Central Texas has a sizable Lutheran presence, dating from German settlement in the mid-nineteenth century, and the Carolina Piedmont is historic home to Quakers, Moravians, and other Protestant dissenters.

Religion has been closely interwoven with other aspects of Southern culture, seen especially in its relationship to the literature and music of the region. Traditional Southern folk culture prized storytelling, which was a reflection of an oral culture that long provided a particular context for regional life and nowhere more so than in religion. Southern Evangelicalism values religious experience, and its characteristic orientation is toward sound. It is a religion of the word. The Bible has occupied a position of central authority in the South. Even when the South had relatively high rates of illiteracy, a pronounced biblical literacy often came through the oral circulation of Old and New Testament stories (Ketchin 1994; Wilson 1999). Lewis Simpson has suggested as well that "the Southern writer has tended to be a kind of priest and prophet of a metaphysical nation," representing the South's experience as a journey toward the human desire for moral meaning within history (Simpson 1972: 190). From another perspective, Southerners made religious music a part of everyday life from the days of the frontier, and few topics show so well the cultural creativity, based in a dynamic of tradition and innovation, that the region fostered.

Although evangelical religion came to dominate the South, the Anglican church represented authority in this late colonial society, and the eighteenth century saw Anglicans in the Southern colonies develop such symbols of status as stately houses, courthouses that they dominated as county justices, and elegant churches. The churches and homes in Virginia expressed the values of the gentry, who early blurred the line between the sacred and the secular. Anglican churches were prime progenitors of an enduring Southern elite, rooted in slave and land ownership, skilled in political leadership, and adept at incorporating yeomen into a social system that would be flexible enough to preserve their essential authority despite generations of change. Anglicanism gave initial spiritual authority to this system (Upton 1986).

Anglicans in the late colonial period faced a dramatic challenge from emerging evangelicals who referred to themselves as a counterculture to that of the gentry. Rhys Isaac's Pulitzer Prize-winning *The Transformation of Virginia* (1982) showed religious dissenters, beginning with the Presbyterians in the 1740s and then the Baptists and Methodists in the two decades from 1760 to 1780, questioning the gentry culture that dominated society. Evangelicals, as the dissenters became known, saw religious conversion, the New Birth, as a truly transforming event, leading to an egalitarian fellowship with the like-minded redeemed. These early evangelicals embraced an individualistic faith, centered on personal sinfulness and the saving power of God's grace, which led to new spiritual communities that enforced considerable moral austerity. Thus appeared the Southern evangelical dynamic of community and individualism. The Great Revival launched a new phase of evangelical growth, beginning on the frontier, first in 1799, in Logan County, Kentucky. The largest revival was at Cane Ridge, Kentucky, in 1801, bringing together some 25,000 worshipers to hear weeklong preaching, including that of black preachers (Boles 1972). Early Southern evangelicals, in general, targeted conversion of young people, empowered black exhorters and young itinerant ministers, and allowed women considerable leeway in prophecy and prayer. These were radical actions in a society that prized order and hierarchy. Evangelical behavior threatened family stability. The household was a central institution in the South, but evangelicals demanded that God be first, above even family (Heyrman 1997).

One historical landmark in the evangelical role in Southern culture was the compromise of its early egalitarianism in the first decades of the nineteenth century, seeking to gain greater influence in Southern states that were, at the same time, achieving a new cultural cohesion. Southerners moved west in these same years, extending the Cotton Kingdom into the Old Southwest and creating new familial and ideological bonds across the expanding South. Evangelicals gradually abandoned their hostility to slavery and restricted black preachers, itinerant preachers became more settled and assumed conventional responsibilities as husbands and fathers, family life emerged as the new evangelical ideal, and churches began restricting the public role of women in worship services. As a result of such accommodations, the evangelical ethos became more socially acceptable and came to suffuse Southern life by the third decade of the nineteenth century (Heyrman 1997).

African-American religion was a shaping force on Southern regional religion from late colonial times. Africans brought considerable spiritual baggage to the New World, including traditional African religions, Africanized Islam, and Africanized Christianity. African Americans reimagined their religious lives, combining elements from varied African religious influences with Anglicanism and, later, evangelical Protestantism. Robert Farris Thompson makes the crucial point that West African religious influence was very prominent, not in specific rituals or formal institutions that survived, but in aesthetics and philosophical inclinations that took root in folk culture. The slave quarters, with its secret praise service, was a likely hearth of African religious influence, including conjure, a system of spiritual influence that combined African herbal medicine with magic and the ring shout (Raboteau 1978).

Although the evangelical denominations had softened their egalitarian message by the 1830s, their continuing appeal for slaves included a worldview that promised spiritual if not earthly equality; a style of worship that resonated with the religious ecstasy of the danced religions of Africa; the early Baptist and Methodist antislavery stance; and licensing of black preachers. Slaves and African Americans in general found status in churches that was unavailable anywhere else in Southern society (Mathews 1977). Black Baptists helped shape Evangelicalism, participating in common revivals with whites and creating separate congregations and an evangelical identity in places throughout the early South. Blacks worshipped sometimes in biracial churches, as well, dominated by whites but with surprising social authority for themselves as church members. For a brief moment in time, blacks and whites were often in the same ritual and spatial setting, hearing sermons, sharing communion, participating in church disciplinary proceedings, and even burying in the same graveyards. While such gatherings were typically segregated, the cultural interchange that occurred among them is the foundation for later religious commonalities among black and white church people of the South.

One of those cultural exchanges was surely in music. Religious music was an expression of Southern culture that provided cohesion across the region in the early nineteenth century. The Methodists popularized the hymns of Isaac Watts, nurturing a new form of singing heard in camp meetings and worship services. Songs such as "Amazing Grace" and "There Is a Fountain Filled with Blood" date from this era, popular among both black and white evangelicals who attended biracial and multi-denominational revivals and created a musical language of religion that would long abide in the South. Southerners typically learned religious songs through the shape-note system, with the shape of the note representing its musical pitch. The *Sacred Harp* (1844) conveyed these songs and it came to rival the Bible for popularity in Southern households (Cobb 1978).

The spirituals became the distinctive black religious music of the antebellum era, expressing a slave identity as God's chosen people. In the spirituals, liberation from this world's troubles might be in the next world, but it could also inspire rebels like Nat Turner, whose 1831 slave rebellion came out of Turner's sense of divine judgment on slavery (Epstein 1977).

Slaves were part of the early nineteenth-century migration of planters and yeoman farmers into the Old Southwest of Alabama, Mississippi, Louisiana, and Arkansas, and this movement had dramatic effects on Native Americans in this area, most of whom the government forced to move west by the end of the 1830s. William McLoughlin's studies of the Cherokees during the early nineteenth century explored the clash of old and new religious systems and the response of Indian religion to attacks on Indian cultural identity. The Cherokee Ghost Dance Movement (1811–13) was a turning point in that tribe's history, when the Christian ideology of whites replaced traditional Indian religion. *Ghost Dance* described the Cherokee apocalyptic vision that predicted that the Great Spirit would destroy whites and return stolen land to the Cherokee (McLoughlin 1984). Evangelicals entered the scene in this period, as Baptists first sent missionaries to the Cherokee Nation in 1819, and Methodist circuit riders began preaching in late 1823. Evangelical concern for spiritual experience in preference to doctrinal rigidities; a relatively informal worship style; the use of Cherokees as exhorters, evangelists, and even ordained ministers; and the congregational autonomy of evangelical religion, all promoted Cherokee acceptance of the faith. The Baptist ritual of water baptism was particularly significant in winning Cherokee converts because it resembled the traditional Indian ceremony of purification, Going to Water (McLoughlin 1984).

Evangelical Protestant ministers thus spread the gospel word to Indians as well as slaves, but religion proved equally significant in this era in sanctifying the dominance of some evangelical believers over others. Mitchell Snay's *Gospel of Disunion* (1993) traced the religious defense of Southern society from the response to William Lloyd Garrison's moral attacks on slavery, to the development of biblical proslavery, the regional separation of evangelical churches, and religious support for Southern nationalism and secession. At the heart of this religious justification for slavery was the development of a slaveholder's ethic, which became the basis of a patriarchal, paternalistic society (Genovese 1974). Of particular significance was the appearance of regional religious institutions in the 1840s, well before the nation's political institutions divided regionally. When Northern Baptists and Methodists in the mid-1840s placed restrictions on slaveowners' participation in their denominations, Southerners in those groups withdrew and founded the Southern Baptist Convention and the Methodist Episcopal Church, South, and Southern Presbyterians would similarly secede from their parent church when the Civil War began. These regional religious institutions were thus central carriers of a self-consciously "Southern" ideology and identity before the Civil War (Goen 1985).

Writers helped to construct a regional civic identity with religious underpinnings by mythologizing the South and its agrarian life. Thomas Jefferson, in *Notes on the*

State of Virginia (1787), had earlier captured the ironic dilemmas facing a South just beginning to think about its peculiar destiny. He pictured his home state as a redemptive pastoral community of plain yeomen farmers. Drawing from biblical and classical elements, Jefferson's vision projected a virtuous America but one rooted specifically in his home state and an emerging "South." Jefferson saw slavery producing not harmony but "the most boisterous passions, the most unremitting despotism on the one part, and degrading submissions on the other." Moreover, Jefferson even projected an apocalyptic nightmare for his people: "I tremble for my country when I reflect that God is just." He feverishly imagined that the positions of slave and master might be reversed – it "is among possible events" and "it may become probable by supernatural interference!" (Peden 1955: 161–3). *Notes* portrayed the underlying tension, potentially, in the redemptive role of the South in defining its role in the new nation – as the location of a pastoral yeoman arcadia and as the site of an apocalyptic transformation of blacks toppling their white masters. After 1830, with Southern slavery under moral attack from the North, Southern writers portrayed the South as a plantation pastoral, with masters as Old Testament-like patriarchs and slaves as contented workers in a morally well-ordered hierarchy with deep roots in Western biblical tradition.

As the crisis of the Union proceeded, Southern ministers, as well as writers, gave vital support for secession. They blessed the troops going off to war against the Yankees, using the same crusader language Northern evangelical churches were using for the opposite cause. Southern ministers comforted the bereaved and continued to urge steadfast support of the Confederate cause, remaining crucial to Southern morale to the end. Ministers developed a rhetoric of civil religion, sacralizing the Confederacy as a righteous cause, fighting against an American Union that had become so heterogeneous that alien religious "isms" were said to flourish there instead of the old-time faith. *Religion and the American Civil War* (Miller, Stout, and Wilson 1998) collects essays from a 1994 conference, and the contributors to the volume analyze, among other topics, religion's role in the coming of the war, the centrality of the Bible to North–South justifications for their war efforts, disagreements among preachers about whether to support secession, the definition of a masculine piety in the Confederate armies, the assumption by women of new spiritual roles during the war, and comparisons of the American Civil War's religious elements with those from other civil conflicts.

The Civil War was a time that rallied religious groups in the region behind the war effort. For Roman Catholics and Jews, the Civil War was the culmination of experiences that had made them distinctive Southerners. The rural character of Southern life, regional complexities of French Catholicism in Louisiana and Anglo Catholicism in Kentucky and Maryland, the dearth of priests and parishes, and the relatively small number of Catholic immigrants to the South, produced a Catholic church in the region that was different from that elsewhere. Catholics faced suspicion and hostility from many Southerners who portrayed the Catholic church as embodying European moral decadence, superstition, and magic. The Catholic church adapted to slave society, though, sanctifying the political order of slavery and states' rights and eventually blessing Confederate armies (Miller and Wakelyn 1983).

Jews had a similarly long presence in the South, with some of the nation's earliest Jewish communities being in the Southern colonies. Most Jewish immigrants to the South were originally Sephardic Jews from the Iberian Peninsula, with Ashkenazi Jews coming from central Europe in increasing numbers after 1840. Jews accepted such aspects of Southern life as slavery, the code of honor, dueling, and states' rights politics and were active in Southern political and civic life throughout the nineteenth century. Thousands fought for the Confederacy, and Judah P. Benjamin served as its secretary of war and secretary of state. Intolerance of Jewish Southerners was also part of their history in this era, with the crisis of wartime exacerbating anti-Semitic influences with critics blaming them for profiteering.

Postwar Reconstruction had its religious dimensions, making the years 1865–77 key ones in the history of religion in the South. In a study of evangelicals in Georgia and Tennessee, Daniel Stowell identifies three religious visions in the postwar South. The Confederate vision saw divine purpose in the result of the war, namely the purification of white Southerners for a future righteous cause. A second vision was that of Northern missionaries and a few Southern religious allies who sought reconciliation of North and South and a conversion of white and black Southerners to a "truer" religion than that they had known before the war. The third vision was that of evangelical freedpeople who created separate religious denominations from those of whites, institutionalizing their dreams of ecclesiastical independence (Stowell 1998).

The Confederate vision became the triumphant "Southern" position, with the religion of the Lost Cause. The Lost Cause had saints like Robert E. Lee and martyrs like Stonewall Jackson and grew stronger as powerful organizations like the United Confederate Veterans and the United Daughters of the Confederacy used religious rhetoric to further sacralize the Confederacy and leave their permanent mark on the Southern landscape through monuments that speak of the cause that "goes with God." The sanctification of the Confederate experience after the Civil War became one of the orthodoxies at the heart of the "Southern way of life" (Wilson 1980). Lewis Simpson sees defeat in the war leading white Southerners to clarify their understanding of "the cause of Southern civilization: redemption from the ever-increasing power of modern materialism." The image of the redemptive South changed from its predominantly Arcadian image to one more rooted in Christian eschatology (Simpson 1972: 203, 206).

White churches affirmed a second orthodoxy of the postbellum South as well: white supremacy. Historian Rufus B. Spain ranked "theories of race" as being as important to early twentieth-century Southern Baptist thought "as the Virgin Birth or the Second Coming." Donald Mathews sees an underlying theological foundation for a particularly white Southern racism. He argues Southern white theology rested in an understanding of the centrality of atonement, Christ's sacrifice, as essential for salvation and the maintenance of a moral order, and white Southerners transposed that understanding into racial segregation. The blackness of sin, in this view, could become a fearful obsession with "blackness" itself, which led to a preoccupation with purity and the black threat to it. The moral and social order rested "on distancing blacks from whites in order to sustain the purity of the white race" (Mathews 1998: 321). The concern for purity was expressed not only in racial matters but also more broadly in an effort to define strictly public and private morality, with prohibition on the sale of alcoholic beverages becoming the preeminent public moralistic movement (Link 1992).

The Progressive era produced a social gospel tradition in the nation, but scholars disagree over how widespread it has been in a South famous for its "cultural captivity" (Flynt 1998). In his study of Richmond, Virginia, Sam Shepard (2001) argues the city's churches dealt with such social issues as education, public health, woman suffrage, prohibition, child labor, and prison reform. Beth Schweiger (2000) goes even further, challenging the idea that religion in the South has been as culturally captive as earlier studies suggested and arguing that ministers generally saw the need to make religion relevant to a changing society. "Uplift" was a term representing a forward-looking ideology among black and white women and reformers in general in the late nineteenth and early twentieth centuries. Rooted in middle-class culture, the uplift ideology frowned on emotional folk religious expression, promoted the Protestant work ethic, and campaigned effectively to gain resources otherwise hard to find in the poverty-ridden, segregated South (Higginbotham 1993).

The Reconstruction era had seen black religion, in general, take permanent new directions, establishing new orthodoxies in African-American religion. Blacks withdrew from biracial churches, seeking to control their own religious destinies and institutions. The folk spirituality that had flourished in the ring shout ritual and the spirituals of the slave quarters merged after the war with the denominational churches that had existed in the antebellum South or new ones brought to the region by Northern missionaries after the war. The black church showed differing responses to the social, political, and economic restrictions of blacks in the late nineteenth century, with some leaders championing a social separatism and others expediently embracing accommodation, but "uplift" surely became the key orthodoxy of the interdenominational "black church" (Montgomery 1993).

Black and white Christians thus established racially separate denominations in the South, institutions which, despite the segregation of their church life, shared much theology, doctrine, and style, especially when compared to the more religiously pluralistic religious systems elsewhere in the United States. Paul Harvey's *Redeeming the South* (1997) looks at white and black Baptists from the end of the Civil War to the 1920s. He finds both denominations in these years becoming well-organized bureaucracies, with ministers pushing for and achieving professional status. Harvey identifies tensions and contradictions in this process, with rural church members continuing to worship in ways that did not reflect modern currents. His chapters are organized as parallel studies of these two Baptist groups, rather than one integrated narrative, suggesting the shared nature of much Southern religious practice and history yet the racially separate institutional structures that characterized the

Southern faith. Most Southerners after the Civil War lived in rural areas, and Ted Ownby (1990) explores the sacred–secular tensions that characterized life among white Southerners. Examining leisure and recreational patterns, he finds a tension between male and female worlds making for an emotionally charged region.

One of the most significant religious changes by the early twentieth century was the emergence of the Holiness/Pentecostal tradition. Holiness churches emerged from Methodism, seeking to regain the passion of Wesleyan piety in what seemed now overly formal Methodist churches. Pentecostalism, in turn, grew out of the Holiness movement and pushed toward additional spiritual manifestations. It was a national movement, but Cleveland, Tennessee became one center of it, producing the Church of God. Another leading Pentecostal group, the black-dominated Church of God in Christ, was founded in Memphis in 1906. Grant Wacker's *Heaven Below* (2001) is a landmark study recreating the experience of being Pentecostal in the early twentieth century. It combines theological understandings with social history.

Pentecostals grew out of Evangelicalism, but their sectarian, predominantly working-class status early in the twentieth century created an identity that was outside mainstream Southern evangelical churches. Catholics were even more outside the evangelical circle, making them vulnerable to Protestant suspicions and, worse, leading to violence that killed nineteen Italian immigrants in the 1890s and Ku Klux Klan intimidation in the 1920s. Nativist opposition after 1890 limited the Catholic role in politics. At the same time, they had become well incorporated into the local places in which they lived. Catholics dominated in south Louisiana and along the Gulf Coast, and the church accommodated to the South's social system, instituting, for example, its own version of Jim Crow segregation in its schools. Devotional societies, recreational agencies, recruitment of native Southern priests, and above all, parochial schools, enabled Catholics to preserve their identity in the Protestant South (Anderson and Friend 1995).

Immigrants from Eastern Europe reinvigorated Jewish life in the South after the Civil War. Southern Jews experienced the ethnic tensions among themselves often found in American society, but living in the South made for special demands. Anti-Semitism was at its worst in the decades from 1890 to 1930 and again during the civil rights years after World War II. The lynching of Leo Frank in 1915 symbolized the dangers of living in a sometimes-violent society, and in this same era, Jews who had long held political office throughout the region saw a diminished political role. The Ku Klux Klan targeted Jews among other groups for persecution in the twentieth century (Evans 1973). Jews in the South practiced their religion but often did not emphasize their cultural and ethnic distinctiveness (Malone 1997).

The South experienced a long struggle to come to terms with modernity, and its religious culture has long reflected the tensions of increasing secularization. Protestant fundamentalism appeared at the turn of the twentieth century as a response to the modernization and secularization of culture, particularly fears of liberal theology. Fundamentalism was both a set of beliefs and an organized movement. It grew out of a Protestant revivalistic heritage, a new late nineteenth-century stress on personal holiness, the spread of premillennialism (a pessimistic view that civilization was now so corrupt that only Christ's second coming could redeem it), and an assertion of orthodox doctrines like the literal truth of the Bible in the face of liberal theological challenges to such orthodoxy. William R. Glass argues that, despite the South's theological conservatism, the organized fundamentalist movement had difficulty taking root in the region. Believers seeing themselves as "fundamentalists" fought in the South as elsewhere for control of their denominations in the 1920s, but Southerners retained allegiances to their own regionally based denominations, which limited their active role in national fundamentalist groups (Glass 2001). The Scopes Trial in 1925 symbolized the conflict between modernism and traditional religious faith, a dramatic trial that fostered across the nation the image of the South as a backward, benighted Bible Belt (Larson 1997).

Partially in response to the Scopes Trial, the Vanderbilt Agrarians issued their symposium, *I'll Take My Stand* (1930), which defended the South as a spiritual bastion against the soulless materialism of American and Western culture. It was a defense of religious humanism, advocating an agrarian outlook, with spirituality posited against materialism in an idealized, humane society. Allen Tate's essay on religion in the volume argued that the Old South failed partly because it never produced a medieval form of religion that would have more closely suited the society the Agrarians believed had typified the antebellum South. Another of the Agrarians, John Crowe Ransom, in *God without Thunder* (1930), posited an orthodox God in contrast to the abstraction of modern American religion.

Southern writers in the twentieth century, including the Agrarians, were generally uncomfortable with the religiosity and emotionalism of Evangelicalism and the authoritarianism of fundamentalism. They often did see issues of spirituality as central ones in the modern world, though, and they believed the Southern historical experience, including Confederate defeat and postwar poverty, represented a resource to use in restraining American materialism. Lewis Simpson sees the creative talents of the Southern literary renaissance seeking to be literary priests. World War I drama-tized for them the "apocalypse of modern civilization: the revelation of the horror of a scientific-industrial-technological machine which is completely dependent on endless consumption, and is in fact consuming the world" (Simpson 1972: 206). Robert Brinkmeyer (1985) doubts, however, that writers fully embraced the role of artist as literary priest. Brinkmeyer sees them trying to reinvigorate their identities, combin-ing their aesthetics as modern artists with the knowledge they brought out of a Southern tradition that seemed in modern criticism to be backward and dated.

Several writers from the Southern literary renaissance were particularly significant for their treatments of religion. William Faulkner explored the impact of Calvinism on his Yoknapatawpha County characters, seeing the abstraction, fatalism, and temptation toward self-righteousness in Calvinism as problems for them. His own sympathies were with characters representing a simple folk religion, more than with those in comfortable mainstream churches (Fowler and Abadie 1991). Like Faulkner, Erskine Caldwell was concerned with the effects of Calvinism on his characters, but he usually portrayed a Calvinism embodied in sectarian, popular religiosity. He typically used it for comic effect, but did suggest that religion helped the poor accept their position in life and vent their emotions. Sin haunts Caldwell's characters in novels like *Tobacco Road* (1932) and *God's Little Acre* (1933).

Richard Wright chronicled religion as part of his early life in *Black Boy* (1940). His grandmother, with whom he lived off and on, was a Seventh-Day Adventist, a millennial group, and young Wright heard a fabulous "gospel clogged with images of vast lakes of eternal fire, of seas vanishing, of valleys of dry bones, of the sun burning to ashes, of the moon turning to blood, of stars falling to the earth." He appreciated the vivid language of the sermons but was too street wise to accept the faith; nonetheless, he learned while growing up important lessons from religion about storytelling and the importance of the black church. Zora Neale Hurston studied and wrote about folk religion expressed in storytelling, sayings, conjure, and songs. In *Mules and Men* (1935) Hurston showed the tensions between the earthy folk black culture and the sometimes hypocritical self-righteousness of church people.

Flannery O'Connor drew from religion more than any Southern writer has done. She was an outsider, an intellectually rigorous Roman Catholic in the evangelical South stricken with a fatal disease in her young adulthood. Grace, rather than good deeds, is the way to transcendence for her characters, evoking the mystery she saw as humans strive to understand the divine. Moments of epiphany mark her stories, revelations usually achieved through violence that can lead to conversion. Her characters are frequently poor, in possessions if not in spirit. O'Connor portrays Southern characters coming out of rural culture, often uneducated and religiously passionate. Middle-class people ridicule these primitivists, but her main characters reject modern society and cling to evangelical religion, actively proselytizing the masses (Brinkmeyer 1986).

The Southern literary renaissance thus made religion and spirituality major issues in modern Southern culture, but the creativity of the years between the world wars suggests the region experienced a Southern cultural renaissance, which made religion a revealing indicator of continuities and changes in that era in areas other than literature. Gospel music emerged full blown in the 1930s, a new body of religious music that combined rural folk spirituals with a lively, more urban style. Religious music had long provided a common folk language of melodies and lyrics across denominational boundaries in the South, and the appearance of the radio and recording industries commercialized gospel music among whites and blacks in separate but parallel movements (Goff 2002).

"Southern gospel" was the term that referred to white performers, especially quartets like the Blackwood Brothers from Mississippi, who began appearing on radio in 1936, and the Chuck Wagon Gang from Texas, whose recording career lasted from 1936 to 1977. New songwriters like Albert Brumley wrote such songs as "Turn Your Radio On," which went beyond the old themes of shape-note books and expressed a modern outlook for spreading the gospel word. Pentecostals embraced the rhythms and spirit of gospel music, including new instruments, and Pentecostal composers wrote enduring songs in the South, such as "The Great Speckled Bird" and "When the Saints Go Marching In." Black gospel music's "jubilee quartets," such as the Fairfield Four, the Swan Silvertones, the Dixie Hummingbirds, and the Golden Gate Quartet, were widely popular by the mid-1930s, and Mahalia Jackson would become gospel's most famous performer. The father of black gospel, Thomas Dorsey, helped organize the Gospel Singers Convention, shaped the distinctive piano style that characterized modern black gospel, and wrote such classics as "Peace in the Valley" and "Precious Lord, Take My Hand" (Harris 1992; Lornell 1988).

The folk culture that produced gospel music remains vital in parts of the South. Appalachian religion, for example, remains a distinctive form of the Southern religious pattern, with more emphasis on such sacraments as communion and sometimes foot-washing ceremonies, German pietistic fervor, and Calvinist theology than among mainstream churches in the larger Southern region (McCauley 1995). Early sociological studies portrayed religion in the mountains as simply compensation for economic deprivation (Photiadis 1978). Contemporary folklorists have provided extensive ethnographic information on local congregations and particular traditions, which show the self-understanding of religious people who are often stereotyped by mainstream culture as eccentric and backward. Jeff Todd Titon's *Powerhouse for God* (1988) studies one minister, John Sherfey, and his congregation, the Fellowship Independent Baptist Church, near Stanley, in Page County, Virginia. An accompanying record album provides the voices of the congregation, and the unusual depth of documentation includes also a film that came out of Titon's fieldwork. One spiritual phenomenon of the Upland South, snake handlers, are undoubtedly the most dramatic but thoroughly atypical representation of Southern religion. David Kimbrough (1995) participated in over 300 services among snake handlers in eastern Kentucky, and he showed snake handling as an extreme version of the fundamentalist and experiential aspects of Protestantism that have long characterized Southern religion in general.

African-American folk religion in the contemporary South is perhaps best seen in Voodoo, Vodun, hoodoo, and conjure, which are all expressions of black Southern folk practice that use the magic of herbs, animism, ancestor reverence, divination, belief in immortality, and spirit intervention to achieve a balance between the material and spiritual realms and to affect human behavior. This tradition comes from West Africa, where Voodoo was a system of religious belief and ritual, in which gods could possess humans who then danced to the movements of the gods. Slaves brought the system to the Caribbean and then to the American South after the Santo Domingue revolution in the late eighteenth century. Ritual aspects gradually diminished, and the system of magic became predominant. Hoodoo and conjure became the common terms to refer to this extranatural magic, which often combined with Catholic devotionalism in south Louisiana. Yvonne Chireau (2000) shows how conjure entered certain churches themselves, especially Spiritualist churches in New Orleans, which combined elements of Catholicism with such aspects of conjure as roots, potions, chants, lighted candles, and bodily possession.

The most recent example of the sacred in Southern creative expression, visionary art, draws from the folklife of black and white Southerners. Among the most acclaimed of Southern visionary artists are Howard Finster, Minnie Evans, William Edmundson, Gertrude Morgan, James Hampton, and Bill Traylor. They use such long-standing aspects of the predominant Southern style of religion as the special authority of the Bible, stress on individual conversion, traditional morality, and informal worship. Evangelicalism suggests the Holy Spirit is accessible to those who welcome it, and the flash of the spirit through revelations encourages visions among these artists. As with the South's writers and musicians, these visionary artists are storytellers. Adam and Eve, Noah and his ark, the birth of Christ, and his crucifixion – visionary artists often portray all of these seminal scriptural incidents (Yelen 1993).

Religious visions have often occurred to religious folk living through the secularization of the South in the mid-twentieth century, and they are a guide to this new stage of modernization. Southern visionaries have combined biblical images with those from modern life. Howard Finster incorporates Elvis Presley, John F. Kennedy, and Henry Ford into his art, as well as the words and images of religious orthodoxy. Finster's visions of the Apocalypse include not only beasts and demons from the books of Daniel and Revelation, but also the submarines and missiles associated with his era's threat of thermonuclear war (Howorth 1995). The young Billy Graham made apocalyptic fear a staple of his evangelical preaching in the 1950s, and Southern gospel music began using images of nuclear war to remind listeners to "get right with God." Songs like the Louvin Brothers' "The Great Atomic Power" and the Golden Gate Quartet's "Atom and Evil" provided the musical soundtrack to these visionary artists (Wilson 2002).

Southern religion faced one of its most dramatic challenges with the rise of an activist civil rights movement in these same years after World War II. African-American churches produced such leaders of the call for justice as Martin Luther King, Jr., Fred Shuttlesworth, and Ralph David Abernathy. Local churches and lay religious leaders were crucial in animating protest in grassroots efforts that made the movement a true regionwide protest. The protests came out of Gandhian non-violent principles, Christian teachings on social justice, and the traditions of the Southern black church. King himself grew up in the black Atlanta middle-class church, and his eloquence drew from the long heritage of rural religion that had anchored black communities under the harshest Jim Crow regimes. Aldon D. Morris (1984) argues African-American churches played the key organizing role in the movement, drawing from their traditional role as institutions well rooted in local communities.

The civil rights movement made the cause of social change a powerful moral challenge to the white South. White religious leaders typically urged moderation and opposed violence, but all too few actually challenged segregation until the increased violent resistance to change in the mid-1960s. Recent scholarship has illuminated the role of some white religious leaders in courageously championing change in Southern racial mores during the civil rights era. Mark Newman's *Getting*

Right with God (2001) is a thorough study of the range of white Baptist leadership in this era and is especially valuable in showing the role of white moderates in encouraging acceptance of desegregation. Charles Marsh (1997) achieves a rare balance in looking at how advocates and opponents of the civil rights movements used religion. He follows the stories of five religious people in Mississippi during the Freedom Summer of 1964, writing from a theological perspective and exploring how these five people brought differing understandings of God into a time of social change.

The South's struggle with desegregation came at the same time as increased modernization after World War II, with prosperity, a diversified economy, urban anonymity, mass culture, consumerism, corporate business, and social diversity challenging the traditional rural and agricultural ways of the region. The institutional church accommodated to the increasingly secular society, and the South's traditional denominations have continued to dominate the region's spiritual life in a period of enormous change. Beginning in the late 1970s, though, members of the Southern Baptist Convention (SBC), the region's largest church, fought a bitter conflict that resulted in a fundamentalist takeover (Ammerman 1990). Despite these efforts to impose an orthodox Protestant religious attitude on the contemporary South, change continues. Northerners moving south have also brought to the region denominations once little known there. The Mormons, Seventh-Day Adventists, and Unitarians all have a significant presence in the region and are growing. New immigration in the 1990s dramatically increased the presence of Roman Catholics among Hispanics in the region. The South contains noticeable numbers of Muslims and smaller numbers of Hindus, Buddhists, Sikhs, and other representatives of world religions not earlier seen in the region. In 1999 one in five Southerners identified with a non-Protestant faith, whether Catholicism, Judaism, Hinduism, Buddhism, or Islam (Tweed 1997, 2002).

All of these new Southerners and others in the region live now in an impersonal, bureaucratic world, based on the capitalist economy, which has brought spiritual as well as material relief from the poverty that afflicted generations of Southerners, but this new modern South has lost the old sense of community and personalism that suffused evangelical religion as not just a church force but a societal one. Walker Percy succeeded Flannery O'Connor as the Southern writer who most deeply explored the spiritual crisis of the region, now as part of a postmodern complex of thought. He was less self-consciously than she dealing with a "Southern" regional culture, and he was widely read in European existentialism. In 1946 he became Roman Catholic, like O'Connor, and found in it a stable worldview and framework for belief. *Love in the Ruins* (1971) was revealingly subtitled "The adventures of a bad Catholic at a time near the end of the world." In his novels, he wrote about characters rooted in remnants of a Southern tradition but facing the anomie, moral meaninglessness, and spiritual barrenness of contemporary life (Samway 1997).

In the contemporary South, writers wrestle with a changed regional context, yet religion remains a shaping force on their imaginations, as with musicians and folk artists. V. S. Naipaul visited the South in the late 1980s and that seasoned traveler wrote that his "great discovery" was that "in no other part of the world had I found people so driven by the idea of good behavior and the good religious life." He added: "that was true for black and white" (Naipaul 1989: 164). Southern writers themselves still know, as Faulkner did, that religion is "just there," a compelling part of the landscape in which they live. Some writers see in the sometimes dramatic spiritual phenomena of the South glimpses of a spirituality that is an anchor in a global world that is connected but often anonymous, materialistic, superficial, and dysfunctional – a breeding ground for spiritual questing, with the South a major spiritual landscape of the imagination.

References and further reading

Ammerman, Nancy Tatom (1990) *Baptist Battles: Social Change and Religious Conflict in the Southern Baptist Convention*. New Brunswick, NJ: Rutgers University Press.

Anderson, Jon W. and Friend, William (eds.) (1995) *The Culture of Bible Belt Catholics*. New York: Paulist Press.

Boles, John B. (1972) *The Great Revival, 1787-1805: The Origins of the Southern Evangelical Mind*. Lexington: University of Kentucky Press.

Brinkmeyer, Robert (1985) *Three Catholic Writers of the Modern South*. Jackson: University of Mississippi Press.

Brinkmeyer, Robert (1986) "A Closer Walk with Thee: Flannery O'Connor and Southern Fundamentalists", *Southern Literary Journal*, 3–13.

Chireau, Yvonne (2000) *Black Magic: Dimensions of the Supernatural in African-American Religion*. Berkeley: University of California Press.

Cobb, Buell E., Jr. (1978) *The Sacred Harp: A Tradition and Its Music*. Athens, GA: University of Georgia Press.

Eighmy, John (1972) *Churches in Cultural Captivity: A History of the Social Attitudes of Southern Baptists*. Knoxville: University of Tennessee Press.

Epstein, Dena J. Polacheck (1977) *Sinful Tunes and Spirituals: Black Folk Music to the Civil War*. Urbana: University of Illinois Press.

Evans, Eli N. (1973) *The Provincials*. New York: Atheneum.

Flynt, J. Wayne (1998) *Alabama Baptists: Southern Baptist in the Heart of Dixie*. Tuscaloosa: University of Alabama Press.

Fowler, Doreen and Abadie, Ann J. (eds.) (1991) *Faulkner and Religion*. Jackson: University of Mississippi Press.

Frey, Sylvia R. and Wood, Betty (1998) *Come Shouting to Zion: African-American Protestantism in the American South and British Caribbean to 1830*. Chapel Hill: University of North Carolina Press.

Genovese, Eugene D. (1974) *Roll, Jordan, Roll: The World the Slaves Made*. New York: Pantheon Books.

Glass, William R. (2001) *Strangers in Zion: Fundamentalists in the South, 1900–1950*. Macon, GA: Mercer University Press.

Goen, C. C. (1985) *Broken Churches, Broken Nation: Denominational Schisms and the Coming of the American Civil War*. Macon, GA: Mercer University Press.

Goff, James R., Jr. (2002) *Close Harmony: A History of Southern Gospel*. Chapel Hill: University of North Carolina Press.

Gwynn, Frederick L. and Blotner, Joseph L. (eds.) (1959) *Faulkner in the University: Class Conferences at the University of Virginia, 1957–1958*. Charlottesville: University of Virginia Press.

Harris, Michael W. (1992) *The Rise of Gospel Blues: The Music of Thomas Andrew Dorsey in the Urban Church*. New York: Oxford University Press.

Harvey, Paul (1997) *Redeeming the South: Religious Cultures and Racial Identities Among Southern Baptists, 1865–1925*. Chapel Hill: University of North Carolina Press.

Heyrman, Christine Leigh (1997) *Southern Cross: The Beginnings of the Bible Belt*. New York: Alfred A. Knopf.

Higginbotham, Evelyn Brooks (1993) *Righteous Discontent: The Women's Movement in the Black Baptist Church, 1880–1920*. Cambridge, MA: Harvard University Press.

Hill, Samuel S., Jr. (ed.) (1984) *Encyclopedia of Religion in the South*. Macon, GA: Mercer University Press.

Hill, Samuel S., Jr. (1985) "Religion and Region in America," *Annals of the American Academy of Political and Social Science*, 132–41.

Hill, Samuel S., Jr. (1998) *Southern Churches in Crisis*. New York: Holt, Rinehart, and Winston.

Howorth, Lisa (1995) "Fear God and Give Glory to Him: Sacred Art in the South," *Reckon*, 1: 41–50.

Isaac, Rhys (1982) *The Transformation of Virginia, 1740–1790*. Chapel Hill: University of North Carolina Press.

Ketchin, Susan (1994) *The Christ-Haunted Landscape: Faith and Doubt in Southern Fiction*. Jackson: University of Mississippi Press.

Kimbrough, David L. (1995) *Taking Up Serpents: Snake Handlers of Eastern Kentucky*. Chapel Hill: University of North Carolina Press.

Larson, Edward J. (1997) *Summer for the Gods: The Scopes Trial and America's Continuing Debate Over Science and Religion*. New York: Basic Books.

Levine, Lawrence H. (1977) *Black Culture and Black Consciousness: Afro-American Folk Thought from Slavery to Freedom*. New York: Oxford University Press.

Link, William (1992) *The Paradox of Southern Progressivism*. Chapel Hill: University of North Carolina Press.

Lornell, Kip (1988) *Happy in the Service of the Lord: Afro-American Gospel Quartets in Memphis*. Urbana: University of Illinois Press.

McCauley, Deborah Vansau (1995) *Appalachian Mountain Religion: A History*. Urbana: University of Illinois Press.

McLoughlin, William (1984) *Cherokees and Missionaries, 1789–1839*. New Haven, CT: Yale University Press.

McLoughlin, William, with Walter H. Couser, Jr. and Virginia Duffy McLoughlin (1984) *The Cherokee Ghost Dance: Essays on the Southeastern Indians, 1789–1861*. Macon, GA: Mercer University Press.

Malone, Bobbie (1997) *Rabbi Max Heller: Reformer, Zionist, Southerner, 1860–1929*. Tuscaloosa: University of Alabama Press.

Manis, Andrew M. (1999) *A Fire You Can't Put Out: The Civil Rights Life of Birmingham's Reverend Fred Shuttlesworth*. Tuscaloosa: University of Alabama Press.

Marsh, Charles (1997) *God's Long Summer: Stories of Faith and Civil Rights*. Princeton, NJ: Princeton University Press.

Mathews, Donald G. (1977) *Religion in the Old South*. Chicago: University of Chicago Press.

Mathews, Donald G. (1998) "'We Have Left Undone Those Things Which We Ought to Have Done': Southern Religious History in Retrospect and Prospect," *Church History*, 67: 305–25.

Miller, Randall M. and Wakelyn, Jon L. (eds.) (1983) *Religion in the Old South*. Macon, GA: Mercer University Press.

Miller, Randall M., Stout, Harry S., and Wilson, Charles Reagan (eds.) (1998) *Religion and the American Civil War*. New York: Oxford University Press.

Montgomery, William E. (1993) *Under Their Own Vine and Fig Tree: The African-American Church in the South, 1865–1900*. Baton Rouge: Louisiana State University Press.

Morris, Aldon D. (1984) *The Origins of the Civil Rights Movement: Black Communities Organizing for Change*. New York: Free Press.

Naipaul, V. S. (1989) *A Turn in the South*. New York: Alfred A. Knopf.

Newman, Mark (2001) *Getting Right with God: Southern Baptists and Desegregation, 1945–1995*. Tuscaloosa: University of Alabama Press.

Ownby, Ted (1990) *Subduing Satan: Religion, Recreation, and Manhood in the Rural South, 1865–1920*. Chapel Hill: University of North Carolina Press.

Peden, William (ed.) (1955) *Notes on the State of Virginia by Thomas Jefferson*. Chapel Hill: University of North Carolina Press, 1955.

Photiadis, John D. (1978) *Religion in Appalachia: Theological, Social, and Psychological Dimensions and Correlates*. Morgantown: Center for Extension and Continuing Education, Division of Social and Economic Development, Office of Research and Development, West Virginia University.

Raboteau, Albert J. (1978) *Slave Religion: The "Invisible Institution" in the Antebellum South*. New York: Oxford University Press.

Samway, Patrick (1997) *Walker Percy: A Life*. New York: Farrar, Straus, and Giroux.

Schweiger, Beth Barton (2000) *The Gospel Working Up: Progress and the Pulpit in Nineteenth-Century Virginia*. New York: Oxford University Press.

Simpson, Lewis P. (1972) "Southern Spiritual Nationalism: Notes on the Background of Modern Southern Fiction." In H. Ernest Lewald (ed.) *The Cry of Home: Cultural Nationalism and the Modern Southern Writer*. Knoxville: University of Tennessee Press.

Snay, Mitchell (1993) *The Gospel of Disunion: Religion and Separatism in the Antebellum South*. New York: Cambridge University Press.

Stowell, Daniel (1998) *Rebuilding Zion: The Religious Reconstruction of the South, 1863–1877*. New York: Oxford University Press.

Titon, Jeff Todd (1988) *Powerhouse for God: Speech, Chant, and Song in an Appalachian Baptist Church*. Austin: University of Texas Press.

Tweed, Thomas A. (1997) *Our Lady of the Exile: Diasporic Religion at a Cuban Catholic Shrine in Miami*. New York: Oxford University Press.

Tweed, Thomas A. (2002) "Our Lady of Guadeloupe Visits the Confederate Memorial," *Southern Cultures*, 72–93.

Upton, Dell (1986) *Holy Things and Profane: Anglican Parish Churches in Colonial Virginia*. Cambridge, MA and New York: MIT Press and the Architectural History Foundation.

Wacker, Grant (2001) *Heaven Below: Early Pentecostals and American Culture*. Cambridge, MA: Harvard University Press.

Wilson, Charles Reagan (1980) *Baptized in Blood: The Religion of the Lost Cause, 1865–1920*. Athens, GA: University of Georgia Press.

Wilson, Charles Reagan (1995) *Judgment and Grace in Dixie: Southern Faiths from Faulkner to Elvis*. Athens, GA: University of Georgia Press.

Wilson, Charles Reagan (1999) "Flashes of the Spirit: Creativity and Southern Religion," *Image*, 24 (fall): 72–86.

Wilson, Charles Reagan (2002) "Apocalypse South." In David Steel and Brad Thomas (eds.) *Reverend McKendree Robbins Long*. Davidson: Davidson College and the North Carolina Museum of Art.

Wright, Richard (1945) *Black Boy*. New York: Harper and Brothers.

Yelen, Alice Rae (1993) *Passionate Visions of the American South: Self-Taught Artists from 1940 to the Present*. New Orleans, LA: New Orleans Museum of Art.

15

African-American Fiction and Poetry

R. J. Ellis

These stories were ... not always beautiful nor their behavior pleasant ...
Zora Neale Hurston, *Moses, Man of the Mountain*

While some critics have considered African-American Southern writers alongside white ones (notably, Fred Hobson, Patricia Yaeger, Richard Gray, Anne Goodwyn Jones, and Susan Donaldson), attempts to trace Southern African-American writing's development remain scarce. Consequently, as Thadious Davis suggests, Southern writing has become "whitened" and African-American Southerners "deregionalized." In Michael Kreyling's words, a "whitened" Southern literary "tradition" results, hostile to African Americans. Yet Southern African-American writing plainly exists. For example, Charles Chesnutt's novels carefully particularize which part of the South their characters inhabit: *Mandy Oxendine* portrays a North Carolina of relative racial tolerance, underpinned (not so contradictorily) by a ready recourse to lynching. The novel's double-edged portrait of a lynching's abandonment after the victim's innocence is proved by a white preacher's confession illustrates the elusive tone and vernacular character of much Southern African-American writing:

> "I dunno," said Skinner stubbornly. "Pears like a pity ter buy this rope ... fer nuthin'. It's true the nigger didn' kill Utley, but he said he did, an' it kind er goes ag'in the grain fer me ter hear a nigger even *say* he killed a white man."
> "*Don't* be so onpatient, Jeff," said Peebles. "We ain't goin' ter hang the wrong man just to please you, even if he is a nigger. After all, he's a pretty white nigger. You kin save the rope; you may have a use for it some other time."
> "What's the matter," said a gruff voice ... "with hangin' the preacher?"
> "No, gentlemen," said Peebles ... "I purtest ag'in the si'gestion. Every man should have a fair trial."

In this painfully comic recognition of racism's fatal powers a "complex consciousness" emerges (to use Langston Hughes's term). It pervades Chesnutt's fiction, making his *oeuvre* a plausible place to begin my survey.

A chronologically better starting point, however, must be William Wells Brown's *Clotel*, the first African-American novel. Published in 1853, *Clotel* possesses a disconcerting generic fecundity, drawing upon not only fictional models, but also abolitionist documents, sermons, and slave narratives. *Clotel's* register constantly changes. In the space of a few pages, a "sentimental abolitionist" representation of a white female's demise ("There sat the Liberator, – pale, feeble...with death stamped upon her countenance, surrounded by the sons and daughters of Africa") gives way to a pastiche of blood-sports reportage, a description of a yellow fever epidemic taken from John R. Beard's biography of Toussaint L'Ouverture, and a "sentimental gothic" account of attempted seduction ("the young girl...was immediately removed to his country seat...remote, in a dense forest spreading over the summit of a cliff...in...desolate sublimity"). Such disconcerting stylistic prolixity is, however, underpinned by didactic purpose, as when exploring how interracial relationships multiply the mixed-race population, blurring the boundary between white and black. *Clotel's* eponymous heroine is described as being "as white as most...wish[ing] to become her purchasers" at a slave auction. Barbed color-line ironies result, only to be refigured in subsequent versions of *Clotel*. Both *Miralda; or, the Beautiful Quadroon* (1860–1) and *Clotelle; A Tale of the Southern States* (1864) are more militant rewritings of *Clotel*, responding to the changing nuances of contemporary color-line politics. *Clotelle* even alters two of *Clotel's* characters: George Green, "as white as most white persons," becomes Jerome Fletcher, "perfectly black...an African," while William Green is described not as a "full-bodied Negro" but a "full-blooded African." Brown's alertness to shifting ideologies of color underlies such revisions. Accordingly, in *Clotelle: or, the Colored Heroine* (1867), *Clotel's* symbolic "tragic mulatta" metamorphoses into proactive agent: where Clotel drowns herself in the Potomac before the White House, Clotelle ends up educating emancipated slaves.

Clotel is repeatedly paradigmatic. Firstly, it establishes migration as a central theme of African-American Southern fiction. Secondly, it foregrounds folk: folk anecdotes vitalize both African-Americans' commodification ("he is bin gambling all night, so I don't know who owns me dis morning") and resistance (an African-American refuses to pay more than the baggage rate when banished to the baggage car). Thirdly, *Clotel* employs sophisticated intertextuality. It is preceded by Brown's personal slave narrative, underlining how *Clotel's* African-American protagonists step beyond white abolitionism's sanctioned "slave narrative" frames. *Clotel* also responds to *Uncle Tom's Cabin*: plot parallels highlight *Clotel's* more overtly political dimensions, hinging on Clotel's illegitimate descent from Jefferson, architect of the Declaration of Independence.

Uncle Tom's huge antebellum impact makes such intertextuality inevitable. Indeed, Martin Delany's serially published novel, *Blake* (1859), stands as a full-blooded riposte, offering a bitter attack on white Christianity and a dangerous militancy.

Blake, an "intelligent slave," escapes not to flee North but to ferment revolution, traveling "From plantation to plantation...sowing...ruin to the master and redemption to the slave." Only then does he takes his family North, before returning to his birthplace, Cuba, undertaking an extraordinary voyage to Africa and back on a slaver and finally supervising preparations for a black Cuban rebellion. *Blake* fictionalizes Delany's activist concerns: promoting African-American militancy and fostering brown/black alliances by rebutting the color line's representation of blacks as subhuman.

Such radicalism is anticipated by Frederick Douglass's *The Heroic Slave* (1853) – a response to the 1850 Fugitive Slave Act. Another riposte to *Uncle Tom*, inspired by Madison Washington's successful 1851 slave mutiny, Douglass's historical novella bestows oratorical dignity upon its slave rebel. It powerfully asserts that slaves must both be granted the "natural right" to freedom and claim this right themselves: "My resolution is fixed. *I shall be free.*" An introductory frame underlines this, bestowing upon Washington the status of heroic statesman and describing his escape from slavery in a fictional revisioning of slave narrative, before depicting his shipboard mutiny. Douglass's, Brown's and Delany's fiction each possesses an arresting generic hybridity, mediating the "complex consciousness" bearing upon Western narrative modes. Each also negotiates with antebellum Southern African-Americans' beleaguered consciousnesses by featuring characters, gifted in oratory, denouncing oppression and advocating liberty. Such alertness to *performance* is always central to Southern African-American writing.

Soon after Brown and Douglass began writing fiction, they were joined by the first published female fiction writer, Frances E. W. Harper (her story, "The Two Offers," appearing in 1859). Harper's achievement requires emphasis because three of her four postbellum novels, the first published by a *Southern* African-American woman, offer a female perspective on racism and slavery's legacies. *Minnie's Sacrifice* (1869), *Sowing and Reaping* (a "*Temperance Story,*" 1876–7), and *Trial and Triumph* (combining Southern African-Americans' postbellum experiences with a temperance theme, 1888–9) were only serialized; *Iola LeRoy* (1892), however, appeared as a book: the African-American female Southern novel had definitively arrived.

Focusing on the pervasive influence of the color line, *Iola* has been highly praised. Fusing quasi-documentary reportage with the sentimental, this historical novel explores how antebellum race relations are repeatedly defined along a symbolic South–North axis. "If our Northern civilization is higher," asserts a Northern white ally of Iola, the mulatta hero, "then we should...stamp ourselves on the South and not let the South stamp itself on us." Harper understands that this sectional emphasis overlooks the "glamour" that slavery's racial divisions have cast "over the Nation." To foreground this, the first four chapters of *Iola*, set during the Civil War, make no mention of Iola, instead stressing racism's repressive impact through a series of folk anecdotes. Only then does Iola's story unfold in nationwide migrations striving to reunite a family divided by slavery. *Iola*, like *Clotel*, identifies how "South" *and* "North" are, as *a national whole*, forced by racism down divisive lines: "You have created in this country an aristocracy of color," Iola observes fiercely, in what also stands as an excoriating attack on 1890s racism. Iola resists mulatta stereotyping and its "tragic" figurations (seduction, rape, death), spurns the temptation of passing, urges race pride and rejects passivity in favor of activism: "I intend . . . to cast my lot with the freed people as a helper, teacher and friend." *Iola* may be clumsily plotted and lean too much on stilted conversations. It may also be heavily sentimental, albeit with the aim of drawing upon the sentimental's capacity to *move* its audience away from entrenched racial attitudes. But it justifies its subtitle (*Shadows Uplifted*) in Iola's vision: "beyond the shadows I see the coruscation of a brighter day and we can help usher it in, not by answering hate with hate . . . but by striving to be more generous, noble and just."

Iola, Harper's most famous novel, reads less well than the more strongly plotted *Minnie's Sacrifice*. Set in the mid-nineteenth century, this traces the lives of two mulattos, Minnie and Louis, so pale that their families pass them off as white. Even the pair themselves are ignorant of their mixed race origins. The novel explores how Minnie and Louis discover and then accept their black identities, refusing to pass because of the "loss of . . . self-respect" this entails. Less focused upon feminist themes, *Minnie's Sacrifice* climaxes not with the end of the Civil War, nor with Minnie's marriage to Louis, but with her darkly *political* murder by the Ku Klux Klan (though the key chapter remains unrecovered, the serial's final installment establishes this), so foregrounding the enduring racist legacies of the South's "peculiar institution."

Whatever the relative merits of *Iola*'s progressive racial politics compared to *Minnie's Sacrifice*'s greater realism, Harper's novels are of immense significance. In 1892 Anna Julia Cooper, in *A Voice from the South*, attacked the silencing of Southern African-American women – and her legitimate anger indicates how important Harper's voice was during the second half of the nineteenth century. It is true it was joined in 1885 by Clarissa Minnie Thompson Allen's *Treading the Winepress*, exploring the tension between race loyalty and color elitism. It is also true that, unknown to anyone, Hannah Crafts had penned her extraordinary novel, *The Bond-woman's Narrative*, sometime during the period 1853 to 1861 (most probably between 1859 and 1861). This thrilling tale of racial persecution in the slaveowning South and of escape North revolves around the treatment of Southern African-American women as commodities, the constant dangers of exposure if seeking to pass, and the sly traps that could be laid in the society that resulted. The central white male character is emblematically named "Trappe," with obvious allegorical intent. *The Bondwoman's Narrative*, like Brown's and Delany's antebellum novels, is a *tour de force* of generic hybridity. Crafts's experimental fusion of the slave narrative with the sentimental and sensational (William and Ellen Craft's narrative of their escape from slavery, and E. D. E. N. Southworth's novels, are important influences) makes it obvious how inventive aesthetic agility is one hallmark of early Southern African-American fiction. But Crafts's novel lay unpublished until the twenty-first century, vindicating Anna Julia Cooper's anger even more, while *Treading the Winepress* remained relatively unremarked compared to *Iola*, which went through four reprints within a twelve-month period during 1892–3.

Iola definitively gave female Southern African-American writers a widely heard voice. But Harper's whole career demands attention – not least because of its sheer duration – right from its beginnings, her pioneering first story, "The Two Offers." Its sharp fictional focus upon the need to resist women's recurrent complicity in their commodification is matched by her later writing's depiction of repetitions of this pattern along the color line. Harper's *oeuvre* makes clear how race and gender discrimination can together generate that kind of overdetermination where one ideological apparatus in significant part replicates (and so reinforces) the hierarchicalizing processes of another. Her writing demands a politicized commitment to resisting such interpellative combinations.

Such resistance is also integral to Harper's antebellum verse, such as "The Slave Auction," "The Slave Mother," and "Bury Me In a Free Land" – titles indicating how they draw upon abolitionist discursive conventions. Harper brings to these an arresting directness. A skilled orator, she *commands* attention through rhetorical devices (opening *in media res*; using rhetorical questions). These are found in both her abolitionist verse (in opening lines like "The sale began" and "Heard you that shriek?") and in feminist-themed poems like "A Double Standard": "Yes, blame me for my downward course, / But oh! Remember well, / Within your home you press the hand / That led me down to hell." Harper's poems mostly work within the parameters of the sensational ballad, but *Sketches of Southern Life* (1872) features six narrative poems describing "Aunt Chloe's" relationship to Uncle Jacob and how she learns to read, becomes politicized, and works for the black community. The verse incorporates a richly textured folk discourse, "you'd think them full of kindness / As an egg is full of meat" ("Aunt Chloe's Politics") – a texturing also found in her fiction, as when a cruel slaveowner is described thus: "De debil in dat woman as big as a sheep" (*Minnie's Sacrifice*).

Like Brown, Harper integrates "folk" into her writing. She draws upon its directness, memorability, clarity, and layered meanings, by which, for example, a spiritual can become a militant abolitionist paean by variably stressing its repeated phrases:

> When the *saints* go marchin' *in*
> When the saints *go* marchin' in
> *I want to be in that number*
> When the saints *go marchin' in*

Given James Baldwin's assertion "It is only in his music...that the Negro in America has been able to tell his story" ("Many Thousands Gone," 1951), African-American song must be seen as formatively integral to Southern African-American writing (see also chapter 11 of this *Companion*). The importance of song constantly emerges: Walter White's 1926 description in *Flight* ("a wild, plaintive, poignantly simple melody...a giant metronome...as...pickaxes were plunged into red clay... / Lawd, I wish'd – hunh! / – never been bawn – hunh!") had been anticipated: by Chesnutt's praise of "plantation song" for "its plaintive... note of vague longing" (*The Colonel's Dream*); by W. E. B. Du Bois's reflections on sorrow songs in *The Souls of Black Folk* ("Ever since I was a child these songs have stirred me strangely"); and by Harper's mention of "weird and plaintive melodies" (*Iola*). These in turn were anticipated by Delany's *Blake* (describing slavesongs as "made to reach the sympathies of others... apparently cheerful but in reality wailing lamentations") and, most famously, by the *Narrative of the Life of Frederick Douglass, an American Slave* (1845).

Particularly important is the multifold syncretism that results – as, for example, when antiphonal songs of African heroes journeying (flying) in search of supernatural powers interface with biblical stories. So "Go Down, Moses" reworks the story of Moses along African lines to establish that, as David Walker's antislavery *Appeal* (1829) puts it, God is a *"God of justice."* In such syncretism, also, the secular (labor) and sacred (appeals to God) coalesce in a meeting of despair, affirmation, and hope of deliverance, as African call and response melds with Christian liturgy – with the emphasis on lines of African descent. The resulting texts often bear, like palimpsests, coded messages aiming to alleviate suffering and convey means of escape – archetypically, from slavery (Douglass claimed his escape was partly inspired by "Run to Jesus").

Consequently, African Americans are accustomed to finding their cultural resources laced with subtleties of language and covert meanings – in Ralph Ellison's words, "a rhetorical canniness." *Iola*'s first chapter, "Mystery of Market Speech and Prayer Meeting," foregrounds this: the "mystery" stems from coded conversations because "It won't do to let the cat outta the bag." Harper's sentiment is anticipated by Delany: "The slaves, from their condition, are suspicious; any evasion... [is] read with astonishing precision." African-American literature repeatedly demands such "precision." Its representational and semantic *masking* requires intellectual sorting. Southern African-American fiction and poetry pick up on these characteristics with *interest*. Yet integrating the oral does more than this; it also effects a triple preservation: of continuity with the past; of integrity faced with persecution and oppression; and of modes of resistance and subversion.

"Orator poets" take up these legacies: Albery Allson Whitman, for example, at his best in two romantic-epic verse-narratives, "Not a Man, And Yet a Man" (1877) and "The Rape of Florida" (1884), addresses the (over-gendered) question, "Is manhood less because man's face is black?" and demands heroism: "Oh, let me see the Negro night and morn / Pressing and fighting on." Perhaps, then, it would have been appropriate to begin this essay not with Chesnutt or Brown but with their precursor, the first Southern orator-poet, George Moses Horton. A slave until Emancipation, Horton developed a paradigmatic desire to write and to achieve recognition as a writer in a society contriving to keep slaves illiterate. Horton put together *Hope of Liberty* (1820), covering not only such conventional subjects as love, religion, and death but also, in his best poems, slavery and his hope of leaving for Liberia. Denouncing slavery's "foul oppression," Horton uses forms influenced by the Bible and hymnal

("Come liberty.../ Roll through my ravished ears, /.../ And drive away my fears") and achieves sophisticated rhetorical effects, as when considering how a slaveowner's death inevitably harbingers "The day of separation" at the auction block ("the trembling pinnacle") "on which we soon must stand" before "tumbl[ing] on / The right or left forever." Horton's final image conflates the sunderings of a slave auction with the day of judgment, illuminating how the poem's title, "Division of an Estate," refers to "man's estate" as well as the dead slaveowner's estate – thereby hinting at the latter's damnation at the hands of a just God.

Such "rhetorical canniness" in encoding militant sentiments is typical. It is promoted, Henry Louis Gates has argued, by the African tradition of celebrating the trickster, often in animal tales advancing contradictory messages, as morality and rules of conduct clash. But trickery did not depend solely upon African legacies, as Douglass's *Narrative* shows in its account of a slave punished because he told the truth to his dissembling master: white mendacity demands reciprocal subterfuge. This is a persistent theme. In 1861 Harriet Jacobs's *Incidents in the Life of a Slave Girl* describes Linda's grandmother countering Linda's owner, Dr Flint's attempts at deceit, and Linda feigning sleep while Mrs. Flint bends over her hoping to hear her speak in her dreams. Ninety-one years later, Ralph Ellison, in *Invisible Man*, depicts an African-American youth trying to manipulate the contest he is tricked into fighting for worthless tokens tossed down by Southern whites.

An array of folk resources evolve, to be drawn upon as the Southern African-American "trickster" uses psychological ploys to counter whites' capacity for deceit. Jacobs illuminates the power plays involved in her brilliant phrase describing the slaveowning Flint: "The old sinner was politic." Signifying politics are a necessary riposte, even if moral compromise results. It is a prerequisite for survival – especially in slavery. Again, Jacobs puts it succinctly: "the condition of the slave confuses all principles of morality, and... renders the practice of them impossible." Perhaps the resulting necessity for temporizing helps account for the recurrence of a confessional mode – as taken up from the slave narrative – paradoxically searching for an *uncoded* honesty. For example, though Jacobs's *Incidents* is fictionalized to the extent that some "incidents" are altered and some characters given pseudonyms, "Linda Brent" struggles to tell the truth in the face of interdiction (moral condemnation). This constrained, beleaguered confessional structure is passed down the decades – emerging, for example, in the next century in Bigger's death-cell confession in Richard Wright's *Native Son* and Celie's desperate letters to God in Alice Walker's *The Color Purple*.

But, as *The Color Purple* also shows, folk narrative's signifying obliquity provides an alternative resource for exploring Southern African-Americans' psychological dilemmas. Deployed even in slave narrative "confessions," signifying was to be turned to more self-consciously in the postbellum period, when the institutionalization of interest in oral folk traditions mushroomed, and as the Port Royal experiment's publication of *Slave Songs of the United States* (1867) and the work of the American Folklore Society (1888ff.) impacted on Southern African-American culture. Such an emphasis stimulated writers like Chesnutt and James Weldon Johnson to carry out related research and, again, a chain of interest develops. So Zora Neale Hurston carried out folk research in Florida; then Alice Walker's *In Search of Our Mothers' Gardens* recorded her search for Hurston, while Toni Morrison's Milkman Dead, in *Song of Solomon*, deciphers children's nursery rhymes. Walker's and Morrison's work reminds us that the confessional and folk modes often combine, despite their apparently distinct ontologies (truthful revelation–trickster dissembling). Uniting them in "paradoxical hybridity" enables a versatile exploration of the contradictions that pervade the color line's apparently "commonsense" metonymy – contradictions embodied in those acts of "passing" featured by Brown, Crafts, and Harper. In one perilous, ideologically fraught sense, passing is the ultimate trickster device.

Charles Chesnutt decisively took up the issue of passing, and the need to return to him highlights his pivotal position in the evolution of Southern African-American writing. His achievement is substantial. Though sometimes marred by a fondness for plot coincidence's facile ironies, his "passing" fictions grip the reader with their *in media res* openings and establish patterns of leaving and returning that, in the systole and diastole of their passion and despair, expose the interweave of class and caste lacing the color line. Early in his career Chesnutt deals with passing fairly straightforwardly, but his first two novels, *Mandy Oxendine* (published posthumously) and *House Behind the Cedars* (1900), take up the theme compellingly. *House* is better known, but its oratorical redolence seems at times ponderous when set beside the dark levity of *Mandy* – arguably the better novel. *Mandy* has been criticized for awkwardly conjoining a layer of social realism (the politics and ethics of passing) with a (late-arriving) suspense plot. Yet the latter serves to drive home how equivalent the conditions of poor white and poor black Southerners ironically are, and how lynching in particular, and racism generally, serve to stave off this recognition. An early attempt to rape Mandy by a "fine gentleman," even though he believes her to be white, leads up to this, as does Mandy's conversation with her black ex-lover:

> "Who is this fine [white] gentleman that will marry [you,] a sand-hill mulatto?"
> "You forgit . . . I'm passin' for white."
> "Who is this fine [white] man . . . who will marry a sand-hill poor white girl?"

Poor white/poor black parallels are made blatant. Mandy, by trying to escape such poverty and so "declar[e] her independence, her revolt," seeks to be an active agent – more positively than *House*'s Rena, a "tragic mulatta" whose attempt to pass is made at her brother's behest.

Like *Mandy*, *House* explores both the "sad tangle" of antebellum relations across the color line (though the echelon of black society seeking to pass is more affluent), and how ideology can "confine" race "unconsciously, and as a matter of course . . . within the boundaries of . . . the customs of the country." By its end *House* has become near-allegorical: Rena stands alone at a point where paths cross; down one advances a white man, her ex-fiancé, who renounced her on discovering her mulatta identity; down another advances a mulatto – attracted by her status as a "bright mulateer." Rena here symbolizes the color line's labyrinthine concatenation of class, caste, sexuality, and desire. Though the effect is powerful (Rena meets her folk-fabled "devils" at the crossroads), it is, nevertheless, beclouded by Rena's objectification in her final, quasi-allegorical role.

Chesnutt's fictions repeatedly explore how "passing" catalyses central issues concerning the color line, but they always display another characteristic of turn-of-the-century Southern African-American writing: political engagement. His story, "The Wife of his Youth," for example, focuses on how the color line interacts with another political line: that between the Northern urban sophisticate and the Southern agrarian field-hand – a line shadowed by history. Chesnutt shows how relations between Northern and Southern African Americans, as well as skin shades, determine membership of a Northern mulatto "Blue Vein" society. In the story's melodramatic denouement, one of the leading "Blue Veins" symbolically chooses to embrace his black Southern past (the "wife of his youth") rather than renounce it (her), as he easily could.

However, Chesnutt's most political text is *The Marrow of Tradition* (1901), a novel provoking controversy upon publication, since white Southerners regarded its portrait of white supremacist violence during the 1898 Wilmington race riot as libelous. In fact, the book's treatment of turn-of the-century racial politics is one of its strengths: *Marrow* displays Chesnutt's sophisticated understanding of how consensual hegemony rests upon repression – whether threatened or imposed (prisons; lynchings; rioting). Repressive apparatuses are revealed as the nurturing *marrow* of hegemony, itself fleshed out by "traditional" discourses of racism. Chesnutt gives a full account of hegemony's processes: "this is the age of the crowd and we must have the crowd with us." Chesnutt's final novel, *The Colonel's Dream* (1905), takes up these political themes. Again controversial, this time because of its preparedness to work from within "sympathetic white" viewpoints, *Dream* explores the dimensions of "the survival of the spirit of slavery" through a startling counterpoint, setting whites' plangent nostalgia for the Old South alongside harrowing depictions of slavery's vitriolic postbellum legacy: racist oppression.

Chesnutt's representations of hegemony's processes have been seen as a pessimistic acceptance of the inevitability of white supremacy. But such an emphasis neglects Chesnutt's subtle deployment of free indirect discourse, shading in and out of different points of view, and enabling, for example, an even-handed treatment of *Marrow*'s black "badman," Josh's resistance to white violence. Similarly, in *Dream*, the failure of the eponymous white colonel's philanthropic dreams is in part attributable to his interior weaknesses. Overall, Chesnutt is far from upbeat – surely because of his shrewd political grasp:

> Cartaret [a newspaper editor] . . . held out to . . . Republicans . . . the glittering hope that, with the elimination of the Negro vote, a strong white Republican party might be built upon the New South . . . [but his] promised result is still in the future . . . The nation was rushing forward with giant strides towards colossal wealth and world-domination.

Chesnutt is an astute explorer of Reconstruction's aftermath – Jim Crow's rise during the 1870s, Northern troop withdrawals after the Hayes-Tilden Compromise (1877), and growing racist oppression by an increasingly imperial white America.

Yet Chesnutt's chief importance resides in the way he explores how folk resources enable African Americans to explore repression *cunningly*. This can be seen best in his complexly framed hybrid narratives in *The Conjure Woman* (1899). Partly aimed to draw upon Uncle Remus's large readership, Chesnutt's tales in fact provide a sharply ironic commentary on Chandler Harris's amiable constructions. "The Goophered Grapevine," the first tale, introduces the collection's folk-anecdote mode. Its white frame-narrator introduces a trickster figure, the internal narrator-cum-storyteller, Julius, an ex-slave trying to retain the income he illicitly obtains from a vineyard abandoned since the war. He fails (the white frame-narrator buys the vineyard despite Julius's story about a conjure-woman's spell blighting it). In subsequent episodes, however, Julius's tale-spinning succeeds in gaining him advantage while each tale carries coded messages: hidden fierce satirizations of antebellum African-Americans' objectification, in which slaves are "conjured" into hams or lumber, signifying both their commodification in slavery and, simultaneously, their almost equivalent plight in postbellum America.

The Wife of His Youth (1899), a second collection of stories, also takes up folk forms in its quietly ironic anecdotal style, often overlain by a vein of broad humor. For example, the accomplished "The Passing of Grandison" depicts two generations of Southern whites comically outmaneuvered by their slave, who steals his whole family from under their eyes through ingenious trickery. Indeed, most of Chesnutt's fiction draws on folklore. So, for example, Josh in *The Marrow of Tradition* owes a debt to "badmen" like Stagolee, and his speech rings with oral cadences. Chesnutt in these ways helped promote the literary exploration of folk modes for their linguistic resourcefulness and formal virtuosity.

As the nineteenth century came to a close, such exploration became well established, if sometimes difficult to pin down, since folk often inheres in what James Weldon Johnson called "the elusive undertone...not heard by the ears." Established folk modes, like the moving oratory of sermons, remained influential ("he knew all the arts and tricks...the modulation of the voice...the pause for effect, the rise...to the terrific, thundering outburst" – *The Autobiography of an Ex-Colored Man*). But now they were joined by a significant awareness of emerging forms, such as jazz and (especially) blues – commercially arranged and published by Hart Wand, Arthur "Baby" Seals, and W. C. Handy, self-nominated "Father of the Blues." Symptomatically, Handy noted all his sources, recognizing how cultural recovery was important: African-American art was increasingly being regarded as a means of "preserv[ing]...manners and customs" (Pauline Hopkins, 1900). Literature itself became subject to recovery: Victoria Earle Matthias in 1895 called for "an earnest and systematic effort" to preserve "Our Race Literature." In this process, cultural politics becomes inextricably entangled with any understanding of Southern African-American writing.

Chesnutt almost personifies this trend because of his recurrent subvention of political themes into folk forms. Such integration of folk with politics also occurs in the work both of earlier writers, like the disturbing minor poet, J. Mord Allen (1875), who attacked "de lynchin's in de South" and the pretensions of a growing Black bourgeoisie (in "Eureka" and "This Race's Benefactor"), and of contemporaries, like Alice Ruth Moore Dunbar-Nelson. In *Violets and Other Tales* (1895) and *The Goodness of St. Rocque and Other Stories* (1899), Dunbar-Nelson explores Creole culture and history in impressionistic experimental cameos (like "The Praline Woman") and plangent stories (like "The Stones of the Village," a tale of "successful" passing). Yet feminist concerns repeatedly emerge, as in "Sister Josepha," whose eponymous heroine cannot leave her convent because, penniless and beautiful, she is vulnerable to male predation. Dunbar-Nelson's biggest mark was made by her 1920s anthologizing, yet at her best she emerges as a committed and clear, if minor, writer:

> . . . [Douglass] was no soft-tongued apologist,
> He spoke straightforward, fearlessly, uncowed;
> The sunlight of his truth dispelled the mist,
> And set in bold relief each dark-hued cloud;
> To sin and crime he gave their proper hue,
> And hurled at evil what was evil's due.

Setting aside the awkward repetition (of "hue"), Dunbar-Nelson's selection of her subject, Douglass, is symptomatic of the way politics often dominated during these "decades of disappointment" following Reconstruction's breakdown in the South.

No one manifests this propensity more than Sutton E. Griggs, who published five highly political novels between 1899 and 1908. Griggs lacks Chesnutt's subtlety, but his novels, published at his own expense and aimed unswervingly at an African-American audience, are a militant response to Southern racism. His melodramatic plots contain startlingly direct accounts of white racism and the need to establish coordinated resistance to such oppression.

The most interesting of Griggs's five novels is his first, *Imperium in Imperio* (1899). Owing debts to the gothic, this *bildungsroman* traces the lives of two African Americans concerned to promote the "equality of the race" through the establishment of an *imperium in imperio*, an autonomous nationwide organization. However, one (Bernard) comes to regard the Imperium as the militant path to black nationalist independence, while the other (Belton) remains intent on achieving equality. It is difficult to assess whether Griggs sides with Belton or the revolutionary Bernard. *Imperium* presents itself as a set of documents bequeathed to Griggs by "Berl Trout," the Imperium's deceased secretary of state. Since the book's "Introduction" records that Trout is "noted for his strict veracity and . . . his conscience," this seems to imply that Griggs endorses Trout's decision to betray the Imperium following Bernard's execution of Belton for opposing his plan to take over America. This would match the stance in Griggs's later novels, which generally favors Belton's more moderate line. Yet Griggs's opening "endorsement" of Trout echoes the "framing" endorsements found in slave narratives. Since such endorsements were mostly furnished by whites, the suspicions of Griggs's target African-American readership concerning Trout (his *fishiness*) will arguably be aroused. This mistrust might then be compounded by the way *Imperium's* thematic earnestness is regularly undercut by a disconcertingly jocose tone – especially in anecdotes describing how Belton relies upon signifying trickery to survive. *Imperium* should perhaps be read less straightforwardly than Trout's integrationist frame apparently advocates. Its message may be more incendiary.

Griggs's writing is certainly deeply politicized. But an even clearer signpost of what is to come is the work of James Weldon Johnson. Johnson rose to prominence by composing the "Negro National Anthem" ("Stony the road we trod, / . . . / Yet with a steady beat, / Have not our weary feet / Come to the place from which our fathers sighed") and by the success of his blues-based lyric, "Sence You Went Away" ("Seems lak to me de sun done loss his light, / Seems lak to me der's nothin' goin' right / Sence you went away"). Early influences – the Ohioan dialect poets Paul Dunbar and James Edwin Cabell and the Southerner Daniel Webster Davis, who composed African-American satirizations of white minstrelsy – are evident in Johnson's collection, *Fifty Years and Other Poems* (1917). Johnson's best poems, like Davis's, incorporate an encoded militancy, as when "O Black and Unknown Bards" praises the spirituals that Johnson would archive in the 1920s – "Steal Away to Jesus," "Jordan Roll," "Swing Low," and "Go Down, Moses": "Mark [their] bars, / How like a mighty trumpet-call they stir / The blood."

Both Johnson's treasuring of folk and his themes clearly exhibit black consciousness and race pride, marking him out as a progenitor of what was to consolidate in the 1920s as the New Negro Renaissance. He constitutes a self-consciously transitional intellectual, building on contemporary developments. Thus, when his *Autobiography of an Ex-Colored Man* (1912) explores the theme of passing, it is indebted to Du Bois's contemporaneous insistence on the formative importance of "the color line." When Johnson's near-white first-person narrator discovers he is a mulatto, his reflections echo Du Bois: "every colored man in the United States . . . is forced to take his outlook . . . from the viewpoint of a *colored* man . . . all . . . must run through the narrow neck of this one funnel. . . . This gives to every colored man . . . a sort of dual personality." *Ex-Colored* is a psychological exploration of this issue: Johnson's narrator details how he at first embraces his newly discovered mulatto identity but then decides to pass. A sense of placelessness results, rehearsing Southern African-Americans' anxieties about their location as Reconstruction broke down and they were systematically excluded from their democratic rights – their identities forcibly "passed" out of the USA's *demos*. To this end the narrator, X, is left nameless. Interpolated documentary-style commentary foregrounds these political considerations, so promoting recognition of social allegories embedded in the text – as when X is compelled to play ragtime endlessly by a white millionaire, until it "took a superhuman effort to keep . . . going" and the millionaire "seemed . . . some grim, mute but relentless tyrant." This symbolizes both the exploitation of black labor and the prurient extraction of cultural capital – prefiguring white "tourist slumming" during the New Negro Renaissance.

Johnson's mistrust of white tourist "primitive folk" enthusiasms underpins his rejection in the 1920s of dialect as "an instrument with but two full stops, humor and pathos." Instead, Johnson turned to folk *forms* – particularly the sermon, which he felt provided a way of "express[ing] the racial spirit by symbols from within," since "The old-time Negro preacher... [gave] people of diverse language and customs... their first sense of unity." His *God's Trombones: Seven Negro Sermons in Verse* (1927), begun in 1918 with "The Creation," explore "the... varied range of emotions encompassed by the human voice" and draw upon black sayings, idioms, and other folk forms – especially the spiritual (Johnson published two collections of spirituals in 1925–6):

> And the echo sounded down the streets of heaven
> Till it reached away back down to that shadowy place,
> Where Death waits with his pale, white horses.

Johnson's *oeuvre* constitutes a wobbly bridge (his views on dialect were rarely shared) to a new sort of sociocultural consciousness marked by the emergence of a "New Negro," as defined by Alain Locke in 1925, and as mentioned before him by such writers as Rollin Hartt (1921), William Pickens (1921), Booker T. Washington (1900), and Sutton Griggs (1899).

The "New Negro" sharpened the emphasis on "cultural heritage," following Johnson's lead ("slave music will be the most treasured heritage of the American negro," 1912). But the nature of this emphasis changed. Bernard Bell called it "ancestralism": a process in which urban (based, if not born) artists looked back to an earlier, "pre-urban" heritage – an American *and* African folk-retrospect interplaying, sometimes uneasily, with a maturing black cultural nationalism and a desire to be contemporary – typically by interacting with modernist experiment (especially in the visual arts). Negotiating these tensions proved to be both fruitful and fraught – for example, in the way "New Negro" reworkings of the celebration of primitivism by modernists like Picasso and Gauguin wrestled uneasily with the shades of "cultural tourism."

These debates centered on Harlem, but the "New Negro Renaissance" occurred nationwide, taking in Georgia Johnson in Washington, Anne Spencer in Lynchburg, and John F. Matheus in Tallahassee. Interchange between North and South was inevitable: the Great Migration, generated first by a collapsing Southern agrarian economy and then World War I's restricting of European immigration, had further promoted such exchange. The beleaguered position of Southern African Americans – signaled by a continuing rise in the number of lynchings – became a core theme of the writing of this period, as part of a reestimation by African Americans of their position. Indeed, post-World War I white persecution of African-American soldiers – repeatedly attacked if appearing in uniform – drove home to African Americans their separateness, as both Walter White's *The Fire in the Flint*, and Richard Wright's

"Long Black Song" record: "them white folks beat up a black sojer yestiddy... jus in from France... still wearin his sojers suit." Race riots followed, in 1919, accompanied by African-American demands for change, and a growing sense of alienation. Consequently, black art was even more resolutely used as a political instrument promoting African-American unity. One result was a burst of Southern African-American writing – Walter White, Zora Neale Hurston, and Sterling Brown, all born in the South, were central Renaissance figures. In their work the art of poet and musician, novelist and folklorist conjoined – as in Sterling Brown's blues-ballad "Ma Rainey," its different voices twined in dialogic unity:

> I talked to a fellow, an' the fellow say,
> "She jes' catch hold of us, somekindaway.
> She sang Backwater Blues one day:
> It rained fo' days an de skies was dark as night...
>
> Thundered an' lightened an' the storm begin to roll
> Thousan's of people ain't got no place to go.
>
> Den I went an' stood upon some high ol' lonesome hill,
> An' looked down on the place where I used to live.
>
> An' den de folks, dey natchally bowed dey heads an' cried..."
>
> Dere wasn't much more de fellow say:
> She jes' gits hold of us dataway.

Such interdisciplinary integration promoted an explosive increase in cultural activity – especially in music: boogie-woogie, gospel and, above all, jazz and blues variants. More secularly, toasts (tortuous narratives, often in couplets, using obscene and vulgar language – a source of rap) drew on the tradition of signifying to counter persecution, harm, or "capture" – as in "The Signifying Monkey":

> Monkey hollered, Ow!
> I didn't mean it Mr. Lion!
> Lion said, You little flea-bag, you,
> ...
> I wouldn't a-been in this fix a-tall
> Wasn't for your signifying jive.

Such developments were intertwined with the continuing recovery of African-American culture promoted by figures like Weldon Johnson, Arthur Schomberg (who urged in 1925 that "The American Negro must remake his past") and, especially, Zora Neale Hurston.

Believing, as she phrased it in "Characteristics of Negro Expression," that "Negro folklore is not a thing of the past" but "in the making," Hurston researched and assembled *Mules and Men* (1934), a collection of folktales acutely sensitive to Southern

African-American vernacular culture. For some critics, like Sterling Brown, the collection was insufficiently "bitter," but this verdict neglects Hurston's understated fierceness about the position of African-American females, as when "Big Sweet" is humiliatingly defeated in a "signifying" contest by Joe Willard and his male friends. The collection, though, also offers extraordinary warmth. If lapsing at times into loose sentimentality, *Mules* mines (somewhat derivatively) an important folk seam – drawing on folktales like "All God's Chillen Got Wings" to depict "High John de Conquer," crossing "like the albatross" from Africa to protect African Americans through his "brer rabbit" trickery. Hurston's work features a range of traditional folk characters: "High John"; "Daddy Mention" (related to the "bad men" of ballad, like Stackolee); and "Runaway Bill," an escaping "bad slave" ("de Mosser hain't cotch me, / An' he never will," Bill declares in *The Sanctified Church*, 1983). Hurston possesses an acute ear for dialect – as in "De Reason Niggers Is Working So Hard," in which an African-American outraces a white to two bundles lying in the road, in order to leave the smaller to "de white man." Yet this smaller bag contains "a writin' pen and ink," not the work-tools found in the larger one. The anecdote ends with a rhythmic vernacular punch line: "ever since then . . . de white man been sittin' up figgerin, ought's a ought, figger's a figger, all for de white man, none for de nigger." Hurston's use of folk elements gives her stories a startling directness, clarity, and signifying complexity, as in the openly feminist "Sweat" (1926): "'Mah tub of suds is filled yo' belly with vittles more times than yo' hands is filled it. Mah sweat is done paid for this house and . . .' / She seized the iron skillet from the stove . . . 'Ah'm gonter stay right heah till Ah'm toted out foot foremost.'" Hurston's best stories often revolve around such domestic *rearrangements* – social and sexual.

The 1930s and early 1940s witnessed Hurston's finest work. Her first novel, *Jonah's Gourd Vine*, published, like *Mules and Men*, in 1934, recounts the infidelities of a Southern African-American preacher. In 1938, *Tell My Horse*, a second book of folklore (using Caribbean/African-American comparisons) appeared, followed in 1942 by her controversial autobiography, *Dust Tracks on a Road* (with its unpopular insistence that race consciousness be stripped of its shibboleths to prevent its becoming a species of African-American hegemonic repression). All these are significant texts, but *Their Eyes Were Watching God* (1937), her second novel, is in another class.

Again folk-rooted, *Their Eyes* possesses considerable complexity, established by the play between its third-person narrative frame and the story told by the central character, Janie. Her domestic-picaresque account of seeking fulfillment in a male-dominated world is enhanced by a subtle interweave of registers, ranging from poetic point-of-view indirect discourse ("She was a dust-bearing bee sunk into the sanctum of a bloom, the thousand sister-calyxes arch to meet the love-embrace and the ecstatic shiver") to simple folk anecdote: "de white man throw down de load and tell de nigger man tuh pick it up. He pick it up because he have to, but he don't tote it. He hand it to his womenfolks. De nigger woman is de mule oh de world as fuh as Ah can see." Significantly, Janie's embittered grandma utters these words, *not* Janie, whose story eludes what her grandma sees as women's fate. Yet, as Houston Baker points out, economics also forms an inescapable backdrop to Janie's progress. It is the dialectic between her female spiritual rise and this other pressing material reality that fuels the book's thematic complexity (however insecure its feminist credentials might be). Like *Dust Tracks*, the novel is controversial, declining the option of representing "African-American community" as a secure haven to explore instead a more precarious concept: *togetherness*.

Hurston's later works mark a decline. *Moses, Man of the Mountain* (1939), retelling its biblical story as an allegorical African-American saga, and *Seraph on the Suwanee* (1948), a story of poor whites in South Florida (written, she claimed, to show that African Americans could write about whites), dilute her folk concerns – though overall it is precisely Hurston's involvement with folk that remains exceptional. Jean Toomer may have briefly taught in rural Georgia, and there heard black folk songs, whose "gold and hints of an eternal purple" (1922) helped inspire *Cane*'s descriptions, but *Cane* is best regarded as an audacious narrative experiment.

Diverging somewhat from a folk-rooted approach and difficult to characterize, *Cane* is as much of a watershed as *Dust Tracks*. It might be termed a prose/poem/story-cycle hybridly tracing the contemporary migrations of African Americans from Georgia to Washington, Chicago, and back to Georgia. Toomer excels at poetic evocation, as in "Blood-Burning Moon": "A large pile of cane stalks lay like ribboned shadows . . . The scent of cane came from the copper pan and drenched the forest and the hill that sloped to factory town." The overpoweringly excessive sensual depiction of this "fragrance" prepares the way for the deadly argument caused by a woman crossing the color line that follows. Southern African-American females are depicted as in the grip of a dangerous, mythologized sexuality, and a compelling sense of how the rural South's human geography maims relationships results. In this way, "Blood-Burning Moon" is *Cane*'s pivot, contextualizing both the suffocating claustrophobia of the opening Southern stories and the consequent migrations – to Washington and/or the North. "Portrait in Georgia," immediately preceding "Blood-Burning Moon," underlines the latter's pivotal function by constructing a white female body out of the ritualized progress of a Southern lynching: "Hair . . . / coiled like a lyncher's rope / Eyes – fagots / Lips – . . . the first red blisters / And her slim body, white as the ash / of black flesh after flame." This concatenation of violence and death with sexuality rehearses the condensations contained within the Southern signifier, "lynching." *Cane*'s intensity in such moments gives it a power that overrides its sometimes-incoherent grasp of gender politics and its occasional tendency towards over-conventional description.

"Kabnis," *Cane*'s closing fiction, set in the South once more, seals this achievement. It depicts the uneasiness of two Northern African Americans confronted by Southern privations and racist threats in a fiction/drama fusion probing, modernistically, at the consciousness of its protagonists, as they gyrate under the thrall of white racism. "Kabnis" ends with a blind, dying, prophet-figure ("Father John") denouncing the white South for its crimes: "Th sin whats fixed . . . upon th white folks . . . f tellin Jesus – lies. O th sin th white folks 'mitted when they made th Bible lie." *Cane* stands as a compelling achievement. Like John Matheus's stories, "Fog" (1925) and "Clay" (1926 – depicting an African-American knifing a white who accuses him of theft), *Cane* explores the rural South with striking intensity.

Distinct from both Toomer's and Hurston's work is Walter White's – underlining the artistic range that the catchall rubric "New Negro Renaissance" encompasses. White's novels are relatively straightforward. *The Fire in the Flint* (1924) is a pessimistic exposé of lynch law's effects upon "a typical Southern town." Alert to lynching's malodorous impact ("so vast, so sinister, so monstrous"), the novel draws upon White's personal infiltration of white supremacist groups. White could pass for white, and his other novel, *Flight* (1926), explores this issue. *Flight*'s mulatta protagonist, far from any "tragic" conventionalization, resists passivity to secure a quasi-feminist consciousness. Her initial, Whitmanesque determination to "contribute a verse" to humankind's "powerful play" ends up as a *voluntary* decision to cease passing and return to "my own people." White may work within what Arthur P. Davis calls the "lynching-passing" school, but his contribution is ground-breakingly naturalistic.

The clear differences between the aesthetic practices of Hurston, Toomer, and White should not be surprising. A conscious "Renaissance" desire to establish a comprehensive cultural superstructure existed, encompassing, in Alain Locke's phrase, "the development...of literary coteries" debating about varieties of art and literary practice. Central to the variegated flowering that resulted was poetic experimentation, especially that exploring dialect in new ways, as poets responded differently to Weldon Johnson's call for verse to hold onto "the racial flavor...the imagery, the idioms...the distinctive humor and pathos,...but...also be capable of voicing the...highest emotion and aspirations." Despite Johnson's contention that something "larger than dialect" was needed, Sterling Brown, the best Southern poet of this period, responded by developing dialect's *range*. Even Johnson recognized that his reservations had been finessed: "Brown's...is not the dialect of the comic minstrel tradition or the sentimental plantation tradition; it is the...living authentic speech of the Negro." As Brown puts it, "Dialect, or the speech of the people, is capable of expressing whatever the people are" through its "accuracy...flow...color...[and] pungency." Brown, like the Kansas-born Langston Hughes, succeeded in drawing his poetry close to African-American quotidian life without lapsing into local color clichés. Yet, unlike Hughes, Brown also, in Wagner's phrase, gives voice to "the folk" more than "the [urban] masses," as when representing "Slim Greer," a folk-inspired trickster badman ("Talkinges' guy / An' biggest liar," who "Passed for white, / An' he no lighter / Than a dark midnight"). Where Hughes's blues and jazz based poems are rooted in the urban, Brown exhibits a mistrustfully ironic perspective on city culture, as in "Memphis Blues":

> Memphis go
> By Flood or Flame;
> Nigger won't worry
> All de same –

> Memphis go
> Memphis come back,
> Ain' no skin
> Off de nigger's back

Brown here shapes a warning about how (Gomorrahan) decadence during the Renaissance may lead to neglect of the ramifications of everyday racist discrimination. Brown's "take" on the city's bedazzling cultural variety was not entirely negative – his affectionate satire "Sporting Beasley" recognizes its vitality – but he always conveys the actualities of urban African Americans' segregated liminality. Brown skewers not only white racism but also those privileged African Americans offering only an abstract commitment to the race.

Brown's best poems are compressed narratives incorporating folk sensibility, as in "Odyssey of Big Boy" or "Long Gone," which explores the psychology of a rootless, casually sexist railroad worker in a spare blues structure, framed by synoptic first and last stanzas:

> I like yo' kin' of lovin',
> Ain't never caught you wrong,
> But it jes' ain' nachal
> Fo' to stay here long
> . . .
> Ain't no call at all, sweet woman,
> Fo' to carry on –
> Jes' my name and jes' my habit
> To be Long Gone.

Brown's verse narratives characteristically possess a strong socio-historical awareness. So "New St. Louis Blues" combines a disruptive critique of "Renaissance uplift" with criticism of female oppression: "Market Street woman noted fuh to have dark days, / Life do her dirty in a hundred onery ways" (1932). Brown's feminism can startle: when equating a Renaissance "Cabaret" with a slave auction, his depiction of the commodified position of females features a disturbing lack of specificity concerning color: "*Show your paces to the gentlemen. / A prime filly, seh. / What am I offered, gentlemen, gentlemen . . .*" Skewed gender relations (the implicit question being, what color is the "slaveowner" now?) repeatedly generated controversy during the Renaissance. Sexual liberation in the 1920s demanded a revisiting of African-American male/female relations.

Georgia Johnson's best poems (like "The Heart of a Woman") explore this arena, as do, more complexly, Anne Spencer's – probing at female dissatisfactions in an allusive modernist style, interweaving free verse with iambic rhythms. "Before the Feast at Sushan" (1920), Spencer's best poem, has a clear feminist theme: "Slave send Vashti to her king": the male speaker's embedding of an instruction to his woman ("Vashti") in an order to his "slave" dramatizes their interchangeability in his worldview. His voice is overbearingly egotistical. In the final nine-line stanza the word "I" appears seven times; and four successive lines start with the first-person singular, like a strand of barbed wire protecting his arrogance. Similarly, "Letter to My Sister" cautions, "It is dangerous for women to defy the gods...but worse still if you mince timidly." Representing the male as "king" or "god," Spencer establishes a deadly satire on male pretensions while exhorting the female to reject "timid" subjugation. Both Spencer and Johnson (especially in *Bronze*, 1922) echo in verse some of Hurston's themes (though not her style).

The Depression's long economic slump, following the 1929 Wall Street Crash, triggered a series of cultural transitions during the 1930s and 1940s. Southern African Americans were confronted by agrarian decline enhanced by mounting problems – climactic (droughts, boll weevil) or economic (interest rate rises and "tractoring-out") – and their social consequences: racism, further lynchings, and such shocking events as the Scottsboro' trial of eight African-American youths accused of raping two white prostitutes. Brown's blues-based explorations of these difficulties continue to make him a key figure. He also became involved with the New Deal's Writers Project Administration, thus linking him to a new generation – Wright, Ellison – and to a general, albeit uneasy, engagement with socialism and communism. What these writers often possessed in common was anger – clearly evident in *Southern Road* (as in its title poem), it is ever-present in Brown's poetry:

> I talked to Old Lem
> and Old Lem said:
> They weigh the cotton
> They store the corn
> We only good enough
> To work the rows;
> They run the commissary
> They keep the books
> We gotta be grateful
> For being cheated. (1939)

The poem comes to a dead trochaic halt on the final word "cheated," emphasizing its bitterness. But such anger is accompanied by Brown's sense of social history: "Remembering Nat Turner" (1949), for example, records Brown's discovery that Turner's wooden memorial has been used, according to an unreliable "old white woman," as "kindling" by nearby "nigger tenants." Brown's finely nuanced dialect voice provides continuity into the 1960s. He is certainly underrated.

Arna Bontemps provides further – if less experimental – continuity. His poems offer conventional, well-crafted rehearsals of such central Renaissance themes as exile, return, and loss. Similarly, his prose eschews the varieties of experimentalism found in Hurston and Toomer, yet he writes with considerable power in his best work: *God Sends Sunday* (1931), a poetic, risqué account of a jockey's picaresque adventures; *Black Thunder* (1936), a novel about the Virginian Prosser slave insurrection of 1800; and, best of all, "A Summer Tragedy" (1933), portraying an old sharecropping couple's decision to die rather than face an impecunious dotage. As they drive to their joint suicide, the sharecropper's expression resembles "the face of a man being burned" – an image invoking lynching to convey the equivalences of Southern deprivation. This sort of grimly accurate realist writing presages Richard Wright.

Wright, though, stands closer to the category of proletarian writer, as in his first collection, *Uncle Tom's Children* (1938). Though Wright moved to Chicago after publication of his first story, *Uncle Tom's Children* as a whole draws upon his Southern background, as does his final work, *The Long Dream* (1958). Wright's powerful writing possesses an unrelentingly humanistic emphasis upon the centrality of the individual, thinking consciousness – so much so that at times he seems almost proto-existential (indeed, eventually exiled in France, he befriended Camus and Sartre). However, this strain in his work is poorly reconciled with a fundamentally naturalistic determinism: an insistence on the inescapable threats of white oppression. Symbols repeatedly drive home its ominous presence. In "Long Black Song," for example, a young mother, Sarah, allows her baby to batter a broken clock, and when asked why by a visiting white salesman, explains that her farm life has no need for time: "We jus' don' need no time, Mistah." But the baby's beating-out of "time" is menacingly pervasive, just as Sarah's life illustrates that, though her "time" may not need hourly measurement, history cannot be beaten. Her heart's desire has become a World War I conscript in the trenches; her husband, Silas, is tied to the self-defeating vortices of sharecropping; and the legacies of Southern racism are driven home by the salesman's pressing of sex upon her, so causing Silas to kill him and Silas's consequent murder by a white mob. The symbolism is heavy, but effective, and, as always, the writing powerful.

Indeed, Wright often comes close to achieving what he saw in Mencken: "this man was...using words as a weapon" (*Black Boy*, 1945). It fulfils Wright's stipulation in "Blueprint for Negro Writing" that "Negro writers" should "feel" what they write with a "passion and strength that will...communicate...to millions who are groping like themselves." Sometimes this desire for immediacy leads to one-dimensionality, as in the predominance of a male-centered viewpoint (females gain short shrift, even when raped). However, Wright takes a trait of protest novels that Baldwin saw as a weakness – the way they "mirror...confusion, dishonesty, panic, trapped...in the sunlit prison of the American dream" – and makes it a strength. His confused, constrained characters struggle with their ideologically molded consciousness and the resulting patterns of bitterness and frustration. "Bright and Morning Star," added to *Uncle Tom's Children* in 1940, matches *Native Son* (1940) in its concentrated exploration of how white-sourced solutions, such as communism, will prove wanting. Repeatedly, as in "Big Boy Leaves Home," Wright's characters are forced by some "transgression" imposed by circumstance to desert the normative white world's sanctioned social locations (sharecropping; ghetto life) for a precarious *hiding*. Such hiding recurs: in his early stories, in *Native Son*, and in "The Man Who Lived Underground" (1944). The latter offers the symbolic formulation, "He knew he could not stay here and he could not go out" – a paradox glossed in Wright's sharecropper's tale, "The Man Who Saw the Flood": "Ef we keeps on like this the white man'll own us body and soul ... Ef we try to run away they'll put us in jail." Wright's last novel, *The Long Dream*, takes up this theme: the South's repressive stranglehold on African Americans makes their lives a "crucifixion" and self-respect impossible, so that when a black businessman, undertaker, and racketeer rebels against his servile collusion with a corrupt white police chief, the latter unhesitatingly has him killed.

Wright's pessimism concerning Southern African-Americans' situation was vindicated during World War II by African-Americans' segregation in the armed services. Resistance led to its limited amelioration, but this only rendered postwar Southern segregation more offensive (as depicted in Junius Edwards's *If We Must Die*, 1961). Continuing ideological repression also needed to be contested – particularly that resulting from the ideological reflex, inherited by McCarthyism, of equating African-American intellectualism with communism. Such legacies proved enduring – despite McCarthy's 1954 discrediting – promoting Southern African-American writing's increasing engagement with rising black nationalism. Combined with strengthening institutional support for black culture, this opened up new aesthetic approaches (with Howard University serving as a fulcrum). Complex fusions were fostered, like Melvin B. Tolson's poetry: "I, as a black poet, have absorbed the Great Ideas of the Great White World and interpreted them in the ... idiom of my own people. My roots are in Africa, Europe and America." Modernism, African-American folk history, and black nationalism fuse in Tolson's poem "Dark Symphony" (his best work):

> Black slaves singing *The Crucifixion*
> In slave pens at midnight,
> Black slaves singing *Swing Low, Sweet Chariot*
> In cabins of death,
> Black slaves singing *Go Down Moses*
> In the canebrakes of the Southern Pharaohs. (1939)

Tolson's modernism always recognized the formative significance of history: "the New Negro ... sprang from ... Nat Turner ... Joseph Cinquez ... Frederick Douglass ... Sojourner Truth" ("Woodcuts for America," 1943).

Margaret Walker also offers a blend of "folk" and "fusion," though her focus in *For My People* (1942) falls upon voicing a communal sense of African-American heritage, as in her tribute to Nat Turner, Denmark Vesey, and John Brown ("The Ballad of the Free"). Typically, she employs the first person plural, as in "The Struggle Staggers Us": "Out of this blackness we must struggle forth; / From want of bread, of pride, of dignity." Walker is a key figure in the transition between pre- and post-World War II Southern African-American writing, most distinctively in her folk-based ballads like "Poppa Chicken," "Molly Means," and "Kissie Lee" and in race-affirmative poems like "We Have Been Believers," "Delta," and "For My People." These lace Whitmanesque/

Sandburgian catalogues and the tropes and rhythms of non-conformist sermons with black-nationalist sentiments: "For my people everywhere singing their slave songs . . . For my playmates in the clay and dust and sand of Alabama backyards . . . For the cramped and bewildered years we went to school . . . For my people thronging 47th Street in Chicago and Lenox Street in New York and Rampart Street in New Orleans . . . Let a new earth rise. Let another world be born. Let a bloody peace be written in the sky." Love of the South, protest against discrimination, and a compassionate desire for wholeness constitute Walker's core themes. That she also engages with the position of black women and their heritage secures her status as a pivotal influence on Southern black writing:

> My grandmothers were strong.
> They followed plows and bent to toil.
> . . .
> They touched earth and grain grew.
> They were full of sturdiness and singing.
> . . .
> My grandmothers are full of memories
> Smelling of soap and onions and wet clay
> . . .
> They have many clean words to say. ("Lineage")

Poems like this and "A Patchwork Quilt" influence Alice Walker's womanism and Toni Morrison's "re-memory." Margaret Walker projects a deep faith in black people's potentialities, as in her historical novel, *Jubilee* (1966), a sometimes over-freighted but compelling attempt to fashion a riposte to Southern apologists' renderings of an old golden South by fictionalizing the experiences of Walker's great-grandmother during slavery, the Civil War, and Reconstruction. Walker forcibly makes plain how "money . . . land . . . votes . . . power" structure her great-grandmother's experiences.

Other transition figures using folk forms and themes (like migration) include George Wylie Henderson in *Ollie Miss* (1935) and *Jule* (1946), Waters Turpin – from *These Low Grounds* (1937) and *O Canaan!* (1939), through *The Rootless* (1957) – and, above all, Ralph Ellison – like Tolson, a key modernist/folk fusion figure. His early story, "Flying Home" (1944), features a black icarus-aviator who, climbing his plane too steeply, strikes a buzzard, crashes, is taunted to the point of madness by an old black laborer, and ends up incarcerated in a mental institution by a local white landowner. An obvious allegory, the story fuses different genres – realism, surrealism, folklore, Greek myth – in its symbolic exploration of African-American Southerners' wartime social position. This sort of fusion reemerges in another early story, "Invisible Man" (*Horizon* 23, 1947), republished in 1952 as the first of *Invisible Man*'s opening seven chapters. Together, these chapters (preceding the narrator's migration North) constitute a set of symbolic illuminations of Southern African-American experience. The first depicts the unnamed protagonist's graduation speech to white dignitaries (paraphrasing Booker T. Washington), following an extraordinary sequence of rigged fights (a "battle royal") between a group of black youths after they have been forced to watch a white female stripper, in fear for their lives. The next six chapters, set in an African-American Southern college, adapt *Without Magnolias* (1940), Bucklin Moon's portrait of a Florida college whose founder is attacked by a sociology professor from Washington, DC for peddling minstrel stereotypes to help secure the college's finances. Ellison's novel takes up Moon's themes with advantage. His cynical college principal, Bledsoe ("You're black and living in the South – did you forget how to lie?"), contributes to a chain of betrayals of the main protagonist, so personifying Ellison's conviction that "constant acts of betrayal" are "implicit" in black leaders' "roles." The unnamed "Nigger-Boy" is thus kept "Running" through a picaresque *bildungsroman* moving from dark Southern oppression to ambivalent metaphysical underground Northern illumination (a neon-lit cellar). Ellison fuses trickster tales, folk, and blues with Dostoevskean dialogism, European modernism, and parody (principally of Wright and Faulkner) to portray its protagonist growing into the recognition that "people refuse to see me... I have been surrounded by mirrors of hard, distorting glass."

Given Ellison's constant "reaching for artistic perfection" (Davis), the decision to publish the uncompleted *Juneteenth* posthumously (even the title is not Ellison's) was controversial. Set in the South, *Juneteenth*'s action occurs "on the eve of the [civil] rights movement, but it forecasts the chaos that would come" (Ellison). The novel takes *Invisible Man*'s intertextual fusions further. A slew of influences – from the Bible through Twain, Weldon Johnson, and Faulkner to Joyce – interlace with African-American folk forms (revival meetings, sermons, call and response, conjure tales, blues), as *Juneteenth* inchoately probes at the color line. The focus is an act of passing: a racist senator, raised by a black charlatan preacher and uncertain of his racial identity ("just nothing definite"), summons his ersatz father to his deathbed, following an assassination attempt. There, both men rehearse their memories in monologues, streams-of-consciousness, and dream. An almost archetypal Southern modernist *bildungsroman* results – intermittently powerful, and better than generally allowed.

Such fusion has not always been admired. John Oliver Killens considered that, since "Art is functional," *Invisible Man* was "decadent," a "vicious distortion of Negro life." Instead, social protest and realism underpin his novels of racial tension in the South. Both *Youngblood* (1954), portraying a struggling black family in Georgia at the start of the twentieth century, and '*Sippi* (1967), intertwining the 1954 *Brown vs. Board of Education* decision on segregation with the breakdown of an interracial marriage, are rooted in social protest and realism. '*Sippi*'s themes signal how, in the second half of the twentieth century, militancy came to a head: in civil rights campaigns and debates about how blacks should react to white provocation. The resulting explosively contradictory events, brilliantly represented in Alice Walker's novel *Meridian* (1976) and reaching a bloody climax in Martin Luther King's 1968 assassination, saw the emergence of new African-American aesthetics, even more demanding in their politics. Paradigmatic of this was what Larry Neal christened the Black Arts Movement (1960–74), within which black cultural nationalism became a *sine qua non*. Addison Gayle, Jr. described it as black people's "de-Americanization." More persuasively, Sonia Sanchez described it as "a slow/painful/upward journey still not completed." A surge in writing and publishing results, part of what has been called a "new Black Renaissance" stimulated by these troubling, vital times – an upsurge taking this essay beyond its remit.

This has been a difficult essay to write; there is no accepted "canon" of Southern African-American writers. Who to include has proved problematic. Should Pauline Hopkins be included? Or Langston Hughes? And what of Victor Séjour's "Le Mulâtre" (1837), since Séjour was born in New Orleans, though his story is set in Haiti and written in French?

Yet perhaps some sort of characterizing definition of "Southern African-American fiction and poetry" emerges – if only by degree. For example, a particularly robust sociocultural thematic can be identified, fueled by confronting the acute marginalization of Southern African Americans resulting from slavery's retention in the antebellum South and postbellum oppression of "free" blacks via segregation, discrimination, and lynching. Consequently, Southern African-American writing persistently avails itself of the slippery resources of narrative experimentation and hybrid performance, recurrently set within signifying "framing," to secure a cultural "space." (This approach of course endures beyond my remit, emerging in Alice Walker's epistolary novel *The Color Purple* and Morrison's incandescent *Beloved*, for example.) Within such formal and thematic experimentation reside navigations of, in White's words, "the tortuous paths the Negro must follow to avoid giving offence to the dominant white sentiment . . . the repressions . . . when talking with . . . any white man in the South." For Richard Wright, African Americans were consequently "locked down in the dark underworld of American life . . . [where] we . . . made our own code[s]." Southern African-Americans' subtle handling of these representational challenges and aesthetic demands took the form of an outflowing of linguistically complex formal experimentation – over and again to exhilarating, disturbing effect.

References and further reading

Andrews, William (1986) *To Tell a Free Story*. Urbana: University of Illinois Press.

Baker, Houston A., Jr. (1984) *Blues, Ideology and Afro-American Literature*. Chicago: University of Illinois Press.

Bell, Bernard W. (1987) *The African-American Novel and Its Tradition*. Amherst: Massachusetts University Press.

Bone, Robert A. (1965) *The Negro Novel in America*. New Haven, CT: Yale University Press.

Carby, Hazel (1987) *Reconstructing Womanhood: The Emergence of the Afro-American Woman Novelist*. New York: Oxford University Press.

Christian, Barbara (1980) *Black Women Novelists: The Development of a Tradition, 1892–1976*. Westport, CT: Greenwood Press.

Cooke, Michael (1984) *Afro-American Literature in the Twentieth Century: The Achievement of Intimacy.* New Haven, CT: Yale University Press.

Davis, Arthur P. (1974) *From the Dark Tower.* Washington, DC: Howard University Press.

Davis, Thadious (1996) "Expanding the Limits: The Intersection of Race and Region," *Southern Literary Journal*, 20, 3: 3–11.

Foster, Frances Smith (1993) *Written by Herself: Literary Production of Early African-American Writers.* Bloomington: Indiana University Press.

Gates, Henry Louis, Jr. (1986) *The Signifying Monkey: A Theory of Afro-American Literary Criticism.* New York: Oxford University Press.

Gayle, Addison (ed.) (1971) *The Black Aesthetic.* Garden City, NY: Doubleday.

Gray, Richard (2000) *Southern Aberrations.* Baton Rouge: Louisiana State University Press.

Jones, Anne Goodwyn and Donaldson, Susan V. (eds.) (1997) *Haunted Bodies: Gender and Southern Texts.* Charlottesville: University Press of Virginia.

Jones, Gayl (1991) *Liberating Voices.* Cambridge, MA: Harvard University Press.

Kreyling, Michael (1998) *Inventing Southern Literature.* Jackson: University of Mississippi Press.

MacAlpine, Carole (1985) *Prologue: The Novels of Black American Women, 1891–1965.* Westport, CT: Greenwood Press.

Miller, R. Baxter (ed.) (1986) *Black American Poets Between Worlds, 1940–1960.* Knoxville: University of Tennessee Press.

Redmond, Eugene B. (1976) *Drumvoices: The Mission of Afro-American Poetry.* Garden City, NY: Anchor Press.

Stepto, Robert (1991) *Behind the Veil: A Study of Afro-American Narrative.* Urbana: University of Illinois Press.

Wagner, Jean (1963) *Black Poets of the United States from Paul Laurence Dunbar to Langston Hughes*, trans. Kenneth Douglas. Urbana: University of Illinois Press.

Yaeger, Patricia (2000) *Dirt and Desire: Reconstructing Southern Womanhood, 1930–1990.* Chicago: University of Chicago Press.

16

Southern Drama

Mark Zelinsky and Amy Cuomo

Perhaps more than any other region of the United States, the South evokes a rich mythography of discordant imagery. One thinks of the grand antebellum plantations signifying tremendous wealth and power, alongside weathered, tin-roofed, one-room shacks lacking electricity or running water. The unsettling symbiosis between whites and blacks simultaneously exhibits an uneasy interdependence and intense mistrust. As with African Americans, the Old South vilifies and honors women alternatively. Like blacks, women must know their place or risk censure should they demonstrate independent thought or sexuality. The agrarian tradition and simple country living are giving way more and more to the pressures of modern urban centers and multinational corporations. The South, loser of the Civil War, harbors the historic regrets of the only Americans, prior to the Vietnam War, ever defeated in an armed conflict. The region calls forth associations from literature and history, politics and sociology. It is Scarlett O'Hara and Rhett Butler, Little Eva and Uncle Tom, pecan pie and jambalaya, mint juleps and sweetened iced-tea, Christian tent revivals and the Ku Klux Klan, red dirt roads and snake-infested bayous, freedom riders and lynchings, rolling hills of bluegrass and fields of cotton, Jimmy Carter and Jesse Helms, and so on. The region, in short, sparks disparate imagery, things in conflict, the essence of theatre – a protagonist struggling against antagonistic forces from within and without. It is not surprising that the South, a region so fraught with tension between sharply divided interests, should also be the birthplace of some of the United States' most significant playwrights. But what qualifies a writer as Southern?

A major factor for inclusion in this essay is a given writer's place of birth and the region in which they spent their childhood. One could argue that such biographical details have little bearing upon one's work, but this collection of essays suggests that the South does, indeed, influence and shape an artist in a strikingly singular way. Thus, geography plays a major factor in our analysis. Playwrights from the North, such as Charles Fuller and Pearl Cleage, who have written plays about the South, have been excluded. Furthermore, although some of America's most important living theatre figures hail from the South, among them, Tony Kushner, Suzan-Lori Parks, and George Wolfe, their work rarely focuses on the region as a culturally shaping force and they, too, have been excised. Even within these parameters, due to length limitations, many important writers have been omitted.

For the purposes of this essay, a Southern playwright concentrates on not only the American South as principal setting, but also on transforming its unique dynamics and polarities into an experience that can be appreciated by international audiences, including theatre-goers of today, those of the past, and those of the future. This work focuses on a group of writers that bring the mythologized South to the stage; keeping it alive in the human imagination and reaffirming its continuing significance to shape our perceptions of a culture that vanishes more and more with each passing day. The South lives in the works of these playwrights, whose dramas may one day hold the last glimpses of a region quickly being undermined by the forces of a global economy.

The roots of theatre in the United States originate in the South, reaching back to the seventeenth century with Virginia court documents from 1665 providing the earliest evidence of a play performance in the colonies. Three Virginians were brought before a judge for acting in *The Bear and the Cub*, a work no longer extant. The actors were eventually cleared and their accuser paid court costs; thereby, although rather dubiously, the beginning of the American theatre and free artistic expression were established (Richardson 1993: 3). The first permanent theatre in what would become the United States was constructed in Williamsburg, Virginia in 1716, and the city also hosted the first performance by professional actors when the Hallam family appeared there in 1752.

Until the devastation of the Civil War, theatre in the South remained vibrant. By the 1790s Charleston, South Carolina had become a significant theatrical center and troupes originating there eventually toured through the Carolinas and as far north as Richmond, Virginia. In the 1830s, flat-bottom boats were converted into performance spaces and floated down the Ohio and the Mississippi rivers, providing entertainments in riverside communities from Kentucky to Louisiana. At about the same time, New Orleans had become a thriving theatre center boasting a venue illuminated with gas lighting – two years prior to any New York theatre being similarly fitted.

Early nineteenth-century American drama favored stereotypical characters, perhaps the most famous being the Native American as "noble savage" and the "Yankee," an idealized version of the common American male. Though perhaps not as common in the literature of the time, the South contributed to this tradition with two additional types: the "happy Darkie" and the "tragic mulatto." The former reached great popularity through the minstrel show, caricaturing African Americans as faithful servants, entertaining whites as comic buffoons. The type remained apparent well into the twentieth century, as evidenced by the house servants in *Gone with the Wind*. Though some historians argue that minstrel shows developed into the African-American musical, today one might read the "happy Darkie" as an attempt to mediate white Southern guilt over its participation in and perpetuation of slavery, demeaning the African as foolish, childlike, and in need of "protection." The "tragic mulatto," perhaps most famously rendered by Dion Boucicault in *The Octoroon* (1859), could be similarly interpreted. A drop of African-American blood prohibits the title character from entry into white society, never mind that her black female ancestor likely had no choice in her coupling with the white male. Both types hint at not only the suppression of African-American and female voices, but also at a cartoonish, demeaning invocation of the South itself.

In reality, the South's African-American community fostered a rich tradition of plays and playwrights. These writers often exposed the racial prejudices of a culture that, in many respects, defined them. Their works share several common themes, including lynching, miscegenation, the barbarism of slavery, social and economic repression, and segregation. Not surprisingly, many black playwrights fled the South, searching for freedom from strict racial taboos. Others remained in the South. Regardless, collectively their dramas reflect the black Southern experience and a desire to change it.

Born in Atlanta, Georgia, Georgia Douglas Johnson (1886–1966) became the dramatist of seven plays. *Blue Blood* (1926) explores the effects of miscegenation on the children of mixed marriages and was performed by the black New York acting troupe, Krigwa Players. Her three anti-lynching plays: *Safe* (ca. 1929), *Blue-Eyed Black Boy* (ca. 1930), and *Sunday Morning in the South* (1925) were not published during her lifetime; however, they gained performances "in church halls, lofts, and schools in the Washington, DC area" (Brown-Guillory 1990: 12). These plays exposed audiences to a horrific practice that enabled Southern whites to repress blacks through fear and intimidation. After years of erasure thanks to prejudice, Johnson's work has returned to the forefront of contemporary cultural studies.

Zora Neale Hurston (1891–1960) grew up in the all-black town of Eatonville, Florida, destined to become one of the finest writers of the Harlem Renaissance. While her greatest achievement is the novel *Their Eyes Were Watching God* (1937), Hurston wrote several plays, including *Color Struck* (1926) and *Mule Bone* (1931), the latter in collaboration with Langston Hughes. *Color Struck* concerns Emma, a dark-skinned African-American whose jealousy of light-skinned women destroys her relationship with John, the man she loves. Hurston demonstrates the shaping force of the South on the black psyche as Emma has internalized the racism of her environment. John returns from a seventeen-year absence in the North to find Emma caring for her dangerously ill daughter, a mulatto. He advises Emma to find a doctor, but she hesitates to leave, fearing that John has taken a sexual interest in her light-skinned daughter. Emma's hesitation costs the young girl's life. In juxtaposing Emma's self-hatred with John's open-mindedness, Hurston implies that racism becomes an environmental poison that can only be escaped in leaving the South. Several of Hurston's short stories were adapted by George Wolfe for the stage in *Spunk* (1990).

Like Hurston, Alice Childress (1916–94) was a displaced Southerner who found a home in Harlem. Born in Charleston, South Carolina, Childress credits her grandmother for sparking her interest in theatre. The civil rights movement transformed the South and its writers, and her work reflects these changes. Her first play, *Florence*

(1949), takes a railway station in a small Southern town as its location and recognizes that blacks may have to leave their tight-knit communities in order to break the color barrier. The plot introduces us to Mama as she waits for a train to New York, planning to bring her daughter, Florence, back South. Florence struggles to make it as an actress, but her lack of success worries Mama. A conversation with a white woman, Mrs. Carter, makes Mama realize that if Florence does not succeed as an actress and returns home, her only employment opportunities will be positions as a domestic. At the play's conclusion, Mama sends a note north encouraging Florence to "Keep on tryin'" (Brown-Guillory 1990: 121). Thus, even unemployment and struggle in New York represent greater hope for the African American than life in the South.

Set in South Carolina in 1918, *Wedding Band: A Love/Hate Story in Black and White* (1966) tells the tale of a black woman, Julia, and a white man, Herman, forbidden by law to marry. The play focuses on the inflexible roles of black servant and white master in the post-Civil War South, revealing the bias of both the black and the white communities against interracial couples. In an argument with Herman, Julia rebukes her lover for defending his father, once a member of the Ku Klux Klan. Although treated sympathetically, Herman's white heritage prevents his understanding of Julia's precarious position. Because of their relationship, Julia remains ostracized by both the white and the black cultures that surround them. Childress's work provides an African-American perspective on how white Southerners exploited blacks, impeding integration through worn out social codes. Once again, Childress reiterates the need to escape the South in order for blacks to achieve equality. Flight from the South was a central motif for many African-American playwrights, but white writers also used the racial tension of the South as an important theme, perhaps none more famously than Paul Green.

Born in Harnett County, North Carolina, Paul Green (1894–1981) contributed numerous plays with Southern themes, such as miscegenation, racial injustice, the collapse of Southern aristocracy, and religious fundamentalism. From a poor farming family, Green is said to have read books while plowing the fields. He began college at twenty-two, but suspended his formal education when he enlisted to serve in World War I. After the war, he graduated from the University of North Carolina, later returning there to teach philosophy and dramatic arts. He is credited with creating symphonic drama: historic plays focused on enlightening the audience that use a chorus, dance, and music to further the plot. Green's most popular symphonic drama, *The Lost Colony* (1937), still gets annual performances each summer in Manteo, North Carolina.

Charles Watson notes, "Green proved himself a comprehensive dramatist of southern life by portraying three major social types: the Negro, the poor white, and the aristocrat" (1997: 103). No play captures these three characters more fully than *The House of Connelly* (1931). Performed as the initial offering of the Group Theatre's first season, *The House of Connelly* portrays the tragic fall of Southern aristocracy. The plot focuses on a white aristocrat, Will Connelly, and his ineffectual attempts to escape poverty as a penniless plantation owner to become a businessman of the New South.

Will falls in love with a poor, white, sharecropper's daughter, Patsy Tate, who has a head for business and a desire for success. Will and Patsy face powerful forces opposing their union in Will's aristocratic family, and the former slaves of the plantation who see Patsy as "poor white trash." The couple wed, but, in a twist of events, two "old sibyl-like Negro women, Big Sis, and Big Sue," smother Patsy. Green's message is apparent: the Old South maintains an economic, cultural, and racial stranglehold on the New South. The play contains references to miscegenation, as Will's father hanged his own child, a mulatto. This theme of the tragic mulatto is treated sympathetically and recurs in other works; however, Green's most famous rendition of the mulatto is in his Pulitzer Prize-winning *In Abraham's Bosom*.

First performed by the Provincetown Players in 1926, *In Abraham's Bosom: The Tragedy of a Southern Negro* is a conglomeration of early folk plays about Negro Life. The plot centers on the title character, the son of an African-American woman and a plantation owner. Set during Reconstruction, Abraham struggles against social constraints as he tries to educate himself and subsequently open a school for blacks. The white townsfolk conspire against Abraham, preventing his starting the school. Confronted by his father's white son, Lonnie, and berated for his lack of work in the field, Abraham kills him and is himself later shot for this murder. Green demonstrates that white prejudice can often be fatal to those of mixed heritage.

While many of Green's most famous works are now rarely, if ever, performed, they still provide a richly layered portrait of the life of poor white Southerners and blacks. Both *House of Connelly* and *In Abraham's Bosom* now seem dated; however, Green's dedication to presenting Southern African-Americans' plight on stage made him a precursor to many black playwrights who fought to develop more genuine black characters. Green's lengthy career as a playwright and theatre practitioner influenced the art for over fifty years.

Green's dramas were an early reading interest for Horton Foote (1916–). Born in Wharton, Texas (a state part of the Confederacy but, with the exception of the southeastern portion, resembling the West today more than the South), the town became the model for the fictional Harrison, Texas where many of Foote's plays are set. Influenced by Southerners' love of storytelling and the folk music of African-American workers, Foote's plays frequently take on characteristics of these varied forms with plots evolving out of several characters' perspectives and themes that echo the simple lyricism from the repeated patterns of routine, day-to-day activities. Foote captures the slow and steady rhythm of the South, exposing the universal in the mundane and revealing the dignity of his characters as they suffer the common losses of life which we all endure, calling our attention to the plight of regular working Southern men and women.

In *The Trip to Bountiful* (1953), perhaps his best-known work and originally written for television, elderly Carrie Watts flees her claustrophobic existence living with her son and daughter-in-law in a cramped Houston apartment and returns to the town of her youth, Bountiful, Texas. Just like the dependent, displaced women Tennessee Williams so often created, Foote's Carrie attempts to escape the modern New South and return to simpler, happier days, but the town she recalls no longer prospers, having become virtually abandoned. Her past has disintegrated, leaving only memories because Carrie has been dispossessed of everything else. Carrie's journey mimics that of any Southerner of her generation; she witnesses a way of life disappear, haunted by its ghost. Foote intensifies the spiritual elements of the play through Carrie's love of Christian hymns. Like any true believer in Christ, Carrie finds her spirit is restored at the play's conclusion.

The playwright earned his only Pulitzer Prize for *The Young Man From Atlanta* (1995). Set in Houston in 1950, Foote resurrects Will Kidder and Lily Dale, characters who appeared in three of the dramas comprising the nine-play cycle collectively known as *The Orphan's Home*. Will and Lily have suffered the recent suicide of their only child, 29-year-old Bill, and the play focuses on discerning what led him to this act. The title character, Bill's former roommate, never appears, but he provokes an atmosphere of fear and worry through his communications with the older couple. The play implies the young men were lovers and shows how people cope with uncomfortable realities. Though the product of the poor, rural South, Will prides himself on competing to become a wealthy wholesale grocer and plans to build a big new home despite the fact that he and Lily live alone and are nearing retirement. Reared to be dependent on men, Lily remains childlike despite her age. Each character's indirectness about the cause of Bill's suicide, their inability to discuss or label it, captures Southern discretion and willingness to deny painful realities. Bill and Lily accept differing realities at the play's conclusion, itself a reflection of Southerners coexisting with wildly varied perspectives, notably, although not an issue in this play, the black experience of the South versus white existence.

Though critics such as Crystal Brian argue Foote's dramaturgy resonates with existential and transcendental themes, others such as C. W. E. Bigsby devote no critical attention to him at all. The playwright does not even earn mention in the latter's *Modern American Drama 1945–2000* (2000). Foote garnered two Academy Awards for screenplays and this threatened to overshadow his work as playwright, but during the last fifteen years his plays have earned more attention and productions than ever before. In addition to winning the Pulitzer Prize, his dramas were offered as the entire season for the Signature Theatre in 1994, and, more recently, three regional theatres joined in producing *The Carpetbagger's Children* (2001), featuring the beloved actress Jean Stapleton, as part of each company's repertoire. A fiftieth anniversary production of *The Trip to Bountiful*, also featuring Stapleton, was slated at two regional theatres for the 2002–3 season, but one wonders if the actress becomes the draw rather than Foote's works. His attention to common people in simple situations, use of everyday language, and lack of dramatic action harkens to a theatre rapidly being outdistanced. When produced well, his plays have the power of Chekhov, but, like the Russian master, a rather limited and diminishing audience. As our attention spans shrink further it seems unlikely that Foote's elegant and simple works will earn a lasting place on international stages. The more melodramatic effects of Lillian Hellman's works may fare better.

Born in New Orleans, Lillian Hellman (1905–84) captivated audiences with her depiction of dysfunction, corruption, and greed in the South's families. Both Hellman's parents were Southerners; her mother came from a wealthy Jewish family who had settled in Demopolis, Alabama, and her father was a shoe salesman whose own father had emigrated to New Orleans from Germany before the Civil War. Living in New Orleans until she was six, Hellman returned frequently thereafter, with the family dividing each year between New York and the Crescent City. When in Louisiana, the family lived with Hellman's two paternal aunts, who ran a boarding house.

The South left an indelible imprint on the playwright, and two of Hellman's plays characterize the region, revealing the underbelly of a New South which has lost the honor, integrity, and high-minded ideals that characterize the antebellum period. She captures the Southern codes of courtesy in which a charming exterior masks a variety of ugly and unpleasant emotions. Her families appear well-mannered and close-knit, but remain highly combative.

Little Foxes (1939) explores the extremes of avarice in a turn-of-the-century Southern household. Conflicts between the Old and New South manifest themselves in arguments about profit and money. The Hubbards – Ben, Oscar, and Regina – try to exploit local townspeople by establishing a cotton mill that will earn high revenues from cheap labor. As a woman of the New South, Regina fixates on securing enough capital in order to do as she pleases. Very much like Scarlett O'Hara after the Civil War, Regina will lie, cheat, or steal in order to choose her own destiny (see Charles Watson's insightful discussion of this subject). Her husband, Horace Giddens, represents the Old Southern gentility that Regina can no longer afford. Rejecting the Hubbard family's methodology, Horace chooses to uphold traditions that put family, honor, and integrity above profit. Horace opposes his wife's profit-making plan and he dies because of this opposition. Greed begets murder and Regina allows her husband to die, triumphing through manipulation and blackmail to become a heroine of the New South.

In *Another Part of the Forest* (1946), Hellman returns to the Hubbards in a prequel to the earlier play. Set in 1880, in Bowdon, Alabama, the drama clarifies the conflict between the pre-Civil War aristocracy and the nouveau riche. We discover the origin of the Hubbards' preoccupation with money. Marcus Hubbard, in his single-minded focus on profit, inadvertently led Union troops to a Confederate encampment. Just as Regina's avarice leads to the death of her husband, her father's greed causes the death of several Southern compatriots. The family begin to turn on each other, and greediness, like a disease, spreads from one generation to the next. Discovering the source of his father's wealth, Ben bankrupts the patriarch and assumes control of the family using the older man's tactics.

Hellman also examines the destruction of the Old South's aristocracy. After his ascent to power, Ben arranges a marriage between his Klan-loving, violent, and stupid younger brother, Oscar, and Birdie Bagtry, the daughter of a respectable landed family. Money equals power in the New South; its misuse oppresses those without it. The play's most sympathetic character, Birdie, symbolizes the Old South. She hails from a genteel but now impoverished family and romanticizes her understanding of the South: a place where civility and manners set a standard for living with honor prized above all. Birdie does not understand that the loss of the Civil War meant the South changed forever. Rather, her experience of the Old South, when times were better, provides her with the faith that the old ways will endure forever. Ironically, Birdie's destruction does not come at the hands of Yankees, but rather thanks to the greed of New Southerners like Regina, Ben, and Oscar, who have a penchant for business and will sacrifice anything or anyone to get what they want.

Although Hellman's Southern plays now seem melodramatic, her work represents an understanding and portrait of "Southern progress." The microcosm of Southern culture represented by the Hubbard clan mirrors a misplaced focus on money over compassion. Although a universal vice, the avarice perpetuated by the Hubbards remains particularly Southern; the loss of the Civil War looms over all of them, influencing each character's behavior. The beauty of the Southern setting reflects the outward gentility of the characters; however, the once glorious country estate now conceals a nest of vipers. Hellman's portrait of the new wealthy Southerner amounts to an indictment of materialism. Concern for the dispossessed runs throughout her work, and, much like Tennessee Williams, Hellman became the conscience of the South.

It is difficult, if not impossible, to argue that any figure dominates Southern theatre more than Tennessee Williams (1911–83), whose works have maintained a prominent place in the international repertoire for over fifty years. In one of the first book-length studies of the man and his work, Signi Falk questioned the "stature" of his contribution to what she termed the "Southern Renaissance" in American literature, but the passage of time has confirmed his place in the highest ranks of theatrical artists worldwide (1961: 25). As Lyle Leverich noted, "There is scarcely a literate person who does not know the name" (1995: 6). Williams is that rare artist who enjoys continuing popular and critical success, and his plays (thanks, in part, to numerous film and television adaptations) have become virtually synonymous with the South.

Williams was born in Columbus, Mississippi to parents embodying the South's duality. A descendant of Tennessee frontiersmen, his father, a traveling salesman, seemed strict and distant to his son, indulging in bodily pleasures, such as drinking and womanizing. His mother, daughter of an Episcopalian rector, was puritanical, forthright in upholding tradition, and overprotective of him and his older sister, Rose. Williams treasured his childhood years in the home of his beloved maternal grandparents; however, when the family moved to St. Louis in 1918, Williams's happiness was shattered. He felt disconnected in the claustrophobic tenement houses of this Northern city, becoming more and more withdrawn. In the South, Williams had an extended family rooted in a rural small-town community where roles were carefully defined by class and race, but the North offered no such comforts. Williams and his family became new members of the faceless masses in the industrial North, suspect thanks to their Southern accents and old-fashioned manners. Williams escaped the isolation he experienced in his new home (a city he grew to hate) by writing. Not surprisingly, he turned to his beloved South for material.

Certainly, not everything that Williams produced is situated in the South, but many of the most enduring and best-known works are set there. He claimed the region was his inspiration for writing and noted: "the South once had a way of life I am just old enough to remember – a culture that had grace, elegance . . . an inbred culture . . . not a society based on money, as in the North. I write out of regret for that" (quoted in Leverich 1995: 54).

Thus, Williams writes about a South that even during his own life was past, already a part of America's history. His South remains a world not necessarily of fact, but, rather, of myth. He celebrates a place and time when seemingly innate, civilized Southern values reigned. Like Hellman, he rejects the materialist atmosphere of the North and its grasping after status-symbol possessions in favor of a South clinging to an elusive, dying culture. The suppression and destruction of old traditions and values by new cultural dynamics constitute a primary tension in many of Williams's plays; however, he often condemns characteristics of this mythologized South, acknowledging the value of change.

In *A Streetcar Named Desire* (1947) Williams creates a powerful metaphor for these worlds in collision with the play's setting in New Orleans's French Quarter and descriptions of the DuBois's family estate, Belle Reve. Vividly evoking the French Quarter through the use of language, scenic requirements, supernumeraries (notably the Mexican Flower Seller), and music, Williams's depiction of New Orleans represents the rise of the New South. Despite the oppressive humidity, the city bustles with life, celebrating it joyously with open sexual abandon, excessive consumption of food and alcohol, and jazz echoing from the streets. Juxtaposed to this steamy exuberance are memories of the lost Belle Reve, "the place in the country," as Stanley notes (Williams 1971, I: 270). Once supporting the DuBois family in style, the plantation was lost, according to Blanche, thanks to the "epic fornications" of male relatives, until nothing remained save the house and a small parcel of land, "including a graveyard, to which now all but Stella and I have retreated" (284). Unlike the Kowalskis, the secretive sexual adventures of the DuBois family produce suffering, decay, and ultimately death.

Blanche's own romantic entanglements mirror this pattern, from the suicide of her young husband, to her anonymous encounters at the Hotel Flamingo, to the affair with her high school pupil, the event propelling her to New Orleans. She viewed the city as a sanctuary, but Blanche is too mired in the family tradition of clandestine misadventures to adapt to the open physicality of the French Quarter. While Williams clearly empathizes with Blanche, his French Quarter and Belle Reve imagery suggest an appreciation for the former's frankness and condemnation of the latter's isolation and secrecy. He champions the old order, appreciating Blanche's love of literature, art, and culture, while simultaneously valuing the new order represented by Stanley's physical strength, drive, and willpower, despite his unnecessary violence. Williams vilifies brute force in later works and demonstrates that while some wealthy

Southern families, like the DuBois clan, have become impotent, others exercise their power in a self-serving and destructive fashion.

Set on the Gulf Coast, *Sweet Bird of Youth* (1959) includes one of Williams's least sympathetic characters, Boss Finley, a man who regards himself as all that "stands between the South and the black days of Reconstruction" (Williams 1971, IV: 72). Boss Finley operates a political machine designed to stamp out desegregation using methods not unlike the Ku Klux Klan and has the play's protagonist, Chance Wayne, castrated to prevent a renewed romance with his daughter. In Finley, Williams suggests the corruption of the South's privileged class, a force that remains not only racist, but also willing to accomplish its goals through any means, no matter how violent. The play implies an unwholesome alliance between the Boss, the state's governor, and an oil corporation, suggesting Finley is motivated by money (a Northern vice, according to Williams) rather than preserving the Southern way of life.

Violet Venable, the matriarch in *Suddenly Last Summer* (1958), offers another portrait of the dangers inherent in the South's upper class. Set in the genteel, old-money New Orleans neighborhood known as the Garden District, the Venable home décor favors the exotic, with luxurious antique furnishings and a tropical garden concealing carnivorous plants. Violet's methods, although less direct than Stanley's, are just as violent. If Williams was unwilling to condemn Stanley, thanks in part to his directness, he is unforgiving of Violet. Through manipulation, economic black-mail, and bribery, Violet buys the silence of her relatives and Dr. Cukrowicz so as to conceal the facts of her son's death by insisting the only witness to his murder, her niece, Catharine, be lobotomized. While *Suddenly Last Summer* can be fruitfully evaluated through a biographical lens (with Williams as the murdered Sebastian, his sister as the victimized Catharine, and his mother as the destroyer, Violet) the play also presents a harsh critique of capital in the hands of a hypocrite interested in half-truths and the preservation of family reputation. Like Boss Finley, Violet unleashes all her resources in an effort to maintain her dominance. While she is uninterested in upholding the racist creed of the nineteenth-century South, as is Finley, she will protect the Venable family reputation at any cost. Not only would Garden District society be scandalized by the cannibalization of Sebastian, but it would also condemn him for his homosexuality. Though Violet appears to win out, Williams does not sanction her victory, once again suggesting that economic manipulation for the stake of outmoded ways or family vanity becomes perhaps the greatest sin.

With Big Daddy in *Cat on a Hot Tin Roof* (1955) Williams presents a very different view of great wealth, this time linking candor to economic power. Owner of an enormous Mississippi Delta plantation, "over twenty-eight thousand acres of the richest land this side of the valley Nile," Big Daddy searches for the reason his favored son, Brick, destroys himself with alcohol (Williams 1971, III: 110). Mistrust-ful of the grasping, hypocritical relatives that surround him, Big Daddy believes he can reach Brick because they represent the two people in the Pollitt family "that never lied to each other" (111). Act two concludes in a powerful revelation for both characters: Brick reveals that he drinks because he could not face his friend Skipper's homosexual longings for him and that Big Daddy is dying of cancer. Raging against the family for concealing his illness, Big Daddy howls, "CHRIST – DAMN – ALL – LYING SONS OF – LYING BITCHES" (128)! Unlike *Sweet Bird of Youth* and *Suddenly Last Summer*, where economic corruption emanates from the heads of families, here the patriarch remains unspoiled while most of those around him have been tainted by greed; however, in all three plays Williams suggests that economic might corrupts, destroying lives and promoting hypocrisy and falsehood in its wake. Grand antebellum plantations with their wealthy families are primary symbols of the Old South, but Williams roundly condemns the racism, violence, and mendacity that they breed.

While critical of the South's wealthy, Williams famously champions the region's disenfranchised and outcasts: women, poets, artists, and the sexually marginalized populate his plays. Although the South tolerates eccentricity more than the North (the often repeated saying goes, Northerners hide their eccentrics in the cellar, but Southerners put them on the front porch), Williams advocates a more prominent place for social outsiders. His fugitives rarely succeed, but he never fails to highlight them, demanding that we respect their perspectives and suggesting we have much to learn from those on the fringes of culture.

Williams sympathizes with Blanche's plight, creating a woman of intelligence, refined in her tastes, and appreciative of culture. Blanche's duplicity is a survival tactic thanks to a culture that does not appreciate female intellect, but rather the female form. She gains further sympathy in her overwhelming guilt over pushing her husband, Allan Grey, to suicide because of her homophobic response to discovering him with another man. Certainly, Blanche's homophobia is the product of her time and place, but Williams demonstrates its destructive consequences for gays and straights alike, implying that hatred of the unusual and the strange produces unintended consequences for the victim and the perpetrator. Tolerance breeds harmony.

As a young man, Big Daddy was given a job by the former owners of the plantation, Jack Straw and Peter Ochello, who were clearly lovers. While Brick exhibits nothing but contempt for them, calling the couple a "pair of old sisters," Big Daddy exhibits appreciation for the opportunities they gave him and seems unperturbed that they were gay (Williams 1971, III: 115). While Brick's sexual identity is debatable, he is clearly eaten up with homophobia and guilt because of Skipper's death. Big Daddy's attitude brings him peace of mind, allowing him to approach his son with understanding as he delicately inquires if Brick too might be homosexual. Straw and Ochello remain unseen, but it could be argued they represent the most successful romantic couple Williams created. Regardless, Big Daddy's attitude makes it clear that we should accept things in an attempt to understand them, rather than denying them (116). The action of *Orpheus Descending* (1957) suggests the opposite of Big Daddy's tolerance, presenting a community clinging to hatred and fear of change.

Set in a small Southern town (textual references suggest Mississippi), the play reworks the Orpheus and Eurydice myth with plentiful allusions to the Christian tradition. Lady Torrance operates her dying husband Jabe's general store. Years earlier she led a happy existence, assisting her father in his orchard and wine garden at Moon Lake. The Mystic Crew burned down the business when Lady's father made the mistake of serving blacks. He died in the fire, set, although Lady does not know it, by Jabe and his men. Val Xavier, a potent, attractive musician drifting from New Orleans, arrives in town and takes a job in the shop. Many of the townswomen are attracted to Val, inspiring envy and suspicion in the men, and Lady and Val become sexually involved. Learning that Jabe was involved in her father's murder, Lady decides to recreate the wine garden in the remodeled confectionery as revenge on her dying husband, but Jabe shoots her, blaming the crime on Val whom the town hunts down and lynches with a blowtorch. The play is Greek in its violence, and the materialistic, racist Southerners represented by Jabe and his men snuff out the freedom of expression that Val promotes in the backward town. Lady's new independence of thought and sexuality earns severe punishment. As Bigsby (1984: 97) notes, the play, "recasts the South as hell." Williams juxtaposes hell, a place ruled by the murdering Mystic Crew who fear blacks with rights, sexual expression, and female independence, with an idyllic image of paradise embodied in Lady's description of Moon Lake. She attempts to recreate it in the confectionery:

> I got it all planned . . . Artificial branches of fruit trees in flower on the walls and ceilings! – It's going to be like an orchard in the spring! – My father, he had an orchard on Moon Lake. He made a wine garden of it. We had fifteen little white arbors with tables in them and they were covered with – grapevines and – we sold Dago red wine an' bootleg whiskey and beer. (Williams 1971, III: 263)

Lady's description of Moon Lake emphasizes life, regenerative and pure with secretive nooks to conceal lovers in courtship. It summons up Bacchanalian abandon, imbibing fermented grapes and outlawed spirits. Conversely, this lake is the scene of the violent murder of her father, destroyed in a fire by racist thugs. Over and over, Williams refers to Moon Lake, perhaps the most potent fictional location he created out of actual places in and around Clarksdale, Mississippi (Leverich 1995: 54). Williams's mythical Moon Lake, where Amanda Wingfield of *The Glass Menagerie* (1945) lost a favorite beau in a gun fight on the dance floor (Williams 1971, I: 149); where Blanche danced with Allan and unwittingly pushed him to suicide at the water's edge (355); where John takes Alma to a cockfight and they almost make love in a secluded arbor in *Summer and Smoke* (Williams 1971, II: 192–204); and where Maggie and Brick will hunt deer with bow and arrow as soon as the season starts (Williams 1971, III: 36). Moon Lake remains simultaneously the actual South and Williams's mythical South, full of promise, hope, and life, yet threatening and deadly, an irreconcilable duality.

   With the exception of *Vieux Carré* (1977), set in a French Quarter boardinghouse during the late 1930s, Williams's renderings of the South grew less concrete over time. While realism remains a vital form on the American stage and probably will for some time, Williams's career mirrors the American theatre's drift toward anti-realistic playwriting and stagecraft. Nevertheless, some of the most popular playwrights from the late 1970s to the present favor a realistic style, exploring the eccentricities of a region where change comes slowly.

After graduating from Southern Methodist University, Beth Henley (1952–), born and raised in Jackson, Mississippi, initially pursued a career in acting, but returned to playwriting, which had been a college interest. She chose Mississippi for her themes and locales. While the towns where she sets her plays differ, they are "essentially the same small town, whatever the particular play set within its strangling boundaries" (Nightingale 1984: 3). Despite name changes, each setting exerts the same pressures on her characters. These pressures arise from the constraint placed upon women even in the contemporary South where "keeping up appearances" retains greater value than dealing honestly with heartfelt pain and tortuous losses. Like precursors such as Blanche DuBois, Henley's women reap rewards for beauty and the appearance of chastity.

Henley's Pulitzer Prize-winning *Crimes of the Heart* (1981) begins shortly after Babe Botrelle, the youngest of the three Magrath sisters, has been arrested for attempting to murder her husband. Set in the small town of Hazelhurst, Mississippi, regional dialect and local color give rise to the play's humor. Lenny has joined a dating club, the Lonely Hearts of the South; Meg tries to open pecans by stomping on them; immediately after shooting her husband, Babe makes lemonade because her mouth feels "bone dry" (Henley 2000: 31). With rampant gossip regarding current and past events, racial taboos, and an insistence on the importance of family ties, *Crimes of the Heart* captures the idiosyncrasies of life in a small Southern town.

As the play unfolds, the audience realizes that the eccentricities of the characters conceal a deeper pain caused, in part, by their Southern heritage. Though only thirty, Lenny regards herself as a failure because she remains unmarried and unwanted; her distress is exacerbated by her concern over a "shrunken ovary" which she feels makes her less desirable. Babe shoots her husband because he discovers her affair with a black teenage boy. Confined by a narrow definition of Southern womanhood, Lenny and Babe reflect radically opposing responses: the former accepts the Southern stereotype that to be thirty, unmarried, and childless means one is an old maid, while the latter refuses to endure a bad marriage, taking dramatic steps to change it. Henley's play differs from those of her predecessors in that Babe's transgression goes unpunished. Rewarded for her sins of adultery and attempted murder, Babe wins freedom and still manages to escape from her abusive husband. The difference between what becomes of Babe Botrelle and Blanche DuBois reflects a changing attitude in the South toward women.

Even more so than the earlier play, *The Miss Firecracker Contest* (1984) explores feminine beauty and feminine expectations. Protagonist Carnelle Scott attempts to win the annual Fourth of July beauty pageant. The play's humor derives from the outlandish characters whose odd behavior is reminiscent of those found in the works of Carson McCullers and William Faulkner. Carnelle dyes her hair firecracker red in a vain attempt to impress the judges; Popeye Jackson began her career as a seamstress making outfits for bullfrogs; after challenging a man to a duel, Delmount Williams got incarcerated in a Louisiana mental institution, as unfortunately his weapon of choice was broken beer bottles. As with *Crimes of the Heart*, these characters are not caricatures, but fully developed individuals whose behavior springs from the oppression of their environment. Like Babe, they go unpunished and may further indulge their eccentricities.

The Debutante Ball (1985) also explores the South's obsession with feminine beauty; however, this play provides a deconstructed look at crimes of passion, marriage for money, and the Southern tradition of "coming out." While *Miss Firecracker* is predominantly realistic, *The Debutante Ball* pulses with theatricality in terms of both character and action. Taking place in the upstairs parlor and bath of the Turner Mansion in Hattiesburg, Mississippi, the plot centers on Teddy Parker, a young debutante whose mother, Jen, desperately wants to get her daughter into society. While the dominant theme concerns mother–daughter relationships and secrets, Henley uses the debutante ball to explore the Southern cultural values which ensnare women. Three years before the play's action, Teddy's father "got bludgeoned to death with a cast iron skillet" (276). Hattiesburg society deems Jen a pariah due to suspicions that she killed her husband. Later exposing herself as the killer, Teddy explains she committed the murder in an attempt to protect her mother from her father's violent reaction to Jen's filing for divorce. Teddy hides her crime from her mother, trying to reshape the truth in the same way Jen reconfigures her daughter into a Southern belle. The makeover fails and eventually mother and daughter reject the definitions others have made for them. In the last scene Jen and Teddy share a moment devoid of pretense, as the former bathes and they talk unashamedly. The imposition of the ideal of the Southern lady cannot repress the desire and the spirit of Henley's female characters, yet it channels their behavior into bizarre and often violent actions. Despite this, her plays are hopeful. Babe, Carnelle, and Teddy do not escape the South, but manage to change their lives despite its repression.

While Henley's works are overtly Southern, her contemporary, Marsha Norman (1947–) writes plays in which locale does not immediately appear dominant. Born in Louisville, Kentucky, Norman came from a fundamentalist religious household and her childhood was lonely. Her career began at the Actor's Theatre of Louisville when the artistic director, Jon Jory, encouraged her to write about a subject that frightened her. The result, *Getting Out* (1977), centers on a young woman's release from prison.

Set simultaneously in an Alabama prison and a Louisville apartment, *Getting Out* concerns a woman's transition as she moves out of incarceration. The protagonist bifurcates into two people, Arlene, who has been transformed by her eight-year prison sentence for murder and Arlie, Arlene's younger self. Arlie represents the "redneck," capable of brutality and unrelenting selfishness, while Arlene embodies the socially acceptable woman who, although lacking in Southern charm, behaves. Despite the best efforts of the state, the prison chaplain, and Arlene herself, Arlie refuses to be banished, appearing on stage to respond to the brutality visited upon Arlene: her mother accuses her of promiscuity, the prison guard who brings her home attempts to assault her, her former pimp tries to get her to work for him once again. By the play's conclusion, Arlene recognizes the need for her more violent and determined self in order to overcome the past and survive.

Arlie/Arlene need all the determination and grit they can muster to overcome Louisville and working at a minimum wage job. The odds of building a better life seem slim. The setting reinforces an important theme regarding the poor, often rural, Southerners whose lack of education and role models confine them to menial labor and sometimes prison. Norman's play suggests that self-determination and drive may not be enough to overcome the disadvantages of Southern poverty.

Born in Atlanta, Georgia, Alfred Uhry (1936–) explores what it means to be "the other" in the South, often focusing on Jews and blacks. *Driving Miss Daisy* (1986) depicts race relations and friendship between the two central characters, Miss Daisy, a wealthy matriarch of Atlanta's Jewish community and Hoke, her African-American chauffeur. Covering a 25-year span, the play explores the pre- and post-civil rights South. Extremely popular, *Driving Miss Daisy* presents a sympathetic picture of the difficulties of race. Both Miss Daisy and Hoke are outside of the South's power structure and experience the bigotry that the culture often reserves for those who are different. Yet in Uhry's South prejudice can be overcome by compassion, thus he provides an optimistic and idealized vision of how the region may develop over time.

Another immensely popular work, *Steel Magnolias* (1987), by Louisiana native Robert Harling (1951–), reinforces the icon of the Iron Butterfly. Typified by characters such as Amanda Wingfield, Scarlett O'Hara, and Regina Giddens, the Iron Butterfly is a woman whose gentility masks her inner strength and ability to survive. We may not approve of her actions, but we admire her grace under pressure. Harling's work takes full advantage of the stereotypes: M'Lynn, the stoic, practical, and well-mannered mother and wife; Truvy Jones, the good-hearted "stand-by-your-man" woman; Ouiser Boudreaux, the eccentric Southern woman with a wicked tongue that hides a good heart. These are all stereotypes associated with Southern women.

The play and subsequent film have become cult classics in the South. In some ways, the film version has replaced *Gone with the Wind* in young Southern women's romanticized vision of the South. The South, then, is a place where family ties, friendship, and the pursuit of one's dreams become the norm. These bonds, however, can be as constraining as the restrictions placed upon women in the Old South. Although framed in a positive light, Shelby's desire for motherhood drives her, and she dies fulfilling the ideal of Southern womanhood by producing a son. In some ways, *Steel Magnolias* represents a desperate desire to hang on to a semblance of what it means to be a Southern woman. The play glorifies small-town Southern traditions, a throwback to a more conservative era, and perhaps represents a futile attempt to hold fast to a rapidly disappearing Southern past.

Despite the tremendous popularity of Harling's play, one could argue that the South depicted in it and the works of many of the other authors discussed in this essay become more and more illusory in the postmodern world. While the discrimination that African-American playwrights such as Johnson, Hurston, and Childress addressed still exists in the South, the way in which racial tensions play out has changed significantly. The South's covert discrimination makes it all the harder to erase. In the works of Green, Foote, and Hellman, Southern culture became defined by a set of manners that are now considered false, counterfeit, even obsolete. Even playwrights such as Henley and Uhry write about a South haunted by a past whose traditions remain active today only in small towns. Williams's plays have mythologized the American South so powerfully that one almost expects to meet Big Daddy or Blanche DuBois during a visit there, but even his later works indicate that the myth nears extinction.

The South has begun to disappear as a defining force in dramatic literature. Contemporary playwrights such as Suzan-Lori Parks and Naomi Wolfe (although born in the South) may use the region as a point of origin for themes in some of their plays; however, the South ceases to define the world of their plays or their characters' realities in the same way as their predecessors. While traditional Southern values remain a potent force in the contemporary rural South, the influx of people from other parts of the world and the departure of many natives have changed the region significantly. The once reliably Democratic South has, as evidenced by recent national elections, gone Republican. While the ideal of the pure, attractive, and genteel Southern Belle has not quite disappeared entirely, she slowly edges toward oblivion. We will have to wait and see what future trends emerge in the work of Southern playwrights. Meanwhile, as a myth of the South herself, perhaps we should recall Blanche DuBois's singing during one of her infamous baths: "But it wouldn't be make-believe if you believed in me" (Williams 1971, I: 366). For somewhere this evening, a Southerner's play gains another production and the South lives again in a theatrical performance binding the present to a renewed mythology.

References and further reading

Bigsby, C. W. E. (1984) *A Critical Introduction to Twentieth-Century American Drama 2: Tennessee Williams, Arthur Miller, Edward Albee*. Cambridge: Cambridge University Press.

Bigsby, C. W. E. (2000) *Modern American Drama 1945–2000*. Cambridge: Cambridge University Press.

Brown-Guillory, Elizabeth (1990) *Wines in the Wilderness: Plays by African-American Women From the Harlem Renaissance to the Present*. New York: Praeger.

Childress, Alice (1973) *Wedding Band; a Love/Hate Story in Black and White*. New York: Samuel French.

Demastes, William W. (ed.) (1996) *Realism and the American Dramatic Tradition*. Tuscaloosa: University of Alabama Press.

Falk, Signi Lenea (1961) *Tennessee Williams*. New York: Twayne.

Green, Paul (1963) *Five Plays of the South*. New York: Hill and Wang.

Hatch, James and Shine, Ted (1974) *Black Theatre USA: Plays by African Americans 1847 to Today*. New York: Free Press.

Hellman, Lillian (1971) *Lillian Hellman: The Collected Plays*. Boston, MA: Little, Brown.

Henley, Beth (2000) *Collected Plays Volume I*. Lyme, NH: Smith and Kraus.

Herrington, Joan (ed.) (2002) *The Playwright's Muse*. New York: Routledge.

Leverich, Lyle (1995) *Tom: The Unknown Tennessee Williams*. New York: Crown.

McDonald, Robert and Paige, Linda Rohrer (2002) *Southern Women Playwrights*. Tuscaloosa: University of Alabama Press.

Murphy, Brenda (ed.) (1999) *The Cambridge Guide to American Women Playwrights*. Cambridge: Cambridge University Press.

Nightingale, Benedict (1984) "Stage View: A Landscape that is Unmistakably by Henley," *New York Times*, June 3. Retrieved November 24, 2002 from Lexis Nexis.

Norman, Marsha (1979) *Getting Out*. New York: Dramatist Play Service.

Richardson, Gary A. (1993) *American Drama from the Colonial Period through World War I: A Critical History*. New York: Twayne.

Shafer, Yvonne (1995) *American Women Playwrights, 1900–1950*. New York: Peter Lang.

Watson, Charles (1997) *The History of Southern Drama*. Lexington: University of Kentucky Press.

Williams, Tennessee (1971–92) *The Theatre of Tennessee Williams*, 8 vols. to date. New York: New Directions.

17

Sports in the South

Diane Roberts

On January 28, 1983, tens of thousands of Southerners, black and white, young and old, waited in the cold to watch a funeral procession. They stood on the bleak banks of Interstate 59, watching the hearse make its stately way over the 45 miles from Tuscaloosa, Alabama, where the church service took place, to Birmingham, Alabama, where the burial would be. Many held homemade signs and floral wreaths; many were dressed in mourning black, but still more wore crimson and white, the colors of the University of Alabama.

The funeral of Paul "Bear" Bryant, coach of the Crimson Tide football team, was one of the great public events of the twentieth-century South. In his essay on burying the Bear, the historian Charles Reagan Wilson (1995) says that only the funerals of Jefferson Davis, Martin Luther King, and Elvis Presley compare in size and importance. That a college football coach could command devotion equal to or greater than the former president of the Confederacy, the great martyr of the civil rights movement, and the King of Rock and Roll demonstrates that, in the American South, sports are never just a game.

Paul Bryant was a poor sharecropper's son from rural Arkansas who earned his nickname by wrestling a bear as a child. Such a feat places him in a long line of folk heroes such as Davy Crockett (who, as the song says, "kilt him a bear when he was only three"), men who demonstrate a superhuman mastery of nature. Bryant is revered for being a winner, bringing national championship after national championship to an impoverished Alabama, a state accustomed to being called benighted and backward, a state that had never been first in anything. But Bryant is not merely heroic, he has been practically apotheosized. In an oft-told (and telling) joke, a man parades around heaven, acting terribly important and grand. One awed, newly arrived soul asks St. Peter, "Is *that* Bear Bryant?" And the saint says, "No, that's God. He just *thinks* he's Bear Bryant."

A famous poster depicts Coach Paul Bryant walking on water, and the Bear is said to "help" the University of Alabama win football games when fans pray to him.

Bryant is, as Wilson says, "a modern saint of the civil religion." And sport is one of the South's chief "civil religions," a focus for devotion as profound as that found in any Bible Belt church. Willie Morris concurs in *Terrains of the Heart* (1981), declaring: "Southern football is a religion, emanating directly from its bedeviled landscape."

While football commands the South's deepest pieties (see below), other sports, from hunting to basketball, also express Southern identities. The region's well-defined race, class, and gender roles are displayed in its sports culture. Indeed, Southerners have long been inclined to see their region as the *omphalos* of American sport. The region's legacy of strong Protestantism contributes to a sense of being "chosen." But the Southern cult of honor is also central to the sporting tradition. Mark Twain satirizes the obsession with family prestige in *The Adventures of Huckleberry Finn* with the pointlessly feuding Shepherdsons and Grangerfords; however, the importance of honor in the Southern mind is painfully real. In the 1820s and 1830s, men fought duels; these days, men (and women) choose teams to invest with honor, virtue, and local pride. Sporting affiliation is similar to church denomination: most people are born to one. It is possible to change allegiance, as Methodists sometimes become Episcopalians or Holiness become Primitive Baptist, to convert from being a fan of the University of Florida to Florida State University. People describe themselves as Bulldogs, Seminoles, Tigers, or Volunteers, just as they call themselves Presbyterians or Catholics, and this tribal identification goes just as deep.

The image of the South as a place of leisure is as old as European settlement. William Byrd, in his *History of the Dividing Line* (1727), describes North Carolinians as devoid of any work ethic, addicted to fun: "'tis a thorough Aversion to Labour that makes people file off to N Carolina where Plenty and a Warm Sun conform them in their Disposition to Laziness their whole lives." Daniel Hundley, in his *Social Relations* (1860), confirms Southerners' love of leisure but insists that their use of spare time pursuing sports makes Southern white men bigger and stronger than their Northern counterparts. This self-aggrandizement gave rise to the notion – demonstrated to be incorrect during the Civil War – that one Southerner could "whip ten Yankees."

As in other regions and other societies, sports in the South articulate conventions of gender and race. While the South has produced many first-rate female athletes, including Babe Didriksen Zaharias, gold medalist in hurdles and javelin at the 1932 Olympics – later a champion golfer – track star Wilma Rudolph, and Wimbledon champion Chris Evert, to name but a few, the culture still values "femininity" over strength. Schoolgirls play soccer, softball, tennis, and basketball in increasing numbers; they swim, dive, and run, yet gymnastics and its perkier cousin cheerleading are still deemed the premier sports for young women, especially young white women, in the post-feminist South. Cheerleading competitions are even televised by ESPN, the cable sports network.

On the other hand, blacks of both genders are assumed to be "natural" athletes, a stereotype which grew out of slavery times. Black women were deemed tough enough to pick cotton 12 hours a day, though white ladies were imagined to be too delicate to manage more than tatting some lace in the Big House. Black men in the mind of the white South were considered preternaturally *physical*, able to withstand heat and able to work in the fields when white men would, it was assumed, collapse. Ironically, it wasn't until well into the twentieth century that many blacks had access to leisure or much sports playing. Booker T. Washington, in *Up From Slavery* (1900) says,

> I was asked not long ago to tell something about the sports and pastimes that I engaged in during my youth. Until that question was asked, it had never occurred to me that there was no period of my life that was devoted to play. From the time that I can remember anything, almost every day of my life has been occupied in some kind of labor.

Lately, sports has been credited for complicating old constructions of race and gender in the South, an instrument of the civil rights movement (see below) and a challenger of notions of Southern "ladyhood." Yet sports continue to reveal that the South is almost "another country," still in thrall to rigid definitions of black and white, masculine and feminine. And sports is one of the clearest ways Southern culture articulates itself. Always less affluent, less literate, more violent, more past-obsessed and tradition-minded than the rest of the nation, the South uses sport to show that it is – against all odds – a land of winners.

Old Times

In 1513 the Spanish arrived in the place they named Pascua Florida and found the Tocobaga, the Timucua, and the Apalache playing ball games. These games may have been related to the Aztec ball games witnessed by the *conquistadores* in Mexico: something like handball. The Spanish were looking for treasure and converts, not native recreations, though there's evidence the Apalache played ball games in or near some of the missions set up by the Franciscans across North Florida.

Lacrosse, played with a ball and a netted stick, had been prevalent among native peoples from at least the sixteenth century. Usually thought of as a pastime of the Iroquois and other Northern nations, it also crops up farther South. In his 1775 *History of the American Indians*, James Adair says "the Cherokee" in Florida played with a deerskin ball and two-foot bats, their palm-shaped ends worked with deerskin thongs.

The British brought the sports of the old country with them: falconry, hunting, fishing, horse racing. An engraving of 1619 for Captain John Smith's *Description of New England* shows "Virginia gentlemen" fishing and hunting on horseback with falcons, dogs, and guns. The landscape teems with fauna: stags, birds, and fish, as if to underscore the official story that the "New World" was an Eden of abundant food and recreation. In reality, the colonial project was struggling. The Roanoke settlement of more than a hundred disappeared in 1587. By 1608 only 38 of the original 105 Jamestown colonists were alive. The others died of dehydration, disease, and starvation. In 1611 it was reported back in London that though the residents of Jamestown still had little food, and seemed reluctant to hunt or fish to feed themselves, they managed to "play at bowls" to keep up their spirits.

The early colonial period in the South saw cock fighting, pit dog fighting, quoits, wrestling, nine pins, and fishing embraced by white men of all classes. About the only sport available to women was riding – unless you count card playing. By the 1650s, Virginia, the Carolinas, and Maryland were so settled that, for the planters, at least, hunting became more a leisure activity than a necessity; just as in England, fox hunting was popular with the gentry. There is a story (possibly apocryphal) that in 1730, a Mr. Smith, none too keen on Maryland gray foxes, imported some English red foxes and turned them loose along the Chesapeake.

George Washington was a famous hunter, often riding out (before the Revolution) with Lord Fairfax. Washington's adopted son G. W. Parke Custis says of the general: "We have neither knowledge nor tradition of his having ever been a shooter or a fisherman: fox-hunting, being of a bold and animating character, suited well to the temperament of the 'lusty prime' of his age."

In 1750, Colonel Tasker of Maryland imported Selima, a daughter of the famous "Godolphin Arabian." She won many races and became the ancestress of a long line of champion horses. Virginia and Maryland became known for their horses (this would later expand into the "wild west" of Kentucky and Tennessee) and their races. Before he became president, Andrew Jackson established Nashville as an important racing town. By 1865 the South had 83 racecourses, while the North, with a much larger population, had only 22. Two of the Triple Crown races, the Preakness Stake (begun in 1873) and the Kentucky Derby (begun in 1875), take place in the Upper South, and there are important racetracks now in Florida, Louisiana, Maryland, Kentucky, and Arkansas.

Thoroughbred racing is now a multi-million dollar business in Kentucky, Virginia, Maryland, and Florida, but it was once a class marker, separating the planters from the poor whites. In 1674, James Bullock, a tailor of York County, Virginia was fined 100 pounds, "it being contrary to Law for a Labourer to make a race, being a Sport only for Gentlemen." John Pendleton Kennedy, progenitor of the "plantation novel," describes an old-school Virginia squire in *Swallow Barn* (1832): "Meriwether is a great breeder of blooded horses; and ever since the celebrated race between Eclipse and Henry, he has taken to this occupation with a renewed zeal, as a matter affecting the reputation of the state."

Sporting Anglophilia

The seventeenth-century Puritan governors of New England discouraged most leisure activities. They accepted King James's Bible but burned King James's *Booke of Sports* (1618), which lays out the "harmlesse Recreation" subjects might divert themselves with, including archery, vaulting, races, and "May games." The South did not suffer from this suspicion of amusements. The gentry in the slaveholding colonies followed what they saw as English custom (though much of it was rapidly disappearing from a modernizing, increasingly bourgeois Britain), erecting May poles, holding Twelfth Night celebrations, dueling, flat-racing, steeple-chasing, fox hunts, and even jousts. Sporting Anglophilia among the white elite persisted long after the Revolution; if anything it increased during the 1840s and 1850s, when planters and proslavery apologists wanted to link the South's semi-feudal (though fluid) caste system with the established aristocracy of the country many regarded with cultural, though not necessarily political, nostalgia as the motherland.

William Lloyd Garrison began publishing his abolitionist paper *The Liberator* in 1831. That same year, Nat Turner led a slave rebellion in Virginia, killing 55 whites. States cracked down on the tiny bits of freedom blacks had and proslavery thinkers such as Thomas R. Dew suggested that slavery freed whites to become refined in mind and strong in body — though picking cotton certainly would have been good exercise. So they created an ideologically loaded fantasy, staging ring tournaments and jousts. Mark Twain blamed *Ivanhoe* for this preciousness, sneeringly labeling the antebellum South "Sir Walter Scottland." Scott was the planters' favorite writer, the provider of an embellished vocabulary for their romantic nationalism. The planters grafted Scott's medievalism onto theories of white supremacy and took to calling themselves "the Chivalry."

Most tournaments resembled the one at Fauquier Springs in 1842, when "knights" with *noms de guerre* out of Scott's novels (Ivanhoe, MacIvor, Brian de Bois Guilbert) rode at each other with 11-foot lances, trying to spear a ring about the size of a bracelet. A few tournaments tried to "Americanize" themselves: one in Memphis required knights to gallop in a circle while firing at a board painted with a life-sized Indian. Over-dressed as they may sound, ring tournaments could be hazardous. In 1851, Tallahassee, Florida was hit with a fierce winter storm two days before the Christmas joust was to begin. The fine roan ridden by "El Caballero de Esperanza," also known as William Moseley, son of a former governor of Florida, slipped and did a complete somersault on the ice. Lieutenant Moseley's blue velvet costume was ruined and, almost as bad, he lost the tournament to the "Knight of the Lake," Robert Hall of Lake Hall Plantation, who got to crown Dora Triplett of Lebanon Plantation his "Queen of Love and Beauty."

Spurred on by the mythic status of Confederate cavalry heroes J. E. B Stuart and Nathan Bedford Forrest, "Contests of Honor" persisted. The postbellum ones were rather pale, self-consciously anachronistic ghosts of their Old South selves, with participants calling themselves "Knight of the Lost Cause," "Knight of Lost Hope," etc. By the early part of the twentieth century ring tournaments had nearly disappeared, though a few straggled on, even using bicycles and cars in a weird attempt to update an activity that had not been taken seriously for four hundred years.

Other equine English customs persist in the South, from the wearing of Ascot-style hats to the Kentucky Derby to modern day fox hunting, though the vast empty acres where Washington and Fairfax rode have now been covered with highways, subdivisions, and malls. Robert Brooks of Maryland imported the first pack of hounds to Maryland in 1650 and hunting-dog breeding is practiced all across the South today, exemplified by the famous Midland Fox Hounds in Midland, Georgia. Some hunts, especially those in the swampier parts of the South, have been democratized in that they no longer require pink coats, shiny boots, or even horses. Men (and some women) go out just with dogs and guns to stalk foxes. But there are still hunts that William Byrd and the old squires of the plantation novels would recognize, with their stirrup-cups, Masters of Hounds and all. When William Faulkner moved to Charlottesville in the late 1950s, he was invited to ride with the Keswick Hunt. Being accepted into this aristocratic Virginia pastime flattered him so mightily he had his portrait taken in full hunting rig.

Polo is a minority sport requiring even more money than fox hunting, and though the game originated in Persia around 600 BC, Americans always saw it as British. Polo is practiced all over the country, but the most glamorous matches – attracting the likes of the Prince of Wales – take place in South Florida.

In the nineteenth century, shooting, like fox hunting, was a way for the gentry to differentiate themselves from the lower orders through their leisure. Johnson Jones Hooper, one of the leading practitioners of "Southwest Humor" and author of *Some Adventures of Captain Simon Suggs, Late of the Tallapoosa Volunteers* (1845), saw field sports as a gentlemanly pursuit which should not be sullied by bird-netting "negroes" who want them for food or the pot-hunting white trash that populate his fiction. Hooper's *Dog and Gun* (1856) is both a collection of hunting stories and a conduct book on the lines of Castiglione's *The Courtier*. It is also quite funny. Chapter 1, "The Gentleman's Amusement," bellows: *"Rule the First* – call Quail QUAIL!" instead of partridge. Other chapters exhort the hunter to buy only an English gun, preferably by Purday or Westley Richards, only English powder, preferably Curtis and Harvey, and English dogs, preferably pointers.

Quail hunting gave rise to a literature of its own. One of the best practitioners of the quail story was Nash Buckingham. A Harvard-educated Tennessean, his 1936 collection *Mark Right!* extols the pleasures of the Southern countryside, but only for the upper classes who traverse it with well-trained dogs, flasks full of good whiskey, and black servants. Quail hunting remains an upper-class pursuit today. Many of the cotton plantations of South Georgia and North Florida were converted to quail in the late nineteenth century and sold to rich Northerners as hunting estates. In Tom Wolfe's 1999 novel *A Man in Full*, the self-made hero muscles his way to the top of Southern society, partly by means of the quail plantation he bought.

Faulkner and other Southern writers celebrate the more meritocratic (though almost entirely male) world of the hunting camp. In *Go Down, Moses* (1942), the Big Woods is a remnant of the old Southern Eden (without Eve, of course), where the likes of General Compson and Major de Spain, representing the gentry, Boon Hogganbeck, representing poor whites, and Sam Fathers, the last of the Chickasaw chiefs, sit together as near-equals – everyone except Ash, the black cook. Ike McCaslin hunts the magical bear, Old Ben, "not even a mortal beast but an anachronism indomitable and invincible out of an old dead time" in what cannot be seen as a sport but a sacrament, "the men . . . ordered and compelled by the wilderness in the ancient and unremitting contest according to the ancient and immitigable rules."

Other British-derived, British-transmitted sports such as golf and lawn tennis did not become popular in the South until after the turn of the twentieth century, when country clubs, modeled on the English country house (or the plantation – the club house at Augusta, Georgia looks like Tara on steroids), started becoming popular. These sports, again, underlined class differences in the South. It is no coincidence that the once-grand Compsons in Faulkner's *The Sound and the Fury* (1929) sell the last of their plantation land to golf-course developers. The Georgian Robert Tyre "Bobby" Jones, Jr. collaborated with a Wall Street financier and a Scottish course designer to create the Augusta National Country Club. Augusta is lauded by overwrought sportscasters for its azalea-wreathed aura of "Southern tradition." Of course, a lot of that "tradition" included segregation: it was not until 1975 that the first black player, Lee Elder, was invited to play there.

In tennis, the story is much the same, thought of as a middle-class white folks' game played for most of its history at clubs which did not allow blacks or Jews to be members (though blacks could work there as servants). Yet two of the greatest American tennis players were black Southerners, Althea Gibson of North Carolina and Arthur Ashe of Virginia. Both of them came of age in an era of Jim Crow schools and few tennis courts open to blacks, yet managed to excel, complicating the notion that tennis was a "white" game. In the last few decades, the tennis camps of South Florida have been producing champion players, including Chris Evert and Jennifer Capriati, and with colleges offering tennis scholarships, the game has become more egalitarian.

Writers, however, continue to use tennis to signify *haute bourgeois* Southernness. Ellen Gilchrist's short story, "In the Land of Dreamy Dreams," tells how LaGrande McGruder, a racist, anti-Semitic ex-deb, "cheated a crippled girl" out of a match and throws "two Davis Classics and a gut-strung PDP tournament racket" off the Huey P. Long Bridge in a fit of self-loathing. French Edward, the protagonist of Barry Hannah's *The Tennis Handsome* (1983), is himself seduced away from the domineering Southern sport of football to become a champion player and classically unaware jock: "Like that of most natural athletes, half his mind was taken over by a sort of tidal, barbarous desert where men ran and struggled, grappling, hitting, cursing as some fell into the sands of defeat."

Baseball

Cricket was played sporadically in nineteenth-century America but never took hold, even in the Anglophile South. Rounders, however, which in Britain dates back to 1744, gave birth to the sport popularly referred to as "the national pastime." Mark Twain said, "baseball is the very symbol, the outward and visible expression of the drive and push and rush and struggle of the raging, tearing, booming nineteenth century."

The less-than-booming South, uncertain well after the nineteenth century over just how much a part of the nation it really is, did not embrace baseball with the same fervor. Nonetheless, the South produced many prominent baseball players, including Joe Jackson, Dizzy Dean, Hank Aaron, Willie Mays, Jackie Robinson, Satchel Paige, and Ty Cobb, as well as journalists and broadcasters Mel Allen and Walter Lanier "Red" Barber. The culture critic Fred Hobson has said that the South "served the same function in baseball that it served in the nation's economy: It was a colony producing the raw materials."

Until the late 1940s, black players were confined to their own leagues, while white players such as "Shoeless" Joe Jackson and Ty Cobb fit neatly into national stereotypes about the South. Jackson, a talented player from South Carolina who was involved in the infamous Chicago Black Sox game-fixing scandal of 1919, could not read or write. Fans used to taunt him during games, demanding that he spell "cat." As if this weren't enough Jackson, according to sportswriter Joe Williams, "carried his own tonic: triple-distilled corn."

Ty Cobb of Georgia came from the opposite end of the social scale, a great batter from a "nice" family — even though his mother shot his father dead in 1904, saying she thought he was a prowler. He went north to play for the Detroit Tigers in 1905, where he set a number of batting records and impressed everyone with his drawling ferocity as a competitor. John Shelton Reed quotes Cobb's teammate Sam Crawford: "He was still fighting the Civil War. He was always trying to prove he was the best."

The game was probably brought to the South by returning Confederate soldiers, some of whom had learned it in Union prison camps. Ex-slaves learned the game the same way. By the 1880s, the Southern League for white clubs had been established, though it suffered from thin rosters and poor organization. There were baseball teams in New Orleans, Macon, Atlanta, Augusta, Mobile, Houston, and Birmingham, funded by local businessmen, often Jewish merchants. Around the same time, black clubs also sprang up across the South. In most instances, the white and black teams might have occupied parallel universes: they engaged in the same game but used separate facilities, usually in separate parts of town, and did not play each other. There were rare instances of black players on Northern teams as early as the 1870s, but their presence in the South was a source of enormous tension, sometimes violence. Fleet Walker and his brother Welday Wilberforce Walker, who played for Toledo, had to quit the game in 1884 when their team was threatened by a vicious mob in Richmond, Virginia.

Indeed, baseball in the South existed in a virtual state of apartheid until well after World War II. The majors did not come South until 1962, when Houston got a team, followed by the Milwaukee Braves moving to Atlanta in 1966 and the relocation of the Washington Senators (renamed the Texas Rangers) in 1972. Eventually, Florida gained two major league franchises in St. Petersburg and Miami: the Devil Rays and the Marlins. But for most of baseball's tenure in the South, the minor leagues ruled.

White minor league teams flourished in Georgia, Florida, Louisiana, the Carolinas, and Virginia, but even more significant were the Negro League teams, hotbeds of talented players working under harsh Jim Crow conditions. These teams would go "barnstorming," that is, travel around from town to hamlet playing several games a day, sometimes having to sleep on people's floors when there was no "negro" hotel, getting food from the back doors of white restaurants which would not allow them to sit inside. George Giles, who played for the Kansas City Monarchs in the late 1920s, says that in Texas "it was 'nigger this' and 'nigger that' and 'look at that nigger run,'" but things were no better up North: "That was the way it was all over the country... Colorado was just as bad as Mississippi. New York was just as bad as Alabama."

Opportunity to play in the Negro Leagues brought some black players out of the desperate poverty of the rural South. John "Buck" O'Neil learned baseball in Sarasota, Florida during the 1920s by watching the New York Giants, who trained there in the spring. His father was a foreman in the celery fields, but O'Neil eventually went on to play with the Miami Giants. Jack Roosevelt Robinson – better known as Jackie – was brought up in California, but he was born in Cairo, Georgia, son of a sharecropper, grandson of a slave. He played first in the Negro Leagues with the Kansas City Monarchs, drawing even white fans. Then in 1947, along with Larry Doby, he integrated major league baseball. This, however, did not go over well with white Southerners: when Robinson's club, the Brooklyn Dodgers, played in Georgia in 1949, the Ku Klux Klan sent death threats.

Perhaps because of the countrywide league and farm-team structure, baseball anticipated the struggles of the civil rights movement. By the early 1950s, even before the Supreme Court decision reversing school segregation, color barriers in white Southern minor league teams began to be breached, though not without difficulty. In 1950, fearing attempts to integrate Southern sports, the city council of Birmingham, Alabama passed an ordinance declaring: "It shall be unlawful for a negro and a white person to play together or in company with each other in any game of cards, dice, dominoes, checkers, baseball, softball, football, basketball or similar game." In 1953 a Mississippi club refused to play one from Hot Springs, Arkansas because they had a black pitcher. Nonetheless, in that same year, a 19-year-old player from Alabama named Hank Aaron was brought into a white South Atlantic League farm team. He had been with the semi-professional Mobile Black Bears and the Negro League Indianapolis Clowns. Aaron would go on to play for the club that became the Atlanta Braves, breaking Babe Ruth's long-held record of 715 home runs. Though white fans in Augusta, Georgia once threw rocks at him and shouted "Nigger, we're gonna kill you," and Georgia Governor Marvin Griffin declared that race-mixing in sports meant that "the South stands at Armageddon," Aaron is now a New South icon, a symbol of graciousness and sportsmanship.

Even with this history of accomplished players both black and white, even with the way baseball's story parallels the story of race in the South – not to mention its in-built pastoralism – baseball has not become a great theme of Southern literature. The Nashville Agrarians did not employ baseball as an emblem of the pre-industrial

Southern Arcadia. There's no Southern Ring Lardner with his baseball stories. Twain, Faulkner, Welty, Ellison, and Styron have not used baseball as a metaphor for the lost Eden, childhood, or even the complexities of manliness – at least not like Bernard Malamud in *The Natural*, Robert Coover in *The Universal Baseball Association*, or Philip Roth in *The Great American Novel*. In Faulkner's *Sanctuary* (1931) Temple Drake and Gowan Stevens are supposed to be on their way to watch the University of Mississippi play Mississippi State University when they wash up at the Old French-man Place, but the baseball game itself is incidental. Jim Randolph in Thomas Wolfe's *The Web and the Rock* (1939) starts out playing baseball in a Georgia mill town but moves up, in both social and sporting terms, to football.

Baseball may now be the broadest church in American sports, at least in its rosters, with players who are Anglo, black, Latino, and Asian. Ownership and management of teams are still largely white. Still, while Southerners of all backgrounds follow the game (and play it, too), baseball still seems like the sport that happens when there is no football. It may be that baseball simply did not fit the post-Civil War need for a resurgent, if displaced, Southern militarism, giving the defeated white South wars to fight where no one actually died. Many of the major league teams have spring training camps in southern Florida, where they go to practice before the regular season. But this is weather-driven (it's still snowing where many of these teams play) and much of their following in Florida comes from transplanted Northerners and Midwesterners. With the recent successes of the Atlanta Braves and the Florida Marlins, however, this could change. And college baseball teams are receiving more attention (and more funding) than before. Florida State University, and the Universities of Miami, Alabama, Auburn, and Florida among others, have highly successful baseball programs, often making appearances at the College World Series. Perhaps as the South becomes more multicultural, baseball may become more integrated into Southern sporting identity.

Basketball

Invented by James Naismith, a physical education instructor in 1891, basketball, like baseball, is more a part of the national culture than Southern culture. Again, like baseball (and football), the professional game came late to the South and flourishes mainly in areas without a strong "Southern" identification, such as Orlando and Miami. But, unlike in many other parts of the country, basketball in the South was never considered an urban game. Indeed, by the 1920s, high school boys all over the rural South played basketball, one reason being that it was so much cheaper than football: all you needed was some hard-packed dirt, a couple of hoops, maybe an old stop sign or sheet of tin for a backboard. In Faulkner's *The Hamlet* (1940) Labove the football star (who hates football) makes Will Varner build a basketball court at his country school. The boys of Frenchman's Bend take to round ball like hogs to corn, winning game after game under Coach Labove until "he carried the team to Saint

Louis, where, in overalls and barefoot, they won a Mississippi Valley tournament against all comers."

By the 1950s, basketball had become a marquee sport for colleges in the mountain South, where titanic coaches ruled. Adolph Rupp coached at Kentucky for over forty years and invented the "fast-break," making the game more aggressive, more exciting. Rupp built a basketball dynasty in this poor, coalmining state, producing a number of famous players who later entered the pros. He himself became the center of national attention, famous for his brown suits and his irascibility. Though a native of Kansas, Rupp transformed himself into a Kentucky gent, known as "the Baron." He once told a newspaper: "The legislature ought to pass a law that at three o'clock every afternoon any basketball coach who is seventy years old gets a shot of bourbon. These damned bouncing, bouncing, bouncing basketballs are putting me to sleep."

Impressive as Kentucky's basketball program has always been, the state of North Carolina has dominated the game in the South for the last half century. In 1946 North Carolina State University hired a coach called Everett Case from the Midwestern basketball powerhouse Indiana University. By 1950, attendance at NC State Wolfpack basketball games annually was over 230,000 – the largest in the country. The basketball teams at Duke, Wake Forest, and the University of North Carolina also grew in prominence. Along with NC State, they saw themselves as the center of the basketball universe – "Tobacco Road" where every year one or more of them were likely to play for a national championship. Football rules in the lower South, but in North Carolina, basketball rules. Team loyalty is fierce. Jim Valvano, the New Yorker who coached from 1980 to 1990 at NC State, was amazed that even the school "colors could evoke such unbridled wrath or joy in people." The uninitiated visitor wearing Carolina blue in Duke territory or Duke blue in Wake Forest territory will quickly find out how important tribal identification can be.

College basketball integrated about the same time as college football, and black players had to endure some of the same indignities and difficulties. In 1963 Mississippi State's Bulldogs were due to play Loyola University in a prestigious tournament. Because Loyola had one black player, Mississippi Governor Ross Barnett actually had a court injunction issued barring Mississippi State from traveling to the game. However, the sheriff charged with delivering the order turned out to be a fan and so "failed" to deliver it to the university. MSU got to play on the national level and one more of the South's color lines was crossed.

Things were nonetheless tough. In 1967 Perry Wallace, the first black player to start for a Southeastern Conference team (Vanderbilt University in Nashville), was taunted by University of Mississippi fans and had rebel flags waved at him. At the University of North Carolina, however, the legendary coach Dean Smith who coached at Carolina for over thirty years made it a point to aggressively recruit black players in both the North and the South. In his early days as a head coach, Smith insisted that players go to the church of their choice on Sundays, but invited his first black player, Charlie Scott, to his own church. Smith also took mixed groups of players to restaurants which had been "white only." His prestige (his Tar Heels won numerous

Atlantic Coast Conference titles, had 27 consecutive seasons with 20 or more wins, made 11 trips to the Final Four and won 2 national titles) helped to change racist attitudes in North Carolina and across the South.

These days, big-time basketball is the province of African-American athletes such as Michael Jordan of Wilmington, North Carolina, who played for Smith at Carolina. Jordan broke all basketball records at North Carolina and went on to break NBA records playing for the Chicago Bulls. Indeed, white players are now seen as a minority in a sport dominated by 7-foot-plus black men.

Women's basketball has become an important collegiate sport in the South, with the University of Tennessee in particular producing championship teams. Even before professional women's basketball, there were some officially amateur but dominating women's basketball teams. In the 1940s and 1950s the Southern Textile League gave women a chance to play sports. These were teams from various mills and vocational schools which provided working-class women with some of the few non-domestic jobs in the South. These games were so popular, even in a South which resisted women's sports, that in 1947 the Winston-Salem newspaper declared their city "the new women's cage capital." In 1951 North Carolina's Hanes Hosiery team beat the Flying Queens of Wayland College, Texas, for the Amateur Athletic Union Championship. Now high-school girls are encouraged more and more to take up the sport and attendance at women's basketball games, both at the professional level and collegiate level, is growing, a mark of late but welcome changes in Southern gender roles.

Football

Football, especially college football, is the South's premier sport. There are areas of Georgia, Florida, and Texas where a match-up between two county high schools can seem like the Super Bowl. H. G. Bissinger's *Friday Night Lights* (1991), about a year in the life of two young teams in the economically depressed town of Odessa, Texas, tells how the year's big game could draw 20,000 people. Games at the larger universities in Georgia, Florida, Alabama, Louisiana, Texas, and Tennessee attract crowds of 80–90,000, with television audiences in the millions. College coaches can earn up to $2 million a year (almost ten times what the president of the United States makes) and become community celebrities, appearing in advertisements for everything from Ford trucks to Golden Flake potato chips.

Professional football did not arrive until 1960, when the Dallas Cowboys and Houston Oilers were established, followed in the mid-1960s by franchises in Atlanta, Miami, and New Orleans, then later, Tampa, Jacksonville, Carolina, and Tennessee. But the pro teams have never achieved what television commentators call "the pageantry" (by which they mean the marching bands, mascots, cheerleaders, flag corps, and near-liturgical rituals), much less the emotional sway, of the college game.

Football migrated south from New England. Princeton and Rutgers played the first US match in 1869; the first Southern scrimmage was in 1877 when the Virginia

Military Institute took on Washington and Lee. Back then, the game was much closer to rugby: no pads, no downs, no helmets. Players were encouraged to grow a thick head of hair to soften the inevitable blows. But it didn't take football long to become hugely popular in the South and innovative Southern coaches such as John Heisman of Auburn and Georgia Tech spiced up the plays. And it did not take the South long to mythologize football: the famous Sewannee "Iron Men" of 1899 played six road games in six days from Texas A&M to the University of Mississippi, and, to the amazement of sportswriters across the nation, won every one.

Indeed, football was supposed to breed "iron men." The long-ingrained, highly articulated Southern cult of white masculinity embraced football. In 1926 S. V. Sanford, president of the University of Georgia, declared: "Football meets that unforgotten need of the race which in the days of chivalry had to be satisfied by the tournament and the joust."

Football underlines the South's precise gender roles: men are to be large, strong, and violent when necessary. Women are to be on the sidelines – literally. At best, a few women work as "trainers" feeding high-energy drinks to the players or toweling off the balls. At worst, they are cheerleaders in short skirts, majorettes in tight costumes, or "Homecoming Queens" in tiaras. It is not, however, unusual for Southern women to be expert in football and as committed to their teams as men. *Southern Living*, an aspirational lifestyle magazine about home decoration, gardening, and cooking, published in Birmingham, Alabama and read mostly by middle-class Southern women, runs an annual feature on Southern football, usually right next to a spread of recipes for a tailgate party – the back-of-the-car picnic spectators hold before games.

Though football remains the one sport women do not habitually play in high school or college, in 1999 a young woman called Ashley Martin was accepted onto a college football team as a place kicker. This generated a ferocious debate in the South as the usual lesbian jokes were made in bars and preachers inveighed in the pulpit against females violating God's law in the same way they rage against abortion and women in the army. Girls playing softball and basketball do not seem to bother them. That there was this much uproar shows that in gender terms the South is still quite traditional: everyone knows his or her ordained place. As Nanci Kincaid, a former homecoming queen and wife of a football coach, says in her 1998 novel *Balls*: "In football, the rules are the rules are the rules. So everybody can go crazy and relax all at the same time."

Football is a violent sport, embracing a sort of Victorian muscular Christianity, perhaps a legacy of its descent from an English public school game. Many coaches and players belong to an evangelical group called the Fellowship of Christian Athletes, where members preach, witness, and generally promote both muscles and Jesus. It is not uncommon for those players who score a touchdown to kneel in the endzone and pray. Nor is it considered odd for college teams to have their own chaplains.

In Southern literature as in Southern society, football is the sport most likely to be used as a metaphor. The game can be a signifier for war, a way to discuss the Southern fetish for honor, and a medium to express the most conservative version of masculin-ity, or, sometimes, the fragility of masculine identity. Brick Pollitt in Tennessee Williams's *Cat on a Hot Tin Roof* (1955) is tormented by his feelings for his best friend Skipper, who has committed suicide. Skipper may or may not have been a homosexual, and Brick may or may not have known it. In any case, Brick and Skipper's shared passion for football aggressively excludes Brick's wife Maggie, who is herself a sportswoman, fond of "bow-hunting at Moon Lake."

The tortured football player in Southern literature and film goes back at least to Thomas Wolfe's *The Web and the Rock* (1939) and Jim Randolph, a football hero in decline. More recent examples of the football player as sacred king, vessel of the ideals and terrors of his culture, include the running back in Don DeLillo's novel *End Zone* (1972), who becomes existentially paralyzed by the thought of nuclear war, and Gavin the "Grey Ghost" (played by Dennis Quaid) a brilliant player who has trouble adjusting to his ageing body in *Everybody's All-American* (1988). Joe Lon Mackey, Harry Crews' murderous, priapic monster of a protagonist in *A Feast of Snakes* (1976), cuts a swathe of physical and emotional devastation through his small Georgia town, appropriately named Mystic. In the end, though, the community exorcises the demon, throwing him into a pit of snakes.

Football embedded itself in Southern culture as if the game had been invented there. As early as 1928 a three-volume *History of Southern Football* by Fuzzy Woodruff appeared, with blow-by-blow accounts of every scrimmage since Princeton beat Virginia 116-0 in 1890. In Faulkner's *The Hamlet* (1940) Yoknapatawpha has its own early twentieth-century football star in the aspiring lawyer and schoolmaster Labove, a country boy who gets a scholarship to the University of Mississippi because he can score touchdowns. His employer, Will Varner, is unimpressed by the game: "I hear it aint much different from actual fighting."

Playing football in college was a badge of courage, as seeing combat at Chick-amauga or Vicksburg had been two generations before. Fuzzy Woodruff describes two of the stars of the 1890 game between the University of Georgia and Auburn University as if they were Achilles and Hector:

> In the line was the gigantic Shafer, years later the city attorney of Selma, Alabama, physically the biggest man I've ever seen outside of a sideshow and a perfectly propor-tioned athlete. On one side of him was Blondy Glenn, whose name has become a tradition at Auburn.

Football has always appropriated military language. Long passes are called "bombs," the coach is often referred to as a "general in the field." In 1996, when the emotionally fraught annual game between Florida State University and the University of Florida was going to determine who played for the national champion-ship, one Florida paper ran a headline screaming, in huge type, "WAR."

The particular war with which white college football is mythically entangled is, of course, the Civil War. In 1920, when Centre College of Kentucky and Georgia Tech were playing "Yankee academies," a sportswriter called it "the most serious invasion of the North since Lee was stopped at Gettysburg." When the University of Alabama faced the University of Washington in the 1926 Rose Bowl – the first time a Southern team had been invited to this prestigious game – Woodruff uses the rhetoric of the Lost Cause to report: "the score stood Washington 12, Alabama 0, and the Southern Cause looked more hopeless than ever."

During the game, white crowds gathered at one end of Dexter Avenue in Montgomery where they had also congregated to celebrate secession in 1861. When news of Alabama's 20-19 last-minute victory came over the wire, the citizens set off fireworks and celebrated in the streets. As if to underscore the connection between "the War" and football, the next year, when Alabama went to the Rose Bowl again, the governor of the state sent a message to the Crimson Tide: "Alabama's glory is in your hands. May each member of your team turn his face to the sun-kissed hills of Alabama and fight like hell as did your sires in bygone days."

The South's slaveholding history is still a factor in college football. Montgomery, Alabama – first capital of the Confederacy – hosts the annual "Blue-Gray Game," pitting stars from Northern colleges against stars from Southern ones. In *Mississippi* (1996) Anthony Walton reminds us that the nickname of the University of Mississippi – "Ole Miss" – is what slaves called the senior white lady on the plantation, and that it is still common to see Confederate battle flags waved during games:

> I was unable to escape Mississippi's unsubtle reminders of past pain; and that sense of the blood of history that at times seemed would be with me all day – from tailgate parties there in the Grove, with molasses-accented belles offering me hors d'oeuvres and barbecue, to the Ole Miss Marching Band's playing of "Dixie" to celebrate the day's victory – clashed in a kind of double vision with the festivities and high spirits. With the exception of the two football teams, there were very few blacks in sight.

College football in the South has largely been separate and *unequal*. Traditionally black colleges fielded their own football teams, usually in facilities that had a fraction of the resources of traditionally white colleges. However, as in baseball and other sports, blacks proved their athleticism in ways that attracted the attention of whites. In the 1950s and 1960s Jake Gaither of Florida Agricultural and Mechanical University, and Eddie Robinson of Grambling University, were two of the most successful coaches of all time. Robinson won over 400 games in his career. They recruited brilliant players which white colleges in the South would not, of course, even consider, though white fans would attend games (sitting in their own little segregated section) to watch players like Bob Hayes, the only man to win an Olympic gold medal *and* play in the Super Bowl.

Despite the 1954 *Brown vs. Board of Education of Topeka, Kansas* decision by the US Supreme Court ending segregation in schools, and despite the obvious wealth of black football talent around, white colleges in the South were slow to admit blacks as students and players. But the more often integrated Northern, Midwestern, and

Western teams beat all-white Southern ones, the more even die-hard defenders of the "Southern way of life" saw the logic of recruiting black men to play for "their" universities. Though he coached for the University of Alabama that Governor George Wallace had vowed to keep segregated, Paul "Bear" Bryant was one of the first white major college coaches to give scholarships to black players and, as a result, won a number of national championships. The rest of the Southern football powers swiftly followed. So now, while black colleges still field largely black teams, so do predominantly white ones. Football (like basketball and baseball) can be a way out of poverty. Good college players go on to the pros and command contracts worth millions. And yet there is something reminiscent of the plantation in affluent white spectators being entertained on a football field by black students of modest means – as if African Americans can only find a place in society if they can sing, dance, or play sport.

Fishing

Fishing – as a leisure activity and as a living – has been central to the South since long before Europeans ever arrived. It could hardly be otherwise, since the South contains more than one-half of the contiguous US coastline as well as important estuaries such as the Chesapeake Bay and the Gulf of Mexico – the latter an astonishingly rich source of grouper, mullet, shrimp, crab, sea bass, and the best oysters in the world. Over 60 percent of Southerners live within a two-hour drive of the Atlantic or the Gulf. Until the suburbanization of twenty or thirty years ago, every Southern child, black or white, was taken fishing, whether with crab trap, sein net, cane pole, or casting rod, and fishing remains a popular – and populist – sport. North Carolina State University even has a course on sport fishing.

It was also a focus of exaggerated pride from early on. In his *Carolina Sports by Land and Water* (1846), William Elliott boasts that he once took 120 bass in one day. Indeed, Elliott's account, subtitled "Including Incidents of Devil-Fishing, Wild-Cat, Deer and Bear Hunting," depicts the South as one large fishing and hunting estate, stocked for the recreation of gentlemen such as himself. He prides himself on his erudition, citing Jean Ribaut's 1562 expedition to the Carolina coast where he went after "Devil Fish," and quoting Linnaeus' *Systema Naturae*, which called the creature the "vampire of the sea." That Elliott's lyrical waxings were not mere fish-tales is evidenced by his elegant, witty account of "devil-fishing" in the *Southern Literary Journal* of 1838, signed "Piscator."

> Elliott's favorite fish is *the bass* par excellence – *Corvina oscellata* – weighing thirty or forty pounds, three feet and upward in length, elegantly shaped, brilliant with silvery and golden hues, and distinguished by one or more black spots on the tail.

The bass is still the South's favorite fish, as well as a multi-million dollar business and a source for country music songs to boot. Bass fishing is now no mere leisure activity but an entire – largely masculine – culture. However unfair the stereotype, bass fishing is now associated with white guys who chew tobacco and cherish a permanent crush on Dolly Parton. The reality is, of course, far more complex, though those men seem to populate the syndicated bass fishing television shows. Bass is now big business. Ray Wilson Scott formed the Bass Anglers Sportsman Society (BASS) in 1967, spawning an empire of television shows, tournaments, and *Bassmaster*, a magazine with readership in the millions.

Bass fishing has become a freshwater pastime of the middle-class South (the working classes still go for catfish or bream with cane poles while the gentry fish for trout), and a way for men to spend money. You have to have a bass boat (which has an enormous motor), a "fish finder," a temperature gauge, maps, tackle, a trailer to haul the thing on, and lots of beer in the cooler. Bass fishing has its own verbs: "bassin'" or "to bass." And when the champion fish is caught, it must be photographed, then stuffed and mounted (in a dynamic hook-fighting curve) to be hung in the fisherman's den. Some bass even taste good, but that is no longer the point.

Ocean sport fishing is driving out the traditional commercial fishing in much of the South, especially along the upper Gulf Coast where the oystermen, shrimpers, and mullet fishermen of Apalachicola Bay face environmental restrictions owing to over-fishing – as well as lobbying by the richer, more powerful sport fishing industry. Their way of life is gradually disappearing as fishing becomes something for people of leisure – a true sport, in William Elliott's sense.

Stock Car Racing

Like bass fishing, racing has become one of the biggest sporting businesses not just in the South but in all of America. Still, most of the important tracks are in the Carolinas, Florida, and Alabama. There are some old-fashioned dirt-tracks in red clay corners of the rural South where freelancers can practice turns and skids. However, the powerful National Association for Stock Car Auto Racing, NASCAR, controls the "official" races and regulates the drivers, who make millions both from the races themselves and product endorsements.

Stock racing began as a skill related to what was technically a crime: moonshine running. Early stock car drivers such as Junior Johnson of Wilkes County, North Carolina, learned their trade evading government agents out to catch them for transporting illegal liquor. 'Shine runners would soup up their engines and make other modifications to help them drive mountain roads faster than the "revenuers." They became Robin Hoodesque heroes to poor white Southerners who resented federal interference in their God-given right to run a still. The romantic 'shiner outlaw went national in the 1958 Robert Mitchum film *Thunder Road*, in which he plays Luke Doolin, a sullen (yet sexy) corn liquor-running anti-hero.

By the time Burt Reynolds made a spate of movies in the 1970s which involved low-slung American cars with huge engines and a boot full of untaxed alcohol (*White*

Lightning, Gator, The Cannonball Run, and *Smokey and the Bandit* films), NASCAR was drawing audiences in the tens of millions to tracks at Darlington, South Carolina (the first purpose-built stock car venue), Daytona, Florida, and Talladega, Alabama. North Carolina continues to be the heart of NASCAR, headquarters of various teams and home of the tobacco companies which sponsor them. The Winston Cup is the greatest prize in NASCAR, awarded to whomever gets the most points in various races.

NASCAR culture is almost entirely white, Southern, conservative, and Christian. Drivers (almost entirely male, though a few women have ventured into the sport) stress family values and capitalism: their cars and their clothes are covered in corporate logos for everything from Red Man tobacco to Lucent Technologies. They are treated like rock stars. Richard Petty, who is, as John Shelton Reed points out, one of the three figures in the South known as "the King" (the others being Jesus and Elvis), grew up in rural North Carolina, the sort of "good old boy" who typifies racing. Younger drivers, such as Jeff Gordon, are beginning to project a more Yuppified, middle-class image, and NASCAR is making inroads into the middle classes. But it remains, despite the vast sums of money involved, a working-class sport, the point of which is to watch people fulfill the American Dream of being able to drive as fast as you can without fear of a cop. The darker side of the sport is that it is extraordinarily dangerous and while the fans surely do not want to see anyone die, they do like a wreck now and then. In a 1965 *Esquire* article, Tom Wolfe dissected the sociology of stock car racing, but Rick Bragg, the Pulitzer Prize-winning journalist, gets to the heart of racing's appeal in his memoir, *All Over But the Shoutin'* (1997):

> They ran bumper to bumper and door to door at 200 miles an hour, and now and then one of them would die. Usually, but not always, it would be some no-name driver in second-rate equipment who just could not handle the speed, that fantastic speed. He would wobble a little on the turns that were banked so steep it was hard to even walk up them, and spin out, and meet Jesus on the wall or on the bumper of a car that hit him broadside, what they called "gettin T-boned."

Violent Sports

With the possible exceptions of basketball and baseball, it could be argued that most sports in the South are violent, involving shooting something, hooking something, or hitting someone. But some sports – boxing, cock-fighting, and wrestling – have violence as their *raison d'être*. In Augustus Baldwin Longstreet's *Georgia Scenes* (1835), the backwoods citizenry enjoys a good knockdown, drag-out bare-knuckle fight: "I looked and saw that Bob had entirely lost his left ear and a huge piece from his left cheek. His right eye was a little discolored and the blood flowed profusely."

Muhammed Ali, born Cassius Marcellus Clay in Kentucky, is the most famous Southern boxer, winning a gold medal at the 1960 Olympics and going on to become heavyweight champion of the world. His refusal to be drafted for the Vietnam War (he said he was not going to go off to Asia to kill poor people when poor people were being killed in America) and his conversion to Islam made him long unpopular with whites and a hero to blacks. Ali is part of a long line of black Southern boxers, beginning with Tom Molineaux, an ex-slave who in 1810 nearly beat the mighty English champion Tom Cribb.

Wrestling (or "rasslin'") has usually been seen as boxing's country cousin, growing out of gouging matches. Twain's *Life on the Mississippi* features a champion Arkansas wrestler called "Sudden Death and General Desolation." These days wrestlers have names like The Rock, Stone Cold Steve Austin, Chyna and Farouk, the *nom de guerre* of ex-Florida State football star Ron Simmons. Wrestling is still a big arena sport in middle-sized Southern cities (along with truck shows and tractor pulls), but has gone bigtime with television shows such as *Smackdown*.

Dueling has died out, but another ancient European sport, cock-fighting, persists, especially in South Carolina and Louisiana. Though it is illegal, cock-fighting can be found (if you know who to ask) in most rural areas of the South, a hold-over of the old days, another ghost from the South's insistent past.

References and Further Reading

Adelson, Bruce (1999) *Brushing Back Jim Crow: The Integration of Minor League Baseball in the American South.* University of Virginia Press.

Benyo, Richard (1977) *Superspeedway: The Story of NASCAR.* Mason/Charter.

Bissinger, H. R. (1991) *Friday Night Lights.* Harper Perennial.

Elliott, William (1846) *Carolina Sports by Land and Water.* Burgess and Jones.

Faulkner, William (1940) *The Hamlet.* Random House.

Faulkner, William (1942) *Go Down, Moses.* Random House.

Feinstein, John (1998) *A March to Madness.*

Higgs, Robert J. (1981) *Laurel and Thorn: The Athlete in American Literature.* University of Kentucky Press.

Holway, John B. (1991) *Black Diamonds: Life in the Negro Leagues from the Men Who Lived It.* Stadium Books.

McElroy, James T. (1999) *We've Got the Spirit: The Life and Times of America's Greatest Cheerleading Team.* Knopf.

Manchester, Herbert (1968) *Four Centuries of Sport in America.* Benjamin Bloom.

Menzer, Joe (1999) *Four Corners: How UNC, NC State, Duke and Wake Forest Made North Carolina the Center of the Basketball Universe.* Simon and Schuster.

Morris, Willie (1981) *Terrains of the Heart and Other Essays on Home.* Oxford, MS: Yoknapatawpha Press.

Rader, Benjamin G. (1990) *American Sports from the Age of Folk Games to the Age of Television.* Prentice-Hall.

Reed, John Shelton and Reed, Dale Volberg (1996) *1001 Things Everyone Should Know About the South.* Doubleday.

Roberts, Diane (1998) "50,000,000 Fans Can't be Wrong," *The Oxford American*, 23: 25–36.

Whitehead, Charles Edward (1860) *Wild Sports in the South*. Derby and Jackson.

Wiggins, D. K. (1997) *Glory Bound: Black Athletes in a White America*. Syracuse University Press.

Wilson, Charles Reagan (1995) *Judgment and Grace in Dixie: Southern Faiths from Faulkner to Elvis*. University of Georgia Press.

Woodruff, Fuzzy (1928) *A History of Southern Football, 1890–1928*. Walter W. Brown.

Wyatt-Brown, Bertram (1982) *Southern Honor: Ethics and Behavior in the Old South*. Oxford University Press.

18

The South Through Other Eyes

Helen Taylor

The South is possibly the most feted, demonized, and scrutinized region of the USA. From the scandalized perspective of nineteenth-century Harriet Beecher Stowe's *Uncle Tom's Cabin* (1852) to the contemporary festivals across the world celebrating New Orleans jazz, blue grass, and country music, the South has long been that "other country" which is both part of, and differentiated from, the rest of the nation. Its peculiar cultural formations and perceived exoticism have drawn to it the eyes of the world. This essay will attempt to explore the ways its meanings and resonances have been transformed by those eyes.

The South is often characterized as insular, digging around its own backyard and obsessed with its indigenous history and character. Many a barbed reference is made to the incestuous nature of Southern relations – be they of family members or religious and political communities. The way Southerners protect their legacy and build defenses against outside influence provides humor in literature and film alike – from the antics of the wholesome Waltons and failed Southern belle Florence King's advice from her grandmother that, whichever sex she slept with, she should never smoke in the street, to the eccentric grotesques who inhabit the novel and film of *Midnight in the Garden of Good and Evil* about that most backward-leaning, inward-looking city, Savannah (King 1985; Berendt 1994). Largely because of its slave economy and violent, divisive history, it is described as another country, an alien, gothic, or exotic site, a region in which a jealously guarded sense of place is paramount, and whose refusal to engage with the wider world and its concerns has locked it into a morbid past.

This is only part of the truth, however, since the South – as much as other regions of the United States – has evolved through huge waves of immigration, the mingling of ethnic and racial groups, and ongoing dialogue with global cultures. The South can too easily be crudely parodied with terms like "Bible Belt," suggesting a homogeneous and rigid grouping of peoples whom modernity has passed by. It is wise to remember that this region has changed in character through several centuries, passing into different national hands, and absorbing (sometimes violently, other times creatively) many different racial and ethnic groups. This is nowhere truer than in the cultural arena. The regional parochialism associated with the South of nineteenth-century Secession, the Civil War and its aftermath, as well as resistance to twentieth-century civil rights movements, can obscure the many links actively maintained between Southern cultural producers and their counterparts in other countries and regions.

Recent scholarship in Southern studies has tracked a dialogic transatlanticism and circumatlanticism (the three continents of Africa, America, and Europe). The influence of Southern music and musical movements on other regions of the US and indeed the world music industry has long been acknowledged, but reciprocal influences from the Paris Conservatoire and Scottish folk music have been less prominently explored; the malign influence of Sir Walter Scott on Southern romanticism has been deplored, but the importance of Scott to Southern culture, and other literary and dramatic exchanges between Southern writers and writers/directors in other nations, have received meager attention. The contemporary South has acquired a significant global reputation largely through a series of cultural dialogues with which other continents, especially Europe, have engaged. These dialogues are increasingly complex, and while disseminating understanding and illumination, can often involve considerable mythification, misrepresentation, and misunderstandings on both sides of the pond. In recent years, among others the Southern Studies Forum, the Institute for Southern Studies, University of South Carolina, and the Midlo International Center for New Orleans Studies have done important work on the reciprocal French, Spanish, and African cultural ties with the South, while Europe-based scholars have examined European social and cultural exchanges (Hook 1999; Ostendorf 1997; Taylor 2001).

Post-World War II European culture has focused closely on the American South. Through a series of real and metaphorical journeys between the continents of North America, Africa, and Europe, the South and Southernness have acquired new cachet; the South has indeed "risen again." This resurgence has come about largely because of the national and global impact of its cultural industries and products (from Coca-Cola to new country music), enhanced by a lively series of intercontinental exchanges. A cultural circumatlanticism has produced new understandings, appropriations, and versions of Southern products and texts that have kept them alive, revivified them, and/or radically transformed their transatlantic and global reception. Transnationalism, transatlanticism and transatlantic studies are dominating current scholarly discourse, reacting against a notion of globalization that offers a "postnational" world transcending national identity. Instead, they focus on what Paul Giles has described as "the frictions and disjunctions brought about by the slow but inexorable erosions of national formations along with the various reactions and tensions which this process produces" (2000: x).

Transatlanticism emphasizes the importance of circulating and dynamic, rather than fixed, cultures, and it explores the dissonances, disruptions, and dislocations inherent in that process. In the work of Edward Said, Paul Gilroy, Berndt Ostendorf, and others, the search for "roots" has been replaced by debates about "routes." The contemporary South is a region that has benefited from the hybridization produced by such real and imaginary journeys and intersections of cultures. This is especially so since the post-1945 decline of Northern "Rust Belt" cities and the rise of the "Sunbelt" South, strengthened by the growing world influence of Southern cultural movements and industries. Once economically poor and politically demonized for its racial attitudes and practices, the South has engaged in productive dialogues with the national sociopolitical mainstream. While in 1974 John Egerton published his influential book outlining such mutual influences, *The Americanization of Dixie: The Southernization of America*, by 1996 Peter Applebome was arguing a case for a stronger one-way traffic, *Dixie Rising: How the South is Shaping American Values, Politics and Culture*.

In *Circling Dixie: Contemporary Southern Culture through a Transatlantic Lens* (2001) I explored and fleshed out this argument through a discussion of five of the most globally celebrated postwar Southern cultural phenomena that have engaged in economic, cultural, and critical dialogue with Europe and Africa, enjoying especially strong relationships with Britain. These are the novel, Margaret Mitchell's hugely influential *Gone With the Wind* and its African-American counter-text, Alex Haley's *Roots*, with their film and television versions; the cosmopolitan and profoundly Europeanized city, New Orleans; the dramatist who put that city on the map with his iconic *A Streetcar Named Desire*, Tennessee Williams; and the utopian internationalist autobiographer–performer, Maya Angelou. While exemplifying the global reach of Southern culture in recent decades, these instances are not unique; successful transnational, transatlantic relationships and mutual influences have long antecedents, and are far from simple or transparent. While most complex since the mid-twentieth century, such hybridity has always characterized the nature and influence of Southern cultures. In order to illustrate this further, this essay will focus on two case studies, the longstanding love affair between New Orleans and Paris, and secondly the Celtic South, with its particular significance in postwar and contemporary popular romance fiction. In both these discussions, my concern will be to demonstrate the elaborate network of connections and allusions that inform transatlantic and circumatlantic dialogues and produce a polyphonic response to the meanings of the South.

New Orleans and Paris

It is hard to think of two cities in the United States and Europe linked so closely as Paris and New Orleans. Historically, one city was founded by members of the other; groups, families, and individuals crossed between the two cities from the early eighteenth century to the present day. Long after the Louisiana Purchase transformed New Orleans into an apparently "American" city, its cuisine, language, architecture, street names, and social and artistic practices were all saturated in Frenchness and particularly owed their provenance to the *Ur*-city. If you walk along New Orleans streets today, Parisian-style perfumiers, fashion shops, cafés, restaurants, wrought-iron balconies, and small bookshops will remind you at every step that this is "like a shrunken Paris" (Russell 1999: 30).

In 1875 Edward King wrote these words after a long trip through the South, beginning in New Orleans:

> Louisiana today is Paradise Lost. In twenty years it may be Paradise Regained . . . You must know much of the past of New Orleans and Louisiana to thoroughly understand their present. New England sprang from the Puritan mould; Louisiana from the French and Spanish civilizations of the eighteenth century. The one stands erect, vibrating with life and activity, austere and ambitious, upon its rocky shores; the other lies prone, its rich vitality dormant and passive, luxurious and unambitious, on the glorious shores of the tropic Gulf. (King 1972: 17, 20)

King was a journalist who had been sent to Europe in 1867 to cover the Paris Exposition and then produced a first naive book, *My Paris: French Character Sketches* (1868), but he had recently returned from a stint as journalist and war correspondent, covering the 1870 Franco-Prussian War and the subsequent events of the Commune. Like two other figures relevant to my argument, Edgar Degas and Kate Chopin, he was witness to a dramatic and bloody episode in Parisian history – his account of which earned him the reputation to ensure a commission from *Scribner's Monthly* to produce a series of articles. After difficult times in Paris, like many visitors to Louisiana and especially New Orleans, he wanted to find a comforting, embracing, feminine Southern city, so was readily enchanted by the city and state, instantly idealizing and feminizing it – contrasting "erect" New England with "prone, passive" New Orleans. He was not the first, nor the last. For many American and French writers, especially in the nineteenth century, each place became a key city of the imagination – yearned for, a focus of nostalgia and desire, a metonymic motherland or female lover.

In a 1995 tourist pamphlet produced by the New Orleans Convention and Visitors Bureau, similar images appear:

> In 1717, she was a mere flicker in the eyes of the French. A year later she was christened on the banks of a great river – a Creole princess born in the new Louisiana territory . . . That little waif on the waterfront was named New Orleans, and she grew up to be the European Queen of the Mississippi.

The pamphlet's emphasis on Frenchness ("Vieux Carré" for the French Quarter and so on) remind us of the city's foundation in the swamps by Frenchman Jean-Baptiste le Moyne, Sieur de Bienville. The feminine creature evoked here is a reminder of that other tourist city, Paris, which was dubbed as early as 1900 "the West's most seductive city . . . 'essentially a city of pleasure and amusements'" (MacCannell 1976: 61). When it comes to Paris and New Orleans, the license and decadence of both are always enlarged within the imaginations of repressed puritan Anglo-Saxons, on either side of the Atlantic.

Of course, Paris and New Orleans are not alone in having their imaginative geography configured in terms of the sensual body. Urban spatiality has become in Edward Soja's words "recharged with multiple sexualities, eroticisms, and desires... [Cityspace] is literally and figuratively transgressed with an abundance of sexual possibilities and pleasures, dangers and opportunities" (1996: 112). In terms of North America, the South is especially so. From earliest days, it was orientalized and eroticized, particularly because of the associations of African slaves with sexuality itself, and the mythified system of *plaçage* (mixed-race informal marriages arranged at "quadroon balls"), the infamous Storyville area of prostitution and jazz, and the city's longstanding reputation as a place of sexual license and laissez-faire.

Today, despite the designation of southwest Louisiana as "America's Caribbean Coast," tourist literature and journalists' articles tend to yoke New Orleans firmly to its European, rather than other cultural and racial, roots. The New Orleans Tourist and Convention Commission refers to "America's European Masterpiece." European-ness still carries the main burden of historical weight and profundity, the very associations that are seen as central to New Orleans's "difference." And who can blame the commercial sector for marketing New Orleans as European? From the nineteenth century, despite its Anglo-Saxon and Hispanic legacies, it is the Vieux Carré's French Catholic Creole culture and lifestyle, infused and enriched by African cultural influences, that have attracted writers and visitors – from Mark Twain and Lafcadio Hearn to Zora Neale Hurston, Jewell Parker Rhodes, and Fatima Shaik. All have sought that combination of what Lewis Lawson claims Walker Percy liked, "an Anglo-Saxon seriousness of purpose and a Mediterranean mellowness" (Lawson 1992: 53). Tourist leaflets call it the Big Easy, the City That Care Forgot, where you should *laisser les bons temps rouler*, a city of "naughty entertainment and an ongoing celebration of the joy of life." Often, Northern characters or references remind us strongly that it's "a different language down here."

This "different language," all this wickedness, was thus often associated with its foundation as a *French*, thus feminized city, one associated with "feminine" frivolity and pleasure-loving naughtiness. Tourist brochures refer to it as "the Queen of the Mississippi" and "the Queen City," a "carefree lady [with] a fabulous flair for gracious entertaining." Grace King, a Protestant writing of her native city as early as 1895, saw New Orleans as "not a Puritan mother, nor a hardy Western pioneeress... simply a Parisian" who was "tyrannical in her loves, high-tempered, luxurious, pleasure-loving" (1895: xvii, xx–xxi). Thirty years later, in his *New Orleans Sketches*, William Faulkner noted many of the same qualities, though for him this Parisian lady was a "courtesan, not old and yet no longer young... [who] lives in an atmosphere of a bygone and more gracious age... a courtesan whose hold is strong upon the mature, to whose charm the young must respond" (Collins 1958: 13–14). In 1962 novelist Hamilton Basso, who was born and lived in New Orleans through the 1920s, described the city as "a Creole version of the Left Bank," claiming he had "Paris in [his] own backyard" (1962: 11). And although the African-American "Creole" presence is widely celebrated in terms of music and cuisine, there is a far stronger

European flavor to the city's literary culture and promotional materials. New Orleans, now a major convention and gambling city, markets itself as European, and particularly French, both in order to emphasize its sophistication, old-world dignity, and charm, precisely to avoid the racy, criminal associations of port cities, and in order to downplay the influence of Afro-American culture via the Caribbean (not to mention that uncomfortable part of New Orleans's slave history). For predominantly white US and European tourists, analogies with North Africa, Marseilles, and the West Indies may prove a disincentive to visit; a feminized Parisian-style Catholic bohemian jewel set within a patriarchal puritan Protestant nation is probably easier to sell to the international tourist and convention set.

So both Paris and New Orleans are feminized, albeit in rather dubious, though seductive ways. For which lover of culture and pleasure can really celebrate an upright/uptight Protestant city? Cities of feminine frivolity are – it must be admitted – much more fun. However crude or stereotypical the gendered images of New Orleans as lazy whore, the fact remains that this is a city, like Paris, associated with women, prostitution, romance, and sexual transgression of various kinds. It is also a city renowned – like Paris – for its prominent female historical figures, fictional and historical (Longfellow's Evangeline, Baroness Pontalba, Madame Lalurie, Marie Laveau, Alice Dunbar-Nelson, Blanche DuBois, and Anne Rice). In any examination of the transatlantic cultural exchanges and conversations between Old and New Worlds, New Orleans's sociocultural history is associated with diasporic movements of women, be they from French and Spanish colonial families, slaves from Africa and the West Indies, or French Acadians from Nova Scotia. One of the most repeated stories of the city's early history relates to the shipment of orphan girls brought from France in 1727 as wives-to-be for young men of the highest reputation – thus themselves usually from distinguished French families. Known as *"les filles à la cassette,"* because of the little trunk containing their trousseau, given by the Company of the West, they became a romanticized group of women symbolizing French colonial ideals and aspirations, ensuring the continuity of national/ethnic purity.

Manon Lescaut

A story of such a deportation has proved one of the most enduring narratives of the transatlantic relationship between Paris and New Orleans. The novel, *Manon Lescaut* (1731), by Jesuit soldier and priest Abbé Prévost, was published just ten years after the foundation of the city of New Orleans as capital of Louisiana, and thus addressed urgent contemporary issues of colonization and the problems of ensuring a French Catholic community in an alien land. Because of its subject matter, it was immediately banned, became a *succès de scandale*, and was translated rapidly into English. Manon is a much-desired, beautiful but impoverished orphan who has been forced to live off a rich patron but loves a young impoverished Parisian student, the Chevalier des Grieux, with whom she runs away from the convent. Des Grieux is an aristocrat who falls foul of his father and social class because of his obsessive love for the poor girl Manon, whose capital lies in her beauty which is traded for profit. Desperate for money, he takes to gambling and she to prostitution, and as a result she is deported to Louisiana as a *fille à la cassette* while he talks his way onto her ship. They land together, claim to be married, and plan to settle into the French colony, where women are in short supply for the French colonists. Des Grieux badly injures a suitor for Manon (whose unmarried status leaves her vulnerable to the governor's command), so they run away from New Orleans and she expires on a cold Louisiana night. Des Grieux is punished but rescued by a friend who returns him to Paris, a chastened man. The class brutality and hypocrisy to which the lovers are subjected in Paris is set against an America – specifically New Orleans – of apparent classlessness and freedom. In fact, Manon moves from one form of exploitation to another, victim of the crude sexual auction pertaining in the early days of the colony. The fact that Prévost gives the real New Orleans of swamps and forests an imaginary landscape of desert, mountains, and treeless plains does not obscure his understanding of the reasons vulnerable Manon had to die there while her lover survives to be rescued by his aristocratic friends and returned to safety in France.

Manon Lescaut has remained a popular text since first publication, and – the first of a series of notoriously enigmatic, sexually compromised femmes fatales in European culture – proved particularly attractive to nineteenth-century opera composers. Six productions on the theme appeared from 1836 to 1890 – by Balfe (*The Maid of Artois*, 1836), Auber (1856), Massenet (1884 and a one-act sequel, *Le Portrait de Manon*, 1894), and (the most celebrated) Puccini (1890–2). There was a further production by Henze in 1951, *Boulevard Solitude*, and a film version in 1949 by H. G. Clouzot, *Manon* – the latter set in post-liberation France, with Manon as collaborator, involved in the black market, passing from man to man until she is shot by Arabs in the Sahara desert. This story's tragic transatlantic theme, repeated in countless editions and productions to the present day, clearly appeals to audiences on both sides of the Atlantic.

Grace King saw through the myth of the transatlantic trade in female flesh, romanticized in those nineteenth-century operatic versions. Scathing about the French who sent young women to the colony, she describes the "hell of lust, passion, and avarice that reigned in Paris during the last days of the System there," leading to "scouring at night" of streets for "human refuse; the contents of hospitals, refuges, and reformatories" (1895: 38), and the loading of ships sailing for the New World, resulting in the dumping of many on the Gulf Coast to become sick and die. To make her case, she quotes the opening chapter of *Manon Lescaut*, in which the narrator witnesses a dozen girls fastened together with chains and wearing soiled clothing, having been removed from hospital to be deported (39–42).

The close relationship between convent and brothel, nun and whore, is one with which many New Orleans writers and artists have engaged in order to explore the city's muddled and complex class and race structure. All too often in its early history, as Manon's story demonstrates, it was impossible to draw clear borders between respectability and illegitimacy, wife and mistress, independent female pedestrian and woman of the streets, and of course black and white. All those terms for different levels of mixed race – mulatto, griffe, quadroon, octoroon, and so on – have deeper and more significant meanings in this city of hybridities than any other. Its historical shifts from French to Spanish, back to French, then to American ownership, followed by occupation during the Civil War and a racially explosive period following that war (remember *Plessy vs. Ferguson* is a New Orleans-based test case) testify to a troubled passage through colonial and postcolonial cultures. Sexual relationships between the races were a feature of this racially mixed and, in American terms, relaxed or at least co-mingled society, a city boasting more free people of color than any other before the Civil War. Indeed, this troubled passage is something cultural producers found compelling within both cities.

Edgar Degas and Kate Chopin

One Parisian artist whose own mixed-race personal and family experiences are mirrored by those of New Orleans is Edgar Degas, the only major French Impressionist painter to travel to the US to paint. Degas's mother was raised in New Orleans as a member of a prominent Creole French family, and hated her married life in Paris – complaining of never going to a ball, "or even to the smallest party" (Benfey 1997: 10). Depressed and consumed with nostalgic longing for her native city, she died when Edgar was thirteen. New Orleans was for him, therefore, a locus of imagination and desire. Some years later, both his brothers moved to New Orleans and, just as brother René's first child was expected, Edgar went to visit for five significant months in 1872. He had just served in the National Guard during the Prussian siege of Paris, and the post-1871 slaughter associated with the Commune, and was feeling exhausted and uncertain of his future direction. In transition, rethinking his life and work, he visited a city itself in transition, in post-Civil War trauma, and – among the French Creole community – a state of social fragility attached to a fast-disappearing cultural heritage.

Degas himself came from a family of both white and black lines – the white Degas-Mussons and the free people of color, the Rillieux. His mother's cousin, the free man of color Norbert Rillieux, inventor of a sugar evaporator and other technological advances, was one of the best-known New Orleanians in France, and now lies in Paris's Père La Chaise Cemetery. In more ways than one did Degas feel uncomfortable in the city – saying that his eyes were troubling him as the light was too strong, and the models too restless. From 1863 to 1873 Degas was preoccupied with the subject of women suffering in times of civil war, and (as Christopher Benfey argues) in New Orleans Degas explored, through family portraits, one of his great subjects: "the woman pushed by circumstances to the margins of her life" (Benfey 1997: 61). He focused on indoor portraits of postbellum women without men – fatherless, widowed, deprived of their sons, women on balconies, with flowers and children, in mourning. Despite writing in letters about his fascination with black nurses, he painted only one image of an almost-effaced nurse in his *Children on a Doorstep (New Orleans)*. His own family racial secrets prevented him from confronting this area of the city's life in his own work – as did his involvement with the Musson family firm which became a center for the establishment of the Crescent City White League, a Ku Klux Klan-style organization that would engage in a bloody racist battle in 1874 to prevent racial integration in the city.

The writer Kate Chopin also became part of this network. Her husband Oscar Chopin's cotton business was next door to the Musson cotton firm on Carondelet Street, and biographer Emily Toth speculates the exiled lonely painter and the solitary walker, Edgar Degas, and art lover and writer Kate Chopin, would have been bound to meet (Toth 1999). They had much in common – both away from their homes, both linked to complex and close Creole families in the Cotton Exchange, both linked in different ways to hardening racial politics in the city, especially via the White League, both keen on gossip, art, and music. Furthermore, both had been in Paris to see the imperial government collapse and the Garde National take over – Kate briefly on honeymoon, Edgar in the National Guard. For both, Paris was a memory of war, bloodshed, disturbance; New Orleans similarly, but with familial and domestic pleasures that gave both of them material for their art. Toth makes further connections that are persuasive. One of Degas's dearest friends, painter Berthe Morisot, had a close woman friend with whom she painted until that woman's marriage in 1869 – an unfulfilling relationship which always led to regret. The unhappily married artist was called Edma Pontillon – a name extraordinarily similar to the chosen name of Chopin's unsatisfactorily married and frustrated artist heroine in *The Awakening*, Edna Pontellier. Furthermore, Toth points out that one of Edgar Degas's New Orleans neighbors, Léonce Olivier, had a wife, América, who eloped suddenly to Paris with his brother René de Gas – and never returned. This scandal was the talk of the town, especially as Léonce was a decent if dull husband. In Chopin's novel, the abandoned husband is called Léonce Pontellier, and the more exciting if unstable lovers Arobin and Robert Lebrun. (Since Chopin had a tendency to use or approximate real people's names, these connections – queried by some scholars because of a lack of firm evidence – are by no means far-fetched.)

Like Degas, Kate Chopin was living in New Orleans at a time of racial unease and violence simmering beneath the surface, in a city recovering slowly from a civil war it was still waging – not only between Federal and Confederate factions, but also between the dying French Creole order and the American homogenizing political and economic forces. Degas painted widows and women mourning losses of family, status, ethnic power, and influence, reflecting the precarious state of the cotton factor business by which his family and the Chopins would be financially burned; Chopin meanwhile was gathering material for a novel that would reflect the divided houses, waning Creole power bases, and radically shifting nature of class, gender, and race relations in the postbellum city. She did this by an insistent ironic reference to the Frenchness of her city and adopted community, a Frenchness that was no longer dominant or at ease in a postcolonial, postbellum American city.

Throughout her work, France is an imaginary and exotic site of nostalgia, yearning, and aspiration. Frenchness signifies desire, the illicit and sexual pleasure – in stories such as "A Point at Issue" and "Lilacs" as well as her first published novel, *At Fault*, and her second, destroyed novel, which began with a Parisian scene, and was apparently strong meat. In *The Awakening*, there are clear intertextual references to Maupassant and other French writers in terms of a feminized version of city streetwalking, Edna transformed into a female flâneur. However, unlike Baudelaire's classic anonymous and marginal Parisian man, Edna Pontellier can only masquerade as flâneur. She walks through the city, but never with that relaxation or easy openness to erotic encounter of her lover Arobin or the city-dweller celebrated by Walter Benjamin.

New Orleans was very much a city of the street, full of spectacular, olfactory, and musical delights, a walker's heaven, as the young married Kate Chopin and the fictional Edna Pontellier discovered. But, like other nineteenth-century cities, it also tried to refuse those delights of the street to respectable women. The desire for and pleasure in walking and free movement were central to this writer and many of her key characters. But she, and they, could only play at having the freedom of the streets and perform the role of flâneur (a term which is firmly a masculine noun). Despite being celebrated as a feminine city, Parisian-style "Queen of the Mississippi" New Orleans was a perilous site for women in public space. A white woman's sexuality and racial and biological destiny meant that to be *on* the streets suggested, however indirectly, to be *of* the streets. Edna gained the freedom of the city for a while, then, recognizing the limits of that freedom in terms of her race, class, and gender, left town rather than going meekly home, and swam to her death. Chopin transformed that Baudelairian figure of the solitary, disillusioned, aimless male flâneur into a complex, "daring and defying" female walker who symbolically challenged the gendered meanings of *fin-de-siècle* urban space (Taylor 1999). Both she and Degas used the solitary, marginalized New Orleans woman to explore the meanings of this transatlantic city and its hybrid culture.

I have focused on nineteenth-century connections between the cities of Paris and New Orleans, because it was during that century that the relationship was most intense, but also most near to breaking point after the Louisiana Purchase. In the twentieth century the racial and sexual issues so carefully encoded, implied, and suppressed within painting, photography, writing, and music, exploded in ways that have engaged with and included European concerns and enthusiasms. Cultural traffic has gone both ways. The New Orleans cuisine, mixed to reflect its ethnic and racial mixtures (gumbo, café au lait, jambalaya) is now served in Parisian and other European restaurants. Fiction writers, from Sherwood Anderson to Anne Rice, have drawn deeply from the racial secrets and transatlantic crossings between the cities, and there has been a steady flow of musicians between the continents. Among others, Sydney Bechet (in whose name there is now a biennial conference), Duke Ellington, Claude Bolling, and Kid Ory all went to record in Paris, and were much feted there. In 2001, at one of Europe's largest jazz festivals, the New Orleans Jazz Acona (in its seventeenth year), the headline act was Paris Washboard.

There is new research and fictional exploration of the role of writers, photographers, painters, Voodoo/hoodoo practitioners, and chefs – many of them women or with important female patrons or muses – who made transatlantic connections between the cities. New Orleans and Paris are linked by cultural forms, mutual admiration and desire, long after colonial links have loosened or been assimilated/hybridized. Cultural travelers have linked the two imaginatively, sustaining their mutual reputations as feminized sites of pleasure, eroticism, and a somewhat haughty and dangerous European sophistication, that suit real and virtual travelers to both places very well indeed. My next case study is also about fantasy and romantic projection, but unlike the New Orleans/Paris nexus, this one has had more troubled and racially reactionary outcomes.

The Celtic South

There is a strong affection between the South and Britain, both in terms of socio-historical roots and ties and of cultural and mythic connections. In terms of demographic influence, it is not a specifically *English* connection, of the kind that exists in New England and other Northern states, which saw a great deal of English immigration. The earliest census in 1790 (albeit disputed by some historians) established that the European majority in the Southern states were *Celts* rather than English – Scottish, Irish, Scotch-Irish, Welsh, and Cornish – and by the time of the Civil War the South's white population was over three-quarters Celtic. From the late seventeenth century to the American Revolution, the Southern backcountry was flooded with one of those groups, the Scotch-Irish, and it has been said that their heritage and style are the characteristics most associated with Southerners over the last two centuries: herding rather than tilling, leisurely, musical, tall-taletelling, violent, clannish, family-centered, fiercely Protestant, with a strong sense of honor (McWhiney 1988). Indeed, the term most used, usually pejoratively, to describe poor white Southern frontiersmen from the mid-1700s is the Scottish term for a noisy, boasting fellow, a "cracker."

Andrew Hook's (1999) work is a reminder of the strong Scottish influence on American culture in all its forms. He draws a parallel between Scotland/England and the South/North by describing the uneasy tension between region and nation, center and periphery, union and separation, in which the subordinate or marginalized region exists in tension and/or conflict with the colonial or dominant power. He also underlines the demographic and thus sociocultural role of Scottish immigration in the creation of the Southern character, and its reactionary appropriations by such bodies as the Ku Klux Klan and the League of the South. This relationship has flourished through cultural projections: "Both Scotland and the South have become visible to the outside world largely as a result of an immensely powerful and highly romanticized version of their historical pasts" (196). Mark Twain famously deplored the malign influence of Sir Walter Scott on the South, blaming his "jejune romanticism of an absurd past that is dead" for the Civil War (Twain 1904: 347), though a generation earlier the New York writer J. K. Paulding had argued the same line. In 1917 H. J. Eckenrode described the South as "Walter Scottland," and this is now conventional wisdom – though rather neglected in terms of scholarly exegesis. William Faulkner's Scottish ancestry, noted by biographer Joseph Blotner, is reflected in his choice of name for his Oxford home, Rowanoak (drawn from Frazer's *The Golden Bough*), and also themes and characters in his fiction and journalism.

The role of Hollywood in this myth-making is paramount. The classic film, D. W. Griffith's *The Birth of a Nation* (1915), which is credited with reviving the moribund Ku Klux Klan in many states during the 1920s, was based on Thomas Dixon's novel, *The Clansman* (1905). This novel, celebrating as it does the founding of the Klan as the savior of the Aryan race, is dedicated to Dixon's uncle, "Grand Titan of the Invisible Empire Ku Klux Klan," and claims that a "young South" was led by "the reincarnated souls of the Clansmen of Old Scotland" – thus reifying racial violence with recourse to ancestral history. Both novel and film draw on imagery related to rituals and practices of Scottish clans as celebrated in Scott – the blood-soaked Fiery Cross being the most resonant and, ominously, the one emulated by members of the Klan rededicated on Stone Mountain in 1915. The Celtic cross has since become a symbol of a rash of "patriot movement" groups in the South, from Christian Identity to Neo-Nazis.

The neo-Confederate, white supremacist League of the South, given apparent academic credibility by academics such as Grady McWhiney (1988), was set up to defend the notion of the true South as Celtic, thus by definition white; other Souths (notably African-American) thus become illegitimate and inferior. Arguing euphemistically for "heritage not hate," among other things the League has declared a wish to return to British spelling, seeing the American Webster's dictionary as an example of "cultural ethnic cleansing." The Celtic card is being played belligerently against what is perceived as a politically correct celebration of multicultural Southern diversity. Leftist Celtic organizations such as the Scottish Nationalist Party and Welsh Plaid Cymru are embraced for their nationalist separatism, which is (mis)interpreted as conservative supremacism. In defiance of Twain, W. J. Cash, and others, Walter Scott's notions of chivalry and honor are invoked simplistically to support a Cavalier Myth, as well as exclusionary notions of hierarchical social relations and xenophobia. In the case of Scots nationalism the movies *Rob Roy* and *Braveheart* are highly recommended; the latter is the film the League website recommended all "Southrons" (Walter Scott's pejorative term) should go see – a recommendation also endorsed strongly by the Ku Klux Klan and John Birch Society.

It is no coincidence that, in the late 1990s, Maya Angelou became a champion of a very different kind of Celticness, that represented by poet Robert Burns. She traveled to Scotland to celebrate him because she found connections between the Scots and her own race, between Burns's poetry and African-Americans' suffering. In *Angelou on Burns*, a film made for the BBC and Scottish Arts Council, she paid particular tribute to the poem "A Slave's Lament," written remarkably by a man who had neither visited Africa or America nor met a slave, and which she claimed most demonstrates the close ties and parallels between this quintessentially Scottish poet and her race: "It is because of my identification with Robert Burns, with Wallace, with the people of Scotland for their dignity, for their independence, for their humanity, that I can see how we sing, 'We Shall Overcome'" (Taylor 1997).

The *Gone With the Wind* Sequel Saga

In 1991 the Celtic Southern theme was given a major international boost from an unexpected source. In direct contravention of Margaret Mitchell's wishes, her Estate commissioned a sequel to *Gone With the Wind*. *Scarlett*, by Southern romance writer Alexandra Ripley, was a huge commercial success, followed by an internationally produced TV mini-series that was screened across the world (1991). Since Ripley claimed to have read widely in Southern historiography and boasted of her Southern credentials, it is most unlikely she would have been ignorant of *Cracker Culture* and its associated political groupings. She certainly adhered to its ideological line fairly closely, and produced a romantically charged fictional version of the thesis. In many ways, the novel attempts to legitimize those Celtic Southern myths of origin and centrality (a very white version that excludes other ethnic groups, especially African Americans) and also to confirm white Southerners' sense of themselves as semi-aristocratic descendants of Irish kings. Indeed, the first half of the novel may be read as setting up the competing national cultures within the South in order to establish a kind of authenticity within Ireland itself, near the historic site of Tara, where Scarlett settles and establishes a new dynastic line with daughter Katie (Cat). After burying Melanie and Mammy, Scarlett socializes with Rhett's (very English) Charleston-based mother, Eleanor Butler, and tries unsuccessfully to fit into demure Anglo ways, later moving on to Savannah and her maternal grandfather, the French Pierre Robillard, who demonstrates the rigid *froideur* of the French, from which she flees. Finally, triumphantly, Scarlett discovers her paternal heritage by going to meet a bunch of Irish cousins living in genteel poverty in Savannah, providing an occasional base for another cousin, the priest and Fenian gun-runner Colum, who persuades her to return to her father's native land.

Irishness, in Savannah and later in County Meath, constitutes the "bit of rough" Scarlett has always craved: physical ease and sensuality, simple pleasures like music and dance, and a chaotic and friendly intergenerational family life. For the white Southerner who wishes to validate an authentic vernacular Southern style that has no associations with the region's slave history, a celebration of folk culture to the tune of "Peg in a Low-Back'd Car" or "The Wearing of the Green" must have seemed a shrewd alternative. And Gerald O'Hara's choice of the name "Tara" for the plantation he won at poker invites a reworking of Celticness, returning Scarlett to her father's homeland that is essentially a female space ("to anyone with a drop of Irish blood in them the land they live on is like their mother," as Gerald reminds her). It is there that she is converted to the Fenian cause, persuaded of the parallels between her own desire to restore Tara to "rightful" hands after the imperialist ravages of the Union army, and the desire of Irish nationalists to throw off the tyranny of English Home Rule and get back Ireland for its "own" people. Colum tells his wide-eyed cousin:

> Remember your South, with the boots of the conqueror upon her, and think of Ireland, her beauty and her life's blood in the murdering hands of the enemy. Do you but think of it now, Scarlett, when your Tara was being taken from you. You battled for it . . . With all your heart, all your wit, all your might. Were lies needed, you could lie, deceptions, you could deceive, murder, you could kill. So it is with us who battle for Ireland. (Ripley 1991: 565)

Thus Ripley draws on the two very disparate histories to link together the two main parts of Scarlett's story, and to elevate her heroine's individual quest into an epic one. By taking Scarlett back to the real Tara, and the real rather than yearned-for birthplace of her father Gerald, Ripley animates a whole mythic space that gives the land and the plantation Tara their suggestive resonance in the original work, and ensures a receptive readership from Irish Americans, especially perhaps in the South. Furthermore, this schematic parallelism allows Ripley to tap into a mass international readership with facile historical lessons. During the 1990s, when the "Troubles" in Northern Ireland and Noraid's fundraising were at their height, her transatlantic romance fed into the most simplistic colonialist model of power relations.

While a commercial success as both novel and TV series, *Scarlett* proved a critical flop, attacked by both *Wind* fans and detractors, with one critic speaking of a "Disney World" Ireland and African-American critic Alvin Poussaint predicting "the white thing will be reawakened, without much critical outlook." However, that reawakened white thing was to come under increasingly serious challenge around the Millennium. In the mid-1990s the Mitchell Estate commissioned a second sequel by sophisticated, ironic Scottish writer Emma Tennant with a view to attracting the critical acclaim that had eluded it with *Scarlett*, but then sacked her after finding she had failed to honor their thematically restrictive agenda. Tennant's subsequent contempt for the Estate was echoed by Southern novelist Pat Conroy, who in 1998 announced his own sequel, *The Rules of Pride: The Autobiography of Capt Rhett Butler*. His "companion" to the original was intended to kill off Scarlett O'Hara and – in defiance of the Estate's proscription of any whiff of homosexuality or miscegenation – would open with the sentence, "After they made love, Rhett turned to Ashley Wilkes and said, 'Ashley, have I ever told you that my grandmother was black?'" The novel has apparently been abandoned, but upstaging Conroy's mischievous approach, an important intervention in the *GWTW* saga hit the headlines in 2001. Alice Randall's "parody" novel, *The Wind Done Gone* (2001), was taken to an Atlanta court by the increasingly overbearing Mitchell Estate for violating copyright laws with "blatant theft" of Mitchell's novel's themes and characters; US District Court Judge Charles A. Pannell, Jr. agreed and banned publication. Leading intellectuals and writers led an outcry against the Estate, claiming censorship of free speech. Randall's publishers, Houghton Mifflin, successfully appealed the decision on the grounds the novel was a "political parody" and thus protected by the First Amendment, as well as presenting a new perspective on the original story. In June 2001 the novel appeared to considerable critical and public interest, with blurb endorsements from Tony Earley and Jay McInerney that claim it as "the connective tissue that binds the fairy tale of *Gone With the Wind* to the gothic nightmare of *Absalom, Absalom!*," and "a brilliant meditation on a modern myth."

The narrative is a diary "discovered" in the 1990s in an assisted-living center outside Atlanta, written by Cynara, named after the eponymous Ernest Dowson poem from which the "Gone With the Wind" title derives. She is half-sister to Other (Randall's neatly-reversed racial stereotyping of Scarlett), daughter of Planter (Gerald O'Hara) and Mammy, who all inhabit Cotton Farm, Tata (Tara). Cynara's diary records her story for posterity, partly to challenge *Uncle Tom's Cabin* ("I didn't see me in it"), partly to testify to a particular slave history that would otherwise be forgotten – as with Frederick Douglass, who is named, and Toni Morrison's "rememorying," which is echoed in key passages. Events progress the story after Rhett has abandoned Scarlett and she has returned to Tara and Mammy; the original novel's characters, themes, and phrases are intertextually referenced throughout. *The Wind Done Gone* documents the deaths of both Mammy and Other herself – the literary murder planned by Pat Conroy, whose gay scenario is also echoed in Randall's bisexual Ashley. These deaths produce in Cynara a crisis of confidence and direction, resulting in her confused marriage to her long-term lover and Other's widower, a bewildered, broken "R." (Rhett Butler).

Increasingly, Cynara and R. are driven apart by their different responses to memory: when they live together in R.'s Atlanta house, R. tells her, "Don't bring your past into this house," while she is acutely aware he has brought into it "his history." The novel traces her painful past as a mixed-race slave whose family is both riddled with longstanding miscegenation secrets and secrecy, and whose life is blighted by her attempts to come to terms with them and to move on in an uneasily multicultural nation. The lack of love between Cynara and her real mother is contrasted with the passionate bonding between her and "Lady" (Ellen O'Hara), the latter explained in terms of Lady's own mixed-race heritage which prevented marriage to a beloved cousin. The companionate and sexually charged love between R. and Cynara is challenged by Other's death and R.'s subsequent return to Cotton Farm and white Southern traditional values; she meanwhile escapes that alien past by moving to Washington, DC for an unmarried liaison and baby with a black Congressman, before contracting lupus from which she eventually dies.

Part of this escape from a fraught past is reflected in Randall's revisionary view of European values and qualities – the very elements that are so mythified in Mitchell's original and Ripley's sequel. With ironic echoes of the Paris sojourn of Jefferson and Sally Hemings, Cynara is sent on a "Grand Tour" of European cities, crossing the ocean on the *Baltic*, a ship that carried supplies for the relief of Fort Sumter. Cynara hates her journey, discovering a fear of seawater that recurs in her stay in European cities on rivers. R. plans to take her to London where they will marry and live as a "passing" white couple. However, Cynara's resistance grows as she considers herself part of "a sailed people" who crossed to America, so that fear of "crossing the water" is the only thing she retains of her mother's and grandmother's, described with echoes of the Middle Passage section of Toni Morrison's *Beloved* as "a heavy lump of an unexplored thing, like a clod of brown-red mud giving off some old mother heat." Cynara's only European yearning is for London, a city known through her reading of the inevitable Walter Scott and Jane Austen (the latter loved only for *Mansfield Park* because "Fanny hated slavers").

Neither Europeanness nor Celticness is celebrated as in *GWTW* and *Scarlett*, nor is Gerald O'Hara's mystical relationship with Irish land and heritage. Europe is signified by the luxuries enjoyed by Cynara's white father, Planter: "We [slaves] had both dusted and mopped and washed too many fine things, too much Limoge [*sic*], too much Wedgwood, too many times, to retain awe." Ireland is described only as a country from which Planter fled from the law, wanted for murder and theft. Cynara's Irish heritage is not the red soil of Tara but (as Lady warns her) the reddening face and thickening nose characteristic of the drinking Irish. For Alice Randall, the Atlantic crossing, and transatlantic connections, were bringers not of nostalgia or celebration but rather of terrible racial memories and fears.

Until the end of the twentieth century, *GWTW*'s characters, images, key scenes and phrases were constantly recycled in popular novel, magazine, TV show, and colloquial conversation. Publishers, filmmakers, and writers quoted and parodied its various elements, straining to titillate new markets. The commercial success of the Ripley sequel and 1994 TV version seemed to ensure a robust continuation of the novel's ideological work. And indeed, its power must not be underestimated. *GWTW* was able to hold its own as a world cultural icon throughout two-thirds of the twentieth century. The Celtic theme of the Ripley sequel and the choice of British stars for the European–American joint-funded mini-series gave a millennial boost to the story for transatlantic, indeed, global reader-viewers. The manifold global circulations and reinterpretations of the story have coincided with, and imaginatively played into, a rise in reactionary movements such as the League of the South and the new academic challenge to multiculturalism, "White studies," together with neo-fascist groups in many European countries. As with Southern groups' appropriations of *Braveheart*, *Gone With the Wind* – the romantic epic that has appealed so widely to international audiences – received in *Scarlett* a new Celtic transatlantic spin that urged millennial readers to forget that work's negative and oppressive influence on representations and aspirations about race and gender throughout the twentieth century.

Alice Randall, of mixed-race heritage with a Confederate general ancestor, reminded the world that there is another story to tell, and that is a story of miscegenation, promiscuous histories, and loyalties that must be addressed before the myth of Tara can be laid to rest. Her novel was written to "help more healing to occur," and its affirmative, semi-utopian conclusion – in which Tata is bequeathed (albeit by a now-crazy R.) to his black butler and all its black, white, and mixed-race inhabitants are buried together – offers a gesture of national reparation and conciliation. It is perhaps a reflection of the persistence of certain conservative Southern icons that this novel – despite a much-publicized court case involving major supporters such as Toni Morrison – has made little critical or commercial impact.

These brief case studies indicate some of the complexities and contradictions of the transatlantic and circumatlantic crossings between cultures. Southern cultures draw on the region's multifarious racial and ethnic groups, and maintain lively engagement with other world cultures, demonstrating in music, literature, architecture, cuisine, and so on those multicultural, international roots, influences, and dialogues that enrich the region's output. The explosion of tourism in recent decades – transforming cities like Atlanta, Memphis, and Savannah, and offering economic salvation to the South Carolina Sea Islands and Louisiana Cajun towns – has produced new formations and audiences for Southern cultures. While divisions and conflicts remain, all these open up the possibilities of that creative hybridization celebrated by white musician Jack Teagarden to legendary Louis Armstrong at their first meeting: "You're a spade. I'm an ofay. Let's blow" (Joyner, in King and Taylor 1996: 12).

References and further reading

Applebome, P. (1996) *Dixie Rising: How the South is Shaping American Values, Politics, and Culture*. New York: Random House.

Basso, H. (1962) "William Faulkner, Man and Writer." *Saturday Review*, July 28, 1962: 11.

Benfey, C. (1997) *Degas in New Orleans: Encounters in the Creole World of Kate Chopin and George Washington Cable*. Berkeley: University of California Press.

Berendt, J. (1994) *Midnight in the Garden of Good and Evil: A Savannah Story*. New York: Random House.

Collins, C. (ed.) (1958) *William Faulkner: New Orleans Sketches*. London: Chatto and Windus.

Egerton, J. (1974) *The Americanization of Dixie: The Southernization of America*. New York: Harper and Row.

Giles, P. (2000) "Foreword." In W. Kaufman and H. S. Macpherson (eds.) *Transatlantic Studies*. Lanham, NY: University Press of America.

Gilroy, P. (1993) *The Black Atlantic: Modernity and Double Consciousness*. London: Verso.

Hook, A. (1999) *From Goosecreek to Gandercleugh: Studies in Scottish-American Literary and Cultural History*. East Linton, Scotland: Tuckwell Press.

Kennedy Toole, J. (1980) *A Confederacy of Dunces*. Baton Rouge: Louisiana State University Press.

King, E. (1972) [1875] *The Great South*. Baton Rouge: Louisiana State University Press.

King, F. (1985) *Confessions of a Failed Southern Lady*. London: Michael Joseph.

King, G. (1895) *New Orleans: The Place and the People*. New York: Macmillan.

King, R. and Taylor, H. (eds.) (1996) *Dixie Debates: Perspectives on Southern Cultures*. London: Pluto Press.

Lawson, Lewis (1992) "Pilgrim in the City: Walker Percy." In Richard S. Kennedy (ed.) *Literary New Orleans: Essays and Meditations*. Baton Rouge: Louisiana State University Press.

MacCannell, D. (1976) *The Tourist: A New Theory of the Leisure Class*. London: Macmillan.

McWhiney, G. (1988) *Cracker Culture: Celtic Ways in the Old South*. Tuscaloosa: University of Alabama Press.

Ostendorf, B. (1997) *Creolization and Creoles: The Concepts and their History with Special Attention to Louisiana*. Odense, Denmark: Odense University Press.

Prévost, A. (2001) [1731] *Manon Lescaut*, trans. S. Larkin. Sawtry, Cambs.: Dedalus.

Randall, Alice (2001) *The Wind Done Gone*. Boston: Houghton Mifflin.

Ripley, Alexandra (1991) *Scarlett*. New York: Warner Books.

Russell, J. (1999) *Yellow Jack*. New York: W. W. Norton.

Said, E. (1993) *Culture and Imperialism*. London: Chatto and Windus.

Soja, E. W. (1996). *Thirdspace: Journeys to Los Angeles and Other Real-and-Imagined Places*. Cambridge, MA: Blackwell.

Taylor, E. (1997) *Angelou on Burns* (dir.) BBC and the Scottish Arts Council.

Taylor, H. (1999) "Walking through New Orleans: Kate Chopin and the Female Flâneur." *Southern Quarterly*, 37 (spring–summer 1999): 21–9; longer version in *Symbiosis*, 1, 1 (April 1997): 69–85.

Taylor, H. (2001) *Circling Dixie: Contemporary Southern Culture through a Transatlantic Lens*. New Brunswick, NJ: Rutgers University Press.

Toth, E. (1999) *Unveiling Kate Chopin*. Jackson: University of Mississippi Press.

Twain, M. (1904) [1883] *Life on the Mississippi*. New York: Harper.

19

The South in Popular Culture

Allison Graham

Like the western United States, the American South has existed largely as an imaginary landscape in the nation's popular arts. Mass-produced and commercially circulated images over the last century and a half have borne little relationship to the history – or even geography – of either region. The West, however, seems to have escaped the kind of creative paralysis that has plagued representations of the South by evolving – especially on film – as a resonant setting for social and political crises. Westerns have spoken to contemporaneous racism in the 1950s; corporate monopolies and the Vietnam War in the 1960s and 1970s; and gender relations, outdated machismo, and the cultural obsession with violence in the decades since. Moreover, westerns have proven to be highly compatible with other popular genres; the classic western formula turns up in films set anywhere from medieval China to outer space. Despite the dominance of white males in western narratives, women and men of other races have replaced them seamlessly over the past several decades. Popular representations of the South, however, have lacked the western's mutability, its transhistorical and transcultural adaptability.

The American South, it seems, is frozen at its exoticized apex and nadir, relegated by tacit national consensus to a heaven-and-hell diptych of social types: sleepwalking belles and gentlemen of the Old South, and rampaging crackers and hillbillies of the Benighted South. But whether it is depicted as an agrarian idyll of Lost Causes and mistily rendered Belle Reves or a backwoods nightmare of lynch mobs and graphically sketched Tobacco Roads, the South of post-World War II popular imagination has embraced not only the polarized rural connotations of the "country," but also, ironically, "*the* country" itself. Howard Zinn claimed in 1964 that "the Southern Mystique" was in fact simply an exaggeration of regrettable *American* traits; thirty-three years later, in *The Redneck Manifesto*, Jim Goad put it more crudely: the South, he said, is "America's cultural nigger rendered in geographical terms." The "dark" underbelly of the nation, the reversed image in the mass-media mirror, the South was and is America's repellent yet all too compelling Other.

However phrased, when white Southerners in the 1950s began to defy federally ordered desegregation in full view of television cameras, the "country" of the South – its red clay hills, swampy bayous, and Delta floodplains – became a politically recharged setting for the nation's ongoing melodrama of race and social class, and its most vocal and violent inhabitants – working-class white men – became emblems of national shame. Since the rise of the modern civil rights movement, representations of the South have undoubtedly reflected the nation's shifting definitions of American whiteness, and the spectacle of the "redneck's" alternating villainy and buffoonery (in fictional films as well as news footage) continues to provide rhetorical grist for politicians, humorists, screenwriters, and advertisers into the twenty-first century. As one of the most exploited stereotypes in American politics to this day, the poor white Southerner may be the most durable and marketable popular "product" of modern Southern culture.

Pre-War Typology

Before World War II, Hollywood films, the major purveyors of popular cultural images, consistently emphasized the dichotomy between plantation-styled "civilization" and rural Southern vulgarity. Films like *The Birth of a Nation* (1915), *Secret Service* (1931), *Cabin in the Cotton* (1932), *Operator 13* (1934), *The Little Colonel* (1935), *The Littlest Rebel* (1935), *So Red the Rose* (1935), *Jezebel* (1938), *Show Boat* (adapted from the 1927 stage play in 1929 and 1936), *The Lady's From Kentucky* (1939), and, of course, *Gone With the Wind* (1939) recycled familiar Old South characters ("flirtatious belles," "cheerful darkies," and "noble gentlemen") and iconography (moonlight and magnolias, hoop skirts, steamboats, Spanish moss, gala balls in white-columned mansions). The Benighted South was the setting for films focused on the barbarous and/or comic misadventures of hillbillies, rednecks, and crackers; J. W. Williamson, in his *Hillbillyland: What the Movies Did to the Mountains and What the Mountains Did to the Movies*, counts 71 "violent Southern 'actioners'" (i.e., movies about moonshiners or mountain feuders) released in 1914 alone. Later, films like *I Am a Fugitive From a Chain Gang* (1932, based on Robert E. Burns's autobiography of the same year, *I Am a Fugitive From a Georgia Chain Gang!*), *Hell's Highway* (1932), *They Won't Forget* (1937), *Boy Slaves* (1939), *Dust Be My Destiny* (1939), and *Swamp Water* (1941) showcased the indigenous population of the Southern backwoods as either "natural-born" killers, sadists, or (at best) mentally deficient fools.

National reporting on the 1925 Scopes trial in Dayton, Tennessee, certainly played a role in establishing the notion of a primitive Southern mountain culture working against the modernizing, progressive forces of the nation (H. L. Mencken's widely quoted descriptions of Tennesseans as "morons" and "halfwits" alone carried immense resonance). Whether intentionally or unintentionally, documentary photographers of the Depression era reinforced this sense of a hellish counter-America below the Mason Dixon Line. Chief among them was Margaret Bourke-White, whose images from the rural Deep South evoked a nightmarish landscape of ruined fields, mutant faces, and broken bodies.

At the same time that Americans outside the South were becoming aware of the ravages of starvation and poverty in the region, however, they also found themselves being entertained by comical stereotypes of hillbillies. Paul Webb's Mountain Boys, Al Capp's Li'l Abner, and Billy De Beck's Snuffy Smith all made their first appearances in magazines or newspaper comic strips in 1935, the same year in which major movie studios began to release animated and live action "hillbilly" films. Because ignorance and laziness were the defining features of these characters (and of their communities, like Li'l Abner's Dogpatch, a word that became synonymous with shacks, ditches, and tilting outhouses), their unapologetic fecklessness offered an implicit defense of the failing economic system: after all, the bumpkins seemed primarily responsible for their own rundown environments. By the time most Americans realized that the US would be entering World War II, though, the image of the incompetent hillbilly would undergo a radical transformation, one that was specifically geared to a different kind of ideological project.

The story of Sergeant Alvin York's heroics in World War I had been publicized for two decades when producer Jesse Lasky persuaded the lauded veteran to endorse the production of a film biography. Directed by Howard Hawks, *Sergeant York* (1941), starring Gary Cooper, depicted the Tennessee mountain boy as a "natural" sharpshooter, an instinctual killer whose Christian pacifism had been overcome by God-fearing patriotism. Grounding the character in the same elemental physicality that defined the stereotypical hillbilly, Hawks and Cooper converted country-boy naivety and ignorance into powerful rhetorical tools, suggesting that those closest to nature and "God's ways" (i.e., rural white Southerners) were not only inherently prowar but also inherently physically gifted. The same argument would be recycled 53 years later in the immensely popular film *Forrest Gump*, in which a mentally deficient rural Alabama white man became a football hero, war hero, and folk hero by simply running faster and farther than anyone else. (Gary Cooper and Tom Hanks, it should be noted, both won Oscars for Best Actor for their performances in these films.)

The popularity of Alvin York's story offers a dramatic example of the rhetorical power of regional stereotyping – in this case, a patronizingly positive reinforcement of the essential "goodness" of country people. In the next decade, however, the stereotyping of rural Southern white men would differentiate between two "strains" of the genus: the harmless hillbilly and the violent redneck. The latter would become the dominant image of Southern culture in mass media for the next sixty years.

Post-War Distinctions: Hillbillies and Rednecks

After the Supreme Court's *Brown vs. Board of Education* decision in 1954, and especially after the Little Rock, Arkansas, desegregation crisis of 1957, television networks and their commercial sponsors backed away from programming that carried even remote Deep South connotations. The hillbilly became a politically safe representative of the South; a naive, slow-talking native of the predominantly white Appalachian or Ozark mountains (and therefore inherently non-racist, or so his behavior implied), the character was an "innocent" signifier of a region of escalating racial turmoil. Entertainers like Tennessee Ernie Ford and Andy Griffith achieved national stardom in the 1950s as featured "hick" performers on television programs and eventually the stars of their own eponymously titled series. *The Real McCoys* (which revolved around the adventures of a poor West Virginia family transplanted to California) became a hit comedy series on CBS from 1957 to 1962, followed by the immense success of *The Beverly Hillbillies*, which premiered in 1962.

Americans clearly delighted in the consistently comic media display of an archaic subpopulation, but the hillbillies' "charming" ignorance of modern institutions and mores was not simply due to a lack of formal education. Like rednecks, their regional cousins from the lowlands, hillbillies seemed incapable of modern learning – not just uneducated but uneducable. Their ignorance appeared to border on stupidity, and suggested a genetic flaw – a flaw particular, it seemed, to one social class within one geographic region. The political ramifications of such stereotyping were obvious in national news reporting from Little Rock during the Central High School desegregation crisis. *Time* and *Life* magazines portrayed segregationist Governor Orval Faubus as a "slightly sophisticated hillbilly" from Greasy Creek, Arkansas, who "belched gustily" with "milk dribbling down his chin" as reporters watched in amazement. One *Life* reader later wrote to the magazine's editors that their coverage of Faubus "couldn't have been better if Al Capp [creator of the Li'l Abner comic strip] had done it." This kind of stereotyping would later be cannily embraced by Southern politicians like George Wallace, who would galvanize national – not just regional – support for their "common sense" mockery of "pointy-headed intellectuals."

The early career of North Carolina native Andy Griffith illustrates the way in which the notion of hillbilly ignorance, although shrewdly exploited by white Southern performers, worked against the seriousness with which many Southern artists' work would be treated by critics. Griffith rose to fame with a series of recorded comedy routines in which he adopted the persona of a country yokel encountering football games, Shakespearean drama, and opera for the first time. He then went on to earn glowing reviews for his performance as Georgia hillbilly Will Stockdale in the television, stage, and film versions of Mac Hyman's *No Time for Sergeants*. Despite his Chapel Hill degree in music, Griffith found his hick persona consistently mistaken for his off-screen and off-stage personality. Magazine and newspaper profiles referred to his "backwoods Tarheel" demeanor; in everyday life, he was, they claimed, "true to his mountain nature." When cast in director Elia Kazan's film *A Face in the Crowd* in 1957, the "real Li'l Abner" (as his first agent referred to him after their first meeting) found himself cast off-screen by Kazan and screenwriter Budd Schulberg as a "one-dimensional" naif with "quaint backwoods expressions." Under Kazan's tutelage in Stanislavski-inspired Method acting (so the publicity claimed), Griffith "lived the part" of egomaniacal Lonesome Rhodes, ruining his marriage and suffering, he later recalled, "a real, genuine nightmare." Kazan's "genius" instincts had sensed that Griffith felt insecure about his Southern country-town background, and with this quasi-Freudian "key" to his actor's repressed emotions, the director made a practice of whispering "white trash" to Griffith before volatile scenes. Kazan may have been pleased with the results, but Griffith's near-breakdown exposed a crucial lack of mental training. No distancing of performer from performance seemed possible for the country boy: "I can't just play-act a part; I have to *be* it," he claimed, verifying his "natural," uncomplicated, and essentially *inartistic* sensibility. The ingenuous yokel who simply "acts naturally" is hardly a candidate for advanced training in the manipulation and articulation of emotion. Rural artistry, in fact, is often perceived as guileless skill, the product of tradition rather than inspired invention – *folk* art, in other words.

Like Andy Griffith, Elvis Presley would be depicted in the mass media as a performer who just "acted naturally." Throughout the late 1950s and early 1960s, as non-Southern Method actors like Marlon Brando and Paul Newman won critical accolades playing a succession of mainly working-class Southern characters, Elvis, who aspired to their level of artistry, was trapped in one rapidly produced, embarrassingly vapid movie after another (31 in all). As a "real" working-class Southern white man, he was, it seemed, incapable of *dramatizing* that condition. His standard role as a woman-chaser with "a very average brain" (his characters' avowal of their own mental mediocrity being a convention of Elvis movies) only reinforced the popular perception not just that rural white Southern men were a distinctive cultural group, but that they might also constitute a distinctive biological category as well. In terms of political expedience, this was most certainly an ideological *effect* of the mass-produced stereotype.

Complicating the Elvis phenomenon was his *specific* regionalism: 1955 was not an auspicious year for white Mississippians seeking national acclaim, especially poor white *Delta* Mississippians. Elvis's signing of his first recording contract with RCA that year had been preceded by the horrific murder of Emmett Till in Money, Mississippi, about 100 miles from both Tupelo (Elvis's hometown until age thirteen) and Memphis (Elvis's next, and permanent, hometown). The trial in Sumner, Mississippi, of white half-brothers J. W. Milam and Roy Bryant for the killing of the 14-year-old black boy was the first Southern race story covered by national television, and Till's Chicago mother's decision to publish a photograph of her mutilated son's face in *Jet* magazine, coupled with the men's rapid acquittal by an all-white jury, provoked global condemnation of the state of Mississippi. Although white Mississippians rallied around the men during the trial, asserting that theirs was "the most lied about state in the Union," those of higher class standing than the working-class brothers eventually shunned the embarrassing crackers. Even their Princeton-educated attorney ridiculed his clients as slow-witted "rednecks," but admitted the usefulness of their class: "peckerwoods," he observed to writer William Bradford Huie, would "fight our wars and keep the niggahs in line." The theory of a regionally based (and regionally bred) standing army of unschooled, violent race-warriors had, ironically, been placed before the American public by outraged NAACP President Roy Wilkins when he first learned of Emmett Till's murder. "You know," he said to television reporters, "it's in the virus. It's in the blood of the Mississippian. He can't help it."

Like the hillbilly, the redneck was doubly debased, a primitive even in the most primitive section of the country, an unschooled and unschoolable mental incompetent. Even the most defensive promoters of Southern culture and "tradition" were quick to acknowledge an overpopulation of "low-down fellows" in the region. South Carolina journalist William Workman, for example, wrote in his 1960 apologia that "the South has its share aplenty of individuals who think with their fists in the absence of anything else to think with." Both the hillbilly and the redneck were quick to rile (especially, as Workman observed, when "inflamed by liquor, by fleeting passion, or by occasional mob psychology"), but the redneck seemed, at least in the 1950s, to carry a stronger tendency toward violence. His savagery was "in the blood." "Whereas the hillbilly and the yahoo pointed to a place on the map," Jim Goad writes in *The Redneck Manifesto*, "'redneck' could be said to designate a place in the *heart*, most commonly an attitudinal aneurysm pulsating with suicidal stubbornness and poisonous hatred."

If hatred was never a subtext of the Elvis persona, danger – to the culture, to his race, to himself (his own "suicidal stubbornness"?) – certainly was. It is this sense of lurking, barely controlled danger that most clearly distinguishes the public images of Andy Griffith and Elvis Presley, two white Southern contemporaries who once shared the stage on *The Steve Allen Show* in 1956. Goad's description of "the poor white" in the US as a Janus-faced entertainer, "a hillbilly clown" and "a redneck villain," who "walked a tightrope between amusing the audience and murdering it," succinctly suggests a motivation for the unrelenting, career-long denigration of Elvis Presley's personal taste and habits. An unreconstructed and unapologetic working-class Southerner, Elvis flouted America's embrace of class mobility and mainstream assimilation. More than that, of course, he consciously blurred the conventional markers of race through his early admiration and adoption of particular styles of black performance, music, and clothing (even dyeing his naturally light-brown hair its famous glossy ebony). He was, as his white Southern critics claimed, a "race mixer" glorying in the "mongrelization" of white American culture.

In the process of "mixing it up," however, Elvis also reinforced the racist underpinnings of the term "white trash." Contaminated by their social, economic, and even cultural proximity to the black communities of Jim Crow segregation, rednecks, crackers, and peckerwoods could be easily dismissed as racial debris by their racial "superiors." Ironically, they would be the most vocal opponents of integration, defending an ideal of white racial purity that they themselves could never attain. The class-bound vulgarity of "white trash" consigned them to the ranks of foot soldiers in the "second Civil War." Exploited and "inflamed" by those who stood to gain the most from continued racial oppression, they became the unwitting scapegoats of white guilt.

American popular culture since the early 1950s has perpetuated the notion that racism is a peculiar feature of poor Southern white life. Once Hollywood movies dared to treat the subject of racism, they established a durable narrative framework for explaining centuries of injustice. White acceptance of responsibility for racism turned out to be fairly painless when the culprits were barely "white" to begin with. By depicting criminality as an inherent characteristic of class rather than race, the movies culturally redeemed whiteness itself and affirmed the decency of American law. The twentieth-century South, according to popular narratives, was an arena of white – not black – heroism, and the modern civil rights struggle an essentially *intra*racial saga in which "good" white people battled "po' white trash" for the reclamation of the race and the region.

Civil Rights and the Hollywood South, 1950–1962

In the late 1940s a number of movies attempted to deal somewhat realistically with contemporary racism, chief among them *Pinky, Lost Boundaries*, *Home of the Brave*, and *Intruder in the Dust* (all released in 1949). Strikingly, only two of these four "social problem" films were set in the South; one (*Lost Boundaries*) was even set in New England. By the next decade, however, American racism would be portrayed by filmmakers as a mainly Southern phenomenon. Westerns would displace issues of race onto Indian-Anglo tensions on the nineteenth-century frontier, but their central white characters would often be Southerners or ex-Confederate soldiers.

By 1957 Hollywood had established a fairly consistent narrative strategy for alluding to the nation's mounting racial tensions. Central to the strategy was the generic figure of the white Southern criminal, a character similar to the emerging "juvenile delinquent" of American teen culture. Rebels without causes like James Dean's troubled characters, Marlon Brando's biker in *The Wild One*, or the slum kids in *Blackboard Jungle* were national problems, and their crises warned of deepening "generation gaps" in all-American homes. "Real-life" Southern rebels, however, *had* a cause: the century-old Lost Cause. News footage from the Deep South had made their angry faces and demeanors familiar television sights; by transplanting the rebels to fictional settings, filmmakers could present liberal morality tales without appearing to "preach."

Avoidance of white Southern offense (and lost revenue from the region) necessitated such displacement, yet television brass demanded even greater accommodation of Southern sensitivities. With many Southern stations refusing to broadcast programs featuring black performers, anxious corporate sponsors feared the power of groups like the Louisiana-based Monitor South, which coordinated regional rejection of television programs with "anti-South" (antisegregationist) bias, and the threat of individual state censorship. A notorious example of network and sponsor intimidation occurred in 1958, when Rod Serling was forced to rewrite his teledrama based on the Emmett Till case to remove all references to the South. The setting was moved to New

England, the murder victim became a white European, and even bottles of Coca-Cola (that most Southern of beverages) were removed from the set.

In contrast, the South was by far one of Hollywood's favorite settings. Even the contemporary South was not off-limits as long as race remained unspoken and unproblematic. In the waning days of the Production Code, filmmakers were old hands at encoding – even overloading – films with sexual and political connotation. The Southern outlaw story quickly became the major vehicle for expressing liberal "race messages" and its plotline offered two resolutions: punishment or redemption (although redemption might follow punishment). The Hollywood morality tales insisted that white Southern criminals be reeducated in middle-class social values and become functioning members of "progressive" America or risk humiliation, imprisonment, even death. Either ending – reformation or purgation – affirmed the ultimate moral purity of white America.

Not surprisingly, Elvis Presley's first films were cautionary tales about the price of poor white Southern rebellion. Extreme punishment was meted out to the star only once, in his movie debut, *Love Me Tender* (1956). Cast as an east Texas farm boy who missed out not only on fighting for the Confederacy but also on finding true love, he shot his luckier older brother in a jealous rage before being killed by a band of ex-Yankees. In subsequent "pre-army films," or those made before the star was drafted into military service, Elvis would be spared such harsh punishment, but nevertheless be forced to learn "civilized" behavior the hard way. Although his post-army films were little more than cartoonish travelogues, Elvis revisited his Southern criminal persona in *Wild in the Country* (1962), playing an Appalachian delinquent with the "mark of Cain" on him. Doomed by poverty and "wildness" to a life of fighting and drinking, he managed to make it to a college campus, where we were to believe he would be reformed and reeducated. Elvis was Robert Mitchum's original choice to play his younger brother in the 1958 film *Thunder Road*, probably the most well-known Southern rebel film of the era. Although the casting did not materialize, the sight of Elvis openly admiring a moonshine-running, law-defying hillbilly would have been an ironic leavetaking of the screen before his induction into the army.

A Face in the Crowd offered another fairly explosive punishment scenario, with Andy Griffith's Southern television demagogue exposed on the air to the nation as an arrogant con man, almost literally falling from fame and grace while weeping maniacally on the balcony of his New York penthouse. Another Southern psychotic, ex-Confederate soldier Ethan Edwards (played by John Wayne) in John Ford's *The Searchers* (1956), suffered from such deep-seated racism that he was eager to find and kill a niece who had been kidnapped by Indians and had, no doubt, endured the "fate worse than death." Edwards's sudden, merciful sparing of the girl's life at the end of the film was unconvincing, but the redemption of American hero John Wayne from the spectacle of savagery was a cultural necessity.

The most blatantly rhetorical of the 1950s Southern redemption films was Joshua Logan's 1957 adaptation of James Michener's novel *Sayonara*. An epic-length story of Southern army officer Lloyd Gruver (played by Marlon Brando) confronting his own racism, the film, set during the Korean War, made no attempt to disguise its contemporary message. His merciless mockery of Japanese women silenced by an attraction to a former geisha, Gruver would make a 180-degree turn from Southern racism to a critique of "the Great White Race." As a West Point-educated general's son from Virginia (facts repeated throughout the film), Gruver had the class and training to generate his own moral and political conversion without external coercion. Southern white men of a different class, however (like Paul Newman's rural drifter in *The Long, Hot Summer*, 1958), had to be either *taught* or *forced* to change.

White Southern women were taught lessons as well. Those mired in Old South fantasies, like Blanche DuBois in Tennessee Williams's *A Streetcar Named Desire* (adapted to the screen in 1951) or Susanna Drake in *Raintree County* (1957), simply went mad. Those whose whiteness was sullied by their loose sexuality, like Ruby Gentry in the film of the same name (1952), or those who "passed" as white, like Julie LaVerne in *Show Boat* (last adapted to the screen in 1951), Monique Blair in *Kings Go Forth* (1958), and Sarah Jane in *Imitation of Life* (1959 version), encountered similarly bleak fates (alcoholism, suicide, and romantic abandonment). Movies about racial "passing," in fact, offered contradictory political messages, seeming on the one hand to condemn racism by chronicling its devastating effects on black characters, yet insisting on the inescapable tragedy of blackness itself.

White Southern women whose only "flaw" was ignorance and poverty were suitable candidates for reeducation, but their enlightenment could occur only through outside intervention. *The Three Faces of Eve* (1957) traced in almost allegorical fashion the path out of Southern benightedness toward the "light" of progressive, modern America. The film told the story of a working-class Georgia woman (played to rave reviews by Joanne Woodward) tormented by two warring personalities, dreary housewife Eve White and vampy playgirl Eve Black. While the character's names were exploited for their biblical and sexual connotations, the racial social class subtext was close to the surface. In fact, the solution to her traumatically *segregated* "selves" turned out to be social, not psychological, in nature. With the patronizing guidance of her sophisticated, non-Southern psychiatrist, the woman learned that neither downtrodden country girl Eve White, who was married to a working-class simpleton, nor white trash tramp Eve Black was an "acceptable" middle-class personality. Sweeping her psyche clear of these Dogpatch squatters, she produced a new character, "Jane." A 1957 model of the modern American woman, Jane betrayed no trace of her former hillbilly "selves"; her brand-new accent was mid-American, and her grammar, grooming, and decorum perfectly "correct." The reborn, suddenly reeducated Southern woman found her biographical anchor in memories of schoolteachers, classrooms, and Shakespearean sonnets.

Other desperate white women would follow "Jane" out of the Benighted South during the 1950s and early 1960s with the help of educated outsiders: rural Tennessean Carol Garth in Elia Kazan's *Wild River* (1960), who married and moved north with a racially tolerant, liberal federal official; Helen Keller, who in the television (1957), stage (1959), and screen (1962) versions of *The Miracle Worker* was guided out of the permanent night of blindness and deafness (and her Alabama family's claustro-phobic and racist home) by Boston teacher Annie Sullivan (while the real Helen Keller would follow Sullivan north to Radcliffe College); and Tammy Tyree, Missis-sippi shanty-boat heroine of the "Tammy" novels (1948–65) of Cid Ricketts Sumner and their popular film adaptations (*Tammy and the Bachelor*, 1957; *Tammy Tell Me True*, 1961; and *Tammy and the Doctor*, 1963), who left the swamp, went to college, and was liberated from backwater ignorance by her English professor. Little Rock native Nellie Forbush in *South Pacific* (adapted from the stage musical in 1958), who called herself "a little hick," had to travel all the way to Polynesia to be reeducated in racial tolerance by a "cultured Frenchman" with multiracial children.

Movies like these insisted that poor white men and women were the major impediments to social change in the South. Just as clearly, change could only be effected through "outside agitation" and, that failing, harsh punishment. But by the early 1960s films focusing on Southern reeducation had run their course of remarkable popularity and a new narrative focus began to emerge, one that would attempt to address the escalating legal and political crisis that the South posed for the rest of America.

Television, Movies, and the Redemption of Southern Justice, 1960–1980

In 1955 many Americans who lived outside of the South got their first televised glimpse of a Southern lawman when Harold Strider loomed into view on the brief news reports from the Emmett Till murder trial. The obese, tobacco-chewing sheriff of Sumner County, Strider became the template for a series of more famous colleagues: Bull Connor of Birmingham, Jim Clark of Selma, Lawrence Rainey and Cecil Price of Philadelphia, Mississippi. Before Southern police commissioners, sheriffs, and dep-uties developed an awareness of the power of nationally circulated images and a consciousness of themselves *as* images, they were prone, like Jim Clark, to assault news photographers verbally and sometimes physically. Behavior of this nature easily translated as an attack upon television viewers and newspaper readers, and exacerbated the estrangement of national audiences from white Southern authorities. The butt of countless jokes and routines by Northern satirists like Tom Lehrer, Mort Sahl, and Lenny Bruce, the Southern lawman of the mid-1960s was easily the most despised figure on the national scene. Strangely, however, a fictional Southern sheriff of the era was embraced and adored by millions of Americans.

In the fall of 1960 *The Andy Griffith Show* premiered on CBS, and would rank in the top eight prime-time television series until its final season in 1968. Andy Griffith had already established his comic reputation as a North Carolina country boy, and the series allowed him to age and refine this persona into the wise character of Andy Taylor, sheriff of the fictional Mayberry, North Carolina. With his inept deputy Barney Fife, played by Don Knotts, Taylor presided over a world which bore almost no resemblance to images of Southern life which were currently filling the nightly news broadcasts. Andy and Barney alone contradicted the stereotype (which was certainly based in fact) of Southern lawmen. Peaceful, friendly, ethical to a fault, Andy did not chew tobacco, was not overweight, and carried no weapon but his common sense. Barney toted a gun, but was ordered by Andy to keep his one bullet buttoned in a shirt pocket.

The timing of the show could not have been more ironic, for it premiered just months after black students in Greensboro, North Carolina, launched the lunch counter sit-in movement. Mayberry itself was modeled upon Griffith's hometown of Mt. Airy, North Carolina, which was only 60 miles north of Greensboro. Entirely white and almost untouched by contemporary social or political upheavals, Mayberry offered a weekly testament to a nostalgic (white) ideal of American life, a fact not lost on Griffith and Knotts, who, Griffith has said, were intentionally evoking their memories of the 1930s South.

The Andy Griffith Show was not an isolated instance of popular displacement. The year of its premiere also saw the publication of Harper Lee's novel *To Kill a Mocking-bird*, a story explicitly set in the South of the 1930s. The parallels between the works are startling: both were set in fictionalized versions of their creators' small hometowns (Lee's Maycomb was actually Monroeville, Alabama) and both focused on decent, mild-mannered, widowed fathers who were men of the law (Lee's Atticus Finch was a lawyer) – a formula, incidentally, which would be closely followed thirty years later in the much-lauded NBC series *I'll Fly Away*. Maycomb, however, had black residents, and the region's racism was not elided.

Despite its reliance on historical displacement (and a child narrator) to soften its critique, *To Kill a Mockingbird* seemed to be a timely indictment of Southern (in)justice. Yet here, as in the reeducation and punishment films of the day, the book and the film aimed their strongest moral ammunition at individuals, not institutions – and more importantly, at individuals of a particular class. The villain of the story was white trash, dump-dwelling Bob Ewell, a man whose "face was as red as his neck." It was his violence, alcoholism, racism, sexual abusiveness, and, finally, attempted murder of children that created the narrative's racial crises to begin with. To much of the rest of America, "Southern law" was an oxymoronic phrase, yet Lee's idolization of Atticus Finch implicitly exonerated the law, as well as the white male power structure of the Deep South; even Boo Radley turned out to be the gallant savior of Jem and Scout. His slaying of the redneck restored peace and harmony to Maycomb. (Billy Bob Thornton would recycle this formula in his 1996 film *Sling Blade*, even casting Robert Duvall, who had played Boo Radley, in a cameo role.)

Gregory Peck won an Oscar for his portrayal of Atticus Finch, but in 1962 he had also played a similar role in the film *Cape Fear*. As a modern-day attorney in North Carolina, his Sam Bowden confronted yet another cracker from hell, this time Max Cady, played by Robert Mitchum. Forced to save his family of women by wrestling the rednecked demon to the death in a primeval swamp, the Southern man of law emerged both morally inviolate and physically superior.

Finally daring to portray contemporary Deep South racism in 1967 (now that the urban North had become the new setting for racial conflagration), Hollywood trumpeted the production of *In the Heat of the Night* as an act of political bravery. In truth, although it co-starred black and white actors and allowed a fair amount of relatively "frank" race talk, it nonetheless followed the pattern established by previous Southern films. Small-town Mississippi police chief Bill Gillespie (played by Rod Steiger, who won an Oscar for his portrayal) looked and moved like the stereotypical Southern lawman, but he turned out to be fair-minded and even respectful of the Northern black police officer (Virgil Tibbs, played by Sidney Poitier) who had been wrongly accused of murder. Although a wealthy upholder of Old South customs came under suspicion for the crime, the "real" criminal in town was the racist redneck who worked behind the counter at a backroads diner.

The characters of Andy Taylor, Atticus Finch, Sam Bowden, and Bill Gillespie accomplished a seemingly impossible feat: they created not just a positive image of Southern law, but a heroic (or, in the case of Andy, admirable) image of its enforcers. It should be remembered that white Southern resistance to federal law posed a threat to the legitimacy and authority of the nation and its Constitution. If the reeducation and punishment films attempted to redeem white America, the figure of the reinvented lawman worked to redeem American law, and to affirm the idea that "the system" worked. The newly cleansed, groomed, and educated lawman provided another invaluable service to the nation: he was helping to reclaim the South as American, not Confederate, territory. The redneck, then, retained his ideological significance in the new narratives of brave Southern lawmen. An inherent criminal by "nature," he would violate taste, decorum, and the law (which, according to the movies, was not problematic to begin with). His rampages and crimes, like those of Bob Ewell, would be the primary cause of regional turmoil.

The Redemption and Collapse of White Southern Authority: 1970–1992

As white trash grew more monstrous in the movies, Southern lawmen grew more respectable. Herschell Gordon Lewis's "splatter film," *Ten Thousand Maniacs* (1964), followed Harper Lee's notion that backwoods monsters are Southern Halloween characters (Bob Ewell attacks Jem and Scout on Halloween night and is killed by a real-life "ghost," Boo Radley), and imagined its rampaging, rural villains as Confederate ghosts. Ten years later "Southern gore" was firmly established as a subgenre of the horror film with *The Texas Chainsaw Massacre*. Louisiana crackers senselessly murdered all three main characters in *Easy Rider* and Texas rednecks raped Joe Buck and his girlfriend in *Midnight Cowboy* (both 1969), but John Boorman's 1972 film adaptation of James Dickey's 1970 novel *Deliverance* managed to integrate the evolving conventions of Southern horror into mainstream drama, creating what for many viewers was an entirely too convincing image of crackers from hell. And if the prison wardens and

Texas Rangers of the popular films *Cool Hand Luke* and *Bonnie and Clyde* (both 1967) were hardly representative of the trend toward respectable Southern lawmen, the peace-and-non-conformity-laden subtexts of the films encouraged a reading of the characters as primarily symbolic of Texan Lyndon Johnson's "Establishment" – specifically, the military establishment – in their mindless assertion of power and control.

As if the major branches of popular culture were being orchestrated by extremely early supporters of Jimmy Carter's presidential aspirations, "country" began to shed its backwoods connotations and enter the mainstream. Folk and rock musicians forged a new path to Nashville, beginning with Bob Dylan, who recorded his 1969 *Nashville Skyline* album there; within a decade groups like Lynyrd Skynyrd and the Eagles would elevate "country rock" into a distinctive genre. The "art house" aura surrounding *The Last Picture Show* (1971), Peter Bogdanovich's black-and-white homage to classical Hollywood films, made Hank Williams fashionable among people who knew almost nothing about country music. An even more prestigious and critically celebrated film, Robert Altman's *Nashville* (1975), set its Bicentennial critique of American political and entertainment culture in a city formerly considered anything but "typically American." "Redneck chic" became a marketing gimmick, with citizen's band (CB) radios, associated primarily with long-distance trucking, springing up in urban apartments and luxury sedans, and CB argot ("Ten-four, good buddy") casually dropped into conversations – all aided by Jimmy Carter's brother Billy, who played the redneck clown for a briefly adoring nation (and for whom a momentarily popular canned beer was named).

While white Southern-inspired fads proliferated during this period, images and ideas associated with the black liberation movement were also claiming space in the national imagination. Both trends found themselves ironically linked in January 1977 when the inauguration of Georgia peanut farmer Jimmy Carter to the presidency preceded by three days the premiere of American television's most highly rated event to date, ABC's eight-night broadcast of *Roots*. With white Southern authority now officially redeemed, 130 million Americans became absorbed in the story of an African family's epic struggle to survive centuries of slavery and oppression in the South.

Not surprisingly, perhaps, Hollywood's Southern lawmen were, like Jimmy Carter, unimplicated in the region's criminal history. Early in the decade, James Dickey had taken a role for himself in the film adaptation of *Deliverance* – that of a cannily perceptive (and seemingly honest) rural Georgia sheriff. Real-life County Sheriff Buford Pusser, who had become a Tennessee legend for his relentless pursuit of regional mobsters in McNairy County, achieved national fame in the *Walking Tall* movies (1973, 1975, 1977). Southern sheriffs even became comic figures, an unthinkable image in the 1960s (except to satirists), in the *Smokey and the Bandit* installments (1977, 1980, 1983) and the CBS television series *The Dukes of Hazzard* (1979–85).

With Jimmy Carter's failure to win reelection in 1980, the South lost much of the ground it had won in the campaign for national redemption and retreated to its familiar role as America's shadow self, its moral and psychological Other. The victor that year, Ronald Reagan, had ensured as much when he proclaimed his commitment to states' rights at the Neshoba (Mississippi) County Fair, a traditional stomping ground for hard-shell segregationists. Indirectly pitching a rhetorical appeal to attitudes which had only, it now seemed, been hibernating during the Carter years, the Reagan and Bush administrations (1981–93) rode the crest of reawakened racism, but also provoked scholarly and creative interest in a yellow-dog South that had suddenly turned Republican.

What emerged from this scrutiny was a revisitation and reappraisal of the modern civil rights movement, beginning in 1987 with the PBS broadcast of the six-hour documentary *Eyes on the Prize*. The next year Hollywood ignited national controversy with the release of *Mississippi Burning*, a film based on the 1964 murders of three civil rights workers in Neshoba County which egregiously distorted both Southern and civil rights history. Its distortions, however, were the generic features of "Southern movies" that had been established thirty years before. The commercially successful recycling of this formula ensured that *Mississippi Burning* would be the new *ur*-text of Southern and civil rights films.

Bubba, Grisham, and the Hardening of Cliché

From a cultural perspective, Bill Clinton's election to the presidency in 1992 undoubtedly owed a great debt to four decades of Southern redemption imagery, especially given its appeal to both liberal and conservative sensibilities. In an intriguing conjunction of political and cultural events, in fact, the rise to national fame of the Arkansas lawyer paralleled the similar rise of another Southern lawyer: John Grisham. The immense commercial success of Grisham's legal mystery novels and their highly profitable film adaptations throughout the 1990s founded a veritable white Southern redemption industry. During the Clinton years, television and movie screens were inundated by Southern biographies and autobiographies; retellings of Southern historical crises (chief among them Ken Burns's multi-part PBS documentary, *The Civil War*); Southern comedies; and civil rights melodramas, detective films, and courtroom dramas.

For all of this revisitation of the region and its past, however, the conventions established in the 1950s and refined in the 1960s continue to shape popular understandings of race and social class. The white working class still produces criminals, the black working class still produces victims, and white lawyers and law enforcers still produce social and political progress. These understandings, though, are shot through with ambiguity and contradiction. Nothing offers greater proof of this than the volatile public responses to Bill Clinton's assumption of power in the 1990s.

As a relatively progressive governor of an underprivileged state, and a lawyer as well, Bill Clinton was not just a symbol of the reclaimed South; he was himself a redeemed Southerner. He was a fatherless (some said illegitimate) child whose mother, a woman of flagrantly working-class (some said trashy) tastes, was abused by an alcoholic second husband, and whose half-brother could have been the inspiration for comedian Jeff Foxworthy's career-making one-line jokes that began, "You're a redneck if..." Clinton's all-American rise from the boondocks to Oxford, Yale, and finally the presidency should have provided a modicum of immunity to regional and social class stereotyping. But, as Greil Marcus has written, Clinton, like Elvis Presley, "reaped all the rewards available in American society except one: moral citizenship." The first twentieth-century president with no family money or estate to inherit, Clinton was an easy target for Washington tastemakers. One 1993 political cartoon, Marcus notes, contrasted the libraries of other presidents with Clinton's probable archive: "a country shack with the sign 'Adult Books' on the roof and a pickup truck parked out back."

White Southern males, Marcus observes, are "perhaps the last group in our society that can be comfortably denigrated as such by the sort of liberals who would never say a public word against blacks, women, Asians, or Hispanics." This seems undeniable, yet to the degree that Americans outside the South have insisted upon the otherness of the region, so too have white Southerners. "What is it about Southern women that is as intoxicating to men as a sniff of homemade peach brandy?" asks Ronda Rich in her 1999 book, *What Southern Women Know (That Every Woman Should)*. "Simply put, Southern women have the ability to survive in a man's world while wrapped in a pouf of flowery femininity and gracious, thoughtful manners." Granted, this kind of moonlight and magnolia imagery has long since passed into camp, but while its demystification is nothing new in Southern fiction, it has become the distinguishing characteristic of an outpouring of Southern autobiographies published since the 1990s. Sometimes called white trash memoirs, these often compellingly written narratives have assembled their own battery of predictable conventions: alcoholism, sexual abuse, drug addiction, beatings, violent death, hopeless poverty, traumatic humiliation. The popularity of the genre might suggest that the South continues to function as a repository of national repressions, as the benighted area "down there" whose exposure to the light is unfailingly horrifying and thrilling.

The "Natural" Paradox of the Crossroads

The point at which the demystification of place became professional Southernism is debatable; the profitability of the phenomenon is not. Although James Cobb worries that "this obsession with idiom and idiosyncrasy threatens to turn the South of popular perception into nothing more than a homegrown caricature of itself," one would have a difficult time arguing that popular perceptions of the region have ever been free of caricature – or that almost any region made self-conscious through art or tourism does not eventually become a well-tended caricature of itself. Like the raw, painfully recalled memoirs of growing up in the "anti-South," though, the pain itself can become fetishized, and the social underbelly perceived as more "real" than those

Plate 6   A shotgun shack at the Shack Up Inn, Clarksdale, Mississippi.

well-tended caricatures, especially by a prosperous population intent on discovering "authenticity" amid simulations and virtual experiences.

Which brings us to the Crossroads. On Highway 61, just south of the intersection with Highway 49 in Clarksdale, Mississippi, the Shack Up Inn does more business than the clean, cool, security-monitored chain hotels that line the major throughway back in town. Perched in the middle of a muddy field, five shotgun shacks, formerly the homes of sharecroppers on the old Hopson Plantation, rent for a starting price of $100 per night, and now boast electricity and running water (along with televisions, VCRs, and a Moon Pie on each pillow). In front of one shack is a bottle tree; inside another is a drawer from the dresser of the last sharecropper to live there. Sometimes the beds have no sheets. Guests come from around the world, most of them on "blues pilgrimages" in the Delta. In October 2001 a visitor from London told a Memphis reporter that "the beauty" of the Inn was "the primitive surroundings in which you find yourself." Making the circle of irony complete is the fact that the proprietors have barely advertised their property; hearing about or stumbling upon the shacks fulfills the visitor's dream of authentic authenticity.

But the Shack Up phenomenon begs a question for the cultural inquisitor: is Elvis's plastic-filled, kitsch-filled Graceland any less "real" than a shotgun shack, any less "authentic"? Apparently so, for the South, it seems, is trapped in the same catch-22 as Elvis: shamed for being "natural" and "primitive," yet granted cultural legitimacy precisely for the defect.

References and Further Reading

Allison, Dorothy (1995) *Two or Three Things I Know for Sure*. New York: Plume.

Blount, Roy, Jr. (1998) *Crackers*. Athens, GA: University of Georgia Press.

Cagin, Seth and Dray, Philip (1988) *We Are Not Afraid: The Story of Goodman, Schwerner, and Chaney and the Civil Rights Campaign for Mississippi*. New York: Macmillan.

Cripps, Thomas (1993) *Making Movies Black: The Hollywood Message Movie from World War II to the Civil Rights Era*. New York: Oxford University Press.

Cripps, Thomas (1993). *Slow Fade to Black: The Negro in American Film, 1900–1942*. New York: Oxford University Press.

Daniel, Pete (2000) *Lost Revolutions: The South in the 1950s*. Chapel Hill: University of North Carolina Press.

Goad, Jim (1997) *The Redneck Manifesto: How Hillbillies, Hicks, and White Trash Became America's Scapegoats*. New York: Touchstone.

Guralnick, Peter (1994) *Last Train to Memphis: The Rise of Elvis Presley*. Boston, MA: Little, Brown.

Henderson, Brian (1985) "'The Searchers': An American Dilemma." In Bill Nichols (ed.) *Movies and Methods, Vol. 2*. Berkeley: University of California Press.

Hollis, Tim (1999) *Dixie Before Disney: 100 Years of Roadside Fun*. Jackson: University of Mississippi Press.

Kirby, Jack Temple. (1986) *Media-Made Dixie: The South in the American Imagination*. Athens, GA: University of Georgia Press.

Kirby, Jack Temple (1995). *The Countercultural South*. Athens: University of Georgia.

MacDonald, J. Fred (1992) *Blacks and White TV: African Americans in Television Since 1948*. Chicago: Nelson-Hall.

Marcus, Greil (2000) *Double Trouble: Bill Clinton and Elvis Presley in a Land of No Alternatives*. New York: Picador.

Morris, Willie (1998) *The Ghosts of Mississippi: A Tale of Race, Murder, Mississippi, and Hollywood*. New York: Random House.

Reed, John Shelton (1986) *Southern Folk Plain and Fancy: Native White Social Types*. Athens, GA: University of Georgia Press.

Soderbergh, Peter A. (1965) "Hollywood and the South, 1930–1960." *Mississippi Quarterly*, 19: 1–19.

Sundquist, Eric (1995) "Blues for Atticus Finch." In Larry J. Griffin and Don H. Doyle (eds.) *The South as an American Problem*. Athens, GA: University of Georgia Press.

Whitfield, Stephen J. (1988) *A Death in the Delta: The Story of Emmett Till*. Baltimore, MD: Johns Hopkins University Press.

Williamson, J. W. (1995) *Hillbillyland: What the Movies Did to the Mountains and What the Mountains Did to the Movies*. Chapel Hill: University of North Carolina Press.

Wray, Matt and Newitz, Annalee (eds.) (1997) *White Trash: Race and Class in America*. New York: Routledge.

Part III
Individuals and Movements

20

Edgar Allan Poe

Henry Claridge

Whether Edgar Allan Poe (1809–49) is a Southern writer or a writer who merely happened to reside in the South is a question frequently addressed but rarely answered. To begin with, it is worth reminding ourselves of the extent of Poe's Southern upbringing. Edgar Poe was born in Boston (on January 19, 1809), was soon after taken by his parents, both itinerant actors, to Baltimore, and on the death of his parents (his father deserted his wife and children in July 1811 and died in December of the year, and his mother died in the same month), was entrusted to the care of John and Francis Allan. Allan, who had been born in Scotland, was a partner in a tobacco exporting and general merchant business in Richmond, Virginia and it was to Richmond that he and his wife took Poe (now Edgar Allan, his foster-father expressing his parental responsibilities through Poe's new middle name, though Allan never adopted Poe legally) in early 1812. Poe received some private tuition in Richmond before the Allans removed to England for some five years. The family returned to Richmond in August 1820. Poe remained in the Allan household until March 1827, interrupted by a year and a half of uncompleted studies at the University of Virginia. After a quarrel with his foster-father in March 1827 he left home and returned to Boston. But Poe was back in Richmond by the summer of 1835, there to take on an assistant editorship of the recently founded *Southern Literary Messenger* and to begin a new career as a literary journalist. Much of Poe's short life was, therefore, spent in the American South, but we should not conclude from this that he had, as a consequence, a strong identification with the South and its manners and mores. Equally, however, it would be wrong to assert that the South did not in some ways, no matter how imprecise and resistant to explanation they may be, mold and define his character and his work. After all, did not Poe himself write in a letter to Frederick W. Thomas of July 1841: "I am a Virginian, at least I call myself one, for I have resided all my life, until the last few years, in Richmond"? (Ostrom 1948, I: 170)

The Richmond of Poe's youth was one of the South's most aristocratic and most English of cities, and it is difficult to see how its gentrified and urbane atmosphere did not reshape the sensibility of someone who was, outwardly at least, an intelligent and sensitive English schoolboy. Perhaps Poe as an intelligent child noted more in the way of continuity than discontinuity between his years in Stoke Newington in north London (then more or less a village) and the world of Richmond. Those who had settled Virginia in the seventeenth century had sought to duplicate in the New World the life they had enjoyed in the Old. But Virginia was a slaveholding state and much of the evolution of Virginia's society of aristocratic planters was dependent upon the increasing demand for African slaves that followed the British government's restrictions on the sale of white indentured servants after 1665. But Virginia successfully disguised its slave-based economy in outward forms of pastoral contentment and agricultural efficiency. Though Virginia was aristocratic and oligarchic, the strong sense of the obligations of public service among landowning and plantation classes did much to tie the traditions of the English legal system, particularly those concerned with property rights, and constitutional forms of government to the increasing prosperity of the state. The acquisition of land brought social esteem. Virginia's dependence on tobacco, however – a plant notorious for its capacity to exhaust soil of its vital nutrients – meant that the unceasing demand for land pushed the colony's frontier westwards and, as a result, towns and, latterly, cities grew only slowly, and industrial development of the kind seen in New England in the late eighteenth century was virtually unknown. With industrialization come the forces of democracy, and where New England was a seedbed of radicalism and reform, Virginia remained in many respects socially and politically conservative.

Little has been made of Poe's years in Virginia and their putative relationship to his writings, and it is understandable for literary historians to be skeptical of using genetic explanations of the evolution of certain kinds of writing (or certain kinds of attitudes in writing), much as modern biographers are skeptical of genetic explanations that invoke childhood experience as determinants of adult behavior. However, it has been conjectured by some of Poe's biographers that Poe felt himself to be something of an outcast in the company of those who enjoyed both the old, and the new, wealth of born-and-bred Virginians. Too little is known of Poe's social affairs in the Richmond years of the early 1820s for this to amount to more than intelligent speculation, despite the irresistible temptation to impute the resentments of his adult years to the child's sense of his inferiority among those known to be his social "betters." The early, and impressive, poem "Alone" (now generally attributed to him, though long thought a poem of doubtful authority) certainly articulates a strong sense of "otherness" through its echoes of Byron's *Manfred* (specifically *Manfred*, II, ii, 50–6):

> From childhood's hour I have not been
> As others were – I have not seen
> As others saw – I could not bring
> My passions from a common spring –
> (Mabbott 1969: 146)

However, the sentiments here might be an expression of psycho-pathological anxiety as much as what Daniel Hoffman calls "the neglect of a materialist bourgeois society" (1973: 33), and certainly they give us no direct cause to link this kind of alienation with the rejections of the gentrified classes of Virginia. The poem, like so much of Poe's major writings, is enigmatic about its causes, and, indeed, itself announces the mystery that it enacts:

> *Then* – in my childhood – in the dawn
> Of a most stormy life – was drawn
> From ev'ry depth of good and ill
> The mystery which binds me still –
> (Mabbott 1969: 146)

If Poe was to play the Southern gentleman in his later years (and it's a big if), as some of his commentators have argued, then early verse such as "Alone" offers little in the way of adumbration of it. Rather, as I hope to show below, the emphasis on sensibilities engendered by solitude and the invocation of the romantic sublime (the "torrent, or the fountain" and the "red cliff of the mountain" of lines 13–14) is, above all, Byronic in character, and is a consequence of Poe's reading and not his environment. But I do not doubt that his reading and his environment may have coalesced in some sense, though one I find difficult to explain.

Modern critics, therefore, are right to question the degree to which Poe's writings, particularly his imaginative writings, are related to his ostensible "Southernness." Robert D. Jacobs, for example, argues that Poe's "insistent lyricism was congenial to the Southern temperament, but probably his penchant for the brief lyric derived from the early German romantics rather than the Cavalier tradition so honored in the South" (Rubin et al. 1985: 135). Similarly, G. R. Thompson, contrasting Poe with William Gilmore Simms, points out that "few of Poe's works feature Southern locales and characters, and virtually none has distinctive Southern themes" (Elliott 1988: 264). Even Richard Gray, a critic sympathetic to the view that Poe's writings bear the imprint of Poe's life in the South, concedes that most of his discussion "of Poe's 'Southernness' has been concerned with the particular *persona* he tried to construct for himself in his private and public writings" (Lee 1987: 186). G. R. Thompson notes that in "his reviews of Southern authors, Poe usually ignored or played down the Southern element" (Elliott 1988: 264). For reasons such as these it is hard to agree with a critic like Joan Dayan, for whom "the romance of the South and the realities of race were fundamental to his literary production" (Elliott 1991: 93). He does not, as Dayan suggests, "perpetually return to his sense of the South" and, indeed, we might legitimately wonder what his "sense of the South" is, and where we can find it expressed. If we want to find out what is Southern about Poe we might look for the evidence elsewhere. It is a commonplace that in his criticism Poe held appeals to nationalistic and regionalist characteristics in literature in low regard. The "Drake-Halleck Review" (about which I shall have more to say below) is commonly read as an attack on American literary provincialism. There is, of course, no other way to read it, but to assume that debates about Poe's "Southernness" begin and end there is fallacious. The sense that the literature of the new republic was merely a subdivision of a larger and better-established literature with English as its mother tongue was strong in Poe for reasons that might be very directly attributable to his years in Virginia. For Poe, the promotion of American literature was very much bound up with the promotion of American democracy, and his distaste for democracy (it comes across, above all, in his science fiction, particularly in tales such as "The Colloquy of Monos and Una," 1841, and "Mellonta Tauta," 1849) reflects the anti-egalitarian tradition of Tidewater Virginia conservatism. Though he studied briefly at Thomas Jefferson's university (the University of Virginia at Monticello opened in March 1825 and Poe was, therefore, one of its first students) he shared none of Jefferson's faith in human perfectibility, progress, and other doctrines of human and social improvement. Some of this is, no doubt, the alienated artist's reaction to the spread of literacy, the rise of the popular press, and, more narrowly, to those excesses of popular sensationalism that David S. Reynolds has so ably discussed in *Beneath the American Renaissance* (1988). But Poe's disdain of the achievements of democratic culture is, arguably, more deeply rooted in the South's strong traditions of Whig opposition (often led by John Marshall, chief justice of the Supreme Court from 1801 to 1835 and a Virginian) to political and constitutional reform. In this respect, therefore, we can argue that while Poe evinces no outwardly Southern "prejudices" with respect to subject matter or locale, his emphasis on imaginative literature's necessary transcendence of the capricious demands of place and time reflects, paradoxically, a very Southern disposition.

We can draw stronger evidence of Poe's political and social affiliations from his career at the *Southern Literary Messenger*. His brief period of editorship (1835–7) was, first of all, commercially successful: he increased the magazine's circulation from 500 copies when he arrived to 3,500 when he left – characteristically, he himself gave the figure as closer to 5,500 copies – and he helped establish the *Messenger* as the leading Southern critical journal. His own contribution to the magazine exceeds a hundred reviews and editorials, in addition to the stories and poems he published therein. When it came to Southern causes the *Messenger* was sympathetic to slavery, especially where the issue of slavery was intimately bound up with the defense of Southern rights and interests. Its cultural politics might, therefore, be described as those of a paternalistically nostalgic conservatism. Poe left the magazine before the more heated debates of the 1840s and there is little evidence that his own views surfaced on the editorial pages (his own comments being largely confined to literary matters) but, equally, it is likely that he shared and endorsed the *Messenger's* appeal to the leisured class – a class made possible by the very existence of the "peculiar institution" of slavery – for its support.

As I have said, Poe's low opinion of arguments for regionalist or nationalist "theories" of literary culture is evident from his important review of the poetry of John Rodman Drake and Fitz-Greene Halleck. The review, which appeared in the *Southern Literary Messenger* in April 1836, has become known as the "Drake-Halleck

Review" (as which it is frequently reprinted); the poets themselves are rarely read, and, indeed, little of the significance of the essay attaches to what Poe has to say about them. Instead, it has become known as the first important essay in which Poe addressed what he saw as the limitations of literary provincialism and, therefore, sought to put a brake on the persistent calls for a national and indigenous literature. Poe's conservative, anti-republican stance is apparent in the early paragraphs of the essay:

> We are becoming boisterous and arrogant in the pride of a too speedily assumed literary freedom. We throw off, with the most presumptuous and unmeaning hauteur, *all* deference whatever to foreign opinion – we forget, in the puerile inflation of vanity, that *the world* is the true theatre of the biblical histrio – we get up a hue and cry about the necessity of encouraging native writers of merit – we blindly fancy that we can accomplish this by indiscriminate puffing of good, bad, and indifferent, without taking the trouble to consider that what we choose to denominate encouragement is thus, by its general application, rendered precisely the reverse. In a word, so far from being ashamed of the many disgraceful literary failures to which our own inordinate vanities and misapplied patriotism have lately given birth, and so far from deeply lamenting that these daily puerilities are of home manufacture, we adhere pertinaciously to our original blindly conceived idea, and thus often find ourselves involved in the gross paradox of liking a stupid book the better, because, sure enough, its stupidity is American. (Poe 1984: 506)

We might want to argue that there is something inescapably "Southern" about these sentiments, though we would find Poe unlikely to agree with us. Much of the demand for a national literature, one that would ultimately compel comparison with that of the "mother country," was of New England manufacture and found its greatest expression in Ralph Waldo Emerson's essays. Poe conducted a long-standing (and many would say successful) campaign against literary Puritanism and its philosophical offshoot, Transcendentalism. We see it, above all, in his rejection of transcendental optimism, his relentless "sniping" at the New England establishment (one expression of which finds articulation at the end of his review of Nathaniel Hawthorne's *Twice-Told Tales* and *Mosses from an Old Manse* in *Godey's Lady's Book* for November 1847; usually reprinted under the title "Twice-Told Tales," though the review is considerably longer here than in the first version that appeared in *Gentleman's Magazine* in April 1842), and his assertion of something close to Melville's idea of "innate depravity" in tales such as "The Black Cat" and "The Imp of the Perverse" (the one, indeed, is a variation on the theme of the other). His relentless assault on the writings of Henry Wadsworth Longfellow – regrettably, it deteriorated into an obsession and alienated some of his "Northern" allies, such as James Russell Lowell – is a further instance of his waspish dismissal of what he called "Frogpondium," Boston's literary elite.

Poe restated his skepticism about regionalist or "Americanist" theories of literature in the *Broadway Journal* in October 1845, a magazine for which he acted as editor and publisher. Here he reaffirmed his belief that the idea of a *national* literature was not tractable to definition (in part, one assumes, because American writing was ineluctably in fealty to the English language) and, moreover, was an expression of ideological, not aesthetic, requirements:

> Much has been said, of late, about the necessity of maintaining a proper *nationality* in American Letters; but what this nationality *is*, or what is to be gained by it, has never been distinctly understood. That an American should confine himself to American themes, or even prefer them, is rather a political than a literary idea — and at best is a questionable point. We would do well to bear in mind that "distance lends enchantment to the view." *Ceteris paribus*, a foreign theme is, in a strictly literary sense, to be preferred. After all, the world at large is the only legitimate stage for the authorial *histrio*. (Poe 1984: 1076)

In a collection of essays the late David Marion Holman (1995) has argued that while the literature of the Midwest is what we would ordinarily characterize as social realism, the literature of the South is "romantic." While generalizations such as this are often betrayed by the very facility with which they are made, Holman is broadly correct in saying that Southern literature shows a marked disposition towards the romantic. And to argue this is not merely to isolate for comment the sentimental romanticism of post-Civil War writing such as that of Colonel William C. Falkner (William Faulkner's grandfather) or Thomas Nelson Page, bound up as it is with its evocation of the decline of a chivalric and heroic ideal. The South had a cult of Byron as much as it had a cult of Scott, and the pervasiveness of Byron's influence in Southern letters in the years before the Civil War has been widely remarked. That Byron's particular "version" of Romanticism should be so influential in the South might seem odd, given his cult of the self, his rebelliousness, his "diabolism" (as T. S. Eliot termed it in his 1937 essay on Byron, reprinted in *On Poetry and Poets*, 1957), and his promotion of the revolutionary ideal. But Byron's was an aristocratic kind of revolutionary Romanticism, as much nostalgic and esoterically pagan as it was radical. Solitariness, day-dreaming, worlds of escape, the infatuation with the capricious or fanciful are as much distinctive features of Poe's writing as they are of those of the early Byron. Poe's poetry is often trance-like and hypnotic, its language seeking aural effects often at the expense of rational meaning. It is that which probably led him to elevate Tennyson's verse so highly, calling him the "most ethereal" of poets and making ethereality a necessary condition of what Poe called (rather unhelpfully) "pure poetry." In his marginalia for the *Democratic Review* of December 1844 he discourses on the virtues that inhere in "indefiniteness":

> I *know* that indefinitiveness is an element of the true music — I mean of the true musical expression. Give to it any undue decision — imbue it with any very determinate tone — and you deprive it, at once, of its ethereal, its ideal, its intrinsic and essential character. You dispel its luxury of dream. You dissolve the atmosphere of the mystic upon which it floats. You exhaust it of its breath of faery. It now becomes a tangible and easy

appreciable idea – a thing of the earth, earthy. It has not, indeed, lost its power to please, but all which I consider the distinctiveness of that power. (Poe 1984: 1331)

The emphasis on the necessary conjunction of the "sister arts" of poetry and music entails a devotion to the "supernal beauty" that art, alone, can engender. Since musical meaning is a matter of expression and, unlike poetry, there is no semantic structure in a piece of music, the meaning of music is finally a matter of perception. For Poe, poetry, like music, is an aesthetic experience of the beautiful. When Beauty becomes the province of the poem the didactic and the moral are left behind. Poe's theoretical thinking about poetry draws extensively on ideas borrowed from Coleridge and Wordsworth, and his readings in the English translation of A. W. Schlegel's *Dramatic Lectures*. Behind all three lies the influence of Immanuel Kant, and Kant's division of the world into pure intellect, taste, and the moral sense. But Poe's analogy of poetry with dream and music is ultimately an expression of "art for art's sake" that Kant would have contested. Much of Poe's insistence on the non-utilitarian character of art is an implicit rejection of the tendency towards the moralistic and allegorical in New England writing, especially that of the transcendentalists. But the *posture* Poe adopts has, above all, its roots in his reading of Byron.

We must never underestimate the extent to which Poe's *whole* career was "Byronic." He wrote verses while at Joseph H. Clark's school in Richmond between the years 1820 and 1823, that is, in his early teens. Mrs. Mackenzie, who acted as foster-mother to Poe's sister, Rosalie, on the death of their parents, is reported to have described the early poems as "worthless imitations of Byron blended with some original nonsense" (Mabbott 1969: 4). The earliest surviving poem attributed to Poe, "Oh, Tempora! Oh, Mores!" (dated 1825 by Mabbott; the title is an echo of Cicero), has features that connect with eighteenth-century satirical verse, but its wit, though feeble, is characteristically Byronic in its admixture of malice and mockery. By 1827, however, with the publication of *Tamerlane and Other Poems. By a Bostonian*, Poe's first volume of verse, published anonymously in Boston when Poe was just 18 years old, the model of Byron is so pervasive as to be disabling. *Tamerlane* itself is Byronic both in its subject matter and its style. The model is Byron's poetic drama *Manfred* (1817) and its appropriation of ancient myths to a cult of the self (itself derived, in part, from Goethe's *Faust*), the method a tightly contrived set of poetic variations (some having stanzaic regularity, others closer to narrative verse forms) that, as is so characteristic of most of Poe's verse, seek to provide musical, or aural, pleasures as much as sentimental ones. The themes are beauty, death, love, pride, and suffering, and while, ostensibly, Tamerlane is a historical subject, Poe took very little from historical sources and so shaped his narrative around events in his own life (particularly his abortive engagement to his Richmond sweetheart, Sara Elmira Royster) that the poem is a disguised autobiography. The "orientalism" of the poem bespeaks Byron's influence through its exoticism and its aestheticism.

Knowing something of the background to its composition, one might argue that one of the most "Southern" of Poe's works is *Politian* (1835), his unfinished verse drama, five scenes of which were published in the *Southern Literary Messenger* in issues during 1835 and 1836 – Mabbott conjectures because the magazine needed copy – but which Poe subsequently abandoned despite his having planned a conclusion. Poe drew on the infamous events in Franklin County, Kentucky in 1825 when Colonel Solomon P. Sharp (sometimes given as "Sharpe") was murdered by Jeroboam O. Beauchamp (or "Beauchampe"): Beauchamp had married Ann Cook, a girl who had been seduced by Sharp and who had borne him a child that subsequently died. On her marriage she requested Beauchamp to avenge her and a few months after their marriage Beauchamp (who had challenged Sharp to a duel) stabbed Sharp to death. After Beauchamp's conviction the married couple attempted suicide, but only Ann died and Beauchamp was hanged the following day. What became known as the "Kentucky tragedy" has figured in other works of Southern literature, notably in Thomas Holley Chivers's *Conrad and Eudora* (1834), William Gilmore Simms's *Beauchampe* (1842) and, more recently, in Robert Penn Warren's *World Enough and Time* (1950). Poe probably knew of Beauchamp's own *Confession* (published in 1826, the year of his hanging) and he probably had also read Chivers's poem, but his only remark on the tragedy occurs in his brief article on the New York editor and author Charles Fenno Hoffman, where he refers in passing to Hoffman's "Greyslaer" as "a romance based on the well-known murder of Sharp, the Solicitor-General of Kentucky, by Beauchampe. W. Gilmore Simms (who has far more power, more passion, more movement, more skill than Mr. Hoffman) has treated the same subject more effectively in his novel 'Beauchampe'; but the fact is that both gentlemen have positively failed, as might have been expected" (Thompson 1984: 1208). But, ironically, what most strikes us about Poe's adaptation of the events of the tragedy is how little interest he has in *historicizing* the material or, to put it another way, how *un*Southern it all is. Poe sets his drama in late fifteenth, early sixteenth-century Rome (he left the date blank in his manuscript), recasts the figures in Shakespearean and Marlovian identities, and translates the whole into sub-Byronic sensational melodrama. *Politian*, above all, shows how Poe's particular version of the romantic imagination inclines heavily towards the macabre and the grotesque. It is inconceivable, for example, how Act X (in T. O. Mabbott's text of the play), where San Ozzo "converses" with the corpse of the servant Ugo, could be acted with any degree of seriousness:

> SAN OZZO. Ah! – very well! – then I shall tell your master
> That you're defunct – or stop suppose I say –
> I think there would be more of dignity
> In saying "Sir Count, your worthy servant Ugo
> Not being dead, nor yet to say deceased,
> Nor yet defunct, but having unluckily
> Made way with himself – that's felo de se you know –
> Hath now departed this life."
> (Mabbott 1969: 284)

But we can see here an adumbration of the style of some of the early stories: the grim humor that approximates to a kind of self-conscious facetiousness, the delight in rhetorical excesses and the frequently florid and sonorous language, all these properties feature, in one way or another, in his stories and lend them an identity that is uniquely his.

One of the ironies of the whole effort of *Politian* is that, as Mabbott tells us, "both Beauchamp and his wife wrote Byronic poetry" (Mabbott 1969: 290), thus suggesting that Poe was never to shake off the English poet's influence, despite his having written in 1829 "I have long given up Byron as a model." (In one of the many attacks he launched on his long-standing adversary in American letters, Henry Wadsworth Longfellow, Poe accused Longfellow of plagiarizing a scene in his *The Spanish Student* from scene IV of *Politian*, "the coincidences" being "too markedly peculiar to be gainsayed" (Poe 1984: 755), though given Poe's nearly endless "borrowings" in an age when copyright was virtually non-existent and quotations from other authors seen as a mark of respect and admiration, his demand for "credit" from Longfellow may seem a little unrealistic.)

If Poe is, indeed, one of the *least* regional of nineteenth-century American authors, both in his imaginative writings and their subject matter and locale, and his prescriptive remarks on literature, why is it that he is so frequently appropriated to accounts of Southern literature and culture, as is evidenced by the very volume in which this essay appears? Put simply, this can be attributed to his "Gothicism" and to the perceived continuities this has with the work of twentieth-century Southern writers such as Faulkner, Carson McCullers, Flannery O'Connor, and Cormac McCarthy, and, of course, with American literature more generally. Literary criticism has done a disservice to Poe's greatest tales by so frequently invoking their Gothic features in accounts both of their genesis and effects. This has been inevitable perhaps, given that one dominant strain in the American criticism of American fiction has been that concerned with identifying, and explaining, the pervasiveness of anti-realist (or romantic) conventions in American writing. By pointing to the Gothic qualities of Poe's writings his tales take their proper place alongside other central expressions of the American disposition towards the romantic and the fanciful in works such as *The Scarlet Letter* and *Moby-Dick*. Poe himself warned us against such a reading of the sources of his narrative art. In his 1840 preface to *Tales of the Grotesque and the Arabesque* he tries to defend himself against the charge that his work is "Germanic":

> I speak of these things here because I am led to think it is this prevalence of the "Arabesque" in my serious tales, which has induced one or two critics to tax me, in all friendliness, with what they have been pleased to term "Germanism" and gloom. The charge is in bad taste, and the grounds of the accusation have not been sufficiently considered. Let us admit, for the moment, that the "phantasy-pieces" now given *are* Germanic, or what not. Then Germanism is the "vein" for the time being. Tomorrow I may be anything but German, as yesterday I was everything else. These many pieces

are yet one book. My friends would be quite as wise in taxing an astronomer with too much astronomy, or an ethical author with treating too largely of morals. But the truth is that, with a single exception, there is no one of these stories in which the scholar should recognize the distinctive features of that species of pseudo-horror which we are taught to call Germanic, for no better reason than that some of the secondary names of German literature have become identified with its folly. If in many of my productions terror has been the thesis, I maintain that terror is not of Germany, but of the soul, – that I have deduced this terror only from its legitimate sources, and urged it only to its legitimate results. (Mabbott 1978b: 473)

(The "single exception" it might be noted, is "Metzengerstein," Poe's first published work of prose fiction, which appeared in the Philadelphia *Saturday Courier* of January 14, 1832; not only does the title betray its Germanic character, despite its Hungarian setting, but also Poe himself subtitled it "A tale in imitation of the German", though scholars have tended to find its source in Horace Walpole's *Castle of Otranto*, 1764.) Poe is here seeking to distance himself from the views of early reviewers such as Joseph C. Neal and James E. Heath, both of whom had isolated the "German cast" or "German school" of "The Fall of the House of Usher" on its appearance in *Burton's Gentleman's Magazine* in September 1839. These critics sought to point to the affinities Poe's prose writings had with those of E. T. A. Hoffmann and Ludwig Tieck and, more generally, with the German *märchen* tradition. In his famous review of Nathaniel Hawthorne's *Twice-Told Tales* and *Mosses from an Old Manse* Poe argues that Tieck's manner "in *some* of his works, is absolutely identical with that habitual to Hawthorne" (Poe 1984: 579) and chided Hawthorne for his lack of originality. Since Poe's reference in the preface to "the secondary names of German literature" encompasses both Hoffmann and G. A. Burger, we can only assume he was eager to educate his readers to the position that his own work was superior to theirs by virtue of its very avoidance of the vein of "Germanism." There are those like Thomas Ollive Mabbott who doubt Poe's candor in the preface, but the evidence of the tales speaks, largely, for itself. Poe invites us to understand his effects of the grotesque and the macabre as merely the framework on which a darker psychological drama is enacted. No reading of what is arguably his greatest short story in this style, "The Fall of the House of Usher" (1842) that insists on its Gothic properties at the expense of its other aspects can do full justice to what D. H. Lawrence calls Poe's "ghastly psychological truth" (Lawrence 1971: 85). Some of the stock conventions of the Gothic are, admittedly, firmly in place in the story, but they are quickly transcended. Where Mrs. Radcliffe, for example, might summon up a supernatural mystery and then interrogate it for its rational explanation, for its causes and consequences, Poe sustains the sense of the mysterious and the inexplicable, that which in poetry, as we have seen, he calls the indeterminate, throughout. His formal techniques are, therefore, governed by the requirements that what is mysterious and inexplicable in the tale has internal consistency. This consistency, of course, is realized in his use of the first-person narrator. The somber landscape and "the melancholy House of Usher"

(Mabbott 1978b: 397) that greet the eye of the solitary horseman (a convention in itself) at the beginning of the tale quickly yield to the more complex registers that result from the narrator's attempt to understand the images before him by means of rational and commonsensical analysis. But the narrator finds himself the victim of the very atmosphere of the house that so shapes Roderick Usher's, and his sister's, destiny, and he begins to submit to the fantasies Roderick himself suffers. One of the "legitimate sources" of Roderick's delusions lies in his belief in "the sentience of all vegetable things," the evidence of which is to be found in "the gradual yet certain condensation of an atmosphere of their own about the waters and the walls." It is this that has created that "terrible influence which for centuries has moulded the destinies of his family" (Mabbott 1978b: 408). The modern reader might, understandably, resist this notion of the sentience of organic things (D. H. Lawrence, however, in his essay on Poe, does not and, moreover, he writes that it surely must apply also to the inorganic) as being beyond empirical demonstration and thus conclude that it is all rather a lot of pseudo-scientific persiflage. Rationalist critics like Yvor Winters dismiss Poe precisely because the experience of the work, and the sense of excitement it may elicit, is not understood or evaluated; the experience is presented for its own sake. Thus, for Winters, insofar as Poe has nothing to say, all his techniques are techniques of diffusion, and effects exist at the expense of thought. Winters holds that madness, or the descent into madness, or, more loosely, what Allen Tate calls the "disintegration of personality" (Tate 1968: 408), places the action of the tales firmly in the realm of inexplicable feeling. The charge is a considerable one but, in effect, it bypasses Poe's own defense of the legitimate sources of his terror and is insensitive to the technical accomplishment of the major tales. Our interest, Poe insists, should lie in the effects of tale, the experience it offers, rather than in its analysis. These considerations do not admit of any interventions from the arguments for realism. Thus the objection to Poe's stories that "these things don't tend to happen" (so similar to David Hume's objections to the belief in the Christian miracles) is misguided, but it *would* be a compelling objection if Poe's tales were narrated by some objective, disinterested, reliable third-person voice, if, in other words, they invited us to think of their truthfulness as lying in some empirically observable realm. The first-person is Poe's "alibi" and throughout his major tales, including many of those that found their way into *Tales of the Grotesque and Arabesque*, such as "Morella," "Ligeia," and "William Wilson," it is his use of an unreliable narrator (by which I mean someone whose very character invites us to be skeptical of what he witnesses) that should warn us against both the fanciful and the literal in their interpretation.

I have tried, therefore, to argue that we should not get carried away by arguments that seek to locate Poe's Southern "credentials" in his Gothicism and the supposed continuity this has with later Southern writing. Poe's attempt to refute the charge that his prose writings are "German" seems all of a piece with his internationalist, anti-regionalist critical stance. Paradoxically, of course, if he had conceded that the stories *were* German in cast those who argue for his "Southernness" would be confronting another seemingly insurmountable obstacle in the paths of their argument. Poe's critics are quick to admit that there is nothing outwardly Southern about "The Fall of the House of Usher," but they nevertheless read it as a story that is pervasively Southern in its inner life. It becomes a kind of allegory of the Old South, with Roderick Usher as its introverted and sensitive Southern hero and Madeline as its Southern belle. But this is to read Poe through our experience of the literature of the South that followed him. For Poe, there was no "Old South" and very little sense of the region beyond Virginia comes through in his writings. The Virginia of Poe's childhood, as I have tried to show, was an extension of England into the New World and it seems to have elicited in his writings very little sense of its "specialness" beyond that more generalized, and editorially motivated, desire to encourage Southern writers (though in this respect, interestingly enough, his advocacy of authorship as a profession was at odds with the cultivation of gentlemanly amateurism in the arts). In his review of Augustus Baldwin Longstreet's *Georgia Scenes* that appeared in the *Southern Literary Messenger* for March 1836, Poe remarks on Longstreet's "discriminative and penetrating understanding of *character* in general, and Southern character in particular" (Poe 1984: 778). But very little in the review is attentive to the regional distinctiveness of Longstreet's descriptions, and Poe's pleasure, above all, comes from Longstreet's gift for humor. One of the few occasions when we do see a landscape and a world that is recognizably that of the South is in "The Gold-Bug," the second of Poe's "ratiocinative" tales (tales of detection), which first appeared in Philadelphia's *Dollar Newspaper* in June 1843. Poe's story was published in two installments, each of them accompanied by engravings by the artist Felix C. O. Darley, a form of publication that is contrary to his statement that the effects of a tale (or a poem) are only properly experienced by a continuous, uninterrupted reading. "The Gold-Bug" has a factual setting, Sullivan's Island, off Charleston Harbor in South Carolina, which Poe knew from his United States Army battery having been stationed at Fort Moultrie in October 1827. Poe evokes the landscape and the seascapes around Sullivan's Island in his opening paragraphs, but the setting is left largely inert and naturalistic, unlike that at the beginning of "The Fall of the House of Usher," which quickly takes on symbolic properties. Beyond its compelling interest as a tale of detection, however, it is distinctive for its rare excursion into local color, especially his portrayal of Jupiter, the black servant to William Legrand. Jupiter's very name, of course, reveals something of the pseudo-classical pomposity of Southerners (and the names they gave to those they owned) and Poe seems eager to employ him as something like a stock comic figure from nineteenth-century minstrel shows. Poe's ear, however, for Jupiter's way of talking is almost Twain-like in the accuracy of its transcriptions, as, for example, when Jupiter is explaining his master's illness to the narrator:

Why, massa, taint worf while for to git mad bout de matter – Massa Will say noffin at all aint de matter wid him – but den what make him go about looking dis here way, wid he head down and he soldiers up, and as white as a gose? And den he keep a syphon all de time. (Mabbott 1978b: 811–12)

Interest in Poe's supposed racism tends to surface in discussions of his one complete novel, *The Narrative of Arthur Gordon Pym of Nantucket* (1838), in which critics sometimes see the black versus white polarities of mid-nineteenth-century America reflected in the racialist polarities that structure the island of Tsalal. Some attempt has even been made to relate the adventures of the novel to the slave rebellion of Nat Turner in Southampton County in Virginia in August 1831 (Poe was in Philadelphia at the time). These accounts of the *Narrative* and the putative attitudes of Poe reflected therein are contextually interesting, if unpersuasive, but it is odd that so little interest of this kind has arisen in discussions of "The Gold-Bug." The story, for all its detective interest, is locally Southern and seems a more appropriate place to investigate Poe's politics and his Southern "heritage" than a novel that even its more sympathetic readers consider an elaborate hoax.

Poe's nineteenth-century admirers, particularly those in France, took little notice of any pretension he might have to being a Southern writer. Stéphane Mallarmé saw Poe's struggle with his contemporaries as a heroic story, and Charles Baudelaire identified with Poe and his assertion of the supremacy of beauty over all other things in art (including, of course, moral *desiderata*). The French symbolists, above all, saw his relationship with society as one in which the imaginative writer struggles, unsuccessfully, with the debased demands of an ignorant and benighted public. Poe thus becomes a paradigm of the Alienated Artist. For Baudelaire, Mallarmé, and Valéry, Poe extended imaginative writing beyond the boundaries of scientific and empirical knowledge, thus challenging the very idea of literature as a rational activity. Poe's alleged "supernaturalism," therefore, services not the inferior demands of "Gothic" convention but instead brings into question both the nature of our knowledge of ourselves and of the world, and the very limitations of that knowledge. The true poet is someone who is closer to a seer than a realistic recorder of what is about him, and Baudelaire particularly isolates in Poe those moments where the act of writing is itself a form of knowledge, the knowledge being realized intuitively and imaginatively rather than intellectually and empirically. With which version of himself would Poe have most readily identified? That which sees him as a literary child of the South, anti-regionalist and anti-localist in his prescriptive criticism, but unavoidably articulating Southern prejudices and attitudes, whether they be social, political, or racial? Or that which sees him as a transcendent genius rising above the capricious demands of a writer's responsibilities to his region and assuming his place in the canon of Western imaginative literature? I have tried to show that while Poe reflects the opinions and values of the South, and that his Virginia years left a significant mark on him, there are dangers in trying to read him as a Southern writer. And there can be no question that of the two versions of himself I have outlined above, he would have preferred the latter.

REFERENCES AND FURTHER READING

Allen, Michael (1969) *Poe and the British Magazine Tradition.* New York: Oxford University Press.

Auerbach, Jonathan (1989) *The Romance of Failure: First-person Fictions of Poe, Hawthorne, and James.* New York: Oxford University Press.

Bell, Michael Davitt (1980) *The Development of American Romance: The Sacrifice of Relation.* Chicago: University of Chicago Press.

Bonaparte, Marie (1949) *The Life and Works of Edgar Allan Poe: A Psychoanalytic Interpretation.* London: Imago.

Brooks, Van Wyck (1944) "Poe in the South." In *The World of Washington Irving.* New York: E. P. Dutton.

Chai, Leon (1987) *The Romantic Foundations of the American Renaissance.* Ithaca, NY: Cornell University Press.

Clarke, Graham (ed.) (1991) *Edgar Allan Poe: Critical Assessments*, 4 vols. Robertsbridge, East Sussex: Helm Information.

Davidson, Edward H. (1957) *Poe: A Critical Study.* Cambridge, MA: Harvard University Press.

Eliot, T. S. (1965) "From Poe to Valéry." In *To Criticize the Critic.* London: Faber and Faber.

Elliott, Emory (ed.) (1988) *Columbia Literary History of the United States.* New York: Columbia University Press.

Elliott, Emory (ed.) (1991) *The Columbia History of the American Novel.* New York: Columbia University Press.

Fagin, N. Bryllion (1949) *The Histrionic Mr. Poe.* Baltimore, MD: Johns Hopkins University Press.

Fiedler, Leslie A. (1966) *Love and Death in the American Novel.* New York: Stein and Day.

Halliburton, David (1963) *Edgar Allan Poe: A Phenomenological Reading.* Princeton, NJ: Princeton University Press.

Hoffman, Daniel (1973) *Poe Poe Poe Poe Poe Poe Poe.* New York: Doubleday.

Holman, David Marion (1995) *A Certain Slant of Light: Regionalism and the Form of Southern and Midwestern Fiction.* Baton Rouge: Louisiana State University Press.

Kennedy, J. Gerald (1987) *Poe, Death, and the Life of Writing.* New Haven, CT: Yale University Press.

Krutch, Joseph Wood (1926) *Edgar Allan Poe: A Study in Genius.* New York: Alfred A. Knopf.

Lawrence, D. H. (1971) *Studies in Classic American Literature.* Harmondsworth: Penguin Books.

Lee, A. Robert (ed.) (1987) *Edgar Allan Poe: The Design of Order.* London: Vision Press.

Levin, Harry (1958) *The Power of Blackness: Hawthorne, Melville, Poe.* New York: Alfred A. Knopf.

Mabbott, Thomas Ollive (ed.) (1969) *Collected Works of Edgar Allan Poe: Poems.* Cambridge: Belknap Press of Harvard University.

Mabbott, Thomas Ollive (ed.) (1978a) *Collected Works of Edgar Allan Poe: Tales and Sketches, 1831–1842.* Cambridge: Belknap Press of Harvard University.

Mabott, Thomas Ollive (ed.) (1978b) *Collected Works of Edgar Allan Poe: Tales and Sketches, 1843–1849.* Cambridge: Belknap Press of Harvard University.

Muller, John P. and Richardson, William J. (1988) *The Purloined Poe: Lacan, Derrida and Psychoanalytic Reading.* Baltimore, MD: Johns Hopkins University Press.

Ostrom, John Ward (ed.) (1948) *The Letters of Edgar Allan Poe*, 2 vols. Cambridge, MA: Harvard University Press.

Poe, Edgar Allan (1984) *Essays and Reviews.* New York: Library of America.

Quinn, Arthur Hobson (1941) *Edgar Allan Poe: A Critical Biography.* New York: Appleton-Century.

Quinn, Patrick (1957) *The French Face of Edgar Poe.* Carbondale: Southern Illinois University Press.

Reynolds, David S. (1988) *Beneath the American Renaissance: The Subversive Imagination in the Age of Emerson and Melville.* Cambridge, MA: Harvard University Press.

Rubin, Louis D., Jr., Jackson, Blyden, Moore, Rayburn S., Simpson, Lewis B., and Young, Thomas Daniel (eds.) (1985) *The History of Southern Literature.* Baton Rouge: Louisiana State University Press.

Silverman, Kenneth (1991) *Edgar Allan Poe: Mournful and Never-Ending Remembrance*. New York: Harper Collins.

Silverman, Kenneth (ed.) (1993) *New Essays on Poe's Major Tales*. Cambridge: Cambridge University Press.

Symons, Julian (1978) *The Tell-Tale Heart: The Life and Works of Edgar Allan Poe*. London: Faber and Faber.

Tate, Allen (1968) "The Angelic Imagination." In *Essays of Four Decades*. Chicago: Swallow Press.

Thompson, G. R. (ed.) (1984) *Edgar Allan Poe: Essays and Reviews*. New York: Library of America.

Wagenknecht, Edward (1963) *Edgar Allan Poe: The Man Behind the Legend*. New York: Oxford University Press.

Walker, I. M. (ed.) (1986) *Poe: The Critical Heritage*. London: Routledge and Kegan Paul.

Williams, Michael J. S. (1988) *A World of Words: Language and Displacement in the Fiction of Edgar Allan Poe*. Durham, NC: Duke University Press.

Winters, Yvor (1947) "Edgar Allan Poe: A Crisis in the History of American Obscurantism." In *In Defense of Reason*. New York: Swallow Press and William Morrow.

21

Southwestern Humor

John M. Grammer

Southwestern humor is the name conventionally given to a tradition of prose narrative, composed mainly during the 1830s, 1840s, and 1850s, set somewhere near the frontier line of the South as it moved from the Appalachian mountains to the Mississippi River and beyond. The characteristic form of this tradition is the humorous sketch, a form reflecting both the modest ambitions of most Southwestern humor and its modest origins, in the magazine or newspaper account. Typically, a Southwestern sketch is a first-person account by an Eastern gentleman who has entered some unsettled district on an errand of business or sport. There he encounters a group of rustic characters whose antics, and particularly whose speech, supply the humor: the effort to render the dialect of rural Southerners, usually by a fairly standard and limited repertoire of orthographic tricks, is a nearly infallible identifying mark of Southwestern humor. This fiction has a fairly narrow range of subjects, which are treated over and over: brawling, hunting, sharp trading, violent practical jokes, militia musters, "frolics" (rural dances), and the effort to practice some civilized profession – law, medicine, or schoolteaching – in an inhospitable environment. The sketches were published in small-town papers, in metropolitan dailies like the *St. Louis Reveille* and the *New Orleans Picayune*, and in popular national magazines like *The Spirit of the Times* – but also, occasionally, in highbrow quarterlies like the *Southern Literary Messenger*. Their audience was surely mostly male, but was otherwise pretty varied, spanning North and South and including both city-dwellers whose tastes also ran to the "true crime" narratives of *The Police Gazette* and, as one editor claimed, "gentlemen of standing, wealth and intelligence – the very corinthian columns of the community," who raised race horses and devoted their leisure to the hunt (Yates 1957: 15). The authors themselves – all of them white and male, all of them Southern by either birth or choice – often came from the latter class; they were planters or professionals whose literary tastes were quite respectable and whose stories were sometimes praised by such serious *literati* as Edgar Allan Poe.

Southwestern humor still carries this ambiguous status: it is a lowborn literature that occasionally finds itself in polite company. Students of American writing have never been able wholly to overlook it. Its most remarkable practitioners – say, Thomas Bangs Thorpe, Augustus Baldwin Longstreet, and George Washington Harris – achieve a power that makes them hard to ignore. And in any case its place in literary history is guaranteed by nepotism: the tradition's important inheritors, including Mark Twain and William Faulkner, confer a retroactive significance on it. And yet some of these students have never got over regretting that American genius should appear in such shabby harlequin. Edmund Wilson's famous comment about *Sut Lovingood's Yarns* – "by far the most repellent book of any real literary merit in American literature" (1962: 509) – typifies the ambivalence polite letters has displayed toward this body of writing.

The name "Southwestern humor" can tell us a few things about it. "Southwest," of course, is the opposite of Northeast, the direction from which issued most of the American literature that could be recognized as such between the mid-seventeenth century and the mid-nineteenth. And "humor," promising pleasure first and only later, if at all, moral instruction, seems the opposite of the morally upright literature that emerged from the villages and cities of Puritan and post-Puritan New England. That New England literary culture is the one gently satirized by T. S. Eliot in "Cousin Nancy":

> Upon the glazen shelves kept watch
> Matthew and Waldo, guardians of the faith,
> The army of unalterable law.
> (1917: 22)

Matthew, of course, is Matthew Arnold, who gave literature in English the job it has never quite managed to resign from, that of quasi-religious moral instruction. At times Southwestern humor seems to have anticipated this commission: one of the functions of the Southwestern sketch is the Arnoldian one of defending Culture against Anarchy. Sometimes, indeed, the humorists seem to be asking a question like the one Arnold asked in 1861, in his famous report to the government about education: "What influence may help us to prevent the English people from becoming, with the growth of democracy, *Americanised*?" (1962: 16). Many Southwestern humorists were gentlemen who would have identified themselves fully with the cultural elite for whom Arnold spoke, and who, like Arnold, were fascinated and alarmed by the twin prospects of democracy and "Americanization."

In this they were scarcely unique. The history of American literature, at least through the nineteenth century, was a long tug of war between British tradition and American innovation, the former seeming both noble and tyrannical, the latter both vulgar and liberating. In 1837 Ralph Waldo Emerson (the "Waldo" on Cousin Nancy's bookshelf), from a lectern at Harvard College, had cast his vote for "Americanization," instructing his country to listen no more to "the courtly muses of

Europe" (1983: 70). He assumed that their place would be filled by cultivated American voices like his own, but two years earlier Augustus Baldwin Longstreet, in the book usually identified as the first specimen of Southwestern humor, had suggested another possibility. This is what one listener, a moralist who might have bought tickets for Emerson's lyceum speeches, heard from behind a hedge near a roadside in Georgia:

"You kin, kin you?"

"Yes, I kin, and am able to do it! Boo-oo-oo! Oh, wake snakes, and walk your chalks! Brimstone and — fire! Don't hold me, Nick Stoval! The fight's made up, and let's go at it. — my soul if I don't jump down his throat, and gallop every chitterling out of him before you can say 'quit!'"

Then a few more threats and oaths, the sounds of violent struggle, and finally, "in the accent of keenest torture," "Enough! My eye's out!" (Longstreet 1971: 10, 11).

The voices summoned by the Southern humorists can help make up a useful dialogue with the cultivated ones, already exercising the privileges of an official literature, that issued from places like Emerson's Concord, Massachusetts. The relationship is not simple opposition: Southwestern humor sometimes seems to be carrying out a morally regulatory function, like the one assumed by Lyman Hall, the passerby in Longstreet's "Georgia Theatrics." Overhearing the horrible brawl, he responds with righteous indignation: "Come back, you brute! And assist me in relieving your fellow-mortal, whom you have ruined for ever!" But here as in many a Southwestern sketch, the joke is on the moralist: peering behind the hedge, Hall discovers not two combatants but a single young man, who has played both parts in what turns out to have been a mere rehearsal: "You needn't kick before you're spurr'd," he says. "There a'nt nobody here, nor ha'n't been nother. I was jist seein' how I could 'a' *fout*." The situation is complicated: we are indeed to be alarmed by the moral unruliness (symbolized by the grammatical unruliness) of the young man, whose thumb prints, "plunged up to the balls in the mellow earth, about the distance of a man's eyeballs apart," remind us of the potential for real horror pent up in his violent imagination. But is not Hall a fool to suppose that he can do something about it? And what of the reader? Caught between horror and helplessness, we are supposed to laugh, betraying ourselves in the process. Southwestern sketches are usually moral fables, in that they propose situations that summon a moral response from the characters and from us. Their interest arises from the tension between that response and the other one also summoned, the amoral impulse to laugh. The Southwestern humorists often seem like men assigned the job of whitewashing the fence of culture and morality; but they often engage us most deeply in the moments when, with the turn of a joke, they slip away from this hot work and obey the subversive impulse of pleasure.

One of the original forms of the Southwestern sketch, and thus one of the places where we can begin, is the hunting story, in which the pursuit of game brings a genteel narrator into contact with the backwoods and its inhabitants. These stories, popular throughout the nineteenth century, were often not so much funny as simply fantastic, tall tales that stretch credibility (the specialty, for example, of the bear hunter and sometime writer David Crockett). But the best of them push beyond mere boastful exaggeration, crossing a kind of discursive frontier line and achieving a kind of backwoods romanticism, a recognition of an American wilderness too large and mysterious to be comprehended by straightforward reporting. That line defines the distinction of one of the very best Southwestern tales, "The Big Bear of Arkansas" (1841), by Thomas Bangs Thorpe. It is a hunting story, and also a boasting "tall tale" about the prodigious men and beasts to be found on the American frontier. The tale is introduced by a nameless gentleman who, in the "social hall" of a Mississippi river steamboat, encounters Jim Doggett, an Arkansas hunter, "a man of perfect health and contentment – his eyes... sparkling as diamonds, and good natured to simplicity" (1841: 113). Doggett is leaving the urban wilderness of New Orleans, whose sophisticated citizens have dismissed him as "green," and gladly returning to his home in the Arkansas forest. He is indeed green, a figure of pastoral innocence who first gets the narrator's attention with his guileless boasts – amounting to a kind of dialect eclogue – about his home, the "creation state... where the *sile* runs down to the centre of the 'arth, and government gives you a title to every inch of it" (114). His Arkansas is an Eden, and Doggett's recognition of its wonders ultimately has as much to do with Thomas Cole's painterly renderings of an American sublime as with the "half-horse, half-alligator" bragging of Crockett. Arkansas, he explains, is "a state without a fault" ("even the mosquitoes is natur, and I never find fault with her"), and as for his favorite quarry, the black bear, "I loved him like a brother" (120). So perfect is Doggett's identification with wild nature that he has taken the name of his most elusive prey: "the Big Bear of Arkansas" is Doggett's own nickname as well as that of the bear he pursued in his most remarkable hunt.

Doggett tells the tale of that hunt, a pursuit, carried out over several months, of a particularly formidable and elusive bear. At one notable turn Jim has chased his quarry, never losing its trail, to a place where he can take aim and fire, apparently killing the beast. Then he finds, as he approaches its fallen body, that he has actually brought down "*a she-bear, and not the old critter after all*" (121). The chase, that is, has led Doggett into a fully enchanted natural world. The Big Bear, he declares – which could appear "*like a black mist*" and disappear at will, could cross trails and apparently exchange identities with lesser bears, could consistently leave confused dogs and hunters behind him – was nothing less than a "creation bar," an "unhuntable" creature which, "if it had lived in Sampson's time, and had met him, in a fair fight... would have licked him in the twinkling of a dice-box" (122). By preying on his imagination, Doggett explains, the bear "*hunted me*, and that, too, like a devil, which I began to think he was" (119). And yet, as Doggett prepares for one last, all-out pursuit of the "old critter," it suddenly appears unbidden at his farmhouse, looming up from underbrush and virtually offering itself as a target. Doggett shoots straight and the "creation bar" falls dead – but not because of the hunter's prowess. Rather, the Big

Bear *"died when his time come"* (122), leaving his executioner to wear his name and tell his story. Like Faulkner's "The Bear," to which it has often been compared, "The Big Bear of Arkansas" is an elegy for vanishing wilderness and for lost innocence, a reminder of the frontiersman's ironic fate of killing the thing he loves "like a brother." Doggett's auditors seem to get the point: while his colorful boasting made them laugh, the ending of his story induces only an awed silence.

That silence, marking the end of wilderness, is what Southwestern humor existed to fill. As Richard Slotkin (1985) has noted, the setting of these sketches is usually not the frontier itself, where a deadly Indian or fearsome bear might be encountered, but rather "the backwash of the frontier" (127), a place recently passed by the frontier line, where savage instincts still linger, but with no savage men or beasts to vent them on. And the tone of Southwestern sketches, therefore, is not heroic or sublime but satiric. Take, for example, a kind of sequel to "The Big Bear" which maps one corner of this "backwash," William Gilmore Simms's "How Sharp Snaffles Got His Capital and His Wife," published in *Harper's Magazine* in 1870. Like its predecessor, it is a hunter's tall tale, framed by the introductory remarks of a genteel narrator. He is a gentleman recounting a hunting trip to the North Carolina mountains, on which he and his two equally genteel friends are guided by a group of local hunters, including Sam "Sharp" Snaffles. On Saturday evening comes "liar's camp," when the locals entertain their clients with "long yarns" about their adventures afield. The first performer is Snaffles, explaining how he acquired a wife, a fortune, and his nickname.

The story is one of frustrated love: young Sam Snaffles, though an honest farmer and noted hunter, has been rejected by Squire Hopson as a suitor for his daughter Merry Ann. Inviting Sam to look at himself in a full-length mirror, the squire asks if "you're the sort of pusson to hev *my* da'ter!" Sam answers indignantly: "I'm as tall a man as you, and as stout and strong, and as good a man o' my inches as ever stepped in shoe-leather" (1996: 247). To the squire, however, "eyes and mouth and legs and airms don't make a man." This would have been news to Jim Doggett, but the squire inhabits a different world, more akin to the jaded New Orleans Doggett regretted visiting than to the innocent wilderness from which he came. Manhood in the squire's world requires not strength or skill or virtue, but "capital" (247).

What follows is a "long yarn" indeed: on a single lucky hunting trip, Sam explains, he trapped a flock of 40,000 wild geese, found a hollow tree containing 10,000 gallons of honey, and killed a prodigious bear weighing at least 450 pounds, not counting hide, bones, and tallow. He carefully quantifies his success because the trophies of this hunt are more than proofs of his skill: the wild geese brought him 60 cents apiece, the bear meat 10 cents a pound, and the honey 50 cents a gallon. Sam has learned a new kind of hunting, one that transforms wilderness into capital and Sam himself into not just a "man" but also a speculator who ends up holding, in delicious revenge, the mortgage on Squire Hopson's farm. He gets the girl of his dreams, money in the bank, and the respect of his shrewd father-in-law, who gives him a new name. "Sharp" Snaffles, now known for his economic opportunism, is still a hunter, but a "professional" whose real trade is guiding and entertaining wealthy gentlemen for a fee. He is a happy man and still a likable one, but no longer a hero; like Jim Doggett, he has been diminished by his success.

The post-heroic world he now inhabits is essentially the one in which most Southwestern sketches are set. To place it in literary geography, we should take our bearings not from the frontier romances of Fenimore Cooper but from something like *A New Home – Who'll Follow?*, Caroline Kirkland's wry 1839 memoir of the Michigan frontier, perhaps the sole classic work of "Northwestern humor." Kirkland's subject was not the heroic struggle for survival but the comically inept, though no less strenuous, struggle for wealth and gentility. Her Michigan settlers have come west not to hunt bears but to speculate in real-estate – another method for turning wilderness into capital – and their imaginations are kindled only by "the talismanic word 'land,'" more interesting to the speculator of 1835–6 than it ever was to the ship-wrecked mariner" (1965: 58).

Kirkland was writing, after all, about one of the newly opened Western territories that Henry Nash Smith called "the fee-simple empire," the vast expanse of arable acres that were expected to extend the blessings of landownership to Americans for generations to come. For an appreciation of the humor inspired by the "backwash of the frontier," it is important to recall what those blessings were. In the 1830s, in most American places, landownership had only recently ceased to be a legal requirement for voting and continued to be an important symbol of full citizenship. The old requirement had arisen from an idea, deeply rooted in republican political theory, that citizens must be economically self-sufficient and thus able to resist the tendency of government to turn them into dependent subjects. Republicanism, according to the historian J. G. A. Pocock, was "a civic and patriot ideal in which the personality was founded in property [and] perfected in citizenship" (1975: 507). The survival of the republic depended on its virtuous citizens, who depended in turn on land.

Land, that is to say, was a symbol and practical guarantor of Culture, a principal bulwark against the political and moral nightmare of Anarchy. It was a talismanic word indeed, even to the most high-minded idealists. But Kirkland's project, like that of most Southwestern humorists, was to note divergences from the ideal and to ask where they would lead. In their settings, often, land was not the firm foundation of civic identity but just a short-term investment, like stock shares for a modern "day trader" – buy low and on credit today, sell high to a gullible newcomer tomorrow, and move on. What kind of citizenship could be erected on the foundation of credit and fraud rather than land itself? Their answers to these questions inevitably took the form of satire, the literary mode designed for the exposure of fraud and error. Almost literally, humor appears in Southwestern narrative when wilderness disappears. It comes, in fact, to occupy, formally, the *place* of wilderness: humor often becomes the lawless presence which, by tugging against the civilizing imperatives of culture and morality, generates conflict in the stories.

Sometimes, to be sure, it is a pretty tame wilderness. Consider one of the most enduringly popular works in the tradition, William Tappan Thompson's *Major Jones's*

Courtship. It originally appeared serially in the *Southern Miscellany*, a Georgia weekly edited by Thompson, was published in book form in 1843 and kept being reissued, in response to public demand, throughout the nineteenth century. In form it is a series of letters purportedly addressed to Thompson by Joseph Jones, a well-off farmer and militia officer from the village of Pineville. They concern the awkward squire's effort to court a local belle, Mary Stallings. Though once "plain as a old shoe," Mary has been transformed, since her matriculation at the "Female College" in Macon, into a marvel of breeding and grace, "jest like some of them pictures what they have in *Appleton's Journal*" (1973: 18). But despite her evident superiority and her seeming indifference to him, Jones doggedly pursues her, reporting to Thompson on his progress.

What the letters record is, in a sense, the familiar tussle between Culture and Anarchy – the tobacco-chewing, grammar-mangling major representing the latter and Mary, prize scholar of the Female College, the former. But it is of course only a mock-struggle, for Mary's alma mater is a very modest monument to Culture, and as for Jones, he is (obviously to everyone but himself) one of nature's noblemen, fully equipped to become the gentleman planter he aspires to be. By the second letter he has "quit chawin tobacker and tuck to writin literature," being after all "termined to do what I kin to raise the literature of Pineville" (24–5). His pretension to literature is amusing, of course, like his clumsy efforts at courtship; but in the end he actually does "raise the literature of Pineville" at least a bit, becoming one of the *Miscellany*'s most popular correspondents. And in the end he does win Mary's hand. The major is the kind of lovable fraud who eventually becomes the things he has pretended to be. Thompson would eventually make Jones the spokesman for his own Southern and Whiggish politics, an embodiment of the planter class that he began by clumsily parodying. The hero's wedding to Mary is the erotic version of a Whig compromise between Eastern Culture and backwoods Anarchy, a synthesis made possible by Thompson's gentle irony, which has softened the contours of both.

Another enduringly popular Southwestern title, one that left those contours a bit sharper, was *Georgia Scenes*, whose author, Augustus Baldwin Longstreet, was a friend and mentor to Thompson. Born in Augusta, Georgia in 1790, educated at Yale, he had a remarkably varied career as a lawyer, judge, minister, and college president. But he is known today for his modest sketches of life in Georgia during "the first half century of the republic." The stories in *Georgia Scenes* are all recounted by one of two fictional narrators, Lyman Hall and Abram Baldwin, natives of the rural district where the sketches are set, to which they have returned after an education in the East. The humor of the sketches arises mainly from the contrast between their cultivated minds and the rough customs and characters to which they are reintroducing themselves. Sometimes Hall and Baldwin end up endorsing, in the language of the sentimental pastoral, the pleasures of country life, but quite as often they express dismay at the savage impulses it frees and announce with palpable relief that law and religion have at last arrived to cage them. In "The Fight," for instance, a dirt-eating poor white named Ransy Sniffle goads two good-natured champions into a horrible brawl simply because he wants to watch it. Thanks to his handiwork, and to the complicity of an entire community that gathers to cheer the mayhem, Bob Durham (the winner) loses an ear, a finger, and a chunk from one cheek; Billy Stallings loses part of his nose, and his face is "so swelled and bruised that it was difficult to discover in it anything of the human visage" (1971: 64). But the humanity of the two combatants is less in doubt than that of Ransy and the gleeful spectators. There is no putting a virtuous face on their savagery, and Hall contents himself with hoping that, "thanks to the Christian religion, to schools, colleges, and benevolent associations, such scenes of barbarism and cruelty as that which I have been just describing are now of rare occurrence" (64).

But it is another tale of conflict, the oft-reprinted "Horse Swap," that finally brings Longstreet up against the limits of his power to arrange a convincing compromise between civilization and its backwoods antithesis. Set not in "the old days" but just "three weeks ago," the sketch describes a contest between two champion horse-traders, "the *Yellow Blossom* of Jasper" and Peter Ketch, to decide which of them can get the better end of a trade. The horses in question are brought forth and examined with care, offers and counter-offers are made, and finally a bargain is struck. Then the two men begin to discover what they have got by trading. Most readers remember the discovery made by Ketch, the "winner" of the exchange: that the energetic demeanor of his new horse is due not to excellent breeding but to the saddle's pressure on "a sore on Bullet's back-bone . . . six full inches in length and four in breadth, [that] had as many features as Bullet had motions." Hall is duly appalled at the cruelty of Bullet's seller: "My heart sickened at the sight; and I felt that the brute who had been riding him in that situation deserved the halter." But his "sickness" and its chief symptom, a blurred vision that makes it hard once again to make out the humanity in his backwoods protagonist, pass quickly. For the horrible discovery and Hall's judgment do not, oddly, form the story's conclusion: the narrative moves briskly past the disturbing disclosures of Bullet's back and his owner's brutality and towards its official punch line, when the brute who saddled Bullet gets his comeuppance: the Yellow Blossom finds that the admirably imperturbable nature of *his* new horse is due to its being completely blind. The story had become one of real horror – horror committed, as is often the case in Southwestern humor, against an animal, and containing the even more disturbing implication that man and animal are not so distinct as we had assumed. But the ending takes it all back. It puts the blanket back over Bullet's sore, as it were, and restores the sketch to its proper generic and moral limits. "The Horse-Swap" becomes again a conventional and comic tale about the con man conned. The stakes again seem minor, financial rather than moral, and the justice done at the end – the embarrassment suffered by the Blossom when he accepts a blind horse in exchange for a sick one – is presented as fully sufficient to the situation. Hall draws back from the possible implications of the scene he has witnessed and declines to go beyond the formal boundaries he has established for himself. "The Horse-Swap" remains just a funny sketch, its horror subsiding to its appointed place as a minor element of plot.

That is its place in many Southwestern sketches, which often conceal horror as the Yellow Blossom concealed Bullet's sore, distracting us with funny dialect and the comedy of the con game. But the horrors are there nonetheless, waiting to be discovered – often by the funny con man himself, when the moment is right. So it is, for instance, in *Adventures of Captain Simon Suggs, Late of the Tallapoosa Volunteers*, published in 1844 by the Alabama writer Johnson Jones Hooper. Unusual in being a continuous, book-length narrative rather than just a series of funny sketches, Hooper's book takes the form of a political campaign biography composed to honor Simon Suggs, a successful scoundrel who has risen high in his backwoods Alabama world and seems likely to go higher still.

Hooper's protagonist, like many dishonest men in the literary Southwest, is a land speculator, operating in a particularly likely corner of the fee-simple empire: the Alabama wilderness still being vacated by the dispossessed Creek Indian tribe. The setting is important. Andrew Jackson had defeated the Creeks in a war waged from 1813 to 1814, and as president sponsored the Indian Removal Bill of 1830, which compelled them to surrender their land and migrate westward. This circumstance creates most of Simon's economic opportunities. Though he contrives to be appointed captain of a militia company assembled to fight any Creeks who might resume the warpath, he emphatically inhabits a post-heroic age. Its representative figure is not the scout or the soldier, but "the industrious speculator... kept unceasingly at work in the business of fraud" (1969: 65). The initial victims are Indians, compelled to sell their lands for a fraction of their actual value; later, the speculators fall to defrauding one another in a furious free-for-all of duplicity. And of course all these minor thefts take place under the shadow of the massive theft by the US government of ancestral Indian lands. It is in this milieu that Simon makes the discovery that secures his place in American literature: that "it is good to be shifty in a new country" (8).

The narrative bears this out over and over, as Simon manages, despite his lack of learning, experience, capital, or common decency, to prosper financially and win the approbation of his neighbors. Those neighbors are for the most part distinguishable from Simon only in being less competent scoundrels and are, along with him, the objects of Hooper's satire. Most of them deserve what they get, from Simon and from the author. Thus the Suggs stories cut closer to the bone than Thompson's or Longstreet's, exchanging their confident or cautious meliorism for a comprehensively satiric vision that exposes not just rural buffoonery but some of the sacred myths of American experience. The progressive, republican narrative of Western settlement is revealed as an affair of theft and fraud, and the citizens it has yielded are just the sorts of scoundrels one would expect. *Adventures of Captain Simon Suggs* bears out as well as any work in the tradition Lewis Simpson's provocative characterization of Southwestern humor as "an antipastoral allegory of American history," "carrying the force of a treasonous political statement" (1983: xii). The political campaign biography of a transparent but popular scoundrel, whose career has been devoted principally to real estate fraud, is the ideal form for such treason.

Of course, satire usually implies some sort of moral norm: to attack the perversion of an ideal is to declare loyalty to the ideal itself. So it is with *Simon Suggs*, whose tongue-in-cheek narrator, so confident in judging and condemning his characters and the errors they represent, must be expressing moral insights lost on them but shared with us. But how far can we be trusted to share the narrator's moral vision, to join him in condemning the crooked protagonist? At times it is hard to avoid being on Simon's side. Consider the book's first episode, describing a formative moment of Simon's boyhood. He is about to be beaten by his father, a "hard shell" Baptist preacher, for the sin of playing cards. Thinking quickly, the boy tempts his father into betting that he, young Simon, cannot produce the Jack of Hearts from a shuffled deck. The elder Suggs agrees, despite his moral objections to gambling, because he needs the 11 dollars that Simon offers as a stake and feels sure the boy cannot pull off the trick. Of course, Simon succeeds, having prudently secreted the needed card up his sleeve; thus he cheats his own father, who was trying to cheat him. The result astonishes Reverend Suggs, who declares the outcome must have been divinely "fixed," and Simon agrees that the matter was *"predestinated,"* though his reference points are not theological (Hooper 1969: 25).

This moment of uneasy concord is interrupted when Simon suddenly laughs "until he [is] purple in the face." He laughs alone, since "the obtusity of Reverend Suggs prevented his making any discoveries" (25). But Simon is the opposite of "obtuse"; he is defined by the quality that assured Sam Snaffles's success, though it is not immediately clear what kind of "discovery" his sharpness has enabled. His laughter, though, is a clue: moralist and con-man can recognize the same Calvinist world of predestined results, in which the depravity of a son who would cheat his father, or a father who would cheat his son, is in the normal course of things. But only the latter witness finds it funny, just as he does the next day when – leaving the pious home in which he no longer belongs and shedding a sentimental tear over the mother who gave it warmth – he again shatters the mood with a laugh. He has suddenly imagined what will happen when the dear old lady next lights her corncob pipe and discovers his parting gift to her, a charge of gunpowder hidden therein. Simon's sense of humor keeps working in the same way throughout the book: as the vehicle of his escape from Victorian sentiment and morality – from the influence of Matthew and Waldo, one might say – and his access to a cheerful nihilism that will serve him well in his home terrain.

It matters that Simon, unlike Major Jones or even Ransy Sniffle, laughs: that he is a humorist himself, indeed operates as a kind of rival to the humorist telling his story. That narrator, with a heavy-handed irony that never lets up, condemns Simon for defrauding his neighbors, for encouraging an Indian-scare so as to get himself elected "captain," for cheating his father and booby-trapping his mother's pipe. No doubt we should as well, and should laugh only as the narrator does – *at* Simon's transparent yet successful frauds. But what if, in addition to that sanctioned response, we also laugh *with* him? It is a dirty trick he plays on his father, no doubt – but the old man is a hypocrite, after all. It is not hard to join Simon in laughing at his discomfiture, is indeed harder not to, since keeping a straight face will mark us, like the Reverend Suggs, as obtuse. But if we do laugh, we have, at least temporarily, switched sides, been seduced away from morality and culture and recruited to Suggs's own nihilism. One of the things Simon's sharpness discovers, then, along with his father's willingness to gamble when the odds seem favorable, is our willingness to be thus recruited. This discovery threatens to undermine the moral function of Hooper's satire. The weapon of humor has fallen into the wrong hands.

The writer who otherwise most nearly resembled Hooper parted company with him in this particular: Joseph Glover Baldwin was careful not to let himself be similarly disarmed. *The Flush Times of Alabama and Mississippi* is a memoir of the author's own years as a young Southwestern lawyer, establishing himself in a district near Hooper's chosen setting. Baldwin, who by the time his book appeared had flourished as a lawyer, judge, and state legislator, admired Hooper and paid tribute to him in one of his sketches, entitled "Simon Suggs, Jr., Esq.: A Legal Biography." In it Simon's son demonstrates his own sharpness by recognizing, as many of Baldwin's characters do, that the true profession for a scoundrel is not real estate but law. The old Creek and Choctaw lands where he lives are, after all, a "sunny land of most cheering and exhilarating prospects of fussing, quarrelling, murdering, violation of contracts, and the whole catalogue of *crimen falsi* – in fine, a flush tide of litigation in all of its departments, civil and criminal" (Baldwin 1987: 48). And the lawyers have come, "armed with fresh licenses which they had got gratuitously...and standing ready to supply any distressed citizen who wanted law, with their wares counterfeiting the article" (52).

The lawyer most expert at counterfeiting jurisprudence, though, is not young Suggs but Ovid Bolus, Esq., one of the great confidence men in American literature. Yet to set Baldwin's most memorable character down as a con man belittles the range of his accomplishments and also the moral significance of his career. Baldwin, tongue in cheek, identifies him as an imaginative genius for whom "the truth was simply too small," merely the ore from which he fashioned the "Sheffield razor" of his public self (3, 4). Bolus is indeed sharp, and as his name implies, he is also master of metamorphoses, able to assume by turns the shape of a military hero, a political insider, a tragic lover, and a successful lawyer who "would as soon lie for you as for himself" (6). As with his predecessors, Bolus's sharpness promises not only financial success but also some kind of discovery, which will be shared with the reader: his career, says Baldwin, was a series of "experiments upon credulity" (4). What do these experiments reveal? Certainly that "credulity" is in plentiful supply on the Alabama–Mississippi frontier; certainly that fraud is no peculiar gift of lawyers, since during the Flush Times "the clients were generally as sham as the counselors" (52). But he shows more than that; in his singular liberation from the tyranny of truth, Bolus embodies his age, "that halcyon period, ranging from the year of Grace 1835, to 1837, when shinplasters were the sole currency; when bank-bills were 'as thick as Autumn leaves in Vallambrosa,' and credit was a franchise" (1). Fraud is the essence of Baldwin's world: confidence men pass for lawyers, "shinplasters" – often worthless paper money issued by state banks or private businesses – pass for currency, and a forged land deed, bought on credit, is indistinguishable from land itself, held in fee simple. The law still calls that kind of property "real," as in "real estate," but "reality" itself is a disputed category in Baldwin's Southwest. There, forest and canebrake have recently given way not to civilization itself but to a crude simulacrum thereof, uncouth and predatory though full of pretensions to gentility and virtue, whose numberless counterfeits are the main objects of Baldwin's satire.

The Flush Times is another comprehensive satire, nearly another "treasonous political statement." Is anybody who he seems to be in Baldwin's Southwest? Does anybody's virtue, or even identity, seem "real" after the author's satire has done its work? Baldwin is careful to answer the question clearly and affirmatively, thus preserving for his book an essentially optimistic and progressive social vision. He includes straightforward portraits of a few admirable men like "The Hon. Francis Strother," who as Commissioner of State Banks was able to impose order on the chaotic and criminal finances of Alabama. And more importantly he creates a narrator, whom we may as well identify with the author himself, who personifies the civilized virtues. The narrator is manifestly a learned and honest man, unsullied despite his immersion in the world of Ovid Bolus and undeluded by the frauds perpetrated there, and he writes about the Flush Times retrospectively, from a present in which his sort of decency has generally prevailed. His narrative voice, elegant, ironic, heavily spiced with legal jargon, proves just the instrument for peeling back the pretensions of that vulgar and lawless time, revealing its true nature, and – the final test of sharpness for Johnson Jones Hooper – laughing at the result. Baldwin's narrative voice somehow combines sharpness with virtue. It shows us what civilization sounds like. The narrator imposes order on his stories as Francis Strother imposed order on Alabama, forcing chaotic places and amoral people to yield up ethical meanings. Insisting that all the bad examples be recognized as such, Baldwin's narrative voice makes *The Flush Times* the most disciplined satire – the one whose fire is directed most accurately, with the fewest unintended casualties – in the tradition of Southwestern humor.

The tension between narrative action and narrative voice, so prominent in Hooper and Baldwin, is in fact a nearly invariable stylistic feature of Southwestern humor. This recognition formed the basis of the most influential hypothesis yet advanced about Southwestern humor, the one proposed by Kenneth Lynn in his book *Mark Twain and Southwestern Humor* (1959). Noticing this formal feature – many Southwestern sketches are introduced and concluded by a civilized narrator, whose remarks enclose a confusing tangle of lawless behavior and ungrammatical speech – and noticing as well that many of the humorists were Whig critics of Jacksonian democracy, Lynn concluded that the typical Southwestern sketch is an anti-Jacksonian parable. The morally and grammatically proper narrators, he said, create a stylistic *cordon sanitaire* that contains and judges the excesses of backwoods democrats. The form of the sketches symbolized what Whigs considered the proper social and political hierarchy. Lynn's theory is out of fashion now, often mentioned only to be disparaged; and it does oversimplify its subject, imposing a single meaning on a quite varied body of literature. But its basic insight – that in many sketches we find two conflicting moral propositions (the ones I have been calling Culture and Anarchy), symbolized by two modes of speech – is indisputable and important. Perhaps instead of his metaphor of the *cordon sanitaire*, with its unvarying and merely political meaning, we could think in terms of a permanent tension, an unresolved tug-of-war, between genteel narrators and rough-hewn characters, with our sympathies in the balance. As I have suggested, the misbehaving characters can exert a powerful appeal: they are bold, imaginative, and undaunted, and they tend to be surrounded not by moral paragons who make them look bad but by hypocrites who make them, in their unabashed crookedness, look perversely honest. And they get good lines to speak: the vivid expressiveness of their dialect is itself an attraction. The genteel narrator is condemned to the job of pulling against that appeal, an occupation in which it is hard to avoid looking priggish and impotent. He must remind us of a better world somewhere to the east, or in the future, in which Simon Suggs would be not funny but indictable; but we know that when that world arrives, the fun will be over. He must thus be the enemy not only of his characters' lawless behavior but also of our lawless reading. He is the story's enemy, so to speak, and he may become ours if we start enjoying the story in the wrong way.

Sometimes, of course, we do not. Baldwin, as I have suggested, keeps us pretty well in line – partly by the expedient of keeping his villains quiet (he prefers to paraphrase rather than quote Ovid Bolus), and in part by cultivating a memorably expressive and funny voice of his own, the most distinctive in the tradition. The humorists who did not employ this prudent strategy risked the moral clarity of their narratives, but in some cases the risk could be run safely. Major Jones does almost all the talking in Thompson's sketches, supplying both the funny dialect and the moral norm and becoming, so to speak, his own Baldwin. The silence of "Mr. Thompson," the nominal delegate from the world of letters and manners, puts us technically on the wrong side of the *cordon sanitaire*, but in *Major Jones's Courtship* we do not really mind: the neighborhood seems safe enough.

We enter a very different kind of neighborhood, however, when we take up the career of the last and perhaps the greatest of the humorists, George Washington Harris. If, as Yeats says, "things reveal themselves passing away," then we might expect Harris's work to distill something essential and revealing about Southwestern humor, for he comes at the very end of the tradition's history. His *Sut Lovingood's Yarns* appeared in 1867, after the Civil War, after Hooper and Baldwin were dead. And in many ways Harris did both adopt the mannerisms and tendencies of Southwestern humor and take them farther than anyone else had. By the time he began writing the Lovingood sketches, in 1854, the formal properties of this fiction were well established, and he duly honored these. The sketches are all introduced by a genteel narrator, "George," who seems a projection of the author himself. And once George steps aside, we enter as usual a moral and grammatical wilderness – the most impenetrable one in the tradition, as it happens – expressed in the voice of Sut Lovingood, an east Tennessee farmer and "nat'ral born durn'd fool." But in the

Lovingood stories we do not emerge from that wilderness. Sut is just the sort of unruly backwoodsman – ignorant, violent, and lawless – whom Lynn's *cordon sanitaire* was meant to contain, but he proves too powerful for that feeble barrier. George opens each story, but is quickly silenced by the voluble and expressive Sut, who does nearly all the talking thereafter and usually gets the last word. The genteel narrator, far from being Sut's moral censor, becomes simply his Boswell, faithfully recording his pithy and outrageous utterances. It is Sut, "a queer looking, long legged, short bodied, small headed, white haired, hog eyed, funny sort of a genius," who gives the sketches their moral orientation (Harris 1966: 33).

This is to say that they have none, because Sut systematically demolishes all the possible sources for such an orientation. Augustus Baldwin Longstreet had counted on "the Christian religion, schools [and] colleges" (1971: 64) to supply morality and order to the Southwest, but Sut is happy to tell us that "I haint got nara a soul, nuffin but a whisky proof gizzard" (138), and that "plannin an' studdyin... am ginerly no count" (63). The Victorian age hoped that virtuous women, marriage, domestic life, and churchgoing would restrain the worst impulses of men, but Sut has declared war on all these civilizing influences. His admiration for women is frankly carnal, stirred not by their piety but by such attributes as Sicily Burns's bosom: "two snow balls wif a strawberry stuck but-ainded intu bof on em" (69). When Sicily cruelly rebuffs his affections and marries another, Sut responds by making an enraged bull break through the wall of her house during the wedding dinner, wreaking havoc on the tables, the food, and the groom's aged and blameless mother. He takes similar pleasure in disrupting Mrs. Yardley's quilting bee, a wholesome domestic ritual by most nineteenth-century lights, but a target of opportunity for Sut, who regards Mrs. Yardley as a censorious busybody and quilting bees as a mere pretext for flirtation and erotic foreplay. He causes a wall-eyed horse tied outside to crash through the door of the Yardley house, destroy several quilts, and trample Mrs. Yardley, whose consequent death Sut conspicuously declines to regret. The hero takes particular delight in pouring "seven or eight pot-bellied lizzards" (54) down the trousers of Parson John Bullens, who has interfered in his relationship with another girl. The terrified Bullens stops his sermon, strips down to "low quarter'd shoes, short woolen socks, an' eel-skin garters," and screams to his shocked congregation that "Hell-sarpints" (56) are attacking him.

Which, if there were any hell-sarpints, they might well do, for Bullens is a hypocrite, a liar, and a distiller of inferior moonshine, fully deserving of his fate. Sut has performed the satirist's function, literally "discovering" the pious fraud to his formerly deluded congregation. Indeed, many of Sut's victims have their victimhood coming to them, a fact which might seem to redeem his cruelty by giving it a moral function: he is brutal, yes, but only to brutes. *Does* Sut's full-contact satire imply a moral norm? He is against hypocrisy, along with chastity, sobriety, and piety, but what is he for? Nothing, so far as one can tell, but honesty – which means being, like Sut himself, openly rather than secretly depraved, owning up to what he calls "the hell-desarvin nater ove man" and making the most of it (58). To say that Sut's victims usually deserve their punishment is therefore true but nearly meaningless: in Harris's world *everybody* deserves it. Sut's moral system — call it Calvinism without grace — is not an instrument for making distinctions between virtue and vice, Culture and Anarchy. His insight is *too* sharp; he doesn't just see through the genteel disguises that obscure those distinctions but through the distinctions themselves. Virtue is just vice undiscovered, and Sut is just the man to discover it; Culture is merely Anarchy deferred, and Sut will be happy to hasten it along.

What is the point, then, of Sut's ferocious, sometimes lethal social criticism? He is defending, it seems to me, not a moral idea but a vision of reality. What, to quote the catechism, is the chief end of man? Sut knows the answer:

> Men wer made a-purpus jis tu eat, drink, an' fur stayin awake in the yearly part ove the nites: an' wimen wer made tu cook the vittils, mix the sperits, an' help the men du the stayin awake. That's all, an' nuthin more, onless hits fur the wimen tu raise the devil atwix meals, an' knit socks atwix drams, an' the men tu play short kerds, swap hosses wif fools, an' fite fur exersise, at odd spells. (77)

Sut is outraged by anybody who resists this ferociously materialist view of life. When you see an innocent baby searching for his mother's breast, Sut demands of George, don't you just want to slap it, "rite ontu the place what sum day'll fit a saddil, ur a sowin cheer," just to let it know how unpleasant life will be? To deny the impulse, Sut warns, is simply bad faith: "Yu may be shamed ove hit, but durn me ef hit ain't thar" (186).

By Sut's lights the most honest man in the book is his father (whom he also acknowledges as "king ove all durn'd fools": 77), particularly as he appears in the first Lovingood sketch ever published, "Sut Lovingood's Daddy, Acting Horse." Dad's horse, Tickytail, has starved to death. After skinning the lamented steed, Dad looks around at his wife and nineteen children and wonders how he will feed them without a horse for plowing. For a time he waits, "hopin sum stray hoss mout cum along," but such strokes of providence are unknown in Harris's world (35). Then the answer comes to him: "Sut, I'll tell yu what we'll du: I'll be hoss *mysef*, an' pull the plow whilst yu drives me" (35). Dad takes his place in the harness, frolics, champs at the bit, and tries to kick his wife, who has noted that he makes a better horse than husband. The plowing goes well for a time, but then Dad blunders into a hornet's nest and is compelled to bolt, still horse-fashion, and plunge into the creek. Sut stands on the bluff above making fun of his father, for "hit were pow'ful inturestin, an' sorter funny," though "Dad cudent see the funny part frum whar he wer" (37).

It is a complicated episode. Losing their horse is of course a potentially life-threatening disaster to the Lovingoods, and there really is nothing for it but to substitute human for animal labor. Desperation, that is, makes Dad look steadily at the troubling possibility of which some of the earlier humorists had caught an occasional glimpse: that raw Southwestern life has simply erased the difference between man and beast. Jim Doggett named himself after a bear; Davy Crockett claimed to be "half horse and half alligator," Longstreet's Hall wanted to place "the Yellow Blossom" in a horse's halter. Dad finally wears one, conceding at last that religion and culture have lost their battle against wilderness. This is, of course, what Sut has been saying all along: that we are beasts, made to eat, drink, fight, and suffer. Southwestern humor nearly always mocks pretense of some sort, but Harris's work isn't content to expose backwoods squires who consider themselves gentlemen, or even crooked land speculators posing as statesmen. His satire is aimed directly at the fond but fraudulent claim that our humanity importantly distinguishes us from the beasts. All the hand wringing of his predecessors about culture, religion, and morality was for naught. Matthew and Waldo were wrong, and Dad has finally shown us our place.

The Lovingood stories insist on a grim, hopeless, materialist world – but it is a world nonetheless full of mystery and even a certain kind of wonder. Anybody who has read much of Harris has noticed one of his favorite mannerisms: the moment when conventional plot, an orderly sequence of causes and effects, suddenly explodes into a bizarre, surreal, all but inexplicable tableau. In "The Widow McCloud's Mare" a character named Stillyards, concluding a complicated business deal, mounts his newly acquired horse, ties a grandfather clock to its back, and fastens his dog's leash to the pommel. Then Sut, who dislikes Stillyards for being a Yankee, frightens the horse. It bolts, the clock begins striking wildly, the dog is horribly dragged, "a string of innards" (47) trailing behind it, until the whole unlikely assembly collides with another group of travelers, leaving dead animals, maimed men, and demolished property scattered across the countryside. A woman who saw Stillyards go by tries helplessly to account for the spectacle: it cannot be the millennium, because there were not any hymn tunes, nor the circus, for the horse was not spotted – "but hit mout be the Devil arter a tax collector, ur a missionary on his way tu China" (50). To Sut, though, wide-eyed with wonder, it is just an amazing and funny episode – vandalism, vehicular assault, animal cruelty, and all. Evidently this is the right response to the utter, random unpredictability of experience, to Anarchy such as Matthew Arnold never dreamed of, Anarchy at the molecular level: don't make sense of it, just find the vantage point from which you can "see the funny part." The way to take the world is not morally but aesthetically; look not for meaning but for pleasure.

Dad gives us a hint of this when he transforms his moment of near-hopeless despair into a riot of the comic imagination, by acting horse. But here Sut is the master: the "sort of . . . genius" he possesses is for just this kind of aesthetic appreciation. Here he is searching for the metaphor by which to render Sicily Burns's beauty, and his own visceral response to it:

> I'se hearn in the mountins a fast rate fourth proof smash ove thunder cum onexpected, an' shake the yeath, bringin along a string ove litenin es long es a quarter track . . . an' I felt quar in my in'ards, sorter ha'f cumfurt, wif a littil glad an' rite smart ove sorry mix'd wif hit.

I'se seed the rattil-snake squar hissef tu cum at me, a sayin z-e-e-e-e, wif that nisey
tail ove his'n, an' I felt quar agin – mons'rous quar. I've seed the Oconee River jumpin
mad frum rock tu rock wif hits clear, cool warter, white foam, an' music . . . the rushin
warter dus make music; so dus the wind, an' the fire in the mountin, an' hit gin me an
oneasy queerness agin; but every time I look'd at that gal Sicily Burns, I hed all the
feelins mix'd up, ove the litenin, the river, an' the snake, wif a totch ove the quicksilver
sensashun a huntin thru all my veins fur my ticklish place. (70)

In a passage like this Sut surely becomes the apotheosis of the dialect narrator. It
anticipates certain moments in *Huckleberry Finn*, like Huck's famous description of a
storm on the Mississippi, and reminds us of James M. Cox's compliment to Mark
Twain: that in his hands dialect became not something to look *at*, but something to
look *with*. So it is with Sut, whose dialect in this passage helps us see two things,
which are versions of the same thing. He is describing his own experience of sexual
longing, one of the many powerful appetites against which he is powerless. And he is
likening that experience to another kind of overwhelming power, that of the beautiful
and terrifying wilderness he inhabits. He is helpless before "the litenin, the river, an'
the snake," just as he is helpless before his own violent and carnal nature. Sut makes
explicit, that is, the analogy that Southwest humor circled around, sometimes
unconsciously, from the beginning: the one between the wilderness mapped by scouts
and hunters and the dark corners of human nature which are discoverable only by
humor. With Sut we are back in Jim Doggett's forest, experiencing the surge of terror
and exhilaration provoked, according to aesthetic theory, by "the sublime." But the
wilderness that provokes this response is now an interior one, a durable Anarchy that,
so far as Harris lets on, is unlikely to be tamed by Culture. The discovery of that
wilderness is the lasting achievement of Southwestern humor.

REFERENCES AND FURTHER READING

Arnold, Matthew (1962) [1861] *The Popular Education of France*. In *The Complete Prose Works of Matthew Arnold, Vol. 2, Democracy and Education*. Ann Arbor: University of Michigan Press.

Baldwin, Joseph Glover (1987) [1853] *The Flush Times of Alabama and Mississippi: A Series of Sketches*. Baton Rouge: Louisiana State University Press.

Blair, Walter (1960) [1937] *Native American Humor*. New York: American Book.

Cohen, Hennig, and Dillingham, William B. (1994) *Humor of the Old Southwest*, 3rd edn. Athens, GA: University of Georgia Press.

Cox, James (1973) "Humor of the Old Southwest." In Louis D. Rubin (ed.) *The Comic Imagination in American Literature*. New Brunswick, NJ: Rutgers University Press.

Eliot, Thomas Stearns (1970) [1917] "Cousin Nancy." In *Collected Poems, 1909–1962*. New York: Harcourt, Brace and World.

Emerson, Ralph Waldo (1983) [1837] "The American Scholar." In *Ralph Waldo Emerson: Essays and Lectures*. New York: Literary Classics of the United States.

Harris, George Washington (1966) [1867] *Sut Lovingood's Yarns*, ed. M. Thomas Inge. New Haven, CT: College and University Press.

Hooper, Johnson Jones (1969) [1844] *Adventures of Captain Simon Suggs, Late of the Tallapoosa Volunteers.* Chapel Hill: University of North Carolina Press.

Inge, M. Thomas (ed.) (1975) *The Frontier Humorists: Critical Views.* Hamden, CT: Archon Press.

Inge, M. Thomas, and Piacentino, Edward J. (eds.) (2001) *The Humor of the Old South.* Lexington: University of Kentucky Press.

Kirkland, Caroline M. (1965) [1839] *A New Home – Who'll Follow?* Albany, NY: New College and University Press.

Longstreet, Augustus Baldwin (1971) [1835] *Georgia Scenes: Characters, Incidents &c., in the First Half Century of the Republic.* Atlanta, GA: Cherokee Publishing.

Lynn, Kenneth S. (1959) *Mark Twain and Southwestern Humor.* Boston, MA: Little, Brown.

Pocock, J. G. A. (1975) *The Machiavellian Moment: Florentine Political Thought and the Atlantic Republican Tradition.* Princeton, NJ: Princeton University Press.

Reynolds, David S. (1988) *Beneath the American Renaissance: The Subversive Imagination in the Age of Emerson and Melville.* New York: Alfred A. Knopf.

Simms, William Gilmore (1996) [1870] "How Sharp Snaffles Got His Capital and His Wife." In *Tales of the South*, ed. Mary Ann Wimsatt. Columbia: University of South Carolina Press.

Simpson, Lewis P. (1983) "Preface" to *The Dispossessed Garden.* Baton Rouge: Louisiana State University Press.

Slotkin, Richard (1985) *The Fatal Environment: The Myth of the Frontier in the Age of Industrialization, 1800–1890.* New York: Atheneum.

Smith, Henry Nash (1950) *Virgin Land: The American West as Symbol and Myth.* Cambridge, MA: Harvard University Press.

Thompson, William Tappan (1973) [1872] *Major Jones's Courtship.* Atlanta, GA: Cherokee Publishing.

Thorpe, Thomas Bangs (1841) "The Big Bear of Arkansas." In *A New Collection of Thomas Bangs Thorpe's Sketches of the Old Southwest*, ed. David C. Estes. Baton Rouge: Louisiana State University Press.

Wilson, Edmund (1962) *Patriotic Gore: Studies in the Literature of the American Civil War.* New York: Oxford University Press.

Yates, Norris W. (1957) *William T. Porter and the Spirit of the Times: A Study of the BIG BEAR School of Humor.* Baton Rouge: Louisiana State University Press.

22

Mark Twain

Peter Stoneley

Mark Twain, or rather, Samuel Langhorne Clemens, was born on November 30, 1835, in the "almost invisible" village of Florida, Missouri. His parents, John Marshall Clemens "of Virginia" and Jane Lampton "of Kentucky," were both a little vain of their antecedents. The Clemenses were supposed to have been in Virginia "stretching back to Noah's time." Tradition linked them with the Geoffrey Clement who was among those that sentenced Charles I to death. The Lamptons, on the other hand, claimed descent from the Earls of Durham. Twain, then, was born into a family of some pretensions, that had enjoyed some success, and that was above all a "good family." His father was a lawyer who, in the prosperous parts of his career, owned several slaves. He had moved west in the hope of capitalizing on new opportunities, and had bought 100,000 acres in Tennessee. Although the family was beguiled by the idea that one day this investment would make them rich beyond all imagining, the land was actually very poor. At the time of Twain's birth, John Clemens was running a small country store with his wife's brother-in-law, John Quarles. While this was modest work, Clemens had plans to make the village of Florida grow. But his hopes were ended with the national financial crises of 1837. The family moved to Hannibal, Missouri, a larger village that, being on the banks of the Mississippi, could withstand economic downturns. Over the next two decades Hannibal would become increasingly successful and many men would make fortunes, but John Clemens would not be among them. He incurred large debts with his initial investments (a hotel, a store, and some rental property), and never recovered. The family was forced to make a series of retrenchments, and was eventually left with nothing but debts. John Clemens had been a taciturn figure before his failure, and over the years he became at once more distant and more oppressive. When he died in 1847, his son got a gruesome image of his father to add to that of overbearing failure: Twain was a secret witness to his father's autopsy.[1]

It would be simplistic and misleading to impose a biographical interpretation on Twain's various and complex writings on the South, but his childhood provides many clues to adult preoccupations. His memories and fictional reconstructions – and it is often hard to distinguish between the two – would be split between an idealizing tendency on the one hand, and feelings of shame and horror on the other. In the autobiographical dictations he gave towards the end of his life, he recorded at great length and in close detail the natural beauty of the scenes of his childhood. Above all, he gives an intense, lyrical account of the countryside around his Uncle John Quarles's farm:

> I can call back the prairie, and its loneliness and peace, and a vast hawk hanging motionless in the sky, with his wings spread wide and the blue of the vault showing through the fringe of their end feathers. I can see the woods in their autumn dress, the oaks purple, the hickories washed with gold, the maples and the sumachs luminous with crimson fires, and I can hear the rustle made by the fallen leaves as we plowed through them. I can see the blue clusters of wild grapes hanging among the foliage of the saplings, and I remember the taste of them and the smell. (*Autobiography*: 13–14)

This passage, which runs on much further than this quotation, is marked by the sense of unfailing abundance, and this is matched by a moral and behavioral freedom. He remembers the "stain" that blackberries and walnuts make on his clothes, and of how pilfered maple sugar tastes better than any that is honestly come by, "let bigots say what they will" (14). The safety and abundance of his uncle's realm contrasts with Twain's writing about Hannibal or its fictional alter ego of St. Petersburg in *Adventures of Tom Sawyer* and *Adventures of Huckleberry Finn*. There, the father is barely mentionable, or he is simply dead, and boys are always in trouble. While his father seldom features in his writing, his mother and her fictional counterparts are described at some length: their warm-heartedness, good intentions, wit, and foibles. He also gives affectionate attention to men other than his anxious, domineering father. Above all, there is Uncle John Quarles – "I have not come across a better man than he was" – who reappears in the fiction as a series of friendly, guileless, dependable uncles.

But in life and in fiction, there was another genial paternal presence, another man who was everything his father was not, and this man was black:

> We had a faithful and affectionate good friend, ally and adviser in "Uncle Dan'l," a middle-aged slave whose head was the best one in the Negro quarter, whose sympathies were wide and warm and whose heart was honest and simple and knew no guile. He has served me well these many, many years. I have not seen him for more than half a century and yet spiritually I have had his welcome company a good part of that time and have staged him in books under his own name and as "Jim," and carted him all around – to Hannibal, down the Mississippi on a raft and even across the Desert of Sahara in a balloon – and he has endured it all with the patience and friendliness and loyalty which were his birthright. (*Autobiography*: 6)

While his own father was demanding (for all that he failed to live up to his own ambitions), in Uncle Dan'l Twain found a senior, wise, protective figure, and one who was not in a position to make demands on Twain or on any white person. Similarly, Jim enters Huck's life in early adolescence – the point Twain had reached when his father died. While Pap Finn could hardly be more different to John Clemens, there is in *Adventures of Huckleberry Finn* that same exchange of the domineering, failed white father for the loving black. Most tellingly, Twain's comments on Uncle Dan'l indicate that his representations of black people served a series of particular, personal needs. The Uncle Dan'l–Jim figure does not change, wherever Twain takes him and whatever difficulties Twain places him in. The black man continues to "serve" through the years, long after Emancipation. Twain makes believe that this is the black man's "birthright." In keeping with broader political and cultural pro-black sympathies, he suggests that all black people are friendly and loyal because that is their racial characteristic. But there is also a near-recognition that Twain's – and other white people's – preferred idea of blackness may be opportunistic, that it may serve their own psychological and literary requirements. For this reason, the Dan'l–Jim figure, though based on a real man, is actually little more than a "stock" character: he is the trustworthy counterpart to "Mammy," and will always play the same reassuring role in whichever story you find him.

When Twain remembers and recreates his past, he evokes the key Southern issues of slavery and the Civil War. It is sometimes suggested that we see Twain not as a Southerner but as a Westerner, coming from the border state of Missouri. But Twain recognized himself as a Southerner, and there is a sense in which he was always in flight from the South. Although he traveled extensively throughout his life, he seldom went South after 1861, and his idyllic recollections were always to be matched by horrors. He would always be drawn to and appalled by those twinned spectacles of failure and dismemberment: his father's, and that of the South. And he would never be rich enough or famous enough to trust that he had finally left the shame of his Southern past behind. He effectively transformed himself into a wealthy Northern liberal; but even as a rich man, he needed to be richer, until, of course, he reproduced his father's failure in his own life with unwise investments and bankruptcy. Let's focus for now, though, on Twain's life in the South and his escape from it.

After his father's death, Twain continued his schooling for a time, but at the age of 13 he was apprenticed to a local printer and newspaper editor, Joseph Ament of the *Missouri Courier*. Twain worked as a printer, often for his older brother Orion, throughout the early 1850s. The boundary between printer and writer or journalist was quite blurred for much of the nineteenth century, and as a printer Twain also wrote sketches and jokes for his brother's paper and others. But this was "backwoods" stuff, and Orion could seldom afford to pay the wages he had promised. Twain made very little money, and his ambitions were soon directed elsewhere. This was the golden age of steamboating; the traffic on the Mississippi was of economic importance to the whole nation, and vital to towns and cities from Hannibal down through St. Louis into the Deep South. Twain was drawn by the glamour of the steamboats, and longed for the authority and affluence of a pilot or a captain. He first attempted to become a cub-pilot in 1855, but he did not get very far until 1857, when he was taken on by Horace Bixby. He received his piloting license in 1859, and spent the next two years earning good money and enjoying his hard-won status. But the outbreak of war put a stop to river traffic and Twain spent the next few weeks in confusion. Then, while on a visit to Hannibal, he joined a Confederate outfit, the Marion Rangers. It is hard to know precisely what happened when Twain was a soldier, not least because his own accounts were almost certainly embroidered to serve later literary and social circumstances. The sympathies of Missourians were divided between the Union and the Confederacy, and the state, though slaveholding, never finally declared for the Confederacy. Missouri was soon in the possession of the Union, and Twain and the Marion Rangers spent a few weeks in fear of attack. They did not encounter any Union troops, and soon disbanded. Meanwhile, Orion, who had campaigned hard for Lincoln in 1860, got his reward in the form of Secretary to the Nevada Territory. He did not have the money to get to Nevada, so Twain decided to pay for the trip and go along as secretary to the Secretary. In a matter of weeks, Twain had lost his career, become a rebel, abandoned the Confederate cause, and become a functionary of the Union. Both deserter and turncoat, he would use his time in the Far West to attempt to become someone else.

Twain tried his hand at mining and prospecting in California and Nevada, but was soon back in the newspaper business, working for the *Virginia City Territorial Enterprise*. He reinvented himself with the pen name of Mark Twain in 1863, and developed a reputation as a humorist. This transformation continued as he traveled the world as a famous sketch-writer and lecturer, and also when he married into a wealthy, genteel, abolitionist New York family. He secured his reputation as a popular writer with *Innocents Abroad* (1869) and *Roughing It* (1872), neither of which dealt with Southern material. However, having disencumbered himself of the poverty, fear, and shame of the South, he returned to it in his work from the mid-1870s onward. The South would be a crucial feature of the work of his middle years, with "A True Story" (1874), *Adventures of Tom Sawyer* (1876), "Old Times on the Mississippi" (1875) and subsequently *Life on the Mississippi* (1883), and *Adventures of Huckleberry Finn* (1885). The South is indirectly present in *A Connecticut Yankee at King Arthur's Court* (1889), and fully present in *Pudd'nhead Wilson* (1894). He would never live in the South again, and would only visit on a couple of occasions, but as an imaginary locale the South was compelling. Indeed, it was the idea and the memory of the South that helped him to sustain the intensity, momentum, and assurance of his career. This endless return is a testament to his fascination with the South, but also to his constant need to renegotiate his relation to his own past and his public image. I want now to explore his major writing on the South, and to relate this in turn to his continued development of the real and fictitious identity of "Mark Twain."

A key text in the evolution of Mark Twain's South is "A True Story, Repeated Word for Word as I Heard It." The scene is the porch of a hilltop farmhouse in the North, at twilight in summer. A leisured white family is joined by one of their black servants, who sits "respectfully below our level, on the steps." This tells us two things: that the family welcomes the servant as a fellow social being, but that a decorous hierarchy is maintained. The servant, Aunt Rachel, seems to be the typically "happy darky" of Northern and Southern stereotype: "She was of mighty frame and stature; she was sixty years old, but her eye was undimmed and her strength unabated. She was a cheerful, hearty soul, and it was not more trouble for her to laugh than it is for a bird to sing." But the narrator, whom Rachel identifies as "Misto C—," makes the mistake of presuming that this happy persona is the only and complete truth of Rachel's life. He asks her how it is that she has "lived sixty years and never had any trouble?"[2] Rachel's role is to laugh good-naturedly at the teasing she receives "without mercy" from the family, but her acquiescence vanishes in an instant: "She stopped quaking. She paused, and there was a silence." Rachel asks Misto C— "without even a smile in her voice" if he is in earnest. Misto C— is "surprised" and "sobered" by what is effectively a sudden shift in power relations. It is now her comments that are pointed, and the white man who squirms under scrutiny. Rachel tells him and the rest of the family how she had been born a slave in the South. Even though her story will be that of all that was taken away from her, her goal in telling it is to claim her full measure of feeling and dignity. She says that the man she married was "lovin' an' kind to me, jist as kind as you is to yo' own wife." They had seven children who were just as keenly loved. When her mistress fell on hard times, Rachel, her husband, and her children were sold off at an auction in Richmond. She talks of the pain this caused her, and goes on to explain how, by extraordinary coincidence, she was reunited with her youngest son, Henry, during the War. Among other signs, she identified him by the scar on his wrist that he had acquired in early childhood, and her conclusion, expressed with triumphant irony, is that she has experienced both extremes of feeling: "Oh, no, Misto C—, *I* hain't had no trouble. An' no *joy!*" (84).

This relatively short and simple piece is curious for a variety of reasons. The plot resembles numerous abolitionist fictions, not least *Uncle Tom's Cabin*, and suggests Twain's willingness to use what Neil Schmitz has characterized as "Unionist discourse."[3] As it happens, this somewhat "contrived" story was based on the experiences of a black servant in Twain's wife's family, Mary Ann Cord – it is indeed a "True Story" – and it is highly probable that Cord related the story on the porch of the family's summer home, Quarry Farm. But it is most useful here for what it reveals about Twain's self-positioning in terms of his social and professional identity. It was first published in the prestigious Boston-based *Atlantic Monthly*, and although by this time Twain was one of the most famous writers in the United States, it was a coup for him to place something in this "highbrow" periodical. The *Atlantic Monthly* was edited by his friend William Dean Howells, and Twain offered it, with self-deprecating pride, at preferential rates: "You can pay as lightly as you choose for that, if you want it, for it is rather out of my line."[4] It is "out of [his] line" in that it lacks the crude, vagabond humor that was a feature of his early bestsellers. It is a sincere, even a sentimental tale, and it represents Twain in an aspirational moment. He had often complained – and especially to Howells – that he was tired of playing up to the public's image of him as madcap humorist. Not only did he send this story to the *Atlantic Monthly*, but he also identified himself not as Twain but as the more sensitive, more earnest, more "True,"

Mr. Clemens ("Misto C—"). But it would be naive to give more credence to this "real," "sincere" Clemens as opposed to the popular trickster that was Mark Twain. There are various sleights of hand in this "True" story. He identifies himself emphatically with his wife's family – Rachel is one of "our servants" – and seems indistinguishable from them. As Arthur Pettit has suggested, Twain is playing a role in this sketch as much as in any of his other sketches, but the role has changed from Southwestern joker to Yankee tenderfoot. Misto C— needs to be told about black life in the South as though he had never been there, and we see here the emergence of the genteel and implicitly Northern, liberal Clemens, the man who would go on to write moralistic and sentimental novels such as *The Prince and the Pauper* (1881) and *Personal Recollections of Joan of Arc* (1896). That he could not shake off his actual Southernness so easily is indicated by the moment when Rachel tells of how she recognized Henry by the scar on his wrist. At that moment in her narrative, she reenacts the event by grabbing Misto C— by the wrist. It is as though, at a subliminal level, the fake Yankee's Southern past has reached out to reclaim him.

There are other significant features to the story, not least the sustained use of the vernacular. Although this is a frame narrative, in that Rachel's excitable and "incorrect" language is mediated by the standardized perfection of Misto C—'s introduction, Rachel is allowed to take over. In this respect the story is a precursor of *Huckleberry Finn*, which is given over entirely to the vernacular figure. Also, it is precisely the adherence to and confidence in a local or racialized way of speaking that will produce the happy ending. Henry recognizes his mother when she utters one of her favorite sayings, a piece of wordplay that she had picked up from her mother: "I wa'n't bawn in de mash to be fool' by trash! I's one o' de ole Blue Hen's Chickens, I is!" (84). Twain values and accedes to this black Southern voice, but other aspects remind us of why Twain's representations of blackness have been the source of endless debate. The story seems to affirm the idea of a black person as someone who moves between laughter and tears with no finer, more intellectual shadings.[5] Her ultimate "joy" seems to compensate for her "trouble," so that at the end Rachel is not a person whom we need "trouble" ourselves about. There is also a suggestion of the paranoid excitement that so often featured in white writing about black people. When Rachel passes from laughter to silence, to questioning the white master, this is accompanied by another "uprising": "Aunt Rachel had gradually risen, while she warmed to her subject, and now she towered above us, black against the stars" (81). This seems to anticipate Twain's most dangerously subversive character, Roxana in *Pudd'nhead Wilson*, who is described in a similar moment: "She rose, and gloomed above him like a Fate" (112).

What "A True Story" indicates above all is how complex Twain's response to the South and Southern material would be, especially when he chose to incorporate the racial theme. But in his bestselling work – and his first novel without a collaborator – his preoccupations were different. *The Adventures of Tom Sawyer* (1876) has not drawn as much critical attention as some of Twain's other works, but it has had a phenomenal presence in American culture. There is a strong sense that Tom's childhood is representative of the essential American boyhood, and indeed of America's essential boyish innocence.[6] Although the novel is not without its gruesome and terrifying moments, it is taken to memorialize boyhood as idyllic, and the American boy as mischievous and independent, but ultimately "good." We learn of Tom's wild ambitions, of his fights, his boredom at Sunday School, the intensities of calf love, and so on. But through all these "scrapes" the overriding, humorous narrative voice reassures us that no trial is to be taken too seriously. Tom will always be smart enough to emerge unscathed from the dramas that he creates or that befall him. There are only occasional references to slaves, and there is nothing of the tragic dimension of Southern institutions that we find elsewhere. To create a stronger element of tension, Twain relies on melodramatic plotlines of the kind that we might find in a dime novel: the villainous Injun Joe kills a young doctor in a grave-robbing incident, and there are some brilliantly realized episodes describing Tom and Becky's bewilderment and misery when they are lost in the caves. Soon all is happily resolved, and Tom has not only Becky's love, but also $6,000 in gold that he and Huck find in the cave.

Tom Sawyer presents the South as idyll much as we find in Twain's autobiographical descriptions of his uncle's farm or his mother's oppressive but good-hearted ways. This relatively simple and innocent treatment would be complicated, though, by events of the late 1870s and early 1880s. Perhaps the most significant event was Twain's return to the South in 1882. He had long thought about writing a book on the Mississippi and his experiences as a steamboat pilot, and he wrote a series of sketches that were published in seven installments in the *Atlantic Monthly* as "Old Times on the Mississippi." These sketches caught the glamour and the excitement of steamboating in its heyday, and also the mysteries of the river and the expertise required to navigate it. "Old Times" represents a pleasurable imaginative return, and it is deliberately focused on steamboating rather than on a broader view of Southern society and culture. When he decided to make a book from the same material, he knew that he would have to expand the field of vision. He began to research the Mississippi through others' books, and went down the river again himself in the spring of 1882. The resulting book, *Life on the Mississippi* (1883), provides an altogether more fraught and diverse point of view. One of the recurrent themes is the sheer violence, brutality, and backwardness of the South. Twain recounts the existence of feuds and vendettas in which whole families are destroyed and where no one can even remember what provoked the initial disagreement: "Some says it was about a horse or a cow."[7] Twain portrays the South as an intensely inward place, in which all kinds of cruelty and degradation are prolonged for the lack of any moderating outside influence. He punctuates his narrative with violent incidents, and at one point includes a lengthy footnote made up of newspaper extracts which report mindless shootings and stabbings. *Life on the Mississippi* amounts to a sustained and direct attack on the social culture of the South.

The critique is extended to slighter matters. Twain notes a lack of basic decency in Southern behavior: Southerners spit, use uncouth language, and have poor table manners. Even college-bred "country gentlemen" use a grammar that is "blasphemous" and "debauch[ed]" (196) (though Twain's distaste for this incorrectness tends to be ignored by those who want to praise his "vernacular values" and his supposed love of diversity). His key indictment of the South is for its pretentiousness. His footnote on the various slaying incidents is used to offset the prospectus of a Kentucky "Female College" which proposes "the Southern to be the highest type of civilization this continent has seen" (286). Ultimately, Twain argues that it was the South's enslavement to un-American, Romantic delusions that led to the Civil War. The South adopted a lot of decorous rituals from the fiction of Sir Walter Scott, but this excessive *politesse* served to mask the actual "semi-barbarism" of Southern life. Twain overstates his case with his stock-in-trade bravura diatribe, and as it happens Scott was as popular in the North as he was in the South. For Twain, the war had been produced by a degraded culture, and not by a complex of economic, political, and cultural problems. His view of the South as obsessed with the past and decayed forms was affirmed by the aftermath. The war would remain the pivotal fact and topic: "In the South, the war is what A. D. is elsewhere: they date from it...It shows how intimately every individual was visited, in his own person, by that tremendous episode" (319).

For Twain, the South was ensnared by a series of perversions which were only confirmed by the war. He seems to displace his personal anguish or shame over his own antecedents; he admits he "was born in the South" (316), but clearly he no longer identifies as Southern. His treatment of the race issue was correspondingly simplistic at this stage of his career. Slavery is seldom mentioned in *Life on the Mississippi*, and Twain's South is a predominantly white place. Black people are effectively relegated to a crude rhetorical gesture at the expense of white people:

> I missed one thing in the South – African slavery. That horror is gone, and permanently. Therefore, half the South is at last emancipated, half the South is free. But the white half is apparently as far from emancipation as ever. (332)

Twain returns once more to the lawlessness of the South at this point, and the violence that he describes is white on white, not white on black.

If his representation of the South is in some respects rather narrow, it also bears signs of a fascinating contradiction. Much as Twain dwells at length on the boorishness of the South, he also finds within that a pleasing roughness and heterogeneity. If the South appalls and shames him with the crudeness of his own past, it also appeals to him as an escape from his genteel Northern present. In a chapter called "The Art of Inhumation," he tells us of a meeting with a Southern undertaker. This man discusses his business with a worldly frankness that is inappropriate, but also vigorous and impressive:

> "We don't like to see an epidemic. An epidemic don't pay...when there's an epidemic, they rush 'em to the cemetery the minute the breath's out. No market for ice in an epidemic. Same with Embamming. You take a family that's able to embam, and you've got a soft thing. You can mention sixteen different ways to do it – though there *ain't*

only one or two ways, when you come down to the bottom facts of it – and they'll take the highest-priced way, every time. It's human nature – human nature in grief. It don't reason, you see." (311)

Twain's humor – the energy and drive of his narrative – depends on his willingness to engage with this kind of impolite material. His work confronts embarrassment, and there is a necessary sympathy or tolerance in his encounter with the incongruous – the pleasure would be lost if he offered the more severely discriminatory response of wit or satire. This ambivalence, this sense that the "backward" and provincial can take attractive *and* disgusting forms, would feature in *Huckleberry Finn*, as would a more complicated take on the racial politics of the South. In *Life on the Mississippi*, however, the balance is firmly in favor of a modern, utilitarian, and orderly nation that is identified as Northern. He makes no attempt to hide his sense of returning to a more congenial, "home" environment as he is carried further back up the Mississippi:

> This is an independent race who think for themselves, and who are competent to do it, because they are educated and enlightened; they read, they keep abreast of the best and the newest thought, they fortify every weak place in their land with a school, a college, a library, and a newspaper; and they live under the law. (397)

Twain's future, and the nation's future, lie with this place and its values. In the event, though, Twain would not jettison the South so completely. As Thomas Sargeant Perry wrote in an important early review of *Huckleberry Finn*, in that novel "we acquire full knowledge of the hideous fringe of the civilization that then adorned that valley; and the book is a most valuable record of an important part of our motley American civilization."[8] Elsewhere it has been argued that the violence that Twain identifies as specifically Southern should be seen as more generally "American," or possibly as "frontier." But the crucial point for me is that the South, with its "motley" and "hideous" life, is what stimulated Twain's most vibrant and powerful work.

Adventures of Huckleberry Finn does new and significant things, but we can also map it onto what we have established as the key aspects of Mark Twain's South. There is the ambivalent response to both the "civilized" and the "backwoods." Critics have tended to overemphasize Huck's rejection of the priggish constraints of society. Certainly, he finds his life as the adopted son of the Widow Douglas "dismal regular and decent" (7). He feels at home on the raft with Jim, living hand to mouth, with long days spent naked and lazy in the river mud. The adopted Huck sweats in his new clothes, and is oppressed by constant commands not to scratch, yawn, or smoke. He has to come to dinner when a bell is rung, and he notes that the food is cooked "by itself." His own idea of good cooking involves odds and ends being thrown together in a barrel so that "the juice kind of swaps around, and the things go better" (7). Huck's preference for things that have been thrown together is something that Twain extends to the nation as a whole: America is vital and interesting – and superior to Europe – because things "swap around," because America is not dominated by the rigid social and behavioral hierarchies, doctrines, and forms of the Old World. But the fear of Southern frontier roughness is still present. While Huck loves the "natural" freedoms of the raft, nature appears in disgusting, threatening guise in the form of his father. Pap Finn represents the ghastly underside of the natural:

> He was fifty, and he looked it. His hair was long and tangled and greasy, and hung down, and you could see his eyes shining through like he was behind vines. It was all black, no gray; so was his long, mixed-up whiskers. There warn't no color in his face, where his face showed; it was white; not like another man's white, but a white to make a body sick, a white to make a body's flesh crawl – a tree-toad white, a fish-belly white. As for his clothes – just rags, that was all. (20)

Food may be better when "things get mixed up," but Pap's mixed-up qualities signify dirt, incoherence, and crudely manipulative violence. In him, many otherwise positive resonances of the natural are reversed. While Huck may love to wear his own "old rags," when he sees his father in "just rags" he sees a future that terrifies him.

The novel explores the possibilities of both wildness and civilization, and the narrative derives impetus from Huck's fear of and attraction to both. He wishes to avoid what the Widow *and* Pap represent, but he also wishes to avoid the alienation that would ensue if he were to remain caught between opposing possibilities. He has Jim, and so he can have company and abandon it; but Huck likes and needs white people, and constantly seeks contact beyond his friendship with Jim. Even so, the relation between Huck and Jim has probably provoked more critical debate than any other relationship in American literary culture. Early in the history of the novel's reception, Twain was seen to have written a benevolent novel in the abolitionist tradition. Jim's humanity is affirmed, in that we learn of his love for his children, and we see his selfless care of both Huck and Tom. But later generations of readers, and especially those in the second half of the twentieth century, have tended to deplore Twain's characterization of blackness. Jim, the argument goes, is nothing more than a minstrelsy or blackface stereotype. He is gullible, ignorant, effeminately "mothering," and he has not the wits of the 13- and 14-year-olds who choose to feature him in their pranks. In fact, it is hard to know the precise nature of the power relation between Huck and Jim (and Twain seems to reinvent that relation without too much regard for consistency). In the second chapter, Jim falls asleep beneath a tree, and Tom hangs Jim's hat on a branch. Jim later claims that witches put him in a trance and rode him all over the state, leaving the hanging hat as a sign. Jim is a deeply superstitious fool who also happens to be vain and boastful. But then again, in chapter 4, Jim seems to return the trick. Huck asks Jim to get his hairball to tell the future, but the hairball will not respond. Jim tells Huck that "sometimes it wouldn't talk without money," so Huck gives Jim a counterfeit quarter, without telling Jim about the genuine dollar that he also has. So Huck is duped into paying for a prediction, but Jim is duped into taking a counterfeit quarter when he might have received a proper dollar. There is a sense at times that Jim is rather more clever than he is willing to let on, but this exchange is still very like the knockabout routines performed by double acts in the minstrelsy shows. Far from being a full and complex character, one might say that he is an interesting match of two stereotypes: the minstrelsy's "happy darky" and the sexless paragon of sentimental fiction.[9]

The argument that Jim is a new and important character in white fiction perhaps finds more justification in the middle part of the novel. When he and Huck are separated in the fog, Jim thinks he has lost Huck, and falls asleep with exhaustion. Huck returns and pretends to have been asleep himself – he tells Jim that Jim must have dreamt the separation. But Jim reasons out what actually happened, and pours scorn on Huck for such a callow trick. Huck apologizes to Jim and tells us that he "didn't do him no more mean tricks, and I wouldn't done that one if I'd a knowed it would make him feel that way" (72). The relationship becomes momentarily fractious, but develops as a result. Huck finds – almost reluctantly – that he has responsibility for how Jim thinks and feels about him. When he later feels a strong "moral" compulsion to betray Jim so that Jim can be returned to his "rightful" owner, he finds that he cannot do it. In what Twain characterized to Howells as the struggle between "a sound heart and a deformed conscience," it is the heart that wins. This cross-racial alliance would be the novel's triumph, if the novel ended at that point. But Huck will renew his friendship with Tom, and Jim will once more become the hapless dupe of white boys' games.

Ultimately, it might seem that Twain is locked into nostalgia for his own youth, in which white boys were smart and black men were strong and loving. But perhaps this is only partly true. *Huckleberry Finn* is set in the period of Twain's youth, but it also makes sense to read it in the light of the events of the 1870s and 1880s. Lou Budd has suggested that we read the novel for its contemporary significations, and this is a strategy that Neil Schmitz has also found persuasive. In the final parts of the novel Jim is once again in captivity, and tormented by the possibility of a freedom that he had seemed, briefly, to realize. This can be read as a sideways view on the "nightmarish agony" of Reconstruction, as the rights of the emancipated slaves – that Reconstruction was meant to protect – were gradually taken away once more. Similarly, there is a strong anticipation of the Civil War, with Colonel Sherburn facing down the mob as a version of General Grant facing down the South. Budd, though, offers a reading of the novel that applies directly to Twain. Budd titles his chapter on Twain's mid-career writings on the South "The Scalawag." In general usage a scalawag is a rascal, but it also has the implication of political opportunism. In the postwar era, a scalawag was a white Southerner who accepted and approved of Reconstruction. Twain is a scalawag in that in the 1870s, at least, he sided with the victorious North. But Budd sees *Huckleberry Finn* in a slightly different light, in that Twain was writing in the literary context of the "glamorizing of the Old South" that took place in the 1880s. The grotesqueness and violence of *Huckleberry Finn* serve to counteract the emerging idea of the Old South as plantation idyll. Far from being locked in autobiographical nostalgia, Budd's Twain moves skillfully between antebellum and postbellum contexts. Above all, Budd reminds us that Huck's willingness to live so intimately with Jim should be seen as an obvious objection to the "rising tide of Jim Crowism."[10]

We are left with a series of contradictions that prove more apparent than real. Twain was a progressive political thinker who used his work to critique racism in the postbellum South. But he wrote, as Budd puts it, out of a "sympathy for the freedman [that] had a condescending base" (105). We cannot say that Twain's South is ever as politically correct as we might wish it to be, and while he was not altogether imprisoned by a deeply personal engagement with the South, the biographical factor remains an important one. Small wonder, perhaps, that Huck is as restless at the end of his novel as he was at the beginning.

Twain turned aside from the South and Southern material for much of the next decade, and returned to it with *Pudd'nhead Wilson* in 1894. This novel offers some of the earlier contradictions, but in starker form and in keeping with some of Twain's growing obsessions. The novel is satirical but seldom humorous, and suggests Twain's increasing pessimism. The main character, Roxana, is white in color but is a slave because she is known to have some black blood. She wonders why her white baby should grow up despised and powerless, when her master's baby will be educated, privileged, and free. She changes the babies' identities so that her son will grow up as Thomas a Beckett Driscoll, while the real Thomas will grow up as the enslaved Chambers. This plot allows Twain to explore a series of related and timely questions. In a period of intense white paranoia – of segregation, lynchings, and disenfranchisement – Twain uses Roxana to explore the difference between "black" and "white." Her color is a comment in itself. Lynching was often justified as a deterrent to black men who might otherwise rape white women, but Roxana's white blackness is testament to white male predation on black women. Also, Twain was preoccupied at this stage with free will and determinism. He accepted that human beings are little more than the product of their social environment, and yet this idea so appalled him that he returned to it time after time. In *Pudd'nhead Wilson* Tom grows into an arrogant and domineering man because he has been encouraged by custom to value himself above others, and especially above the true son and heir, Chambers. Chambers, who ought to fulfill his white identity and be masterful, is equally the creature of his environment in that he is perceived as black and grows to be subservient. The point must be that social training accounts for behavior, and that free will or genealogical inheritance counts for nothing. But Tom is not the courtly and honorable gentleman he was raised to be: he has a "native viciousness" that is in keeping with the fact that his mother is "a born slave."[11] Roxana herself veers from one stereotype to another, being both mammy and spiteful white belle. Twain's interest in determinism falls away, and we are left with two mulattoes as the indisputably "bad" characters. For all its interest in the self as social construct, the novel could also be read as a warning of the dangers of miscegenation.

Twain found it increasingly difficult to finish any text towards the end of his life. *Pudd'nhead Wilson* caused him endless problems, and perhaps it is remarkable that the novel is not more incoherent, given that Twain's personal fortunes were collapsing as he worked on it. He would not produce much that would alter our sense of his South, not least because his South was usually a static, prewar South. But what about Twain's representations of himself – Mark Twain the public persona – and what about his reception in the South? As far as reception is concerned, there is frustratingly little evidence. He remained aware that there was a Southern readership, and from time to time he censored his work to make it palatable to that readership. At the height of his fury over Southern lynching, he projected a book on the subject, but only got as far as the introduction, "The United States of Lyncherdom." But he gave it up on the basis that it would ruin his reputation in the South. As he wrote to his publisher, "I shouldn't have even half a friend left down there, after it issued from the press."[12] So in 1901, at least, he seemed to think that he still had a significant following in the South, though he lost enthusiasm for many projects and may have been using the notion of a Southern readership as an excuse for dropping this one. Southern reviews of *Life on the Mississippi* and *Pudd'nhead Wilson* are scarce, but one review of *Pudd'nhead Wilson* gives us a clear sense of the offense the novel must have given. Martha McCulloch Williams, writing in the *Southern Magazine* in 1894, suggests a better title for that novel would have been "The Decline and Fall of Mark Twain." She comments that the "much-advertised serial is tremendously stupid." Williams deplores the fact that Twain deals in all the clichés of the fictional South, with gentlemen who "overstep the color line." Such is Northern ignorance on the topic, she claims, that Northerners have asked her "if there were still any pure blacks at all, or any pure-blooded whites." She thinks that Twain and others are set on "gleaning the full harvest of 'Uncle Tom's Cabin.'" She observes, "So far as I know, all that the South has ever done to Mr. Clemens has been to buy his books, when it had precious little money to buy anything, and to set him upon a pedestal as the very prince of humorists." She knows that Twain is not in error through ignorance, and has therefore been "unveracious for revenue only." Williams concludes that Twain has found out "the sort of book that sells best."[13]

Williams confirms the assumption that Twain endangered his white Southern reputation with his major writings on the South. But it is important to remember that Twain was probably more famous as a personality than as a writer as such. There were several Mark Twain impersonators doing the rounds (there still are), and there was the notion, as defined by Andy Hoffman, that "Mark Twain" was "a detachable persona, a stock figure invented by one man but playable by many."[14] How did Twain deploy this persona in relation to the South? He played up his Southernness after 1906 with the wearing of white suits, but an earlier and more important intervention was his appearance at veterans' rallies. His defining public statement on his own Civil War experience began as the Putnam Phalanx Dinner Speech, given in Hartford in 1877, a speech that would be reworked as a sketch, "The Private History of a Campaign That Failed." This would be published in the *Century* in December 1885 as part of a series on Civil War leaders and battles. In the final, printed version, Twain presents himself and other "boys" in a series of comic misadventures, until a dramatic night when they are terrified by reports of Union advances.

A lone horseman approaches through the gloom, and in fear and panic the boys shoot him. The man dies muttering of a wife and children. Having discovered that war is "the killing of strangers against whom you feel no personal animosity," Twain tells us that he "resolved to retire from this avocation of sham soldiership while I could save some remnant of my self-respect." But as Pettit and others have pointed out in their studies of the speech and the sketch, the "boys" were in their twenties and thirties, and the moral superiority that emerges from this "Private History" is rather suspect. The "cowardice" or "treachery" of Twain's desertion is turned into a proof of his humanity and wisdom, while at the same time he seeks to avoid condemning the military men whom he adored.[15] Also, our sense of this otherwise noble admission of "private history" is complicated by the fact that the shooting of the stranger was almost certainly invented.

With a touching but still comic after-dinner turn before generals and other veterans, or with a sketch in a series on battles and leaders, Twain uses his "Private History" to relocate himself within the events that, in reality, he had sidestepped (if sidestepped is not too small-scaled an expression for going all the way to Nevada). As he does so, he becomes part of what Nina Silber has described as the "romance of reunion."[16] But while Twain was happy to be on the top table, hobnobbing with the generals and being part of the rebonding of American manhood, he did not enter into this romance in an unthinking way. Silber points out that the most conclusive force for reunion was the United States' imperialist venture into the Philippines. This gave new life to the ideology of Anglo-Saxonism that "could finally bridge the bloody chasm of the Civil War" (196). Twain, though, deplored American imperialism and was energetic in attacking it. For Twain, a reunion with the South would always be an impossibility, even as he entered into the spirit of masculine postbellum sentiment. His South was a childhood idyll that was lost in an aftermath of shame and guilt. He evinced hopelessly entangled impulses of affection and anger, and felt a compulsion to return to the scenes that both stimulated and defeated him. Twain, from his own hopelessly time-bound vantage point, succumbed to the feeling, but not to its political deployment. For him, the South had indeed become a "Private History"; or rather, it had become too specific and too personal a mythology to be amenable to latterday concerns.

Notes

1   For Twain's description of the "almost invisible" Florida and of his family's ancestral pretensions, see Charles Neider (ed.) *The Autobiography of Mark Twain* (New York: Harper and Row, 1975), pp. 1, 17. For biographical accounts, see Dixon Wecter, *Sam Clemens of Hannibal* (Boston, MA: Houghton Mifflin, 1961) and Andrew J. Hoffman, *Inventing Mark Twain: The Lives of Samuel Langhorne Clemens* (London: Phoenix, 1997). Scholars have long assumed that Twain witnessed at least part of his father's autopsy: in a collection of notes, "Villagers of 1840–3," there is the unexplicated remark, *"The autopsy."* See *Huck Finn and Tom Sawyer Among the Indians, and Other Unfinished Stories* (Berkeley: University of California Press, 1989). As Dahlia Armon and Walter Blair note in the California edition, Twain recalled the incident in his notebook of 1903, but disguised it: "1847. Witnessed post

mortem of my uncle through the keyhole." See *Indians* 286; as Wecter notes in his *Sam Clemens of Hannibal*, no uncle died in 1847, but this was the year of his father's death (116). Wecter also notes the correspondence with William Dean Howells that relates to Orion Clemens's account of this episode.

2   Mark Twain, "A True Story," in *Tales, Speeches, Essays, and Sketches*, ed. Tom Quirk (New York: Penguin Books, 1994), p. 80.

3   Neil Schmitz, "Mark Twain's Civil War: Humor's Reconstructive Writing." In *The Cambridge Companion to Mark Twain*, ed. Forrest G. Robinson (Cambridge: Cambridge University Press, 1995), p. 81. For a recent and interesting reading of this story and also of the sketch dealing with Twain's Civil War experiences, "A Private History," see Peter Messent, *The Short Works of Mark Twain: A Critical Study* (Philadelphia: University of Pennsylvania Press, 2001).

4   Mark Twain to William Dean Howells, September 2, 1874. See Henry Nash Smith and William M. Gibson (eds.) *Mark Twain–Howells Letters*, 2 vols. (Cambridge, MA: Harvard University Press, 1960), vol. 2: p. 22.

5   I am thinking here of Richard Wright's review of Hurston's *Their Eyes Were Watching God*: "Her characters eat and laugh and cry and work and kill; they swing like a pendulum eternally in that safe and narrow ambit in which America likes to see the Negro live: between laughter and tears." This review first appeared in *New Masses* for October 5, 1937; it is reprinted in *Zora Neale Hurston: Critical Perspectives Past and Present*, ed. Henry Louis Gates, Jr. and K. A. Appiah (New York: Amistad, 1993), pp. 16–17.

6   See, for instance, Louis J. Budd, *Our Mark Twain: The Making of His Public Personality* (Philadelphia: University of Pennsylvania Press, 1983).

7   Mark Twain, *Life on the Mississippi* (New York: Penguin Books, 1984), p. 194.

8   Thomas Sargeant Perry, review, *Century*, 30, 1 (May 1885): 171–2; reprinted in *Adventures of Huckleberry Finn* (New York: Norton, 1977), pp. 289–90.

9   For more on the cultural incoherence of Jim and of other black characters, see Eric Lott, "Mr. Clemens and Jim Crow: Twain, Race, and Blackface," in *The Cambridge Companion to Mark Twain*, ed. Forrest G. Robinson (Cambridge: Cambridge University Press, 1995), pp. 129–52. For a fascinating study of *critical* incoherence with regard to race, and canon, see Jonathan Arac, *Huckleberry Finn as Idol and Target: The Functions of Criticism in Our Time* (Madison: University of Wisconsin Press, 1997).

10   Louis J. Budd, *Mark Twain: Social Philosopher* (Bloomington: Indiana University Press, 1962), p. 103. Budd's choice of phrase seems to offer an ironic slant on racist fears over the "rising tide of color."

11   Mark Twain, *Pudd'nhead Wilson and Those Extraordinary Twins*, ed. Malcolm Bradbury (Harmondsworth: Penguin Books, 1986), p. 105.

12   Mark Twain to Frank Bliss, August 29, 1901; quoted by Justin Kaplan, *Mr. Clemens and Mark Twain: A Biography* (New York: Simon and Schuster, 1966), p. 365.

13   Martha McCulloch Williams, "In Re 'Pudd'nhead Wilson,'" in "Books and Writers," *Southern Magazine* 4 (February 1894): 99–102. My source is the photocopy in the Budd Archive, housed in the Center for Mark Twain Studies at Elmira College. Professor Budd told me that he did not include this review in his *Mark Twain: The Contemporary Reviews* (Cambridge: Cambridge University Press, 1999) because Williams is, after all, basing her review on the first two installments of the serial publication.

14   Hoffman, *Inventing Mark Twain*, p. 230. See also Budd, *Our Mark Twain*, for a sense of Twain's currency.

15   Schmitz, "Mark Twain's Civil War," notes that Twain's dereliction becomes "a moral act" (81). "Private History" is reprinted in *Tales, Speeches, Essays, and Sketches*.

16   Nina Silber, *The Romance of Reunion: Northerns and the South, 1865–1900* (Chapel Hill: University of North Carolina Press, 1993).

23

Ellen Glasgow

Julius Rowan Raper

The most trumpeted dimension of Ellen Glasgow's literary career has been the campaign of "blood and irony" she conducted as a realist and feminist against the nostalgic fiction created by Thomas Nelson Page, Joel Chandler Harris, and others of the generation dominating Southern writing in the 1890s when she began to publish. If one approaches her work, however, with the South's diversity in mind, it becomes clear that her contributions to an enlarged understanding of the region stretch beyond her pioneering Southern realism and feminism to include the ways she focused attention on such conflicts as the Anglican–Puritan, planter–farmer, and Tidewater–Valley divisions in Southern life, as well as aspects revealed by approaching the seemingly unified South from the Darwinian, naturalistic, feminist, Marxist, psychoanalytic, and modernist perspectives that emerged during her five decades as an author.

Difficult Beginnings

The month of Glasgow's birth (on April 23, 1873) marked the eighth anniversary of the conclusion of the American Civil War, the national trauma that froze her region in the posture against which she would direct the truth-telling that marks her fiction. Despite the original heterogeneity of the states that after 1820 began to cohere around the defense of slavery and states' rights and in 1861 formed the confederation that would wage war with the United States, the eventual defeat of these once-independent states shocked them into the defensive and elegiac monolith called the South. This entity, at least as psychological in nature as political, dedicated itself to certain cherished if neurotic ideals – among these, the Old South of Edenic plantations, the Lost Cause of noble soldiers, and the superiority of white aristocrats – ideals that came to exist not only in the collective sensibilities of the wounded region but also in the pages of the generation of popular writers that Thomas Nelson Page represented.

Through its internal divisions, Glasgow's childhood family refuted key elements of the monolithic past that traumatized Southerners around her were constructing, and these challenges to the region's mythology would appear in her fictions in various ways. The glaring contrasts between her parents, who married in 1853, belied the ethnic and social homogeneity of the antebellum South. While Mrs. Anne Jane Gholson (1831–93) was, in truth, a descendant of the Tidewater Anglo-Episcopal plantation aristocracy, with connections to the Randolphs, Woodsons, de Graffenrieds, and other leading Virginia families, her line back to Virginians of distinction was a relatively weak one, running through two orphaned women and suggesting thereby the fragility of class claims. Her husband, Francis Thomas Glasgow (1829–1916), by contrast, was a strict Scotch-Irish Presbyterian and an emerging Southern industrialist.

Although Francis Glasgow lived most of his first two decades in the Shenandoah Valley of Virginia between the Blue Ridge Mountains and the Alleghenies, his family in no way matched the once familiar stereotype of Scotch-Irish mountaineers as violent, whiskey-making cracker-hillbillies. When his grandfather, Arthur Glasgow (1750–1822), and family arrived from Ulster in 1766, they took possession of four or five thousand acres that today include the small towns of Buena Vista and Glasgow, south of Lexington, Virginia. Coming from a prosperous family, Francis graduated from Washington College (now Washington and Lee University) in Lexington before moving to Richmond to study law. It was through his mother's brother, Joseph Reid Anderson, that he in 1849 joined the Tredegar Iron Works of Richmond, a firm in which Anderson served as president and which would become the most important manufacturer of the South once the Civil War began.

Although the marriage of women from the planter group to industrialists was a familiar pattern of the antebellum period, it was not a prominent element in the mythology of the Old South dominating Southern literature when Glasgow came of age. Nor did the violence Southern industries used to put down slave rebellions against the companies for which they were compelled to work figure as a favorite theme of Thomas Nelson Page and his idealizing associates, but it loomed large in the Glasgow family's recent past. The sexual relationship of men of Francis Glasgow's standing with African-American women was another detail omitted from the fictional record popularized by Page's *In Ole Virginia* tales (1887) and Harris's *Uncle Remus* sketches (1876–80), a record that Ellen Glasgow knew, even from her relatively sheltered childhood, avoided the harsh truths of the South in which she lived.

Consequently, her earliest stories build on sexual misalliances that cross class barriers and picture scenes of racial and class violence. For example, in her first published fiction, "A Woman of Tomorrow" (1895), a young woman emerges as candidate for associate justice of the Supreme Court years after she leaves behind her the heir of a rundown aristocratic family who sacrificed himself to rural desolation in order to take care of his mother. Two years later, Michael Akershem, the protagonist of Glasgow's first book, *The Descendant*, starts as an illegitimate son of a "poor-white" Virginia woman and a wandering stranger. Much later, following a crisis with his mistress, a Bohemian artist named Rachel Gavin, Akershem kills a writer for the free-thinking newspaper *The Iconoclast* that Akershem edits in New York. Glasgow's second novel, *Phases of an Inferior Planet*, published in 1898, features a frustrating marriage between Mariana, a Southern woman in revolt, and Anthony Algarcife of New York, an apostate Episcopal minister turned Darwinian scientist and teacher. Economic straits and the death of their child destroy their tie and drive Algarcife back to the church, where he becomes a powerful but disillusioned and hypocritical clergyman.

When Glasgow turned her critical eye directly upon the South in her third novel, *The Voice of the People*, published in 1900 as though to signal the coming of a New South for the new century, she made hostility between the classes her central concern. The protagonist Nicholas Burr follows a familiar American pattern, that of a poor young man born in a log cabin who, with early help from a member of the local gentry, ascends in politics to become a hero of the people. Although this model was good enough for Andrew Jackson and Abe Lincoln, Nicholas Burr finally seems not good enough for the aristocrats of Kingsborough, Virginia. After Nicholas becomes governor, his humble birth combined with class prejudice blocks his union with the blue-blooded woman who once agreed to marry him. Nonetheless, his conduct in office earns him the title "The Man of Conscience," and a chance to advance to the national Senate. Nicholas dies, however, attempting to protect a Kingsborough African-American who stands in grave danger of lynching. In this way, two years before Thomas Dixon began his prejudiced study of racial conflict in the South with *The Leopard's Spots*, Glasgow presented the tragedy of lynching in a fashion as dramatic as, but far more balanced than, Dixon's. While neither of her two early New York novels found Virginia's class and racial prejudices suitable for full treatment, both themes would become recurring elements of the many Virginia novels to follow Burr's unfortunate story.

Early Success

Compared to themes Glasgow experimented with in *The Voice of the People*, those of her third novel, *The Battle-Ground*, published in 1902, represent an apparent step backward. The qualities that made it a popular book of its time are those it shared with costume novels about the American Civil War, especially its battle heroics, romantic clichés, and evocations of a courteous serene antebellum South. Even so, it indicates directions in which she will move in the future, for its early plantation romance – 260 pages of the 512-page novel – chiefly provides a contrast to and target for the realism that follows. The first half emphasizes the protective walls and traditions that the foppish protagonist Dan Montjoy has to relinquish when he faces the savagery of war. In contrast to Anthony Algarcife in *Phases of an Inferior Planet*, Montjoy manages to survive outside the shelter of moribund traditions and in the process discovers what he is when free of his family heritages: beneath his class trappings waits the man that his beloved Betty Ambler says is his true self. Not only does the war strip him of his habitual cleanliness and foppish wardrobe, but it also forces him to wear rags, eat green corn, uncooked bacon, and other fare formerly reserved for tables of the slave population. He exchanges his romantic view of the South's war for a sense of shame regarding the vulgar waste it has caused. Wounded and recovering in a makeshift hospital, he witnesses his father face death with great dignity and manages to overcome his feeling of inferiority about the paternal side of his family. In his expanded awareness, he finds himself depending on the various classes, races, sexes of his region, even on generous Union soldiers at Appomattox. His greatest humiliation, however, in the wake of defeat proves to be having to rely on a member of the once-sheltered sex, Betty Ambler.

Betty anticipates the women that Glasgow's novels to come will picture the South turning to for insight and energy after the Old Order experiences the irreversible devastation of 1861–5. Along with the social and emotional struggles of gifted men like Nick Burr to emerge from the lower classes, characters resembling Betty Ambler will embody central themes of the important novels Glasgow writes after 1902: the multiple problems that "new women" of the South encounter as they confront the surviving patriarchy in their efforts to reinvent themselves. Glasgow will view such women through the changing ontological lenses the new century provides, chiefly those adapted from the biological and psychological sciences. Although not the first of Glasgow's new women, Ambler deserves special attention because she is on the scene at the moment when roughly one-third of Southern men have been killed, one-third wounded, and the remaining third largely demoralized.

Two earlier female characters exhibited traits of the emancipated Southern woman who interested Glasgow, but they dwelt outside the South. In *The Descendant* Rachel Gavin, despite her "soft Southern accent," is a "jolly little Bohemian" living in Akershem's apartment building. Even though she has earned respect as an artist, her social audacity contributes to her falling victim to his distaste for marriage. In *Phases of an Inferior Planet* Mariana Musin, a Southern girl in revolt, likewise meets her lover, Algarcife, in a New York apartment hotel. Although she marries him and they have a child, the death of the child and Algarcife's jobless destitution provoke Mariana to run off to sing in a traveling comic opera. Eventually she remarries, but the second husband dies, leaving her sufficient wealth to assist Algarcife. His desperate return to the Episcopal ministry so overawes her, however, that she hesitates – and ultimately dies of pneumonia. Although Eugenia Battle, in *The Voice of the People*, initially possesses the social boldness to become engaged to Nicholas Burr, at the first sign of trouble she hurries, as already noted, to the safety of her own class and so does not qualify, like Betty Ambler, as one of Glasgow's new Southern women. In fact, none of Glasgow's first three "heroines" have, according to her Darwinian standards, much survival value once they venture beyond the shelters of the Old Order. Betty Ambler, however, has no choice, for the established Southern way of life vanishes before her eyes.

Betty proves her endurance, later termed the "vein of iron" by Glasgow, not only by assisting Montjoy's recovery while caring for members of the older generation, but also by managing two plantations. Certain sources of her extraordinary resilience go back to family members, for she possesses (much like Glasgow herself) her "father's head and her mother's heart." She also draws, however, on a will to survive that appears to have small precedent in the world she inherits. In contrast to her sister Virginia, a pretty, prim, bashful, and finally doomed belle, Betty proves herself resolute, defiant, assertive, competitive, saucy, spirited, independent; she also acts on a well-developed sense of compassion. The latter as much as her passion leads her to take on the destitute, but it is her intelligence backed by fortitude that enables her to do so. Heroines of equal determination whom Betty anticipates will inhabit many of Glasgow's most admired novels; they include Dorinda Oakley (*Barren Ground*), Ada Fincastle (*Vein of Iron*), and Roy Timberlake (*In This Our Life* and *Beyond Defeat*).

Along the way to her major phase, however, Glasgow would create a number of other women styled after the Betty Ambler model, as well as various male protagonists resembling the wounded Dan Montjoy or the aspiring Nick Burr, and would pass each of them beneath the light of the new century's evolving vision. One of the most powerful of her transitional novels, *The Deliverance*, published in 1904, focuses on Christopher Blake, who might have been the heir of Montjoy had the latter had no Betty to minister to his body and spirit, for Blake belongs to the generation of demoralized Southern men who came of age following the Civil War. While living in what was once his family's overseer's house, the morose and illiterate Blake struggles to feed two sisters, an uncle, himself, and his mother, an elderly woman traumatized into blindness by the sounds of the approaching Northern army. The latter character survives on the illusion that she still lives in ancient Blake Hall and can expect her daily portions of sumptuous food and drink, but her offspring, in truth, scrape by on cornbread, bacon, and back-breaking labor. Blake's rage to take revenge on Bill Fletcher, the Blakes' one-time overseer now occupying Blake Hall, leads to the deaths of Fletcher and Christopher's mother and to Christopher's eventual imprisonment.

In Blake's recovery, the role of feminine sustainer falls, strangely, to Fletcher's daughter, Maria. Her function in the story is to nourish, redirect, and give new impetus to the considerable emotional power Blake once squandered on hatred, so that after his prison stay he realizes that the "vision through which he . . . regard[s] the world" has altered and finds himself able to perceive "the abundant physical beauty of the earth." This shift in Blake's vision parallels an earlier alteration in Maria's view of things and, like Mrs. Blake's psychogenic blindness, reflects Glasgow's growing appreciation of her characters' psychological processes. At the same time Maria's change reveals her creator's continuing interest in Darwinian issues, for it illustrates the novel's overarching theme that "environment more than inheritance determines character." To the genteel attorney whom Glasgow uses as a distorting "reflector" during the opening chapters, Maria gives an appearance of grace and quiet elegance, but her poise seems inauthentic – not hers by family right. In his prejudiced eyes, she is "a dressed-up doll-baby" with the "natural things squeezed out of her" by the artifice of a Northern boarding school. Yet she has the "making of a woman . . . after all." It takes six years of a wretched marriage and a return to rural life to open up her nature. The desolate wildness of Virginia mirrors and liberates the defiant vital force within her. In this way she not only becomes the figure of light who draws Christopher out of his morose inner darkness but also, in Glasgow's canon, establishes the possibility that individual women from the non-aristocratic classes may recreate themselves in as positive fashion as do such self-made men as Nicholas Burr — that like the new men the new women, in contrast to Betty Ambler, need not emerge from the once-aristocratic group.

Transitions and Achievements

Although Glasgow did not again write a novel with the energy of *The Deliverance* until *Virginia* in 1913, her intervening works continued to expand the range of Southern fiction by dealing with untraditional subject matter. As the language used to describe the metamorphosis of Maria Fletcher suggests, by the time Glasgow was finishing Maria's story she was taking a new interest in the philosophical problems of free will. In fact, much of her reading in this period dealt with this and other metaphysical questions, including God and immortality, that reach beyond the largely scientific positions on which she built her first five novels. As the mystical vision of Laura Wilde that concludes *The Wheel of Life*, published in 1906, indicates, Glasgow's new theology and eschatology owed more to Hindu, Buddhist, and pantheistic texts than to mainstream Occidental religious authorities.

The novelty of *The Ancient Law*, from 1908, resides chiefly in its treatment of factory conditions among white workers in the Virginia textile industry, a subject that Glasgow knew less about than she would have known, through her father's profession, about Virginia iron manufacturers or, by its ubiquity, about the manufacture of tobacco products, a topic that crops up in *The Deliverance* and her later works. In 1909 she published her only novel written in the first person and that the point of view of a man, attempting, unsuccessfully it turned out, to compensate with technique for what she lacked in a deeper understanding of masculine psychology. Even so, Ben Starr of *The Romance of a Plain Man* advances Glasgow's social program by climbing from Dickensian poverty to succeed in the railroad business and to wed the blue-blooded Sally Mickleborough, thereby triumphing where Nick Burr had failed — though, in Starr's marriage, business often displaces domestic intimacy.

Of the innovations Glasgow introduced in the works between *The Deliverance* and *Virginia*, the one that contributed most to her growth as a novelist appeared in *The Miller of Old Church* (1911). Admittedly, the protagonist Abel Revercomb, a miller, follows the by-now well-trod path of Nicholas Burr, for Revercomb, the fastest-rising self-made man and foremost citizen of his area, finds himself burdened by an unwise marriage in the political career he planned, after being blocked in his long-lasting love for Molly Merryweather. Molly, however, emerges as a more complex character than Burr's Eugenia Battle. Her own claim to social status, for example, is tenuous, since she is the illegitimate child of an aristocratic soldier of fortune and his overseer's daughter; consequently, Revercomb's own mother, a joyless Calvinist, sees Molly's coquetry as proof that she has inherited the sinful nature of her parents. Other passages, however, bring out the multiple sources of her behaviors. These include the flirting and fickleness that resemble the impulsiveness of her father's family and a cruel teasing taught her before she was ten by her man-hating mother. She also possesses a pattern of growing dissatisfied with any goal she attains. This perversity may owe something to a sense of gender inferiority, but early on it also supports her will to remain free to reject the commonplace and pursue the adventurous. When she comes into an inheritance from her father, she feels swayed by upper-class attitudes, but her automatic defiance of social pressures keeps her free of the snob attitudes and aristocratic sweetness in which her father's family, the Gays, attempt to smother her. Glasgow's interest in the *over*determination of Molly's attitudes and actions marks a breakthrough from the simple positivism of her earlier novels, where character was too often the arithmetic product of instinct and environment. This depth, along with other elements in the novel, shows Glasgow moving steadily back toward realism and away from the mysticism that had often marked her works since creating the romance of Christopher Blake and Maria Fletcher.

An accomplished instance of the author's renewed realism appears in *Virginia*, published in 1913, a novel that builds on her earlier themes while embodying her deepening appreciation of the psychological dimensions of characters. As early as *Phases of an Inferior Planet* she dealt critically with the evasive thinking accompanying the sheltered life of a hypocritical clergyman; and in Eugenia Battle, Virginia Ambler (Betty's beautiful and helpless sister), and Mrs. Blake, she dramatized ways that class sheltering permits individuals to suppress their knowledge of reality when the truth turns ugly. With her new heroine, Virginia Pendleton, however, she places evasive idealism at the center of her fiction and asks Virginia's bad faith to serve as a metonymy not only for her state and region but also for the mind of her nation in the year in which the self-proclaimed idealist Woodrow Wilson, himself a Southerner, took office as the representative American. Through Virginia's perspective Glasgow explores the causes, the nature, and ultimate disaster of viewing life through a single, unquestioned, unchanging set of mind, in this case through the veil of idealistic false consciousness. While the novel provides a number of less idealistic characters, including the oppressive New South industrialist Cyrus Treadwell and his pragmatic and self-protective daughter Susan, Virginia with her artificially nurtured duty to sacrifice herself to the ideals of family, or to anyone who needs her to do so, dominates the novel. In the rounded portrait of its title character and its setting, *Virginia* stands as the culminating fiction of Glasgow's first two decades as a published writer.

The Long Transition

Having attained a certain novelistic mastery in *Virginia*, Glasgow began after 1913 to move more deeply into the occulted realms that the modern psychologists, Sigmund

Freud and especially Carl Jung, were rapidly illuminating. While her 1916 novel *Life and Gabriella*, in contrast to *Virginia*, reworks the Betty Ambler mold of self-reliant woman, it updates the type by making her a contemporary figure, carries her from the gloomy Victorian parlors of Richmond to various New York settings, and commits its more than five hundred pages to an exhaustively realistic analysis of a single character, Gabriella Carr. Despite its commonplace surface, the chief energies in the book arise from the way Glasgow uses mirrors, both literal and figurative, to turn Gabriella inside out and thereby dramatize the otherwise hidden movements of her psyche. Gabriella projects her needs and anxieties upon the only creatures she knows that seem to possess extraordinary powers – the series of men who pass through her life. Her sexual encounters trigger dreams of new possibilities, or a fresh reality, a new life to live. In this complex process of anticipation followed by either disillusionment with, or incorporation of, traits that each male possesses, Gabriella's phantasies become as compelling a test of reality as reality was a test of phantasies in Glasgow's earlier books. Her dreams show her the way she must grow.

The experimental use of mirroring characters to explore things concealed in the psyche would continue through the series of short stories Glasgow wrote from 1916 through 1923, a group that includes magazine romances, ghost tales, and her most familiar short fictions, especially "The Professional Instinct," "The Shadowy Third," and "Jordan's End." As she suggests in one of the ghost stories, "Whispering Leaves" (1923), these short pieces are experiments in which she seeks to recover fiction's birthright, misplaced during the age of realism – its stock of words for the invisible things contained in the "sunken garden" of the mind. For as the chief male character says in *The Builders*, her 1919 novel, something has "knocked a big hole in reality. We can look deeper into things than any generation before us, and the deeper we look, the more we become aware of the outer darkness in which we have been groping." For the protagonist, World War I created the hole and the darkness is external. For his creator, psychological discoveries made the new opening, and the darkness that groups of mirroring characters convert into light lies within.

The Builders and the novel that followed it in 1922, *One Man in His Time*, fill the gap in reality in somewhat different fashions. The first of the two centers on Caroline Meade, a private nurse with some of Betty Ambler's vigor and resilience, who finds herself choosing between the two sides of the divided family in which she cares for the ailing daughter. On the one side, Angelica Blackburn, the wife, comes across as helpless, self-pitying, and manipulative; her husband David, on the other, has a reputation for treating his wife badly but emerges as an energetic, intelligent leader given to theory, idealism, and hope for the future. Although David Blackburn seems the latest avatar of Nick Burr and Ben Starr, he owes a great deal to Glasgow's tie to Henry W. Anderson, a successful Richmond attorney, and candidate for the Republican vice-presidential nomination, to whom Glasgow found herself engaged for a short period, a man who in his relatively humble beginnings and spectacular rise in the law, railroad business, and politics might have stepped out of one of her early books. Although the longest-lasting of Glasgow's three major affairs, that with

Anderson appears to have had the worst effect on one of her novels; for *The Builders* devolves finally into mere political tract.

One Man in His Time also looks back to the Nick Burr pattern of a popular political leader who rises from humble origins (the new character's mother ran away from her good Virginia family to marry a circus performer) to become a paragon of civic virtue – in this case, a golden mean between romantic and realistic temperaments, between progressive and conservative political forces. All this before a gun shot kills him as he tries to end a fight between extreme factions. Gideon Vetch, however, remains a relatively secondary figure in the novel for which he seemingly serves as the eponymic character. Indeed, Vetch's true time may have been the Age of Lincoln, or Andrew Jackson, or the Virginia of the revolutionary period; in which case the character who best represents the modern epoch would be Stephen Culpeper, a Southern Prufrock. The two worlds between which Culpeper wanders are the dead world of his pity-collecting mother and old-fashioned family traditions, and the still unborn future of impulsive freedoms and violent candor that repels and attracts him when he perceives it embodied in Vetch and Vetch's daughter Patty. In this novel's advance over *The Builders*, Culpeper emerges as Glasgow's most psychologically complex character since at least Virginia Pendleton – or would emerge thus had the author not decided to shift the focus too often to the point of view of Corinna Page, a character (bearing the name of Glasgow's beloved publisher, Walter Hines Page, who had died four years earlier) so given to moral abstractions that she could have wandered from the closing pages of *The Builders*. While Culpeper styles himself a prig, he comes across as less so than Corinna, whom the author attempts to represent as generous and open to life. The interposition of Corinna's perspective between the reader and the more compelling characters finally dooms *One Man*, despite its superior elements, to much the same fate as *The Builders*, both novels lost to political propagandizing.

Promises Fulfilled

The three flawed novels that span from *Gabriella* in 1916 through *One Man* in 1922 proved to be partial successes, for the three, along with the short stories already mentioned and collected as *The Shadowy Third and Other Stories* (1923), constitute the experiments leading to Glasgow's period of masterworks that began with *Barren Ground* (1925) and culminated in *The Sheltered Life* of 1932. Each of the four books from this latter period demonstrates important advances in Glasgow's powers as a novelist. Whereas *Barren Ground* features her most completely realized Southern woman, a woman of the soil, *The Romantic Comedians* of 1926 is both her best comic novel and contains her most successfully rounded male protagonist, a Southern gentleman challenged to transcend the old patterns to which he is heir. *They Stooped to Folly* (1929) contains her most biting satire and prepares the way for *The Sheltered Life* in 1932, her damning picture of the South's evasive idealism, her most tragic novel, and, with *The Romantic Comedians*, her most nearly perfect fiction.

The heroine of *Barren Ground*, Dorinda Oakley, possesses so many facets, and such contradictory ones, that she lends herself to contrary interpretations. To many feminists, she appears an epitome of woman's triumph over adverse circumstances and over the weaknesses of men, chiefly those of the handsome doctor who seduces her, marries another woman, and leaves Dorinda pregnant. To other readers, because the traumatic failure in love has hardened Dorinda, she seems one of life's victims: while she succeeds in restoring her family's depleted farm and lifting it to a prosperity it has never known, she turns her back on a series of men who would love her and settles instead for a *mariage blanc* to an unchallenging but good and practical farmer-businessman. Whereas her toughness, sexual repression, and ambivalence about men, including her early lover, elicit Freudian readings, the imagery of the novel, including that of her most "Freudian" dreams, seems to call for the assistance of Carl Jung, whom, according to Glasgow's autobiography, she favored over Freud. For example, Dorinda's seducer's name, Jason Greylock, by bringing to mind Jason and the Golden Fleece, introduces the Medea theme of feminine revenge that structures the novel roughly in the manner of Joyce's mythic method in *Ulysses* three years earlier, one of the major breakthroughs of modernism. The allusion to Medea also explains Dorinda's richest dream, that of plowing Jason-faced thistles from the barren field of her emotions, a passage paralleling her rage to Bronze-Age Jason's desire to slay the earthborn giants who sprang from the dragon's teeth. The Jason–Medea archetype is but one of several uses Glasgow makes of symbols provided by the story's setting, the most fully realized rural scene in any of her novels.

The book also contains one of her most realistic treatments of Southern racial problems in its contrast between the sensational exploitation of black women by Jason Greylock's physician-father, a relationship echoing Old South patterns, and Dorinda's rather cool and understated but practical relationship with Fluvanna, the African-American woman who becomes a mainstay of Dorinda's dairy business. In short, the rich texture of *Barren Ground*, the harvest of Glasgow's long writing career, calls for repeated readings and rewards many of the most productive critical approaches subsequent critics have brought to Southern writing.

While not as epical as its predecessor the year before, *The Romantic Comedians* is an equally rich work, mythic in its own way, and a more perfectly constructed novel. In her preface to the book, Glasgow points out that with it she finally transcended the limits of surface realism by discovering "that the truth of art and the truth of life are two different truths." In her new work she eschewed the record taking of "external verisimilitude" for "the more valid evidence of the imagination," a choice that enabled her to create a "sound psychology" for her aging Southern gentleman, Gamaliel Bland Honeywell. Psychology presented a challenge she now found "more important, and incidentally more interesting, than [the] accurate geography" of her previous fictions, including, one would infer, *Barren Ground*. Although the sexual inclination of the newly created widower that prompts him to wed Annabel Upchurch, a girl young enough to be his granddaughter, quickly evokes a Freudian reading for the book, the "sounder psychology" Glasgow preferred here appears to have been the Jungian theory that suggests men continuously project their own *anima*, their inner woman, a hardwired archetype quirked by the male's mother, upon each woman who excites or repels them. Bottled-up Honeywell, who has had woman troubles for as long as he remembers, discovers, but only after his fickle new wife has plucked and abandoned him, that the nurse who succors him during his recuperation from the Annabel debacle reminds him of the young mother of his childhood and is "the woman [he] ought to have married!" In contrast to Honeywell, his sister Edmonia Bredalbane has seldom allowed her scruples to distract her from her appetites: with four husbands and other company she is the living heir to the Wife of Bath, just as her brother and Annabel descend directly from Chaucer's January and May. All this makes for a sad but hilarious, occasionally ribald, comedy, one that Glasgow ties with precision to the pre-moral but vital force of the seasons, chiefly spring, that nurture the characters' being.

Like the two novels before it, *They Stooped to Folly* aligns itself with a season appropriate to its tone and structure, in this case winter, the season for irony and satire, modes that permit little movement for limited, even flawed, individuals. The year is 1923–4, a period in which World War I has given America an excuse for the first wholesale exportation of its way of life under the missionary cover that it is saving the world for democracy. This impulse Glasgow would have associated chiefly with the Red Cross success of her erstwhile fiancé, Henry Anderson, and her brother, Arthur Glasgow, while rescuing Rumanians from the ravages of hunger and disease during the Great War. In the novel this pressure takes the form of the Republic's "oligarchy of maternal instincts" that drives Americans into an orgy of self-sacrifice as they attempt to reform the world. Although the author fills the novel with the obligatory war nurses, rescuers, and disgruntled idealists, the central sacrificer of self proves to be Virginius Littlepage. To penetrate Littlepage's thick defenses, Glasgow again uses the modified Cubist, solidly Jungian, method with which she conveyed various feminine dimensions of Gamaliel Honeywell.

As Littlepage's brother Marmaduke, a painter, says, Littlepage has four secret lives, all mirrored in the "jolly purple shadows" that Marmaduke, who usually produces purple nudes, has been painting in his study of his brother's face. As the novel develops, a number of candidates emerge to serve as carriers of Littlepage's shadow and anima projections. The most obvious of the contrasexual figures is Amy Paget Dalrymple, "one of those fair, fond, clinging women whom men [Littlepage, at any rate] long either to protect or to ruin" and in whose company he finds himself at the moment a call comes to inform him that his own wife Victoria has died of a heart attack. His clearest Shadow, or same-sex carrier, is Marmaduke, the bohemian brother who states the anti-matriarchal theme of the book.

The other two characters who reflect concealed sides of his psyche evade easy detection. The reader must work at penetrating Littlepage's defense of gentility in order to discover traits he shares with his cynical son-in-law Martin Welding, whom he regards as an "unmitigated cad." Yet when Martin says that he is in hell, that he has had enough of women, that he wants "to get away from every woman on earth," Littlepage understands all too well, for he too wants to find a place "where woman, even as an ideal, could not hope to survive." The most completely hidden of Littlepage's secret-sharing doubles may be his secretary Milly Burden, for he knows that Milly bore Martin an illegitimate child (it did not live) before Martin met Littlepage's daughter; consequently, Littlepage cannot help seeing Milly as a fallen woman and a threat to other women in his office. At the same time, Milly's helplessness stimulates his pity, in part because while his own daughter Mary Victoria was away as a nurse saving the Balkans, Milly displaced Mary Victoria in his emotions. Milly thus picks up and combines the disparate feelings he has for his daughter and for Amy Dalrymple, the other "fallen woman" of his affections. Consequently, the psyche of this Southern gentleman resembles a jungle at war with itself. There are numerous other interrelationships and conflicts in the novel, but the most devastating twist Glasgow gives her assault on the nation's matriarchy must be that elements of the story imply that men like Littlepage have created their own prison, governed by ostensibly perfect ladies, in order to escape from the freedom to which nature has condemned them — into unending boyishness. Because this is one vice to which Southerners have no special claim, Glasgow's satire in *They Stooped to Folly* targets a large group of Americans, both male and female.

Although the projective approach of Glasgow's previous two novels also structures *The Sheltered Life*, its ironic tone and tragic structure differ significantly from the salubrious comedy of *Comedians* and the stinging satire of *Folly*. It is difficult for an empathetic reader not to feel pity and fear for its four enmeshed central characters, Eva and George Birdsong, Jenny Blair Archbald and her grandfather, General Archbald. In weaving their stories together, Glasgow created her most moving and nearly perfect embodiment of the evasive idealism that, now and again since *Phases of an Inferior Planet*, she had pictured ravaging her region and nation. Whereas in *Barren Ground*, *Comedians*, and *Folly* she focused each of her stories through a single well-developed character, in her new novel she elected to have Jenny Blair and the General share the instrument of vision, yet managed to round out each of them. This she was able to do because by 1932 she had gained full control of her projective method. Malleable young Jenny Blair, for example, has a troupe of reflecting characters, but the most important are the Archbalds' next-door neighbors Eva and George Birdsong. Jenny takes Eva, the former beauty of Queenborough, as her symbol of order, beauty, and perfection, but she cannot explain what impulse causes her to blurt out that Eva will be slow about making out her will or what force leads her to respond to Eva's life-threatening operation with an unmanageable mixture of terror and ecstasy. For in her worship of the older woman she will not acknowledge, even to herself, that Eva is her rival for George, the only man who stimulates her virginal wild desire for mystery and delight and kindles the passion to which she wants to resign her will. Her extended flirtation with George cannot entertain the possibility that he also is filling the emotional vacuum left by the death of her father when she was five, or acknowledge that George has added a sexual dimension to her childhood need for a father who might satisfy her fundamental need for feelings "of security, rightness, fulfillment."

The complexity of Jenny Blair nearly matches that of the General, whom Glasgow represents as the creator of the sheltered social garden in which his family and the Birdsongs live. Because they are his "creatures" they also mirror him. While Jenny Blair and George respectively repeat his youthful rebellion against tradition, on the one hand, as well as his imprudent generosity and youthful adulterous impulse on the other, all the supporting characters efficiently echo aspects of his long life and layered personality. The most important of these, however, proves to be Eva Birdsong, and the role he asks her to play costs the four of them dearly. Glasgow portrays the General as a good man and a prosperous attorney but also as a man who lives almost completely on the surface of his being. His buried, truer life he channels largely into his worship of Eva, the only woman lovely and lovable enough to carry his continuing need for the "fulfillment, completeness, perfection" that he equates with "what men call Divine goodness." The false role Eva takes on in serving as the General's and Queenborough's ideal means that for forty years she has not been herself and that for twenty of those years she has been "somebody else." These are her discoveries shortly before she finds George with Jenny Blair in his arms and murders him with his hunting gun. At this juncture, the General rushes in to invent a cover story, withdraw his secret self from Eva, and transfer it to his granddaughter, who hysterically insists she "didn't mean anything in the world" in surrendering herself to the enduring evasions of the sheltered life that they, as modern Southerners and Americans, all share.

Falterings

Following *The Sheltered Life*, Glasgow's novels reveal a gradual falling off in focus, intensity, and store of energy available for the creative process. Even so, *Vein of Iron*, published in 1935, offers her most sustained depiction of a community made up of Southern Calvinists, the prize-winning *In This Our Life* constitutes her most daring exploration of Southern racial hypocrisy, and its sequel, *Beyond Defeat*, which appeared twenty-one years after her death, provides her simplest, most serene picture of the good life.

For the setting of *Vein of Iron* Glasgow moved back to her paternal roots among the descendants of Scotch-Irish Presbyterians who first came to the Valley of Virginia during the second half of the eighteenth century. In assessing this half of her heritage, she was reevaluating one of the major sources of American culture in as much as the Southern Puritans shared key values with those in New England. To be sure, this once-dominant element of the nation's life includes, as the book shows, much that is objectionable; but it also embodies a number of virtues that Americans would do well to salvage, Glasgow implies, during the economic crises of the 1930s. The inhabitants of Ironside, Virginia, seem to be both victims and beneficiaries of their doctrine-ridden way of life. Their neglect of the senses and the emotions, for example, produces families who are unhappy although they are strong, and individuals who cannot articulate love even though they feel it. They value independence above solidarity and practice a charity more prudent than generous. For these and numerous parallel reasons, a reader may conclude that Glasgow's portrait of the Valley culture achieves a balance that is both penetrating and appreciative, yet damning.

The same reader may admire the balanced mix yet feel disappointed by the chronicle's major characters. Much the way the culture at large in the novel looks back to the maternal ancestors of Dorinda Oakley in *Barren Ground*, Ada Fincastle appears to be another Dorinda, pregnant and abandoned. In contrast to Dorinda, who lost her baby in an aborting accident, Ada accepts the adversities of living as an unwed mother and an outsider to the Ironsiders' community. She eventually weds the lover with whom she conceived the child, but he is a man repeatedly kept from her by another woman, the Great War, or the Great Depression, and Ada must continuously adjust her dreams to a world plagued by war, mass culture, and depression. Her father, John Fincastle, deals with that world in a very different but equally thwarted fashion. He appears to be another General Archbald, equally sweet but with a rural crustiness; the author clearly intends him, however, as an F. H. Bradley living the life of a Virginia mountain man. As his story unfolds he evolves from his post-Kantian idealism to become a Nirvana-seeking mystic. He comes closest to realizing this goal at the moment he dies outside the house in which he fancies he sees the face of his mother, long dead. Ultimately, despite its brilliant record of Southern Scotch-Irish life, *Vein of Iron* is too diffuse, sentimental, and didactic to rank among Glasgow's finest fictions.

The interval between *Vein of Iron* and Glasgow's next book, *In This Our Life*, would be six years, the longest between any of her novels. A number of factors explain this delay, chiefly that in 1934 she began writing *The Woman Within*, the autobiography that she ordered be published only after she died, and would work on it intermittently until 1943, two years after *In This Our Life* appeared. She was also crafting the critical prefaces for the second collected edition of her novels, *The Virginia Edition of the Works of Ellen Glasgow*, twelve volumes that Scribner's brought out in 1938; the collected prefaces themselves would appear, along with that for *In This Our Life*, as *A Certain Measure* in 1943. A third intrusion on the time she could spend with the last novel published during her lifetime was her rapidly failing health, the two heart attacks that prevented her taking the book through her customary third draft. In spite of this loss of physical strength, her late sixties became a period of considerable creative activity allowing her to journey into territory new to her – although Jean Toomer, William Faulkner, Zora Neale Hurston, and other American writers preceded her there.

In This Our Life, which won Glasgow a Pulitzer Prize and promptly became a Bette Davis film, is a double-barreled novel, one in which the subplot threatens to overwhelm the main. The central thread of this family story follows the competition of two sisters, Roy and Stanley Timberlake, chiefly over men. The supporting thread pictures the intellectual ambition of Parry Clay, a young man of mixed blood surreptitiously related to the Timberlake sisters, and the way he becomes the sacrifice that would save Stanley from a fate she deserves. While Roy follows the Betty Ambler–Dorinda Oakley model of strong Southern women, Stanley extends the helplessness of Virginia Ambler, as well as the selfish innocence of Annabel Upchurch Honeywell and Jenny Blair Archbald, into the realm of criminality. First, spoiled Stanley (soon to be the Bette Davis character) runs off with her sister's husband, Peter Kingsmill, whom she then drives to suicide. In the meanwhile, Roy finds herself attracted to Craig Fleming, the fiancé Stanley jilted when she decided to take Kingsmill from her sister. Although he grows to love Roy, Fleming, a well-meaning radical attorney, cannot free himself from his impulsive attachment to her sister, and after Stanley, following Kingsmill's suicide, runs down a young girl with her car, Fleming joins the larger family's plot to shelter Stanley by foisting her guilt onto Parry Clay.

Visibly white but legally black, Clay is another of Glasgow's natural aristocrats with a native potential equal to that of Nick Burr. The social and internal gravity, however, of the African part of his heritage (he also carries Native American genes as well as sets from both the maternal and paternal sides of Stanley's family) creates the force that dooms his admirable ambitions. Clay thus provides a mirror of the conscience of the family, of Virginia, and, by implication, of America. He would have been forced to take on Stanley's just fate, did not Asa Timberlake, the father of Stanley and Roy, break rank with the family by uncovering the truth and sharing it with appropriate officials.

Asa's decision to act in this manner represents an important personal triumph, and because he, along with Roy, usually serves as the point-of-view character, his internal conflicts dominate the novel. He finds himself torn between the largely progressive characters in the novel – chiefly Roy, Clay, and Fleming, but also Kate Oliver, Asa's soulmate mistress – and those comprising the plutocratic matriarchy that rules his family and region. Each of the supporting characters has a claim on part of Asa's personality, much the way General Archbald found himself ruled by his various dependents. Asa's chief difference from Archbald arises from the role William Fitzroy plays. Called the foremost robber baron of the South, Fitzroy is the financial power behind Asa's tyrannizing invalided wife Lavinia and stands as a considerable presence in Asa's own household, especially for his spoiling Stanley, around whom Fitzroy behaves as impulsively as Honeywell did with Annabel Upchurch. It is against this nexus of familial, uxorious, and financial instincts that Asa struggles when he finally elects to stand with Clay and other progressive forces in the novel, including Roy. Relative to the struggles of Clay and Asa, Roy's sibling rivalry and her troubles with men seem a bit minor, though they take up a large part of the book. And the resolution she reaches after Fleming reverts to Stanley, her touching but hopeless one-night encounter with a young Britisher running off to World War II, resolves nothing.

Endings

What their encounter does, however, is leave the door open for a sequel. *Beyond Defeat* begins three years later when Roy brings Timothy, the child she conceived during her night with the death-bound boy from Canterbury, back to Queenborough, after having remained out of touch during the intervening years spent working in New York department stores. In these matters, she travels the road Dorinda avoided through aborting her child. Roy is desperate: she has no money, no friends, no hope, but she has contracted pneumonia and must find someone to care for her son while she undergoes medical care. In the ritual-like rhythm of the novel, she appeals for help to various family members, but her mother, Craig Fleming, and William Fitzroy's wealthy widow all have reasons for not accepting Timothy. Fleming she finds happier and much steadier now that he has joined Kate Oliver's agrarian commune. Asa also belongs to the commune, living there, Lavinia says, in sin. Asa, it turns out, has found his long-deferred freedom with Kate, as part of "something bigger than one person – or than two persons." Asa promises that Timothy will somehow be looked after, a vow he can keep only because Kate – a tall upright Gaea–Demeter–Dorinda figure who moves in harmony with the "earth or air" – generously backs it up. With a vision more mature than his daughter's, Asa views Kate's farm, Hunter's Fare, as the simple place where he experiences the total circumambience of the natural world and feels "caught and held in some slow drift of time." Although Roy intuits that her freedom and strength have their source in Asa and his in the earth of Hunter's Fare, she does not yet comprehend the adequacy of his expanded insight. Time alone will enable her to grasp the rest.

With Asa's strangely illuminating vision of family, time, place, and repose, Glasgow's rich, fifty-year literary life comes to an end. She died November 21, 1945. *Beyond Defeat* finally appeared in print in 1966, as a new generation of scholars and academic critics were taking over the work of evaluation begun by journalists and reviewers during her long lifetime. Only as we step back from her period can we begin to appreciate all that she contributed to writing the American South into being. Today, self-made Southern men, independent-minded Southern women, and talented, determined black Southerners may seem commonplaces of Southern literature and life. They were not so when she began. Nor had any Southern writer done the critical work needed to put Southern aristocrats, complacent patriarchs, white supremacists, self-pitying professional Southern victims, evasive idealists, and patronizing practitioners of noblesse oblige in their place so that the underprivileged classes, races, and gender could begin their ascents from backwoods and depressed farms to make appropriate contributions to the life of their region and nation. It was Glasgow's job to clear the weeds from the barren land of the South, and to make it, if not virgin again, at least fit soil for all its inhabitants. Readers are still discovering how well she succeeded.

REFERENCES AND FURTHER READING

Auchincloss, Louis (1964) *Ellen Glasgow*. Minneapolis: University of Minnesota Press.

Glasgow, Ellen (1902) *The Freeman and Other Poems*. New York: Doubleday, Page.

Godbold, E. Stanly (1972) *Ellen Glasgow and the Woman Within*. Baton Rouge: Louisiana State University Press.

Goodman, Susan (1998) *Ellen Glasgow: A Biography*. Baltimore, MD: Johns Hopkins University Press.

Holman, C. Hugh (1966) *Three Modes of Modern Southern Fiction: Ellen Glasgow, William Faulkner, Thomas Wolfe*. Athens, GA: University of Georgia Press.

Inge, M. Thomas (ed.) (1976) *Ellen Glasgow: Centennial Essays*. Charlottesville: University of Virginia Press.

Kelly, William W. (1964) *Ellen Glasgow: A Bibliography*. Charlottesville: University of Virginia Press.

MacDonald, Edgar E., and Inge, Tonette Bond (eds.) (1986) *Ellen Glasgow: A Reference Guide*. Boston, MA: G. K. Hall.

McDowell, Frederick P. W. (1960) *Ellen Glasgow and the Ironic Art of Fiction*. Madison: University of Wisconsin Press.

Matthews, Pamela R. (1994) *Ellen Glasgow and a Woman's Traditions*. Charlottesville: University of Virginia Press.

Meeker, Richard K. (ed.) (1963) *The Collected Stories of Ellen Glasgow*. Baton Rouge: Louisiana State University Press.

Parent, Monique (1962) *Ellen Glasgow, Romanciere*. Paris: Nizet.

Raper, Julius Rowan (1971) *Without Shelter: The Early Career of Ellen Glasgow*. Baton Rouge: Louisiana State University Press.

Raper, Julius Rowan (1980) *From the Sunken Garden: The Fiction of Ellen Glasgow, 1916–1945*. Baton Rouge: Louisiana State University Press.

Raper, Julius Rowan (ed.) (1988) *Ellen Glasgow's Reasonable Doubts: A Collection of Her Writings*. Baton Rouge: Louisiana State University Press.

Rouse, Blair (1962) *Ellen Glasgow*. New Haven, CT: College and University Press.

Rouse, Blair (ed.) (1958) *Letters of Ellen Glasgow*. New York: Harcourt, Brace.

Rubin, Louis D., Jr. (1967) *The Curious Death of the Novel: Essays in American Literature*. Baton Rouge: Louisiana State University Press.

Scura, Dorothy (ed.) (1992) *Ellen Glasgow: The Contemporary Reviews*. Cambridge: University of Cambridge Press.

Scura, Dorothy M. (ed.) (1995) *Ellen Glasgow: New Perspectives*. Knoxville: University of Tennessee Press.

Taylor, Welford Dunaway, and Longest, George C. (eds.) (2001) *Regarding Ellen Glasgow: Essays for Contemporary Readers*. Richmond: Library of Virginia.

Wagner-Martin, Linda (1982) *Ellen Glasgow: Beyond Convention*. Austin: University of Texas Press.

24

Fugitives and Agrarians

Andrew Hook

I

The South's regional or sectional distinctiveness in the context of the rest of the United States has generally been taken for granted. When I was a student at Princeton University in the 1950s I frequently encountered the view that the South was still a foreign land. Caroline Gordon and Allan Tate, then living in Princeton, were sufficiently intrigued by my Scottish accent to insist that I read Burns aloud for them; I was too young and too polite to let it be known I found their Southern voices equally different and equally intriguing. But from the time of the South's origins until the 1920s – when the so-called Fugitives and Agrarians emerged – there is at least one area of normal cultural life in which the existence of a distinctive Southern contribution is at least problematic. That area is intellectual life. Did the traditional South ever sustain an intellectual class? Did the South ever provide the kind of communal or civic context in which an acknowledged intellectual elite could flourish?

Those who have inclined towards a positive response to such questions have until recently tended to focus on the early periods of Southern history in the eighteenth and early nineteenth centuries. Certainly, when the case began to be made in the late 1920s that the South and Southern tradition offered a viable alternative to the reductive materialism and spiritual aridity of modern American society, it was in that early period of Southern history that its superior culture was seen to be located. At a time when Southern statesmen were vying with New Englanders for the leadership of the newly created USA, there was clearly a Southern contribution to the culture of the American Enlightenment. Nonetheless, as early as 1816, George Tucker was attempting to explain Virginia's backwardness in cultural matters by referring to the structure of its social life: the scattered plantations, and the absence of cities, combined with a preference for foreign authors and a preoccupation with practical pursuits, had produced a situation in which a native literature could not be expected to flourish. Near the end of the nineteenth century, Thomas Nelson Page advanced almost the same arguments to explain the South's failure to develop a significant literary culture; in *The Old South* (1892) Page suggested that the failure was a consequence of the South's non-urban, agrarian society, the resulting absence of printing houses, and the failure to develop a reading public within the South for Southern authors. However, to these sociological explanations Page added the equally conventional one that all of the intellectual powers of the Old South had been used up by the worlds of politics and polemical controversy, and that it was the existence of slavery that had led to "the absorption of the intellectual forces of the people of the South in the solution of the vital problems it engendered."[1] Certainly, there is a case to be made for the view that in the antebellum period the way ahead for any ambitious young Southerner was through politics or the law, rather than through any form of purely cultural study. This at least is very much the implication of a letter that Dickens received from Thomas Ritchie of the *Richmond Enquirer* in 1842: "The *forte* of the Old Dominion is to be found in the masculine production of her statesmen, her Washington, her Jefferson, and her Madison, who have never indulged in works of imagination, in the charms of romance, or in the mere beauties of the *belles lettres*".[2] Equally clear is the evidence from the lives of those authors whom the Old South did produce: William Gilmore Simms, for example, the Old South's best novelist, found little support in his native South Carolina. Simms had many more readers in the North than in the South, and had to undertake frequent visits to New York to meet other writers, editors, and publishers, and so establish himself as a writing professional. Other Southerners such as John Pendleton Kennedy and Edgar Allan Poe found that their only way to pursue a literary career was by leaving the South altogether.

There is then some evidence to support the analysis provided by Tucker at the opening of the nineteenth century, and by Page near its end, in explanation of the South's failure to develop a truly significant literary and intellectual culture. But the roots of the South's failure to produce a genuine and recognizable intellectual class perhaps lie deeper. I have noted the suggestion that if there was ever a time when the South enjoyed a tradition of culture worthy of admiration it was in the period before, during, and after the winning of American independence: at a time, that is, when the South's sectional identity was less clearly defined than it was soon to become. The South did not invent itself in its final form until the 1830s, when the slavery issue began to dominate the American political stage. It was the slavery question and its ramifications that largely united the slaveholding states. But the source of this increased sense of Southern identity was not one favorable to the continuing development of a Southern intellectual class. That is because the most striking feature of the cultural life of the Old South after the early 1830s is its intolerance of criticism. In such crucial areas as the institution of slavery, states' rights, and relations with the North, freedom of debate more or less ceased to exist. Southern opinion had taken its stand on these issues; there was no room for further argument. Under pressure from the North, nothing was required but unswerving defense of Southern ideology. Intellectual or literary challenges to mainstream

Southern attitudes and values were unacceptable. Conformity, not criticism, was what was demanded: not, then, the kind of circumstances in which intellectual freedom and exchange could flourish. In *A Sacred Circle: The Dilemma of the Intellectual in the Old South, 1840–1860* (1977) Drew Gilpin Faust explores the lives and works of five antebellum Southern intellectuals, including Simms, but the story told is essentially one of intellectual isolation and alienation. Even more significantly, Faust indicates that the only issue on which her sacred circle of five was widely attended to in the South was its readiness to come to the defense of slavery.

Defeat in the Civil War changed nothing. Southern society in the postbellum period became if anything less tolerant of criticism from within or without than it had been before. Thomas Nelson Page, Thomas Dixon, and a great many others were soon engaged in what Mencken called "sentimentalizing the civilization that had collapsed and departed... All conceivable human problems were precipitated into platitudes. To question these platitudes became downright dangerous to life and limb."[3] In the post-Reconstruction period it was the South's attitude to the question of race that above all remained beyond criticism. When G. W. Cable tried to raise the race issue in his fictions he was soon compelled to leave New Orleans and settle in New England. Fred Hobson in *Serpent in Eden* (1974) provides a list of other Southerners who were compelled to make their careers in the North because they had dared to be critical of Southern society: Walter Hines Page and John Spencer Bassett of North Carolina, William Garrott Brown of Alabama, and William P. Trent of Virginia and Tennessee. W. E. B. DuBois was right to suggest in *Crisis* in 1926 that "What the white South has needed for a hundred years is frank and free self-criticism."[4] Such self-criticism would have been the task of a free-thinking Southern intellectual class. But from the 1830s to World War I the South had made it impossible for such a class to exist.[5] After the war there were some within the South who were beginning to agree. In 1920 the young Thomas Wolfe was writing in his personal notebook about the "puerile nature of intellectual life"[6] in the South, while in 1925, in an essay in the *Nation*, Allen Tate agreed the South "was never greatly distinguished for a culture of ideas."[7] The New Orleans *Double Dealer* in 1921 had been more forthright:

> Is there in any newspaper of the South any evidence whatever of an interest on the part of its readers in literature – which is to say, in thought? For reading the daily press of the South who could divine that the people of the South ever heard of a book ... There is no indication, or very little, that Southern people think or read, or that they are hospitable to thinkers, or writers, or artists.[8]

These comments on the intellectual deficiencies of the South, like those by Wolfe and Tate, are of course made in a new, postwar Southern context. This is a time when notions about the need to think about change in the South, even the abandonment of cherished Southern traditions, are at last beginning to be aired. Much more specifically, these comments are made in the specific context of H. L. Mencken's notorious onslaught on what he regarded as the egregious weakness and worthlessness of Southern culture and Southern tradition. Mencken's views were expressed most famously in the essay in *Prejudices, Second Series* (1920) which he called "The Sahara of the Bozart." The South, Mencken, argued, once the most civilized section of the United States, had by 1920 become "almost as sterile, artistically, intellectually, culturally, as the Sahara Desert." And he goes on, with great panache, to list the South's deficiencies:

> In all that gargantuan paradise of the fourth-rate there is not a single picture gallery worth going into, or a single orchestra capable of playing the nine symphonies of Beethoven, or a single opera-house, or a single theatre devoted to decent plays... but when you come to critics, musical composers, painters, sculptors, architects and the like, you will have to give it up, for there is not even a bad one between the Potomac mud-flats and the Gulf. Nor an historian. Nor a sociologist. Nor a philosopher. Nor a theologian. Nor a scientist. In all these fields the south is an awe-inspiring blank.[9]

Mencken had begun his attacks on the South long before the "Sahara of the Bozart" essay, and he would continue his unrelenting onslaught to the end of the 1920s and beyond. But from the beginning there was an element of a love-hate relationship in his condemnation of the South. Having been brought up in Baltimore, he regarded himself as a Southerner, and he was among those who believed that the South he excoriated had in the antebellum past represented a civilized and cultural ideal. In the *American Mercury* in 1930 he even argued that the victory of the South in the Civil War would have produced a Southern society without those elements that disfigured its current reality. If the Confederacy had won, he suggested, "no such vermin would be in the saddle, nor would there be any sign below the Potomac of their chief contribution to American *Kultur* – Ku Kluxery, political ecclesiasticism, nigger-baiting, and the more homicidal variety of Prohibition... The old aristocracy... would have at least retained sufficient decency to see to that."[10]

Mencken's anti-Southern prejudices do then seem to have coexisted with some degree of sentimental romanticizing of the Old South. But what has to be recognized is that in the new South of the 1920s Mencken's views do appear to have made a major impact. This is the central thrust of Hobson's monograph *Serpent in Eden*. Obviously, there would have been major changes in Southern society in the 1920s had Mencken never existed. But his attacks do seem to have focused Southern minds, sparking reactions whether positive or negative. The educated South at least could not just ignore the "Sahara of the Bozart" essay. Hobson cites evidence from the University of Virginia, the University of North Carolina, and Vanderbilt University, all suggesting that Mencken's views were very much the flavor of the month. So much so that there were soon those prepared to argue that it was Mencken's impact that was responsible for the sudden increase in cultural and intellectual activity in the New South. Jesse Wills, for example, a member of the Fugitive group itself, recalled that the magazine was established at "a time when the late H. L. Mencken was the idol of the students.

Even Allen [Tate], before he found T. S. Eliot, used to carry Mencken around under his arm."[11]

Even if it is possible to debate the precise importance of Mencken's contribution, what is not in dispute is that the 1920s did see the beginnings of the emergence of an intellectual class in the so-called New South. That class was composed of academics, writers, editors, and journalists. It included Howard Odum, Gerald Johnson, Julian Harris, Paul Green, and W. J. Cash. The University of North Carolina was its intellectual heart. What united these new Southerners was their belief that traditional Southern attitudes and values had to change, that in some directions at least the South had to modernize. The 1920s, that is, saw the emergence in the South of what it had resisted for a hundred years: an intellectual class willing to look critically at its traditions, and prepared to discuss and debate ideas both new and old. These critics and commentators were not outsiders – though most of them had had experience of the world outside the South – they were not in any sense enemies of the South, but they were prepared to grapple with the South's problems, criticize its weaknesses, and condemn its evils. Academic and intellectual analysis of the South and its traditions was at last becoming possible.

Soon, too, there were other signs of movement and change within Southern culture. A flourishing literary culture seems to require the existence of publishing outlets for new and challenging work. That role has often been taken by so-called "little magazines," small circulation, avant-garde publications in which new and established authors can find an outlet for work not appealing to a commercial publisher. In the 1830s in Richmond, Virginia, Edgar Allan Poe had tried to turn the *Southern Literary Messenger* into a cosmopolitan, high quality literary magazine in defiance of the norms of Southern provincialism. But Poe's attempt was short-lived and he had no successors. None, that is, until the 1920s, when the New South suddenly began to produce a range of little magazines. Two of these – the *Reviewer* and the *Double Dealer* – strongly supported by Mencken, were soon pursuing an agenda very much in line with that of the New South intellectuals; the Southern literary renaissance they were seen to be promoting involved, that is, a conscious rejection of the romanticized sentimentality of traditional Southern writing. In fact the early issues of the *Reviewer*, edited and published in Richmond from 1921, were traditional enough, but influenced by Mencken, it soon moved in new and more challenging directions. It published new young Southern writers such as Julian Peterkin, Frances Newman, Paul Green, Gerald Johnson, and Allen Tate, and began to provide a platform for increasingly bold and radical criticism of Southern society. At the end of 1924 the editorial base of the *Reviewer* moved from Richmond to Chapel Hill, where it continued to provide a platform for writers hostile to Southern traditionalism. A year or so later, however, financial problems led to the *Reviewer's* merging with the *Southwest Review*. In the early 1920s there can be no doubt that the *Reviewer* helped significantly in the creation of a new Southern intellectual class.

If the *Reviewer* performed this function in the Upper South then the *Double Dealer* did the same in the Deep South. Established in New Orleans in 1921, for the following five years the *Double Dealer* flourished as a little magazine publishing an impressive range of American authors, both Southern and non-Southern. Thus its contributors included Sherwood Anderson, Hemingway, and Hart Crane, as well as John Crowe Ransom, Allen Tate, Robert Penn Warren, and Donald Davidson. Compared with the *Reviewer*, the *Double Dealer* always remained a more purely literary magazine; and it was always more interested in promoting good, modernist writing from any source, than in specifically advancing a new Southern literature. Yet the *Double Dealer* was harshly critical of Southern provincialism and cultural stagnation, so that it too should be seen as contributing significantly to the emergence of a new kind of intellectual culture in the South.

II

It is within this context of the problematic cultural and intellectual history of the South, and the specific developments beginning to occur in the New South of the 1920s, that the emergence of those writers and thinkers who have come to be known as Fugitives and Agrarians has to be placed. What has to be recognized is that these writers and thinkers broadly shared the view of the South's intellectual history that the Southern magazines just quoted adopted. Indeed, one of them – Allen Tate – played a highly significant part in propagating and establishing that view. The result is that the revisionist work of more recent writers on the South and its intellectual history is not relevant to the Fugitives and Agrarians. In the last twenty-five years or so historians such as Michael O'Brien and Richard King, backed up by detailed studies of individuals and groups in the nineteenth-century South like Drew Gilpin Faust's *A Sacred Circle* and E. Brooks Holifield's *The Gentlemen Theologians: American Theology in Southern Culture, 1795–1860* (1978), have attempted to show that the traditional account of the South as a kind of intellectual desert is simply wrong. Michael O'Brien, in particular, has moved away from the position he took in *The Idea of the American South 1920–1941* (1979) and in *Rethinking the South: Essays in Intellectual History* (1988) has challenged all those commentators and historians in both the nineteenth and twentieth centuries, Southern and non-Southern, who have been dismissive of the South's intellectual life in the century preceding the Southern renaissance of the late 1920s and 1930s. In the present context, however, the rightness or wrongness of O'Brien's position is not the issue, because Fugitives and Agrarians alike tended much more towards Tate's view of the South's literary and intellectual past than towards O'Brien's current revisionist case.

Fugitive was a poetry magazine published in Nashville between 1922 and 1925 by a group of Southern writers closely associated with Vanderbilt University. The putative originator of the Fugitive group was Sidney Hirsch, and the original membership included John Crowe Ransom, Allen Tate, Walter Clyde Curry, Stanley Johnson, Merrill Moore, Donald Davidson, Alec Stevenson, Jesse and Ridley Wills,

James Frank, William Y. Elliott, and William Frierson; Robert Penn Warren, Laura Riding, and Alfred Starr subsequently joined the group, to make a final total of sixteen members. Most of the major figures in this list – Ransom, Tate, Warren, and Davidson – eventually became identified with the Southern Agrarian movement. But it is important to recognize that *Fugitive* itself was in no sense an Agrarian publication. It was a poetry magazine and nothing more.

When most of the Fugitives got together for a three-day reunion at Vanderbilt in May, 1956, this point was underlined. Alfred Starr, for example, pointed to "the confusion that exists between the poetry that the Fugitives wrote and a different era entirely – the succeeding era, which coincided roughly with the great economic depression, the political era of the prose writers, the Agrarians. I think a sharp separation should be made in our minds – surely for posterity, if for no other reasons – between these two things." Merrill Moore strongly agreed: "There were two distinct movements, even though one grew into another...the greater majority of the Fugitive group was not interested in the Agrarian movement, or the Neo-Agrarian movement; and I, for one, would strongly emphasize that fact." Near the end of the meeting Moore felt the need to reiterate his point: "I want to make it clear that in my humble opinion the so-called 'Fugitives' refer to the period of 1922 to 1925 and relate primarily to pure poetry – if there is such a thing." Allen Tate, a Fugitive who did become an active Agrarian, agreed that the original aims of the Fugitives were specifically only poetic: "the Fugitives' objective was the act of each individual poet trying to write the best poetry possible." Even as a poetry magazine, *Fugitive* had little in the way of a specific agenda. Its contributors were united by a commitment to poetry; beyond that they had no shared aims, values, or beliefs. They all happened to be Southerners, but their Southern identity had nothing to do with what brought them together. As Louis D. Rubin, Jr. said in 1962, "during the early 1920s the Fugitives were not particularly interested in their identity as Southerners."[12]

In all these respects *Fugitive* has little in common with the *Double Dealer* and even less with the *Reviewer*. Not even *Fugitive*, however, could remain wholly insulated from the cultural context in which it was being produced. In its very earliest publicity material, it announced itself as "The Fugitive in the 'Sahara of Bozart.'" "Its output," it asserted, "is not radical nor yet reactionary; it is not committed to the modern cerebral doctrine of poetry on the one hand, nor the school of the Heart-strings on the other." And "the editors are working to stimulate the growth of a true poetry in the South." Subscribers are told that the way to "keep in touch with literary development in the South, is to read *The Fugitive*."[13] The references here to Mencken's essay, and to a new kind of poetry being written in the South, make it clear that the group were perfectly aware that in publishing their new magazine they were engaging in the ongoing debate about the direction of Southern culture. Again, in the foreword to the first issue of their magazine, there is an emphasis on the need for change in the direction of Southern writing:

A literary phase known rather euphemistically as Southern Literature has expired, like any other stream whose source is stopped up. The demise was not untimely: among more advantages, "The Fugitive" is enabled to come to birth in Nashville, Tenn., under a star not entirely unsympathetic.[14]

Over a year later *Fugitive* was still referring disparagingly to what had been regarded as the Southern tradition in poetry: "We fear to have too much stress laid on a tradition that may be called a tradition only when looked at through the haze of a generous imagination."[15] Much later Allen Tate would confirm that the Fugitive poets did see themselves as breaking with the past: "The literary tradition in the United States, and particularly in the South at the end of the First World War, was not usable; that is, we couldn't take off from our elders: there was nothing there."[16] The Fugitives, then, committed only to the writing of poetry, and in no way involved in a critical examination of the state of Southern society, were nonetheless aware of what was new, different, and challenging — at least in terms of a traditional Southern literature — about their endeavor.

The Fugitives' own intentions were probably not the determining factor in any assessment of their contemporary impact on Southern culture. How they were perceived counted for more. Mencken himself appears to have been ambivalent about the new poetry magazine. Writing in the *Baltimore Sun*, he declared its contents "constitute, at the moment, the entire literature of Tennessee." Even the local Nashville newspapers were uncertain how to take this remark: "The lay mind is left in uncertainty as to whether Mr. Mencken was taking a genial or vicious poke at the State or was handing 'The Fugitive' a compliment."[17] At the very least Mencken's remarks helped to make *Fugitive* known to a wider American public, and both Vanderbilt and Nashville were soon ready to welcome the notice the magazine was gaining. "English writers praise 'The Fugitive'" announced the *Nashville Tennessean* in August, 1922: "Robert Graves, Frederick O'Brien, Coppard, Kournos and others of a literary school centering around Oxford, have written to the editors their opinion that *The Fugitive* is one of the most promising things being done in America at the present time."[18] A little later the same paper appeared with the headline: "Internationally Known Poets Contribute to Nashville's Verse Magazine."[19] The contributors in question were Witter Bynner, Louis Untermeyer, John Gould Fletcher, and L. A. G. Strong. Later headlines ran "Fugitives add to Literary Honors of Tennessee"; "Nashville Poets are Heralded at Home and Abroad," and "Critics of World Pay Recognition to Local Group."[20] In April 1923 the *Vanderbilt Hustler* was telling its readers that the university, thanks to the success of *Fugitive*, was "commanding recognition in the literary world." "Tennessee has gathered the highest poetic laurels in the South."[21] And as in all these examples of public recognition, much is made of the fact that the Fugitive poets were winning approval from critics and commentators from outside the South. Nashville was now known in different parts of the world as "the city in Tennessee where *The Fugitive* is published."[22] The note here of a kind of provincial pride in all these commendations is unmistakable. A long article in a Sunday issue of the *Nashville Tennessean* in May 1923 even listed all 32 of the states in the US and the three foreign countries (Britain, Germany, and Canada) where subscribers to *Fugitive* were to be found, as well as naming every magazine and newspaper that had made favorable comment on the poetry magazine. It is as though the people of Nashville have to be reminded that it really is true that the publication of *Fugitive* has brought them fame and distinction.

The same article does concede that "*The Fugitive* has had its defamers here in this city" but argues that that was only to be expected as the group had "set at nothing" the traditions of Southern poetry in particular.[23] Such contemporary reactions to the appearance of *Fugitive* do not always emphasize its special significance in the context of Southern culture as a whole, and while there were always those who saw the magazine as an answer to the Mencken-inspired assault on Southern backwardness and cultural sterility, there is no way in which *Fugitive* and its contributors can be seen as consciously engaged in the debate over the desirable direction of Southern society and culture as a whole. As we have seen, the Fugitive group chose not to emphasize its Southernness. It was their shared interest in poetry that had brought the group together – nothing else. In his recollections of *Fugitive*, written in 1962 and published in *Memories and Essays* (1975), Allen Tate makes explicit the sense in which the group was not concerned about its Southern identity in the years when the magazine was actually being produced: "Not at that time, not in fact until about 1927, did we become consciously historical and sectional."[24]

III

Allen Tate's comment indicates that things changed around 1927. What he means is that in the second half of the 1920s, after the poetry magazine had ceased publication, some – but by no means all – of the original Fugitive group metamorphosed into Southern Agrarians. About them there can be no dispute: John Crowe Ransom, Donald Davidson, Allen Tate, and Robert Penn Warren would all contribute to the Agrarian manifesto *I'll Take My Stand* (1930) and taken together they unquestionably represent the emergence of a powerful force within the South's intellectual life, even though the views they espoused were largely hostile to those of the editors, journalists, academics, and writers who, earlier in the 1920s, had emerged as the New South's intellectual class. In his memoir Tate seems to argue that the potential for the emergence of a Southern consciousness, perhaps even for a defense of Southern tradition, had always existed in the Fugitive group, even though nothing had surfaced at the time:

> I would call the Fugitive an intensive and historical group as opposed to the eclectic and cosmopolitan groups that flourished in the East. There was a sort of unity of feeling, of which we were not then very much aware, which came out of – to give it a big name – a common historical myth.[25]

In fact at the Fugitives' reunion a few years earlier William Y. Elliott, arguing that the Fugitives were a more unified group than similar poetry groups at Oxford, Harvard, and California, had already made this point. But where Tate speaks of a unity of feeling based perhaps on a common historical myth, Elliott emphasizes a sense of community based on a shared regional background plus actual family relationships:

> Now I think undoubtedly there is something in the South, and there is particularly something in the fact that many of us were kin to each other several generations back. I believe I am a distant kinsman of both Johnny (Ransom) and Andrew (Lytle). And we have a sense of community that goes far deeper than probably most people have in that kind of sense – the people who grew up in this region and grew up as boys together, like the Starrs grew up with me.[26]

And Elliott goes on to insist on the key role played in the early Fugitive days by Sidney Hirsch, whose commitment to a dimension of mysticism and philosophy "was one of the most timely bonds among us."[27]

In fact Hirsch's interests seem to have had little or nothing to do with the South or with the state of Southern society and culture, either in the past or the future. And reading the poetry of the Fugitives in their magazine provides little in the way of evidence of either Tate's shared historical myth or Elliott's regional kinship. In other words the gap between the Fugitives' original commitment to poetry, and the subsequent commitment of some of their number to Southern Agrarianism, is perhaps more obvious than is any compelling sense of continuity. Given this situation, one might well ask why is it that the Fugitives have come to be so closely identified with Southern Agrarianism, an ideological movement focused not on literature, but on society and economics? The simple answer is that the identification came about because the members of the original Fugitive group who moved on to become advocates of Southern Agrarianism happened to be those most gifted in purely literary terms: after *Fugitive* ceased to appear in 1925, the poets who went on to make the most significant contribution to America's twentieth-century literary culture were Ransom, Tate, Penn Warren, and Donald Davidson – and all four of these became contributors to the primary manifesto of Southern Agrarianism: *I'll Take My Stand*, published in 1930.

I'll Take My Stand consisted of an introduction headed "A Statement of Principles" followed by twelve essays on different aspects of Southern society and economics. Apart from the four former Fugitives the contributors included two novelists – Stark Young and Andrew Nelson Lytle – two historians – Frank Lawrence Owsley and Herman Clarence Nixon – the poet John Gould Fletcher, a professor of English, John Donald Wade, a journalist, Henry Blue Kline, and Lyle Lanier, a psychologist. All the essays were intended to demonstrate that the Southern tradition, and the Southern way of life, based on its agricultural economy, somehow offered a desirable alternative to the modern, industry-based society that had come to characterize the rest of the

United States. The immediate occasion of the volume was the notorious Scopes trial in Tennessee in 1925. Centered on the issue of teaching evolutionary Darwinism in Tennessee public schools, the trial had brought the South a mass of unwelcome and hostile publicity. A book like the proposed collection of essays would represent a counter-attack against such negative images of the South. John Crowe Ransom suggested that the origins of the book paralleled the origins of *Fugitive*: it emerged naturally out of the discussions and meetings between friends. "Wouldn't it be fair to say," said Ransom, "that the *I'll Take My Stand* group began precisely in the way that the old Fugitive group had begun – with discussions – long before there was a policy?"[28] The title itself, however, taken from "Dixie," that unofficial anthem of the South, was controversial from the first. It was suggested by John Donald Wade, and Ransom and Donald Davidson accepted it. Robert Penn Warren and Allen Tate, however, were not impressed. Tate obviously felt that such a title could be seen as endorsing a kind of Southern atavism. "It is an emotional appeal to ill-defined beliefs," he wrote, "it is a special plea. The essays in the book justify themselves *rationally* by an appeal to principle. It thus falsifies the aims of the book."[29] Tate's objections seem soundly based, but clearly were not allowed to prevail.

What then are we to make of *I'll Take My Stand*? Given that it is no more than a collection of essays by writers from different professional backgrounds and of differing degrees of personal intimacy, it is hardly surprising that the volume's overall coherence is problematic. In Richard Gray's suggestive description the volume, however, "only hovers on the edge of confusion."[30] Perhaps the nature of that potential confusion is best indicated by the uncertainty the reader has over how far *I'll Take My Stand* is about a literal social and historical South, and how far the volume offers an actual economic policy for the future of the South involving both resistance to the industrializing policies of the New South and promotion of the South's existing agrarian tradition. Certainly, some of the essays in the volume make this kind of case. But taken as a whole, *I'll Take My Stand* also advances an alternative argument in which the South of the past, present, and future becomes only a grand metaphor or image of a superior, more civilized community than anything the contributors can discover in the materially obsessed, business-driven, industrialized and spiritually empty Western culture that increasingly surrounds them. In this account *I'll Take My Stand* seems to be more about moral values and religion than history and sociology. These two strands of meaning can of course be read as mutually supportive; but such possible linkage does not eliminate the tension between them.

At the Fugitives' reunion in 1956 those who had gone on to become Southern Agrarians were inclined to play down their commitment to a policy of resisting any kind of change in Southern society or the Southern economy. Part of the problem was their need to show that there was indeed an evolution from their role as Fugitive poets to their role as Agrarians. Inevitably, this was easier to do if the Agrarian movement itself could be defined more in metaphorical than social or historical terms. John Crowe Ransom was ready to agree that the Fugitives had not been much interested in society and politics: "Well now, the Fugitives were very green in public affairs.

I certainly can testify to that for myself. I had very little interest in public affairs."[31] And Allen Tate insisted that for him even the Agrarian policy "never seemed . . . to be a political program."[32] Davidson and Warren were inclined to agree. Davidson's view was that *I'll Take My Stand* "can be taken just as much as a defense of poetry as it can be taken as a defense of the South."[33] For Warren, the book was essentially a form of protest "against certain things: against a kind of de-humanizing and disintegrative effect on your notion of what an individual person could be in the sense of a loss of your role in society."[34] Frank Owsley also saw the volume in terms of what it was repudiating: "Summing up briefly, then, I think our revolt was against materialism – the same thing, in a way, that the Fugitives had revolted against – and against stereotyped forms of living and thinking."[35]

Despite all the protestations, made a quarter of a century after the event, it is impossible to read *I'll Take My Stand* without finding in it not just metaphors of protest but affirmations of the superiority of the historical South and the Southern way of life over the modern alternatives available elsewhere. Donald Davidson's articulation of such views may be seen as representative. Near the beginning of his contribution he insists that plans for the industrialization of the South should be subjected to "a stern criticism," and that "a contrary program, that of an agrarian restoration," should be upheld, because "the South, past and present, furnishes a living example of an agrarian society, the preservation of which is worth the most heroic effort that men can give in a time of crisis."[36] Such questioning of the value of industrializing the South, and endorsing of its agrarian tradition, runs through all of *I'll Take My Stand*. Towards the end of his essay, Davidson also supplies a summary of most of the reasons why the South's agrarian-based civilization is assumed to be superior to the industrial alternative. Having argued that the Civil War itself was essentially a conflict between agrarianism and industrialism, and that the postbellum South, led by such men as Walter H. Page and Henry W. Grady, allowed itself to be temporarily seduced by "'new south' doctrines subversive of its native genius," Davidson suggests that it is only now, at the end of the 1920s, that the South has given "any general promise of following the industrial program with much real consent." And such consent can only be dangerous:

> So far as industrialism triumphs and is able to construct a really "new" South, the South will have nothing to contribute to modern issues. It will merely imitate and repeat the mistakes of other sections. The larger promise of the South is in another direction. Its historic and social contribution should be utilized.

And Davidson goes on to define what the actual "historic and social contribution" of the South is:

> It offers the possibility of an integrated life, American in the older rather than the newer sense. Its population is homogeneous. Its people share a common past, which they are not likely to forget; for aside from having Civil War battlefields at their doorsteps, the

Southern people have long cultivated a historical consciousness that permeates manners, localities, institutions, the very words and cadence of social intercourse. This consciousness, too often misdescribed as merely romantic and gallant, really signifies a close connection with the eighteenth-century European America that is elsewhere forgotten. In the South the eighteenth-century social inheritance flowered into a gracious civilization that, despite its defects, was actually a civilization, true and indigenous, well diffused, well established.

This Southern civilization had other admirable features: "a fair balance of aristocratic and democratic elements," "diversity within unity" "leisureliness, devotion to family and neighborhood, local self-sufficiency and self-government," and of course "the South was agrarian, and agrarian it still remains very largely."[37]

The account of the Southern past that Davidson provides is clearly a highly selective one. Presumably the reader is expected to identify slavery as no more than one of the "defects" that Davidson allows Southern civilization to have possessed. And this is perhaps the point at which to stress that only one of the twelve Southerners who contributed to *I'll Take My Stand* even attempted to address what one might have imagined was the South's most divisive and overwhelmingly significant problem: the place of the African-American community, scarcely two generations away from slavery, within Southern society. Warren's essay, "The Briar Patch," discusses the place of the negro in the modern South, but as far as the other writers are concerned the whole issue is virtually air-brushed out of the picture. And at this early stage in his career, even Warren's essay is hardly a liberal tract. Its tone is indicated by his conclusion, which suggests that the Southern white "wishes the negro well," and "wishes to see crime, genial irresponsibility, ignorance, and oppression replaced by an informed and productive negro community."[38]

Selective or not, Davidson's account of Southern civilization and the Southern tradition touches on almost all the notes that his fellow-contributors underline in their accounts of what it is in the South that needs to be preserved and built upon. In all these accounts Southern agrarianism is superior to industrial capitalism as the basis for a way of life. Industrial capitalism is destructive of human community and thus of the kind of civilization that has flourished in the South. Hence the South's need to resist the siren calls of so-called progress and industrialization. In the words of Herman Clarence Nixon, "it is time for Southerners to say affirmatively that the South must cultivate its provincial soul and not sell it for a mess of industrial pottage, that the section can and should work out its own economic salvation along evolutionary lines." "The human civilization now based on Southern agriculture," he goes on, "is in no little peril, and industrial civilization under the capitalistic system does not offer a satisfying substitute in human values."[39] Stark Young agrees:

> It would be childish and dangerous for the South to be stampeded and betrayed out of its own character by the noise, force, and glittering narrowness of the industrialism and progress spreading everywhere, with varying degrees, from one region to another.[40]

But it is Andrew Nelson Lytle in "The Hind Tit," an essay which sets out in fine detail what the actual life of a Southern farmer following strict agrarian principles would be like, who best encapsulates what dissent from the materialism of the idea of economic progress really means: "A farm is not a place to grow wealthy; it is a place to grow corn." And again: "A stalk of cotton grows. It does not progress."[41]

Perhaps it is in this context of rejection of naive ideas about the inevitable forward march of a scientifically based progressive materialism and industrial capitalism that the Southern Agrarians can be seen as something more than isolated voices of their time and place. The idea that non-industrialized regions of the world could offer a viable alternative to the wasteland vision of modern society, so prevalent in modern art in general, particularly in the post-World War I period, was one that had considerable currency in the early part of the twentieth century. If the characteristic image of so much twentieth-century art is the lonely, isolated, deracinated figure desperately seeking identity and meaning in a contingent, God-abandoned universe, then a return to the traditional values of a region outside the mainstream of modern, industrial society could be seen as offering the artist a possible alternative. Out of a regional context, that is, the civilized values, seen as disappearing or in retreat in the surrounding, dominant culture, might still be affirmed and asserted. Writers as diverse as Hardy, Yeats, Synge, Ford Madox Ford, and D. H. Lawrence may all be seen as regionalists in this precise sense. It is within this regional-minded worldview that Southern Agrarians may be seen as taking their place. As regionalists, they insisted that the South, and the Southern tradition, preserved a way of life in which there was order and stability, the correct adjustment between men and nature, between the individual and his community, which was fast disappearing from the rest of American society. Writing in 1935 of the background to the appearance of *I'll Take My Stand*, Donald Davidson stated: "Uppermost in our minds was our feeling of intense disgust with the spiritual disorder of modern life – its destruction of human integrity and its lack of purpose."[42] Not exactly a feeling unfamiliar in the context of twentieth-century art in general. This is the sense in which Ransom, Tate, Warren, and Davidson can be seen as taking their stand in defense of those values that a great many modern artists have also chosen to defend. And this is the sense in which Davidson in 1956 could insist that "*I'll Take My Stand* was as much a defense of poetry as a defense of the South." But to see the Agrarians as positive regionalists in this way is to give them the benefit of a great many doubts. The region upon which they were apparently taking their stand was much more deeply flawed than they were prepared to admit. As Richard King has said: "Whatever the validity of their critique of the modern world, most of the Agrarians avoided hard questions about the South itself."[43] Avoiding these hard questions is what finally negates the positives of Southern Agrarianism.

I'll Take My Stand nevertheless remains a provocative work. As an actual program for the ordering of society, economics, and politics it has little to offer the South or anywhere else. It is surprisingly Eurocentric. The ideal of the ordered society the Agrarians celebrate seems to originate in an England or France of their imaginations.

Ransom even endorses Scotland's distinctive position within the United Kingdom as a model for the South to follow in the context of the rest of the United States. Yet the volume's attacks on laissez-faire capitalism, on Marxism and industrialism, on rampant materialism, on naive progressivism – as well as its brief vignettes of alternative ways of living – still continue to echo down increasingly eco-conscious decades. *I'll Take My Stand* almost certainly changed nothing in the 1930s South. But contributing to the volume certainly made the creative writers among the Agrarians reassess their role as Southerners. Without Fugitives and Agrarians both, the twentieth-century Southern literary renaissance would have taken longer to emerge.

NOTES

1   Thomas Nelson Page, *The Old South* (New York, 1892), p. 59.
2   See Louis D. Rubin, Jr., *The Writer in the South* (Athens, GA: University of Georgia Press, 1972), pp. 12–13.
3   See Fred C. Hobson, Jr., *Serpent in Eden: H. L. Mencken and the South* (Chapel Hill: University of North Carolina Press, 1974), p. 81.
4   Ibid, p. 81.
5   In his *The Idea of the American South 1920–1941* (Baltimore, MD): Johns Hopkins University Press, 1979), Michael O'Brien agreed that after the Civil War "there were, indeed, few Southern intellectuals" (p. 7).
6   See Hobson, *Serpent in Eden*, p. 30.
7   Ibid, p. 77.
8   Ibid, p. 51.
9   Ibid, pp. 14–15
10 Ibid, p. 18.
11 See Rob Roy Purdy (ed.) *Fugitives' Reunion: Conversations at Vanderbilt May 3–5, 1956* (Nashville, TN: Vanderbilt University Press, 1959), p. 92.
12 See Twelve Southerners, *I'll Take My Stand: The South and the Agrarian Tradition* (New York: Harper Torchbooks, 1962), p. vii.
13 See Merrill Moore, *The Fugitive: Clippings and comment about the magazine and the members of the group that published it* (Boston, MA, 1939), p. 7.
14 Ibid, p. 14.
15 See Hobson, *Serpent in Eden*, p. 73.
16 See Purdy, *Fugitives' Reunion*, p. 132.
17 See Moore, *The Fugitive: Clippings and Comment*, p. 132
18 Ibid, p. 17.
19 Ibid, p. 17.
20 Ibid, p. 30.
21 Ibid, p. 29.
22 Ibid, p. 31.
23 Ibid, pp. 33–5.
24 Allen Tate, *Memoirs and Opinions, 1926–74* (Athens, OH: Ohio University Press, 1975), p. 33.
25 Ibid, p. 33
26 See Purdy, *Fugitives' Reunion*, p. 90.
27 Ibid, p. 91.
28 Ibid, p. 201.

29   See Richard Gray, *Writing the South: Ideas of an American Region* (Baton Rouge: Louisiana State University Press, 1997), p. 128.
30   Ibid, p. 143.
31   See Purdy, *Fugitives' Reunion*, p. 59.
32   Ibid, p. 212.
33   Ibid, p. 181.
34   Ibid, p. 210.
35   Ibid, p. 206.
36   See Twelve Southerners, *I'll Take My Stand*, p. 30.
37   Ibid, pp. 52–4.
38   Ibid, p. 264.
39   Ibid, p. 199.
40   Ibid, p. 328.
41   Ibid, pp. 205, 207.
42   Donald Davidson, "*I'll Take My Stand*: A History," *American Review*, 5 (1935): 309.
43   Richard King, *A Southern Renaissance: The Cultural Awakening of the American South, 1930–1955* (New York: Oxford University Press, 1980), p. 56.

25

William Faulkner

Richard Godden

A Map and a Problem

Early in his unfinished study of Flaubert's life and work, Sartre notes that those engaged in literary lives should begin with a problem, presumably so that a diverse range of writings, biographical events, and historical pressures may be drawn together in what he elsewhere describes as a constellation of difficulty. The problem is the constellation, the constellation maps the life. At first glance, mapping Faulkner is unproblematic. Born in a small town in northern Mississippi (New Albany, 1897), he died in a slightly larger town in northern Mississippi (Oxford, 1962), having lived in Oxford since he was five. Of his nineteen novels all but five are set, in large part, in a notional county (Yoknapatawpha), at whose nub lies Jefferson, spatially and architecturally mirroring Oxford. Non-Yoknapatawpha elements in the fiction may range from Utah (*If I Forget Thee, Jerusalem*, 1939) to Tibet (*A Fable*, 1954), but do so briefly and with intent to return: more typically, material that quits the county does so for Virginia (*Soldiers' Pay*, 1926) or New Orleans (*Mosquitoes*, 1927; *Pylon*, 1935). Indeed, at the back of *Absalom, Absalom!* (1936), Faulkner turns cartographer, identifying his county in terms of the location of his various stories.

Like his fiction, Faulkner traveled but did not depart: to Europe (1925–6); to Los Angeles, spasmodically on screen writing contracts, involving more and less lengthy stays (1932–51); to Stockholm to receive the Nobel Prize (1950), and to Brazil (1954) and Japan (1955), as a cultural envoy for the State Department. The list sketches the pattern of a particular literary life; Paris for youthful modernism; Hollywood for mid-career cash, as the novels went out of print and the short stories commanded insufficient fees; Sweden and the global dimension, when, during the late career, with his idiosyncratic syntax largely stalled, Faulkner's style was misappropriated as Cold War evidence for national "individualism," and the author was caught up in the triumph of US corporate interests as those interests toured the world for markets. But, even in Japan, the interviews address Yoknapatawpha.

The map at the back of *Absalom, Absalom!* remains the best map, particularly if read alongside the Chronology and Genealogy that precede it. Sites like "Sutpen's Hundred," "Old Bayard Sartoris' Bank," or "Compsons where they sold the pasture to the Golf Club so Quentin could go to Harvard," tie place to family name – which names recur across various novels, linking them via traceable genealogies and coherent (if at times erroneous) chronologies. But, as Foucault has noted, "genealogy is for cutting, not for understanding": his point being that the sheer linearity of family trees (such as those scrupulously drawn up for Faulkner by Cleanth Brooks) make plain by excision, using descent to omit awkward matters – the bastard, the servant, the shady deal – upon which a family's life may so often depend.

The core omission on the map, and one that takes me to my mapping problem, is encoded in Faulkner's demographics. In 1936 he lists the population of his county as "Whites 6,298" and "Negroes 9,313," yet none of his storied places features an unambiguously black event. So, tangentially, to my problem; or to two closely linked problems, by way of a version of their solution. Why is it that a continuing strand of Faulkner's characters appear unable to stop talking or to stop thinking, while another and equally persistent strain are vocally impaired and to differing degrees cognitively damaged? The driven talkers seem legion and span the career, from the chattering aesthetes of *Mosquitoes*, through the erotic fantasist Horace Benbow (*Flags In the Dust*, 1973, published in a cut version as *Sartoris*, 1929; and *Sanctuary*, 1931), to Gavin Stevens with his wearied inability to remain silent on virtually any topic (*Intruder in the Dust*, 1948, and *The Town*, 1957). Mute or almost mute idiots arrive early with Donald Mahon, cerebrally maimed in *Soldiers' Pay*, and Benjy Compson, able only to bellow in *The Sound and the Fury* (1929). They persist via Ike Snopes, limited to self-identification as Ike H-mope (*The Hamlet*, 1940), before mutating to holy fools (Sam Fathers, in *Go Down, Moses*, 1942) and silent devils (Flem Snopes, in the Snopes trilogy, 1940–59); the last two assume a taciturnity tantamount to vocal impairment, though for very different reasons.

One explanation for the talkers who talk too much or too little is to be found in Addie Bundren's diagrammatic dismissal of voice, in her section of *As I Lay Dying* (1930), one of the 59 monologues, from 15 viewpoints, that make up the novel. On her deathbed, Addie notes:

> I would think how words go straight up in a thin line, quick and harmless, and how terribly doing goes along the earth, clinging to it, so that after a while the two lines are too far apart for the same person to straddle from one to the other. (117)

Her geometry proposes that language is "just sounds" having little relation to action or "doing." As "vessel[s]" "profoundly without life" (116), signifiers cannot contain their signifieds, so that when Addie thinks of her family, "*Anse*...*Cash* and *Darl*...Their names would die and solidify into a shape and then fade away...And I couldn't think *Anse*, couldn't remember *Anse*" (117). Here, the substance of the sign puts at risk the very person or referent it nominates, before, itself, fading away.

Modernism, Language, and Shopping

The dematerialization of the sign, predominantly as signified but in Addie's instance also as signifier, is a key feature of Anglo-American modernism, prefigured by Mallarmé and the French Symbolists, and variously exemplified by Joyce's linguistic turn(s), Eliot's espousal of difficulty, Imagism's instruction, "direct treatment of the thing," and Hemingway's allied mistrust of abstraction and veneration for the concrete. Faulkner translated Verlaine (four poems in 1920), took Mallarmé's title, "L'Apres Midi D'un Faun," read *Ulysses* (probably in 1924), and borrowed sustainedly from *The Waste Land* and from Hemingway. Yet Addie's dispersal of the referent and Faulkner's more general and apparent mistrust of language (his talkers tend just to talk, while his mutes are associated with moral value), do not finally fit the modernist model.

J. M. Bernstein (1995) offers a useful summation of those modernist poetics in which Faulkner was so thoroughly grounded, noting of modernist work that it "continually disclaims itself," in order to offer "a thematics of writing which operates a refusal of representation" (166, 167). One inflection of modernist scholarship would add that representation is refused because the things represented have changed; most notably, they have been priced and placed in the shop-windows of a burgeoning commodity culture. In 1929 Helen and Robert Lynd noted of their representative small American city, Middletown, "more and more of the aspects of living are coming to be strained through the bars of a dollar sign" (1929: 81); as bodies pass through those bars, by way of the consumption imperative, they are transformed. Put crudely, during the first third of the twentieth century, American culture became a culture orientated increasingly to "the viewpoint of exchange" (Haug 1986: 15), where the seller's view is the pervasive view. Seen from the perspective of sale, things and their consumers grow double bodied. Haug argues that, for the seller, an object's use is a "transitory phase" or "lure," existing merely to accomplish the vital activity of exchange. For this to happen, the use of objects and persons must be subordinated to their appearance, in advertising terms, to their capacity to carry an image. It follows that any commodity's function as part of someone's needs is secondary to that item's ability to propose a "promise of use," ensuring purchase. In effect, "use," taken to market, atrophies, becoming a promissory "appearance of use" or "impression of use" (12–44). What I, care of Haug, am calling atrophy of use, amounts to a receding referent and good cause for modernism's mistrust of those signs, objects, and persons caught up in modernity.

Faulkner knows as much and is critically responsive to the expansion of consumerism with its offers of a "capitalist reality" (Marchand 1985: xviii) constructed from promise and wish. To read *If I Forget Thee, Jerusalem* (1939) is to watch the failed attempt of Harry and Charlotte to live outside the theatre of just such an economy. Indeed, Faulkner turns the working of that economy against his own writing: he wrote his first book, *Marionettes* (a brief poetic drama), six times in long hand.

Marionettes reappear in *If I Forget Thee, Jerusalem* as show-puppets, "almost as large as small children" (556), blasted with syphilis and being made by Charlotte (a sometime New Orleanian shop-window dresser) for magazine covers. Plainly, by 1939, Faulkner has his doubts about the use of an artist's work, and the efficacy of the handmade in an age of accelerating mass consumption.

But Middletown is Muncie, Indiana; and during the 1920s and 1930s the South remained predominantly rural and low waged, in a predominantly industrializing and high-waged national economy. Rural workers, black and white, tended, during the first three decades of the century, not to own the land they worked. As tenants, they lived on credit out of the commissary store, a debt paid, or left owing, from an agreed share of the crop, at the growing season's close. Not being paid in cash, tenants lacked the means to become consumers. State statistics are revealing: during the 1920s and 1930s in Mississippi, a smaller percentage of the population owned radios and telephones, possessed registered motor vehicles, or used electricity in their homes, than in any other state. Last in state listing for per capita wealth, its figures for per capita retail sales were 34 percent of the national average. Given the economy of Mississippi, and of Yoknapatawpha county, Mississippi, modernist explanations of Faulkner's modernist mistrust of language are unpersuasive.

Labor, Language, and Modernism

Why then do so many of Faulkner's narrators find it so difficult to stop talking, and why do several of his mutes carry the attributes of Christ? One answer, at least to the first part of the problem, and at least for the long decade of Faulkner's major work (1929–42), lies encoded in the map at the back of *Absalom, Absalom!* Just as, demographically, the county is predominantly black yet, by weight of story, predominantly white, so the narrators of Sutpen's story go on about Sutpen and his very white house because they know, but cannot acknowledge, that Sutpen, his house, the plantocracy, and they as its descendants and inheritors (Shreve excepted) are created by black work. Put aphoristically, the white narrators and their subjects are blacks in white face, talking about much except what they know – their own dependency on a bound population who make them what they are. But I run ahead of myself, without offering the ghost of an argument.

Glossing even the plot of Faulkner's most canonical and modernist text is hard: *Absalom, Absalom!* tells the story of Sutpen, five times. Three versions are framed and revised by Quentin Compson in conversation with his Harvard roommate, Shreve, the fifth teller. Circa 1827, Sutpen, a poor white from west Virginia, quits his family as they migrate into the Delta. Arriving in the West Indies, he puts down an uprising among slaves on a French sugar plantation on Haiti. As due recompense, he marries the owner's daughter and achieves a son (1829). For reasons unspecified, but much speculated upon, he sets the marriage aside – eventually reaching northern Mississippi with a handful of Haitian slaves and sufficient capital to "buy" a hundred square miles of Indian land. A marriage and a plantation are made, only for the denied and (by Sutpen) never acknowledged son of the first liaison (Charles Bon) to come to the door, court the daughter, and bring the house down. Incest and miscegenation did it, at least according to the five narrators as they work through, fill in, and guess at the story. Much is fabricated, compulsively and at length, but the impact of Bon is central and reiterated.

The name "Bon" deserves annotation. Quentin Compson, citing his father and his father's father on the subject of naming, notes, "Father said he [Sutpen] probably named him himself Charles Bon. Charles Good ... Grandfather believed, just as he named them all – the Charles Goods and the Clytemnestras" (219–20). Bon: Good: Goods – the pun is cruelly obvious yet it remains critically unheard. That single syllable retains the novel: retains rather than contains, because "Bon" makes its subterranean narratives available by withholding them. We are told little about why Sutpen repudiated his first born, beyond a reference to a first wife's Spanish blood (208) in its capacity to "mock" his "design" (218). If "Spanish" is a euphemism for "dark" and so for "African," as seems likely on Haiti, then Bon is black, and would technically and in antebellum Mississippi be a slave. Hence his repudiation, on grounds of an initial and unwitting miscegenation, later compounded by his proposed witting and incestuous miscegenation – or so runs the disputed and combined argument of the five narrators (as revised by Shreve and Quentin). Except that Sutpen's transmission of the name "Bon" suggests that at some level blood, whether Spanish or African, is a false clue, and that the planter set his son aside (in the last instance) for proprietorial reasons; because in him he recognized his own white property (that substantive "good" which makes him a master) as black "goods." The recognition that white owners are all but black is, of course, unbearable to those who own, and must be put aside ... but must return (as does Bon), being inherent in the labor structure of the planter's substance. Put another way: should the Southern planter absolutely deny that which makes him what he is (his "good" in the form of his "goods"), he will cease to be Southern, and ceasing to be what he is – he will die. Witness what happens when Henry Sutpen kills his half-brother Bon at the gates to the Hundred in 1865. Since Henry is his father's heir, and the murderer of his father's (and of his own) substance (Bon), he must die. Having killed that which makes him, he does indeed vanish – much to the consternation of the narrators – returning, all but a corpse, to the ruined shell of the Hundred, to die in 1909.

Generically speaking, Sutpen shares the conundrum of a Southern owning class which founds itself on constrained labor. Again, the conundrum runs: if the white "good" of the owning class depends on the "goods" that the black makes, the owning class must deny it, while retaining that "good" (that Bon) in which their very substance resides. I would stress that the narrators of Sutpen's story (with the honorable exception of the Canadian, Shreve) are all inheritors of planter property (Quentin's Harvard place is paid for by the sale of land deriving from plantation wealth). They, like their subject, are caught in class contradiction: their substance, whether as body, property, land, or language, is haunted by black labor, a shade that must be repressed *and* embraced. Their solution is stylistic – a way of talking which buries the bound man alive in the language of those who own. Dead and buried, the bound man conceals the master's means to mastery. Alive and acknowledged, he troubles the master's independent consciousness. As a linguistic presence (a revenant *in language*), operating at the lower levels of the narrator's consciousness, and consequently at the outer reaches of his or her language, the bound man's trace (*almost* readable) ensures that the consciousness of the class (and of its narrators) will retain its peculiar substance. The word "Bon" is just such a revenant in language: keeping the "goods" hidden in the "good" and obscuring both by translation.

Such an account faces at least a double objection: that it overrates the capacity of a "peculiar" economic system to bind and blend black and white, and that consequently it ignores alternative sources of ethnic interdependency – most notably the region's sexual pathology (so much the substance of what the narrators have to say). The first objection may be briefly and historically met. Mark Tushnett, a historian of slave law, draws a useful distinction between "partial relations" in a free market and "total relations" under slavery (1981: 6). His point is that where wages are paid, employer – employee connections are partial: because the wage payer pays only for the working part of a worker's day, the ties that bind are limited. Within the "peculiar institution," relations between binder and bound extend to the whole life of the slave and through the whole life of the master – dependency is absolute. Moreover, the dominance of dependency for the culture should not be attributed simply to the region under slavery. The net effect of the Emancipation Proclamation (1863) was to modify rather than to dispense with the binding of black labor in the South.

Defeated in war, the plantocracy did not lose its lands to redistribution; instead, it revived the plantation mode of production under newly coercive rules, rules that, in the words of the labor historian Jay Mandle (1992), left black workers "not slave... not free." Chattel slavery gave way to sharecropping, a system whereby landowners constrained tenants (black and white) by debt. Dependency persisted from the antebellum South through the premodern (because "not free") South of the 1930s. *Absalom, Absalom!*, a book about a planter, may be read as expressive of the cognitive consequences of a labor-driven ethnic inseparability for the South's landowning class in 1936.

Race, Sex, and Cultural Pathology

Yet it remains the case that the narrators of *Absalom, Absalom!* cannot stop talking about incest and miscegenation, topics which I have cast as their way of *not* talking about labor. Undoubtedly, sexual pathologies that turn on racial typing feature widely in Faulkner's writing. *The Sound and the Fury* (1929) may be taken as exemplary, not least because it enables me to address the cultural sources of Faulkner's enduring preoccupation with forms of sexual crossing, while eventually making a case for the connection between sexuality and economy. In addition, the novel features

Faulkner's "star" idiot, and so allows the recovery of the second strand of my initiatory problem. Benjy, among other things, is mute and (like Christ at the time of his death) thirty-three on the day of his interior monologue. Like *Absalom, Absalom!*, *The Sound and the Fury* consists of multiple narratives: three brothers (Benjy, Quentin, and Jason Compson) take a section each to think about a sister (Caddy), and more particularly about her virginity and its loss. A fourth section is narrated by an authorial voice. That the sister's hymen is the text's focal object is made plain by Faulkner's accounts of the novel's source. On several occasions he insists that the novel began with a mental or "symbolical . . . picture" of Caddy's soiled undergarments up a tree; under which tree, two brothers watch the stained drawers ascend (Stein 1987: 240). All of which begs the question, "Why should a sister's hymen matter quite so much?"

From a first reading of *The Sound and the Fury* it is clear that each of the brothers has difficulties getting over his sister; her "honor" and its loss is central to them all. I have space only to outline the case: Benjy frequently shares Caddy's bed, at least until he is thirteen, and bellows at her departure. Quentin spends a fair part of his Cambridge day trying to restore an immigrant girl to her parental house; he calls her "sister," and in memory circles back to events surrounding Caddy's protracted loss of "honor." He appears to believe that incest might serve if not to heal the hymen at least to involve the incestuous pair in shame so great as to "isolate" them from "the loud world" (101). For Jason, too, the question of a sister's virginity is inseparable from incest. He must have noticed that Caddy chose to call her fatherless child Quentin. Fearing that his niece is "too much like" her mother (262), he insists on at least a semblance of respectability, but his sanctions are no match for her kimono: "I'll be damned if they don't dress like they were trying to make every man they passed on the street want to reach out and clap his hand on it" (232). The three brothers, with very different degrees of self-consciousness, "want to reach out" to their sister. Strangely, doing so involves each of them in forms of more or less recognized miscegenation.

Benjy becomes "bluegum": confronted with evidence of Caddy's loss of virginity, and only apparently lacking cognitive control over time, he immediately turns to a scene in which he is told about second-hand impregnation among bluegums:

> Caddy came to the door and stood there . . . I went towards her, crying, and she shrank back against the wall and I saw her eyes and I cried louder and pulled at her dress. Her eyes ran.
>
> *Versh said, Your name Benjamin now. You know how come your name Benjamin now. They making a bluegum out of you. Mammy say in old time your granpaw changed nigger's name, and he turn preacher, and when they look at him, he bluegum too. Didn't use to be bluegum, neither. And when family woman look him in the eye in the full of the moon, chile born bluegum.* (69)

Late in the summer of 1909 Caddy lost her virginity. Benjy recognizes the loss – an insight which need not involve mysterious intuition – Caddy's eyes are probably moving far too fast. Upon discovering her loss Benjy goes back almost nine years to November 1900, when his name was changed. The shift appears to have no mechanical trigger, yet there is evidence of a narrow imagination producing at least partially conscious comparisons. Caddy's sexual change is associated with Benjy's name change in an essentially cultural analogy involving two impurities: loss of virginity is likened to loss of a first or maiden name. In effect, Benjy counters a disturbing insight by recalling a particular story about multiple names. A Mississippi bluegum is a black conjuror with a fatal bite. Versh's bluegum has the additional gift of magic eyes, a gift that seems to have resulted directly from a name change. Simply by looking at his congregation the bluegum preacher can make them all, even unborn children, bluegum too. As a bluegum, Benjy can look into Caddy's shifty eyes and reimpregnate her in an innocent incest which involves no penetration. According to the story, Benjy is the father of Caddy's child. That Benjy should play bluegum at this precise moment suggests that even a person with a mental age of perhaps three, albeit in a 33-year-old body, knows the preplots of his time. By means of a black mask Benjy, at some level, intends to get his sister back.

Quentin's desire for incest is altogether more articulate; nonetheless it too is shadowed by intimations of miscegenation. By contemplating sex with his sister he joins the other suitors, all of whom are "blackguards" (the epithet is carefully chosen and much repeated). To elevate the presence of the word "black" within "blackguard" into a case for the interdependency of white and black male potency may look like ingenuity of the worst kind. However, Quentin cannot divorce his own sense of Caddy's sexuality from the sexuality of black women: "*Caddy? Why must you do like nigger women do in the pasture the ditches the dark woods hot hidden furious in the dark woods*" (92). Given that Caddy acts like "nigger women" in "the dark woods," it follows that those who come to her may well be "dark" or even "black," and so deserving of the term "blackguard." A similar fear of racial crossing haunts Jason's recognition that Miss Quentin is of his "flesh and blood." Both Mrs. Compson and Caddy use this phrase when urging him to support his niece (181, 209), and in each case the wording triggers, within the space of a page, metaphoric acts whereby Jason is associated with a "slave" because he works so hard. Once used, the term sticks. The "slave" Jason is attracted to his niece, whom he likens to "a nigger wench" (189), believing that she "act[s] like [a] nigger" (181) because "it's in her blood" (232). Since he shares her blood, it is a short step from his claim that "blood always tells" (181) to the recognition that what it tells may be a tale of mixed race. He does not take this step, however, perhaps because the blood that beats in his head gives him blackouts.

"Slave" thus joins "bluegum" and "blackguard" as covert forms of blackface, by means of which the brothers achieve displaced penetration of their sister. I have traced these submerged plots through the novel's verbal latencies to suggest how, for the brothers, the sister's hymen is also a color line. In taking Caddy's virginity, no matter at what distance, each of them, metaphorically, turns "black"... but why? Any reading of Jim Crow establishes that a fearful conjunction of race and sex disturbed the Southern white imagination during what has been called the Radical era (1889–1915). Faulkner was born in 1897, Quentin in 1891, Jason two years later, and Benjy two years after that. The creator and his characters grew out of a period of acute and specific racism, during which white and black sexuality became inextricable. Until the black, the virgin, and the incestuous brother are put into the Black Belt at the turn of the century, their centrality for Faulkner will not be understood. To make the case that Faulkner's plots lie in the Southern politics of race and gender (1890s–1910s), a brief history of that racial pathology is necessary. To the conservative Southern mind the end of slavery in 1865 posed a key problem: how to position blacks in their organic place (at the bottom, as the hands of the system) without the educational benefits of the benevolent institution of slavery. "Freed," the black "child" could all too easily turn against the recently sustaining father (the antebellum planter as patriarch). By the mid-1880s the problem appeared to have worsened, in that a generation of young blacks was coming to manhood without the "civilizing" effects of slavery. All of which prepared the way for the rise of the Radical mentality, which signaled the South's "capitulation to racism" between 1890 and 1915. Whereas the conservative sought to "protect" and "preserve" blacks by assigning them their proper place in the "natural order," the Radical was obsessed with the failure of that order. He feared that the angelic black child of slavery, released from the school of the peculiar institution, was becoming the demonic black adult of freedom. To the Radical, the weaponry of Jim Crowism (disenfranchisement, segregation, lynching) supplied the only means to subordinate blacks as they degenerated. One image especially focused the issue of black regression: "the black beast rapist." Joel Williamson makes the case that, faced with a deepening agricultural depression and the failure of political action to foster economic reform, white Southerners turned to racial action as an area in which they might at least appear to be managing their lives. Neither Faulkner nor the Compson children would have escaped apprenticeship to Radicalism's pathologies. Williamson notes:

> When they were through with the Radical era, there was hardly a facet of life in the South in which the whites had failed to respond to the black presence, and the nature of that response gave Southern white culture in the twentieth century its basic shape. (Williamson 1984: 318)

White self-images turned on the image of the black male. The plot runs as follows: during the antebellum period, Southern white males of the owning class idealized womanhood, by raising the female gentry on pedestals above the reality of interracial sex between slave women and slaveowners. In the words of one Southern historian, the white woman became "the South's Palladium... – the shield-bearing Athena gleaming whitely in the clouds, the standard of its rallying... She was the lily-pure maid of Astolat... And – she was the pitiful Mother of God" (Cash 1971: 89). By means of propriety, husbands, fathers, and sons whitewashed their property and its sustaining institutions. The cult of Southern womanhood raised the standard of the unbreachable hymen precisely because miscegenation breached the color line throughout the prewar South. Plainly, if the iconic figure was to withstand the iconoclastic force of the realistic evidence, it needed support – support which white males found in the incest dream. Where the hymen stores the family "blood," protecting it from any risk of contamination through crossing, incest ensures that where crossing has occurred it shall be between like "bloods."

As the pathology whitened key whites, it blackened key blacks, producing a mythological dark couple, the woman as sexual "earth mother" and the man as "black beast rapist." Emancipation had changed the obsessional map. Freeing the slaves blocked white access to the quarters. In the white mind, since the "freed" man now served the libidinous black female, his nature shifted from child ("sambo") to satyr. By definition a satyr cannot be sated, and, unsated, he will necessarily seek the white women earlier denied him. Within this pervasive fantasy, white men, having impeded their own intimacy with white women, projected onto the black male extravagant and guilt-free versions of the sexual behavior they were condemning and denying to themselves.

By 1915, Radicalism was dead as a political idea, but not before its plots had entangled those raised among its extremities. Witness the sexual and narrative habits of the Compson brothers, each of whom attempts to enter his sister (or some version of her) in an incest that will shore up the integrity of his family and class, but can do so only in blackface, since white potency is inextricable from black forms. Of the three, Benjy's consciousness best preserves the sister's purity since his minimal linguistic options ensure that she remains uncomplicated, while a fragmented temporality allows him to keep her to himself, in or near childhood. Of the some 106 bits of underorientated time making up his interior monologue, the majority occur prior to 1910, the year in which she lost her virginity. Given that Benjy can be in 1898, as Caddy climbs the tree, or in 1910 as Caddy marries, and prefers to be as close as possible to the former – he can, in effect, regrow his sister's hymen. Such a reconstruction of sororial innocence is abetted by linguistic poverty. Benjy is the ideal bolt-hole for the hymen and for the values that it embodies, hence Faulkner's decision to start *The Sound and the Fury* from his perspective. Within Benjy, and for Faulkner as his vocalist, white and black can all but be kept apart, in the teeth of the region's sustained and fearful experience of their ethnic codependency.

The Pathology Deconstructed

Faulkner's post-publication statements indicate that he intended to tell the Compson story from within a single consciousness, but failed; adding viewpoints one after another to produce what he describes as his "most splendid failure." That "failure" is ensured by his decision to follow Benjy's day with Quentin's, insofar as Quentin acts as the historian of the very pathology whose "utopian" aspect structures Benjy's muteness. The case for Quentin as analyst of that which the iconic hymen represses can only be sketched.

At the close of June Second, 1910, Quentin, a freshman at Harvard, kills himself by jumping into the Charles River. An adolescent suicide, the critical consensus blames him for his repetitive, deeply incoherent, and rigidly fixed patterns of memory. Behind the unflattering portrait lie two commonplaces. The first is that for all readers June Second is oppressively the day of its narrator's death; the second assumes Quentin's inability to transcend the past by means of the present. Sartre's is the most famous statement of this temporal trap. Since "everything has already happened," Quentin can only and compulsively repeat a past which "takes on a sort of super reality" (Sartre 1987: 255). I have my doubts about both assumptions. Quentin's day is filled with much more than provision for suicide: first, second, and third time readers may well find that the flatiron purchase pales in significance before the Boston Italian community, child abduction, court cases, and Caddy. The consensus might counter that the events of the busy day are directed to the terminal event, insofar as they replay obsessions centered on incest. Such a case rests on a particular version of "repetition" in which any event is a "substitute" bound by a chain of substitutions to an original object. Although not denying that the section features high levels of analogy, as Quentin moves mentally between Boston and Mississippi, I would nevertheless argue that analogy involves radical revision rather than repetition.

Quentin experiences the Boston Italian community as central to his day. Encountering a seemingly lost Italian girl, he struggles to find her family. When he calls that child "sister" he creates for himself an "enigma" with which the immigrant girl's proximity (her smell for instance) and Caddy's remoteness (the odor of honeysuckle) both resist and yield to one another; their compatibility rests on incompatibilities of class, race, time, and odor which will not lapse into resemblance (before passing from resemblance to repetition). Rather, the "sister" is a disturbing hybrid that creates for Quentin a conceptual need to challenge earlier versions of what sisters are and do. Where the Southern sister could (at least for a time, and at least in Quentin's head) be subjected to a "flame" that would "clean" her hymen (176), her Northern counterpart is dirtied with industrial fires (her face is "streaked with coal dust": 147). My point is that, on looking at the unnamed immigrant child, he does not see Caddy, he sees the collapse of what Caddy meant to him. Whereas, in the South, the very idea of incest involves a form of cultural heroism – raising the standard of the virgin – in the North, Quentin's return to that idea is deemed child-molestation, worthy of a six dollar fine. Quentin, accused of interfering with his charge, is taken before a local magistrate.

The main events of the Italian subplot turn on the arrest and trial, prior to which Quentin's habits of mind and language tended to warrant critical unkindness. His thoughts were often claustrophobic and almost impenetrably private. However, his day, centering on the public accusation that he has molested a child, features a clear shift in mental habit. At every point, events leading up to the trial and the trial itself form an external representation of an inner drama (the incest fable), in which Southern tragedy, relocated, comes back as a Northern farce that precipitates Quentin into historical revision. Externalization does not involve a return of the repressed, but rather requires that Quentin see key scenes in the regional fantasy of his class from below. Caddy, a somewhat soiled Palladium, becomes a dirty immigrant girl; the South's aristocratic champion, still "Galahad," albeit "half-baked" (110), reappears in the guise of an Italian worker, as worried about wages as about family; the judicial father – aptly named Squire – recomposes the Southern patriarch as a barely literate figure who writes in something resembling "coal dust" (142).

During the second half of June Second, Quentin dismantles his own historical model. Time reemerges from the archetypes of a particular cultural pathology and the creative responsibilities of the historian begin. Those responsibilities are finally beyond him because, with the sustaining narrative of one "was," that of redemptive incest, gone, he has no meaningful context in which to place his new information. At a loss for history, not oppressed by it, he kills himself.

The events of Quentin's day give him good reason to break from cultural appren-ticeship to a pathology associated with the sister's honor. By revising a sister and the space of white sexuality structured by her image, he gains an alternative sister and loses himself. Yet Faulkner reverses the suicide, resurrecting Quentin to frame the narratives of *Absalom, Absalom!* As a trainee historian of a Southern pathology, Quentin comes primed to struggle with the labor trauma from whose awkward ethnic proximities the region's racialized sexual pattern arise.

Agricultural Revolution and the Loss of a Subject

Much of what I have said rests on the determining force of a coercive regime of accumulation, grounding a premodern culture of dependency. But during the second half of the 1930s the regional form of labor, which in binding the black to the land bound him also to the land's lord, was transformed. A revolution in labor use, driven by federal funds, effectively exorcised black from white. To read sociological commen-tators in the 1930s addressing Southern agriculture, is to hear black tenants described as "virtual slaves," held "in thrall" and subject to "almost complete dependence, (Johnson 1934: 11, 4). The postbellum agricultural worker lived most typically under forms of constraint, at least until New Deal programs unbound him from the white owner. The historian Jonathan Wiener (1979) describes provisions put in place by the Agricultural Adjustment Administration (1933–42) as constituting the South's "second Civil War," during which masters were freed from mastery to become employers who paid a wage, and the unfree were freed to become un- or under-employed. Between 1933 and 1938 the influx of federal funds into the South produced systematic eviction and enclosure, while drastically increasing both cropper mobility and regional out-migration. Between 1933 and 1940 the Southern tenantry declined by more than 25 percent. All of which occurred as Faulkner wrote *Absalom, Absalom!* Economically, black and white were taken apart, one consequence of which was that white need never be as black again. Another and literary consequence was that Faulkner lost his problem, and with it a central tension from which much of his major work was forced.

Working briefly on two of Faulkner's more crucial post-1940 texts, I shall use my final sections to explore his reaction to losing the generative subject of so much of his writing. Declining powers and increased drinking, explanatory aphorisms concerning late Faulkner, do scant justice to the works in question. In *Go Down, Moses* (1942) Faulkner interweaves short stories, preoccupied, in large part, with different ways of taking value from Southern land. One strand, focusing on Lucas Beauchamp, a black worker, engages with cropping and the plantation; another, dealing with Ike McCaslin, a member of the plantocracy who has set aside his inheritance, addresses hunting and the big woods. The proprietorial position of Beauchamp exactly expresses Faulkner's difficulty in situating black and white after their separation by economic change.

Lucas, the descendant of a miscegenous union between the planter Lucius Quintus Carothers McCaslin and a slave, Tomasina (Lucas's grandmother and Lucius's granddaughter), works as a tenant on the Carothers plantation. Faulkner specifies that he does not own the land he works. The current owner attempts systematically to manage Lucas's labor: that Lucas ignores all such advice, does not mean that he works as a free economic agent. Yet we are assured that he has over three thousand dollars banked in Jefferson (in part a "legacy" against guilt, paid by the McCaslin estate). Financially "free," Lucas chooses to labor within "unfree" forms. He is a contradiction in terms — committed to "unfree" structures of feeling, while possessed of access to their displacement. To compound his unlikely economic and emotional hybridity, by day he attends to his crop, while by night he seeks to extract buried treasure from an Indian mound, with the aid of a metal detector. The residual or prehistoric (the mound) and the emergent or modernistic (the machine, "efficient and business-like and complex with knobs and dials": 63) meet and clash in his activity. In effect, Lucas is an anomaly whose creation allows Faulkner to retain his subject (dependency) even as he faces aspects of those forces (cash and technology) that have displaced it.

Ike McCaslin compounds Lucas's archaism via an impulse to regress from the racialized problematic of Southern history as a whole. In repudiating his inheritance and retreating as often as possible to the big woods, Ike turns from human history (embodied in his grandfather's sexual abuse of bound labor) and towards nature (represented in the hunting camp). In effect, he would recast himself as a natural, being aided in this by an education in wilderness skills, care of Sam Fathers, whose ancestry is part Chickasaw, part black, and part white (with an emphasis on the Native American strain). Revisiting Sam Fathers' burial plot, where the bones of a dog and a bear's paw intermingle with the corpse, "not in earth, but of earth... Myriad, one" (244), Ike almost treads on a snake, "more than six feet of it... and old" (246). He experiences double vision, so that the snake exists in two times: in the time of the story's setting (circa 1888) and in a prehistoric space marked by spectral evidence of rudimentary limbs:

> The elevation of the head did not change as it began to glide away from him, moving erect yet off the perpendicular as if the head and that elevated third were complete and all: an entity walking on two feet and free of all laws of mass and balance and should

have been because even now he could not quite believe that all that shift and flow of shadow behind that walking head could have been one snake. ("The Bear": 245)

It should be recalled that in Genesis the serpent went "upon [its] belly" only after God's discovery of its offense: prior to the Fall, possessed of its own feet, it too was unfallen. Ike, "without premeditation," addresses the monster as "Chief," "Grandfather" (245). His attribution is genealogically interesting, and open to at least three interpretations. Strictly speaking, if Ike is addressing a serpentine grandfather, and since Theopholus McCaslin or Uncle Buck is his biological father, we must assume that he casts his grandfather, Lucius Quintus Carothers McCaslin, as the snake that, historically speaking, he very much was. The bestial name fits, but its Chickasaw form, tone, and unfallen accessories suggest that Ike has a different grandfather in mind. Let us assume that, given Sam Fathers as an adopted father, Ike looks through the reptile to Sam's father, Ikkemotubbe, also known as Du Homme/The Man. But this option is not without problems. Ikkemotubbe was a poisoner who fell from the grace of his Indian title, to be called Doom: in which case, he too is just too beastly to warrant prelapsarian markers. A third genealogy can be traced from the name: let us suppose that Ike, "speaking the old tongue which Sam had spoken" (245), speaks for, or as though he were, his mentor, Sam. If so, the line would run from Sam to Ikkemotubbe, The Man/Doom. Since the most doomed man is Adam, and Adam's father is God, Ike in addressing his grandfather (through Sam) is talking to God. There is, however, an ancillary option: Sam's Chickasaw name means Had-Two-Fathers, one Indian, the other quadroon slave. It follows that, in order to talk to God, with Sam's tongue and via a divine snake, Ike must both revise Genesis *and* suppress an alternative black lineage (with its attendant history). Ike's projections and omissions are complex: he becomes an ethnically cleansed Sam so that he may project, through the mulch where Sam lies with the animals, a revisionist reptile. The snake contains post- and prelapsarian times; but Ike's "Oleh" renders the earth rife with Eden, into which Ike, by way of Sam's word, all but degenerates. His archaic usage allows him to regress along a genealogical line to its fount – discovering an alternative Grandfather, happy as God to make men from prelapsarian mud.

The ingenuity of Ike's self-revision should not disguise its moral and political evasiveness. Faulkner recognizes Ike's dubiety (see "Delta Autumn") but, as with Benjy, he remains imaginatively drawn to simpletons among whose perceptual and cognitive processes he may bury secrets of elusive and narrowed value – an innocent grandfather, a virgin land, a hymenial sister. Skeptical appraisal of such opaque residues does not entirely disperse their affective power.

An Allegory for Modernity

Between 1943 and 1954 Faulkner worked on what he considered would be his *magnum opus*. *A Fable* is, arguably, his last "great" book. An allegory, set during

World War I and addressing the Cold War, it is, bar a single section, located outside the South, predominantly in France, but with forays into Africa (Senegal), Asia (Tibet), and Eastern Europe (Poland). One small strand is set in Alabama. One character, briefly central, is black. In his discussion of Walter Benjamin's version of allegory, Max Pensky (1993) notes, "the allegorical mode of apprehension always arises from a devalued appearance world"; or, as Benjamin would have it, "the heart of the allegorical way of seeing involves the recognition that, everything about history . . . is expressed . . . in a death's head . . . Because death digs most deeply the jagged line of demarcation between physical nature and significance" (1977: 165).

Faulkner turns to the painfully protracted creation of a global allegory at the historical moment when *his* South, held together by issues of dependency, comes apart; when its incoherently cohering center, a regime of accumulation founded on coerced labor, is abruptly modernized by a regional shift towards a waged economy. The Snopes trilogy, consisting of *The Hamlet* (1940), *The Town* (1957), and *The Mansion* (1959), may be read as Faulkner's attempt to trace the slow rise of a new and monied bourgeoisie, a proto-professional middle class of urban officials, bankers, and pornographers – but *A Fable* stands as his most considered and melancholic response to Yoknapatawpha's and his own drastic loss of meaning.

The allegory is timetabled around Passion Week, and turns on a mutiny whose leader is marked for Christ. Late in May 1918, at the instigation of one man, who converted twelve, a division of French foot soldiers disobey an order to attack. Their refusal initiates a ripple effect along both lines of trenches, so that the "whole front stopped" and by sundown "there was no more gunfire in France" (676). The ripple has an economic extension, in that the unexpected cessation of hostilities threatens to stop military production. One allusion will have to serve for sustained argument. General Granyon, commander of the mutinous regiment, has a systemic sense of a single bullet. For Granyon, the bullet that each of his three thousand men deserves is the structural cornucopia of militarized production. One bullet contains, among other things, his military training, the mining, smelting, and munitions industries, prime ministers, cabinet members, board chairmen, bankers, lobbyists . . . The single sentence detailing what makes a bullet runs for virtually two pages (880–1).

Granyon and Faulkner comply with C. Wright Mills, who in 1956 was to argue that "war lords," "corporate chieftains," and the nation's political executive had formed a "power elite," whose interlocking directorates were responsible for "the great structural shift of modern American capitalism toward a permanent arms economy" (123). The figures at mid-century were compelling: since the run-up to war in 1941, the element of the national budget marked for military purposes had not dropped below 30 percent. By 1954, 85 percent of government expenditure on research (some two billion dollars – twenty times the prewar rate) was for "national security." But if the structure of a "national security" state was to work, military production had to continue to be devalued by use: in effect, the mutiny instructs the old Marshal (Allied Supreme Commander) in how to "fix" armaments so that they can continue to be made, perhaps forever. In order to ensure a conference with his German equivalent, he has to tamper with munitions along a lengthy sector of the allied front. At his order, shells are disarmed in secret so that the enemy's commander can fly across allied lines, be shot at from the air and remain unharmed. The greater good of militarized production requires that enemies meet: at that meeting, they agree (presumably) to fire on their own men, if and where any subsequent mutiny breaks out. The runner (John the Baptist to the corporal's Christ) initiates a second refusal, taken up by French and German troops. As the mutineers approach one another across no-man's land, they produce no serial ripple because they are immediately shelled from both sides. Continuing hostility and war production are thereby ensured.

The old Marshal's insight, care of the mutiny, involves the recognition that, like military products, his military workers (the allied forces) should where necessary be devalued so that the permanent arms economy may be ensured permanency. I should add that the corporal turns out to be the old Marshal's son, a familial convolution indicative of how mutiny is seminal to the logic of the militarized state. The corporal enables such states to recognize that, far from being one another's enemies, they are servants of a global system, one of whose priorities is control over national populations, for the greater good of economic production for death. Prior to having the corporal shot, his father describes to him his vision of a technological dystopia in which machines fight machines, and man, reduced to a voice, "endures" only because of his capacity to quit a planet despoiled by war, and to militarize further planets:

> because already the next star in the blue immensity of space will be already clamorous with the uproar of his debarkation, his puny and inexhaustible and immortal voice still talking, planning still to build something higher and faster and louder; more efficient and louder and faster than ever before. (994)

In a rewrite of his Nobel Prize Address (December 1950), entirely in keeping with the financial underpinnings of the Nobel Foundation, Faulkner has the old Marshal insist that mankind's "endurance" is inseparable from the efficiency with which he produces munitions. In 1918, as seen from the perspective of 1953, the old Marshal has a very American point; a point that is also, by 1953, very Southern. War modernized the South. Roosevelt's mobilization agencies used international crisis to drive regional development, ensuring, via defense contracts, that war production moved increasingly South and West. The historian James C. Cobb argues that World War II expanded the South's industrial capacity by 40 percent. Yoknapatawpha could not finally withstand the consequences of federal funding.

Periodization and Conclusion

When Faulkner died in 1962 *his* South, the product of a long counter-revolution, running from the Emancipation Proclamation (1863) to the second Agricultural Adjustment Act (1936), a counter-revolution on behalf of a coercive and racialized economy, was dead. In responding to that economy's workings, to its protracted demise and to the cultural expressions of its processes, Faulkner wrote diverse work of a mainly modernist form, rare in the canon of Anglo-American modernisms for its strained debate with a premodern labor history.

REFERENCES AND FURTHER READING

Benjamin, Walter (1977) *The Origin of German Tragic Drama*, trans. John Osborne. London: New Left Books.

Bernstein, J. M. (1995) *Recovering Ethical Life: Jürgen Habermas and the Future of Critical Theory*. London: Routledge.

Brooks, Cleanth (1974) *William Faulkner: The Yoknapatawpha County*. New Haven, CT: Yale University Press.

Cash, W. J. (1971) *The Mind of the South*. London: Thames and Hudson.

Cobb, James C. (1984) *Industrialization and Southern Society, 1877–1984*. Lexington: University of Kentucky Press.

Faulkner, William (1990) *Absalom, Absalom!* In *William Faulkner, Novels 1936–1940*. New York: Library of America.

Faulkner, William (1990) *If I Forget Thee, Jerusalem*. In *William Faulkner, Novels 1936–1940*. New York: Library of America.

Faulkner, William (1992) *The Sound and the Fury*, new, corrected edition. New York: Modern Library.

Faulkner, William (1994) *A Fable*. In *William Faulkner, Novels 1942–1954*. New York: Library of America.

Faulkner, William (1994) *Go Down, Moses*. In *William Faulkner, Novels 1942–1954*. New York: Library of America.

Faulkner, William (1995) *As I Lay Dying*. In *William Faulkner, Novels 1930–1935*. New York: Library of America.

Gray, Richard (1996) *The Life of William Faulkner: A Critical Biography*. Oxford: Blackwell.

Haug, Wolfgang Fritz (1986) *Critique of Commodity Aesthetics*, trans. Robert Brock. Cambridge: Polity Press.

Johnson, Charles (1934) *Shadow of the Plantation*. Chicago: University of Chicago Press.

Johnson, Charles, Embree, Edwin R., and Alexander, W. W. (eds.) (1935) *The Collapse of Cotton Tenancy: Summary of Field Studies and Statistical Surveys, 1933–35*. Freeport: Books for Libraries Press.

Kartigarner, Donald M. (1979) *The Fragile Thread: The Meaning of Form in Faulkner's Novels*. Amherst: University of Massachusetts Press.

Lynd, Helen, and Lynd, Robert (1929) *Middletown*. New York: Harcourt and Brace.

McMillen, Neil R. (1989) *Dark Journey: Black Mississippi in the Age of Jim Crow*. Champaign: University of Illinois Press.

Mandle, Jay (1992) *Not Slave, Not Free*. Durham, NC: Duke University Press.

Marchand, Roland (1985) *Advertising the American Dream: Making Way for Modernity, 1920–1949*. Los Angeles: University of California Press.

Matthews, John T. (1982) *The Play of Faulkner's Language*. Ithaca, NY: Cornell University Press.

Mills, C. Wright (1956) *The Power Elite*. Oxford: Oxford University Press.

Moreland, Richard C. (1990) *Faulkner and Modernism: Rereading and Rewriting*. Madison: University of Wisconsin Press.

Ownby, Ted (1999) *American Dreams in Mississippi: Consumers, Poverty and Culture, 1830–1998*. Chapel Hill: University of North Carolina Press.

Pensky, Max (1993) *Melancholy Dialectics: Walter Benjamin and the Play of Mourning.* Amherst: University of Massachusetts Press.

Polk, Noel (1996) *Children of the Dark House: Text and Context in Faulkner.* Jackson: University of Mississippi Press.

Sartre, Jean-Paul (1987) "On *The Sound and the Fury*: Time in the Work of Faulkner." In David Minter (ed.) *The Sound and the Fury.* New York: Norton.

Stein, Jean (1987) "William Faulkner (1956): Interview with Jean Stein vanden Heuvel." In David Minter (ed.) *The Sound and the Fury.* New York: Norton.

Tushnett, Mark (1981) *The American Law of Slavery, 1810–1860: Considerations of Humanity and Interest.* Princeton, NJ: Princeton University Press.

Wiener, Jonathan (1979) "Class Struggle and Economic Development in the American South, 1865–1955," *American Historical Review*, 84 (2): 970–1006.

Williamson, Joel (1984) *The Crucible of Race: Black–White Relations in the American South Since Emancipation.* New York: Oxford University Press.

26

Literature of the African-American Great Migration

Kate Fullbrook

The lazy, laughing South
With blood on its mouth...
And I, who am black, would love her
But she spits in my face.
And I, who am black,
Would give her many rare gifts
But she turns her back upon me.
So now I seek the North –
The cold-faced North,
For she, they say,
Is a kinder mistress,
And in her house my children
May escape the spell of the South.
(extract from Langston Hughes, "The South," 1926)

The history of the United States has always been characterized by a succession of heroic and sometimes tragic narratives of shifting populations. From the arrival of the European settlers in the sixteenth and seventeenth centuries, to the great wave of adventurers and pioneers making their way westward in the eighteenth and nineteenth centuries, to the massive influxes of immigrants from Central and Eastern Europe, Latin America, and the Far East in the twentieth century, one basic element of the American adventure has been and remains that of restlessness and mobility, of following one's desire to the possible other life which can only be found elsewhere.

These positive versions of the great American movements of populations have their dark counterparts, such as the driving of Native Americans from their tribal lands and into either death or a kind of internal exile on reservations; or the triumph of agribusiness, which has pushed the small farmer close to statistical extinction in the United States; or the real extinction which has been visited on so many populations of North American plants and animals. And there is no subset of the American population for which the narratives of the mass movements are more important than that of African Americans. The most notorious of these narratives is that of the Middle Passage, the appalling and dangerous sea journey from Africa to the Americas, which brought its cargoes of captured Africans into slavery in the New World. But other narratives of movement are also of crucial importance in African-American history and to African-American literature. The story of the Middle Passage is one enacted on the East–West axis of the Atlantic crossing, with the West representing slavery (in contradistinction to its usual significance of increased freedom in the American geographical imagination) and the East representing an imagined African homeland of respect, rest, and consolation. In contrast, the most typical specifically American geographical imaginary axis for African Americans hinges on the division between the North and the South, with the Atlantic seaboard and the Mississippi River serving as routes to an increase or diminution in freedom.

In all of this the South serves as a literary figure of great complexity, which mirrors the intricacies and complications of the history, experiences, and feelings of its African-American population. In antebellum times the North signified the realm of freedom, the destination of the Underground Railroad that could lead from slavery in the South to liberty in the free states of the North, or to the even greater freedom of Canada. Conversely, the threat of being sold down the river – being sold, that is, further South along the Mississippi, and therefore into grimmer, more deprived, more dangerous forms of slavery than those which generally pertained in the more northerly slave states – also featured strongly in antebellum African-American folklore and music. This imagery was given its own additional blood-drenched confirmation in the American Civil War, with the (largely reluctantly) abolitionist North pitted against the slaveowning South. As a result, and as might be expected, the mythological resonance of the North–South divide is one of the most powerful in the American imagination. That it should be an even stronger part of the African-American symbolic repertoire is scarcely surprising. And that both the articulation and the testing of this mythology should form integral parts of the literature of the Great Migration of African Americans from the South to the North in the twentieth century cannot help but be the case. This essay will examine a number of selected texts as case studies of the ways in which this North–South mythology informs the literature of the Great Migration. Before turning to this writing I want to note some major reasons which prompted the great movement of black Americans from the agrarian, rural South to the industrial, urban North, and radically altered the nature of African-American experience in the course of only a few decades.

The Great Migration

While the fact of the Great Migration is not in dispute, the exact dates of the phenomenon are not yet completely agreed. A good starting point is to note that in 1900 nine out of ten black Americans lived in the South and most worked on the land. By the end of the twentieth century African Americans were overwhelmingly urban, with 80 percent living in cities by 1970. Many of these new urban dwellers, of course, remained in the South. But many did not. The Great Migration refers to a double move with two separate but equally profound elements: from rural to urban and from South to North. In both instances very large movements of population are involved in a short period of time. For example, Alferteen Harrison notes that between 1915 and 1960 "about five million rural Southern African Americans migrated to the Northern industrial cities of America" (1991: vii). They moved along the Atlantic coast from Florida to Pennsylvania, New York and New England; along the Mississippi River and its Illinois Central railroad route which ran from the Mississippi Delta through Memphis, Tennessee to Chicago, and then Detroit, and the other big cities of the Midwest; and along the highways that led from Texas, Arkansas, and Louisiana to California and the West Coast (xvii). The periods of greatest migration from the South were the thirty years between 1910 and 1940, and the 1950s. It is the earlier of these two periods which is most frequently meant when the Great Migration is mentioned, and it is with this period that this chapter will be mostly concerned, though it is salutary to remember that large numbers of African Americans were already moving from the South to the North as early as 1900 and these numbers did not diminish until late in the century. By the 1980s the pattern of migration had reversed, with more African Americans going South than North (this configuration matched the patterns of movement within the United States of other population groups), as the previously successful industrial cities of the North suffered economic blight because of a combination of under-investment in technological research and development and cheap competition to become the problematic "Rust Belt" of the last part of the century.

In the first part of the twentieth century, matters were altogether other. And the factors which decided the African-American population to shift north were complex. They included elements both of repulsion from the South and of enticement from the North. Those who moved did so with great deliberation. The Migration prompted an enormous amount of controversy in all areas of the United States, in ways which all participants regarded as highly politically charged. What it represented, indeed enacted, was the first mass exercise by the black population of the rights of movement guaranteed by its enfranchisement by the Civil War. The Great Migration was the unmistakable signal that African Americans did not "belong" to the South, but to the United States as a whole, just like the rest of its citizens. It was also the sign that this population would no longer tolerate being treated as a pool of semi-indentured rural serfs. With the shift to the North the African-American population also jumped in one move from the quasi-feudal background of the South to the full modernity of the industrial city. In every way it was a radical change, and both the anxiety and the excitement generated by this great alteration mark the literature produced by its participants.

As is usually the case with such dramatic movements of populations, the reasons for the Great Migration were diverse. Many were linked to changes in the fortunes of the preeminent slave crop: cotton. Most importantly, the invention of the mechanical cotton picker undermined the Southern sharecropper system, which had tied African Americans to lives of rural penury since Reconstruction. The decimation of the cotton crop by successive invasions of the boll weevil further undermined Southern agriculture. In 1915 terrible floods hit Alabama and Mississippi. Finally, in 1920, the bottom fell out of the cotton market, leaving large portions of the South facing economic catastrophe a decade earlier than the rest of the nation (Lehmann 1991: 6–7, 15; Meier and Rudwick 1966: 191–2). In addition, the Southern system of segregation, supported by racial violence (with an increase in lynchings at its most extreme), along with a recrudescence of the Ku Klux Klan, became increasingly intolerable for the black population. From this point of view, the mass exodus of large numbers of African Americans from the South represented a stunning collective protest against Jim Crow conditions, a protest which many white Southerners found threatening, insulting, and, given their inability, as James R. Grossman notes, "to recognize blacks as active and rational participants in the historical process," simply baffling (1989: 39).

Despite attempts at persuasion and intimidation by white Southerners to prevent the cheap African-American labor force from leaving the area, and despite a widespread belief that credulous blacks would only leave if lured away by dishonest and unscrupulous labor agents from the North, accounts by African Americans show that the pull of the North was composed of hope regarding the possibilities for self-improvement which have always motivated most Americans. As World War I proceeded and the need for industrial workers in the North grew at the same time that the war cut off European immigration to the States, increasing numbers of African Americans decided to try to better themselves in the North. As Thomas R. Frazier explains, when the "black newspaper, the Chicago *Defender*," (which made its way to the South largely via the African-American employees of the great railroad lines of the Mississippi and its tributaries) "began to encourage blacks to migrate northward and Northern industry began to send labor recruiters to the South, the response was overwhelming' (1988: 230).

Examples of that response, and the reasons behind it, are best illustrated by letters written to the *Defender* by prospective internal immigrants, asking for help and guidance in making their way north, and giving their reasons for wishing to move in the clearest possible way. Parts of these four letters from Georgia, Louisiana, and Oklahoma in 1917 give eloquent tastes of the most common collective motivations:

> *My dear friends:* I writen you some time ago and never received any answer at all. I just was thinking why that I have not. I written you for employ on a farm or any kind of work that you can give me to do I am willing to do most any thing that you ant me to so dear friends if you just pleas send ticket for me I will come up thear just as soon as I receives it I want to come to the north so bad tell I really dont no what to do, I am a good worker a young boy age of .23. The reason why I want to come north is why that the people don't pay enough for the labor that a man can do down here so please let me

no what can you do for me just as soon as you can I will pay you for the ticket and all so enything on your money that you put in the ticket for me, and send any kind of contrak that you send me.

Gentlemens: Just a word of information I am planning to leave this place on about May 11th for Chicago and wants ask you assistance in getting a job. My job for the past 8 years has been in the Armour Packing Co. of this place and I cand do anything to be done in a branch house and are now doing the smoking here I am 36 years old have a wife and 2 children. I has been here all my life but would be glad to go wher I can educate my children where they can be of service to themselves, and this will never be here.

Sir: I am looking for a place to locate this fall as a farmer. Do you think you could place me on a farm to work on shares. I am a poor farmer and have not the money to buy but would be glad to work a mans farm for him. I desirous of leaving here because of school accommodations for children as I have five and want to educate them the best I can.

Dear Sir: I am writing you for information I want to come north east but I have not sufficient funds and I am writing you to see if there is any way that you can help me by giving me the names of some of the firms that will send me a transportation as we are down here where we have to be shot down here like rabbits for every little orfence as I seen an orcurince happen down here this after noon when three depties from the shief office an one Negro spotter come out and found some of our raice mens in a crap game and it makes me want to leave the south worse than I ever did when such things happen right at my door. (Frazier 1988: 238–9)

Better and more just wages, a desire for social justice, the determination to secure a decent education for one's children: these hopeful, purposeful, optimistic points feature in letter after letter and account after account of the reasons which fired the imaginations of the migrants. The reputation of the North as a haven of freedom and of opportunity was so strong that it was still intact in the second half of the century. As Joseph Lattimore, a 50-year-old insurance broker in Chicago, born and raised in Mississippi, explained to Studs Terkel in one of his inimitable interviews in the 1990s: "My idea of Chicago, pre-1962, was almost like going to heaven. It was coming to integration, where you could sit anywhere you wanted on the bus, anywhere you wanted in the theater. Utopia. After I got here, I began to realize there was not the integration I had envisioned" (Terkel 1993: 134). Lattimore described himself to Terkel as "a typical African-American." And his experiences both of hope and of its diminution are, sadly, typical of the Great Migration as a whole. Although Lattimore's personal story is one of real success, with children at college, a thriving small business, and enough money to have left the ghetto behind, the underlying tenor of his life is that of disappointment. "I don't have a lot of faith in a better day coming," he told Terkel. "Being black in America is like being forced to wear ill-fitting shoes. Some people adjust to it. It's always uncomfortable on your foot, but you've got to wear it because it's the only shoe you've got" (137, 136).

It is difficult to overstate the dismay experienced by generations of African Americans as they discovered that the accounts of splendid economic and educational opportunities and of racial harmony in the North, as opposed to the pauperization, disenfranchisement, and racial aggression of the South, were simply dreams. As they moved from the plantation to the ghetto, the African-American migrants reencountered aspects of the racism they had hoped to leave behind. In the North, white workers were hostile to the new entrants to the labor force, and blacks were confined mostly to heavy, unskilled jobs in the industrial labor market. Discrimination increased in all aspects of life in Northern cities as African-American numbers grew. There were race riots in Philadelphia and East St. Louis in 1917, bombing of black homes in Chicago in 1918, and more race riots in 22 cities in 1919. That year, in fact, marks an important point in African-American history in that large numbers of blacks fought in self-defense very publicly against whites in the riots. There is a good deal of truth in Thomas Frazier's claim that the "'new Negro' spoken about so widely in the 1920s emerged from the bloody street fights of the summer of 1919" (1988: 231). The founding of the NAACP (National Association for the Advancement of Colored People) in 1909, and its growing influence throughout all the years of the Great Migration, marked a kind of collective coming of age for an African-American population which now understood that it would have to fight for its rights everywhere. Race, it was understood, could no longer be dismissed as an essentially Southern problem. It was an issue for the whole of the United States, and from this time onward was treated as such (Meier and Rudwick 1996: 188–95).

The Great Migration and the Arts

In one sense, it is fair to say that almost all of the art produced by African Americans in the twentieth century is either dominated or deeply marked by the personal and collective experience of the Great Migration. As the great black Southern rural population came to terms both with the excitement and with the possibilities of the Northern city, as well as the harshness of the conditions within which African Americans were forced to live; as the black folkways of the South altered to suit Northern circumstances; and as the church (particularly the Baptist church) and the extended family worked to hold together a community characterized most strikingly by restlessness, an artistic response of great richness represented, analyzed, and helped to make sense of this experience. That sense included the construction of a new black identity which gloried in the freedoms which had finally been claimed. Movements in the first quarter of the century, like Marcus Garvey's utopian Universal Negro Improvement Association, and the ideal of the Black Metropolis, whatever else might be said about them, were manifestations of this new atmosphere of racial pride and self-help which also informed the artistic practices of what Alain Locke famously identified as the "New Negro" movement of the Harlem Renaissance in the

1920s. This movement can only be understood as an epiphenomenon of the Great Migration. Important figures such as the poets Langston Hughes (1902–67, born in Joplin, Missouri), James Weldon Johnson (1871–1938, born in Jacksonville, Florida), and Countee Cullen (1903–46, born in New York City); novelists such as Arna Bontemps (1902–73, born in Alexandria, Louisiana), Jessie Redmon Fauset (1884–1961, born in Camden County, New Jersey), Nella Larsen (1893–1964, born in Chicago), and Claude McKay (1889–1948, born in Jamaica); essayists, critics, and theorists such as Alain Locke (1886–1954, born in Philadelphia), Charles S. Johnson (1893–1956, born in Bristol, Virginia) , and W. E. B. Du Bois (1868–1963, born in Great Barrington, Massachusetts) all contributed to what is now seen as the legendary modern flowering of African-American art in Harlem in the years following World War I. All drew in important ways on the African-American experience of the South and the ways it had and might be utilized and transformed in the new geographical diaspora.

Literature and history were not the only areas to respond powerfully to the Great Migration. Both in this period and later, black Southern folk materials underpinned the innovations made by jazz, blues, and gospel composers and performers from Duke Ellington (1899–1974, born in Washington, DC) and Louis Armstrong (ca. 1900–71, born in New Orleans), to Bessie Smith (1896–1940, born in Chattanooga, Tennessee) and Ma Rainey (1886–1939, born in Columbus, Georgia), and, later, Big Bill Broonzy (1893–1958, born in Scott, Mississippi) and Muddy Waters (1915–83, born in Rolling Fork, Mississippi), in inventing the only music which has a good claim to be called specifically American. In the visual arts, muralist and graphic artist Aaron Douglas (1898–1979, born in Kansas), painters such as Archibald Motley, Jr. (1891–1981, born in New Orleans), and photographers such as Richard S. Roberts (1881–1936, raised in Florida) and James VanDerZee (1886–1983, raised in Lenox, Massachusetts) produced work that partook simultaneously of black folk art and legend and the high modernism of the day, and which was as sophisticated as the New York City which fostered its development.

As can be seen from the brief notations on their places of origin, many of these artists and intellectuals were born and usually raised in the South. There is not one who does not work tellingly and adventurously with the African-American Southern legacy. That they are rarely cited as Southern artists or thinkers comprises a misrepresentation and denuding of the powerful regional tradition which has had, and continues to exert, a deep influence on the arts in America as a whole. This influence is probably most important in music, particularly in popular music, but it is of crucial interest in literature as well, particularly in fiction and in autobiography. In the remainder of this chapter I want to look in some detail at three of the finest prose works of the Great Migration: Jean Toomer's modernist text, *Cane*; Zora Neale Hurston's memoir, *Dust Tracks on a Road*; and Richard Wright's autobiographical *Black Boy* to illustrate the complexities of the appropriation of and conversation with the culture of the South in important works by three of the most significant African-American writers the Migration produced.

Jean Toomer's *Cane*

Of all the texts which emerged from the Harlem Renaissance, Jean Toomer's *Cane* is usually regarded as the most intellectually demanding, the most complex, and the most significant for subsequent generations of African-American writers. Toomer himself, who was born in 1894 in Washington, DC and died in 1967, was a fascinating individual. Of mixed race parentage, he was raised in the home of his stern maternal grandfather, Pinckney Benton Stewart Pinchbeck, who was regarded as black. Pinchbeck had served as acting governor of Louisiana during Reconstruction and later as a US senator. Toomer's childhood experiences left him decidedly ambivalent about race, and he personally refused traditional racial classification, considering himself a member of the new "American" race. *Cane* represented Toomer's only literary success, and after its publication he turned to Gurdjieff and his teachings in the first characteristic gesture of a revolution in his life that was thereafter concerned with socialism, mysticism, psychology, and, in his later years, the Society of Friends.

As much as Toomer disclaimed racial classification for himself, *Cane* was a product of his meditations on it as a young man. His personal experience of race was complicated. His childhood had been spent in affluent areas of Washington, DC, until he moved in with his beloved uncle, who lived in a black neighborhood, when he was in his mid-teens. After graduating from high school, Toomer moved restlessly between education and employment. He tried to settle in at the University of Wisconsin-Madison, the Massachusetts College of Agriculture, the American College of Physical Training in Chicago, New York University, and the City College of New York. None of the courses for which he enrolled nor the jobs he took to finance them held his interest for long. A breakdown in 1918 and the growth of a serious interest in writing, which included contacts with his new mentor, Waldo Frank, and immersion in the work of other contemporary authors such as Edward Arlington Robinson, Sherwood Anderson, Carl Sandburg, and the Imagists, were crucial ingredients which prepared him for writing *Cane*. After living in Washington, caring for his dying grandfather, and reading and thinking deeply about the conditions of African-American life, the final catalyst for the composition of his classic text came to Toomer when he accepted a temporary post as the head of a black technical school in Sparta, Georgia in 1921 (Turner, in Toomer 1988: 124–9). As Toomer himself explained, the situation was of utmost importance to him as he struggled to find some purpose to his life:

> I had always wanted to see the heart of the South. Here was my chance... The setting was crude in a way, but strangely rich and beautiful. I began feeling its effects despite my state, or, perhaps, just because of it. There was a valley, the valley of "Cane," with smoke-wreaths during the day and mist at night. A family of backcountry Negroes had only recently moved into a shack not too far away. They sang. And this was the first

time I'd ever heard the folk songs and spirituals. They were very rich and sad and joyous and beautiful. But I learned that the Negroes of the town objected to them ... So, I realized with deep regret, that the spirituals would be certain to die out. With Negroes also the trend was towards the small town and then towards the city – and industry and commerce and machines. The folk-spirit was walking in to die on the modern desert. That spirit was so beautiful. Its death was so tragic. Just this seemed to sum life for me. And this was the feeling I put into *Cane*. *Cane* was a swan song. It was a song of an end. And why no one has seen and felt that, why people have expected me to write a second and a third and a fourth book like *Cane*, is one of the queer misunderstandings of my life. (Toomer 1988: 141–2)

Toomer's account of this aspect of the origins of *Cane* might serve as a telling epigraph for the literature of the Great Migration as a whole. It is the passing of a rural way of life, which, whatever else it might hold, contains elements of richness and beauty, and which is being overtaken by the urban, the mechanical, the modern, which concerns Toomer. The liminality of his own position allowed him an extraordinary vantage point from which to view the changes brought about by the Migration. He was an individual who had lived on both sides of the color line in the Southern city of Washington, DC. He had studied and lived in the great cities of the North. And he brought all his urban experience to bear on his reflections on the historical changes overtaking the South as a significant portion of its population moved out of the back-country, out of the past, and into the modernity of the American cities both north and south of the Mason Dixon line.

That Toomer constructed an adventurous, modernist text for his treatment of this moment of coming to modernity for African Americans seems, from this point of view, one of those few uncannily exact literary instances where form makes a precise match with content. *Cane* exhibits some of the traits of modernist-inflected primitivism, and also draws heavily on the kinds of varied portraits of American small-town grotesques which featured in writing that Toomer admired by Sherwood Anderson, Edward Arlington Robinson, and Edgar Lee Masters. However, for the most part it functions as a superb example of the kind of high modernist writing which concentrated on the formation of the clarity of the image to signify the intersection of historical and psychological tension and change. The match with the experience of the Great Migration is both profound and exact, as Toomer's text traces the adventures in consciousness demanded from those whom it most intimately affected. The book, published in 1923, was immediately recognized as the masterpiece of intellectual fiction of the Harlem Renaissance, a reputation it has maintained ever since, despite being out of print from 1927 to 1967.

Cane is divided into three parts, each of which is preceded by a geometrical arc which Toomer meant as the sign of the broken circle of the African-American lives he describes. The first and second sections are made up of poems and vignettes; the third section crosses a short story with a closet drama. The first section is set in Georgia and is concerned largely with failure, danger, and violence, which are linked with sexuality in the South. That South is evoked beautifully and economically through a lyrical deployment of a system of almost ideogrammatic icons of Southernness: whispering pine forests, sawmills, cotton fields, tiny shacks, swamps, red soil, the Dixie Pike, hounds and chickens, heat, a blood-red moon, and religion which is indistinguishable from superstition for both blacks and whites. And, of course, the central symbol of the sugarcane features everywhere with its sweetness, its capacity to enflame as moonshine liquor, and its rustling fields in which to hide clandestine sexual encounters, illegal stills, and unhinged violence. The vignettes of the first section focus on six women and on the ways in which their sex and race make for variations on unhappiness in a postbellum South which tries to regulate desire in ways that promote only suffering. The first vignette, "Karintha," mourns the violation of the young black girl, forced into sexuality too soon, who burns her forest-born baby in the sawdust of the mill. "Becky" traces the melancholy story of the white woman who bears two mixed-race sons and who is rejected by both the white and black communities. "Blood-Burning Moon" features the grotesque outcome of Louisa's inability to choose between her two lovers, one white and one black. By the end of the vignette both die (knifed and lynched, respectively) because of a sickeningly typical violent jealousy in which sex and race are mixed in archetypically Southern fashion. Taken as a whole, the first section of *Cane* delineates the pathologies of the South, while studding its accounts with an iconography of beauty that neither slavery nor Southern racism could extinguish.

The first section, punctuated by the songs of slaves and the folkways of the Old South, closes with the most revolting of Southern practices: the lynching of a young black man. With this archetypal Southern obscenity the text moves from the country to the city. In this new urban context the vignettes are also concerned with the failure of love and sexuality for the African Americans who are damaged by their attempts to adjust to the metropolitan lives which, in their very modernity, strip them of knowledge and hope. The section also plays on encounters between Northern and Southern African Americans in the Southern city of Washington, DC, which forms the setting for all but one of the vignettes (only "Bona and Paul," about the sad failure of an interracial couple, is set in the North, in Chicago). It is the lack of roots which undermines the characters in the vignettes, who nevertheless find some joy and sustenance in the arts of song and dance and theatre which surround them in this section of the text, and which represent an urban variation on and appropriation of the African-American aesthetic traditions which reach back to the times of slavery. The difference between the African Americans made anxious by housing, jobs, sexuality, identity, and purpose in the city and those who are not is encapsulated in a brilliant passage in "Box Seat," in which the central figure, Dan, who is disturbed and disturbing in his luckless pursuit of Muriel, assumes his seat in a theatre next to a woman who does not share his anxieties of displacement:

> He has to squeeze past the knees of seated people to reach his own seat. He treads on a man's corns. The man grumbles and shoves him off. He shrivels close beside a portly Negress whose huge rolls of flesh meet about the bones of seat-arms.

A   soil-soaked fragrance comes from her. Through the cement floor her strong roots sink down. They spread under the asphalt streets. Dreaming, the streets roll over on their bellies, and suck their glossy health from them. Her strong roots sink down and spread under the river and disappear in bloodlines that waver south. Her roots shoot down. (65)

The lyric surrealism of this passage forms a paean to the historical roots which the formalist structures of the modernist text themselves declare superseded is one of the finest and most illuminating moments in *Cane*. What Toomer produces here is a liminal figure caught in a liminal moment, represented by a woman who is simultaneously at home in the modern theatre of the city and rooted in the South of her ancestors, a woman who figures as an icon of the Great Migration itself, and one which further disturbs the anxious protagonist of the vignette.

This disturbance, homelessness, rootlessness, and anxiety are the governing themes of the final section of *Cane*, the section which is the most autobiographical and least successful. In it, Toomer returns to his contemplation of the rural South, with a psychodrama in which a young, Northern African-American man first loses his job as a temporary head of a school in Georgia, and then tries to come to terms with the legacy of the South mediated through a cast of characters who represent various aspects of African-American reactions to it, ranging from accommodation to rebellion to acceptance of the slave heritage. Again the themes of sex and love, pollution and purity, violation and innocence, are set in play in a nightmare world in which the major character cannot come to terms with either the pain of Southern history or the natural beauty of the South, both of which seem to invalidate his lifetime in the North. All this is represented by what the organizing consciousness of the text thinks of as the repeated song of the night winds in Georgia:

> White-man's land.
> Niggers, sing.
> Burn, bear black children
> Till poor rivers bring
> Rest, and sweet glory
> In Camp Ground. (83)

The central character, Kabnis, a typically modernist scarecrow of a man, "an atom of dust in agony on a hillside," can find no redemption, because there is none to be had. There is only the self and the land, history and nature, and the modern America which is in the process of becoming. This America is embodied in Toomer's experimental textual practice, which reflects on the death of the spirit of the premodernist African-American South, and the way it fostered a tragic beauty in the face of grotesque suffering. *Cane* was, as Toomer said, "a song of an end." The book itself enacted, in its themes, icons, and idiom, the historical division marked by the Great Migration, in which the South became for African-American writers not a personal destiny but a cultural repository of extraordinary resonance and possibility.

Zora Neale Hurston's *Dust Tracks on a Road*

If Toomer's *Cane* draws on a Romantic tradition of the South in terms of its presentation both of the horror and of the pleasures embedded in the African-American heritage, and supplements this with modernist tactics of distinctly international and cosmopolitan provenance, Zora Neale Hurston's memoir, *Dust Tracks on a Road*, written in California in 1941 and published in 1942, was concerned with the author's own extraordinary experience of the Great Migration. The book is now regarded as a classic of African-American autobiography, but, like *Cane*, it was out of print for many years, just as Hurston herself, the leading female writer of the Harlem Renaissance, was "lost" until her famous rediscovery by Alice Walker, who published an important article on her in the popular American feminist magazine *Ms.* in 1975. Hurston, who was born in 1891, died alone and impoverished in 1960. Even her grave in Fort Pierce, Florida was unmarked until Walker paid for a memorial for her writerly precursor whose work is now clearly seen, as Henry Louis Gates notes, as important for three literary canons: the black, the American, and the feminist (Hurston 1991: 262). Hurston's novels *Jonah's Gourd Vine* (1936), her most famous book, *Their Eyes Were Watching God* (1937), and *Moses, Man of the Mountain* (1939), as well as a great deal of journalism, a number of short stories, and writing for dramatic performance, precede the composition of her memoirs. Hurston's work was not limited to the literary. She published extensively in the area of African-American history and culture in academic and popular journals. Her anthropological fieldwork in African-American culture both in the United States and the West Indies, begun under the direction of Franz Boas, is also of real significance. Like Toomer, she believed she was recording the folklore, folk songs, folktales, and folkways of the rural slave past just before modernity ensured either their disappearance or their transmutation into something quite other. Her anthropological books, *Mules and Men* (1935) and *Tell My Horse* (1938), inform her autobiography in interesting ways. As well as being a fine novelist, a pioneering academic, and a writer with a deep interest in and talent for the performing arts, Hurston was also and always a thinker with great independence of mind. It is the combination of her multiple abilities, her extraordinarily varied experience, and her confident originality which makes Hurston's account of her own personal experience of the Great Migration in *Dust Tracks* so thought provoking and satisfying.

Hurston begins her memoir by calling attention to the history of the Southern town where she was born. Eatonville, Florida, she explains, was a "pure Negro town – charter, mayor, council, town marshal and all. It was not the first Negro community in America, but it was the first to be incorporated, the first attempt at self-government on the part of Negroes in America" (1). Eatonville seemed an oasis of complete enfranchisement of African Americans in the Jim Crow South. Eatonville's freedom owed a great deal to the behavior of the white founders of the local town, Maitland, who were, as Hurston points out, "to a man, people who had risked their lives and fortunes that Negroes might be free" (5). After a black man had successfully served as Maitland's first mayor alongside a white city council, local African-American activists suggested the founding of a self-governing black town. With the help of the powerful white founders of Maitland, this plan came to fruition and in August 1886 Eatonville was incorporated, "and made history by becoming the first of its kind in America, and perhaps in the world" (6). Hurston's beloved, exasperating, and forceful father left Alabama, sharecropping, and the plantation with his young ex-schoolteacher wife and the first three of their eight children to come to Eatonville. He served as mayor of the town and wrote most of its laws. It is from this starting point, with parents who had already begun the journey from the rural to the urban, from the slave past to the new future, that Hurston began her own life journey. Her much-loved mother, who died when Hurston was only nine, encouraged her children to "jump at de sun," to follow their highest ambitions (13). Ambition for African Americans, as for most Americans, entails mobility. Zora's own passion for wandering is explained by her mother saying "she believed a woman who was an enemy of hers had sprinkled 'travel dust' around the doorstep the day I was born" (23). The "dust" seemingly worked on all the Hurston children. By the mid-1920s, when Zora graduated from Barnard in New York, her siblings were living in Memphis, Tennessee; Decatur, Alabama; Jacksonville, Florida; Brooklyn, New York; with one brother, who trained as a chef, working up and down the east coast of the United States. It is the most American of patterns.

Zora's own trajectory is propelled by her intellectual talent and sheer purposeful-ness. After the death of her mother, her father's quick remarriage to a hated step-mother, her subsequent alienation from her father's household, and her schooling in Jacksonville, she moved north, first to Baltimore, where she completed high school, and then to Washington, DC to Howard University. By 1925 she was in New York, with a scholarship to Barnard and her groundbreaking work with Boas about to begin. A visible presence in the Harlem Renaissance, she worked with Langston Hughes and Charles S. Johnston, while undertaking fieldwork, which she stressed was fraught with danger because of the quick emotions of the simple people among whom she worked.

The later part of *Dust Tracks* is concerned not only with her research findings in such areas as folktales and voodoo, but also with her ideas concerning race. In this – and running against the fashion of the 1930s and 1940s for naturalist writing and sociological explanations of cultural groups of all kinds – Hurston insisted on cutting through the classificatory stranglehold of race to concentrate on the shared humanity (for good or for evil) of both blacks and whites, and on the importance of classifica-tions other than the racial for understanding the minds and imaginations of individ-uals. Throughout her autobiographical narrative, as in her account of the founding of Eatonville, she stressed the importance of the cooperation between black and white Americans. Her own birth was accidentally attended by a white man who served as midwife to her mother and helpful godfather to Zora herself, who he nicknamed "Snidlits," and to whom he gave a repeated warning: "don't be a nigger," which

Hurston explained saying "The word Nigger in this sense does not mean race. It means a weak, contemptible person of any race" (30). Again and again, and despite the controversial nature of her positions, Hurston rejected the idea of the racial subsumption of the individual into a single group. She notes, for example, that it was Africans who sold other Africans into slavery. She takes great care to give credit to those white Americans who had helped her. She says she is tired of the topic of race. "There is no *The Negro* here. Our lives are so diversified, internal attitudes so varied, appearances and capabilities so different that there is no possible classification so catholic that it will cover us all" (172). She believes in no universals at all, whether human or divine. "Being an idealist," she writes, "I too wish the world was better than I am. Like all the rest of my fellow men, I don't want to live around people with no more principles than I have. My inner fineness is continually outraged at finding that the world is a whole family of Hurstons" (206). Expressing universalist sentiments of this order, with a humor that smoothly cites her own African-American family as the exemplar of those principles of individuality and difference, it is no wonder that Hurston's thought was seen, and is still seen, as controversial, problematic, and sometimes traitorous by those who see racial categories and the ethical imperatives which accompany them, as inevitably leading to separatism and division.

Hurston's views make most sense when they are seen in the optimistic light of her experience of the Great Migration. Often placed in situations where she was one of a kind – the only African-American, the only woman, the only educated individual – Hurston herself encountered the varieties of difference that were so important in the formulation of her views. What *Dust Tracks* emphasizes, more than anything, is that the self is composed of crosscurrents of available categories to which one might belong partially or wholeheartedly, as well as containing elements that are private and unascribable to any group membership. The view is an anthropologist's, certainly, but it is also one which opens out the world – in a mixture of freedom and belonging – in ways which might otherwise be occluded by the exigencies of migration. It is for these reasons that Hurston stressed that her own literary imagination was populated as much by the myths of the Greeks and Romans and Norse, by *Gulliver's Travels* and *Grimm's Fairy Tales*, by the stories of Hans Anderson and Robert Louis Stevenson and Kipling as by the tales of Brer Rabbit, Brer Fox, Sis Cat, and Buzzard that she loved to hear the men of Eatonville tell when she was a child. The Bible for Hurston is high literature and folktale as well as an illustration of comparative religious ideology. It is for these reasons, too, that Hurston emphasizes the fact that on going north it was important for her to remember that she "was a Southerner, and had the map of Dixie on my tongue." The "average Southern child," she said, "white or black, is raised on simile and invective" (98). The idiom of the North was different, but it, too, was available to those who troubled to acquire it.

Hurston's tough, funny, intelligent, idiosyncratic, and altogether absorbing account of her own internal migration works in harmony with the American dictum of the importance of the individual. *Dust Tracks* ends with a disclaimer of any feelings of "race prejudice," and a reiteration of universalist principles, and a call for the powerful to "think kindly of those who walk in the dust" (209). That there should be such a triumphant statement of the success of the principles that fueled the hopes of so many who were part of the Great Migration by one of their number is one of the many reasons for the continuing significance of Hurston's memoir.

Richard Wright's *Black Boy*

To move from *Dust Tracks on a Road* to *Black Boy* is to make a profound shift in outlook on the ways in which the African-American experience has been represented. As Henry Louis Gates, Jr. justly remarks, "few authors in the black tradition have less in common than Zora Neale Hurston and Richard Wright" (in Hurston 1991: 260). If Hurston was the leading female figure in the Harlem Renaissance of the 1920s, Wright was the dominant black literary figure of the 1930s and 1940s (Meier and Rudwick 1996: 210). Born in Roxie, Mississippi in 1908, and raised in the South, Wright made his way to Chicago in 1927, where he spent ten years. He moved to New York in 1937. His naturalist novel *Native Son*, the definitive mid-century African-American novel, was a huge success when it was published in 1940. *Black Boy: A Record of Childhood* sold over 400,000 copies in the first few months after it appeared in 1945. These were Wright's two most important books. Although he continued to write after his emigration to France in 1947, his later work, which was heavily influenced by the existentialism in which he had become interested, never captured the danger and excitement of his earlier productions. Wright died in Paris in 1960. It had been a very long migration indeed from Roxie, Mississippi.

Wright, who was a member of the Communist Party from 1933 to 1944, and whose work is heavily inflected with sociological and naturalistic analyses of race in America, was eloquent on the shock caused by the Great Migration. As he stated in 1941 in *12 Million Black Voices: A Folk History of the Negro in the United States*, in a fine example of the portentous, insistent, oratorically inflected prose which is his trademark, the Migration posed the gravest of challenges to its participants:

> Perhaps never in history has a more utterly unprepared folk wanted to go to the city; we were barely born as a folk when we headed for the tall and sprawling centers of steel and stone. We, who were landless upon the land; we, who had barely managed to live in family groups; we, who needed the ritual and guidance of institutions to hold our atomized lives together in lines of purpose; we, who had known only relationships to people and not relationships to things; we, who had had our personalities blasted with two hundred years of slavery and been turned loose to shift for ourselves – we were such a folk as this when we moved into a world that was destined to test all we were, that threw us into the scales of competition to weigh our mettle. (Lehmann 1991: 52)

It is this sense of frightful unpreparedness, of danger in and of fear at the great historical leap from the plantation to the city, that haunts the pages of *Native Son* and

Black Boy alike. If Jean Toomer had chosen the idiom of lyricism and imagism to represent the Great Migration, and Zora Neale Hurston the language of universalist optimism, Wright's account of his personal journey from South to North is one of aggressive, heroic defiance, shaped by notions of the power of rebellion of the oppressed and of the dreams of the downtrodden to remake the world. It was a view of the African-American situation – which was by the 1940s largely an urban one – in harmony with the anticolonialist struggles of the day, and one which would feed directly into the next great surge of African-American political action in the civil rights movement of the 1950s and 1960s.

From the first, Wright figures the experience of race in terms of white violence against blacks. His first glimmers of understanding of race come when his mother tries to explain to him why a white man might beat a "black boy," despite the victim being neither the white man's child nor a boy at all. Wright finds it all "bewildering" and refuses to include himself in the category of those who might be beaten. It is this refusal either to submit to docility or to the punishment which its absence attracts in the South for black men, that fuels Wright's dream of joining the Great Migration. Despite the limitations of his schooling, his dream has two coequal parts: writing books and going north.

> The North symbolized to me all that I had not felt and seen; it had no relation whatever to what actually existed. Yet, by imagining a place where everything was possible, I kept hope alive in me...I knew that I lived in a country in which the aspirations of black people were limited, marked-off. Yet I felt I had to go somewhere and do something to redeem my being alive.
>
> I was building up in me a dream which the entire educational system of the South has been rigged to stifle. I was feeling the very thing that the state of Mississippi had spent millions of dollars to make sure I would never feel...I was beginning to dream the dreams that the state had said were wrong, that the schools had said were taboo. (Wright 1966: 187)

As Wright moved out from childhood, from Jackson, Mississippi to Memphis, Tennessee to Chicago, Illinois he realized, he said, that he was running away from the South rather than toward anything but an amorphous hope. That hope, however, had a great deal in common with the motivations traced by Zora Neale Hurston and shared by the African-American correspondents of the *Defender*. Drawing on his reading of the great American naturalist writers – "Dreiser, Masters, Mencken, Anderson, and Lewis" – Wright believed in their shared vision that "America could be shaped nearer to the hearts of those who lived in it" (283). And it was in "groping toward that invisible light" of hope generated by these writers that Wright says he found the justification for his actions.

Black Boy, which is equally concerned with evoking the texture of early twentieth-century Southern life and its painful difficulty for Wright's poor, ill, and dysfunctional family, ends with the young Wright on his way north, knowing that he "could never really leave the South, for my feelings had already been formed by the South, for there had been slowly instilled into my personality and consciousness, black though I was, the culture of the South." His hope is expressed in a metaphor of himself as a Southern plant, which will be transplanted elsewhere, to see if "it could grow differently" (284). Wright closes his book, which is full of violent passions, with the tenderest of pastoral metaphors, bearing himself with hope and with dignity toward an unknown North.

Conclusion

Wright's combination of hope and shock offers an apt summary of the literature of the Great Migration. In making the move from south to north, as Alain Locke described it, "a railroad ticket and a suitcase, like a Baghdad carpet, transport the Negro peasant from the cotton-field and farm to the heart of the most complex urban civilization" (Rubin et al. 1985: 291). The literature which emerged from this great collective experiment in self-transformation also moved the African-American experience of the South from the margins to the center of America's metropolitan, and therefore national, consciousness. As one of the most important starting points for the Black Arts Movement of the 1960s and 1970s, and for the extraordinary renaissance in African-American women's writing since the 1970s, the literature of the Great Migration has continued to provide both aesthetic and historical directions for some of the finest American literary productions.

KATE FULLBROOK

Kate Fullbrook completed this essay while she was suffering from an illness that proved to be fatal. Despite the obvious difficulties she was under, she showed characteristic determination, cheerfulness, and courage, by insisting on going ahead with the piece. To have produced anything under the circumstances would have been deeply impressive; to have produced something of such quality was and remains an act of genuine heroism. Kate was a person who combined a passionate commitment to the study of literature with real generosity of spirit and imagination. She made those who knew her proud to call themselves her colleagues and friends. She will be sorely, terribly missed.

REFERENCES AND FURTHER READING

Balshaw, Maria (2000) *Looking for Harlem: Urban Aesthetics in African-American Literature*. London: Pluto Press.

Bryant, J. A., Jr. (1997) *Twentieth-Century Southern Literature*. Lexington: University of Kentucky Press.

Frazier, Thomas R. (1988) *Afro-American History: Primary Sources*, 2nd edn. Belmont, CA: Wadsworth.

Gates, Henry Louis, Jr., and McKay, Nellie Y., et al. (eds.) (1997) *The Norton Anthology of African-American Literature*. London: W. W. Norton.

Gilroy, Paul (1993) *The Black Atlantic: Modernity and Double Consciousness*. London: Verso.

Gray, Richard (2000) *Southern Aberrations: Writers of the American South and the Problems of Regionalism.* Baton Rouge: Louisiana State University Press.

Grossman, James R. (1989) *Land of Hope: Chicago, Black Southerners, and the Great Migration.* Chicago: University of Chicago Press.

Hakutani, Yoshinobu and Butler, Robert (eds.) (1995) *The City in African-American Literature.* London: Associated University Presses.

Harrison, Alferteen (ed.) (1991) *Black Exodus: The Great Migration from the American South.* London: University Press of Mississippi.

Hill, Patricia Liggins, et al. (eds.) (1998) *Call and Response: The Riverside Anthology of the African-American Literary Tradition.* New York: Houghton Mifflin.

Hughes, Langston (1994) *Collected Poems of Langston Hughes.* New York: Knopf.

Hurston, Zora Neale (1991) *Dust Tracks on a Road.* Foreword, Maya Angelou; afterword, Henry Louis Gates, Jr. New York: Harper Perennial.

Killens, John Oliver and Ward, Jerry W., Jr. (eds.) (1992) *Black Southern Voices: An Anthology of Fiction, Poetry, Drama, Nonfiction, and Critical Essays.* London: Meridian.

Lee, A. Robert (1998) *Designs of Blackness: Mappings in the Literature and Culture of Afro-America.* London: Pluto Press.

Lehmann, Nicholas (1991) *The Promised Land: The Great Black Migration and How it Changed America.* London: Macmillan.

Lomax, Alan (1993) *The Land Where the Blues Began.* London: Methuen.

Meier, August and Rudwick, Elliot M. (1966) *From Plantation to Ghetto: An Interpretive History of American Negroes.* New York: Hill and Wang.

Powell, Richard J. (1997) *Black Art and Culture in the 20th Century.* London: Thames and Hudson.

Rubin, Louis D., Jr., et al. (eds.) (1985) *The History of Southern Literature.* Baton Rouge: Louisiana State University Press.

Terkel, Studs (1993) *Race.* London: Minerva.

Toomer, Jean (1988) *Cane,* ed. Darwin T. Turner. London: W. W. Norton.

Wright, Richard (1966) *Black Boy: A Record of Childhood and Youth.* New York: Harper and Row.

27

Zora Neale Hurston

Will Brantley

The last entry in the Library of America's edition of the works of Zora Neale Hurston is a letter published by the author in the *Orlando Sentinel* on August 11, 1955. This is the letter in which Hurston famously opposed the 1954 Supreme Court decision to desegregate the public schools. Hurston's views are not unknown to her readers – many of whom would prefer that she had never voiced them – but editor Cheryl Wall must have realized that it was best to let Hurston speak for herself on this issue. As always, Hurston is not without her defining sense of humor:

> I promised God and some other responsible characters, including a bench of bishops, that I was not going to part my lips concerning the US Supreme Court decision on ending segregation in the public schools of the South. But since a lot of time has passed and no one seems to touch on what to me appears to be the most important point in the hassle, I break my silence just this once. Consider me as just thinking out loud.

Hurston then presents her "thoughts": "The whole matter revolves around the self-respect of my people. How much satisfaction can I get from a court order for somebody to associate with me who does not wish me near them?" Hurston compares the court's ruling to "the doctrine of the white mare," wherein the mules of the world unthinkingly follow the white horse that has been let in through a "cunning opening of the barnyard gate" (Hurston 1995a: 956–7).

Hurston's letter does not become more endearing as it progresses – it even contains a diatribe against communists who have attempted to lure blacks with the promise of white mates – and it may be that readers can take some comfort in the fact that it was written near the end of Hurston's life when she was in poor health and when her often conservative views had calcified to the point that she could no longer think through the contradictions of her position. The fact is, Hurston's position on the Supreme Court ruling is in keeping with the sometimes-strident individualism that is a hallmark of her career. As early as 1928 Hurston said that she was not "tragically colored" and that she did not "belong to the sobbing school of Negrohood" (1995a: 827). In her letter to the *Orlando Sentinel*, Hurston reiterates her long-held position: "It is well known that I have no sympathy nor respect for the 'tragedy of color' school of thought among us, whose fountain-head is the pressure group concerned in this court ruling." Hurston calls for "ethical and cultural desegregation" but finds it illogical "to scream race pride and equality while at the same time spurning Negro teachers and self-association" (1995a: 958).

Hurston's often controversial career falls into four distinct stages: her apprentice years in the early to mid-1920s when she was submitting poems, plays, and stories to journals such as the African-American *Opportunity*; her attempts in the late 1920s and early 1930s to establish a "Negro Theatre" with plays such as *The Great Day* (1932) and *Mule Bone*, her combative collaboration with Langston Hughes – a work that was copyrighted in 1931 but not staged until 1991; her great period of the 1930s, the years when she published *Jonah's Gourd Vine* (1934), *Their Eyes Were Watching God* (1937), *Moses, Man of the Mountain* (1939), and two collections of folklore, *Mules and Men* (1935) and *Tell My Horse* (1938). Depending on one's perspective, Hurston's autobiography, *Dust Tracks on a Road* (1942), can be seen as the culmination of her work during the 1930s (she began the autobiography in 1940) or as the work that – even though it was well received upon publication – would signal a decline in creativity. Although she continued to write fiction, Hurston published only one more novel, *Seraph on the Suwanee* (1948), and the publication of this work, which concerns white Floridians, was due in large part to the intervention of her friend Marjorie Kinnan Rawlings. Hurston's final years were marked by financial crises, a series of odd jobs, failing health, and a gradual but near complete withdrawal from public life. She continued to produce pieces for the local *Fort Pierce Chronicle*, but when she died on January 28, 1960, Hurston was buried in a segregated cemetery in what has become one of the most celebrated of all unmarked graves.

No other African-American writer of the twentieth century has produced either a larger body of writing or one marked by as many tensions and unresolved questions. Readers have pondered whether Hurston's deepest identification is with whites rather than blacks; others have remarked upon a too romantic presentation of the South and a willingness to overlook the more glaring displays of the region's racism. Critics continue to debate the extent to which Hurston crafted a fictional autobiography, the extent of her allegiance to the folk community, the value of her later works, and perhaps most significant (because it is ignored by so many of her admirers), the extent to which it is accurate to label Hurston a feminist. Do her justly celebrated creations of strong and independent women characters override other dimensions of Hurston's sexual politics that seem at odds with the defining goals of the feminist movement?

It may be a bit unfair to begin an introduction to a writer with a series of caveats, but Hurston is no longer in need of introduction; she has in fact become the center of a cottage industry and a valuable commodity for Harper Collins and the lucky booksellers who own rare copies of her works (a first edition of *Their Eyes Were*

Watching God alone can command more than several thousand dollars). Since Alice Walker began Hurston's reclamation in the mid-1970s, she has become a staple figure in a wide variety of college courses. Her life has become the subject of plays, media presentations, and at least six children's books, all of which focus on her many achievements and which present her as a racial role model of accomplishment. So Hurston is in much less need of introduction than she was in, say, 1975. What she may be in need of are more readers who can appreciate the full complexity of her life, her art, and her politics.

Hazel Carby is right to caution readers and critics to "question the extent of our dependence upon our recreations" of Hurston (1994: 42). While it is true that she created self-affirming female characters such as Janie Starks, it is also true that Hurston was equally drawn to messianic male characters, ranging from John Pearson, the preacher figure modeled on her father in her first novel *Jonah's Gourd Vine,* to the subject of her final unpublished project – a biography of King Herod the Great. To be sure, Hurston provided many challenges to the notion that women must be passive with needs defined solely by men. In *Their Eyes Were Watching God* Janie eventually finds love with the itinerant Tea Cake, but first she leaves her husband Logan Killicks without divorcing him and then rejects her status as a trophy wife of the powerful Jody Starks; she even exposes Jody's abuse in public. No one could possibly question the value of this novel for Alice Walker and other African-American writers and critics who saw in Hurston a new paradigm: the self-affirming and self-emancipating black woman writer who deliberately wrote outside the framework of white oppression. Still, in their eagerness to embrace Janie's discovery of her own voice, Hurston's critics have often seemed willing to dismiss the ways in which she probes male–female power relationships in the novel. Many of the entries in Rose Davis's annotated bibliography reveal that by the mid-1980s Hurston had become a bedrock of what might be called the "healing" school of criticism. Critics were so moved by Janie's awakening that they tended to ignore the fact that replicating her relationship with Tea Cake might prove problematic for anyone other than Janie – or her creator, Zora Neale Hurston.

It was therefore notable when Deborah Plant, in a study of Hurston's philosophy and politics (titled, appropriately, *Every Tub Must Sit On Its Own Bottom*), challenged Hurston's earlier critics to reconsider her feminism, a term that must be carefully defined or questioned when applied to Hurston. Plant even goes so far as to claim that *Their Eyes Were Watching God* is not really a feminist text, for Janie never behaves as a fully autonomous and independent being. Plant rebuffs earlier critics who have seen in Janie and Tea Cake the complete embodiment of a perfect relationship: "Is life on the muck with a man determined to keep a woman dependent on him a feminist ideal? Is being *allowed* to play checkers and tell stories with this man a feminist ideal also?" (1995: 168). Plant points to one of the most intriguing tensions in Hurston's life and work: while she was drawn to something resembling Virginia Woolf's model of androgyny in her own life, Hurston envisioned in her fiction "an *ideal* traditional relationship of dominance and subordination" (169).

Henry Louis Gates, one of Hurston's major promoters, acknowledges but looks beyond the lure of her "image as a questioning, independent, thoughtfully sensual woman" to argue that Hurston's larger appeal lies in "her command of a narrative voice that imitates the storytelling structures of the black vernacular tradition." "Indeed," Gates explains, "no writer in the African-American literary tradition has been more successful than Hurston in registering the range and timbres of spoken black voices in written form. The language of her characters *dances*; her texts seem to come alive as veritable 'talking books.'" Gates adds, "Almost never do we feel Hurston's hand on our shoulders as we read her texts. Given the historical prominence that the propaganda function has, necessarily, been accorded in the black formal arts, this is no mean achievement" (1993: xii–xiii).

Students who read Hurston for the first time often echo Gates by noting that she makes visible a world of human surprise and frailty that they would not otherwise have seen. But Gates may be too quick to dismiss a propagandistic component of Hurston's work. One of Hurston's chief goals as an artist was to reveal the beauty and wonder of rural African-American culture. Her audience for this enterprise consisted of white readers who dismissed this culture out of hand, as well as African Americans who were not aware that the oral literature they had taken for granted could be seen as constituting a body of art. Hurston was fond of noting that folklore was in fact the art of people who do not know they are producing art. To bring this art to a larger audience, Hurston would produce both works of fiction and nonfiction (she liked to blur the distinction), and she would rely upon that component of her personality that she foregrounds in almost all her work: her sense of humor, which she claimed in her autobiography would always prevent her from seeing either herself, her family, or her community as "the whole intent of the universe" (1995a: 765).

It is thus odd that so little of the large body of commentary on Hurston confronts this key element in her writing. There is one major exception: John Lowe's *Jump at the Sun: Zora Neale Hurston's Cosmic Comedy* (1994), the first sustained examination of Hurston's humor in all its multilayered brilliance. As Lowe observes, Hurston saw language as "a way to show one's love for life; an indirect mode useful in saying the unsayable and in negotiating differences; a wonderful teaching tool and thus a way to bridge the distances between rural and urban, black and white, rich and poor, men and women, author and reader" (51). Nowhere is Hurston's love of humor and play more inviting than in the closing passage of her autobiography:

I have no race prejudice of any kind. My kinfolks, and my "skin folks" are dearly loved. My own circumference of everyday life is there. But I see the same virtues and vices everywhere I look. So I give you all my right hand of fellowship and love, and hope for the same from you. In my eyesight, you lose nothing by not looking just like me . . . Let us all be kissing-friends. Consider that with tolerance and patience, we godly demons may breed a noble world in a few hundred years or so. Maybe all of us who do not have the good fortune to meet, or meet again, in this world, will meet at a barbecue. (1995a: 769)

Hurston might hope for a moral world complete with social equality, but she rather slyly suggests that her readers are equally likely to act upon their demonic impulses and end up in a conflagration that is encoded here as a Southern barbecue. As such an image indicates, Hurston's humor could be at times dark. In this vein, Lowe remarks upon the dark comedy of the hurricane in *Their Eyes Were Watching God*:

> The grim sequence of events that lead to Tea Cake's infection with rabies is chilling, but looked at with a surrealist's detachment, getting bitten by a mad dog that is riding the back of a cow in a hurricane is wildly funny, a scene only a cosmic joker could write. And in fact . . . it seems the biggest joker in the book, on whom all eyes are turned, has to be God. (Lowe 1994: 188)

Lowe has provided what to my mind is the most satisfying explanation of Hurston's overriding goal as an artist – an explanation that links her anthropological fieldwork to her late essays and her more subtle works of fiction. Lowe defines Hurston as a modern descendant of the African griot figure, a poet and musician who was retained by royalty, who knew the legends and history of a given tribe, and who, as a careful mimic and gifted songwriter, could even impersonate the behavior of animals. "Throughout Hurston's works," Lowe writes, "we see inanimate objects, animals, and forces of nature animated and personified, often in a comic manner, beginning with the awkward but interesting sketch 'Magnolia Flower,' which is narrated by a river to a brook, and extending onward through folk proverbs and idioms to the talking buzzards of *Their Eyes* and the philosopher lizard of *Moses*" (1994: 6–7). Lowe makes another intriguing parallel between Hurston and the griots of West Africa, who, as a matter of custom, could not be buried with the people they served. "What an irony, therefore, that Zora Neale Hurston, master of all the griot arts, was indeed buried 'apart,' in an unmarked grave" (8).

Hurston never claimed griot status for herself, but she did possess an extraordinary sense of self and placed great value on her books. While working for the Federal Writers Project in 1938 and 1939, she was assigned to write a chapter on art and literature for *The Florida Negro*, an African-American state history that was not published during Hurston's lifetime. In "Art and Such," a piece that anticipates her later letter to the *Orlando Sentinel*, Hurston surveys what she perceives to be the most significant writing by African Americans from the era of slavery to her own time and including her own work. Hurston accepts the fact that Frederick Douglass, the first great African-American writer, would inevitably champion the progress of his race: "Douglass had the combination of a great cause and the propitious moment as a setting for his talents and he became a famous man." But Hurston has less patience with those disciples of Douglass who have established themselves as "race men," many of whom, she contends, have been overly impressed by their ability to enter and matriculate from a white college. "It was assumed," Hurston asserts, "that no Negro brain could ever grasp the curriculum of a white college, so the black man who did had come by some white folks' brain by accident and there was bound to be conflict between his dark body and his white mind" (1999: 140–1).

It is easy to see that such a critique would be deemed inappropriate to the assignment that Hurston had been given. The essay was made available only in 1999 when Pamela Bordelon published a much-needed edition of Hurston's work for the Federal Writers Project. "Art and Such" is nonetheless central to Hurston's understanding of her own artistic mission. In pondering the effects of so much race consciousness on the literature produced by African Americans in her native state, Hurston asks, "Can the black poet sing a song to the morning? Up springs the song to his lips but it is fought back . . . and he mutters, 'Ought I not to be singing of our sorrows? That is what is expected of me and I shall be considered forgetful of our past and present . . . I will write of a lynching instead'" (1999: 142). Anyone who has read *Their Eyes Were Watching God* will concede that Hurston never resisted her "song to the morning." In her survey of Florida artists Hurston thus devotes more attention to her own work than to that of any other figure, calling attention to her objectivity, to the way she uses the black idiom (a term she always preferred to dialect), and even synthesizing and giving a collective voice to the critical reaction to her first novel: "'Here at last is a Negro story without bias. . . . The characters in the story are seen in relation to themselves and not in relation to the whites as has been the case. To watch these people one would conclude that there were not white people in the world. The author is an artist that will go far'" (1999: 144).

Hurston, of course, did go far; she did, in fact, produce the kind of literature that was always something other and something more than documents of protest or race consciousness. Her aim, as she defines it in "Art and Such," was to achieve "the universal oneness necessary to literature" (1999: 145), and by "universal oneness" she meant something more complex than universality of theme. In *Their Eyes Were Watching God*, for example, Hurston depicts a community that she knew well from her own experience, but she also produced a novel that inscribes the tradition of Voodoo that she observed in the Caribbean while writing the novel, and, as Cyrena Pondrom has shown, she provides a "modern reinterpretation of the ancient Babylonian myth of Ishtar and Tammuz, with syncretic allusion to its analogues, the Greek story of Aphrodite and Adonis and the Egyptian tale of Isis and Osiris" (1985: 182). It is this cultural overlay that one encounters throughout Hurston's fiction; in her third novel, *Moses, Man of the Mountain*, she weaves legends and interpolations from the Bible, from rabbinical literature, from African lore, and from other sources to give readers an image of Moses as a biblical Voodoo priest. It is Hurston's self-affirming and syncretic use of myth that places her squarely within the movement of modernism and that links her to writers such as H. D., Gertrude Stein, and Virginia Woolf, writers who, as Pondrom further observes, "suffered critical banishment to the margins of the literary canon" because their vision seemed so different from that of their male contemporaries (1985: 202).

Ironically, those writers who consciously set out to undermine Hurston's reputation were often her fellow members of the Harlem Renaissance. In a now infamous *New Masses* review of *Their Eyes Were Watching God*, Richard Wright said: "Miss Hurston seems to have no desire whatever to move in the direction of serious fiction," adding:

"her prose is cloaked in that facile sensuality that has dogged Negro expression since the days of Phillis Wheatley." Wright did not stop here; his intention was to wipe Hurston off the map as a serious writer of African-American fiction: "The sensory sweep of her novel carries no theme, no message, no thought...[Hurston] exploits the phase of Negro life which is 'quaint,' the phase which evokes a piteous smile on the lips of the 'superior' race" (Gates and Appiah 1993: 16–17). Alain Locke's review for *Opportunity* is almost tame by comparison. Locke praised the novel for moving beyond "so much local color fiction about Negroes," but he mourned Hurston's apparent refusal to "come to grips" with what he called "social document fiction" (Gates and Appiah 1993: 18).

Fortunately, Wright, Locke, Sterling Brown, and other Harlem Renaissance figures were not Hurston's only jury. Hurston was in fact blessed with enthusiastic and perceptive readers, many of whom drew attention to those features of her work that have become the focus of later critical assessments. Reviewers described Hurston's unenviable task of making folk culture seem relevant to readers who, by their race and social standing, are far removed from that culture; reviewers were also sensitive to Hurston's sometimes precarious position as a critical but subjective ethnographer who chose *not* to write herself out of her works. In its review of *Jonah's Gourd Vine* the *New Republic* noted Hurston's dual and sometimes complicated status as a participant/ observer: "An insider, she shares with her hero the touch of 'pagan poesy' that made him thrill his hearers when he preached. But she is an insider without the insider's usual neurosis" (Gates and Appiah 1993: 7). Although her second collection of folklore, *Tell My Horse*, was less well received than *Mules and Men*, readers could still see that the author was attempting to master a hybrid form of nonfiction that could accommodate the discourses of travelogue, political commentary, personal reminiscence, anthropology, and folklore. The *Saturday Review* described the tension that results from such a multivocal work with its "constant conflict between anthropological truth and taletelling, between the obligation [Hurston] feels to give the facts honestly and the attraction of (as one of her characters says in *Mules and Men*) the 'big ole lies we tell when we're jus' sittin' around here on the store porch doin' nothin'" (Gates and Appiah 1993: 25).

Hurston's obscurity at the time of her death seems especially unjust in view of the legends that have come to define her dramatic personality, including her quarrels not only with Langston Hughes but also with the many academic headmasters for whom she attempted to work and with whom she could not agree. Hurston's obscurity at the end of her life – and her critical neglect for a period of about three decades – should not have been the fate of the child whose mother taught her to jump at the sun and who developed what by any indication was an extraordinary sense of self-worth. It is this profound sense of self that Hurston documents in her much discussed autobiography, the work that inevitably finds itself at the center of debates regarding Hurston's artistic intentions.

Dust Tracks on a Road begins with Hurston tracing her early desire to create and inspire. She covers the years of her upbringing in an all-black and nurturing community where she became uniquely sensitive to the beauty of African-American culture. She then describes the period following her mother's death when she was sent to live with relatives, a time she defines as her "wanderings" (1995a: 618). Hurston describes her intense hatred for her stepmother, her travels as a maid to the female lead in a Gilbert and Sullivan touring troupe, her schooling at Morgan Academy in Baltimore and Howard University in DC, her job as a chauffeur and companion to novelist Fannie Hurst, and her study of anthropology with Franz Boas at Barnard College. Along the way Hurston stresses her self-preserving sense of humor, her will to become part of the artistic world, and her desire for justice in a land that seems always bent on another course. She concludes *Dust Tracks* with a group of self-reflective essays on topics such as love, religion, and race. Hurston finds that her sense of herself as "a precious gift" (1995a: 796) is always complicated by the sexual dynamics that undergird and ultimately undermine relationships. She provides a debunking critique of conventional religion because it is at odds with her intellectual skepticism and essentially pantheistic view of the world. And, as if to highlight her differences with Alain Locke and other African-American intellectuals, Hurston explores the platitudes that have, from her perspective, shaped and often squelched the discourse of racial advancement. *Dust Tracks on a Road* is a remarkable piece of self-disclosure, but because it can also be read as a work of self-concealment, it has become unquestionably Zora Neale Hurston's most controversial work.

Hurston does not shy away from contradictions. The self-image that she presents in *Dust Tracks* is that of a woman in motion, seizing every moment for the experience it might offer. She underscores her strong sense of communal kinship, but she also insists that her bonds to the folk – and to all other people – are always up against her equally strong sense of separateness, what she calls her "cosmic loneliness" (1995a: 598). Here Hurston speaks with the voice of direct statement, but more often she chooses a less direct or more oblique way to suggest her sense of separation. For instance, she recalls the time when as a child she was sent back home from school in Jacksonville. Hurston remembers the boat trip and the captain's pleasure with her spelling abilities: "The captain kept passing through and pulling my hair and asking me to spell something, and kept being surprised when I did. He called out 'separate'...and I spelled it back at him as I went down the gangplank." This incident might seem trivial had the captain asked for another potentially tricky but less racially evocative word. Hurston adds that it looked as if this white man "had some more words he wanted spelled. Then he threw a half dollar that fell just ahead of me and smiled goodbye" (1995a: 631–2). The memory conveys Hurston's sense of separateness – the flip side of her bond with her Eatonville hometown and yet apparently the component of her personality that enabled her to stand apart and render what she perceived to be the essence of this community. The memory also suggests, however subtly, the pattern of patronage that Hurston would find necessary as an African-American woman writing at mid-century. It is not a lengthy recollection (Hurston tends to favor the brief sketch, the short but evocative encounter), and yet it indicates the care with which one must approach Hurston's autobiography.

Indeed, it illustrates her belief that a life emerges only with the participation of a thinking and active reader.

One of the major complaints brought against Hurston's autobiography is that it contains little commentary on her other work. It is true that Hurston provides no sustained analysis of her books or her creative processes, but what she does provide may be equally important: she pinpoints the impulse that prompted her to become a writer who would work outside any given prescriptions. Regarding *Their Eyes Were Watching God*, her most widely praised novel, Hurston notes that it was written during a brief period in Haiti when a relationship had come to a turning point. What she offers the reader is an account of the novel's genesis: it evolved from her attempts to "embalm" all the "tenderness" of her romantic passion into a work of art (1995a: 750). Hurston is content to leave any further analysis to the novel's reader.

Another charge brought against Hurston's account of herself in *Dust Tracks* is that she minimizes the brutality of the South – a region in which African Americans were only rarely part of self-constructed and supportive communities such as Eatonville. In her foreword to the Harper Collins reissue, Maya Angelou claims (somewhat inexplicably) that Hurston "does not mention even one unpleasant racial incident" and that the book, whatever its virtues, was the result of Hurston's "imperious creativity" (1991: x, xii). Hurston's biographer, Robert Hemenway, is less caustic but still claims *Dust Tracks* "is an autobiography at war with itself" (1977: 272–8). In a foreword to Hemenway's biography, Alice Walker remarks, "For me, the most unfortunate thing Zora ever wrote is her autobiography. After the first several chapters, it rings false" (xvii). The book's initial reviews were, by contrast, quite positive and *Dust Tracks* was awarded the *Saturday Review*'s Anisfield-Wolf Award for the year's best book on race relations. The negative reactions from Walker and other critics have been countered by Nellie McKay, Henry Louis Gates, and others, but it is still likely that Hurston's autobiography will never please all her critics. The strong reactions it elicits are further evidence of the ways in which Hurston has been appropriated and even recreated by her readers.

One of the most important events in recent scholarship on Hurston is the Library of America's 1995 publication of a restored *Dust Tracks*, including all the chapters and passages that were omitted by Hurston's publisher, Bertram Lippincott, when the book appeared in 1942. According to Cheryl Wall, Hurston's editors deleted political and sexual commentary and anything that might invite a libel suit (Hurston 1995a: 983). The restored passages – roughly 10 percent of her typescript – provide a more complete picture of Hurston's sense of self and worldview. Here, for example, is a previously omitted passage in which Hurston uses a sexually encoded anecdote to comment on the breach between men and women:

> One afternoon my oldest brother was on the store porch with the men. He was proudly stroking two or three hairs on his top lip. A married man in his late twenties was giving him some advice about growing a big, thick mustache. I went on inside. While I was coming out, I heard something about getting his finger wet from a woman and wiping

it on his lips. Best mustache-grower God ever made. They all grew theirs that way. It was a good thing my brother let them know so he could be told the inside secret. I emerged from the door and the porch fell silent. (1995a: 600–1)

Hurston uses free-indirect speech to convey the interaction of the men on the porch – the scene where many tales unfold in Hurston's world – and to represent herself as a privileged and interpretive observer. Only after she goes to college and studies anthropology does she understand that the men on the porch were initiating her brother into the rituals of manhood. Hurston engages in some playful one-upmanship when she says that "a man's moustache was given him by a woman anyhow. It seems that Adam came to feel that his face needed more decoration than it had. Eve, obligingly, took a spot of hair from where she had no particular use for it – it didn't show anyway, and slapped it across Adam's mouth, and it grew there" (1995a: 601). Hurston's little story is ribald and entertaining in itself, but it also reveals her understanding that the rites of manhood depend upon women and yet exclude them at the same time; it also suggests that she can hold her own in this sometimes-uneven playing field. The story of the moustache is a subtle playing out of the sexual dynamics that Hurston describes at greater length in her chapter on love. Given her affinity with the trickster figure in African-American folklore, it seems odd that many critics would praise the many disguises and modes of indirection in her fiction and yet expect a more prosaic or pedestrian account of her own life.

It is perhaps understandable that a publisher would attempt to avoid libel suits from living persons who might object to Hurston's presentation of their behavior; less easy to understand are the attempts to silence Hurston's political commentary or, rather, her desire to define herself within a political framework. Hurston provided a scathing critique of American imperialism that her Lippincott editors deemed unsuitable for publication during the war years, including a satirical response in the form of an allegory to the question, "Will military might determine the dominant religion of tomorrow?" Hurston casts Franklin Roosevelt, whose liberalism she always contested, as "Sincere Determination," a figure that is capable of deciding which countries "rated crowns of empire and which didn't" (1995a: 761–2). In another excised passage (again one that must have seemed unsuitable during a time of war), Hurston asserts: "while we all talk about justice more than any other quality on earth, there is no such thing as justice in the absolute in the world. We are too human to conceive of it. We all want the breaks, and what seems just to us is something that favors our wishes. If we did not feel this way, then there would be no monuments to conquerors in our high places" (1995a: 765–6). Hurston had a keen understanding of the ways in which power is played out not only in individual relationships but also on international stages. It would therefore seem that she might be more tolerant of Roosevelt's policies in a time of war, but Roosevelt was also aligned with the Left and with its dream of a collectivist society. Given her insistence on human acquisition and the human will to conquer, Hurston could not accept a view of society that would do away with the social hierarchies that emerge not only in relationships between men and women but also in larger communal structures.

Hurston's political views are rooted in her defiant individualism, as are her views on race. She could claim no consciousness of race while simultaneously producing a body of writing that seems conscious of race at every turn. Like the Florida alligator, she seems happy to "muddy the water." It is worth noting, however, that Hurston's ego does not preclude a sense of humility. She claims, in fact, to regret not only her autobiography (which did not say everything she wanted it to say) but her other books as well: "It is one of the tragedies of life that one cannot have all the wisdom one is ever to possess in the beginning . . . Anyway, the force from somewhere in Space which commands you to write in the first place, gives you no choice. You take up the pen when you are told, and write what is commanded" (1995a: 717).

Here Hurston links herself, perhaps unintentionally, to her father and to other ministers who received a similar calling. Like these figures, Hurston carefully shaped a public persona and fully intended for her words to reach an audience. She said as much in her 1934 application for a Julius Rosenwald Fellowship to pursue graduate work in anthropology at Columbia. "It is almost useless," she wrote, "to collect material to lie upon the shelves of scientific societies . . . The Negro material is eminently suited to drama and music. In fact it *is* drama and music and the world and America in particular needs what this folk material holds" (1995a: 970). As an artist, Hurston's goal was to present her folk material in all its fullness; she wanted to make it immediately accessible while she simultaneously conveyed its textual richness and the many ways in which it is embedded within larger patterns of cultural mythology. As Craig Werner remarked, "Hurston projected a dazzling variety of (modernist) personae and (folk) masks. On the few occasions when she encountered individuals aware of the nuances that both connect and distinguish the two phrasings – she never encountered a sizable group who shared her knowledge – they were almost invariably men who were unable to reconcile her ability with their preoccupations concerning women's creative abilities" (1993: 137).

It is safe to say that Hurston would be pleased with the fact that her work has found its audience, one possibly even larger than she could have imagined. Since the late 1970s critics have left few stones unturned. Hurston has been examined within the contexts of documentary and oral storytelling traditions; within the evolution of American ethnic humor; within the social history of gender politics and female sexual freedom; and within debates about colonialism, the African diaspora, black nationalism, and patterns of assimilation. The critical tools of deconstruction, feminist autobiographical theory, reader-response criticism, and psychoanalytical theory have been applied to Hurston's writings, and her works have been examined for what they might reveal about topics ranging all the way from the carnivalesque to black hair styles.

Hurston's importance as a twentieth-century woman of letters cannot be overestimated; less resolved, oddly enough, is her critical standing as a Southern writer. In a symposium on the state of Southern literary study, Eric Sundquist notes that multiculturalism has helped to reconfigure the ways in which Southern literature can be defined and studied. But Sundquist also notes that "aspects of the [Southern] Agrarian tradition are alive and well" and that to acknowledge this presence "is much more honest and revealing than the pretense that, say, Zora Neale Hurston has carried the day" (Sundquist et al. 1999: 687).

That Sundquist uses Hurston as his benchmark is an indication of her importance, but the truth of his statement can be attested to by the fact that only a handful of scholarly articles have attempted to link Hurston to her white Southern contemporaries. The most important of these is Jan Cooper's "Zora Neale Hurston Was Always a Southerner Too." Cooper urges readers to "question exactly how 'white' previously assumed European American traditions may be" (1993: 58–9), and she links Hurston to the very group of writers that she is pitted against by Eric Sundquist – the Nashville Agrarians. Cooper defines Hurston's goal as the preservation of the Southern culture she knew from her own observation, but she also notes that the "urge to preserve a traditional Southern culture because it might contain healing power for the future" is less commonly associated with black writers than with the influential Agrarians (63). Like the Nashville group, however, Hurston was drawn to the "pervasive mythic image" of the agrarian community (61), and in *Their Eyes Were Watching God* she presents "something as close to the agrarian ideal as a modern Southern writer could imagine, a community in which all members have a well-defined role and are fundamentally at harmony with the luxuriant natural world surrounding them" (66).

Cooper's compelling argument challenges the assumption that labels such as "Harlem Renaissance" or "Southern Renaissance" can reveal anything especially useful about a writer as distinctive and as self-assured as Zora Neale Hurston. Though she regarded herself always as a Southerner, Hurston did not confine herself to those concerns that are so often trotted out to define the distinctiveness of (white) Southern writing: a sense of the past in the present, an awareness of evil and human limitations, a respect for the communal order, and so on. These preoccupations appear in Hurston's work, but they seem subordinate to her larger design as a Southern writer – a design she may have inadvertently outlined when in 1938 she was asked by the Federal Writers Project to provide a "Proposed Recording Expedition into the Floridas." One cannot read Hurston's proposal without an awareness of the ways in which it speaks to her work as a whole:

> There is not a state in the Union with as much to record in a musical, folklore, social-ethnic way as Florida has . . . No other state in the Union has had the history of races blended and contending. Nowhere else is there such a variety of materials. Florida is still a frontier with its varying elements still unassimilated. There is still an opportunity to observe the wombs of folk culture still heavy with life. Recordings in florida [*sic*] will be like backtracking a large part of the United States, Europe, and Africa, for these elements have been attracted here and brought a gift to Florida culture each in its own way. The drums throb: Africa by way of Cuba; Africa by way of the British West Indies; Africa by way of Haiti and Martinique; Africa by way of Central and South America.

Old Spain speaks through many interpreters. Old English speaks through black, white, and intermediate lips. Florida, the inner melting pot of the great melting pot America. (1999: 66–7)

Hurston's now-recovered writings for the WPA record the distinguishing and sometimes vanishing characteristics of this distinctive multicultural state. In a sense, Hurston's collected work prefigures the current movement to deprovincialize the study of Southern culture and the region's literature. A brilliant, if at times contrarian, thinker, Hurston is, as John Lowe maintains, a twentieth-century Southern descendant of the African griot. Her status as an important modernist, an influential woman writer, and a major African-American artist is incontestable. In time her status as a *Southern* writer may seem equally crucial.

REFERENCES AND FURTHER READING

Angelou, Maya (1991) "Foreword." *Dust Tracks on a Road*, by Zora Neale Hurston. New York: Harper Collins.

Boyd, Valerie (2003) *Wrapped in Rainbows: The Life of Zora Neale Hurston*. New York: Scribner.

Brantley, Will (1993) *Feminine Sense in Southern Memoir: Smith, Glasgow, Welty, Hellman, Porter, and Hurston*. Jackson: University Press of Mississippi.

Carby, Hazel (1994) "The Politics of Fiction, Anthropology, and the Folk: Zora Neale Hurston." In Genevieve Fabre and Robert O'Meally (eds.) *History and Memory in African-American Culture* (28–44). New York: Oxford University Press.

Cooper, Jan (1993) "Zora Neale Hurston Was Always A Southerner Too." In Carol S. Manning (ed.) *The Female Tradition in Southern Literature* (57–69). Urbana: University of Illinois Press.

Davis, Rose Parkman (1997) *Zora Neale Hurston: An Annotated Bibliography and Reference Guide*. Westport, CT: Greenwood Press.

Gates, Henry Louis, Jr. (1988) *The Signifying Monkey: A Theory of Afro-American Literary Criticism*. New York: Oxford University Press.

Gates, Henry Louis, Jr., and Appiah, K. A. (eds.) (1993) *Zora Neale Hurston: Critical Perspectives Past and Present*. New York: Amistad.

Glassman, Steve, and Seidel, Kathryn Lee (eds.) (1991) *Zora in Florida*. Orlando: University of Central Florida Press.

Hemenway, Robert E. (1977) *Zora Neale Hurston: A Literary Biography*. Foreword by Alice Walker. Urbana: University of Illinois Press.

Howard, Lillie P. (ed.) (1993) *Alice Walker and Zora Neale Hurston: The Common Bond*. Westport, CT: Greenwood Press.

Hughes, Langston, and Hurston, Zora Neale (1991) *Mule Bone: A Comedy of Negro Life*, ed. George Houston Bass and Henry Louis Gates, Jr. New York: Harper Collins.

Hurston, Zora Neale (1995a) *Folklore, Memoirs, and Other Writings*, ed. Cheryl A. Wall. New York: Library of America. Includes *Mules and Men* (1935), *Tell My Horse* (1938), *Dust Tracks on a Road* (1942), and selected nonfiction.

Hurston, Zora Neale (1995b) *Novels and Stories*, ed. Cheryl A. Wall. New York: Library of America. Includes *Jonah's Gourd Vine* (1934), *Their Eyes Were Watching God* (1937), *Moses, Man of the Mountain* (1939), *Seraph on the Suwanee* (1948), and selected short stories.

Hurston, Zora Neale (1999) *Go Gator and Muddy the Water: Writings by Zora Neale Hurston from the Federal Writers' Project*, ed. Pamela Bordelon. New York: Norton.

Kaplan, Carla (ed.) (2002) *Zora Neale Hurston: A Life in Letters.* New York: Doubleday.

Kreyling, Michael (1998) *Inventing Southern Literature.* Jackson: University of Mississippi Press.

Lowe, John (1994) *Jump at the Sun: Zora Neale Hurston's Cosmic Comedy.* Urbana: University of Illinois Press.

McKay, Nellie (1988) "Race, Gender, and Cultural Context in Zora Neale Hurston's *Dust Tracks on a Road.*" In Bella Brodski and Celeste M. Schenck (eds.) *Life/Lines: Theorizing Women's Autobiography* (175–88). Ithaca, NY: Cornell University Press.

Plant, Deborah (1995) *Every Tub Must Sit On Its Own Bottom: The Philosophy and Politics of Zora Neale Hurston.* Urbana: University of Illinois Press.

Pondrom, Cyrena N. (1985) "The Role of Myth in Hurston's *Their Eyes Were Watching God,*" *American Literature,* 58, 2: 181–202.

Sundquist, Eric, et al. (1999) "A Symposium: The Business of Inventing the South," *Mississippi Quarterly,* 52, 4: 659–87.

Werner, Craig (1993) "Zora Neale Hurston." In Elaine Showalter, Lea Baechler, and A. Walton Litz (eds.) *Modern American Women Writers: Profiles of their Lives and Works – from the 1870s to the Present* (137–47). New York: Collier.

28

Flannery O'Connor

Susan Castillo

The Southern novelist Flannery O'Connor once remarked that all of us are grotesque in one way or another, though we rarely realize this about ourselves, and that indeed what is considered normal is often grotesque, while the grotesque itself is the stuff of everyday reality. An example of this are the bizarre road signs which flank Southern highways and which are a source of endless delight for the semiotician. Though it would be difficult to choose a favorite (serious contenders would be "Do not shoot from highway," "Get Right with God," and the truculent "Don't mess with Texas,"), my own personal choice is "Read Signs," spotted near Pelahatchie, Mississippi. Clearly, there is a logical contradiction at work here; if one does not read signs, one is hardly likely to be galvanized into doing so by reading the one in question.

As a person who was born and raised in the American South, I have always been a bit bemused by the to-do over what critics (particularly those who hail from points north of the Mason Dixon line) call the Southern Grotesque or the Southern Gothic. The abundance, in texts by Southern writers, of references to the distorted, freakish, and absurd elements which seem to be woven into the texture of everyday life are, as any Southerner can attest, not mere stylistic devices but rather Aristotelian mimesis of the first water: Southern life really *is* like that. One could of course argue that distortion, freakishness, and absurdity are not exclusive to the South, and indeed one does encounter them in the work of writers from other regions. The uniqueness of the Southern Grotesque, however, is its moral dimension and its attempts to come to terms with unspeakable histories and events; writers such as Flannery O'Connor and Eudora Welty have chronicled this phenomenon not only with amusement but also with a certain compassion devoid of sentimentality or condescension.

In much recent criticism, the terms "gothic" and "grotesque" are used interchangeably. In this essay I shall begin by sketching the history of the grotesque in fiction and by looking at the characteristics of what has come to be known as the Southern Grotesque or Gothic. I then go on to review recent theorization on abjection, with emphasis on the work of Julia Kristeva. I shall then go on to analyze Flannery

O'Connor's novel *Wise Blood* and her short story "The Artificial Nigger" in the light of these concepts.

Colonial texts describe the South as "a delicate garden, abounding with all kinds of odoriferous flower" where making a living demanded "no toil or labor." In a certain sense, subsequent Southern fiction attempts to come to terms with the contradictions between this pastoral vision of the South as idyllic agrarian dream and the historical reality of a patriarchal culture which relied on the extensive use of slave labor. One thinks, for example, of Mark Twain's *Huckleberry Finn* and the contrast between the ideal world of Huck and Jim on the raft floating down the Mississippi and the sordid world of redneck reality on the banks of the river. This ambivalence persisted into twentieth-century Southern writing. The Southern Agrarians, including writers and critics such as John Crowe Ransom, Allan Tate, Robert Penn Warren, and Donald Davidson, reaffirmed pastoral agrarian values and denounced what they perceived as the tainted priorities of an economy based on industry and commerce.

It is, however, in the texts of certain Southern women writers that this division between idyllic pastoral dream and crude historical, economic, and political realities is most clearly apparent. In many ways, the style which critics call the Southern Grotesque can be described as a reaction to the discrepancy between the vision of the South as antebellum pastoral Arcadia on the one hand and the crude historical realities of a patriarchal, racist society on the other. It is thus instructive to wander through the gallery of freaks and deformities which abound in this genre, since they can offer us telling insights into exactly which unpalatable realities the South has repressed in its own vision of itself.

The word "grotesque" is derived from the Old Italian *grottesco*, odd or extravagant, and was originally used to describe the paintings decorating the walls of a grotto or cave. Webster's *New Twentieth-Century Unabridged Dictionary* describes it in the following terms:

> 1. in or of a style of painting, sculpture, etc. in which forms of persons and animals are intermingled with foliage, flowers, fruit, etc. in a fantastic design; 2. characterized by distortions or striking incongruities in appearance, shape, manner, etc.; fantastic, bizarre; 3. ludicrously eccentric or strange; ridiculous, absurd.

Thus, the grotesque is characterized by the juxtaposition of contradictory elements or genres, meant to produce a feeling of alienation or defamiliarization in the reader or spectator in order to present a reality characterized by radical discontinuity, devoid of significance, in which human beings attempt to create meaning in a world which is disjointed and senseless. The German theorist Wolfgang Kayser has suggested that the grotesque is based on a vision of this estranged world:

> Suddenness and surprise are essential elements...We are so strongly affected and terrified because it is our world which ceases to be reliable, and we feel that we would be unable to live in this changed world. The grotesque instills the fear of life

rather than the fear of death. Structurally, it presupposes that the categories which apply to our world view become inapplicable. We have observed the progressive dissolution ... the fusion of realms which we know to be separated, the abolitions of the law of statistics, the loss of identity, the distortions of natural size and shape, the suspension of the category of objects, the destruction of the personality, and the fragmentation of the historical order. The grotesque is a play with the absurd ... an attempt to invoke and subdue the demonic aspects of the world.[1]

The grotesque is thus an aesthetic of extremes. There is indeed a tradition of the grotesque in American literature, dating from the convoluted autobiographies of the colonial period, going on to the work of Charles Brockden Brown and Edgar Allan Poe, and later in that of Ambrose Bierce and Sherwood Anderson. Indeed, F. Scott Fitzgerald's description of the bizarre party guests of Jay Gatsby in *The Great Gatsby* is a *tour de force* of the grotesque, as are the tormented characters which people the fiction of Nathanael West. But it should be said that the South, as a region and a culture of extremes characterized by a certain decadence and by racial and social fragmentation, is especially fertile soil for this genre.

The critic Erwin Panofsky suggests that the grotesque is ultimately an art of acceptance and reconciliation of contradictory possibilities.[2] Indeed, it represents a certain recognition of the fact that amid the essentially chaotic and violent nature of the universe, it is the perception of the individual that orders and gives meaning to reality. It is important to keep in mind, however, that the grotesque/gothic is an aesthetic based on instability, and that the reconciliation of possibilities that Panofsky posits is a contingent and fleeting one at best. At the same time, an essential condition of the grotesque is its comic nature. Gilbert Muller has pointed out that

the subject matter of the grotesque – the raw material which creates the vision – is always potentially horrible, but the treatment of this material is comic: this explains the peculiar complexity of tone, combining both horror and the ludicrous, which characterizes the grotesque as an art form. But our laughter at grotesque figures is always tinged with uneasiness and a certain sense of guilt at our own amusement.[3]

It is this guilty pleasure that distinguishes the grotesque from the surreal; in surrealism, the realm of the irrational is viewed with wonder. Thus, characters in a fiction of the grotesque are always contradictory, with more than a hint of the absurd. The grotesque plot is characterized by exaggeration, comic melodrama, the juxtaposition of the horrible and the ridiculous.

In attempting to understand texts in the Southern Grotesque tradition and the ways in which the irrational and the arbitrary are seen as part of the fabric of everyday life, one of the most useful concepts I have encountered is that of abjection. It is arguable that in the work of certain Southern middle-class writers, the hidden violence of existing social structures (and doubts about their legitimacy) are repressed and then displaced into figures of comic horror: clowns, tricksters, demons, fanatics, pranksters, villains. In these texts, the reader is confronted with spectral, monstrous embodiments of what is unstable or contradictory about their own cultural positions, with "othered" versions of their own nightmares. Clearly, the possibility of complete alignment between a unified self and a stable, essential culture is nothing more than a mirage. But the realization that such a concept is merely a chimera and thus ultimately unattainable provokes fear and pain, and middle-class writers and readers often react by projecting malign intentions onto these grotesque Others who threaten to reveal the fundamental instability of their structures of meaning and hierarchy.

In her recent theoretical work, Julia Kristeva has linked such figures of horror with psychoanalytic concepts of abjection. In *Powers of Horror* Kristeva characterizes the darkness or "maternal blackness" of the womb as a state which is both feared and desired, and which is present (however remotely) in the memory of us all. The moment of birth, in which the child is emerging from the mother's body, is viewed as the site of liminality *par excellence*; the child is both within its mother and outside her, and is simultaneously leaving its prenatal existence and beginning to live towards death. For Kristeva, this primordial division of the self is the situation of radical heterogeneity from which one can never completely escape, but which must be overcome in order to achieve individuation. In this sense, the meaning of the word "abject" is literal; one must throw away or cast aside this multiplicity of selves in order to convert it into a symbol which can in turn be subjected to (and viewed negatively within), not the body of the mother, but the symbolic order ruled by the Law of the Father. This process in turn produces spectral or monstrous Others who embody this state of unstable hybridity and ambivalence, between center and margin, childhood and adulthood, masculinity and femininity.[4] Barbara Creed observes that constructions of the monstrous are often based on religious and historical notions of abjection, in particular sexual immorality and perversion, corporeal alteration, decay and death, human sacrifice, bodily wastes, the feminine body, and incest.[5]

It seems to me that Kristeva's ideas on abjection are particularly useful in the analysis of Southern Gothic texts, given the instability of certain categories that are central to Southern culture and Southern subjectivities. Foremost among these are race, gender roles, and religion. Despite its history of racial segregation, interracial sexual relationships have existed since time immemorial in the South, regardless of Jim Crow laws and the Code Noir. The notion of racial separateness, of the two races coexisting side by side in hermetically sealed divisions and never intermingling, is little more than a fiction: the most cursory of glances at a representative sample of Southerners will reveal that they come in all shades and colors. The physicality of the phenomenon of abjection takes on even greater force when one bears in mind the overpowering importance of bodies in Southern culture. In the South, the color of one's body directly determined whether one was slave or free; even nowadays, race and racial categories play a significant role in delimiting the individual's possibilities of socioeconomic mobility. Gender roles in the South are equally unstable, with contradictory stereotypes of strong women such as the Steel Magnolia coexisting with visions of the Southern Lady as a delicate hothouse flower, particularly after World War II with the entry of increasing numbers of Southern women into the workforce.

Finally, religion and attitudes toward death have always been the most ambivalent of phenomena in the South, with apocalyptic fundamentalists living alongside carefree hedonists who do not identify with any denomination; snake handlers court death on the same streets where funeral parlors prettify corpses with pancake makeup.

Flannery O'Connor, who captures many of these contradictions in her work, was one of the most skilled practitioners of the style which has come to be known as the Southern Grotesque or Southern Gothic. This was not by accident; in her essay "The Grotesque in Southern Fiction" she states that the kind of fiction which can accurately be called grotesque is so because of a directed intention on the part of the author.[6] After discussing the confinements and limitations of the realist and naturalist traditions and invoking Nathaniel Hawthorne's distinction between novel and romance, she goes on to state:

> If the writer believes that our life is and will remain essentially mysterious, if he looks upon us as beings existing in a created order to whose laws we freely respond, then what he sees on the surface will be of interest to him only as he can go through it into an experience of mystery itself. His kind of fiction will always be pushing its own limits outward ... Such a writer will be interested in what we don't understand rather than in what we do. He will be interested in possibility rather than in probability. He will be interested in characters who are forced out to meet evil and grace and who act on a trust beyond themselves – whether they know very clearly what it is they act upon or not. (*CW* 815–16)

Later in the same essay, she adds that a novelist should be characterized not by his function but by his vision.

Flannery O'Connor's dark visions were not always fully understood by her contemporaries. When her first novel, *Wise Blood*, appeared, one obtuse critic declared that the author dwelled on degeneracy in "an insane world, peopled by monsters and submen,"[7] concluding that the protagonist, Hazel Motes, was not credible because he was "a poor, sick, ugly, raving lunatic." John Simons, reviewing it in *Commonweal*, dismissed it as "a kind of Southern Baptist version of *The Hound of Heaven*,"[8] while *Time* magazine, with its usual inane glibness, saw it "as if Kafka had been set to writing the continuity for L'il Abner."[9] In recent decades, however, and particularly after 1980, the outpouring of critical studies on O'Connor's work has assured her status as one of the major writers of twentieth-century American fiction.

By any standard, *Wise Blood* is an extraordinary achievement. The reader first encounters Hazel Motes, its protagonist, traveling by train to the city of Taulkinham. He is described as a young country bumpkin of about twenty, with a broad-brimmed preacher hat, wearing a loud blue suit with the price tag still attached. At first glance, it would seem that O'Connor is setting him up as a figure of fun, but there is something dark and forbidding about Hazel, and death is woven into his story at every turn. On the journey he encounters Mrs. Hitchcock, a garrulous matron, who tries to look into his eyes, described as having "the color of pecan shells" (*CW* 3) and who notices that "the outline of a skull under his skin was plain and insistent." As he lies in his berth on the train, Hazel is haunted by memories of death:

> In his half-sleep he thought where he was lying was like a coffin. The first coffin he had seen with someone in it was his grandfather's. They had left it propped open with a stick of kindling the night it had sat in the house with the old man in it, and Haze had watched from a distance, thinking: he ain't going to let them shut it on him; when the time comes, his elbow is going to shoot into the crack. His grandfather had been a circuit preacher, a waspish old man who had ridden over three counties with Jesus hidden in his head like a stinger. When it was time to bury him, they shut the top of his box down and he didn't make a move . . . Haze had had two younger brothers; one died in infancy and was put in a small box. The other fell in front of a mowing machine when he was seven. His box was about half the size of an ordinary one, and when they shut it, Haze ran and opened it up again. They said it was because he was heartbroken to part with his brother, but it was not; it was because he had thought, what if he had been in it and they had shut it on him. (*CW* 9–10)

This fear of entombment is a staple of Gothic fiction which is directly related to abjection. Hazel's greatest fear is that of being buried alive, a state reminiscent of the liminal moment of birth when the child is both within and beyond the mother, divided between the primordial longing for the blackness of the womb/tomb and the fear of oblivion.

Though Hazel had thought of becoming a preacher like his grandfather, his army experience convinced him that in fact he has no soul. He is nonetheless haunted by the image of Christ, described as moving from tree to tree in the back of his mind, "a wild ragged figure motioning him to turn round and come off into the dark where he was not sure of his footing, where he might be walking on the water and not know it and then suddenly know it and drown" (*CW* 11).

The emphasis on signs throughout *Wise Blood* can be seen as a signal of failed attempts to resolve the situations of liminality that plague Southern cultural subject-ivities. On arriving in Taulkinham, Hazel is assaulted by an apparently meaningless barrage of blinking neon signs: "PEANUTS, WESTERN UNION, AJAX, TAXI, HOTEL, CANDY" (*CW* 15). Following yet another sign (MEN'S TOILET. WHITE) to the segregated toilet, he sits in the cubicle (which he chooses because of a sign on the door with "the large word WELCOME, followed by three exclamation points and something like a snake": *CW* 15) and studies the obscene inscriptions on the sides and door. Finally, he notices a scrawled sign advertising the services of Mrs. Leora Watts, a local prostitute, "the friendliest bed in town" (*CW* 16), and decides to flee from Jesus by actively embracing sin. These seemingly random signs, evoking urban chaos, racial segregation, and transgressive sexuality, present Hazel with conundrums he is unable to solve in a meaningful way.

Hazel thus makes a beeline to Mrs. Watts's house. She is a figure straight from a painting by Hieronymus Bosch, with yellow hair, greasy pink skin, and small pointed teeth flecked with green. After informing her that he is not a preacher, Hazel proceeds to lose his virginity, albeit in highly unsatisfactory and guilt-ridden fashion. He nonetheless continues to feel that he is being stalked by Christ. Once again, Hazel is simultaneously fleeing from and embracing mature sexuality.

On his second evening in Taulkinham, Hazel encounters three characters who will figure prominently in his private drama. He meets the first, Enoch Emery, a country boy like himself, as they watch a demonstration of a miraculous potato peeler. Enoch is one of the Doppelganger figures who populate O'Connor's fiction; he is a vision of Hazel's darker side. At the same time Hazel catches sight of a blind man, who seems to be a preacher and who has allegedly blinded himself as an act of faith. He is led by a young girl, who gives Hazel a pamphlet titled "Jesus Calls You," yet another sign (*CW* 21). When the blind man urges him to repent, Hazel replies defiantly that he does not believe in sin, that Jesus does not exist, and shouts to the crowd which has assembled that he is going to preach a new church, which he calls "the church of truth without Jesus Christ crucified."

Shortly after this incident, Hazel decides to buy a car, perhaps because of his compulsion to flee from the danger of unconditional faith. After buying a decrepit car, he cruises at high speed down the highway, until he is obliged to slow down by a truckload of chickens. The slow pace at which he has to drive leaves him vulnerable to glimpses of the menacing signs which flank the highway: "WOE TO THE BLAS-PHEMER AND WHOREMONGER! WILL HELL SWALLOW YOU UP?" (*CW* 42). Despite his frantic efforts to pass the truck and escape from these signs, he is literally brought to a halt by yet another sign: "Jesus Saves." To this, Hazel reacts by reiterating the doctrine of Original Sin, that this sin has come for any person before the whoremongering and the blasphemy. He adds: "Jesus is a trick on niggers" (*CW* 43).

In an attempt to escape from his Christ-ridden conscience, Hazel then goes to the local zoo in order to find Enoch Emery and through him to locate the mysterious blind preacher and his daughter. He encounters Enoch in a landscape of the absurd, a municipal swimming pool flanked by a hot dog stand called the Frosty Bottle in the shape of an Orange Crush soda. There, he and Enoch ogle a local woman, who again resembles a gargoyle out of a medieval nightmare:

> The woman was climbing out of the pool, chinning herself up on the side. First her face appeared, long and cadaverous, with a bandage-like bathing cap coming down almost to her eyes, and sharp teeth protruding from her mouth. Then she rose on her hands until a large foot and leg came up from behind her and another on the other side and she was out, squatting and panting ... Her hair was short and matted and all colors, from deep rust to a greenish yellow. (*CW* 47)

Sexuality is once again associated with death. The woman's "long and cadaverous" face suggests a death's head, and the comparison of the bathing cap to a bandage and the sharp teeth suggest pain and violence. Traditional stereotypes of delicate Southern femininity are exploded: the woman's foot and leg are large, and her hair is "short and matted" like that of a man; the verbs "squatted" and "panted" suggest an animal quality. This is hardly Botticelli's Venus rising from the waves, but rather a night-marish, liminal male/female aggressor.

Enoch then agrees to reveal the whereabouts of the blind preacher and his daughter, if Hazel will agree to see something which he insists on showing him. Hazel, in exasperation, agrees. Enoch tells him of his "wise blood," a kind of visceral preverbal knowledge which provides him with premonitions: "Enoch's brain was divided into two parts. The part in communication with his blood did the figuring but it never said anything in words. The other part was stocked up with all kinds of words and phrases" (*CW* 49). These premonitions, though non-verbal in nature, are nonetheless interpreted by Enoch as signs impelling him to act:

> "... when I saw you at the pool, I had thisyer sign."
> "I don't care about your signs," Haze said. (*CW* 52)

Hazel has despaired of being able to make sense of the signs which are assaulting him.

Nonetheless, he allows Enoch to take him to the zoo, where he is shown what appears to be a piece of mop with an eye (actually an owl). Vision, as has been stated, is all-important in O'Connor; indeed, one of the only things Hazel had taken along when he went to war were the glasses of his pious mother, "in case his vision should ever become dim"(*CW* 13). To the sinister all-seeing eye of the owl, Hazel repeats desperately, "I AM clean" (*CW* 54). Enoch then presents him with yet another sign, graven in concrete: "MUSEVM." Inside the museum, he shows Hazel a shrunken three-foot man in a glass case. At this vision of a diminished humanity, of the jesus with a small j of the Church without Christ, Hazel throws a rock at Enoch and runs away in terror. Here it could be argued that Hazel Motes is fleeing not only from religion but also from his own sexuality; indeed, religion and sexuality are often conflated in Southern culture. His car is a getaway car in the most literal sense; his escapes, ostensibly from his relentless consciousness of God, invariably follow episodes involving women leading him into carnal temptation. This occurs first of all with Leora Watts. Later, Sabbath Lily Hawkes, the daughter of the false blind preacher Asa Hawkes, entices him into bed, provoking another getaway. Despite his protestations that he believes in nothing, Hazel is confident of his car's ability to whisk him away from the danger of faith in religion or in women, and it is in his car that Hazel's dark side emerges in earnest. As Laura Kennelly has observed, it is dangerous to feel pity for an O'Connor character, precisely because the author often uses it to trap the reader into a sentimental empathy based on condescension. It is usually at this point that she pulls the rug from under the reader and his/her preconceptions by having the pitied character do something revolting or morally repugnant.[10] This is certainly the case with Hazel Motes: just as we are beginning to empathize with his existential quest, he uses his car as murder weapon, running repeatedly over the defenseless body of Solace Layfield, an evangelical competitor weirdly similar to himself, who has tried to steal the idea of the Church without Jesus, but who despite this really does believe in Christ:

The man didn't look so much like Haze, lying on the ground on his face without his hat
or suit on. A lot of blood was coming out of him and forming a puddle around his head.
He was motionless all but for one finger that moved up and down in front of his face as
if he were marking time with it. Haze poked his toe in his side and he wheezed for a
second and then was quiet. "Two things I can't stand," Haze said, " – a man that ain't
true and one that mocks what is. You shouldn't have ever tampered with me if you
didn't want what you got." (*CW* 115)

It is only when a bullying highway patrolman pushes his beloved car (the only thing
in which he seems to have real faith) over an embankment that Hazel deliberately
blinds himself in order to recover his original purity of vision.[11] Shortly thereafter, he
dies while fleeing from his landlady, the terrifying rationalist Mrs. Flood, yet another
predatory, sexually threatening woman.

The Southern Grotesque world of *Wise Blood* is, as has been stated, characterized by
an aesthetic of liminality. Its denizens inhabit a fluid realm in which conventional
borders are effaced or erased or shrouded in mystery, in which ontological or epistemological certainties no longer exist. The usual boundaries between human beings,
animals, plants, and even objects are seen as tenuous. Examples of this abound in the
text: the women on the train are "dressed like parrots" and one of them has a "bold pea-
hen expression" (*CW* 7); Leora Watts, the prostitute, has "a grin as curved and sharp as
the blade of a sickle" (*CW* 37); the cheeks of the false blind preacher, Asa Hawkes, are
streaked with lines that give him "the expression of a grinning mandrill" (*CW* 20); the
bears in the municipal zoo are compared to sedate matrons seated face to face, having
tea. But these perceptions are never fixed, never constant. Enoch Emery is described at
first as "a friendly hound dog with light mange" (*CW* 23), but when he spies on the
woman at the swimming pool, his image takes on more sinister connotations:

> She had a stained white bathing suit that fitted her like a sack, and Enoch had watched
> her with pleasure on several occasions. He moved from the clearing up a slope to some
> abelia bushes. There was a nice tunnel under them and he crawled into it until he came
> to a slightly wider place where he was accustomed to sit. He settled himself and
> adjusted the abelia so that he could see through it properly. His face was always very
> red in the bushes. Anyone who parted the abelia sprigs at just that place, would think
> he saw a devil and would fall down the slope and into the pool. (*CW* 45–6)

This acts to reinforce in the reader the sensation that the physical realm is mysterious
and unknowable, populated by demons and malevolent objects, where nothing is
what it seems and nothing remains what it apparently is for very long. Descriptions
involving reflection, mirrors, and polished surfaces occur throughout the text, but the
images they reflect back are distorted. When Hazel goes to Leora Watts's room,
he sees her reflection, slightly distorted, in a yellowish mirror; when he buys the car,
he sees the sinister blasphemous boy he meets on the used car sales lot through the car
windows: "The two window glasses made him a yellow color and distorted his shape"
(*CW* 38).

As Hazel goes around the city, preaching (unsuccessfully) the Church without Christ, he proclaims his belief "it was not right to believe in anything you couldn't see or hold in your hands or test with your teeth." But this narrow positivistic view of reality is ultimately unsatisfactory, and does not enable Hazel to operate any more successfully in the world. The unreliable evidence of his senses induces him into error, over and over, with his mistaken recognition of the porter on the train, and his idea that the sexually aggressive daughter of Asa Hawkes is an innocent child; as well, he is oblivious to Asa's false blindness. O'Connor skewers the Church without Christ, and its positivist refusal to accept whatever it cannot see, in the advice Asa's daughter Sabbath receives when she writes to newspaper columnist Mary Brittle:

> Then she answered my letter in the paper. She said, "Dear Sabbath, Light necking is acceptable, but I think your real problem is one of adjustment to the modern world. Perhaps you ought to re-examine your religious values to see if they meet your needs in Life. A religious experience can be a beautiful addition to living if you put it in the proper perspective and do not let it warp you. Read some books on Ethical Culture."
> (*CW* 67)

For O'Connor, this is what the church without the vision of Christ crucified and without faith in the resurrection amounts to: a fashion accessory, an addition to living divorced from the meaning of life itself.

The secular world portrayed in *Wise Blood* is one of radical epistemological uncertainty. Names are unreliable; Hazel's competitor, the evangelical con man Hoover Shoats, calls himself Onnie Jay Holy. It is a nightmare world, devoid of meaning; each of Hazel's epiphanic moments is precipitated when he is unable to interpret the signs which constantly crop up in neon, on pamphlets, on roadside billboards. And yet it is when he finally surrenders to the realization of the limitations of his senses by the radical act of physically blinding himself, that he gains a measure of tortured peace. As his landlady looks at his dead face, she glimpses in the blackness of the burned-out sockets where his eyes once were a tenuous, receding point of light.

Katherine Hemple Prown reminds us that O'Connor herself was an ambivalent and often contradictory figure who was attempting to function as a writer and to get her work published in the masculinist literary context of the Southern Agrarians by adopting a literary strategy of misogyny and the denial of female subjectivity. It is indeed the case that in *Wise Blood* emphasis is placed on the male characters, and Hazel's quest for spiritual enlightenment is defined mainly in opposition to the female characters of the novel. However, Prown adds that in manuscript versions of the novel, matters are not quite so cut and dried; apparently there are homosexual scenes in the manuscript of *Wise Blood* which did not make it into the published version. It is unclear whether this was a decision on the part of O'Connor herself, or whether this was suggested by her mentor Caroline Gordon, who adopted similarly masculinist strategies.[12]

It is not only in O'Connor's novels that the South's repressed nightmares resurface in gothic forms. In her story "The Artificial Nigger" the reader is confronted with the instability of racial categories and racialized identities in the South. Its protagonist, Mr. Head, is a man of sixty, described as possessing eyes which had "a look of composure and ancient wisdom as if they belonged to one of the great guides of men. He might have been Vergil summoned in the middle of the night to go to Dante, or better Raphael, awakened by a blast of God's light to fly to the side of Tobias" (*CW* 210). He lives with his orphaned grandson Nelson, who as the story opens is asleep on a pallet on the floor. In an arresting juxtaposition of the divine and the excremental, the room in which the boy is sleeping is portrayed in the following terms: "The slop jar, out of the shadow and made snow-white in the moonlight, appeared to stand guard over him like a small personal angel." We learn that the two of them are going to the city where the boy was born, a trip described as a "moral mission" by the grandfather, who hopes to teach the boy that the fact that he was born in a city is no grounds for superiority and to convince him to stay at home in the country for the remainder of his life.

The two rise early and prepare to hail the train. The relationship between grandfather and grandson is one in which they compete to show who has real authority. When the boy invokes his superior city origins, Mr. Head responds that he may discover that he does not like the city after all because "it'll be full of niggers." When the child makes a face indicating that this might not be such a bad thing, the grandfather retorts that Nelson has never seen a Negro, adding, "There hasn't been a nigger in this county since we run that one out twelve years ago and that was before you was born" (*CW* 213). To this, Nelson replies that he will know one when he sees one.

The two catch the train to Atlanta. The journey is replete with gargoyle images blending human characteristics with those of animals or even of plants in a way that is typical of O'Connor's fiction: the conductor is described as having "the face of an ancient bloated bulldog" and Mr. Head has "white hair that has turned tobacco-colored" (*CW* 214). The grandfather embarrasses the boy by telling all the occupants of the coach that this is his first trip to town. Suddenly, a negro man walks through the car. O'Connor describes him thus:

> A huge coffee-colored man was coming slowly forward. He had on a light suit and a yellow satin tie with a ruby pin in it. One of his hands rested on his stomach which rode majestically under his buttoned coat, and in the other he held the head of a black walking stick that he picked up and set down with a deliberate outward motion each time he took a step. He was proceeding very slowly, his large brown eyes gazing over the heads of the passengers. He had a small white mustache and white crinkly hair. Behind him there were two young women, both coffee-colored, one in a yellow dress and one in a green. Their progress was kept at the rate of his and they chatted in low throaty voices as they followed him. (*CW* 215–16)

The man is not black but brown ("coffee-colored"), and appears well-to-do, as evidenced by his satin tie and ruby pin. His procession down the aisle of the train is kingly; his stomach protrudes "majestically" and he holds his walking stick like a scepter. Such an image challenges not only the boundaries of color and racial stereotypes but also those of economic class; the negro is affluent, while Mr. Head and his grandson are clearly not. This disparity is underlined when, as the "procession" (to use O'Connor's own term) passes them, light glints off a sapphire ring on the man's hand. As the negroes leave the car, Mr. Head asks his grandson, "What was that?" The boy replies, "A man." When Mr. Head insists, asking what sort of man he was, the child replies impatiently that he was a fat one, failing to classify the man in terms of racial category. Mr. Head proclaims, "That was a nigger," and teases the boy that he should have known this, given his city origins. The boy retorts angrily that his grandfather had described them as black, and adds, "You never said they were tan" (*CW* 216). To this, his grandfather replies that he is merely ignorant. The child reacts by deflecting his anger toward the figure of the negro:

> Nelson turned backward again and looked where the Negro had disappeared. He felt that the Negro had deliberately walked down the aisle in order to make a fool of him and he hated him with a fierce raw fresh hate; and also, he understood now why his grandfather disliked them. (*CW* 216)

Racists are not born but made. The boy Nelson, confronted with a figure who contradicts all his previous impressions (that negroes are black and whites are white, that negroes are poor and whites are not), resolves this uncomfortable situation of liminality by abjecting his own fear and anger onto the figure of the other, in imitation of his grandfather. Things become even worse when Mr. Head takes the boy to show him the dining car, described as the most elegant car on the train, where meals are being served by "three very black Negroes in white suits and aprons." Here, the reader thinks, is a representation of African Americans more in accordance with traditional Southern stereotypes of the negro as faithful retainer or servant. But even this is turned on its head when the grandfather, on being asked if they would like a space for two, says loudly that they had eaten before they left; clearly, they cannot afford the dining car. To this, the waiter asks them to stand aside, "with an airy wave of his arm as if he were brushing aside flies" (*CW* 217). The large negro man who had come through the carriage *is* able to afford to eat in the dining car. Mr. Head defiantly explains to his grandson that even so, "They rope them off" (*CW* 217). But racial restrictions on space work both ways: when he asks to see the kitchen, the black waiter refuses to allow them entry. In anger, Mr. Head shouts that this is because the cockroaches in the kitchen would run the passengers out. This provokes a laugh among the white travelers, and Nelson feels pride in his grandfather.

When they reach Atlanta, they are assaulted by a multiplicity of signs as they look out the window. Many of these signs evoke racial and regional stereotypes: Southern Maid Flour, Dixie Doors, Southern Belle Cotton Products, Southern Mammy Cane Syrup. On alighting from the train, they stop to weigh themselves on a scale which also issues tickets with their fortunes. Their weights are wildly inaccurate, but Nelson is told that a great destiny awaits him; however, he is warned that he should beware of dark women. But he loves the city, and cries out in exultation that he was born there and it was where he came from. His grandfather reacts by ordering him to put his head down the sewer:

> Mr. Head was appalled. He saw the moment had come for drastic action. "Lemme show you one thing you ain't seen yet," he said and took him to the corner where there was a sewer entrance. "Squat down," he said, "and stick your head in there," and he held the back of the boy's coat while he got down and put his head in the sewer. He drew it back quickly, hearing a gurgling in the depths under the sidewalk. Then Mr. Head explained the sewer system, how the entire city was underlined with it, how it contained all the drainage and was full of rats and how a man could slide into it and be sucked along down pitchblack tunnels. At any minute any man in the city might be sucked into the sewer and never heard from again. (*CW* 220)

If the city is a space of interracial mingling and transgression, the sewers represent the abjection of this hybrid space, symbolized and cast off as filth and read as repugnant. The sewers are described as "pitchblack tunnels," a womblike maternal darkness into where a *man* (my emphasis) may be sucked at any moment. Nelson is frightened for a moment, but he then retorts that a man can stay away from holes.

As they wander around Atlanta, Mr. Head and Nelson become lost, and suddenly realize they are in the heart of an African-American neighborhood. Nelson suggests they ask one of the negroes the way, and when his grandfather refuses to do so, he asks directions of a woman standing in a doorway:

> Nelson stopped. He felt his breath drawn up by the woman's dark eyes. "How do you get back to town?" he said in a voice that did not sound like his own.
>
> After a minute she said, "You in town now," in a rich low tone that made Nelson feel as if a cool spray had been turned on him.
>
> "How do you get back to the train?" he said in the same reed-like voice.
>
> "You can catch you a car," she said.
>
> He understood she was making fun of him but he was too paralyzed even to scowl. He stood drinking in every detail of her. His eyes traveled up from her great knees to her forehead and then made a triangular path from the glistening sweat on her neck down and across her tremendous bosom and over her bare arm back to where her fingers lay hidden in her hair. He suddenly wanted her to reach down and pick him up and draw him against her and then he wanted to feel her breath on his face. He wanted to look down and down into her eyes while she held him tighter and tighter. He had never had such a feeling before. He felt as if he were reeling down through a pitchblack tunnel. (*CW* 222–3)

Once again, the city is presented as the scene of interracial sexuality and transgression. The negro woman is a disconcertingly ambivalent version of the Mammy stereotype, and Nelson's reactions to her veer between incestuous sexual desire (his response to the sensuality of her voice, her breasts, her fingers laced through her hair) and the wish to be held like a small child in her arms, "tighter and tighter." His feelings are a dizzying mixture of lust and terror of being reabsorbed into this primordial black female space, with the motif of the darkened tunnel reappearing once more.

Nelson's grandfather pulls him away, and the two follow the streetcar lines in order to find their way back to a white area. Finally, the boy becomes exhausted and falls down into a deep sleep. Mr. Head decides to teach him a lesson in order to cure him of what he views as the child's impudence. He abandons Nelson on the pavement and hides in a nearby alley to watch him wake up alone. As time passes and Nelson goes on sleeping, his grandfather bangs on the lid of a garbage can. The boy, in a panic, runs down the street and crashes into an elderly woman, spilling her groceries and breaking her ankle. The terrified Nelson is surrounded by a flock of furious women, and when Mr. Head approaches the boy clings hard to him. But Mr. Head denies his grandson, saying that he has never seen him before. The crowd disperses, and the two walk off, but the boy is hurt and angry, and walks at a distance from his grandfather. Finally, a man in a more affluent suburb tells them how to find the suburban train stop so that they can catch the train to return home. Mr. Head tries every sort of overture to make amends, offering Coca-Cola and water to the boy, who continues to repel his attempts, looking at him with "eyes like pitchfork prongs" (*CW* 227).

Reconciliation between the two finally comes about in the unlikely form of a decaying statue of a negro on the lawn of one of the houses. The plaster figure is about the size of the boy, and is described as having one entirely white eye and holding a slice of watermelon:

> Then, as the two of them stood there, Mr. Head breathed, "An artificial nigger!"
>
> It was not possible to tell if the artificial Negro were meant to be young or old; he looked too miserable to be either. He was meant to look happy because his mouth was stretched up at the corners but the chipped eye and the angle he was cocked at gave him a wild look of misery instead.
>
> "An artificial nigger!" Nelson repeated in Mr. Head's exact tone.
>
> The two of them stood there with their necks forward at almost the same angle and their shoulders curved in almost exactly the same way and their hands trembling identically in their pockets. Mr. Head looked like an ancient child and Nelson like a miniature old man. They stood gazing at the artificial Negro as if they were faced with some great mystery, some monument to another's victory that brought them together in their common defeat. They could both feel it dissolving their differences like an action of mercy...
>
> Mr. Head opened his lips to make a lofty statement and heard himself say, "They ain't got enough real ones here. They got to have an artificial one."
>
> After a second, the boy nodded with a strange shivering about his mouth, and said, "Let's go home before we get ourselves lost again." (*CW* 230)

The image of the negro, with its prominent lips stretched into the *commedia dell'arte* grimace that passes for a smile, provides the two with the reassurance they need. In an urban space of transgression that calls into question the symbolic structure and social hierarchies of their world, this racist image of the watermelon-eating, grinning, oppressed negro corresponds exactly to the traditional picture of the subservient negro against which poor Southern whites have defined themselves. The artificial negro is a kind of specular poor man's version of the equestrian statues of Confederate heroes which exist throughout the South; it is a monument to the victory of another social class, and bears witness to the fact that poor whites and disenfranchised blacks have never been able to make common cause. The ageless image of the subservient grinning black man is an eerie mirror image of Mr. Head and Nelson, who like their darker image are neither young nor old, bending over like suppliants with hunched shoulders and trembling hands. It is only in opposition to this dark Doppelganger that they are able to give their own lives meaning and significance.

In the concluding paragraphs of the story, O'Connor suggests that mercy has been brought to Mr. Head because of the agony he has suffered and the awareness he has gained of his own depravity. As the tale draws to a close, Nelson watches the train disappear into the woods "like a frightened serpent" (*CW* 231). Like Adam, he has been tempted by the serpent in the Garden, but unlike Adam he does not intend to fall again.

In Flannery O'Connor's fiction, the reader is presented with the vision of a region which is attempting to repress the nightmares of its historical past and the racial and social injustices of its present. The South of Flannery O'Connor's Southern Grotesque is a Bakhtinian Carnival of crazed businessmen, quixotic knights-errant, sinister hairdressers, devout ministers, serial killers, con artists, and mad housewives desperately seeking redemption. It is, in short, a reasonably accurate and plausible rendering of Southern reality.

NOTES

1   Wolfgang Kayser, *The Grotesque in Art and Literature*, trans. Ulrich Weisstein (Bloomington: Indiana University Press, 1963), p. 184.
2   Erwin Panofsky, *Gothic Architecture and Scholasticism* (Latrobe, PA: Archabbey Press, 1951), p. 64.
3   Gilbert Muller, *Nightmares and Visions: Flannery O'Connor and the Catholic Grotesque* (Athens, GA: University of Georgia Press, 1972), p. 7.
4   See Julia Kristeva, *Powers Of Horror: An Essay on Abjection*, trans. Leon S. Roudiez (New York: Columbia University Press, 1982), pp. 1–89. For a lucid and extremely useful discussion of Kristeva's ideas, see Jerome Hogle, "The Gothic and the 'Otherings' of Ascendant Culture: The Original *Phantom of the Opera*," in D. Punter (ed.) *Spectral Readings: Towards a Gothic Geography* (Basingstoke: Macmillan, 1999), pp. 177–201.
5   Barbara Creed, *The Monstrous Feminine: Film, Feminism, and Psychoanalysis* (London: Routledge, 1993), p. 9.
6   Flannery O'Connor, "The Grotesque in Southern Fiction," in *Flannery O'Connor: Collected Works*, ed. Sally Fitzgerald (New York: Library of America, 1988), p. 814. Subsequent references to this work (to be included parenthetically within the text) will be abbreviated as *CW*.
7   Isaac Rosenfeld, "To Win by Default," review of *Wise Blood*, by Flannery O'Connor, *New Republic*, July 7, 1952: 19–20.

8   John Simons, "A Case of Possession," review of *Wise Blood,* by Flannery O'Connor, *Commonweal,* June 27, 1952: 297–8.

9   "Southern Dissidence." Anonymous review of *Wise Blood*, *Time*, June 9, 1952: 108–10.

10   Laura B. Kennelly, "Exhortation in *Wise Blood*: Rhetorical Theory as an Approach to Flannery O'Connor." In *Flannery O'Connor: New Perspectives*, ed. Sura P. Rath and Mary Neff Shaw (Athens, GA: University of Georgia Press, 1996), p. 156.

11   The idea of blindness as a prerequisite for insight is present, for example, in the story of St. Paul's temporary blindness during his conversion experience on the road to Damascus (as O'Connor herself states), and in the Oedipus myth as well.

12   See Katherine Hemple Prown, *Revising Flannery O'Connor: Southern Literary Culture and the Problem of Female Authorship* (Charlottesville: University of Virginia Press, 2001), pp. 4–5, 138–46, 170.

References and Further Reading

Anonymous (1952) "Southern Dissidence," review of *Wise Blood*, *Time*, June 9: 108–10.

Kayser, Wolfgang (1963) *The Grotesque in Art and Literature*, trans. Ulrich Weisstein. Bloomington: Indiana University Press.

Kennelly, Laura B. (1996) "Exhortation in *Wise Blood*: Rhetorical Theory as an Approach to Flannery O'Connor." In *Flannery O'Connor: New Perspectives*, ed. Sura P. Rath and Mary Neff Shaw. Athens, GA: University of Georgia Press.

Kristeva, Julia (1982) *Powers of Horror: An Essay on Abjection*, trans. Leon S. Roudiez. New York: Columbia University Press.

Muller, Gilbert (1972) *Nightmares and Visions: Flannery O'Connor and the Catholic Grotesque*. Athens, GA: University of Georgia Press.

O'Connor, Flannery (1988) *Collected Works*. New York: Library of America.

Panofsky, Erwin (1951) *Gothic Architecture and Scholasticism*. Latrobe, PA: Archabbey Press.

Prown, Katherine Hemple (2001) *Revising Flannery O'Connor: Southern Literary Culture and the Problem of Female Authorship*. Charlottesville: University of Virginia Press.

Rosenfeld, Isaac (1952) "To Win by Default," review of *Wise Blood* by Flannery O'Connor, *New Republic*, July 7: 19–20.

Simons, John (1952) "A Case of Possession," review of *Wise Blood* by Flannery O'Connor, *Commonweal*, June 27: 297–8.

29

Eudora Welty

Jan Nordby Gretlund

In many readers' minds "the Mississippi writer" is a special category. To call a writer "a Mississippian" is more than placing her geographically. The categorization is, of course, a qualification of "writer," and it may even be understood as a limitation. But like most limitations it is also, as Flannery O'Connor wrote in a comment about Eudora Welty, "a great blessing, perhaps the greatest blessing a writer can have," because it serves as "a gateway to reality." What Welty always knew was that her imagination was bound to the reality of life in her native state; her fiction came out of a particular landscape and was based on her familiarity with the State of Mississippi and its people.

It was no real surprise to anybody that President Clinton called Welty on April 13, 1994 to congratulate her on her eighty-fifth birthday, for Eudora Welty's reputation as an outstanding twentieth-century American writer is secure among professional critics and the general public, both at home and abroad. Her initial success as a writer was the result of her achievement in the genre of the short story, as demonstrated in the collections *A Curtain of Green, The Wide Net and Other Stories*, and *The Golden Apples*, published in the 1940s, and *The Bride of the Innisfallen* (1955), all gathered – with two later stories – as *Collected Stories* in 1980. While critics do not concur on all aspects of her short stories, the preeminence of Welty's work in this genre remains unquestioned. The majority of her short stories are of great tonal variety, set in the American South, and reflect the language and highlight the culture of her region, but her treatment of universal themes clearly transcends regional boundaries.

Eudora Welty also established a reputation as a critic. Her literary criticism was collected in *The Eye of the Story: Selected Essays and Reviews* and in *A Writer's Eye: Collected Book Reviews*, which were published in 1978 and 1994, respectively. Welty was also a photographer. Beginning in the 1930s, she took ruthlessly honest photographs of her world, which at that time included poverty-stricken Depression victims. The interest in photography not only taught her about frame, proportion, perspective, and light and shade, but also about the everyday lives of Mississippians all over the state. Over the years the photos were made available in several collections, for example *One Time, One Place* (1971), *Photographs* from 1989, with a selection of 226 prints, and *Country Churchyards* from the year 2000, which became the last book to be printed in Welty's lifetime. But her greatest popular success came as a result of three mainly autobiographical lectures at Harvard University in 1983, which became the bestselling *One Writer's Beginnings*. It is a tribute to the author's superb style that the book stayed on the bestseller list for almost a full year. In short, her careers as a writer of short fiction, a critic and reviewer, a photographer, and an autobiographer have received much attention and deserved praise over the years, and her name is still associated with these fields of interest.

Her career as a novelist started in 1942 with the publication of *The Robber Bridegroom*, but Welty's work as a writer of novels has not received the attention it merits, neither from critics nor the reading public. *The Robber Bridegroom*, which was adapted as a successful musical and brings together history and fairy tale, and her second novel, *Delta Wedding*, which is in the tradition of the plantation novel, were upon publication compared negatively with her short fiction. However, today, they are almost unanimously regarded as classics in their special genres of the novel. A similar recognition has not yet been given her last two novels. *Losing Battles*, which is a long hymn to rural life, is also an experiment in narrative technique that critics found too episodic. Although it won a Pulitzer Prize in 1973, *The Optimist's Daughter* was a disappointment in its apparent lack of action, and the novel has only recently begun to come into its own.

In today's literary climate there is an obvious need to consider the historical and cultural background for Welty's achievement. The critical consensus nowadays seems to place Welty as a Jungian postmodernist and as an early feminist. It is not that postmodernistic alienation was unknown to her, but for Welty, alienation was still an indication that something is wrong. Although she came of age at a bad time in the poorest state in the union, and this left an indelible mark on her fiction, she was never the alienated author looking for a better place to live and write.

Eudora Alice Welty was born in Jackson, Mississippi, on April 13, 1909, the first surviving child of Mary Chestina Andrews and Christian Webb Welty. She had two brothers, but was the only daughter. Her mother was from West Virginia and of Virginian descent. Her father was from Ohio and of Swiss ancestry. After graduating from Central High School in Jackson in 1925, Eudora Welty went to Columbus to attend the Mississippi State College for Women. After two years she transferred to the University of Wisconsin, where she majored in English literature and received her BA in 1929. Her father urged her to study something that could help her find employment, so after college she studied advertising for a year at the Columbia University Graduate School of Business in New York. But when she came onto the job market it was at the height of the Depression, and advertising jobs were scarce. So in 1931 she returned to Mississippi. Later that year her father died, which was a heavy loss to her. She got a job editing a newsletter, *Lamar Life Radio News*, for the life insurance company where her father had been president.

Welty also supported herself as a society correspondent in Jackson for the Memphis *Commercial Appeal* and she edited the weekly program for WJDX, a local radio station in Jackson. In 1933 she found a job that became more important for her development as a writer than college classes and techniques of advertising: she became a publicity agent, "junior grade," for the newly founded Works Progress Authority. The job meant that she wrote feature stories on local projects in Mississippi's 82 counties. For three years she traveled throughout her state on publicity assignments for the State Office of the WPA. As a hobby she carried a camera, photographed what she saw in the counties, and she wrote short stories based on her experiences. Her stark photos of unposed country people were shown in Lugene Gallery, a camera shop in New York, in 1936, and the same year her first story, "Death of a Traveling Salesman," was published in a journal called *Manuscript*.

Within two years her stories appeared in such prestigious publications as the *Atlantic* and the *Southern Review*. Robert Penn Warren and Cleanth Brooks, who were the editors of the latter, published more stories by Welty than by any other writer in their periodical. The story "Lily Daw and the Three Ladies" was collected in *Best American Short Stories 1938*, "Petrified Man" won an O. Henry Award in 1939, and the influential Diarmuid Russell, son of the Irish poet known as A. E. (George William Russell), became Welty's literary agent in 1940. With the added help and support of Ford Madox Ford and Katherine Anne Porter, her first collection of stories, *A Curtain of Green and Other Stories*, was published in 1941, the next year brought a Guggenheim Fellowship and her first novel *The Robber Bridegroom*, and by 1943, when the second collection of stories, *The Wide Net and Other Stories*, appeared, Welty had a national audience and her reputation as a writer was established.

Welty worked for half a year on the staff of the *New York Times Book Review* during 1944. She reviewed writers she admired, such as William Faulkner, Virginia Woolf, and Isak Dinesen. She also wrote several reviews under the pseudonym of Michael Ravenna about the art that came out of World War II. Her intimate friend in the 1940s, John Frasier Robinson, was in Italy during the war, and to compensate for his absence Welty focused on the Delta, Robinson's native area. Her first full-length novel, *Delta Wedding*, is dedicated to him and includes elements from his family's history. It was published in 1946 and enlarged Welty's audience considerably. In 1949 she published her best book, both in critical estimation and in her own opinion, the short story cycle *The Golden Apples*, which is the most technically complex and thematically most convincing of her works. She received a second Guggenheim Fellowship and started to receive a virtual flow of prizes and awards. The first honorary doctorate came appropriately from the University of Wisconsin upon the publication of the short novel *The Ponder Heart* (1954), which was dramatized and had a successful run on Broadway; it was adapted as an opera composed by Alice Parker, and became a PBS TV play on October 15, 2001.

A few of her early stories were placed in New Orleans, New York, or San Francisco, but it is with *The Bride of the Innisfallen and Other Stories* (1955) that we see fiction by

Welty reflecting her travels in Italy, England, and Ireland. The title story was written at Bowen's Court, County Cork, Eire, and the volume is dedicated to the Irish novelist Elizabeth Bowen. From 1955 to 1970 Welty published only a children's book, originally written for her nieces, *The Shoe Bird* (1964), which later became a ballet, and two important short stories inspired by civil rights themes. During these years she was nursing her demanding, invalid mother and had little time for writing. But in her mind she was preparing her longest novel, *Losing Battles* (1970), which celebrates the family solidarity and the endurance of poor Mississippi farmers in Tishomingo County during the Depression.

When Mrs. Chestina Welty died in January 1966 her daughter was working on a somewhat autobiographical novel, which was first published as a long story taking up a whole issue of *The New Yorker* in March 1969. When *The Optimist's Daughter* appeared as a novel in 1972 it was dedicated to Mrs. Welty, and it appeared on bestseller lists. A decade later the same material was used in Welty's autobiographical William E. Massey lectures at Harvard University (April 1983), which became *One Writer's Beginnings* (1984). From the end of the 1970s until she died on July 23, 2000, Welty made her life's work available in collections of her essays, short stories, photographs, book reviews, and complete novels. The collections show that the whole of her work is greater than the sum of its parts. She was already during her lifetime one of the most honored of writers. In 1973 William L. Waller, governor of Mississippi, proclaimed May 2 "Eudora Welty Day"; in 1982 Millsaps College, MS, established a "Eudora Welty Chair"; in 1986 the Jackson public library was renamed in honor of Eudora Welty; in Columbus, MS, they celebrate the "Eudora Welty Writers' Days" every year; in 1992 she was awarded the Frankel Humanities Prize; in 1996 she became Chevalier de la Légion d'Honneur; and in 1998 Eudora Welty became the first living writer to be included in the Library of America, with volumes 101 and 102 of the series.

On almost every page she wrote, save the occasional savage attack on religious hypocrisy, Welty expressed her joy of living where she lived. She managed to state our emotions in the concrete terms of a fierce humor that indicates an affirmation and acceptance of life in all its forms, whether we are a jealous sister in China Grove, a defeated mail rider on the Natchez Trace, an old maid shocked out of her habitual thoughts at the ruins of Asphodel, an overseer of common country origin who marries into an aristocratic family in the Delta, a lifeguard at Moon Lake whose successful efforts at resuscitation are not appreciated, a simpleton in the town of Clay who becomes isolated in his community because he is generous, an Irishman who mourns his dead budgerigar, a woman who makes a show of her sorrow at her husband's funeral in Mount Salus, a poor hill farmer in Boone County who is trying to tell a story, or an orphan girl from Morgana who is being ogled by a deacon. These people and their emotions come alive in Welty's redemptive and humorous fiction. Her greatest achievement was that she never falsified an emotion by abstracting it into sentimentality, and her great knowledge of the settings for her fiction helped her remain in the concrete world.

Welty is without doubt, like William Faulkner, her fellow Mississippian, to be seen in the first row of the exponents of the Southern renaissance in literature, but her mentality was very different from that of Faulkner, and possibly more representative of her time and place. It is clear that any assessment of twentieth-century cultural development in the South has to consider Welty's achievement. Her obvious identification with her town, her state, and its people was only augmented by her short periods of living outside the South. The Agrarian ideas, the city experiences, the racial conflicts, the ignorance, the violence, and the clashes of local men and women of her times are reflected in her fiction with a compassion and a sincere concern that made her literary achievement one of international significance.

Welty was never a political conservative in the manner of some Nashville Agrarians; nor were her thoughts programmatic expressions of an ideology, although she might have been much more of a political militant, especially on the issue of race, than it has been supposed. She was always "a literary Agrarian," which simply means that her fiction reveals her emotional inclination toward many Agrarian ideas. In the 1930s Welty wrote in the Agrarian tradition. Like the Nashville Agrarians she opposed an industrialism that isolates the individual by cutting him off from his community and his spiritual needs. In the ideological battle between scientific, industrial values and humanistic, agrarian values, Welty discovered and demonstrated her regional bias. She did not believe in the optimistic notion of continual evolutionary "progress," and the achievement of a national culture based on modern technology and spatial mobility, instead of a traditional culture based on a sense of place, did *not* appeal to the young writer. She saw clearly what John Crowe Ransom meant when he explained that "what is called progress is often destruction."

In her "Place and Time: The Southern Writer's Inheritance," published anonymously in *The Times Literary Supplement* (September 17, 1954), Welty wrote: "The ravishment of their countryside, industrialization, standardization, exploitation, and the general vulgarization of life, have ever, reasonably or not, been seen as one Northern thing to the individualist mind of the South." But she never railed against the defilement of the "old order" or entertained great nostalgia for the Old South, like some Agrarians; she was a regionalist and a traditionalist in subtler ways. In her first volume of stories, *A Curtain of Green* (1941), in stories such as "Death of a Traveling Salesman," "Flowers for Marjorie," and "The Whistle," the enemies are obviously industrialism, commercialism, and materialism. Welty had seen the crisis of the industrial system in both New York and in Mississippi and felt the need for permanence in human values as much as any of the Agrarians. There was no doubt in her mind that eventually her native state would also have to accept the industrial–technological mode of life, and some of her work from the time shows that she was worried about the effect of the consumer society on the quality of life of the rural community.

She spent time in New Orleans, San Francisco, and particularly in New York, and the cities played an important role for Welty's development. If we compare her personal comments on the cities to her treatment of them in fiction, we see that the biographical pronouncements imply an acceptance of the city, whereas city life depicted in her fiction implies a *rejection* in the Agrarian mode. The rejection is so obvious that the cities never fully come to life, especially if we compare the city settings with the topographical verisimilitude of her fictive Southern towns. The scant use of the city in her fiction and the mostly negative image of it have their origin in her Agrarian ideas about place, identity, and a rewarding life. The strength of her fiction is identification in her fictional territory, with both her native area and its people. The area has changed since the 1940s, and although the big-city atmosphere itself is not the focus of the fiction, the New South and its world of big cities are reflected in her work. Her fictional portraits of city life obviously involve a selective process, and the elements selected to represent life in cities are generally so negative that it is impossible to overlook the implicit judgment. The visit of a little girl to an old ladies' home in "A Visit of Charity" reads as a slice of city life, and "The Whistle," "A Worn Path," and "The Whole World Knows" demonstrate that the "progress" the Agrarians encouraged the South to resist arrived long ago.

Humor is one of the hallmarks of the literature of the Southern renaissance, and a happy combination of antebellum Southern humor and modern humor with a view to eternal concerns may be found in Welty's tragi-comic fiction. It ranges from the tall story of Mike Fink as defeated mail rider in the novel *The Robber Bridegroom* to the epic account in *Losing Battles* of dirt-poor Mississippi farmers during the Depression and the chronicle of the comedy of manners in "Why I Live at the P.O.," "Petrified Man," and *The Ponder Heart*. Even though *Delta Wedding* and *The Optimist's Daughter* are serious novels, they are also satires of class prejudice. Welty's sincere concern is obvious behind the pandemonium surrounding a wedding in the Delta and behind the parody of a bourgeois funeral in a tradition-minded community. Her moods range from the acid comment of the puzzled bystander to total compassionate identification. In the stories "At the Landing," "A Piece of News," "No Place for You, My Love," and "The Bride of the Innisfallen," she anticipates the modern debate on societal roles for men and women. Her attack on the norms of conformity in all racial, religious, and gender matters is obvious in "Moon Lake" and "Asphodel."

Welty's fiction is the triumph of an artist who was always "locally underfoot," also as a frequent customer in Jitney Jungle, the local supermarket in her neighborhood. The "sense of place" that became a lecture at Cambridge University in 1954, and later Welty's best-known essay, "Place in Fiction," was developed in her hometown. It is essential to understand this element in her art to grasp the writer's relationship with her community, and it is in her humor that she reveals her Southern roots most clearly. It is a humor that depends on place and community not only for its kind, but for its existence; through her humorous vision we learn about the communities, fictive and real, of Jackson, China Grove, Fairchilds, Morgana, Mount Salus, Boone County, and others along the Natchez Trace. Throughout her works there is a trace of humor based on her understanding of a place and its people. The Faulknerian element of pity for the individual in his misfortune is always present, as in Welty's account of the Ponders of Clay in the short novel *The Ponder Heart*. When we recognize flaws in

Edna Earle and elements of the grotesque in Uncle Daniel, it is probably as reflections of our own limitations. Welty may have satirized the Miss Know-It-Alls and eccentrics she saw about her in Jackson and elsewhere, but the purpose was always to amuse by displaying the folly of humankind and to offer laughter as a means of questioning our concept of "sanity" – it was never to expose or ridicule her own community.

One of the reasons why Welty's fiction is compelling as an expression of its time is that it covers all of her native state and many years of its history. Her thoughts on a changing South come out in her portrayals and interpretations of the family as *the* institution of Southern life. Her preoccupation with a family life that is rooted in community and tradition is brought out in portraits from various parts of Mississippi. The Fairchild family lives in the Delta area of the state. *Delta Wedding* is her plantation novel, and it is full of tensions between blacks and whites. To write plantation novels is a tradition that started early in Southern literary history, and hundreds of romantic plantation novels are still sold through chain stores every year. Welty's novel unmasks the genre while contributing to it. She celebrates the Fairchilds' sense of family, which is the result of a continuous psychological interplay between the family past and present, but she also demonstrates how family traditions and myths clash with disruptive forces and new values, which are represented through outsiders. Some of the threats to the insular and proud Fairchilds are internal. Although they are a charming family enjoying the plantation life that they have lived in the Delta for generations, the Fairchilds are also late representatives of an old caste system, and as Welty shows beyond doubt, bigoted and self-serving.

Welty devoted much of her writing to an evaluation of the values of "the last non-materialist civilization in the Western World," as Richard Weaver described the Old South. The *leitmotif* of *Delta Wedding* is a dramatic episode on a railroad trestle. Appropriately, the most complete version of the incident is told to Mr. Rondo, a local minister, and when the theme is brought up throughout the novel, it is often with new details. George Fairchild risked his life to try to rescue Maureen Fairchild, the half-crazed daughter of his dead brother Denis; her foot was caught in the track. The Yellow Dog, which is the popular name of the Yazoo-Delta train, stopped just short of hitting the two on a trestle. Mr. Doolittle, the engineer of the train, would probably have cursed anybody of his own class who had risked his life so carelessly in front of his train, but his reaction is to apologize to the Fairchilds for having frightened them. The incident demonstrates the stability of the social order in the Delta in the fall of 1923. Even if they knew, no one among the Fairchilds would even dream of considering what the poor whites think about them. Nevertheless, the wedding referred to in the title of the novel is ultimately between classes. The Fairchilds cannot survive in the modern world without relinquishing some of their class and caste privileges. They will just have to hope that the poor whites, in payment for their social ascent, can learn to behave and think like members of the clan and that they will stop identifying with the class of their birth.

Delta Wedding is much more about racial relations than has been maintained in previous criticism. A flaw in the Fairchilds is that they see only stereotypes, they fail to see their black workers as human beings with widely differing psychologies. There is no difference between the women and men in the family in this regard, for the Fairchild women rule the domestics as firmly and efficiently as the men rule the field hands. By adding detail upon detail about the relationship between the races, Welty makes it clear that not for a moment did she think of the plantation as the site for a flawless way of life. The moral shortcomings of the ruling class are thoroughly exposed. *Delta Wedding* is a realistic novel, especially when compared with other novels on the subject. What helps raise Welty's plantation novel above the majority is that it recreates a world that did exist, and that it offers valid criticism of that world. The poor whites may not be the most charismatic characters – they entirely lack the accomplishments, charm, and grace of a cradle Fairchild – but on close inspection they turn out to be the most sensible and realistic people in the novel.

The Fairchilds have aristocratic pretensions and are the landed gentry in *Delta Wedding*. Their opposite in the social scale are the Beecham-Renfros of the northeastern hills in *Losing Battles*, who are as poor as you can be and still survive. As regards social position the lower-middle-class families of *The Golden Apples* are the norm in between these extremes. The need for a strongly united family that Welty showed as a fact of life in the plantation manor also exists in Morgana. The need, or even yearning, for a united family is very much alive, but it remains an ideal. There are no genuinely happy families in Morgana, which is one reason why the people in the town are dissatisfied with their lives. If we compare the MacLains to the Fairchilds, or to the Beecham-Renfros, it is obvious that unlike the others, the MacLains could be used as a model example of what happens to the family in the post-agrarian society, as predicted by the Nashville Agrarians. By 1930 the rural districts of the South had seen about a fourth of the native-born population leave the region. Some went north, others headed for the growing Southern cities, and families were broken up. During the first forty years of this century Welty's fictional town of Morgana remained small and rural, but the lives of many of its families fit the statistics of deteriorating family unity in a changing region. Welty was a regionalist, in the sense that she accepted the inherited environment, history, and tradition of her South, but she never set out deliberately to be the spokesperson of her region. The emphasis in her fiction is always on the individual character and his or her emotions. But the attacks on certain individuals and their middle-class values in Morgana are the most vicious and satirical Welty ever wrote.

The town of Morgana and its people are the main unifying factors of the short stories collected and arranged in *The Golden Apples*. The stories are arranged chronologically in a cycle that begins around the turn of the century and covers more than forty years in the history of the town. Unlike Welty's two earlier collections of short stories, *The Golden Apples* is cyclical. The stories are interlinked, but the narrative is not continuous. It has time gaps, and it has no obvious single central plot. The collection is unified by its choice of the fictional township of Morgana as setting, save in one story, and by the continuous appearance of members of the same town families. Morgana offers its people all the security and resources of a supportive community, but it does not allow privacy and a separate individual identity. There are obviously unstated standards and unwritten rules that encompass all life within the small-town society. Morgana will not leave the MacLains alone, it worries about them, and they find themselves in standing quarrels with the town. Life in the community is sensed as being oppressive, but as some of the MacLains learn the hard way, life outside the town limits does not offer the comfort and security of the native community. Ironically it is the roving MacLains that help define essential facets of the identity of Morgana by struggling with its standards. The town does not reject the MacLains because they go beyond its boundaries by living out their hidden desires, for these may secretly be shared by many in the town. Miss Eckhart, the foreign piano teacher, is rejected because she does not share anything with the community, not even hidden desires. *The Golden Apples* is also the story of Virgie Rainey, who comes to accept that the steadying point in her life is the town. After forty years of restlessness she finally accepts that her identity is firmly situated in her hometown, and with her newly acquired sense of place comes the acceptance of a whole body of thought founded on her situatedness.

Welty also manages to convince us that black people are present and play an important part in the life of the community. They are never just "blacks" or the inhabitants of any town; they are highly individualized Morgana blacks. She demonstrates her ability to recognize the essential humanity of her African-American characters in early stories such as "Keela, the Outcast Indian Maiden," "Powerhouse," "A Worn Path," "First Love," "Livvie," and in her only Civil War story, "The Burning," where two Southern ladies lose heart in adversity whereas their black maid endures and prevails. Some of her black characters are decidedly more conservative upholders of community values than the white people of the town. Blacks appear to be docile and friendly and racial relations seem frozen in rigid formality, so Welty exposes the traditional racist bias of the town as a "natural" and, it seems, permanent quality in all white men and women of Morgana. "Negroes" are the people who most white people "have" to help out around the house, for the blacks in town are generally "real trustworthy." The way people treat their black help (i.e. know how to put them to work) is an indication of social status. But the authenticity of her African-American characters originates in Welty's careful delineation of their individuality, and they are not denied their identity as human beings, nor are they stereotyped.

The event that inspired the short story "Where Is the Voice Coming from?" was the killing of Medgar Evers in Jackson, Mississippi, on June 12, 1963. The murder was committed on the night of President John F. Kennedy's nationally televised address on integration in the South, which Evers had watched. If the story appears to be closer than Welty's fiction in general to the actual event that inspired it, the reason is probably the quick transmutation of fact into art. The first version of the story was written on the night of the murder of Medgar Evers. It was created out of her emotional reaction to an act of perversion in her hometown, and there was no time for a recollection of the murder in tranquility. If a murderer's meaning is defined by what he came out of, he is also a product of where he lives, and in this case the site of the crime happened to be Welty's hometown. The killing in Jackson upset Welty's psychological security in her identity as a Jacksonian, and the racially motivated murder in her own "neighborhood" forced her to question her native sense of identity also in fiction. Her "place" is time made visible, and this is also true of the unpleasant present of June 1963.

The question of the title answers itself. Welty knows where the voice comes from, and finally we will have to admit that so do we. Her target is our calm complacency and smugness, which we are forced to realize and recognize, because the truth shown to us is that the voice is our voice. What makes this story art is not the perfect evocation of a place, a changing community, and a historical period, nor is it the obvious political comment. What makes it art is the analysis of the nature of the murderer with all his serious flaws and total wrongheadedness. Time is his enemy, and the changes wrought by time make it hard for him to love the place where he lives. The insight into the killer's mind is thoroughly informed by Welty's intimate sense of a place and its people. He killed, as she writes, for his own "pure D-satisfaction," he killed for bitterness and despair in an attempt to turn loose the load placed on his shoulders by others. And this is where the voice really comes from, the voice comes from us, and from the character of the culture we live in and have helped create. The art of "Where Is the Voice Coming From?" is in the portrait of the assassin's existential problems, which are universal. Above all he wants to be recognized as an individual by the people of his hometown. Welty shows his humanity, exactly *because* it is so hard to accept. The writing of the story was her way of measuring herself against the enduring identity of her place and all that has happened there, and she showed that existential decisions originate in the individual's sense of place and community and have moral consequences. In the story Welty's creative principles reveal her moral principles, and her sense of place is not finally distinguishable from the ethics of living in a place and finding one's identity in relation to it.

Losing Battles is a novel written almost entirely as dialogue, and lends itself well to Welty's humorous style. It is the story of Jack Renfro's escape from jail and his heroic return to the ancestral home in time to participate in the Vaughn-Beecham-Renfro family's celebration of his great-grandmother on her ninetieth birthday. It is also an epic account of the poor white farmers of northeast Mississippi during the 1930s. Welty placed her longest novel in the hill country of the state. Her own map of Boone County, placed at the beginning of the novel, indicates that the Banner community is located close to the Mississippi–Alabama state line, and the location, which is the southern tip of Appalachia, explains the traditional poverty, the absence of plantations, and the consequent absence of black people in *Losing Battles*. The area is an extension of Middle Tennessee, and the soil in the hills is made up of gravel and sand. In order to escape the misery and the uncertainty of their situation the men and women of the county tell stories that reflect their everyday lives and often in a comic light, but the farmers are not ridiculed in the novel; on the contrary, they are extolled. Although everything is described as leisurely, the description of the desperate situation is realistic enough to imply criticism of farming programs, or the lack of them, at the time. The events of the novel occur during one of the first years of the Depression, and it would be a long time before the situation would improve.

It is tempting to see the family as a communal protagonist of the novel. The poor farmers of the hill country demonstrate an unwavering faith in a strong and united family. Welty tells us that not only does the family matter, but also it is a defining part of our selves. The family past demands attention at the reunion, and its power over the present is reflected in the family legends. The farmers are not, in any manner of speaking, living in the past; on the contrary, they live fully in the present, but for them the present moment always presupposes the presence of the past. The notion is Agrarian in that their feelings are tied up in the family memory of the homestead, and it is a memory that can only be kept alive by being communicated from generation to generation, so the family tell stories to protect their uniqueness against time, change, and adversity. The recitation of remembered stories makes of existence a constantly recurring, recognizable, and therefore comforting pattern of what has always been. In that sense the oral tradition, as an expression of the communal memory, is an Agrarian weapon against changing times and so-called "progress."

Welty's value orientation has always been traditional, and it remains so in *Losing Battles*. The novel from 1970 is as much an endorsement of basic Agrarian ideas as the early stories "Death of a Traveling Salesman," "The Whistle," and "Flowers for Marjorie," and her photographs from the 1930s. In the best Agrarian tradition the family reunion serves in *Losing Battles* as a social occasion that affirms a family's solidarity and their will to resist change, to endure the economic facts of their time and place, and to prevail. Although they do demonstrate their separateness and quarrel with their culture at times, the poor farmers of the novel do not repudiate it. Nor do they think of it as "culture," as they do not abstract their relation with their place. Welty celebrated the poor white farmers for their humanity, particularly the strong women, but she made no attempt to hide the fact that inexplicable evil exists among them. Without trivializing the actual landscape, her preoccupation with Boone County went beyond the precise, identifiably local and mimetic descriptions of life in a corner of her state to intimations of timeless joys and sorrows. The artistic achievement is that the Mississippi landscape of *Losing Battles* comes to encompass everything that happens, has happened, and will happen for as long as landscape and memory and talk exist.

Just how healthy the town of Mount Salus is, or is not, is one of the questions raised in *The Optimist's Daughter*. Laurel Hand, the daughter of the title, now lives in Chicago, and to her old friends in Mount Salus, Mississippi, the city she now calls home seems remote and even somewhat unreal. Laurel had come south because her father Judge McKelva was seriously ill. After three weeks he dies and his body is brought back on the New Orleans–Chicago train to be buried in Mount Salus. The town is probably about the size of Morgana in *The Golden Apples*, and like Morgana it houses a tradition-oriented and class-conscious community. The McKelvas were of the upper class in Mount Salus, but in her hometown Laurel has come to feel that she is an outsider. The McKelva House is no longer "home" in the sense that it provides the foundation of Laurel's identity, and Mount Salus no longer furnishes her with an identity as a member of the community. One of the unwritten laws of Mount Salus life seems to be that when you marry and move out of town, you not only marry a stranger, but also a new place; especially if your new home is also out of state. And Laurel's marriage had been brief and not connected with Mount Salus. Her tragic loss of a husband gets little attention in her hometown, but her loss of Phil is a constant presence in Laurel's mind. When she sees her hometown again the impression interacts with her memory of the past, just as her ability to cope with her present situation depends on her ability to come to terms with the past. The town is still there as a container of all that ever was experienced in that community, but Welty outlines cultural change in the contemporary South. When Laurel was growing up, the physical setting still shaped the social interaction in town, but since she left, the relationship between place and social place has weakened considerably. Her disorientation and feeling of estrangement in Mount Salus are, however, results of a general cultural displacement. The novel implies that the social order is becoming impersonal and increasingly technological, and that a sense of self is no longer necessarily ingrained with a sense of community. The past is "immoderate" in that it devours Laurel's present. Although the troubled woman intuitively knows the whole truth about her parents and herself, she is not ready to accept that knowledge. In her isolation, alienation, and emotional poverty she is very much a woman of the twentieth century. At its best the novel questions one of the old verities of the Southern community: does the past live in the present, and if so, does it enrich the living? The novel is also about the difficulty of being honest and unsentimental about the past and the people who represent it, and it is about the necessity of coming to terms with the past, both the public myth of the past and the family past.

Class is certainly not a new topic in her fiction, but in *The Optimist's Daughter* the clash between social classes becomes a dominant theme. Welty makes it clear that the disagreement in the novel over the choice of a burial plot expresses a profound disagreement between genteel and poor white Southerners about the past, its traditions, and their importance for the present community. The basic difference between Laurel Hand and Fay McKelva, her young stepmother, emerges in their attitudes to the past. The reason why this becomes a vital part of the novel is that Welty supports and censures both the genteel and the poor white parties in the discussion. She seems to say that our changing feelings about the past are valuable, and that we need to free ourselves every so often from the tyranny of the past by remembering that we cannot control it, only recapture it through memory, which is, by definition, always unstable and inconclusive. It should not be forced to fit an already selected pattern, and there must be room for detachment. In fact the past offers a choice of what we want to remember, which is limited only by our honesty and our ability to "freeze" and control memories. Welty gives a positive answer to Allen Tate's despairing question about the capability of the modern individual to draw strength from tradition and to overcome emotional stuntedness by defining, reviving, and repossessing the past.

The novel illustrated Welty's preoccupation with the past, the clash between social classes, and the survival of the community. But it was her search for answers to existential questions that gave her fiction a place in the first order of literature. She was not a sociologist trying to right social wrongs, and not a psychologist trying to explain the origin of psychoses; nor was she a preacher choosing between vice and virtue. She was a novelist offering her vision of how it has always been with us and of how it is with us now. Welty avoided crusading, she even warned against it in her 1965 essay "Must the Novelist Crusade." She did not try to teach us how to behave, but she showed us how we live and helped us up to the point where we could interpret our own lives. She showed how we may find a way out of our psychological isolation by facing our past and accepting it for what it can tell us about the subjectivity of life in time and place. At the end of the brief visit to her hometown, Laurel pins her hair up for Chicago, steps back into her high-heeled city shoes, says goodbye to Mount Salus, probably for the last time, and heads back to a life in a South Side apartment and to her job. Her present project is to design a curtain – for a theatre.

There was always a pronounced out-of-life-into-fiction tendency in Welty's work, and at times the distinction between the genres of fiction and autobiography blurred in her writings. She realized early that by seeing the particulars of her native situation, she could successfully approach the universal. The permanent lesson she learned at the beginning of her career was that to write well, it is not enough to be fascinated with your subject, if you are really ignorant of it. She learned to write on subjects that grew naturally out of her own life, and in *One Writer's Beginnings* she summed up her family with a realism worthy of Jane Austen. In her fiction the view of humankind is not obscured by any crusading for a cause, nor did she in her autobiographical book become blinded by nostalgia for the family past. The book is a realistic account of what it was like to grow up in the Welty family. The writer's account of the family at home is unflinchingly truthful to the double nature of everything, and the Weltys are presented as the marvelous people they were on occasion, but we also see them as the limited human beings they sometimes proved to be. The book's thematic drama is a coming to terms with the memory of the mother, and the portrait of Mrs. Chestina Welty is rich and rounded, but there is no romanticizing in the account of the years spent in the daily company of the awe-inspiring and demanding woman. Welty always saw family and community as they are, and as a writer she saw it as her job to make reality real by revealing the core of our humanity. But *One Writer's Beginnings* is also a postmodern narrative, as it is a fictionalized, distorted, and compensating memoir that offers only unreliable biographical information about the writer.

Eudora Welty was an influential mind of the South throughout her long literary career, from the 1930s through the 1990s, and her fiction is representative of the collective Southern experience from the Depression until today. Over the years she dealt with the historical, political, social, cultural, and ethnic landscape of her South by seeing it in the context of time. Her landscape contains ignorance, poverty, and political conservatism. But it is also a landscape of individuals who identify with their community and revere the traditions of their place. Eudora Welty's work represents a cultural continuity of basic Agrarian ideas, from their origin in the rural South to their present importance in a largely urbanized and Americanized South.

REFERENCES AND FURTHER READING

Appel, Alfred, Jr. (1965) *A Season of Dreams: The Fiction of Eudora Welty.* Baton Rouge: Louisiana State University Press.

Binding, Paul (1994) *The Still Moment: Eudora Welty, Portrait of a Writer.* London: Virago.

Bloom, Harold (ed.) (1986) *Modern Critical Views: Eudora Welty.* New York: Chelsea House Publishers.

Carson, Barbara Harrell (1992) *Eudora Welty: Two Pictures at Once in Her Frame.* Troy, NY: Whitston Publishing.

Champion, Laurie (ed.) (1994) *The Critical Response to Eudora Welty's Fiction.* Westport, CT: Greenwood Press.

Desmond, John F. (ed.) (1978) *A Still Moment: Essays on the Art of Eudora Welty.* Metuchen, NJ: Scarecrow Press.

Devlin, Albert J. (1983) *Eudora Welty's Chronicle: A Story of Mississippi Life.* Jackson: University of Mississippi Press.

Devlin, Albert J. (ed.) (1987) *Welty: A Life in Literature.* Jackson: University of Mississippi Press.

Dollarhide, Louis, and Abadie, Ann J. (eds.) (1979) *Eudora Welty: A Form of Thanks.* Jackson: University of Mississippi Press.

Evans, Elizabeth (1981) *Eudora Welty.* New York: Frederick Ungar.

Gretlund, Jan Nordby (1997) *Eudora Welty's Aesthetics of Place.* Columbia: University of South Carolina Press.

Gretlund, Jan Nordby, and Westarp, Karl-Heinz (eds.) (1998) *The Late Novels of Eudora Welty.* Columbia: University of South Carolina Press.

Harrizon, Suzan (1997) *Eudora Welty and Virginia Woolf: Gender, Genre, and Influence.* Baton Rouge: Louisiana State University Press.

Johnston, Carol Ann (1997) *Eudora Welty: A Study of the Short Fiction.* Boston, MA: Twayne.

Kieft, Ruth M. Vande (1987) *Eudora Welty.* Boston, MA: Twayne.

Kreyling, Michael (1980) *Eudora Welty's Achievement of Order.* Baton Rouge: Louisiana State University Press.

Kreyling, Michael (1991) *Author and Agent: Eudora Welty and Diarmuid Russell.* New York: Farrar, Straus, and Giroux.

Kreyling, Michael (1999) *Understanding Eudora Welty.* Columbia: University of South Carolina Press.

McHaney, Pearl Amelia (ed.) (1999) *Eudora Welty: Writers' Reflection Upon First Reading Welty.* Athens, GA: Hill Street Press.

Manning, Carol S. (1985) *With Ears Opening Like Morning Glories: Eudora Welty and the Love of Storytelling,* Westport, CT: Greenwood Press.

Manz-Kunz, Marie-Antoinette (1971) *Eudora Welty: Aspects of Reality in Her Short Fiction.* Bern: Francke Verlag.

Mark, Rebecca (1994) *The Dragon's Blood: Feminist Intertextuality in Eudora Welty's the Golden Apples.* Jackson: University of Mississippi Press.

Marrs, Suzanne (1988) *The Welty Collection.* Jackson: University of Mississippi Press.

Mortimer, Gail L. (1994) *Daughter of the Swan: Love and Knowledge in Eudora Welty's Fiction.* Athens, GA: University of Georgia Press.

Opitz, Kurt (1959) *Neoromantik als Gestalterin der Prosa Eudora Weltys.* Inaugural dissertation, Freie Universität Berlin, Berlin-Dahlem, Ernst Reuter Gesellschaft.

Pingatore, Diana R. (1996) *A Reader's Guide to the Short Stories of Eudora Welty.* Boston, MA: G. K. Hall.

Pitavy-Souques, Danièle (1992) *La Mort de Méduse: L'art de la nouvelle chez Eudora Welty.* Lyon: Presses universitaires de Lyon.

Polk, Noel (1994) *Eudora Welty: A Bibliography of Her Work.* Jackson: University of Mississippi Press.

Pollack, Harriet, and Marrs, Suzanne (eds.) (2001) *Eudora Welty and Politics: Did the Writer Crusade?* Baton Rouge: Louisiana State University Press.

Prenshaw, Peggy Whitman (ed.) (1979) *Eudora Welty: Critical Essays.* Jackson: University of Mississippi Press.

Prenshaw, Peggy Whitman (ed.) (1984) *Conversations with Eudora Welty.* Jackson: University of Mississippi Press.

Prenshaw, Peggy Whitman (ed.) (1996) *More Conversations with Eudora Welty.* Jackson: University of Mississippi Press.

Randisi, Jennifer Lynn (1982) *A Tissue of Lies: Eudora Welty and the Southern Romance.* Washington, DC: University Press of America.

Schmidt, Peter (1991) *The Heart of the Story: Eudora Welty's Short Fiction.* Jackson: University of Mississippi Press.

Trouard, Dawn (ed.) (1989) *Eudora Welty: Eye of the Storyteller.* Kent, OH: Kent State University Press.

Turner, W. Craig, and Harding, Lee Emling (eds.) (1989) *Critical Essays on Eudora Welty.* Boston, MA: G. K. Hall.

Waldron, Ann (1998) *Eudora: A Writer's Life.* New York: Doubleday.

Welty, Eudora (1941) *A Curtain of Green and Other Stories.* Garden City, NY: Doubleday, Doran.

Welty, Eudora (1942) *The Robber Bridegroom.* Garden City, NY: Doubleday, Doran.

Welty, Eudora (1943) *The Wide Net and Other Stories.* New York: Harcourt, Brace.

Welty, Eudora (1946) *Delta Wedding.* New York: Harcourt, Brace.

Welty, Eudora (1949) *The Golden Apples.* New York: Harcourt, Brace.

Welty, Eudora (1950) *Short Stories.* New York: Harcourt, Brace.

Welty, Eudora (1954) "Place and Time: The Southern Writer's Inheritance," *Times Literary Supplement,* September 17: xlviii.

Welty, Eudora (1954) *The Ponder Heart.* New York: Harcourt, Brace.

Welty, Eudora (1954) *Selected Stories.* New York: Modern Library.

Welty, Eudora (1955) *The Bride of the Innisfallen.* New York: Harcourt, Brace.

Welty, Eudora (1957) *Place in Fiction.* New York: House of Books.

Welty, Eudora (1962) *Three Papers on Fiction.* Northampton, MA: Smith College.

Welty, Eudora (1964) *The Shoe Bird.* New York: Harcourt, Brace, and World.

Welty, Eudora (1965) "Must the Novelist Crusade?" *Atlantic,* 216 (October): 104–8.

Welty, Eudora (1969) "The Optimist's Daughter," *The New Yorker,* 45 (March 15): 32–128.

Welty, Eudora (1969) *A Sweet Devouring.* New York: Albondocani Press.

Welty, Eudora (1970) *Losing Battles.* New York: Random House.

Welty, Eudora (1971) *One Time, One Place: Mississippi in the Depression, A Snapshot Album.* New York: Random House.

Welty, Eudora (1972) *The Optimist's Daughter.* New York: Random House.

Welty, Eudora (1975) *Fairy Tale of the Natchez Trace.* Jackson: Mississippi Historical Society.

Welty, Eudora (1978) *The Eye of the Story: Selected Essays and Reviews.* New York: Random House.

Welty, Eudora (1980) *Acrobats in a Park.* Northridge, CA: Lord John Press.

Welty, Eudora (1980) *Bye-Bye Brevoort: A Skit.* Jackson, MS: Published for New Stage Theatre.

Welty, Eudora (1980) *The Collected Stories of Eudora Welty.* New York: Harcourt Brace Jovanovich.

Welty, Eudora (1984) *One Writer's Beginnings.* Cambridge, MA: Harvard University Press.

Welty, Eudora (1989) *Photographs.* Jackson: University of Mississippi Press.

Welty, Eudora (1994) *A Writer's Eye: Collected Book Reviews,* ed. Pearl A. McHaney. Jackson: University of Mississippi Press.

Welty, Eudora (1998) *Complete Novels*, ed. Richard Ford and Michael Kreyling. New York: Library of America.

Welty, Eudora (1998) *Stories, Essays, and Memoir*, ed. Richard Ford and Michael Kreyling. New York: Library of America.

Welty, Eudora (2000) *Country Churchyards*. Jackson: University of Mississippi Press.

Welty, Eudora, and Sharp, Ronald (eds.) (1991) *The Norton Book of Friendship*. New York: W. W. Norton.

Westling, Louise (1989) *Women Writers: Eudora Welty*. Totowa, NJ: Barnes and Noble.

Weston, Ruth D. (1994) *Gothic Traditions and Narrative Techniques in the Fiction of Eudora Welty*. Baton Rouge: Louisiana State University Press.

30

Oral Culture and Southern Fiction

Jill Terry

Stories should be read in silence, of course, but one should be able to hear them as well.

Toni Morrison (Evans 1983: 341)

What is Distinctively Oral About Southern Writing?

In his foreword to Reed's *Whistling Dixie* (1990), Eugene D. Genovese circles around what for him is the ambiguous essence that is demanded of writing from the South. He uses the terms "true Southern style" and "Southern folkways" to describe something of what he has in mind when he states "Americans need to be reminded that there are good-sized regional differences in this country." What *is* specific to Southern culture and its writing? In the last decade this difference has sometimes been articulated in the term "pastoral." The classification is used to describe an Edenic rural South such as that which W. J. Cash, Richard Gray, and Lewis Simpson have each identified as a feature of Southern literature, which they argue perpetuates a romantic notion of difference in rejecting modernization, and promoting a myth of rural class agrarian origin. Of course, this is only part of a story that largely obscures what is surely an equal determinant of Southern culture, that contributed by the South's African past. In many ways, the cultural products of the black Southerner have always shared the priorities of the "pastoral" white Southerner, insofar as the priorities involved signify similar concerns with origins, albeit different origins. In both the white and black cultures of the South there has been a desire to recapture an idea of identity that is associated with a time before "the modern," and the common pathway to the imaginative roots of identity is by way of the oral tradition. For black writers, this may mean a symbolic South from which their ancestors have escaped. When the oral tradition is represented in fiction, then that fiction frequently speaks of tradition, memory, and therefore identity, rooted in the past. It is significant that the writer most generally lauded by Southern scholars as the "father" of Southern fiction, William Faulkner, is described as one of American fiction's most strongly "voiced," "oral," or "colloquial" writers (Ross 1989: 100). The most important and influential African-American writer of Southern origin, Ralph Ellison, wrote a novel that is celebrated for its oral effects. *Invisible Man* (1952) has been described by the author as a symphonic jazz composition. The anguished theme for both writers is the South's racial history and the resulting condition of black–white relations.

As I write about "Southern oralities," I have in mind a tradition in which both black as well as white writers are able to take their place. Orality – that which has the quality of being spoken or otherwise orally communicated – has had a vital role in representing not only the rooted past, but also the changing places of the South, and the shifting racial dynamics of the South, too. Orality may well be one of the most significant characteristics of writing described as "Southern."

The paternal roles of Faulkner and Ellison in regard to the construction of canons of fiction associated with the South has deflected attention from the contribution of women writers; since the 1970s, as an effect of feminist critical endeavor, the female tradition has attracted critical acclaim. While not exclusively the province of women writers, it is in women's writing concerned with representations of female identity in a historically patriarchal South that orality is especially prioritized. Women are regarded as having the primary role in the passing on of oral cultural forms. With regard to African-American women writers and the oral tradition, Stephen Henderson notes:

> Black women almost by definition have always been involved in the generation and sustenance of our literature and culture in general. One could, in fact, make the case that the founders of black American literature, in a formal sense, were women...One could make an equally strong case for the oral tradition. (Henderson, in Evans 1983)

Representations of Southern dialect, folktales, oral history, and music are all forms of orality exemplified in women's writing to celebrate feminine creativity and women's voices. Accounts of quilt-making are especially important in Alice Walker's work, as is healing in writing by Gayl Jones, Kaye Gibbons, and Lee Smith; all are writers who are referred to in the following discussion as Southern women whose work best exemplifies techniques of literary orality. The creative activities described are presented as emanating from oral traditions of knowledge passed from generation to generation of women, and in their novels the writers effect an extension of those traditions. For example, just as Alice Walker's story "Everyday Use" draws together the fragmentation of folk memory in stitches, so the similar practices of cooking and healing represent pieces of women's culture that are framed within literary forms that mimic oral storytelling.

Literary orality is also present in the way the sounds of Southern voices are evoked in Southern fiction, both in the idioms of Southern speech that are integral to the Southern storytelling tradition, and in representations of Southern oratory drawn from the strong religious life of the South. Analogies to these forms assist fiction in being recognizable to readers, whether or not they have much experience of Southern oralities in their primary forms. Readers respond to "a true ear for speech," "authentic Southern storytelling," "a powerful sense of history in the blood"; these are qualities emphasized by the back-cover blurbs of Southern novels. The ability to "hear" a dialogue, or what Toni Morrison describes as an "analogy" of "the texture" of music in a written text, relies on the ability of a writer to mimic the oral and thus to create the impression in the mind of the reader that the text "sounds" or "speaks" (Morrison, cited in Gilroy 1993: 78). The response elicited from the reader suggests there is already an idea, or a version, of the sounds depicted in their mind. In this sense the readers of Southern literary oralities may be interpellated as the participatory listeners of Southern oral cultures.

An important function of orality in Southern writing is to signify to the reader the region of the South. Eudora Welty is famous for saying that it is characteristic of Southern writing to define Southern place by opening "a door in the mind." Of course, the creative energies deployed in signifying the South emerge as locked in a binary relationship to the North, reflecting a historical (post-Civil War) antipathy and positioning as "other." It is largely the purpose of the places portrayed in Southern fiction to be "in the mind." In their introduction to *Southern Writers at Century's End* (1997), Folks and Perkins suggest the importance of pastoral notions of the South for African-American writers whose "fiction reflects, at least imaginatively, an intimacy with the land, an identification with nature and the physical environment, an emphasis on the necessity of an extended family and a supportive community, and a legacy of struggle against social oppression and a consequent immersion in history" (5). Southern texts enable the reader to imagine a particular world and to restore the memory, or idea, of oral culture and performance. However, as Julius Rowan Raper has noted, "the extraordinary sense of place . . . is a mainstay still of Modern Southern Fiction – but, less and less, of modern Southern life" (1990: 9). Place is a mainstay because the reworking of oral modes in fiction encourages the creation of a "fix" for writer and reader between Southern orality and imagined places, and thus Southern identities. Readers note that they can "hear Southern voices"; they imagine a "particular place," remember the sound of the blues, as a result of fictional techniques devised for the representations of oral forms.

In the last half of the twentieth century there was rapid change in the region of the South. With such change communities are unsettled, and so it becomes more important for connections with others to be reaffirmed, whether by regional or racial ties, and it is the *idea* of shared cultural inheritances that can provide the means for the rooting of a sense of identity. This can be claimed in general for Southern writers notwithstanding the fact that in the antebellum South one group owned the other. That, post-reconstruction, racial equality has never been achieved is the reason why the recognition of shared cultural inheritances has not often extended outside of the racial group. Difference, as opposed to shared Southernness, has been articulated in the formation of separatist canons of Southern writing. It is how what Toni Morrison describes as "literary whiteness" and "literary blackness" is made in the Southern context (1993: xiv). The respective political endeavors of early scholars concerned to establish roots ensured the separatist documentation of lines of cultural descent, and the separately delineated theorization of Southern cultural forms, and literary canons. White scholars such as Richard Weaver and John Shelton Reed reached back to European sources to describe white Southern culture and the "Southern vernacular." It is claimed that this vernacular is represented in a literary tradition arising from Twain's *Huckleberry Finn* (1885) because of Twain's innovation of a dialect/vernacular-speaking child telling his story in his own words. The project of Black Nationalism as espoused by Melville Herskovits and Henry Louis Gates, Jr.'s early work, and adopted in discussions of the "black aesthetic" describes a literary tradition that begins with slave narratives such as developed in the writing of Frederick Douglass. Black scholars have continuously stressed the significance of representations of orality in African-American cultural texts. This is a characteristic of particular prominence in the writing and criticism of the Harlem Renaissance of the 1920s and in the 1960s Black Arts Movement. For the spokesmen who developed the Black Aesthetic and who prescribed the characteristics of an approved black canon, the journey back to Africa as the source of racial identity was through the South. In his 1968 essay "The Black Arts Movement," Larry Neal called for a separate "symbolism, mythology, critique, and iconology," emphasizing the African survival and the oral tradition. Contemporary critics, led by Houston A. Baker and Gates, have reasserted the view that the oral features of African-American writing are intrinsic to its difference. The critical project of these African-American scholars has primarily concerned document-ing features of early slave culture that have distinct origins in Africa as demonstrated by parallels in dialect and elements of tales and proverbs.

Nevertheless, there can be no doubt that people of African and European descent have encountered exposure to one another, albeit in a relationship of inequality, in the South. Contemporary discourse about the processes of hybridity and creolization has brought recognition that colonial and colonized cultures and languages cannot be separated from each other. This has prompted Shelley Fisher Fishkin's question, "was Huck black?" in her rereading of *Huckleberry Finn*. Interrogating precisely those oral features that have established this text as foundational for white American literature, Fishkin (1993) establishes the black vernacular antecedents of Huck's celebrated Southern dialect. As Russell Reising asserts: "the dialogizing of the American canon is an essential project," and an increasing willingness by Southern scholars of history, musicology, and literature to engage in investigations that are not demarcated by race has enabled consideration of the multicultural antecedents of contemporary Southern culture (1986: 236). For example, studies of the religious culture of the South where Euro-American belief systems and African expressive styles converge have produced evidence about the symbiosis of creative exchange in the South. These studies suggest that the mixing of oral cultural traditions has been more important than any other single factor for the extraordinary richness of Southern cultures. This leads William Piersen to assert: "in the South . . . the melting pot really worked far better than most Southerners or modern social theorists have been willing to admit" (1993: 189).

With regard to the literature that has drawn so strongly on its oral antecedents, Thadious M. Davis describes the "literary confluence" of black and white writers who reach "across race and class and time" in their articulation of self-expression in a "spatially defined landscape" (1993: 15, 28, 33). The Southern landscapes imagined by contemporary Southern women writers often retain some fidelity to the pastoral scene, particularly in their rewriting of Southern history from the personal perspective of individual families – for example, Alice Walker's *The Color Purple* (1982) and Lee Smith's *Fair and Tender Ladies* (1988). They also envision the contemporary industrial and commercial landscape of K-marts such as that which forms the setting of Bobbie Ann Mason's *In Country* (1985), and the parodied ghost theme park in Lee Smith's *Oral History* (1983). The fluidity of an imagined Southern landscape is also demonstrated by Gayl Jones's recent accounts of women who migrate in, out of, and across the South. Thus the Southern literary landscape can depict different truths and different, even multiple, Southern places, races, and identities. The long cohabitation of black and white people in the South has ensured that the influences on the developing oral cultures and their literary representations have been reciprocal and dialogic.

The priority of gaining agency in self-representation is intrinsic to writing by black and white Southerners, especially women. This is because, as Richard Gray has argued, "Southerners have always shown how one viable response to feelings of marginalization is to *build* on the margins, to root one's thinking precisely in the sense of being disempowered and different" (1997: 291). Lack of power is notable in roles occupied by the female characters of Southern fiction. While individual contemporary black and white Southern writers of fiction and their critics may prioritize either the concerns of region or of race, they are commonly concerned to interrogate the ways in which Southern identities have been characterized, and caricatured, by dominant voices. In *The Color Purple* Celie recognizes the discrimination that her Southern rural dialect attracts:

> Darlene trying to teach me how to talk. She say US not so hot. A dead country give-away. You say US where most folks say WE, she say, and peoples think you dumb. Colored peoples think you a hick and white folks be amused. (Walker 1982: 193)

The dominant voice of Northern standard American English is framed as representing the repressive ideology against which Celie learns to assert her own cultural pride and voice, but the prejudice Celie feels has earlier been demonstrated in the nineteenth-century dialect writing which helped to establish the Southern literary canon. The function of dialect as shorthand for evoking stereotypes and mocking "primitive" regional characters is described by Gavin Jones:

> Readers could not get enough of black dialect, Appalachian dialect, Pike Country dialect, Maine dialect, New Yorkese dialect – every region was mined for its vernacular

gold, and every predominant ethnic group was linguistically lampooned in popular
poetry and prose. (Jones 1999: 1)

Contemporary literary orality represents a "talking back" to fiction that previously
inscribed negative identity scripts – the "poor white," "the Appalachian hillbilly,"
"the negro." Writers tell stories and claim for characters the ownership of voices of
local communities that have been satirized and marginalized in earlier writing and
have continued to be so in the technological age – for example, the television
programs *The Waltons, The Beverly Hillbillies*, and *The Dukes of Hazzard*, and films
such as the 1972 version of James Dickey's *Deliverance*. By creating diversity in their
many narratives, and disrupting stereotypes, by subverting canonical definitions of
tradition, as well as popular culture myths, Southern writers challenge these negative
and comedic identity scripts. Ironically, they do this by claiming back and utilizing
the very cultural products that are prime elements of those scripts, notwithstanding
the risk that these scripts may appear reinforced. In claiming authorship of their own
regional and ethnic identities, Southern women writers seek to assert authority over
the oral cultural modes that have been used to misrepresent and assert dominance.

The Storyteller

There is general agreement among commentators on the South that one particular
predilection of Southerners is to *tell* stories; whether in the primary oral/spoken form,
or through representations of oral storytelling in the form and content of fiction.
Many Southern women writers have acknowledged the strong influence of their own
exposure to experiences of maternal orality. Like Eudora Welty, who was influenced by
her mother's gossiping sessions, Alice Walker and Lee Smith are among those
Southern women who have noted their own mother's influential oral model. The
past is reconfigured as personal, familial black and white histories and expressions are
reclaimed in imaginative reconstructions that figure communities of women taking
responsibility for passing on memories. These memories are sometimes a debilitating
burden, in particular when the memory is of the experience of slavery, as in Toni
Morrison's *Beloved* (1988) and Gayl Jones's *Corregidora* (1975), but they may also be
the strengthening bond of women in adversity, as in Kaye Gibbons's *Charms For the
Easy Life* (1993), the narrator of which regards her mother and grandmother as being
experienced in "the areas of loneliness, abandonment, betrayal, and other furious
pursuits" (214). For Alice Walker, the maternal tradition of women's writing is
crucial, as she explains in an account of searching for her literary mother, Zora
Neale Hurston, in the garden of the South. The Southern writer Doris Betts argues
that the characteristic contemporary women writer's storytelling tradition applies
whether characters are "from the farm, the mill, the new city, named Vicki or
Elizabeth rather than Norma Rae." Betts recalls Flannery O'Connor's remark about
her Boston cousins: "when they come South they discuss problems, they don't tell

stories. We tell stories" (Betts, in Manning 1993: 269). Lee Smith confirms this view of the distinctively oral life of the South: "we've just got a narrative approach to life. Southerners believe that everything should be told with a story" (Hunt 1994).

The stories that these writers have their characters tell involve matters that are, conventionally, the concerns of women: cooking, health, birthing, childcare, and administering to the dead. They present first person, intimate accounts of women's lives, as in Smith's *Fair and Tender Ladies* (1988), where Ivy narrates her naturalistic account of the sounds of the birth of her child: "I could hear my bones parting and hear myself opening up with a huge horrible screeching noise" (144). The Granny Midwife who attends Ivy is one of a series of elderly figures such as people Smith's fiction. They have their companions in other writing by Southern women, where grandmothers instruct granddaughters in the practices of midwifery and the herbal lore of folk medicine, as in Gibbons's novel. The three-women household in that novel is a favored one for Southern women writers, and especially in the work of Toni Morrison, for example *Song of Solomon* (1977). Storytelling is frequently viewed by writers as an oppositional technique that they can adopt to subvert subjugation by authorized dominant discourses of history. This is because storytelling prioritizes an individual perspective. It also functions as a source of cultural memory, aiding the cultural cohesion of subordinated groups. The weaving together of different time periods is a narrative structure shared by these novels. Familiar from oral storytelling, this structure exemplifies concerns for the contemporaneity of history.

For African-American writers, creating the idea of a speaking voice with which to articulate individual experience effects a response to a history from which their ancestors have often been erased. A history in which the black writer was first denied the instruments of writing and later suffered from the refusal of powerful white voices to accept that their writing was either authentic or literature ensures a radical perspective on their relationship to the region. The assertion of both an oral voice and its representation in the literary form, also responds to racist assertions that white "literate" cultural forms are superior to black oral culture. Standard English literate forms of writing were a means by which slaves sought to assert their humanity and slave narratives were the antecedents to the development of the African-American "literary" voice; a means by which to demonstrate equality of intellect.

Similarly, the claim of the writer to her own polemical and creative voice has been a particularly important impetus for Southern women and is especially notable in the autobiographical genre, as exemplified by Maya Angelou. In a discussion of fictional and autobiographical writing by Ellen Glasgow, Zora Neale Hurston, and Eudora Welty, Lucinda MacKethan has identified a "Southern way of seeing" in which the "acceptance of memory" is "the primary means of knowing" (1990: 10). This impetus to define an individual way of knowing and remembering their "Southernness" is demonstrated by Zora Neale Hurston and Eudora Welty in their autobiographies, *Dust Tracks on a Road* and *One Writer's Beginnings*, and in the fictional works which established them as the literary foremothers of contemporary Southern women writers. In much Southern women's fiction the adoption of a first person narrative voice asserts specific, individual, female subjectivity. Where a voice is speaking of black experience, as in Hurston's writing, this is part of a tradition that began with the earliest written expression in slave narratives such as Harriet Jacobs's *Incidents in the Life of A Slave Girl* (1861), using the autobiographical form to depict the realities of the experience of captivity and enslavement.

The Dialect Speaker

The literary tradition that evolved as the voice of the African-American was inscribed with dialect, the rhythms of black speech, representations of music and oral ritual.

> I'm pore, I'm black, I may be ugly and can't cook, a voice say to everything listening. But I'm here.
> Amen, say Shug. Amen, amen. (Walker 1982: 187)

Henry Louis Gates has argued that, in *The Color Purple*, Celie, from "an erased presence... writes herself into being" (1988: 243). The self inscribed by Celie is a self defined by her own oral expression; as Gates also asserts, "the will to power for black Americans was the will to write; and the predominant mode that this writing would assume was the shaping of a black self in words" (1984: 4). Through creative acts of oral and literary expression, authors and performers have taken control over the production of knowledge about their own life stories and experiences, and have sought to correct dominant misrepresentations and so maintain a black presence in, and influence on, white culture.

The depiction by Southern writers of their characters' dialect speech has occasioned criticism, particularly when the writer is African-American. This is because it is precisely this form that was used by white writers to inscribe the childlike illiteracy of their black characters, and therefore their difference from white characters and narrators whose standard English prose framed and controlled the dialect. Despite being vulnerable to the charge of replaying negative stereotypes in the minstrel tradition, because of Janie's use of dialect within a standard English narrative frame, Zora Neale Hurston's purpose was that of claiming back the black female voice and asserting it against both white and black male repression. *Their Eyes Were Watching God* (1942) is a novel celebrated by the many feminist critics who cite it as a foundational text. For these critics, Hurston is empowered because she achieves her own authorial voice, because she celebrates the act of her female character's narration of her story, and because she values the vernacular dialect of a rural Southern black community.

Several African-American women writers have followed Hurston's lead and have developed techniques whereby the voice of female characters can be directly asserted within a fictional text. Alice Walker is the foremost of these writers and in the pastoral Southern world of *The Color Purple* the protagonist, Celie, manages to express her own black voice, unmediated by the standard English of author or narrator. This voice is particularly emphasized because the representation of her spoken dialect is defamiliarized within the epistolary form of the novel. *The Color Purple* establishes the possibilities for orality and literacy to be mutually constitutive.

Like Alice Walker, the Appalachian writer Lee Smith has described herself as the "medium" through which her characters speak. In her novel *Fair and Tender Ladies*, Smith adopts an epistolary technique comparable to Walker's. The white Southern protagonist, Ivy, writes to her dead sister but, as with Celie's addresses to "dear God" in *The Color Purple*, this has an autobiographical function in which the reader is constructed as the listener to a story composed in vernacular dialect. Similarly, in Smith's novel, dialect is defamiliarized within the representation of the written form of a letter. In her introduction to Mark Twain's *Sketches, New and Old* (1996), Lee Smith claims Twain as an important influence on her development of storytelling: "he told story straight onto the page . . . For me, to be able to write in the vernacular is to be able to write." This objective is similar to that which Gates claims is the imperative for black Americans. In her novel, Smith achieves a range of oral effects with an amalgamation of dialect vocabulary, for example "seed," "oncet," dialect syntax, "Your name is not much common here," and misspellings, for example, "intrest." The latter, paradoxically, emphasizes that this is in fact a written letter – you cannot misspell speech. Ivy's declaration of her desire to be a writer, and her enjoyment of reading, contribute to a continual deconstruction of oppositions between orality and literacy while effectively prioritizing orality as telling "true" stories and literacy as telling fiction. Smith is sensitive to the kind of controversy engendered by Hurston's dialect writing and she is never patronizing in her representations of dialect, nor is there ever any suggestion of a minstrel comedy. Her work, like Alice Walker's, is therefore a development of Hurston's and set apart from the dialect writers popular at the turn of the century who, Gavin Jones states, upheld "an elitist agenda by juxtaposing the 'proper' language of the narrator and the 'improper' language of character" (1999: 39).

Writers must be judicious in their use of dialect representation, using only sufficient phonetic spelling to allow for the imagining of voice without their work becoming the unreadable prose that a precise phonetic transcription produces. Such unreadability was a deficiency of the close phonetic efforts of the nineteenth-century Southern dialect writers, such as the writer of Appalachian fiction Mary Noailles Murfree, who was dismissively labeled a "local colorist." The reader must respond to the oral effect that is mimicked, but not lose this effect through labor; they must be able to "hear" imaginatively. This can be achieved through narrative strategies such as repetition, rhythm, disorganization of narrative voices, the omission of quotation marks, and moderate misspelling to suggest the spontaneity of actual speech.

In Lee Smith's novel *Oral History* the multiple narratives of numerous narrators produce a constant sense that each tale and conversation belongs to an organic body of speech, a continuum of storytelling, as stories knit into one another. The imitation of oral storytelling is produced by what appear to be direct addresses to the reader/

listener which privilege the dynamic vitality of oral storytelling over traditional history. Granny Younger's words are good examples of this effect: "So I am telling how"; "I smoke a pipe too and you know it"; "I'll tell it directly." The reader is constructed as an implied listener who is present at the time of the telling, who is at the mercy of Granny's whim, but who is also given the illusion of the freedom not to listen (Smith 1983: 31, 37). Rather than producing nostalgic representations of monolithic backwoods identity, Smith ensures that she subverts stereotypes by presenting a multiplicity of different Appalachian voices in narration; these often contradict one another, as no one individual knows the whole story. The illusion of polyphony in *Oral History* brings the novel closer to its oral source, while the adoption of dialect indicates the prioritizing of voices in performance over text. Nevertheless, as she seeks to capture the voices and ways of her community, Smith's objective here seems to be a preservationist and "pastoral" one.

In *Corregidora*, which Gates describes as a "speakerly" novel, the African-American writer Gayl Jones developed her procedure for the "transformation" of the oral into a written colloquial narrative. What she describes as "ritualized dialogue" involves "the language, the rhythm of people talking, and the rhythm *between* people talking" (Gates 1988: 181; Jones, in Harper 1979: 359). In her recent novels Jones achieves a comparable polyphonic oral effect to Smith's through the use of multiple voices. Her writing seeks to escape the linearity of a written narrative and this is achieved by the intertextuality and digressions that are reminiscent of an oral experience. The pages of Jones's novel *Mosquito* in some ways resemble Zora Neale Hurston's porch in *Their Eyes Were Watching God*, where the impression of several voices speaking at once is achieved as they interrupt each other in free indirect speech unhindered by quotation marks. However, Jones has gone further than Hurston or Smith in this novel, for as the narrator speaks directly to the reader, she strongly implies the reader's active presence and response as a listener and her voices represent those of the contemporary black Southerner:

> I can't reveal to y'all everything, even them of y'all that is worth listeners, or tell you all the strategies of the new Underground Railroad, at least the strategies I knows about, 'cause I don't know who might be listening to this conversation ... I got to talk to y'all more about that, 'cause y'all keeps asking me this and that about my story. It ain't that I don't trust y'all – I means the ones of y'all that is worthy listeners – but you can't trust everybody with every story. (Jones 1975: 284–5)

The Preacher

The pastoral appeal of Lee Smith's fiction is due in part to its being developed from material from her anthropological collections of the stories and vernacular expressions of people in her home environment. Her novels contain a mix of song, folklore, and dialogue that evoke the sounds of the Appalachian Mountains. Smith's literary strategy is comparable with that of Zora Neale Hurston, who worked for several years as an anthropologist. Hurston returned to her home in the Deep South to collect the folktales and dialect that were the foundation of her fiction. As she described it in her autobiography:

> I was a Southerner and had the map of Dixie on my tongue. They were all Northerners...It was not my grammar that was bad, it was the idiom. They did not know of the way an average Southern child, white or black, is raised on simile and invective. (Hurston 1970: 200)

What Hurston refers to as "idiom," the "simile," and "invective" is in part a result of the strong influence of Southern religion on black and white communities. W. J. Cash credits black preachers with having a primary influence on Southern white oratory:

> In the South there was the daily impact upon the white man of the example of the Negro, concerning whom nothing is so certain as his remarkable tendency to seize on lovely words, to roll them in his throat, to heap them in redundant profusion one upon another until meaning vanishes and there is nothing left but the sweet canorous drunkenness of sound, nothing but the play of primitive rhythm upon the secret springs of emotion. (Cash 1969: 53)

The special role of religion in popular oral culture can be seen most graphically in its influence on both black and white musical forms. Lawrence Levine has documented the ways in which black cultural identity was both developed and asserted by the slave spirituals and gospel music that fed the blues. As with the blues, the importance of religious themes and rhythms is evident in country music and rock and roll from the South and demonstrates the power of religion in the construction of cultural identities. It is in the secondary orality of the technology of radio and television that the music, fundamentalist preaching, and evangelical fervor of Southern churches are most powerfully disseminated throughout the contemporary South and beyond. Through these media non-Southerners hear the sounds of the voices and music that create the expectations of orality for their reading of Southern fiction. Helen Taylor notes that outside the South, both internationally and in the North, "there has been a large appetite for Southern evangelical religion, encompassing gospel music and singers...as well as high profile preachers" (2001: 12). Because the Southern evangelical and Pentecostal traditions foreground performance rather than text, this religious orality is documented in fictional accounts by Southern writers, but their fiction may also have a similar function. Toni Morrison describes the way in which literature should evoke the effect of a black preacher: "it should try deliberately to make you feel something profoundly." The South for these writers is still Christ-haunted in the way Flannery O'Connor described. The Southern phenomenon of evangelical fervor as played out in revival camp meetings is described by one of Smith's characters, Ivy Rowe:

My word, Beulah – they don't meet but twice a month, and so it goes on for ever. They start with singing and Delphi Rolette lines out the words which he has been doing for twenty years, and then there is preaching and then more singing and more preaching. (Smith 1988: 184)

Ivy discovers that such religious fervor is an instrument of patriarchal control when she struggles to avoid her brother Garnie's belt and she hears the words that for him legitimate his repressive ideology:

These things doth the Lord hate, a proud look, a lying tongue, an heart that deviseth wicked imaginations, feet that be swift in running to mischief. (262)

This is a theme taken up in Smith's novel *Saving Grace* (1995), in which the narrator's father, a charismatic, itinerant, serpent-handling preacher, uses his pronouncement that "God will provide" as an excuse to neglect his wife and children. The novel defamiliarizes the narrative of the Southern Bible Belt, reviving the history of a group of people, religious snake handlers, who have been marginalized as "other" to the dominant establishment church; it also examines why such fundamentalist practices have attraction. This is important, as the Appalachian Mountain religions have been read as evidence of the "deficiencies" of the people and Smith's is a sympathetic account of this subculture. The narrator, Florida Grace, who has been subjected to the patriarchal and puritanical tyranny of her father, and to a lesser degree of her minister husband, struggles to find her own identity. Like Hurston's Janie, her achievement in this respect is to find her voice from a first person narrative position in a fictional autobiography that has the quality of a testimony, drawing attention to *telling*:

My name is Florida Grace Shepherd, Florida for the state I was born in, Grace for the grace of God. I am the eleventh child of the Reverend Virgil Shepherd . . . I am and always have been contentious and ornery, full of fear and doubt in a family of believers. Mama used to call me her "worrywart child." (Smith 1995: 3)

While the narrator names herself, thus inscribing her identity, this is not a traditional face-to-face storytelling situation, but has the rhetorical pattern typically associated with orality. The repetition of "I am" suggests a spoken narrative, as does the use of the dialect words "ornery" and "worrywart." Thus signified is the possession of a personal account that displaces any other that might seek to repress it. The story of the ordinary girl takes precedence over the oratory of her famous preacher father and also subverts the emotional restraint placed on her by her husband; ironically, he is named Travis Word, suggesting a travesty of The Word. The striking sound of these men is recounted only by the controlling testimony of Gracie, who discovers her own ability to claim voice in the predominantly feminine practice of speaking in tongues.

As the white Southern churches contribute to both the oral culture of the region and its exemplification in women's writing, so the continuing survival of an oral culture that has part of its roots in Africa has been assured in the secular and sacred oral traditions and in their literary representations. Important foundations of African-American cultural expression lie in the call-and-response forms of the sacred tradition, whereby the black preacher's authority is found in the response of communal voices. From the rhetorical sermons of the black church, the institutional setting for individual and communal affirmation, the power manifested in the speeches of the civil rights movement and contemporary politics developed. This cultural heritage is celebrated in musical expression, from work songs, to spirituals, to blues, jazz, and rap, and what Ellison in *Shadow and Act* described as blues and jazz *impulses* have been recognized as very important and affirming black consciousness influences for literature.

The Musician

Southern religion is frequently represented as a repressive institution which positions other cultural forms as emanating from the devil, yet religious practices are also shown to be empowering for isolated and subjugated individuals and communities whose ancestors have been driven to seek sanctuary in their faith. James C. Cobb notes that, "like the blues, country music also reflected the tension between the teaching of the church and the temptations of the world" (1999: 199). This is an essential part of the conflicting oral culture represented in contemporary writing, for while religious oratory and music make up part of the fabric of Southern women's writing, it is frequently in conflict with the stories and music of a pagan, secular nature. The titles of blues songs such as "Me and the Devil Blues" and "Preachin' the Blues" exemplify a rebellion against the religious community from which they are excluded. The title of Lee Smith's book *The Devil's Dream* (1992) conveys similar connotations for the story of Kate Malone. It is Kate's music which her husband Moses, who "nobody could beat" for praying, considered to be "the voice of the Devil laughing":

> He came busting outen them woods like God Hisself, a-hollering, snatched the fiddle and broke it over the front porch rail, then beat all of them, Jeremiah and Ezekial and May and Kate, too, until the children run off in the woods to get away from him. (Smith 1992: 23, 29)

Religious music is distinguished from the "sinful" music of the secular fiddle and while religious orality has an important role in providing cohesion for the community, this is juxtaposed with the commercial radio and traveling medicine shows that were instrumental in circulating popular music. Due to the historical sweep of *The Devil's Dream*, in covering four generations of a musical family modeled on the Carters, the music of contemporary "hillbilly" bands is characterized not as the natural outpourings of backwoods primitives, but as a media package that is constructed out of fiddle dance tunes and tin-pan alley songs. Disallowing the perception that the music of Appalachia is in any way "pure" or a fossilized remnant of a pastoral utopia, Smith's novel acknowledges orality's role in the contemporary selling of the South as what Richard Gray describes as "a kind of giant theme park or American version of the heritage industry" (2000: 356).

Popular music – blues and jazz, folk and country – is one of the most expressive oral forms of the ordinary Southerner. The most significant export of the South, as James C. Cobb has shown, this music has occupied the same "common economic and cultural terrain" across race in the poor rural South, and each style has absorbed elements of the other (1999: 120). Although music functions as emblematic of racial difference for African-American critics in pursuit of a purely black aesthetic, music historians such as Bill C. Malone have established that the music of white Southerners has been very strongly influenced by African-American blues. The understanding of both black and white popular musical traditions should be complicated by recognition of the multiracial influences on these musical forms. As Paul Gilroy argues, music is one of the "untidy elements in a story of hybridization and intermixture that inevitably disappoints the desire for cultural and racial purity, whatever its source" (1993: 199). Articulating her sense of loss at the cross-fertilization, or appropriation, of black musical form, Toni Morrison suggests that the African-American novel can be the cultural form that has the responsibility for providing the healing momentum of identity assertion:

> For a long time, the art form that was healing for black people was music. That music is no longer exclusively ours; we don't have exclusive rights to it. Other people sing it and play it; it is the mode of contemporary music everywhere. So another form has to take that place, and it seems to me that the novel is needed by African Americans now in a way that it was not needed before. (Morrison, in Evans 1983)

While the hybridization of cultural forms can unsettle the assertion of racial categories applied to literature as "blues" or "jazz writing," due to its long history of enforced orality black culture has remained strongly in dialogue with the hegemony of white discourse. In particular, African-American women writers have underlined the foundational role that music plays in their writing. Alice Walker is "trying to arrive at the place where music already is"; Toni Morrison describes writing as "another form of music" and she says she writes "in order to replicate the information, the medicine, the balm we used to find in music." Gayl Jones describes her "own feeling of connection with the oral storytelling and black music continuum" (Walker 1984: 264; Morrison, in Bigsby 1992: 29; Jones, in Harper 1979: 357). Thomas Marvin summarizes this "continuum":

> By transforming traditional African-American folk materials into powerful contemporary art capable of communicating across cultural boundaries, musicians provided inspiring models for African-American literary artists who wanted to let the voice of the folk community be heard in modern American literature. (Marvin 1996: 587–8)

It is for the "blues aesthetic" of her 1975 novel *Corregidora* that Gayl Jones is best known. In this novel Jones adopts the role of a blues singer. Foreshadowing Walker's character Celie, Ursa Corregidora achieves selfhood through claiming ownership of, and pleasure in, her own sexuality and this is achieved concomitant to her creative self-expression as a singer. Her voice becomes the medium through which she "bears witness" and is empowered:

> *They call it the devil blues. It ride your back. It devil you.* I bit my lip singing. I troubled my mind, took my rocker down by the river again. It was as if I wanted them to see what he'd done, hear it. All those blues feelings. (Jones 1975: 50)

Jones allows for the unsettling of dichotomies of good and evil and brings about the relativity of meaning as it enters imaginative territories beyond the "correct." Ursa's blues singing combines the pain and the restorative effects of a Freudian "talking cure." The novel is an extension of the music it represents in form and in theme. It represents a catharsis that stands for otherwise uncontrollable anger and hatred in ways that are familiar from blues to rap. This exemplifies what Ralph Ellison in *Shadow and Act* termed "to finger the jagged grain." Paradoxically, the pain for Ursa must be relived and the debilitating psychological consequences of this are such that, as Toni Morrison suggests in *Beloved*, the writer must accept responsibility for stories that she can neither "pass on"/overlook, nor "pass on"/transmit.

As with the blues, writers take many ideas for narrative strategies from jazz; for example, in the interplay of voices improvising on the basic themes of a text, as in a "jam session," and jazz associations that are made between key words and phrases, as well as in subject matter, characters, and settings. Gayl Jones describes the ways African Americans translate jazz effects into their writing:

> In literature jazz can affect the subject matter – the conceptual and symbolic functions of a text, translate directly into the jazz hero, or have stylistic implications. The writer's attempt to imply or reproduce musical rhythms can take the form of jazz-like inflexibility and fluidity in prose rhythms... A sense of jazz – the jam session – can also emerge from an interplay of voices improvising on the basic themes or motifs of the text, in key words and phrases. Often seeming nonlogical and associational, the jazz text is generally more complex and sophisticated than the blues text in its harmonies, rhythms, and surface structures. (Jones 1991: 200)

Also a novel about bearing witness and giving testimony, Jones's *The Healing* (1998) exemplifies the effect of jazz improvisation. Engaging with a full range of oral representations and mimicking the idioms of speech, the narrator, Harlan, addresses her audience as listeners in the first person. The mix of cultural referents demonstrates the hybridization of cultures and foregrounds the novel's relationship to jazz as a hybrid, creolized music. Going further than Lee Smith's recognition of the commodification of Southern culture in *The Devil's Dream*, Jones creates a postmodern pastiche of black essentialism:

How does he know I ain't playing myself? Maybe that's who some of us are. Maybe I'm the Archetypal Nigger Entertainer and not the Stereotypical Nigger Entertainer. (Jones 1998: 152)

As a faith-healing narrator, Harlan is placed within a folk culture where oral narratives are privileged and in a role whereby she effectively overturns the patriarchal function of the church as an instrument of oppression. *The Healing* recognizes the polyphony of American culture and is a radical novel in refuting the view of the black community as a cohesive entity as defined by the Black Aesthetic. This perspective is reiterated and reinforced in *Mosquito* (1999). An improvisational bricolage inscribed with the range of music that has been significant to black culture, from spirituals to rap, the novel depicts the contemporary South as a crossroads where legal or illegal aliens from Mexico pass. In both novels the free and direct discourse of the narrators "speaks" to the readers/listeners in metaphorical conversation: "we has got to know that the listener is as important to the story as the storyteller" (Jones 1999: 614). *Mosquito* strives to be what its narrator describes as "a true jazz story" which "reads kinda like jazz in they rhythm" (421). Complicated by discussions of hybrid origins and the social constructions of race, both novels are nevertheless grounded in the blackness associated with specific oralities and the contexts of oral traditions. The call and response performed by Southern black congregations, myths, rituals, folk wisdoms and stories are passed on, in, and by the novels.

Conclusion

The prioritizing of the oral tradition in writing by Southern women reflects concerns with tradition, regionality, and identity; it signals dialogism by virtue of its relation to the dominance of standard literary forms and the rhetoric of universality that excludes gender, race, and class perspectives. However, the success of this as characteristically Southern writing must rely on its relation to the worlds of Southern sounds. There is still a vital relationship between Southern identity and geography for Southern writers, and the large majority of Southern women novelists continue in their emphasis on talk and music. However, despite the dynamic natures of Southern cultures, the particular history and culture depicted in contemporary Southern women's writing and its criticism remains divided by the color line. Where critics do articulate connections between white and African-American women writers who are from or who write about the South, their common concern with gender politics reflects the successes of 1970s feminism.

The South is changing and its cultural distinctiveness is being erased in the growing homogenization of America and technologizing of popular culture. This is good enough reason to continue to inscribe specific individual and group identities with literary oralities. In the contemporary Southern context the difference of dialect becomes an expression of specific contemporary identity rather than inferiority.

Whether the emphasis is on ethnicity or region, whether orality is recognized as performative or not, the common purpose is a response to negative stereotypes and to assert identity positively – as Southern, as black, as female. In this sense the function of oral forms is the same whether in the original or the copy as a strategy of resistance to master narratives. The claiming of the oral voice is always a controllable literary trope and a political act.

REFERENCES AND FURTHER READING

Baker, H. A., Jr. (1984) *Blues, Ideology, and Afro-American Literature: A Vernacular Theory*. Chicago: University of Chicago Press.

Bigsby, C. (1992) "Jazz Queen," *Independent on Sunday*, April 26.

Cash, W. J. (1969) [1941] *The Mind of the South*. New York: Vintage.

Cobb, J. C. (1999) *Redefining Southern Culture: Mind and Identity in the Modern South*. Athens, GA: University of Georgia Press.

Davis, T. M. (ed.) (1993) *Women's Art and Authorship in the Southern Regions: Connections*. Urbana: University of Illinois Press.

Ellison, R. (1964) *Shadow and Act*. New York: Random House.

Evans, M. (ed.) (1983) *Black Women Writers (1850–1980)*. New York: Anchor/Doubleday.

Fishkin, S. F. (1993) *Was Huck Black? Mark Twain and African-American Voices*. New York: Oxford University Press.

Folks, J., and Perkins, James A. (eds.) (1997) *Southern Writers at Century's End*. Lexington: University of Kentucky Press.

Gates, H. L., Jr. (ed.) (1984) *Black Literature and Literary Theory*. New York: Methuen.

Gates, H. L., Jr. (1988) *The Signifying Monkey: A Theory of African-American Literary Criticism*. New York: Oxford University Press.

Genovese, Eugene D. (1990) "Foreword." In John Shelton Reed, *Whistling Dixie: Dispatches from the South*. Columbia: University of Missouri Press.

Gibbons, Kaye (1993) *Charms for the Easy Life*. New York: G. P. Putnam's Sons.

Gilroy, P. (1993) *The Black Atlantic: Modernity and Double Consciousness*. London: Verso.

Gray, R. (1997) *Writing the South: Ideas of an American Region*. Cambridge and Baton Rouge: Cambridge University Press and Louisiana State University Press.

Gray, R. (2000) *Southern Aberrations: Writers of the American South and the Problems of Regionalism*. Baton Rouge: Louisiana State University Press.

Harper, M. S. (1979) "Gayl Jones." In M. S. Harper and R. B. Stepto (eds.) *Chant of Saints*. Urbana: University of Illinois Press.

Hunt, V. (1994). "Interview with Lee Smith," *Southern Quarterly*, 32, 2.

Hurston, Zora Neale (1970) *Dust Tracks on a Road*. Urbana: University of Illinois Press.

Jones, Gavin (1999) *Strange Talk: The Politics of Dialect Literature in Gilded Age America*. Berkeley: University of California Press.

Jones, Gayl (1975) *Corregidora*. New York: Random House.

Jones, Gayl (1991) *Liberating Voices: Oral Tradition in African-American Literature*. Cambridge, MA: Harvard University Press.

Jones, Gayl (1998) *The Healing*. Boston, MA: Beacon Press.

Jones, Gayl (1999) *Mosquito*. Boston, MA: Beacon Press.

Levine, L. (1977) *Black Culture and Black Consciousness: Afro-American Folk Thought from Slavery to Freedom*. New York: Oxford University Press.

MacKethan, L. (1990) *Daughters of Time*. Athens, GA: University of Georgia Press.

Malone, B. C. (1993) *Singing Cowboys and Musical Mountaineers: Southern Culture and the Roots of Country Music*. Athens, GA: University of Georgia Press.

Manning, C. S. (ed.) (1993) *The Female Tradition in Southern Literature*. Urbana: University of Illinois Press.

Marvin, T. F. (1996) "Children of Legba: Musicians at the Crossroads in Ralph Ellison's *Invisible Man*," *American Literature*, 68: 587–8.

Morrison, T. (1993) *Playing in the Dark: Whiteness and the Literary Imagination*. London: Pan Macmillan.

Piersen, W. D. (1993) *Black Legacy: America's Hidden Heritage*. Amherst: University of Massachusetts Press.

Raper, J. R. (1990) "Inventing Modern Southern Fiction: A Postmodern View," *Southern Literary Journal*, 22, 2: 3–19.

Reising, R. (1986) *The Unusable Past: Theory and Study of American Literature*. New York: Methuen.

Ross, S. M. (1989) *Fiction's Inexhaustible Voice: Speech and Writing in Faulkner*. Athens, GA: University of Georgia Press.

Smith, Lee (1983) *Oral History*. New York: G. P. Putnam's Sons.

Smith, Lee (1988) *Fair and Tender Ladies*. New York: G. P. Putnam's Sons.

Smith, Lee (1992) *The Devil's Dream*: New York: G. P. Putnam's Sons.

Smith, Lee (1995) *Saving Grace*. New York: G. P. Putnam's Sons.

Smith, Lee (1996) "Introduction." In Mark Twain, *Sketches, New and Old*. New York: Oxford University Press.

Taylor, H. (2001) *Circling Dixie: Contemporary Southern Culture Through a Transatlantic Lens*. New Brunswick, NJ: Rutgers University Press.

Walker, Alice (1982) *The Color Purple*. New York: Harper.

Walker, Alice (1984) *In Search of Our Mothers' Gardens*. London: Women's Press.

31

Recent and Contemporary Women Writers in the South

Sharon Monteith

There are few spots on the globe as interesting as the South; and perhaps none so rich in startlingly poignant paradoxes...The time has come...to see the region in perspective.

Lillian Smith, *How Am I to be Heard? Letters of Lillian Smith*

"You always explain with a story."
"So do you. We're Southerners."

Mary Lee Settle, *Choices*

The South is home (or adopted home) to a range of women writers, young and old, black and white, lesbian and heterosexual, for whom the region offers a starting point for literary explorations of landscape, heritage and ancestry, class, race, and ethnicity. In rituals of departure and return, Southern women have defined the South against other places. Also, in recent decades, new social and critical movements have impacted contemporary Southern fiction: from the civil rights movement and the women's movement to environmentalism, multiculturalism, and gay revisionism. This essay will examine some of the sea changes that have found their way into Southern novels and stories and argue that region is really the stories that people decide to tell about the place. Its focus is the heterogeneous South or the "Multi-Souths," to borrow C. Hugh Holman's phrasing in his 1983 article "No More Monoliths Please." Many contemporary novels challenge essentialist notions about Southern community and homeplace and novelists self-consciously engage with the myth of a timeless continuity of (white) Southern cultural identity. Writers slough traditional expectations and clichés while expanding our sense of Southern literature.

Recent and contemporary writers self-consciously dramatize rather than crystallize a sense of coherent Southern identity. C. Vann Woodward, looking back over Southern history in *Thinking Back*, asserted that the best Southern novelists "often write about the obscure, the provincial, the eccentric, the tormented, and the humble – the uncelebrated" (1986: 109). Readers are drawn to Southern fiction for its dramatization of the bizarre and grotesque as well as the quietly meditative. Southern women from Carson McCullers to Anne Rice have sought out the strange in familiar settings. Gothic fantasies like Rice's "Vampyre Chronicles" and Poppy Z. Brite's rebarbative and grotesque *Exquisite Corpses* (1996), set in New Orleans, use horror to expose women's marginality, tormented love, and violent eccentricities. These are unlikely to have been the kinds of Southern fictions Woodward had in mind, but at the other end of the fictional spectrum, Jan Karon's Mitford fictions (from *At Home in Mitford* to *A Common Life*) also sit oddly within the representational scope Woodward outlines, while reacting against it. The stories are provincial, taking place in Mitford, North Carolina (population 1,000), a homogeneous white and Christian small town that is stuck in a 1950s fantasy South, reminiscent of "Leave It To Beaver" and "Ozzie and Harriet." Karon's novels are popular with readers who seek a soft-focus South; the narratives exemplify a white housewives' utopia that exudes bland and sweet didacticism and lacks the irony that peppers Southern fiction. The "Hallmark Cards-style" South is, thankfully, largely unsuccessful in its attempt to counter more complicated, acerbic depictions of the region. More writers join in discrediting and demolishing myths, like that of the Southern belle, a graceful if limited presence in Southern culture. Reynolds Price famously described Southern women as "mack trucks disguised as powder puffs." Rather than the willed "Southernness" of Karon's Mitford, Rebecca Wells's Ya Ya Sisters, or Jill Conner Browne's Sweet Potato Queens, a more equivocating Southern lady has entered contemporary fiction – for example, in Mary Lee Settle's work. In *Choices* (1995) the life of "a nice girl," a debutante from the West End of Richmond, becomes a "bloody battlefield." Melinda serves as a Red Cross volunteer in Kentucky and joins Mother Jones in union organizing; she becomes involved in the Spanish Civil War and in the resistance during World War II. Returning to the South, Melinda discovers that the civil rights movement of the 1950s and 1960s is another kind of civil war over which she has guiltily remained silent while fighting for civil rights around the globe. Melinda represents the kind of intelligent, feisty protagonist who energizes recent Southern fiction.

Contemporary writers bring Southern women's voices to the fore. In Lisa Alther's *Kinflicks* (1978) Ginny Babcock flees north from Tennessee only to career from one possible role to another as she plays out the possibilities for a woman coming of age in the 1950s and 1960s. Ellen Burns in Blanche McCrary Boyd's *The Revolution of Little Girls* (1992) dares to be different, becoming her High School's beauty queen while drunk and strung out before coming out as a lesbian. The strength of such novels lies in the first person narrative technique. The dramatic monologue is a form that "takes possession of the speaker," as Eudora Welty describes it in *One Writer's Beginnings*. It is a way of celebrating the self, as in the case of Kaye Gibbons's resilient heroine in *Ellen Foster* (1987), or of allowing a character enough rope to hang herself by virtue of her own words, as in Ellen Douglas's classic short story "I Just Love Carrie Lee" (1963). One writer posits that "Southern" is a language in its own right; Settle's Melinda believes her language is "a polyglot of English, Southern, and war." Southern voices have been subject to stereotype as readily as Southern women, however. A waitress in Dorothy Allison's satirical story "I'm Working on My Charm" tells the young protagonist learning the ropes that women like her "just hold a place in the landscape": as far as visiting "Yankees" are concerned, "once we're out of sight we just disappear." The way to handle the tourists is to drawl slowly and talk like you're from Mississippi, since "Yankees got strange sentimental notions about Mississippi." Allison refuses to let her protagonist disappear into sentimental notions and years later, successful in her career and attending a sophisticated soiree in the North, the waitress's point is proved. The host declares: "Southerners are so charming" with their "two names said as one." The observation is a prime example of what Granny Mattie in another of Allison's stories in *Trash* (1995) calls "Bullshit and applebutter." Even arriving in the Congo, the Price family in Barbara Kingsolver's *The Poisonwood Bible* (1999) is greeted by Northerners who immediately pass judgment on the family's "charming" Southern accent: "She even tried to imitate the way we said 'right now' and 'bye-bye' ('Yay-es the ayer-plane is leavin rot nail!' and '"Bah-bah" like a sheep!')"

In Jill McCorkle's wonderfully irreverent "Your Husband Is Cheating On Us" in *Final Vinyl Days and Other Stories* (1998) a mistress's breathless and darkly humorous monologue is delivered to her lover's wife:

> I have been thinking that we should get rid of Mr. Big. That's right, don't look so shocked until you hear me out. It would be just like in that movie that came out a year or two ago, only I do not want to get into a lesbian entanglement with you. I mean, no offense or anything, it's just not my cup of tea. Actually, I would like some of whatever you're drinking. Diet Coke is fine. Don't slip me a Mickey, okay? A joke, honey. That's a joke. I'm full of them. Probably every joke you heard for the last eight years has been right out of my mouth. Mr. Big has no sense of rhythm or timing – in *anything*, you know.

Humor can be found in the most serious of situations and even in the most desperate and dark aspects of Southern women's fiction. The voices and humorous situations McCorkle imagines often contain seeds of fear and violence as well as comedy. *July 7th* (1984), a novel that superficially resembles Welty's *Losing Battles* (1970), in that generations come together to celebrate elderly Granner's birthday, soon veers off into murkier territory. The murder that opens the novel takes place in a convenience store where an elderly assistant is suffocated with saran wrap in an undignified violation of a quiet life.

Rather than conform to expectations, writers step outside of their own experiences using the form of the dramatic monologue. In Ann Patchett's prize-winning *Taft* (1995), a fascinating study of fatherhood, the point of view is not that of the eponymous Taft, the absent white father at the center of the text, but of John Nickel, a black bartender in downtown Memphis for whom the compelling Taft becomes synonymous with his own crises over parental responsibility. An equally interesting variation on the first person narration is Tova Mirvis's bestselling *The Ladies Auxiliary*

(1999), a comedy of manners set in the same city and at the same time but inside Memphis's orthodox Jewish community. It is distinguished by a narrative "we" in which a chorus of self-righteous though self-searching Southern ladies who pride themselves on their safe if strict community judge the newcomer in their midst. Batsheva is a convert to Judaism and a newcomer to the South. The Ladies Auxiliary assumes she will prove to be as restless and risqué as the flighty women who populate stories by Ellen Gilchrist, but Batsheva proves more intriguing than they surmise. The novel's polyvocality is carefully coordinated as a choral performance in which individual voices feature in different phases of the symphony, but are never allowed to dominate. Old traditionalist Mrs. Levy and young, unhappy Shira Feldman are located at the extremes of a female continuum in which religion acts as a buffer shielding each woman from the outside world ("drink, drugs and the rest"). But their "Jerusalem of the South" is collapsing and the women's voices are slowly modulated in their condemnation of the outsider who accepts their way of life even as they decry her ability to follow their rituals.

In Southern fiction, women characters may be "insiders" like most of the women in Mirvis's first novel or "outsiders" like Batsheva, or young Tabitha's mother in Pat Cunningham Devoto's *My Last Days as Roy Rogers* (1998), set in the 1950s. Tabitha observes that her mother finds it difficult to adjust to life in a small Alabama town filled with her husband's relatives:

> Life in Bainbridge was to Mother like dropping Tallulah Bankhead down in the middle of the Amazon rain forest... Mother could not get it through her head that baking a good cake for the missionary circle was more important than spending an afternoon reading *The Adventures of Tom Sawyer* to us as we huddled in a circle around her rocking chair on the screened porch. Or that visiting Great-Aunt Lizzie on the tenth anniversary of her husband's passing was more important than putting her feet up and reading the editorials in the *Birmingham News*.

Community is a constellation of concerns for contemporary writers. Devoto is beginning to specialize in depictions of small rural communities, but Dorothy Allison presents most effectively the small-minded in small-town Cayro, Georgia. In *Cavedweller* (1998) Delia Byrd reunites with the daughters she abandoned to escape a brutal husband for a new life in Los Angeles. The town has not forgotten her decision and the first person she meets remembers her as "that bitch who ran off and left her babies... don't think that people don't remember." More positively, in *The Ladies Auxiliary* the women begin to unpick the provincial threads that unite them when they realize that the outsider may actually shed new light on community ways; a convert may "see further, as if they were standing on our shoulders" and each woman confides in Batsheva. They wish Batsheva were "more like us" but they also find that "we wanted to become a little more like her." Although it takes friendship with the rabbi's wife to grant her a "kosher seal" of approval, Batsheva's presence in their midst prompts the women to reconsider some of the prejudices that have been heightened by their desire to prevent the closed community from unraveling.

One of the tensions that pull at Mirvis's Memphis community is cross-generational anxiety and the over-protectiveness that obtains when parents delimit the space their children may occupy outside the home. But psychotherapists also refer to "toxic" parents and Southern fiction has its share of abusive fathers and stepfathers (in *Ellen Foster* and Dorothy Allison's *Bastard Out of Carolina*, for example) and irresponsible mothers, like Easter's in Welty's "Moon Lake" (1949) and the brothel keeper in Sheri Reynolds's *Bitterroot Landing* (1994). In *Bastard Out of Carolina* the mother actually withdraws from her daughter precisely *because* she has been abused by "Daddy Glen," the husband she trusted. Marnie in Janice Daugharty's *Like A Sister* (1999) is so recklessly in lust that she leaves her children to the mercy of corrupt social forces, and Christine in Doris Betts's *Souls Raised from the Dead* (1994) deserts her family because she values cosmetics and TV over all else – including her daughter. But there are also irresponsible families like Delia Grinstead's in Anne Tyler's *Ladder of Years* (1995). When Delia walks away from her self-absorbed physician husband and three precocious children, they are unable to recall what she actually looks like when asked to provide an accurate description for the local newspaper. Traditional familial roles are scrutinized by women writers in a variety of contexts.

In *Choices*, Settle's Melinda professes: "A Southerner without a family is like a loose marble," but in contemporary Southern fiction the emphasis is on alternative "family" units that are cross-racial and intergenerational, allowing creative space in which to breathe beyond familial stereotypes. Black Southern writers have been at the forefront of the enterprise. By the end of Alice Walker's *The Color Purple* (1983) Celie and Shug, Squeak and Grady have lived happily together in Shug's house in Memphis and, once back in rural Georgia, Celie and those closest to her settle in the home she inherits, to live out what Linda Tate (referring to Shay Youngblood's *The Big Mama Stories*, 1989) calls "community-as-family" (1994: 34). Such "families" are always woman centered, often spiritual, and closely associated with the landscape itself. In her preface to the tenth anniversary edition of the novel, Walker describes herself as "a worshipper of Nature" and Celie as a "spiritual captive" who "breaks free into the realization that she, like Nature itself, is a radiant expression of the heretofore perceived as quite distant Divine." Although Walker is unusual among Southern writers in her New Age commitment to spiritualism (she thanks the cast of the novel for coming and sees herself as a literary medium), there is a significant number of fictions in which the spiritual and natural merge in distinctively Southern places. Sam in Bobbie Ann Mason's *In Country* (1985) hopes spending the night on the edge of the local swamp in Kentucky will make her feel closer to her father who died in the jungles of Vietnam. In the end she only feels more alone, but Rebecca Florice, who fills her North Carolina garden with healing herbs in Linda Beatrice Brown's *Rainbow Roun Mah Shoulder* (1984), is a figure in landscape around whom others gather; and Gloria Naylor's Mama Day in her "mother wit" can summon lightning and turn flowers into butterflies as easily as she cures a woman's infertility, working roots like a modern-day conjure woman in a fictive landscape steeped in African-American folklore and history.

The Biracial South

Many contemporary women novelists choose to tackle issues of race and racism. In Devoto's *My Last Days as Roy Rogers* Tabitha's best friend during the strained times of a polio epidemic in 1954 is black Maudie May; and in her second novel, *Out of the Night that Covers Me* (2001), Devoto explores what has long been an archetypal interracial Southern friendship, between a young white boy and an old black man, again set in 1950s Alabama. *Water from the Well* (2000) by Myra McLarey focuses on black and white communities in Arkansas through six interconnecting stories that develop out of passion and violence, but there is a distinct tendency in recent fiction for stories of reconciliation and redemption, especially by white writers. Janice Daugharty, whose primary setting is rural Georgia, usually resolves the moral quandaries that charge novels like *Whistle* (1998); and writers who focus on friendships between women in the South frequently imagine redemptive, utopian relationships that resonate with hope for a racially harmonious post-civil rights South.

Black Southerners like Alice Walker and Ann Allen Shockley are often much less conciliatory. In *Meridian* (1976) an interracial friendship is strained by the ramifications of sexual and racial politics, and in Shockley's stories in *The Black and White of It* (1987) the historical roots of gender and sexual conflicts are traced back to slavery. Lesbian love is made symbolic of white women's cultural decadence in astringent stories like "Women in a Southern Time," in which a black maid shelves her ambitions to train as a nurse when she is smothered by her mistress's need for her in her house and in her bed. Interracial love between women is the subject of more hopeful speculation in the novel *Loving Her* (1974). Despite efforts to resolve tensions in fiction that remain problematic in life, in racially polarized Southern towns and cities, white writers like Ellen Douglas in the acclaimed *Can't Quit You Baby* (1988) and Elizabeth Cox in *Night Talk* (1997) pursue complex explorations of the factors that inhibit cross-racial cooperation. Cox has Evie and Janey Louise maintain their friendship beyond childhood and the point at which it is usually curtailed by separate homerooms at school and inculcation into separate friendship groups after school. The girls live together in Georgia in the 1950s and, following their mothers' example, "Over the years, they had learned how to be each other's friend." When Janey Louise falls prey to tragedy and moves away for a time, Evie is bereft: "My room, without Janey Louise, felt like living inside a cube of ice... No one could come into her place." As their relationship twists and turns into the 1990s, the repressed racial antagonism that simmers beneath the surface of their community takes its toll. But Cox has produced a rare work, in which the central friendship eschews utopianism but persists under pressure despite the tired epithets and cruel acts of those who seek to undermine Janey Louise and subvert Evie's attempts to remain close to her childhood friend when her own life is untouched by racism.

The history of Southern race relations has proved a compelling if difficult subject both for established novelists like Douglas and Elizabeth Spencer and new voices like Devoto and McLarey. It remains a source of drama and quiet meditation. Most recently, Melanie Neilson writes a mystery in which the internecine history of race relations skews love and preempts murder in a first novel following her acclaimed memoir *Even Mississippi*. However, *The Persia Café* (2001) is also a lyrical story firmly embedded in Southern folkways and foodways; Fannie Leary, Neilson's protagonist, is a cook who informs us that the story she tells "begins in my nose." It unfolds slowly in a small Mississippi River town, and in its emphasis on the pervasiveness of regret and the impossibility of forgiveness owes much to the "dark fable" of Southern literary history, in which racism disrupts even the smallest and most harmonious of Southern communities.

Replacing the South

From Ellen Glasgow and Eudora Welty to Alice Walker and Ellen Douglas, a sense of place has proved a resonant feature of fiction. Josephine Humphreys asserts "Fiction must *take place*" and in *Rich in Love* (1987) two characters take a tour of Charleston, the city in which they have grown up and which they still call home. They experience what has come to be recognized as heritage tourism ("the smell of bus fuel had become the dominant smell of the city") as they take in Fort Sumter, Boone Hall Plantation, and the Old Slave Mart Museum. One character, Rhody, disguises herself before joining the tourists in order to gain a different perspective on the South she knows so well, otherwise "You get in your way." One way of expanding tropes of one's region is through deterritorialization, as Deleuze and Guattari describe it in *On the Line* (1983). From an estranged, displaced perspective the South is divested of its seemingly generic in dual-location novels where comparative landscapes become symbolic of cultural interaction and exchange. In *The Color Purple* the two sisters spend much of their lives writing back and forth between Africa and Georgia and in *In Country* Sam's fixation on Vietnam extends into a meditation on the temporal and historical connection between Hopewell, Kentucky and Quang Ngai, as signaled in her father's life and death.

In Kathleen Coskan's *The High Price of Everything* (1988) the South becomes striated in unexpected new ways. Coskan, who grew up in Georgia, juxtaposes stories set in her birthplace with others that take place in Ethiopia. Sometimes her characters play at being Margaret Bourke-White photographing everyone they see, but more generally Coskan concentrates on the differences place makes in the lives of her characters. For another writer, Marie Thomas, it is often the similarities that are most striking. In her story of "The Texan" in *Come to Africa and Save Your Marriage* (1987), cultural and corporate imperialism lend a wry note to a sardonic tale. The protagonist notes that the Hilton Hotel in Nairobi is just like the Hilton he remembers in Texas, except that everyone who serves him is black. The observation returns him to the mindset he learned growing up: "That don't bother him. Despite what everyone said about Southerners and their racial views, the Texan lived by one rule; any man that shows me he's at least as good a man as I am; that's all I ask." Thomas's story exemplifies the Southern adage that a good man is hard to find, and this man remains trapped in believing that all Southerners are white and all good people are men.

In her earliest novels Barbara Kingsolver had her characters travel from rural Kentucky to Arizona, in *The Bean Trees* (1988), and to Oklahoma, in *Pigs in Heaven* (1993), but in *The Poisonwood Bible* a family of missionaries leaves the pine-covered Georgia hills for the jungle of the Belgian Congo at the end of the 1950s. In detailing the Congolese fight for Independence in an epic multi-voiced novel, Kingsolver captures, among many other things, the absurdities of transposing Southern etiquette to a context that is so different: "We came from Bethlehem, Georgia, bearing Betty Crocker cake mixes into the jungle," says Leah, one of the daughters of evangelist Nathan Price.

Dual-location novels represent one popular method for reenvisioning Southern mores, but in new immigrant fiction the South, though predominantly biracial, is stretched to include the experiences of those Lan Cao and Susan Choi choose as their protagonists. Women writers are beginning to lead us to think of Southern places in new ways through stories about Vietnamese and Korean immigrants in Virginia and Tennessee, respectively, in *Monkey Bridge* (1997) and *The Foreign Student* (1998). Each novel follows a war-torn refugee for whom the American South becomes home. Each protagonist is positioned by other characters, either as a romantic castaway or, more disturbingly, as an embodied threat to Southern cohesion. Chang (or "Chuck" as he is renamed) and Katherine, a Southerner "born and bred" in *The Foreign Student*, exhibit a similar wariness about the world around them; his learned during the Korean War, hers at the University of the South in Sewanee, where she is estranged from her family and set apart from her peers due to a long affair with a much older professor. Iain Chambers in *Migrancy, Culture and Identity* (1994) describes how the stranger becomes an emblem of the "urgencies of our time" and "a presence that questions our present." Clearly, there are problems when the immigrant is reduced to metaphor, but because the South has historically, if solipsistically, been constructed only as a biracial society, the reader's sense of the region is reshaped, the familiar rethought. Bilingual and bicultural storytellers, like Judith Ortiz Cofer, a Puerto Rican writer and critic living in Louisville, Georgia, remind us that an ethnically diverse South exists in literature as well as in life. Lee Smith has said that the reason black people never figure in her fictions is that she never met a black person until she moved away from her home in southwest Virginia. However, writers who explore the Appalachian region Smith has called "the rugged terrain of my heart" also include Native-American Marilou Awiakta of mixed Cherokee and white Appalachian heritage, whose writing combines environmentalism with issues of equality and diversity (as in *Selu: Seeking the Corn-Mother's Wisdom*, 1993). From Cuban-American writers in Miami to Latin Americans in Austin, Texas, the angle of vision on the South is widening.

The Ecocritical South

While the land has long been the mythos of Southern culture, the history inscribed into landscape can be painful. Black writers in particular have explored the horrors of Reconstruction, as in Margaret Walker's *Jubilee* (1966). And in Marita Golden's *And Do Remember Me* (1992) Jessie Foster's coming of age in the Mississippi Delta is set against the emotionally murky and politically dangerous Freedom Summer of 1964. Another writer who turns to the South in her fiction, Toni Morrison in *Song of Solomon* (1977), exhibits what Wes Berry has called a sense of "blasted pastoral" when Milkman Dead explores his ancestral roots in Southern places (Jones and Monteith 2002), and Lane von Herzen employs pathetic fallacy, anthropomorphism, and heightened symbolism to align the east Texas environment in *Copper Crown* (1991) with her characters' homoerotic friendship. An environmentalist and ranger for the National Park Service, Nevada Barr lets her park ranger heroine Anna Pigeon roam from Texas, in the award-winning *Track of the Cat* (1993), to Mississippi's Natchez Trace Parkway, the setting for *Deep South* (2000) and *Hunting Season* (2002). As Southerners embrace environmentalism, a strong ecocritical concern over Southern places is developing, from eco-tourism supporting conservation in the Florida Everglades, through Dolly Parton's embracing of environmentalism through Dollywood's eagle sanctuary in Tennessee, to environmental health policies in response to Louisiana's "Cancer Alley."

Southern interest in environmental concerns is perhaps best epitomized by Janisse Ray, winner of the Southern Book Critics Circle award for nonfiction in 2000 for *Ecology of a Cracker Childhood*. In one memorable scene Ray skydives into Georgia and a tree "reached out its arms and caught me . . . I was home." Ray merges memoir with environmental history to explore her childhood home on US Highway 1, literally a junkyard in the midst of the Edenic forests of southeastern Georgia. It is in living astride two radically different Souths – the depleted junk wasteland and the sprawling, primeval longleaf pine forests – that Ray finds her true home. She has been described as the South's Rachel Carson and admits to carrying the landscape "inside like an ache," and her memoir is a powerful lens through which to read a burgeoning subgenre of Southern women's fiction. Connie May Fowler's *Remembering Blue* (2000) is a tale of fishermen on Florida's Gulf Coast whose way of life and livelihood are suffering due to environmental pollution and land developers. In earlier novels, like *River of Hidden Dreams* (1994) and *Before Women Had Wings* (1996), Fowler's ecocritical concerns are only one thread bound into stories of matrilineal history or domestic violence. In *Remembering Blue* they are at the forefront: a young widow recalls the fisherman husband she loved who went missing at sea and their life together with his Greek-American family on a small fictional island called Lethe. Lethe has all the lush vegetation of Florida and is reminiscent of landscapes depicted by environmental crusaders and anthropologists Marjorie Stoneman Douglas and Zora Neale Hurston.

For Fowler, as for many other Southern women writers, including Eudora Welty and Mary Lee Settle, mythology is an important feature of writing that explores memory and forgetting. Fowler's narrator, Mattie Blue, explains: "I at twenty-five years of age am left to ponder the world as if I were a woman of eighty. My remembrance, my meditation on Nick Blue – who he was and why his life was important – is a simple act by a grieving wife, yet his story cannot be told to the exclusion of mine." Nor can her story be told to the exclusion of the Florida landscapes and seascapes that so imbue the novel. Fowler enmeshes characters with place like the Chickasaw writer Linda Hogan, who crosses environmentalist activism with a keen sense of mystery in *Power* (1998), also set in Florida.

Ecocritics like Lawrence Buell, and, with more specific resonance for the South, Louise Westling, seek to revive and revise tropes of the American pastoral by studying the ethical relationship between literary texts and physical place. Ecocriticism is a kind of ecological humanism in which paeans to nature mix with political environmentalism in a post-pastoral South. Southern ecocritical writing has specific echoes, not only of the Nashville Agrarians but also of neglected novels like Caroline Miller's *Lamb in His Bosom* (1934), set in rural Georgia, and rediscovered autobiographies like Mary Hamilton's *Trials of the Earth* (1992), which evokes the wilderness of woods and canebrakes in the Mississippi Delta a century ago and the pioneering spirit of women "toiling to blaze a way." Hamilton's story, edited by Helen Dick Davis in the 1930s, has been reintroduced to readers by Ellen Douglas, whose own *The Rock Cried Out* (1979) is indicative of what Suzanne W. Jones calls a "new agrarian" perspective on Southern places (Jones and Monteith 2002). *The Poisonwood Bible* begins by asking the reader to picture a forest and to subsume herself within its cool glades: "I want you to be its conscience, the eyes in the trees... This forest eats itself and lives forever." Similarly, in Kingsolver's *Prodigal Summer* (2000) Deanna Wolfe, a wildlife conservationist, is only one of three central characters for whom the remote Appalachian hills become the fecund, sensuous center of the novel.

Class Finds and Comic Acts

While in *Ecology of a Cracker Childhood* Janisse Ray writes about her loving close family, many novelists deal with poverty, deprivation, violence, and abuse in the family by depicting scarred subjects living wounded lives. Dorothy Allison, Sheri Reynolds, and Connie May Fowler each redeem bewildered white "crackers" who sometimes find solace in nature. Jael in Sheri Reynolds's first novel, *Bitterroot Landing*, is almost feral, living off the land for much of the story. There is a growing subgenre of novels in which epithets like "poor white," "white trash," and "dyke" are no longer terms of opprobrium and there is a keen sense of the absurd and of gentle irony in what Blanche McCrary Boyd has called "the redneck way of knowledge." There is also a commitment to explore class to expose the visceral daily negotiations of working-class women with men and with institutions. In Maureen Brady's *Folly* (1983) a group of women work at a textile plant in North Carolina and live in a trailer park. They come together across their different experiences when a baby dies due to the negligence of the plant and they strike for better conditions.

Overtly political evocations of Southern experience are less rare than one might suppose, but much less well known than they should be. One reason for this may be the difficulties in maintaining a clear sense of story when the political issues one wants to bring to bear are so numerous. Cris South's *Clenched Fists and Burning Crosses* (1984) is a case in point. It is a brave novel that opens with a Klan rally during which a black woman is killed and the white lesbian protagonist, Jesse, who intends to testify against the woman's murderers is beaten and raped by the men involved. Most of the women characters have been sexually abused and anger is one of the tools they use to survive when even a refuge for battered women is invaded by a murderous husband. The clenched fist of the title is at once a salute, a symbol of their reclamation of power from neo-Nazis, and a metaphor for the women's overall endurance; one elderly lady tells of her aunt, who for eight long years clenched her fist so that her thumbnails "had done growed clean through her hands . . . Reckon it could happen to any of us."

The willingness to engage with politics and new social movements alone does not make for powerful writers and Cris South places too many issues on the agenda for a short novel to carry. But Dorothy Allison, like Flannery O'Connor and Carson McCullers before her, maintains a politicized sense of the dark and doomed but never loses her creative nerve either. Wonderfully anarchic but devastatingly dark, Allison's short memoir *Two or Three Things I Know for Sure* (1995) is based around family pictures, the kinds of photographs that are reworked to effect in her stories of love and loss, like "River of Names" (1998) in which the protagonist's litany of dead cousins caught together in a single photograph forces the reader to catch her breath:

> One went insane – got her little brother with a tire iron; the three of them slit their arms, not their wrists but the bigger veins up near the elbow; she, now she strangled the boy she was sleeping with and got sent away; that one drank lye and died laughing soundlessly. In one year I lost eight cousins.

Allison locates women and girls living lives truncated by poverty and low expectations on the jagged edges of small Southern towns. They work with others at the local Winn Dixie or waffle house but they are not joiners – they do not belong to a union or a church. They are stubbornly enduring as well as isolated, but sometimes addicted to the violence that moves beyond the confines of language to characterize their daily lives. Like Mick Kelly in Carson McCullers's first novel, *The Heart is a Lonely Hunter* (1940), doomed to thankless wage slavery in a five-and-ten-cent store, and Evie Decker who suffers from such low self-worth in Anne Tyler's *A Slipping Down Life* (1970) that she carves the name of her pop idol into her forehead, Allison's characters lack a sense of agency.

One of the heaviest burdens Southern women writers carry is the burden of history as it cordons them off from others, in trailer parks on the outskirts of town or in shacks even further into the margins of society.

Public Events and Private Ritual

History is a terrain that Southern women writers have long been reclaiming in very imaginative ways. In Roland Barthes's definition the literary work is always paradoxical; while it may represent history, it simultaneously acts to resist it. This observation seems particularly useful when one comes to consider women writing historiographical fiction. Kaye Gibbons's *On the Occasion of My Last Afternoon* (1998) and Alice Randall's *The Wind Done Gone* (2001) are resistant texts. They are political in the sense that they are revisionist, reworking literary history as parody as well as revisiting periods in the past. As a prelude to Randall's controversial novel set largely during Reconstruction, it is useful to return to Alice Walker's short story "A Letter of the Times" (1983), in which Susan Marie is angered by her white friend Lucy dressing like Scarlett O'Hara for a fancy dress ball. When I first wrote about this story (Monteith 2000: 174) I noted that among Susan Marie's many reasons for irritation was the lack of an iconic black Southern belle in popular culture to counter the resonance of Scarlett O'Hara. Randall fills that gap. In the early 1990s, in an assisted-living facility outside Atlanta, an elderly lady dies. Little is known of her except that her general good health failed on two specific occasions in 1936 and 1940 that coincided with the publication and film premiere of the novel *Gone With the Wind*. The reader discovers that this Southern lady dedicated her life to a failed dream of publishing the diary of her ancestor, Cynara, Scarlett O'Hara's half-sister from whom Scarlett is separated by "a river of notions: notions of Negroes and notions of chivalry, notions of race and place, notions of customs and rage." Cynara was born in the kitchen of the "great house" (not Tara but Tata); reads *Uncle Tom's Cabin* ("I didn't see me in it"); marries R (Rhett Butler); is inspired by Frederick Douglass; and falls in love with a black senator. The literary history that Randall resists and reorients with some success is already myth. Before the case to prevent the publication of *The Wind Done Gone* was turned down on appeal, an Atlanta court issued an injunction against the parody for violating the copyright of *Gone With the Wind*, citing Mitchell's "beloved characters and their romantic tragic world."

Robert Penn Warren famously referred to history as "the big myth we live by, and in our living, constantly remake" and Faulkner said that in the South the time was always really a few minutes before 2 o'clock on July 3, 1863, with General Pickett about to give the fateful order to charge in the midst of the Civil War. Slavery and the Civil War have been the South's strongest public memories and its biggest myths. They underpin Gibbons's *On the Occasion of My Last Afternoon*, in which Emma Garnet Tate Lowell, preparing for death in the year 1900, looks back over the seventy years of her life. She remembers Clarice, the black housekeeper with whom she shared half a century; life on a plantation on the James River; and tending wounded soldiers in Raleigh, North Carolina. At the beginning of a carefully researched novel, Gibbons delineates Seven Oaks, five miles from the Carters' Shirley Plantation, home to General Robert E. Lee's mother. Across the James River is tenth President John Tyler's (1841–5) Sherwood Forest plantation. Gibbons carefully inserts her imaginary family, the Tates, into a famous chain of plantations in Charles City County, VA, not far from Richmond, the capital of the Confederacy.

In Southern women's writing "history" is therefore often understood as an imaginative space, even a domestic space. The Civil War, so crucial in Emma Garnet's life, is reinterpreted from a woman's point of view, a narrative act most famously performed by Louisa May Alcott in *Little Women*. History erupts to crash through the lives of Gibbons's family in the form of the Civil War, and Emma Garnet and her husband Quincy – a Southern woman and a Northern man – attempt to heal the rift in the nation by healing the nation's wounded. Gibbons's epigraphs, Allen Tate's "Ode to the Confederate Dead" and Robert Lowell's "For the Union Dead," the first a Southerner and the second a descendant of the New England Lowells Gibbons refigures in the novel, reinforce her overall thesis. The two poems balance each other, suggesting reconciliation with the bloody, violent past; and a belief in reconciliation continues to animate fiction by women as willing to grapple with the past and its legacy as any of their male counterparts.

Such a Long Memory

According to a character in Josephine Humphreys's award-winning first novel *Dreams of Sleep* (1984), history's "one true lesson" is that it fades: "we can't sustain the things we used to sustain: dynasties, clans, big families; we can't even maintain their monuments. Statues are losing their noses, tombstones their letters." But the stories we tell ourselves about the past merge with a sense of public history in "memory novels" in which an individual meditates on life. The memories of elderly women are a structuring principle for a number of Southern novels, from Elizabeth Hardwick's haunting *Sleepless Nights* (1979) to Gibbons's *On the Occasion of My Last Afternoon* and Mary Lee Settle's *Choices*. In novels that use autobiographical forms, women (like Granny Younger in Lee Smith's *Oral History*) look back over eventful lives that span the nineteenth and twentieth centuries. Kaye Gibbons's protagonist admits: "I had so many bits of ideas waiting for the years to align into some pattern of logic, to be synthesized so that by my adulthood I would have what I often termed to my children as quick-marrow, the living sense, the core of knowledge about the way the world works." The narrator unites her past and present in the desire for story. Events are sifted and scrutinized until it becomes apparent, little by little, that the family "history" she repressed is her testimony.

Southern history is often written on the body of a woman. Where Mary Lee Settle's Melinda feels her body is "a whole history of dancing," in Alice Walker's *Meridian* the eponymous protagonist suffers a mysterious illness that limits her civil rights activism. The illness is presented in enigmatic, if Freudian, terms as a kind of debilitating hysteria because Meridian's body has been in the firing line for many years, under attack literally and psychologically from intransigent white racists. Meridian is the symbolic embodiment of historical civil rights struggles in the rural South; while in Lee Smith's *Black Mountain Breakdown* (1981) Crystal's catatonic state is less equivocal, precipitated as it clearly is by the memory of childhood abuse that overwhelms her in adulthood. In Carol Dawson's *Body of Knowledge* (1994) Victoria's swollen body weighs around 600 pounds. She swallows the plot, digesting the stories of her dysfunctional family until she has consumed the past, its tragedies with its ambiguities. Faulkner famously described Quentin Compson's body as a family vault in *Absalom, Absalom!*: "He was not a being, an entity, he was a commonwealth. He was a barracks filled with stubborn backward-looking ghosts." The military image and the ever-present Civil War are set aside for specifically domestic images in Dawson's novel, so that the women's version of events is brought to the fore. Women writers – Dawson, Denise Giardina, and Ellen Douglas, for example – cite Faulkner's influence on the fiction they write; the shadow he casts is a long one.

The compulsion to recall events and to revisit Southern places and past times animate Southern fiction, whether mordantly witty or hopelessly tragic. For some women characters, it is precisely the machinations of family and memory that lead them to atrophy in lonely houses, as in Eudora Welty's classic story "Why I Live at the PO," where a Southern daughter moves out of a claustrophobic family atmosphere only so far as the similarly domestically enclosed local post office. Houses are often a singular metaphor for loss and disintegration. In Bobbie Ann Mason's *In Country* Sam is acutely aware that the foundations of her uncle's house are unstable, just as his mind wanders back into combat in Vietnam and his nightmares threaten to overwhelm his grasp on reality. In Augusta Trobaugh's *Resting in the Bosom of the Lamb* (2000) four old women living closely together discover that their present harmony is tenuous when evil deeds in their past remain unaddressed; and in Pam Durban's *So Far Back* (2001) events that happened in 1837 continue to affect relationships between women in 1989.

Time is often elastic in Southern fiction. Mary Lee Settle's "The Beulah Quintet" stretches back 300 years and Sharyn McCrumb's recent bestseller *The Songcatcher* (2001) covers around 250 years (from England in 1649 to the South in 1980) in tracking an Appalachian ballad that has passed through seven generations and threatens to die with the country singer whose plane has crashed in mountains bordering North Carolina and Tennessee. Lalita Tademy in *Cane River* (2000) creates a family saga out of her personal search for family records for slaves living in Louisiana from the early 1800s. She traces four generations of black women who gave birth to children by white French planters.

Although Southern fiction is often unflinching in its preparedness to face the past, it is not best known for dystopian science fiction or dazzling fantasy as literary methods for doing so. Nevertheless, there are writers who utilize the idea of time travel in novels that explore slavery and vampirism. In 1976, the bicentenary of the Declaration of Independence, a commemoration that brought to mind the nation's failure to implement the Declaration's principles with respect to huge sections of the South's population, Octavia Butler published a novel called *Kindred*. California-born Butler, the first African-American woman writer to become renowned as a writer of science fiction, locates her protagonist Dana in a time trap that hauls her back from California in 1976 to her ancestors in the early nineteenth-century South and endangers her own life and identity. In *The Gilda Stories* (1991) Jewelle Gomez details an odyssey in which a lesbian vampire begins her life as a slave in the South in the 1850s and moves through two hundred years of life, loves, and persecution. Both writers posit what I would call a psychology of time rather than a chronology. As in other Southern memory novels, time is personal, not physical or fixed. In *Kindred's* structuring, time remains sequential but according to two different systems. Ten days in 1976 become five long years near the beginning of the nineteenth century when Dana is trapped in the past, charged with sustaining her heritage. For her descendants to survive she must save her white great-great grandfather and slaveholder from his own reckless behavior. As she opines: "I am the worst possible guardian for him; a black to watch over him in a society that considered blacks subhuman, a woman to watch over him in a society that considered women perennial children. I would have all that I could do to look after myself." Time and space collapse under the burden that is the weight of history in this novel. Dana is a witness and participant in a narrative that owes much to the genre of science fiction, but she is also a spiritual medium: her empirical introduction into slavery provides the psychological and historical focus for discovering her matrilineage, an idea that Gayl Jones explores in a different way in *Corregidora* (1975) and Alice Walker in *Possessing the Secret of Joy* (1992), in which Tashi seeks for a stronger sense of a female continuum in tribal rites, Jungian theory, and on the sores of Africa and America.

This essay has concerned itself less with the established voices in Southern women's fiction in order to explore those writers who in recent novels and stories reorient our ideas of Southern story. In the introduction to her *Collected Stories*, one established writer, Elizabeth Spencer, defines the role of the writer as walking down "a personal road" that is "always moving on," out of the South, beyond its boundaries and curving back again. Spencer has lived outside the South for much of the time that she has been writing about the region. Sometimes distance stirs Southern writers to look over their shoulders and rest on new features of the literary landscape they have inherited. For example, Mary Lee Settle has frequently described how she visited London Zoo and sat researching in the British Museum, learning about the American brown bears that figure in scenes in *0 Beulah Land* (1956).

When Janisse Ray takes a bird's-eye view of the South, she hopes that Southern forests "may return to their former grandeur and pine plantations to grow wild" and Sheri Reynolds's young protagonist Jael, searching for spiritual salvation, feels she is as likely to find it reflected in a tiny cricket's eyes as in her own faded scars. In *The Poisonwood Bible* Adah, taking the entrance exam for Emory, muses on those questions that require her to select the odd word out of a series: "Given my own circumstances, I find that anything can turn out to belong nearly anywhere." Southern women writers explore an ever-widening web of concerns when they take the region as their subject.

REFERENCES AND FURTHER READING

Bennett, Barbara (1999) *Comic Visions, Female Voices: Contemporary Women Novelists and Southern Humor.* Baton Rouge: Louisiana State University Press.

Chambers, Iain (1994) *Migrancy, Culture and Identity.* London: Routledge.

Deleuze, Gilles and Guattari, Felix (1983) *On the Line.* New York: Autonomedia.

Dyer, Joyce (ed.) (1998) *Bloodroot: Reflections on Place by Appalachian Women Writers.* Lexington: University of Kentucky Press.

Gray, Richard (2000) *Southern Aberrations: Writers of the American South and the Problems of Regionalism.* Baton Rouge: Louisiana State University Press.

Inge, Tonette Bond (ed.) (1990) *Southern Women Writers: The New Generation.* Tuscaloosa: University of Alabama Press.

Jones, Ann Goodwyn and Donaldson, Susan V. (eds.) (1997) *Haunted Bodies: Gender and Southern Texts.* Charlottesville: University of Virginia Press.

Jones, Suzanne W. and Monteith, Sharon (eds.) (2002) *South To A New Place: Region, Literature, Culture.* Baton Rouge: Louisiana State University Press.

MacKethan, Lucinda H. (1990) *Daughters of Time: Creating Woman's Voice in Southern Story.* Athens, GA: University of Georgia Press.

Magee, Rosemary M. (1992) *Friendship and Sympathy: Communities of Southern Women Writers.* Jackson: University of Mississippi Press.

Manning, Carol S. (1993) *The Female Tradition in Southern Literature.* Urbana: University of Illinois Press.

Monteith, Sharon (2000) *Advancing Sisterhood? Interracial Friendships in Contemporary Southern Fiction.* Athens, GA: University of Georgia Press.

Perry, Carolyn and Weaks, Mary Louise (2002) *The History of Southern Women's Literature.* Baton Rouge: Louisiana State University Press.

Prenshaw, Peggy Whitman (ed.) (1984) *Women Writers of the Contemporary South.* Jackson: University of Mississippi Press.

Reisman, Rosemary, Canfield, M., and Canfield, Christopher J. (1994) *Contemporary Southern Women Fiction Writers: An Annotated Bibliography.* Metuchen, NJ: Scarecrow Press; Pasadena: Salem Press.

Tate, Linda (1994) *A Southern Weave of Women: Fiction of the Contemporary South.* Athens, GA: University of Georgia Press.

Westling, Louise (1985) *Sacred Groves and Ravaged Gardens: The Fiction of Eudora Welty, Carson McCullers, and Flannery O'Connor.* Athens, GA: University of Georgia Press.

Westling, Louise (1996) *The Green Breast of the New World: Landscape, Gender and American Fiction.* Athens, GA: University of Georgia Press.

Woodward, C. Vann (1986) *Thinking Back: The Perils of Writing History.* Baton Rouge: Louisiana State University Press.

32

The South in Contemporary African-American Fiction

A. Robert Lee

"You're black and living in the South – did you forget how to lie?"

Ralph Ellison, *Invisible Man* (1952)

John had read about the things white people did to colored people; how, in the South, where his family came from, white people cheated them of their wages, and burned them, and shot them – and did worse things, said his father, which the tongue could not endure to utter.

James Baldwin, *Go Tell It On The Mountain* (1953)

I

Neither of them a Southerner by birth, both Ellison and Baldwin, even so, issue reminders of the accusing memory, the bitter sting, that the South can hold for Afro-America. This is not to overlook in their two landmark novels, as in other black written fiction, a more fondly remembered Dixie of black family and kin and, in the storytelling by Toni Morrison, Alice Walker, and their fellow women authors, of longtime black Southern styles of mothering and sisterhood. Nor does it suggest that these do not link into, or find story form from, the yet wider, and more inclusive, intimacies of the South's black rural communities and townships and each different workplace and church congregation.

But the South in view, and albeit written by the Oklahoma-raised Ellison and by Baldwin as vintage Harlem expatriate, bespeaks a familiar enough equation: one, since the importation aboard a Dutch vessel of "Twenty Negars" as indentured servants, to Jamestown, Virginia in 1619, of black endurance in the face of the long winding course of white hostility. For have not black Southerners, however profoundly implicated in their sense of region, been obliged to face a radical ambiguity? Suborned under slavery as working labor, whether cotton or tobacco, field or house, it has taken the arduous haul since Abolition for them to win recognition as necessary co-citizenry. Yet however often denied they have been inextricable from the making of the South as ongoing history, as a homeland and body of custom and myth, and not the least of things, as a style of talk.

The timeline runs from the early slaveholding plantations of Virginia, Georgia, or Louisiana to the Ku Klux Klan begun in Pulaski, Tennessee in 1865, and from disfranchisement in the wake of Reconstruction to the largely Southern-mandated segregation of the US army during World War II. If the 1960s ushered in key contemporary change in the form of civil rights, voter registration drives, and black power, white racist intransigence also continued. The church bombing at Sixteenth Baptist Church Street in Birmingham, Alabama in September 1963, or the killing of Martin Luther King in Memphis, Tennessee, in 1968, can be thought symptomatic. A celebrated rally like that of Selma, Mississippi, in 1965, however, did double duty as a reminder not only of the South's Colored Only regimes but also of the counter-politics of coming desegregation.

Jim Crow, moreover, in all its myriad bullying and at its worst in each lynching, fire attack, and rape, can be seen to have led to anything but a culture of victimry. Latterday setbacks, often graphic, continue, among the more recent the white-supremacist decapitation of James Byrd, Jr. in Jasper, Texas in 1998. But the strength of body as of spirit, the sheer stamina, which has underwritten black survival in the South, and given rise to each affirming code of language and belief and humor, equally holds. Literary fiction, almost of birthright, was bound to draw from an archive at once so rich, if often ambiguous, in its human drama.

The music of the black South supplies one immediate seam, whether the virtuosity of Mississippi blues and New Orleans jazz or legendary names from Louis Armstrong to Bessie Smith, Muddy Waters to B. B. King. Black Christianity, Bible-Protestant and often millennial in its allusions to the promised land, and full of a dazzling sermonry of call and response and spirituals like "Swing Low, Sweet Chariot," supplies another. Everyday foodways, to include black-eyed peas, corn pone, collard greens, pigsfeet or chitterlings, give their own idiom of black Dixie. Humor is remembered, and restyled, from mockery of the Big House and in performances of the cakewalk during slavery, to Hoodoo, also known as Voodoo or Vodoun, a black and slave belief-system of sympathetic but often capricious African deities and of which Ishmael Reed wittily avails himself in his "Southern" pastiche slave-narrative *Flight To Canada* (1975), to the wordplay of competitive insult like the dozens.

The fund of vernacular folklore, Brer Rabbit or Jack the Bear, Stackolee or High John the Conqueror, necessarily weighs. It won early explicit recognition in collections like Zora Neale Hurston's *Mules and Men* (1935) and *Tell My Horse* (1938). This transposing of the South's black oral tradition into a quite indispensable body of written story continues in the contemporary authorship of, among others, Raymond Andrews in his Muskhogean County novels like *Appalachee Red* (1978), with its ribald, vernacular portraits of black and country Georgia, or A. R. Flowers, raised in Memphis, Tennessee, in *De Mojo Blues* (1985) and *Another Good Loving Blues* (1993), both of which draw with a surest touch from black Delta idiom and blues along with Hoodoo.

The lineage, in fact, is of longstanding, whether Charles Chesnutt's Uncle Julius McAdoo folk pieces like "The Goophered Grapevine" (1897) and his *The House Behind the Cedars* (1900), a classic novel of "passing" set in North Carolina; or Jean Toomer's *Cane* (1923), with its mosaics of Georgia heat and race-fever; or Richard Wright's "Big Boy Leaves Home" and "Long Black Song," the one a Southern-mythic story of black flight and the other of black resistance, to be followed by *The Long Dream* (1958), a parable of black manhood in a white controlled Dixie township. In Hurston's case she famously drew from her own all-black Eatonville, Florida upbringing as well as from the Caribbean and the Carolinas and the South's other sections.

The extracts from Baldwin and Ellison, also, and to be sure, need their due sense of context. In *Invisible Man* the voice belongs to Dr. Bledsoe, a kind of grotesque Booker T. Washington and principal of the Tuskegee-like Deep South College, as he upbraids the eponymous narrator. The slave tactic of "putt'n on ol' massa," with its calculated mock-servility, he is shown to have adapted, however, to his own cynical political interests. The other speaks to the ordeal of consciousness of 14-year-old John Grimes in *Go Tell It On The Mountain* as he wrestles with his preacher-father's hatred of white people, and his own Pentecostal call of spirit over flesh, in the Harlem of the Depression. The effect is to bring the South to the North, Dixie's white violence and fervent backcountry black Christianity carried echoingly into Manhattan's premier black city.

Significant as they are in their own right, both novels, at the same time, offer bearings, a pathway, into how the fiction of contemporary Afro-America more generally has taken to writing the South. For his part, Ralph Ellison, in the two full-length works of fiction to have appeared under his name, and fortuitously as may be, bequeaths a marker for the half-century in play. After much celebrated delay, including the loss of an earlier draft in a fire at Ellison's summer home in Plainfield, Massachusetts in 1967, *Invisible Man* now has its posthumous successor in the novel *Juneteenth* (1999).

If *Invisible Man* deservedly won classic status one factor lies in how its first part depicts Dixie. The Battle Royal scene carries an emblematic reference-back into slave ownership and pugilism. Any supposed magnolia version of the South is undercut by the township's brute racial politics and practices. The Trueblood and Golden Day episodes turn, at times with near surreal dark comedy, upon race-and-sex as the haunting cultural phobia of history south of the Mason Dixon line.

In *Juneteenth*, although the South again constitutes but one point of reference, the view of America's racial plenty, not to say ethnic–racial overlap, and as a resource for strength as against division, again finds expression. Ellison's soaring ventriloquy, together with his use of trickster myth, adaptations of jazz and blues riff, and deployment of the black sermon, adds confirming density, a would-be epic of the national drama of black and white.

Under a title which remembers June 19 1865, when Union troops entered Texas to free it of the baleful reach of Southern slavery, the long aborning *Juneteenth* could not be more ambitious. In its story of Bliss, the seeming white-born Southern child raised as a black preacher by his mentor, the former jazz virtuoso Reverend A. Z. Hickman, it seeks both to give witness to America's history as one hexed, near broken, by its race phobias and fissures, and yet challenged to make good on its shared human occupancy. Bliss as harlequin, in Hickman's plan, is to carry the inner meanings of blackness into the very citadel of America's whiteness. Ellison, thereby, seeks to open black and white as constructs to every kind of interrogation: hue, visage, language, politics, history, an America of the South, the Southwest, and across the regions.

The span of the story runs in time from Lincoln's Emancipation Proclamation in 1863 to Bliss's incarnation as the latterday racist Senator Adam Sunraider of Vermont, and in geography from Oklahoma to New England to Washington, DC. But for all the scenes in "the territories" and elsewhere, it is inevitably the South which supplies a kind of bedrock of reference, whether the episodes of good ol' boy viciousness or Hickman's black Camp revivals and conversions. Bliss's life, from childhood adoption through to his assassination in the Senate chamber, could not be more specific, even singular, and yet, and at the same time, call upon the always larger iconography of memory.

For, to apply a line from the opening chapter of *Juneteenth*, this is the Afro-America, the America, and indeed the South, of a people "embarked upon a difficult journey who were already far beyond the point of no return" (Ellison 1990: 5). The South invoked by Ellison and Baldwin, slavery and after, acts as generic terrain, mythical kingdom. In the black literary fiction between *Invisible Man* and *Juneteenth* there has been no shortage of other contributions, each substantively particular as to cast, locale, and story while remaining linked into a shared general vision.

II

The further names in consideration, no few in number, can still do only selective justice to a genuinely compendious record. It could even be asked whether or not virtually any African-American text, however obliquely, does not bear the footfalls of black memory of the South. But novel, novella, stories single or collected, and by writers both from the South or North, each puts Dixie under its own style of black fashioning. To be sure, there are overlaps of a general temper with the South written into being by Faulkner or Flannery O'Connor, James Dickey or Bobbie Ann Mason. But there can be no overlooking a narrative imagination also different in its grounding, that of an Afro-South as it were, and which gives its own discrete narrative to the overwhelmingly white-told versions of the events, and eventfulness, of the South as a historic American theatre of region.

In all these respects Toni Morrison, born in Ohio and long resident as Random House editor and professor in New York, serves as a key voice, her South summoned in different vignettes, wonderfully vivid panels of story. These find place within the unfolding overall panorama of African-American history she began with *The Bluest Eye* (1970) and its story of Pecola Breedlove's descent into racial and sexual self-hate. Whether, subsequently, given as the "flying African" fantasy and Virginia treasure-hunt, and through the person of the Michigan-raised "Milkman" Macon Dead III, in *Song of Solomon* (1977), or as the "haint" of slavery and the desperate, if loving, hacksaw killing by Sethe Suggs of her own daughter to escape continuing enslave-ment in antebellum Kentucky in *Beloved* (1987), she has sought always to render the South as perfectly literal yet, and at the same time, a dispensation which reverberates in the inner mind and senses.

The same holds for the less acclaimed *Jazz* (1992), told as though a 1920s blues ballad: the love triangle of Violet Trace, her husband Joe, and his passion for the 18-year-old Dorcas who refuses to name him as her killer as she lies dying after he has shot her from jealousy. Harlem may be the setting but it calls up the South of the turn of the century Great Migration, a South if for Violet and Joe the site of their courtship as "a young country couple" from Vesper County, Virginia with the move to Baltimore, Maryland to follow, then also the cause of "a wave of black people running from want and violence."

Morrison's landscape in *Jazz*, overwhelmingly, is the Harlem of Lenox Avenue and 140th Street, its round-midnight clubs, eateries, and storefront churches. In one way it could not be more citied. But with each arriving northbound train, literally segregated into Colored Coaches yet full of mythic resonance, it is also a Harlem which, once again, she shows to have drawn black-Southern country remembrance into its very way of being.

A similar process of adaptation holds for Albert Murray, the Alabama-raised novelist of *Train Whistle Guitar* (1974), *The Spyglass Tree* (1991), and *The Seven League Boots* (1996), his blues-inspired Scooter trilogy which, without downplaying the color-line, respectively, and always affectionately, calls up a South of black boyhood, Tuskegee education, and life as a Swing-era bassist in an Ellington-style orchestra. In his *South To A Very Old Place* (1971), a memoir and half-fictive travelogue, he puts matters with succinct flourish:

> You can take the "A" train uptown from Forty-second Street in midtown Manhattan and be there in less than ten minutes. There is a stop at Fifty-ninth Street beneath the traffic circle which commemorates Christopher Columbus who once set out for destinations east on compass bearing west. But after that as often as not there are only six more express minutes to go. Then you are pulling into the IND station at 125th Street and St. Nicholas Avenue, and you are that many more miles north of Mobile, Alabama, but you are also, for better or worse, back among homefolks no matter what part of the old country you come from. (Murray 1971: 3)

Alice Walker's career as fiction writer might almost be a paradigm in its use of the South as literary context and motif. Its silhouette is everywhere in her language and imagery, whether her Georgia family sharecropper and African-Cherokee origins, cross-marriage to the civil rights lawyer Melvyn Leventhal, activist years in Jackson, Mississippi, or the evolving black feminist ideology of womanism which she would gather into a volume like *In Search of Our Mothers' Gardens* (1983). Both of her first novels, *The Third Life of Grange Copeland* (1970), with its unsparing, and at the time greatly controversial, three-generational portrait of black family fissure, and *Meridian* (1976), with its protagonist Meridian Hill as early womanist figuration in an era of 1960s civil rights, draw upon a Deep South, Georgia specifically, whose race etiquettes and vexations Walker grew up with first hand.

No novel of hers, however, more deservedly came to the fore than *The Color Purple* (1982), its epistolary story of Celie, her sister Nettie, and the flamboyant, red-dressed "Queen Honeybee," Shug Avery, as the crafted expression of different styles of womanhood won against a backcountry South of brutalizing black maleness. Controversy again was immediate. Had Walker perpetuated a stereotype of black-Southern men as rapists and tyrants? Are the Africa scenes too sentimental a foil to the regime which first separates Celie from her sister, makes her the sex commodity respectively of her stepfather Alphonso, an unloving second spouse, and her eventual husband Albert, who withholds Nettie's letters from her, and in the course of which she is arbitrarily separated from her own children?

The novel, in fact, was at once always fuller, and more nuanced, than these reactions suggested. Walker handles the complex sexuality which, under Shug's healing love and guidance, gives self-esteem to Celie with genuine subtlety. Albert and Celie, despite his past ravage, in turn find a new equilibrium as Celie begins her clothes design business in Memphis, a reborn but forgiving weaver-woman or Penelope, as it were. Their relationship, finally, assumes its place within the unsilenced womanism which brings together Celie, Shug, Nettie, the children Adam and Olivia, and the rest of their circle. It represents Southern black womanhood, if not Southern black family at large, imagined under new auspices.

This rite of passage, as Stephen Spielberg was to recognize in his 1985 film with Whoopi Goldberg in the title role, also takes its course against, and within, a finely etched Georgia. Black-centered in family and relationship, it gives only passing references to a white ambient population. Speech is vernacular, Hurstonian. The story gains from a close sense of mule-worked land, climate, household, birthing, dress, food, and the music and dance of blues and the country jukes. *The Color Purple* tells a cautionary, and evidently enduring, tale of gender and dynasty. But no small part of its success lies in the degree to which Walker furnishes Georgia as a South in just the right attentive working detail.

III

A necessary line of recent African-American fiction of the South is to be met with in the varying styles of "historical" novel. As notably as anywhere it came to be a phenomenon most associated with Alex Haley's *Roots: A Family Saga* (1976), whose

TV spin-offs (*Roots*, 1977; *Roots, the Next Generations*, 1979) won an American viewership of well over a hundred million. Gambia to Maryland and Virginia, Kunta Kinte to Chicken George in North Carolina, George's daughter Cynthia (Haley's grandmother) to his own birth and family upbringing in Henning, Tennessee: *Roots* was deemed a unique American genealogy, at once diaspora and homecoming, and with the South as its inevitable turning point.

Haley's canvas embraces Juffure in West Africa as idyll, the trauma of the middle passage, slave auction, Dixie servitude, the freedom trail, the black 1920s and Depression, and a South, an America, eventually obliged to face the shadows of its history. Beginning from the capture, and then transportation, of Kunta Kinte to Virginia in 1767, the story evolves through a vivid gallery of African into African-American clan and no less than seven generations of historical change. Haley's own search for ancestry plays into the momentum, whether the Atlantic journey back through slave ports both in America and Africa, or the final encounter with the griot able to rekindle the story from passed-down oral memory.

Whatever the cavils about inertness of style, or plagiarism, or about the Hollywood studio huts-and-jungle Africa of the TV series, this was widely taken for a "fiction of fact" whose sweep, for good or ill, invited comparison with *Gone With The Wind*, one kind of pageant of the South for another.

Margaret Mitchell's bestseller of 1936, to a considerable extent, was also in the mind of Margaret Walker when she composed her "neo-slave" novel, *Jubilee* (1966). Based upon the life of her great-grandmother, Margaret Duggans Ware Brown, her figure of Vivry, offspring of a white slaveholder and bonded slave, serves as a would-be rebuke to the stereotype of the mammy. Reactions, even so, have varied as to the efficacy of *Jubilee*. In telling the story of the white Dutton plantation, replete in ageing belles like Big Missie and Miss Lillian and the Legree-like poor white overseer Grimes, not to say the replay of Sherman's March on Atlanta, how far does it escape its own kind of formula narrative as magnolia romance or gothic? Is Vivry herself sufficiently invested in imaginative life?

There can be little doubt of a South, a canvas, of high incident. Vivry's girlhood, always open to sexual risk, takes place under the guardian care of older black women. Her life in the quarters is told with circumstantial flair. The unwitting double marriage, first to Randall Ware, her Free Negro blacksmith husband, and then to Innis Brown, her loyal homesteader, and her mothering of Jim, Minna, and Harry, underline slavery's often dire implication for black family life in the South. Few scenes in *Jubilee* carry the frisson of Vivry's witness to the hanging of two black women as alleged murderers. If her rise to elder, and old-time Bible Christian, can look routine, that does not by any means eclipse the former Georgia slavewoman, Margaret Walker's Vivry as lived figuration of a past black South.

In Ernest Gaines, raised on a plantation in Oscar, Louisiana, the South looks to a storyteller of rare triumph. His creation has been St. Raphael Parish, a world of black, Cajun, Creole, and other mixed-race communities and lives with near to hand New Orleans and the bayou country. *Catherine Carmier* (1964) delineates the crossed racial love of Jackson Bradley and the novel's Catherine, a chronicle of the loss, the masquerades and silences, brought on by the Southern hex of race. *Of Love and Dust* (1967) turns on murder, the plantation heritage, and relationships once again pursued in defiance of prescribed race lines with their accusations and taboo. *Bloodline* (1968), five first-person narratives told in voices freighted in vernacular, carries the imprint of yet other kinds of fought-for black selfhood. Given acknowledgment of *In My Father's House* (1978) as a portrait of intergenerational black politics in the South, together with *A Gathering of Old Men* (1983) and *A Lesson Before Dying* (1993), both with their own workings of Southern remembrance, no novel, however, has more won Gaines his reputation than *The Autobiography of Miss Jane Pittman* (1971).

Told as though in the tape-recorded voice of the centenarian Jane Pittman in the early 1960s, that of a one-time slave still living on a Louisiana plantation and who marches for civil rights at the novel's conclusion, it unspools a history, a South, from cotton slavery and the War of Secession to the era of Rosa Parks and Martin Luther King with greatest sureness. Not surprisingly, it led to an acclaimed TV version of 1974, starring Cicely Tyson. Gaines himself, in a 1978 interview with *Callaloo*, speaks with just the right inside appeal, and affection, when he says of the fictional Jane Pittman:

> You have seen Miss Jane, too. She is that lady who lives up the block, who comes out every Sunday to go to church when the rheumatism does not keep her in . . . She sits on a screened-in porch fanning herself in the summer, and in the winter she sits by the heater or the stove and thinks about the dead . . . She knows much – she has lived long. Sometimes she's impatient, but most times she is just the opposite. Truth is what she remembers.

To Jane's friend, Mary Hedges, the book's self purporting editor explains: "I teach history . . . I'm sure [Jane's] life story can help explain things to my students." Mary's response is to ask: "What's wrong with them books you already got?" to which is answered: "Miss Jane is not in them" (Gaines 1971: x). As she calls up the cross-hatch of people who have entered her life, black, white, Creole, Cajun, or mulatto, and all the Louisiana history they bear, Jane, in fact, assumes her own kind of griot voice. The one-time slavegirl, escapee, wife and mother, and eventual community historian, however, remains a black Southerner, a witness to the region as both time and place. "Miss Jane's story is all of their stories, and their stories are Miss Jane's" confirms Gaines's "editor."

She can be as spontaneous, and at times as discontinuous, as each volte-face in her history, and aging memory, all require. These nicely intersect in the editor's further, and not a little Faulknerian, observation that "This is what Mary and Miss Jane meant when they said you could not tie all the ends together in one direction." Built as a quartet – "The War Years," "Reconstruction," "The Plantation," and "The Quarters" – and as much seemingly spoken as written, the novel becomes a tale of the South inextricable from its telling.

"I'm headed for Ohio," says Jane in childhood in the aftermath of the South's defeat. But as her companions are killed by renegades from the "Secesh" forces, in fact, she walks not out of the South but right back into it, a voice of accusation and yet celebration. Each section bears witness. In "The War Years" as Jane and Ned, the son of Big Laura who has been killed in the escape from the plantation, seek to escape northward from the patrollers, they also find their route into literacy and the discard of slave-naming. Jane abandons Ticey, her slave name. Ned calls himself after Frederick Douglass:

> We must have been two dozens of us there, and now everybody started changing names like you change hats. Nobody was keeping the name Old Master had given them. This one would say, "My new name Cam Lincoln." That one would say: "My new name Ace Freeman" . . . Another one standing by a tree would say, "My new name Bill Moses. No more Rufus." (17–18)

Gaines leaves little doubt for the black South of the connection between freedom and name, the twin liberation of escape and word.

"And that was the deal: the Secesh got their land, but the Yankees lend the money" (69). So, in "Reconstruction," Jane cites a contemporary, the era in which she has married the warm, devoted horsebreaker, Joe Pittman (even though, in slave fashion, they have "jumped the broom") and the return of Ned. In this surrogate son Gaines offers a local version of Douglass, also a teacher–orator but whose challenge to postbellum white ascendancy leads to his murder by the Cajun Albert Cluveau. Ned has died for refusing the South's terms ("America is for red, white and black men"). But he dies facing his killer, his blood, like that of black generations before him, sedimented into the Southern soil ("For years and years, even after they had graveled the road, you could see little black spots where the blood had dripped").

In "The Plantation," actually the Samson plantation where Jane spends the early part of the twentieth century, she witnesses a latest twist in the drama of mulattodom. In the love of white Tee Bob Samson for Mary Agnes Lefabre, a Creole woman "tainted" by the merest increment of black ancestry, the most ancient of Southern race taboo is broached. The affair, beautifully told as a courtship, a lost hope, ends in disaster but not melodrama. Jane's is the monitoring voice, against a backdrop of the Klan and the rise of Governor Huey Long. She remembers the sympathetic Cajun, Jules Raynard, first on Tee Bob ("he thought love was stronger than one drop of African blood"), and then on the challenge to transform an old South, and its taboos, into a new South ("The past and the present got all mixed up").

As to "The Quarters," the section centers on Jimmy Washington, the only son of Jane's friend Lena Washington, an early civil rights activist who challenges the preordained racial order by using a whites-only water faucet. He meets his death at the hands of a white Dixie posse. Jane transforms the account of the event she acquires from Robert Samson, the latest scion of the plantation dynasty, into a kind of talking blues. "They shot him at eight o'clock this morning," she intones.

She it is, however, survivor of a past as cruel as any in American history, who best understands Jimmy's sacrifice as she puts her own body, and authority, into the march for civil rights. She does so from the "march" as much of history as any one Southern protest or place. "Me and Robert looked at each other there for a long time," she says, "then I went by him." On this measure *The Autobiography of Miss Jane Pittman* has its title figure "go by" not simply one more white Southerner, but the white South at large. Gaines offers her as legacy to the future.

A shared ambition of scale holds for the novels of Leon Forrest, Chicagoan, from 1969 to 1972 the editor of *Muhammad Speaks* though never himself a convert to Islam, and whose ancestry looks both to Creole Louisiana and its Catholicism and the Mississippi of his father's family and its inheritances of backcountry and Bible Protestantism. Each of his novels, from *There Is A Tree More Ancient Than Eden* (1973), with its vision-haunted passage of Nathaniel Witherspoon as he attends his mother's Chicago south side funeral, through to *Divine Days* (1992), quite the longest novel in the African-American tradition and given over to the life and memory of the writer Joubert Antoine Jones, once more implies the South within the North. This is a Chicago born of black migration, blues, religion, and always remembrance of the dislocations, or in Forrest's abiding metaphor, the orphanings of slavery.

Two novels, especially, focus these "histories" of the South, at once modernist in their telling (Joyce and Faulkner are clear influences) and yet, unmistakably, also indebted to jazz, the warm improvisational talk of black barbershop, kitchen, and street, and always of equal importance, the sermon as its own art of performative rhetoric.

In *The Bloodworth Orphans* (1977) Forrest envisages a Book of Genesis, the huge dynastic chaos begotten of the slaveowning white patriarch Arlington Bloodworth Sr. (1817–1917), and reaching from antebellum Mississippi to modern New Orleans, from Chicago to Africa. Told as a colloquy between Nathaniel (or "Spoons" as he has become) and Noah Ridgerook Cranberry, last of the Bloodworths, Forrest unravels a saga of miscegenation, religious prophets – notably W. W. W. Ford, his conflated trickster version of Elijah Muhammad as founder of the Black Muslims – and a history from its very beginnings in the slave South as near-fantastical as not. The intertextual echoes are many, notably of Faulkner's Quentin and Shreve in *Absalom, Absalom!* or of Ellison's Rinehart in *Invisible Man*. But as imagined world, a dense, contrapuntal portrait of familied orphanry, and of above all of South into North, the novel achieves unique status.

With *Two Wings To Veil My Face* (1984) Forrest creates another vast genealogical web in which Nathaniel becomes scribe, amanuensis, to Great-Momma Sweetie Reed. Her story becomes his, that of another black elder whose origins are to be found on the Rollins plantation in antebellum Mississippi and which approaches its close in an imagined Chicago of 1958. Voices, memories, ledgers, a cycle of pasts, all become the very ply of Great-Momma's passage. They include the South of her mother's rape and murder in 1874; her marriage at 15 to the former escaped slave (and Nathaniel's grandfather), the 55-year-old Jericho Witherspoon, in 1882; and her half-delirious attendance at the memorial service for the 115-year-old in the Memphis-Raven-Snow Funeral Home in 1944. No feature of the story more stands out than the branded letters "JW" on the patriarch's back, each "vivid as a visitation," and in whose de-encrypting Forrest gives his measure of America's slave South, together with its northbound aftermath, as in equal parts literal and ghost history.

Other history-focused fictions in which the South acts if not always as fulcrum, then as an indispensable touchstone, might almost be thought to add up to a litany; four do duty. In John A. Williams's *Captain Blackman* (1972), told as though in hallucination by the injured Abraham Blackman in the Vietnam War, the novel develops a serial portrait of black warriordom from pre-Independence to the Civil War, World Wars I and II to Indo-China and the nuclear age. The South, within this, is caught, vividly, dramatically, in Williams's scenes of slave insurrection and Civil War black regiments fighting in the Union cause.

For Toni Cade Bambara in *The Salt Eaters* (1980), situated in the invented town of Claybourne, Georgia, her story of Velma Henry's attempted suicide and eventual recovery through a politics of black sisterhood and community against a nearby polluting chemical corporation, tells the one Southern story inside another. Layered in different time-shifts, multifocal as to character and not least in Minnie Ranson as faith-healer, and brimming in allusion to the folkways of the black South, it gives witness to past strategies in which black Americans have tricked, duped, and outwitted the white power-structure. Velma's own healing, thereby, becomes the expression of a political well-being of gender and Southern black community at large.

David Bradley's *The Chaneyville Incident* (1981), a decade in the making, makes historical excavation itself the center of his novel. In the research of John Washington, a Philadelphia history professor, and through a dazzling narrative display of black-oral, manuscript, and libraried sources, Bradley tells a story of Southern slave forbears. The figure of C. K Washington acts as a key presence, an insurrectionist leader in the continuum of Gabriel Prosser, Denmark Vesey, or Nat Turner. The role of Underground Railroad stations is given remembrance, not least Chaneyville as the site of a Maseda-like group suicide of slave escapees to avoid recapture. The black–white love relationship of Washington as black historian and his Virginia slaveholder-descended psychologist girlfriend, Judy, further refracts, and gives a possible healing to, this South–North history.

A frequent observation about Sherley Anne Williams's *Dessa Rose* (1987) is that it acts as a riposte to William Styron's *The Confessions of Nat Turner* (1967). However pertinent, that is not to underplay its own unique conception of a neo-slave novel, Dessa as "author" of her own history both in deed as female slave insurrectionist, and in word, despite the would-be possession of her story by the white plantation owner, Miss Rufel, and the white male amanuensis, Nemi. Its scenes of Southern enslavement, escape, revolt, and itinerary sweep as Dessa and other ex-slaves travel the region in a fake minstrel show, work to a double end.

At an immediate level Williams offers well-turned exemplary fare, a slave-woman's vindication of efficacy and inward identity. But, quite equally, *Dessa Rose* seeks to "unslave" the South's very language of ownership and dispossession. Williams's achievement, not unlike Harriet Jacobs's *Incidents in the Life of a Slave Girl* (1861) over a century earlier, cannot be thought less than considerable, the slave South told as at once high narrative drama in its own right, and yet, throughout, as also canny, liberationist counter-text.

IV

In their peopling, and sense of the South as locale and time, the novels of Morrison, Walker, Gaines, and their contemporaries have had plentiful company. William Demby's *Beetlecreek* (1950) offers a symptomatic early marker. Its portrait of Johnny Johnson, adolescent son of a dying, consumptive mother in Pittsburgh, and sent to his aunt and uncle, David and Mary Biggs, in their West Virginia township, suggests race division as always an endgame. Demby, furthermore, does a nice reversal of the Huckleberry Finn–Jim equation. He pairs Johnny with a kindly older white man, Bill Trapp, a one-time carnival performer and a magus of sorts. For all that the story ends on a fatal note of destruction, this is the South as might-have-been, a benign racial garden as against the binaried stasis of white and black.

Trapp's approach to David Biggs in the name of a proposed picnic leads to the latter's sense of racial odds, this particular South a *huis clos* made such by the town's circles of hostility and taboo:

> There was no way to explain to the old man how complicated this story was, how Negro life was a fishnet, a mosquito net, lace, wrapped round and round, each little thread a pain . . . too complicated.

For Johnny, this could not more hold. He sees his life in West Virginia as "an episode in a dream," one of entrapment, betrayal. His mother's hemorrhaging so becomes prophetic of a death-in-life, whether the stillborn child born to the Biggs, or David Biggs's failing marriage and doomed hope of a renewal with the ex-street girl Edith Johnson, or the local gang leader's killing of a baby pigeon as the denial of beginning life.

It is, however, the false rumor of child molestation against Bill Trapp, and the town's temporizing agreement to let things stand, which further perpetuates the deathly status quo. The final burning of Trapp's house, the outcome of Johnny's gang initiation, inverts this South into a wasteland, the ashes of hope for a better Southern order. The novel has sometimes been thought too unrelenting (little wonder that after its publication Demby moved to Italy where *The Catacombs*, his early postmodern, or as he calls it cubist, novel, would be published in 1965). But *Beetlecreek* affords its own kind of achievement, a South modern without having ceased to be accusingly ancient, and whose shadow of racial enmity Demby is able to invest with its own kind of life.

Gayl Jones's *Corregidora* (1975) derives its setting from her native Kentucky, an imagined 1960s-told, and bittersweet, blues story of the South. In Ursa Corregidora, club singer, of Bracktown, Kentucky, there is carried the memory of the original Corregidora as the Brazilian *mestizo* slaver whose monstrous, bewitching sexual rule has bequeathed blight on her and the history to which she belongs. Her own sexual damage – she has had her womb removed after a fall at the hand of her estranged husband Mutt Johnson – gives a grim irony to Southern slavery's self-preserving injunction to "make generations."

Ursa's brief affair with Tadpole, owner of Happy's, the café club where she sings, leads to betrayal with a younger woman. That she finally learns how Great Gram acted in revenge for all four generations of women (Great Gram herself, then Grandmother and Mama – each prostituted by, and the latter two fathered by, Corregidora) by orally dismembering Corregidora, serves, even as she returns to Mutt, to underline her own full awakening to slavery's cost for black womanhood. Jones's South in the novel is one of deepest inherited wound, enslavement in the form of sexual property. Yet, in the blues Ursa sings, and embodies, and in however relative a degree, it is a South reflexively also made subject to rejoinder, a repossession.

For Gloria Naylor, New York raised of Mississippi parents, her *Mama Day* (1988) can be thought a virtuoso tale of two worlds, New York and Willow Springs, the latter a black Southern coastal island between South Carolina and Georgia. The inspired reworking of Shakespeare's *The Tempest* is unignorable – the storm, the island, the title figure Mama, or Miranda, Day as black female Prospero – yet filtered through the African Americanism of conjure, roots, the communing with spirits.

The novel looks back to a first slave woman, Sapphira Wade, who took the island by force from its white first proprietor, and forward to the contemporary failed marriage of Mama Day's great-niece, Cocoa (full name Ophelia), and her now deceased husband George Andrews, with whom, through Mama, she now speaks across the barrier of life and death. The world in view derives from black animist belief and practice, one of interventionary spirits, the supernatural. These spirits act as the guardian signatures of a culture which fuses Africa into Dixie, a source for its people of nurture, meaning, strength, continuity in the face of severance. Willow Springs, and Mama Day as its inspirational avatar, literally embodies that order, a passed-down black sisterhood, a magical black South.

In Randall Kenan and Melvin Dixon the South encounters quite another kind of genuinely enterprising imagination, one not only black but also gay. In Kenan's *A Visitation of Spirits* (1989) he makes over his own background of Chingquapin, North Carolina, into Tims Creek, home of the Cross family, in which Horace Creek, 16-year old cousin of the Reverend Jimmy Greene, descends into breakdown, and eventual suicide, as he fails to come to find a *modus vivendi* for his sexual orientation. The novel has been thought unsparing, too suffused in nightmare, self-accusation. But Kenan writes with a sure touch, whether about Horace's dream of becoming a hawk, a soaring bird, as his bulwark against pathology, or in his portrait of a black religious South whose Calvinist–Lutheran prescription leaves little room for sexual plurality.

In Dixon's *Trouble The Water* (1989) the homocentrism can be thought more mooted. Its story of Jordan Henry, and the call made upon him by his grandmother for the not so obscure oedipal revenge against his father for allowing the death of Jordan's mother, with a setting also in backcountry North Carolina, reviewers were over-quick to term Southern gothic. The command of conjure and folk materials, as of the ways of a complicated sexuality, deserved better.

A. J. Verdelle's *The Good Negress* (1995), a meticulously paced first novel of the coming of age of Denise Palms ("Neesey"), takes place as an interaction of two black family regimes, the one that of her watchful, savvy grandmother in down-home rural Virginia, and the other that of her well-meaning but flighty mother in inner-city and street Detroit. Were another first novel to be offered in comparison it might be Ntozake Shange's *Sassafras, Cypress and Indigo* (1982), a stylish collage of story, poem, and diary given over to three sisters, along with their mother, who carry their exuberant creative sass out of black Charleston into the bohemianism of California.

Neesey's rise to consciousness in *The Good Negress* Verdelle locates within a close-worked context of black family, at once granddaughter, daughter, sister to David and Luke Edward, and above all, a girl moving into possession of her own language of experience. The emphasis falls upon Neesey as homemaker, cook, and cleaner, but also the beginning taker of her own life decisions, whether as high school writer–student or sexual initiate. She both embodies black womanhood as lineage and, in her literal yet always emblematic journeys from Virginia to Detroit, a yet latest South-into-North.

V

The South in the African-American short story has shown a vibrancy quite of a kind with longer fiction. The title story of John Edgar Wideman's collection, *Damballah* (1981), might be thought confirmation, a near exquisite vignette of the early South told as though in several voices, in which the slave, Orion, named Ryan by his owner, refuses any word of English, is beaten for his escapes, and seeks his own transforming life-in-death in the waters of a Southern river. It is water which calls up Orion's memory of a sacral realm, healing, the medium of his ancestral deities. Of these Damballah, to whom he prays, acts as Vodoun father god, the spirit of his own Africa to offset the South's slave America.

Woman-authored short storytelling centered on the South equally weighs. Arthenia Bates's *Seeds Beneath The Snow* (1968) offers gentle fare, story-vignettes of a middle-class black Southern community. Toni Cade Bambara's *Gorilla, My Love* (1972) depicts the black rural South and citied North as bound into an ongoing continuum and through the focus of sorority, women's relationship with each other. Alice Walker's *In Love and Trouble: Stories of Black Women* (1973) pursues lives, Southern for the most part, told in black-womanist voice. Gayl Jones's *White*

Rat (1977), stories edged in violence and set within or against the South, explores cross-sexuality. Opal Moore's "Freeing Ourselves of History: The Slave Closet" (1988), a piece which looks back to Southern slave legacy, looks to the costs as against the gains to Afro-America entailed in assimilation.

A name which has much come to preside is that of James Alan MacPherson, born and raised in Savannah, Georgia, and the justly feted author of *Hue and Cry* (1969) and *Elbow Room* (1977). In the former collection, assured stories like "On Trains" and "A Solo Song: For Doc" call up legendary old-time Pullman porters and waiters, elders usually of Southern origins from the classic American railway era to whom MacPherson gives honoring memorial. In the latter collection a piece like "Why I Love Country Music" depicts the fond, echoing recall of a black New Yorker for his long-ago Southern boyhood and the girl he once partnered at a country dance. "The Story of a Dead Man" turns on black Southern folklore, the feisty, mythic story of Billy Renfro. MacPherson, to be sure, has frequently written of worlds far beyond the South, be it Manhattan or London. But those generated from Georgia, as from other Dixie, carry an especial force of remembrance.

VI

In one sense it cannot surprise that black fiction has put the South, for all the gravity of its history, under fantastical, and even comic-irreverent, rules. How else to account for worlds, lives, so arbitrarily turned upside down? George Schuyler's *Black No More* (1931) was early into the fray, with its zany, take-no-prisoners story of a rogue geneticist's invention of a treatment to change skin color and its "race purity" implications especially for the Deep South. In *Cotton Comes To Harlem* (1965), perhaps the best-known of his Grave Digger Jones/Coffin Ed Johnson Harlem detective series, Chester Himes memorializes the South as cotton-patch in a violent but always fiercely comic and spiraling urban parable.

William Melvin Kelley's *A Different Drummer* (1969), in which the entire black population of a Southern state leaves in a reprise of slave escape, lowers its own boom on supremacist whiteness. John Killens, no doubt mindful of his Macon, Georgia upbringing, in *The Cotillion, or One Good Bull Is Half The Herd* (1971), equally cuts a satiric swathe through Dixie, along with the cities, for all manner of race and class practices.

In Charles Johnson's *Oxherding Tale* (1982) the South is explored as though under baroque phenomenological auspices, appropriately enough in fiction written by a professional philosopher and the author of *Being and Race: Black Writing Since 1970* (1987). In the story of the "black" Andrew Hawkins, of Cripplegate Plantation, who becomes the "white" William Harris, a birthing the result of a drunken wife-swap, Johnson takes aim at all imprisoning identity-by-category and nowhere more ruin-ously than in America's ever color-obsessive South. Is there not, too, a fugitive remembrance of the American South as race theatre in the science fiction, the speculative gender and ethnicity galactic writing, of Samuel R. Delany and Octavia Butler, typically the former's *Return to Neveryon* quartet (1979–87) and the latter's *Patternmaster* (1976) and its sequels?

Rarely, however, has black authorship exhibited quite the brio, the flourish, of Ishmael Reed, born in Chattanooga, Tennessee, raised in Buffalo, New York, and a doyen of the postmodern turn. Whether an early fantasia novel like *The Freelance Pallbearers* (1967), with its tilts at Nixonian America, or *Mumbo Jumbo* (1974), with its Dixie-generated vision of a "Neo-Hoodoo" outbreak of jazz and cultural vitality in the 1920s, the South has throughout supplied a touchstone. But with *Flight To Canada* (1976) it becomes a yet more complete site for Reed's comedy of errors, the South and its mythologies made subject to dark laughter.

Reed tells his story as mock epic, a slave escape decked out in rap, music, jive-talk, even a verse Prologue which explains that this is "secret" narrative, an alternative telling of the South. For all its reference to "Jeff Davis and Lee," mint-julips Dixie, belles and mammies, and the spirit of Sir Walter Scott, time zones can, and do, intersect. Helicopters fly anachronistically over the quarters. The Underground Railroad, antebellum icon, shades into modern form as a jumbo jet no less, seats duly reserved, flies the escapees into Canada.

For in the entourage of Raven Quickskill, slave, penman, trickster, and reverse Uncle Tom, together with Master Swille, plantation owner, and his TV-obsessed wife Ms. Quille, and their slave servants Robin and Judy, not to mention Princess Quaw Quaw Tralararara and the slaves 40s and Stray, this is syncretism writ large. The South becomes "black" black comedy. Abraham Lincoln visits the slave quarters with "Hello Dolly" playing in the background. Harriet Beecher Stowe, Byron-haunted New Englander, makes her entrance in the same sweep as John A. Williams, celebrated African-American author of *The Man Who Cried I Am* (1967). John Wilkes Booth, actor, assassin, is to be heard alongside Harry Reasoner, Texas's gravel-voiced journalist and anchorman. A Native American avian lore of ravens and other spirit birds is shown to overlap with African-American tradition.

One key lies in Reed's use of Edgar Allan Poe as the South's custodial presence, the gothic *symboliste* behind "The Fall of the House of Usher." Poe, or "Eddie Poe" as he becomes in the novel, Reed implies could not more serve as the voice of the South's white psyche, a South outlandish in slaveholding, codes of pseudo-gentry and, always, its self-haunting as to "the war":

Why isn't Edgar Allan Poe recognized as the principal biographer of that strange war? Fiction, you say? Where does fact begin and fiction leave off? Why does the perfectly rational, in its own time, often sound like mumbo-jumbo? Where did it leave off for Poe, prophet of a civilization buried alive, where, according to witnesses, people were often whipped for no reason? No reason? We will never know, since there are so few traces of the civilization the planters called "the fairest civilization the sun ever shone upon," and the slaves called "Satan's Kingdom." Poe got it all down. Poe says more in a few stories than all the volumes by historians. Volumes about that war. The Civil War. The Spirit War. Douglass, Tubman and Bibb all believing in omens, consulting conjure and carrying unseen amulets on their persons. Lincoln, the American Christ, who died on Good Friday. Harriet saying that God wrote "Uncle Tom's Cabin." Which God? (Reed 1976: 18–19; italics in original)

Poe, the South's "whitest" historic author, as forerunner to Ishmael Reed, black contemporary whose life has been lived mostly in New York and California, affords a perfect irony. For in the literary fiction of both writers the American South finds its most fantastical repertoire, a history, a region, nothing if not abidingly familiar, yet, and at the same time, abidingly other.

REFERENCES AND FURTHER READING

Andrews, Raymond (1978) *Appalachee Red.* New York: Dial Press.

Andrews, William L., Foster, Frances Smith, and Harris, Trudier (eds.) (1997) *The Oxford Companion to African-American Literature.* New York: Oxford University Press.

Baker, Houston (1980) *The Journey Back: Issues in Black Literature and Criticism.* Chicago: University of Chicago Press.

Baker, Houston (1984) *Blues, Ideology, and Afro-American Literature: A Vernacular Theory.* Chicago: University of Chicago Press.

Baldwin, James (1953) *Go Tell It On The Mountain.* New York: Alfred A. Knopf.

Bambara, Toni Cade (1972) *Gorilla, My Love.* New York: Vintage.

Bambara, Toni Cade (1980) *The Salt Eaters.* New York: Random House.

Bates, Arthenia (1968) *Seeds Beneath The Snow.* New York: Greenwich.

Bell, Bernard (1987) *The Afro-American Novel and Its Tradition.* Amherst: University of Massachusetts Press.

Bradley, David (1981) *The Chaneyville Incident.* New York: Harper and Row.

Butler, Octavia (1976) *Patternmaster.* New York: Warner Books.

Butler-Evans, Elliot (1989) *Race, Gender, and Desire: Narrative Strategies in the Fiction of Toni Cade Bambara, Toni Morrison and Alice Walker.* Philadelphia, PA: Temple University Press.

Byerman, Keith (1985) *Fingering the Jagged Grain: Tradition and Form in Recent Black Fiction.* Athens, GA: University of Georgia Press.

Callahan, John (1988) *In the African-American Grain: The Pursuit of Voice in Twentieth-Century Black Fiction.* Urbana: University of Illinois Press.

Carby, Hazel (1987) *Reconstructing Womanhood: The Emergence of the Black Woman Novelist.* New York: Oxford University Press.

Chesnutt, Charles W. (1899) "The Goophered Grapevine," in *The Conjure Woman and Other Tales.* Boston, MA: Houghton Mifflin.

Chesnutt, Charles W. (1900) *The House Behind The Cedars.* Boston, MA: Houghton Mifflin.

Christian, Barbara (1984) *Black Women Novelists: The Development of a Tradition 1892–1976.* Westport, CT: Greenwood Press.

Clarke, John Henrik (ed.) (1968) *William Styron's Nat Turner: Ten Black Writers Respond.* Boston, MA: Beacon Press.

Delany, Samuel R. (1979–87) *Neveryon* series. New York: Bantam; Hanover: University Press of Unveryon.

Demby, William (1950) *Beetlecreek.* New York: Rinehart.

Demby, William (1965) *The Catacombs.* New York: Pantheon.

Dixon, Melvin (1987) *Ride Out The Wilderness: Geography and Identity in Afro-American Literature*. Urbana: University of Illinois Press.

Dixon, Melvin (1989) *Trouble The Water*. Boulder, CO: Fiction Collective 2.

Ellison, Ralph (1982) [1952] *Invisible Man*, 30th edn. New York: Random House.

Ellison, Ralph (1990) *Juneteenth*. New York: Random House.

Flowers, A. R. (1985) *De Mojo Blues*. New York: E. P. Dutton.

Flowers, A. R. (1993) *Another Loving Blues*. New York: Viking.

Forrest, Leon (1973) *There Is a Tree More Ancient Than Eden*. New York: Random House.

Forrest, Leon (1977) *The Bloodworth Orphans*. New York: Random House.

Forrest, Leon (1984) *Two Wings To Veil My Face*. New York: Random House.

Forrest, Leon (1992) *Divine Days*. Oak Park, IL: Another Chicago Press.

Gaines, Ernest (1964) *Catherine Carmier*, New York: Atheneum.

Gaines, Ernest (1967) *Of Love and Dust*. New York: Dial Press.

Gaines, Ernest (1968) *Bloodline*. New York: Dial Press.

Gaines, Ernest (1971) *The Autobiography of Miss Jane Pittman*. New York: Dial Press.

Gaines, Ernest (1978) *In My Father's House*. New York: Alfred A. Knopf.

Gaines, Ernest (1983) *A Gathering of Old Men*. New York: Alfred A. Knopf.

Gaines, Ernest (1993) *A Lesson Before Dying*. New York: Alfred A. Knopf.

Gates, Henry Louis, Jr. (1984) *Figures in Black: Words, Signs, and the Racial Self*. New York: Oxford University Press.

Haley, Alex (1976) *Roots: A Family Saga*. New York: Doubleday.

Himes, Chester (1965) *Cotton Comes To Harlem*. New York: Putnam's.

Hunter, Kristin (1978) *The Lakestown Rebellion*. New York: Scribner's.

Hurston, Zora Neale (1935) *Mules and Men*. Philadelphia, PA: Lippincott.

Hurston, Zora Neale (1938) *Tell My Horse*. Philadelphia, PA: Lippincott.

Jablon, Madelyn (1997) *Black Metafiction: Self-Consciousness in African-American Literature*. Iowa City: University of Iowa Press.

Johnson, Charles (1982) *Oxherding Tale*. Bloomington: Indiana University Press.

Johnson, Charles (1987) *Being and Race: Black Writing Since 1970*. Bloomington: Indiana University Press.

Jones, Gayl (1975) *Corregidora*. New York: Random House.

Jones, Gayl (1977) *White Rat*. New York: Random House.

Kelley, William Melvin (1962) *A Different Drummer*. Garden City, NY: Doubleday.

Kenan, Randall (1989) *A Visitation of the Spirits*. New York: Grove Press.

Killens, John O. (1971) *The Cotillion; or, One Good Bull Is Half The Herd*. New York: Trident.

Klotman, Phyllis Rauch (1977) *Another Man Gone: The Black Runner in Contemporary Afro-American Literature*. Port Washington, NY: Kennikat Press.

Lee, A. Robert (ed.) (1980) *Black Fiction: New Studies in the Afro-American Novel Since 1945*. London: Vision Press.

Lee, A. Robert (1983) *Black American Fiction Since Richard Wright*. BAAS Pamphlets in American Studies, No. 11.

Lee, A. Robert (1998) *Designs of Blackness: Mappings in the Literature and Culture of Afro-America*. London: Pluto Press.

McDowell, Deborah, and Rampersad, Arnold (eds.) (1992) *Slavery and the Literary Imagination*. Baltimore, MD: Johns Hopkins University Press.

Mackenthan, Lucinda Hardwick (1980) *The Dream of Arcady: Place and Time in Southern Literature*. Baton Rouge: Louisiana State University Press.

McPherson, James Alan (1969) *Hue and Cry*. Boston, MA: Little, Brown.

McPherson, James Alan (1977) *Elbow Room*. Boston, MA: Atlantic-Little.

Moore, Opel (1988) "Freeing Ourselves of History: The Slave Closet," *Obsidian*, 2: 37.

Morrison, Toni (1970) *The Bluest Eye*. New York: Holt, Rinehart, and Winston.

Morrison, Toni (1977) *Song of Solomon*. New York: Alfred A. Knopf.

Morrison, Toni (1987) *Beloved*. New York: Alfred A. Knopf.

Morrison, Toni (1992) *Jazz*. New York: Alfred A. Knopf.

Murray, Albert (1971) *South To A Very Old Place*. New York: McGraw-Hill.

Murray, Albert (1974) *Train Whistle Guitar*. New York: McGraw-Hill.

Murray, Albert (1991) *The Spyglass Tree*. New York: Pantheon Books.

Murray, Albert (1996) *The Seven League Boots*. New York: Pantheon Books.

Naylor, Gloria (1988) *Mama Day*. New York: Vintage.

Pryse, Marjorie and Spillers, Hortense J. (eds.) (1985) *Conjuring: Black Women, Fiction and Literary Tradition*. Bloomington: Indiana University Press.

Reed, Ishmael (1967) *The Free-Lance Pallbearers*. Garden City, NY: Doubleday.

Reed, Ishmael (1972) *Mumbo Jumbo*. Garden City, NY: Random House.

Reed, Ishmael (1976) *Flight To Canada*. New York: Random House.

Rodgers, Lawrence R. (1985) *Canaan Bound: The African-American Great Migration Novel*. Urbana: University of Illinois Press.

Schuyler, George (1931) *Black No More: Being an account of the strange and wonderful workings of science in the Land of the Free, A.D. 1933–1940*. New York: Macauley.

Shange, Ntozake (1982) *Sassafras, Cypress and Indigo*. New York: St. Martin's Press.

Stepto, Robert (1979) *From Behind the Veil: A Study in Afro-American Narrative*. Urbana: University of Illinois Press.

Sundquist, Eric (1993) *To Wake the Nations: Race in the Making of American Literature*. Cambridge, MA: Belknap Press.

Toomer, Jean (1923) *Cane*. New York: Boni and Liveright.

Verdelle, A. J (1995) *The Good Negress*. Chapel Hill, NC: Algonquin Books.

Walker, Alice (1970) *The Third Life of Grange Copeland*. New York: Harcourt Brace Jovanovitch.

Walker, Alice (1973) *In Love and Trouble: Stories of Black Women*. New York: Harcourt Brace Jovanovitch.

Walker, Alice (1976) *Meridian*. New York: Harcourt Brace Jovanovitch.

Walker, Alice (1982) *The Color Purple*. New York: Harcourt Brace Jovanovitch.

Walker, Alice (1983) *In Search of Our Mothers' Gardens: Womanist Prose by Alice Walker*. New York: Harcourt Brace Jovanovitch.

Walker, Margaret (1966) *Jubilee*. Boston, MA: Houghton Mifflin.

Walker, Margaret (1972) *How I Wrote Jubilee*. Chicago: Third World Press.

Wideman, John Edgar (1981) *Damballah*. New York: Avon Books.

Williams, John A. (1967) *The Man Who Cried I Am*. New York: Doubleday.

Williams, John A. (1972) *Captain Blackman*. New York: Doubleday.

Williams, Sherley Ann (1987) *Dessa Rose*. New York: Berkley Books.

Wright, Richard (1947) *Uncle Tom's Children*. New York: Harper.

Wright, Richard (1958) *The Long Dream*. New York: Doubleday.

33

Writing in the South Now

Matthew Guinn

Any effort to write about a literature still unfolding necessarily involves a high degree of speculation. Postmodern Southern fiction in particular – protean, dynamic, and heterogeneous – renders any critical approach to it into something of a high wire act. Yet diverse as it may be, contemporary Southern writing does offer the critic some solace. If today's authors do not conform to the traditional critical paradigms established by Renascence critics, their work evinces at least a nascent network of themes and approaches to writing about the South that are beginning to gel into as much of a pattern as the postmodern era will allow – providing a net partway knitted below the critic's high wire. My goal here is to survey briefly recent critical performances on the high wire, then to essay my own outline of the creative net now taking shape.

By the mid-1970s it had become clear that all was not serene within the household of Southern fiction. Although such distinctly postmodern authors as Barry Hannah and Walker Percy had been welcomed by the establishment – if, perhaps, grudgingly, on the basis of literary acumen rather than adherence to the traditional Southern aesthetic – a new crop of writers was emerging that frankly defied the belletristic tradition. Two writers in particular embodied significant new trends. Harry Crews, the son of South Georgia sharecroppers, had published a string of powerful novels written from a poor-white perspective that Southern criticism was simply unequipped to evaluate. Another rising star of the era, Cormac McCarthy, portrayed the South in such virulently anti-pastoral images as to provoke Walter Sullivan to declare him an artist "not merely bereft of community and myth," but one who had "declared war on these ancient repositories of order and truth" (1976: 71).[1]

If Sullivan's pronouncement sounds inordinately dire, the future from his vantage point would indeed prove disastrous: as I will argue, "declaring war" on community and myth went on to become one of the defining approaches to postmodern Southern writing. The generation of writers that have followed Crews and McCarthy displays an overwhelming tendency to write about the South critically – often, from the perspective of native sons and daughters of the South orphaned by its culture and mythology. Authors who, like Crews, lacked the Vanderbilt pedigree of Sullivan and his peers proliferated like ragweed throughout the 1980s and 1990s. The roster of significant artists with humble origins is lengthy: Dorothy Allison, Larry Brown, Dennis Covington, Richard Ford, Tim Gautreaux, William Gay, Kaye Gibbons, Bobbie Ann Mason, Tim McLaurin, Chris Offutt, Dale Ray Phillips. Just as important, white writers from the middle and upper classes began to rebel against the conventions expected of literary fiction. With McCarthy as a forerunner, writers such as Hannah, William Hoffman, Josephine Humphreys, and Bret Lott subjected Southern culture to a newly acidic scrutiny. And as if to confirm Sullivan's dour assessment years earlier, these writers have become key figures in postmodern Southern fiction.

As the twentieth century drew to a close it seemed that the traditionalist's only hope for continuity lay, ironically, in the South's African-American writers. Such was Fred Hobson's contention in *The Southern Writer in the Postmodern World* (1991). Hobson discerned a newly broad range of voices among the South's white writers – from lower-class perspectives to urbane contemporary realism – that barely resembled the rural and community tropes of Renascence fiction. It was black writers, Hobson argued, who produced novels most resembling traditional fiction. "Contemporary black writers," Hobson maintains, "tend to be more concerned with community, place, and the past and its legacy – and to ground their fiction more fully in a rich traditional folk culture – than do most of their white counterparts" (92). Hobson goes on to suggest "Afro-American fiction, within contemporary Southern literature, is what, in the 1930s, 1940s, and 1950s, white Southern fiction was within the national literature – a powerful, folk-based, past-conscious, often mythic expression of a storytelling culture within a larger literature" (93).

Although Hobson cites Ernest Gaines and Alice Walker as prime examples of his argument, his thesis has borne up well in the last decade's younger African-American writers. Local history is the core of Anthony Grooms's saga of segregated Birmingham, Alabama, in *Bombingham* (2001), and even such contemporary realism like John Holman's *Visible Spirits* (1998) imbues a late twentieth-century urban setting with a community-based folk culture. And the South's most powerful young black writer, Randall Kenan, fits them all: his *Let the Dead Bury Their Dead* and *A Visitation of Spirits* are a combined *tour de force* of folk-based, mythic storytelling – fully imbued with a postmodern sensibility, but not subjected to it.

Evidently, then, a postmodern Southern literature thoroughly distinct from what preceded it lies elsewhere than with the black writer. According to Robert H. Brinkmeyer it lies altogether elsewhere – outside the South itself. In *Remapping Southern Literature: Contemporary Southern Writers and the West* (2000) Brinkmeyer cites the "diminishment of place as a shaping and creative force in the Southern literary imagination" as paramount in contemporary literature (25). Brinkmeyer discerns a sort of westerly migration begun in earnest with Cormac McCarthy's classic *Blood Meridian* (1985), and cites an impressive list of Southern authors who have set novels in the West, from Hannah to Rick Bass, Frederick Barthelme, Doris Betts,

Clyde Edgerton, Richard Ford, and Barbara Kingsolver. These novels' settings reflect a sense of the South as being at last depleted of artistic resources – and indicate that the frontier may well now be the best landscape on which to play out the themes of the Southern imagination. As Brinkmeyer puts it, "Southern writers have more and more been striking out on their own, moving away from the imaginative shape of 'classic' Southern literature that is so secure in regional place, history, and memory" (26).

While Brinkmeyer is certainly correct in noting that a westward drift is prevalent in recent fiction, I would propose that the most definitive tendency in contemporary Southern fiction is not striking out for the territories, but striking *in*, toward a more incisive and critical interpretation of the South, informed by postmodern currents of thought that interrogate history and culture (and indeed, metanarratives in general) with a new level of scrutiny and distrust. I have argued in *After Southern Modernism* (2000) that the new level of cultural skepticism coheres around two approaches: a resurgence of literary naturalism in lower-class white writers such as Allison, Larry Brown, and Crews; and an iconoclastic spirit I call "mythoclasm" in others such as McCarthy and Kenan that seeks to undermine the South's received notions of community and tradition. Thus the most salient trend in contemporary Southern fiction is one of discontinuity with the immediate literary past, a deliberate effort to break from tradition.

Considered in this light, McCarthy's *Blood Meridian* is indeed important to Southern literature – not for its geographical reorientation, but rather for the new direction it charted for historical interpretation in fiction. McCarthy's blood-drenched saga of the Old West set a new tone for historical fiction by Southerners. No longer was history the source of a more ordered vision of existence (as the Nashville Agrarians saw it), nor a field to be explored to determine just where the culture went adrift, in the manner of Quentin Compson's consideration of Thomas Sutpen in *Absalom, Absalom!* Rather, the new focus uses the Southern past as a prism through which to read the culture's formative period – and its literary tradition – in postmodern fashion, debunking any notion of a golden era, or a set of historical archetypes that might be used, in modernist fashion, to order the chaotic present. One of the epigraphs for *Blood Meridian* demonstrates this new stance with emphatic terseness. Excerpting a news account of an anthropological expedition to Ethiopia, the novel takes as its starting point the report of "a 300,000-year-old fossil skull" that "shows evidence of having been scalped." Although not all recent work embraces such a savage view of the past, the new stance in contemporary Southern fiction nonetheless evinces a broad iconoclasm, suggesting that the noble past long taken for granted never did, in fact, exist. Through class-based, feminist, and cultural critiques, postmodern historical fiction suggests that the mythic Southern aristocracy of modernist fiction – like McCarthy's scalped Neanderthal skull – bears distinct signs of barbarity – if only the contemporary observer looks closely enough.

Consequently, the contemporary novelist's approach to history is analogous to that of the anthropologist, seeking to subject received notions of the past to a scrutiny more resembling that of the social sciences than the mythic paradigms of an oral culture. If this approach is a contemporary form of what Richard Gray has described in *Southern Aberrations* as the long tradition of "Southern self-fashioning" (2000: xiii) in the literature, it is unique in its goal of undermining tradition in general. Michael Kreyling pursues such lines in *Inventing Southern Literature* (1998), his survey of the region's literary criticism. Kreyling persuasively argues that "the South" in literature is a construct, the product of competing ideologies in which a predominantly white and male aesthetic has achieved the upper hand in shaping and interpreting Southern literary output. Most provocative is Kreyling's assertion that Southern literature, despite its frequent use of history, is actually at odds with the past – that the fiction itself is a continual effort to rewrite a benighted history. In Kreyling's phrase, traditional Southern fiction comprises a series of "inventions and reinventions of the South in literature as ways of *keeping history at bay*" (xii; emphasis added).

Indeed, much of postmodern Southern fiction seems to carry on the pattern of holding history at arm's length. Excepting the historical playfulness in the work of Hannah and John Barth – and the dead-earnest historical reckoning in black authors such as Toni Morrison and Gloria Naylor – the Southern postmodern seems largely to be focused on the contemporary or the immediate past, whether through K-Mart realism, "grit lit," or latterday local color. But in the past decade a number of contemporary authors have turned their eyes to the Southern past and produced strikingly iconoclastic historical novels. Charles Frazier's *Cold Mountain* (1997) – arguably the best-received Southern novel of the 1990s – uses the familiar topic of the Civil War as the vehicle of a revisionist approach to Southern literary mythology, following a yeoman protagonist's witheringly critical stance toward the antebellum society. Josephine Humphreys's *Nowhere Else on Earth* (2000) charts the depredations of North Carolina's Lumbee Indians through the same period – and is a marked departure from the contemporary setting of all her previous work. The three writers I will consider here as particularly illustrative of the trend toward historical revision – Bobbie Ann Mason, Kaye Gibbons, and Steve Yarbrough – are especially interesting because their reputations have been secured not on historical fiction, but on work that is widely considered to be quintessentially contemporary. Prior to taking up the past as the subject for *Feather Crowns* (1993), *On the Occasion of My Last Afternoon* (1998), and *Visible Spirits* (2001), none of these writers had set a work farther back than the mid-twentieth century – the end of the Southern Renascence. Thus their compulsion to revisit the past suggests a trend in Southern postmodernism – counter to postmodernism in general – that history is not altogether dead, but rather populated by restless ghosts demanding redress. And in the process of giving those ghosts a hearing, these authors are charting a new course in Southern literary history.

Mason, Gibbons, and Yarbrough are further illustrative of broad contemporary patterns, in that none of them hails from the kind of background that has long been standard for white Southern writers. All were raised in lower-class or blue-collar homes, and all cleave to views of social class, gender, and race that have long been absent in Southern fiction. The revisionist spirit that accompanies such perspectives is nowhere more clear than in their interrogations of the South's fabled past. In their work the familiar dynamic of the past in the present is maintained only superficially, for we are now dealing with a different sort of past – the old South as interpreted by the descendants of those marginalized by it. It may be that Southern fiction at the dawn of the twenty-first century has reached a strange juncture that is uniquely Southern yet also uniquely postmodern – an uneasy moment in a traditionalist literature in which history has returned, under clear-eyed scrutiny, with a vengeance.

By the 1990s Bobbie Ann Mason had secured a prominent place for herself in Southern literature. An astute contemporary realist, her work provides the student of Southern fiction with a unique and perplexing set of questions about late regional culture, foremost among them, whether *Shiloh and Other Stories* or *In Country* represent the ultimate expression of the Southern literary consciousness, either as epitaph or coda to the Renascence. Such questions arise from what is perhaps the most distinct characteristic of Mason's writing: the sense of dissonance that pervades it. She *appears* to be writing a version of late Agrarian fiction in which waning farm communities are contrasted with the emptiness of an ascendant commercial culture – where the local strip-mall K-Mart stands in a kind of cultural chiaroscuro with the cornfields behind it. Yet those readers inclined toward contextualizing Mason within the Southern tradition cast about vainly for authorial commentary, for some controlling ironic perspective, on the cultural state of affairs in her work. Absent from her juxtapositions of urban and rural, commercial and local, is the figure of the author herself. One encounters the materials of a neo-Agrarian vision, but none of the polemic that should accompany it.

This peculiar objectivity is due in part to Mason's minimalist technique and the generic conventions of realism, but its origins run deeper than the matter of literary style. Given her subject matter, one must question why Mason has not adopted the tenor of her predecessors, why her work does not more resemble that of authors taking up similar cultural transitions, from Faulkner's *Go Down, Moses* to Fred Chappell's *I Am One of You Forever*. The answer lies in biography. Although Mason possesses many of the credentials of an agrarian writer, her experience with the agricultural life precludes the nostalgia that lends poignancy to the pastoral as practiced by other Southern writers. Mason makes this distinction clear on the first page of her memoir *Clear Springs* (1999), with the declaration: "I grew up on a small family farm, the kind of place people like to idealize these days. They think the old-fashioned rustic life provided what they are now seeking – independence, stability, authenticity. And we did have those on the farm – along with mind-numbing, back-breaking labor and crippling social isolation." The farming life is for Mason an existence "in steady conflict with nature," and the author claims to have "hated the constant sense of helplessness before vast forces, the continuous threat of failure" – "especially" rural "women's part in the dependence." From a class and gender perspective omitted from *I'll Take My Stand*, Mason offers a newly balanced accounting of the agricultural South.

Mason also adopts an attitude toward tradition that sets her at odds with her predecessors, from the Agrarians to Faulkner and Eudora Welty. Consider her view of the Southern tradition:

> I'm not sure all those qualities of the Old South were all that terrific ... I'm not nostalgic for the past. Times change and I'm interested in writing about what's now. To me, the way the South is changing is very dynamic and full of complexity ... My characters have more opportunities in their lives than their parents did, and even the parents are more prosperous in their old age than they ever were before. That is what's changing about the face of the South – that more and more people are getting in on the good life. (Wilhelm 1988: 37)

Here is explanation for the lack of elegy in Mason's fading communities: Mason's people cannot afford nostalgia and, even more to the point, have no material reason to interpret changes to the South in negative terms. Hence, the progress that Southern literature traditionally decries must be reckoned as something other than the death-knell of an ideal culture. That Mason's stance toward the historical South is determined by a class perspective not incorporated into the canonical literature explains why her treatment of conventional Southern material fails to satisfy conventional Southern readings. Whereas Mason's fellow Kentuckian Wendell Berry, for example, argues in the preface to *Sex, Economy, Freedom and Community* (1993) that the "duty" of the writer is to resist consumer culture at every turn, Mason takes no such stand. Rather, she objectively observes the changing South without attempting to preserve it as a discrete and mythic region. In the process, she effectively demonstrates not only the constructedness of the traditional "South," but also illustrates how the dominant ideology of Southern literature has worked to preserve it.

All this is borne out thoroughly in *Feather Crowns* (1993), which dismantles the Agrarian conception of the historical South through the unassuming material of quotidian detail. On one level the novel resembles an Agrarian saga, or one of Berry's novels. A reading in this vein can be delineated quickly enough: the novel begins on a self-sufficient Kentucky farm in the early twentieth century, which grows more vulnerable to the vicissitudes of a cash-crop economy as its dependence on tobacco increases. With the birth of Christie Wheeler's quintuplets, celebrity and mass culture intrude and the enticements of progress are heeded by the family patriarch, Wad Wheeler. The babies die shortly after their birth, but through Wad's machinations Christie and her husband take their embalmed bodies on a tour of the South in a grotesque combination of chautauqua and sideshow exhibit. With financial gain comes something close to spiritual death, and the organic culture of the novel's opening – the extended family on the farm – is fragmented.

This is an intentionally reductive summary, yet its very simplicity reflects the consequences of an orthodox reading that would render Mason's complex work familiar. Like much of Mason's other fiction, *Feather Crowns* celebrates portions of rural life but, in a subtle yet important distinction from Agrarian practice, it declines to celebrate it entirely. By taking up the *locus classicus* of Agrarian philosophy – the pre-industrial family farm – as its subject, the novel completes an engagement with Southern literary tradition only touched upon in Mason's earlier work. The result is an agrarian novel without myth, rendered in a realistic manner at odds with historical fictions like Stark Young's *So Red the Rose* and Allen Tate's *The Fathers*. Alongside play-parties and fiddle music such as described in *I'll Take My Stand* is material less folkloric, from a fan bearing the advertising image of Jesus standing before a tobacco warehouse, to trading cards imprinted with the trademark logos of pharmaceutical products (Mason 1993: 63, 160). Mason takes pains to depict the material hardships of the culture, which is "filled" with "poor folks" and in which "a child [living] to his tenth year was always a cause of celebration" and one woman of fifty is considered "old" (334, 287, 36). Further, Mason's nineteenth-century South is marked by manifest racism, dotted by "old slave cabins small as corncribs" with blacks living in "desolation" (335, 341). Most damning of all, Mason has her protagonist conclude the narrative on a note pointedly lacking in any Arcadian nostalgia: "You wanted to know how it was back then, but it wouldn't thrill your heart to know" – "don't ever think we lived in the good old days" (449, 452). Popular culture, racism, and hard times are present even in the halcyon era of the Agrarian South, and these elements render the characters of Mason's historical novel not very different in their concerns and limited perspectives from the people of her contemporary settings. The novel demonstrates not only the deficiencies of the traditional mythic Southern past, but also the shortcomings of a cultural perspective that would locate anomie and disaffection solely within modernity. If Mason's work may in some sense be viewed as a dialogue with Agrarianism, her response here seems to be: *Et in Arcadia ego.*

Thus Mason's lasting contribution to Southern literature may be a historical consciousness imbued with an uncommon instinct for realism, a revisiting of the past without the apologia that has so often accompanied it. Without adopting the strident iconoclasm of contemporaries like McCarthy or Hannah, Mason manages to achieve similar effects. Mason focuses on those elements problematic to the program of such mythic novels as those the Agrarians wrote, rendering in detail what the Agrarians embellished or omitted concerning Southern agriculture. Her critical realism exposes the mythical supports of the literary past, undermining the abstraction of traditionalist fiction by observing a great number of troubling social details overlooked by the sweep of narratives intent on a grander scope.

It is a subtle iconoclasm, but an incisive one. As part of the general movement in contemporary Southern literature toward realism, it works against the creative process common to Renascence fiction and imperils the consensus on which Southern literature has long rested. This is nowhere more evident than in a comparison between *Feather Crowns* and one of the more widely acknowledged essays in *I'll Take My Stand*: Allen Tate's "Remarks on the Southern Religion" (1930) and its image of the "half-horse." If a slight twisting of Tate's metaphor may be allowed, it seems reasonable to suggest that the Agrarians themselves fell victim to "the enemy, abstraction," and in doing so rendered their program susceptible to theoretical shortcomings closely analogous to Tate's half-horse (167). As Tate wrote in 1930: "Nothing infallibly works, and the new half-religionists are simply worshipping a principle, and with true half-religious fanaticism they ignore what they do not want to see – which is the breakdown of the principle in numerous instances of practice. It is a bad religion, for that very reason; it can predict only success" (158). The Agrarians fell victim to abstraction; Mason has done the opposite. She does indeed praise those portions of the rural life that are genuinely redemptive – but she does this alongside her chronicle of the "breakdowns" which invariably accompany it. Her lack of adherence to a programmatic Agrarian platform that can predict only success places her within the "whole-horse" perspective that (quoting Tate again) "takes account of the failures" and consequently is "realistic." The result is a vision of the rural South that is in Tate's terminology "mature" and "not likely to suffer from disillusion and collapse" (159). In focusing on the rural and in delving into the Southern past, Mason covers familiar terrain, but she does so while correcting the "short memory of failure" that has marked that well-traveled landscape.

If Mason corrects the short memory of the Southern pastoral, her contemporary Kaye Gibbons seems intent on recovering not what has been merely forgotten by the culture, but what it has repressed. Indeed, Gibbons's career may be read as a prolonged assault on the patriarchal South, her novels a series of efforts to destabilize its authority. From her debut novel *Ellen Foster* – which appropriates motifs from *Huckleberry Finn* to cast a girl as the questing hero(ine) – to her most recent work, Gibbons repeatedly depicts the South as an environment that not only consigns its women to the margins, but also often threatens their very survival. In this, Gibbons follows the pattern of Southern women's writing Patricia Yaeger describes as a chronicle of "the numinous terrors of the everyday" that "exposes the deforming effects of the Southern political tradition upon women, men, and children of color, upon white women and children, and even upon white men" (1997: 288–9).

Considered sequentially, Gibbons's work moves upward through the social hierarchy with each novel, from the "trash" perspective of *Ellen Foster* to the yeomanry of *A Virtuous Woman*; from the vaguely defined middle class of *A Cure for Dreams* and *Charms for the Easy Life* to the landed bourgeoisie of *Sights Unseen*. Given such a progression, it seems inevitable that her most incisive critique of Southern patriarchy would appear in *On the Occasion of My Last Afternoon* (1993), a Civil War novel centering upon the planter aristocracy of the Old South. Yaeger notes "a frequent reprise" in the criticism of Southern women writers is their alleged "lack of thematic, stylistic, or political 'largeness'" (1997: 288). Gibbons negates the criticism by taking as her subject the nucleus of Southern myth, the plantation, and the vast action of the war that arose from it. Exploring such "large" subjects, she operates in territory already mapped by Faulkner, Tate, Young, and other modernists, yet her narrative of a disintegrating feudal patriarchy ascribes blame for the demise of the old order to a source overlooked in the tragic saga of the Renascence: the patriarchy itself. In Gibbons's treatment the key battles of the war are waged on the home front, behind the facade of the big house; the antebellum myth is deconstructed from within.

If Gibbons's aim in the novel is to uncover the historical and cultural bases of her women characters' daunting environments, her choice of patriarchs could not be better. Samuel P. Tate (one notes a rich sense of intertextuality in the name) is a wealthy planter who "had served two terms in the legislature and was known all over Virginia to be an honest, upright, hearty, and earnest Episcopalian" (Gibbons 1993: 2). In spite of his reputation, Tate is haunted by his impoverished childhood, by the fact that he cannot claim the true aristocracy his culture worships. He is clearly one of W. J. Cash's cotton parvenus, of the instant Southern upper class lately arisen from "the strong, the pushing, the ambitious, among the old coon-hunting population" (Cash 1941: 14). Throughout her work, Gibbons's men are the practitioners of repression and restrictive ideology; Tate's yearning for social prominence indicates that this tendency is historic.

> In few words, he needed our neighbors, not for political standing, elected and supported as he was during his legislative terms by those men who used him to speak their fears. The families whose ancestors had disembarked at Jamestown were necessary to complete the picture he craved himself part of, just as he had paid dearly for a visiting, reluctant artist to touch up a fox-hunting scene and place him on the one riderless horse. And then there father was, all of a sudden on the library wall, in the lead on a race across a Scottish moor, wearing a full kit. He also had the man render a coat of arms of the Tates of Edinburgh, the place he fancied that he belonged to have come from had his family – as I found out from the greasy letters of passage sent to me when one of his kin died – not swabbed steerage of vomit and human refuse from Liverpool to Mr. Oglethorpe's debtors' colony in Georgia. (Gibbons 1993: 40)

Time and frontiers, indeed. The lack of the former is only a slight impediment to a man of Tate's coarseness with the means to purchase the myth he seeks. Tate (like his fellow planters, Gibbons implies) is the architect of a culture preoccupied with roles equally false and restrictive – a culture authored by white men for their benefit alone.

From such a culture arises a series of everyday terrors for the women in the novel, best represented by Tate's wife, Alice. With her recurrent "sick head-misery," Alice recalls the quailing Ole Miss of legend, a figure targeted with derision by Old South critics from Harriet Jacobs onward. Yet Gibbons does not attribute her character's ailment to an inherent weakness indulged by a paternalistic society. Rather, it results from the psychological war of attrition fought daily in the Tate household, the product not of a pedestal position in the family, but of the incessant hammering of emotional abuse she suffers from her husband. The novel's narrator, Emma, sees her mother as "a lady who could have enjoyed developing her mind and might have found the same pleasure in using it that she did in reading light magazines and chatting at sewing circles with her friends," but whose "survival" in Tate's home "took the place of whatever mind-work she might have accomplished" (96). The portrait of a planta-tion mistress such as Faulkner's Caroline Compson is tempered by straitened domestic relations akin to those of Charlotte Perkins Gilman's "The Yellow Wallpaper." When Alice finally succumbs to the abuse, her deathbed physician speculates that she "must have been a lady of severe emotion and intense study, for such trauma of mind was evident in her drawn face," and ascribes the cause of her death to "Inflammation of the Brain owing to over-exertion of an organ not constructed by our Maker for life other than that of quiet domesticity" (155, 157). Here the nineteenth-century context makes the culpability of men more evident than in Gibbons's contemporary works, their role in a repressive society more salient – and, given the historical plantation setting, indeed formative in the culture that followed.

This revisionist woman's perspective shapes the account of the Civil War in the novel. The Confederacy is not described in the feminine terms of the historical myth, but through the masculine delusions of Samuel Tate. From his "vehement correspond-ence with every pro-Negro newspaper editor in the South" to his hawkish jingoism, Tate becomes conflated with a social order that represents the apotheosis of repression exerted by white men of power (129). In keeping with Gibbons's conception of patriarchal ideology, the Confederacy thrives on euphemism as an important tool for the maintenance of myth. The culture that insists on substituting the word "servant" for "slave" becomes in the war a patriarchy intent on consciously manipu-lating fact into propaganda: the Southern military initially is depicted as "an army of Natty Bumppos," and battlefield deaths are reported with such rhetorical flourishes as "passed at Manassas" (26, 182). After the tide of war has turned against the Confeder-acy, Tate is "bolstered against all reality by newspaper accounts that diminished truth with such decorous conclusions as: 'Confederate forces were pushed back. Wake County guards performed admirably. Some were lost'" (218). An iconoclastic per-spective emerges in Emma's response to such self-delusion. In a room with other women at the announcement of Virginia's secession, she detects an "unspoken agree-ment that martyrdom was for dead saints" and observes that among the women at least, "nobody was quoting soaring passages from *Ivanhoe*" (173). Her insistence that the war "was a conflict perpetrated by rich men and fought by poor boys against hungry women and babies" further separates her from the dominant ideology of men like her father (164).

But it is through her depictions of Tate that Gibbons thoroughly deconstructs the mythic stature of the war that became a lodestone of modern Southern fiction. As one of his daughters observes, Tate "thinks he himself is the South" (194). It is in this terse observation that Gibbons's challenge to mythic history becomes clear. For Tate "is" indeed the South – the South of the Confederacy, of the antebellum slave economy, of the patriarchy that placed landowning white men in a hegemonic position at the peak of the culture. Yet his complete embodiment of the ideals of this culture is used to turn the mythic Confederacy inside out: the trope of a lost organic South is debunked at its foundations. Gibbons, like Cash in *The Mind of the South*, exposes the crass materialism beneath the aristocratic veneer of the antebellum planter, but she also moves her critique further, into self-conscious literary subversion. As an incarnation of the Confederacy, Tate joins a host of fictive Southern characters who epitomize a vanquished way of life, a vital connection to place and culture that formed the basis of what the dissociated Southern modernists saw as "lost" in twentieth-century society. Consider Allen Tate's description of George Posey in *The Fathers* as a fitting example: George is consumed "by an idea, a cause, an action in which his personality could be extinguished . . . it seemed as if George had succeeded in becoming a part of something greater than he: the Confederate cause" (1977: 180–1). In Gibbons's revision, the extinction of personality through culture – the quaesitum of Southern modernism – is exposed as a patriarchal fantasy. The rewards of being consumed by a historical narrative greater than the individual self are, as the title of Tate's novel makes clear, limited to but a few members of Southern culture. Further, the crucial sacrifice of participating in such a cause is reckoned only in patriarchal terms – not, as Emma observes, in the price paid by women, the poor, and African Americans, who have long suffered a different sort of extinction of personality that can hardly be considered beneficial. With Samuel Tate functioning as the avatar of Confederate commitment, the Southern war appears as but a sweeping example of the violent damage wreaked at home. Hardly a pitched battle for freedom, independence, or Southern sovereignty, it is, from Gibbons's female perspective, a macrocosmic enactment of the male hegemony practiced inside the plantation household.

Consequently, the resolution of Gibbons's Civil War novel departs significantly from its Southern predecessors, even those focused on the home front of the war such as *The Fathers* and *The Unvanquished*. Despite the trials of Reconstruction, the demise of the old order is rather more liberating for Gibbons's characters than tragic. Throughout, *On the Occasion of My Last Afternoon* follows with remarkable accuracy the historical conditions chronicled by Drew Gilpin Faust in *Mothers of Invention*, from the ambivalent morale of Confederate women to the hospital work of the domestic war; the novel also reaches similar conclusions about the lasting social effects of secession. Faust notes that the war "undermined the wealth and political power of the planter elite," transforming the hierarchies of race and class "that had so firmly placed white men at the apex of the social pyramid" (1996: 4). Samuel Tate's dissolution personifies this shift, symbolizing the less than chivalric tribulations of the planter bereft of his feudal prominence. But the profoundly iconoclastic strains of the novel emerge in Emma's reaction to Confederate defeat. Faust observes that "the desire to cling to eroding status remained strong" for those daughters of the Southern aristocracy "who remembered the rewards of class and racial power in the Old South" (254). Emma resists this tendency. Always of "a mind that studied the manner in which people of varying classes dealt with one another," she adapts to the new social order adeptly, seeking to develop and foster in her children the "quick-marrow" that "ignores lines of class hierarchy and race" (Gibbons 1993: 8, 115). Emma claims to be "tired of the accoutrements of high-toned existence," intent instead on discovering "truth, authenticity" (111). As Gibbons's novel demonstrates powerfully, truth and authenticity are to be found outside the mythos of the Old South and its patriarchal regime. From such a vantage point the Old South's displacement by a new, egalitarian society can be reckoned a tragedy only by those orchestrators of the myth that kept them in power.

Faust (1996) concludes her study by citing two enormously influential meditations on Southern history: C. Vann Woodward's idea of "the burden of Southern history" and Gavin Stevens's reverie of Pickett's Charge in *Intruder in the Dust*, asserting that "Southerners burdened with the past Woodward describes, like the Southerners forever poised at two o'clock on July 3, are white Southerners and they are male Southerners. The weight of Southern history is just as heavy for women and for African Americans, but it is constructed rather differently" (256). Gibbons's novel serves a literary function parallel to Faust's history by examining the burden of Southern history for those who did not participate in scripting its dominant narrative. It is intriguing that Gibbons's historical novel concludes by revisiting a genre generally overlooked in the Southern literary canon, the reconciliation romance of the nineteenth century. Her protagonist's marriage to Quincy Lowell of Boston, whose family maintains staunch connections to abolition and Transcendentalism, revives the Reconstruction theme of reunion through marriage in the aftermath of war. It is a romance form rejected by the modernists, yet in Gibbons's treatment it is hardly a format limited by generic conventions. The epigraphs of *On the Occasion of My Last Afternoon* — passages of Allen Tate's "Ode to the Confederate Dead" and Robert Lowell's "For the Union Dead" juxtaposed — lend ironic resonance to the Tate–Lowell marriage within the pages of the novel. Conscious of the ramifications of intertextuality, Gibbons's postmodern reconciliation romance proposes a union not only of North and South, but also between the mythic literary history of a patriarchal South and the dissenting voices silenced by it. Quincy Lowell helps Emma Tate to "drag the past into the present," holding her "steady" as she "maneuver[s] amongst the ruins" of history (174). The familiar dynamic of the past in the present perseveres, but from the Southern women's perspective it accrues Freudian implications of repression and a benighted former existence. Southern history is redeemed only by the outsider's aid — by an accounting of the past outside the terms of Southern patriarchy. Nearing the end of her last afternoon, Emma remarks: "a receipt is only as good as its alterations" (266). Her feminine metaphor may well describe Gibbons's contribution to the postmodern use of the Southern past.

Perhaps the most deeply iconoclastic writer to emerge in recent years is Mississippi native Steve Yarbrough. As the title story of his collection *Veneer* (1998) powerfully demonstrates, the Southern social order is for Yarbrough a uniquely ersatz brand of American culture, in which a superficial gentility barely manages to conceal the fundamental avarice of the rural communities' prime movers: its landholding scions. Indeed, his fiction resonates with a conviction that turning over a spadeful of Delta soil will more often than not reveal the buried bones of a past injustice. Most damning of Yarbrough's excavations is his repeated depiction of African Americans and poor whites as dual victims of Southern capitalism. Yet in all but its darkest moments, Yarbrough's work promises that change is possible, through better understanding the dynamic by which these marginalized Southerners are kept at odds with one another.

Visible Spirits (2001) is a sustained illustration of the Southern upper class as — in the words of one nineteenth-century Southerner — "an aristocracy without nobility"

(Foner 1988: 2). Like Gibbons's Samuel Tate, the patriarch of *Visible Spirits* is ruthless and brutal, but so too are all his peers in the novel, who strive to maintain the status quo of slavery through Reconstruction and into the early twentieth century. Yarbrough's Sam Payne articulates his rapacious philosophy not only to his family (although notably he has, like Gibbons's Tate, driven his wife to an early grave), but also to gatherings of fellow planters who concur with him at every rhetorical turn. Payne's view of Southern economics is both nakedly capitalistic and bereft of any sense of *noblesse oblige*. He argues that "there were not enough riches in this world to go around, and if you meant to have anything, you had to work folks right into the ground. That had always been the truth, it always would be, and anyone who claimed otherwise was a goddamn dreamer," and expresses an atavistic view of landownership: "calling it yours don't make it yours . . . Taking's what makes it yours – and you don't just take it once. You got to take it again and again" (Yarbrough 2001: 211, 202). Ultimately, Payne says, race relations come down to a simple economic dichotomy: "Between the hills and the river, there ain't space enough for both [races] to prosper" (222).

In a more traditional Southern novel, such views would likely be presented as the distorted thinking of an individual incapable of properly appreciating the old order, such as Faulkner's parvenu Thomas Sutpen. But Yarbrough takes pains to show that Payne's views are held by all the community's leaders; no Sartoris-like aristocracy is presented to ameliorate the portrait. When, for example, Payne's prodigal son Tandy returns to Loring after years of rambling dissipation, he finds his own cruelty and grasping selfishness to be perfectly suited to his native community: "He'd been a stranger for so long, in so many different places, that every place had come to seem strange. Except here" (76). Soon enough Tandy has set in motion a series of race-baiting backroom meetings with landowners that results in the ousting of the black postmistress and Tandy's securing her position. When a postal carrier freezes to death on his mail route, Tandy seizes the opportunity to cast the accident as a racial killing, firing his own pistol into the white carrier's body and suggesting that the "murder" was perpetrated by one of Loring's black laborers. And the community is quick to adopt his theory of the guilty party:

> They would have to pin the crime on a Negro, but they could not allow themselves to blame *the Negroes* – of whom, in Loring County, there were four for every white – because those Negroes were necessary. You could get mad at one horse and shoot it, but if you shot the whole remuda, who would pull the plow? (252)

The resultant lynch mob is met by two racial moderates of Loring, Tandy's brother Leighton, the newspaper editor, and Seaborn Jackson, a successful black businessman and proponent of Booker T. Washington's philosophy of assimilation. Leighton is emblematically blinded in one eye by the mob; Jackson is murdered (later, the story will circulate that Jackson had "sold whiskey on the side" and been killed by "two other colored men" when a deal went sour). Tandy Payne is never held accountable for the crime that incites the night's brutality – his place in the community of Loring has been secured by his adherence to its racist ideology.

That *Visible Spirits* ends with such a dark portrayal of the Southern community in general makes it an important landmark in the literary tradition. Yarbrough seems to agree with Seaborn Jackson's assertion that "People who live between a rock and a hard place can afford to go . . . a little crazy. But we live between a rock and a knife" (131). For in fact it is the moderates of the novel – those who would cleave to a middle path in race relations – who are most sorely punished by the community, resulting in a thoroughly dystopian picture of the historical South. Barring the possible exception of McCarthy's *Outer Dark* and *Child of God*, *Visible Spirits* is likely the most negative depiction of the South in the region's literature.

Where, then, to proceed from such a past? Yarbrough offers an answer in *The Oxygen Man* (1999), his finest novel to date and one of the best works of Southern fiction produced at the close of the twentieth century. *The Oxygen Man* is also set in the Mississippi Delta, and though its action spans the years 1972 to 1996, I would like to conclude by considering it briefly as a prime example of the Southern past in the postmodern present. In it agriculture has entered a sort of postmodern phase, with soybean and cotton cultivation replaced by catfish farming in ponds carved out of the Mississippi soil. Its cast of characters is familiar, even if their roles have been altered. Latterday planter Mack Bell, a landowner and catfish producer, resides at the top of the social order, overseeing black laborers who no longer work in fields but tend ponds. The novel's title character, Ned Rose – Bell's "oxygen man" charged with keeping the catfish ponds properly aerated – occupies an uneasy space between them as a kind of contemporary overseer, always reminded of his social superiority over the laborers, yet simultaneously aware that he is perceived by Bell and his peers as "white trash." The narrative Yarbrough constructs from such a social mélange culminates in a striking examination of race and class in Southern life, and finally suggests – with an unprecedented understanding of the South in nearly Marxist terms – that the two are inextricably bound.

Witness, for example, the scene in which Sunflower County's farming elite meets to discuss union activity in the area. The meeting takes place in 1996, but its subject and tenor are old ones:

> "You let a bunch of niggers start singing the same tune," Fordy Bashford said, "and you got you one hell of a racket."
>
> "Need to get one bunch singing gospel," Mack said, "and the other bunch singing soul and all the rest singing the blues. Otherwise, next thing you know we'll be paying tractor drivers fifteen dollars an hour, and it'll cost twenty an hour to get anybody to stick his foot in a pond." (39)

The contemporary flourishes in the scene – among them, that the men are drinking Carta Blanca beer – only underscore Yarbrough's implication that it was ever thus, and further buttress his contention in *Visible Spirits* that those atop the South's social hierarchy are merely the ones who treat Southern life in frankly Darwinian terms. Mack Bell's clear if vulgar analogy expresses a fundamental understanding of ideological manipulation, and his prediction of increased hourly wages makes his profit motive plain. As he has said to Ned earlier, "You know them sons of bitches come to me Monday morning and demanded I raise 'em to six dollars an hour? . . . I told 'em to quit dreaming and start working" (12).

Ned's conscience prevents him from embracing such views, but his very lack of identity – he is white but "different" from Mack Bell in vague but emphatic ways, yet clearly distinct from the African Americans – inclines him to view Mack as a makeshift source of self-definition. This identity crisis expresses itself throughout the novel, from Ned's acquired taste for imported beer to his consideration of buying a used Mercedes, as a pained quest for belonging. Not since Harry Crews's *A Feast of Snakes* has the poor white's uncertain status been so well expressed:

> For some folks, everything in between the beginning and the end was just a fight for breath, just one long struggle to suck in air or water or food, anything to fill the cavities that threatened to expand inside those folks until they themselves were walking raging nothings that couldn't do much but eat and drink, piss and shit, hurt and moan, that lived to writhe and tingle, kick ass and shoot off, that had a hole they could never fill because the hole was them and they were the hole, the sum of their natures null. His momma was that, and his daddy was, and he knew now that he would be too, that there was nothing he could do to avoid it. (104)

It is significant that Ned conceives of himself in such reductive terms (indeed, the poor-white existence here resembles that of the catfish in the murky ponds) at the most crucial juncture of his life. For the passage comprises his thoughts when, as a teenager seeking acceptance from Mack Bell and his peers, Ned stands before a black storeowner who has just refused to sell him a case of beer. With Indianola's young elite waiting outside the store in Mack's Cadillac, "thinking that Ned would fail whatever test this was," Ned strikes the storeowner with an empty bottle and takes the beer out to his friends (104). Whether the blow kills the black man or not is never made explicit, but nonetheless the crime effectively renders Ned indentured to Mack Bell for life.

The act of violence is deeply symbolic and historically resonant, for it represents the poor white enacting violence on an African-American at the behest of the white upper class, another example of the present being not very different from the benighted past. But the resolution of *The Oxygen Man* promises redemption for Ned and, by extension, the poor-white and black South, as well. When the adult Ned learns of Mack's plans to execute the principal black union activist, he kills his employer; it is an act of self-sacrifice that will break the cycle of baronial exploitation practiced by Mack – and also an effort at expiation for Ned's youthful crime. As in Crews's *A Feast of Snakes*, the poor-white's only means of self-declaration would seem to be violence. But where Crews's Joe Lon Mackey strikes out randomly – releasing his pent-up anger indiscriminately – Ned's is a calculated act with justice behind it, with a chance of truly disrupting the social order. The self-hatred expressed in Ned's thoughts is channeled outward rather than toward self-immolation; in Yarbrough's novel, there is a clear focus of culpability: the postmodern incarnation of the old order.

If my brief accounting of *The Oxygen Man* seems only to skirt the issues of race and the past, I will close with Yarbrough's own words, which make the interconnectedness between the poor white, the South's African Americans, history, and the postmodern present manifestly clear. If we may expect more novels like *The Oxygen Man* in the future, we may soon find our conventional conceptions of distinctly "white" and "African-American" Southern literatures to be antiquated – that a proper understanding of the region and its history in economic and class terms will render our old readings of the literature as discrete, racialized parts of a whole archaic. For if there is a redemptive promise in the skepticism of the South's most gifted younger writers, it lies in the refusal to keep history at bay, choosing rather to unearth the past for a full accounting of what has shaped – and more importantly, misshaped – the South. Yarbrough dramatizes this accounting in one of Ned Rose's epiphanies on the entwined nature of race and class. After suffering yet another humiliation at the hands of Mack Bell – who has just tauntingly reminded him of his assault on the black store owner – Ned finds himself in Mack's idling Cadillac, at the highway shoulder, wailing. This is what he hears as his voice echoes across the Delta:

> The sound came again, and Ned was listening to it too, ringing out in the night, this sharp dark piercing sound, he was listening as if it hadn't come from him but from someone else, someone who must have been standing ... across the road in the cotton patch, someone with blood in his eyes, with chains on his legs and welts on his back, standing there in this his second century. (231)

Note

1   Sullivan's comments derived from the 1975 Lamar Memorial Lecture at Mercer University. Two of the other critics I will discuss were also Lamar Lecturers: Fred Hobson in 1990 and Robert H. Brinkmeyer in 2000. The critical trajectory suggested by this brief history of the lecture is nicely illustrative of the literature itself – from the attempt to recover organic wholeness (Sullivan) to diversity (Hobson) to dispersal (Brinkmeyer).

References and further reading

Berry, Wendell (1993) *Sex, Economy, Freedom and Community: Eight Essays.* New York: Pantheon Books.

Brinkmeyer, Robert H. (2000) *Remapping Southern Literature: Contemporary Southern Writers and the West.* Athens, GA: University of Georgia Press.

Cash, W. J. (1941) *The Mind of the South.* New York: Alfred A. Knopf.

Faust, Drew Gilpin (1996) *Mothers of Invention: Women of the Slaveholding South in the American Civil War.* Chapel Hill: University of North Carolina Press.

Foner, Eric (1988) *Reconstruction: America's Unfinished Revolution.* New York: Harper and Row.

Gibbons, Kaye (1993) *On the Occasion of My Last Afternoon.* New York: G. P. Putnam's Son's.

Gray, Richard (2000) *Southern Aberrations: Writers of the American South and the Problems of Regionalism.* Baton Rouge: Louisiana State University Press.

Guinn, Matthew (2000) *After Southern Modernism: Fiction of the Contemporary South.* Jackson: University of Mississippi Press.

Hobson, Fred (1991) *The Southern Writer in the Postmodern World.* Athens, GA: University of Georgia Press.

Kreyling, Michael (1998) *Inventing Southern Literature.* Jackson: University of Mississippi Press.

Mason, Bobbie Ann (1993) *Feather Crowns.* New York: Harper Collins.

Sullivan, Walter (1976) *A Requiem for the Renascence: The State of Fiction in the Modern South.* Athens, GA: University of Georgia Press.

Tate, Allen (1977) *The Fathers and Other Fiction.* Baton Rouge: Louisiana State University Press.

Twelve Southerners (1930) *I'll Take My Stand: The South and the Agrarian Tradition.* New York: Harper and Brothers.

Wilhelm, Albert (1988) "An Interview with Bobbie Ann Mason," *Southern Quarterly,* 26, 2 (winter): 27–38.

Yaeger, Patricia (1997) "Beyond the Hummingbird: Southern Women Writers and the Southern Gargantua." In *Haunted Bodies: Gender and Southern Texts,* ed. Anne Goodwyn Jones and Susan V. Donaldson. Charlottesville: University of Virginia Press, 287–318.

Yarbrough, Steve (1999) *The Oxygen Man.* Denver, CO: MacMurray and Beck.

Yarbrough, Steve (2001) *Visible Spirits.* New York: Alfred A. Knopf.

Part IV
Afterword

34

Searching for Southern Identity

James C. Cobb

By the second half of the twentieth century, the term "New South" connoted long-needed reforms that would destroy the region's most problematic peculiarities and move it at last into the mainstream of national life. As it had emerged in the wake of Reconstruction, however, what Paul Gaston described as the original "New South Creed" had actually promised a swift and sweeping industrial and commercial revolution without the sacrifice of racial, political, and cultural continuity or autonomy. The New South Creed soothed the wounded pride of war- and Reconstruction-weary white Southerners with an extravagantly romanticized vision of the aristocratic antebellum golden age that lay behind them and offered them inspiration and hope in the promise of a prosperous and dynamic industrial golden age that lay just ahead.

Espousing a powerful mixture of myths about the past, illusions about the present, and fantasies about the future, the architects of the New South succeeded in constructing a new regional identity, one so enduring that, as Michael O'Brien observed, "the New South helped to make permanent the very idea of a South." W. J. Cash described the New South as "not quite a nation within a nation but the next thing to it," and in fact, its architects set out to build the kind of "imagined political community" that Benedict Anderson offered as his definition of a nation.

Like constructed national identities from the Third French Republic to Khomeini's Iran, the New South rested on a rigidly proscribed version of the region's past in which antebellum planters were genteel aristocrats and benevolent masters; Reconstruction was an unspeakable horror comparable to rape; the "Redeemers" who overthrew it were the heroic descendants of the old planter class; and finally, segregation and disfranchisement were natural, appropriate responses to emancipation, rooted in the South's peculiar racial history and absolutely vital to restoring and maintaining social stability in the region.

Although the New South Creed quickly became the dominant ideology among late nineteenth-century Southern white political, economic, and intellectual leaders, its contradictions, inconsistencies, and inaccuracies were too blatant to escape challenge altogether. The first generation of postbellum Southern intellectuals generally shared a belief that economic modernization was the answer to a multitude of the region's ills. Still, by no means all of them accepted the romanticized version of antebellum Southern life, nor did all of them embrace the hyperbole and ballyhoo about the era of progress and enlightenment already at hand. In fact, as they challenged the New South Creed, these early critics raised important questions and suggested crucial themes that would ultimately engage many of the leading figures of the twentieth-century Southern Renaissance.

At times, Walter Hines Page could sound a bit like New South apostle Henry Grady. Yet he showed nothing but disdain for the New South's uncritical celebration of the Old South and the Lost Cause, and he urged his fellow Southerners to think more about building schools than erecting monuments to the Confederate dead. A staunch proponent of economic progress, Page nonetheless expressed his doubts about what the New South had actually achieved. Insisting that his native state needed nothing quite so badly as a "few first class funerals," Page sounded remarkably like H. L. Mencken and his South-baiting minions three decades later when he described North Carolina as "the laughing stock among the states" and declared: "There is not a man whose residence is in the state who is recognized by the world as an authority on anything." Describing Page as "a more effective critic of Southern sloth, poverty, and intellectual and cultural sterility than any Southerners of his generation," Fred Hobson explained that when Page "looked at Dixie, what he saw was a problem South, the same South that Howard W. Odum and the social scientists would see and seek to remake thirty or forty years later."

Like most of his white contemporaries, Page saw the "Negro Problem" as essentially unsolvable and more of a problem for whites than for blacks. This was clearly not the case, however, with Charles Chesnutt, who, as Wayne Mixon pointed out, criticized the New South movement "from the perspective of the man most neglected by it, the Negro." Though he lived most of his adult life in Chicago, Chesnutt wrote as a Southerner, and his concerns about the direction in which the New South was headed transcended racial lines. In fact, in his final novel, *The Colonel's Dream*, Chesnutt devoted considerable attention to the plight of the New South's overworked and exploited poor whites. In detailing the frustrated efforts of Colonel French, a chivalrous ex-Confederate, who sought to blend the best of Old South ideals with the economic benefits of New South progress, Chesnutt exposed the conditions confronting many white workers in the New South. When Colonel French asks citizens about conditions in the local mill, a liveryman fairly explodes: "Talk about nigger slavery – the niggers never were worked like white women and children are in them mills."

One of the few of Chesnutt's white contemporaries who challenged the New South's racial arrangements, George Washington Cable, attempted to call forth a "Silent South" of humane, fair-minded whites who would challenge the region's racial code and restore the civil rights of black Southerners. He offered some poetic mockery of Henry Grady's famous New South speech, which had essentially ignored the region's racial problems. Cable was quick to praise the eloquence of "Grady" but equally quick to point out that "on MEN'S EQUAL RIGHTS, The darkest of nights, Compared with him wouldn't seem shady."

Cable's call for racial justice came within the context of his overall critique of the New South movement, and reform-minded Southerners of the mid-twentieth century would echo his call for the South to rejoin the nation and the world at large: "When we have done so we shall know it by this...there will be no South...We shall no more be Southerners than we shall be Northerners." Instead of the "New South," he insisted, "What we ought to have in mind is the No South."

It was hardly surprising that Cable, Page, and several other New South critics eventually took up life in exile outside the region. As transparent and contrived as it may seem in retrospect, the New South Creed was one potent piece of mythology. It painted an almost seamless and undeniably seductive mural in which a glorious past, a reassuring present, and a glittering future were fully integrated and virtually indistinguishable. The Old South legend was the emotional and psychological cornerstone of the New South ideal, but where the antebellum Cavalier had been done in by forces beyond his control or even his comprehension, his New South descendants were firmly in command of their own destinies. As champions of past, present, and future, the New South crusaders were in an all but impregnable position, while those who challenged them were quickly demonized, not just as critics of the status quo, but bipolar subversives bent on undermining both progress and tradition.

Because the New South identity depended on a rigid scripting of both the region's distant and recent past, its orthodoxy weighed so heavily on those who wrote Southern history that, as William E. Dodd pointed out in 1904, "Many subjects" of interest to historians might "not with safety be even discussed." Certainly, "to suggest that the revolt from the Union in 1860 was not justified, was not led by the most lofty minded of statesmen," was "to invite not only criticism but an enforced resignation."

The romance of the Lost Cause was not the only impediment to objectivity confronting Southern historians. There was also the uncritical insistence of the New South Creed on the region's miraculous self-resurrection, omnibeneficent economic progress, and racial and class harmony. As Gaston summarized it, the "central theme" of the writings of early twentieth-century New South historians such as Philip Alexander Bruce and Holland Thompson was "the concept of triumph over adversity, of steel will and impeccable character overcoming staggering problems, often against what seemed impossible odds."

In the hands of many writers, the history of the New South was every bit as romantic as that of the Old. Broadus Mitchell's *The Rise of the Cotton Mills in the South* even promised readers "not only an industrial chronicle, but a romance, a drama as well." As Daniel J. Singal explained, Mitchell's portrayal of the early mill builders as the philanthropic descendants of the antebellum cavaliers demonstrated "the extraordinary power that could be wielded by the New South ideology over one of the most intelligent, learned, and compassionate Southerners of his era."

Trinity College historian John Spencer Bassett had insisted in 1897 that any historian in the South who had ever "departed from traditional views... has been denounced as a traitor and a mercenary defiler of his birthplace." Proceeding to prove his own point, after showing the temerity to challenge the New South's racial and political institutions, Bassett found it prudent to head north to Smith College in 1906. As he departed, he explained "it was the conviction that I could not write history and direct public sentiment too that made me come North" and predicted that it would be "another generation" before the South "will be ready for the scholar or the serious writer of books."

Bassett's forecast proved remarkably accurate, although a bit too optimistic where professional historians were concerned. Singal pointed to the influence of the New South Creed as the principal obstacle to the arrival of intellectual modernism in the region, and in fact, a move to unravel the tangle of myth and inconsistency that lay at the heart of the New South identity did not coalesce until the post-World War I intellectual awakening of the Southern Renaissance.

Tensions between the New South's myths and its realities seemed to reach the snapping point as events such as the Leo Frank lynching, the resurgence of the Ku Klux Klan, the wave of postwar racial violence, and the Scopes trial drew unprecedented attention to the South's problems and deficiencies and raised a multitude of questions about the New South Creed's vision of progress in the region. Published in 1924, Frank Tannenbaum's *The Darker Phases of the South* only reaffirmed growing perceptions of Southern benightedness. In the same year, expatriated former Alabama Populist William H. Skaggs stepped forward in *The Southern Oligarchy* to focus the attention of Americans at large on the plight of "the great mass of white and colored citizens of the Southern States, who are held in political subjection and economic serfdom." Meanwhile, Oswald Garrison Villard repeatedly deplored the barbarity of lynching in the pages of *The Nation*, while W. E. B. Du Bois assailed Southern racial customs in the NAACP's *The Crisis*. H. L. Mencken's mockery of a New South that "for all the progress it babbles of" was "almost as sterile, artistically, intellectually, culturally, as the Sahara Desert" won him a corps of slavish imitators among young journalists in Dixie, including Gerald W. Johnson, Nell Battle Lewis, and Wilbur J. Cash.

Within a few years of Mencken's anointment of the South as the "Sahara of the Bozart," however, observers were referring to a "renaissance" in Southern thought and letters. The most notable explanation for the timing of this flurry of intellectual activity came from Allen Tate, who declared in 1945 that "with the war of 1914–1918, the South re-entered the world – but gave a backward glance... that backward glance gave us the Southern renascence [*sic*], a literature conscious of the past in the present." Earlier, Tate had alluded to a postwar economic transformation in the South, characterizing the Southern Renaissance as "a curious burst of intelligence that we get at the crossing of the ways, not unlike on an infinitesimal scale, the outburst of poetic genius at the end of the sixteenth century when commercial England had already begun to crush feudal England."

Tate's interpretation has been questioned by some latterday critics, but, as Reinhard Bendix has pointed out, in many modernizing societies "changes in the social and political order were apparent before the full consequences of the industrial revolution were understood." Certainly, there is no disputing Richard King's contention that many of the key participants in the Renaissance shared "a pervasive, subjective sense that *something* fundamental had changed in and about the South." Thomas Wolfe would eventually set his classic novel *Look Homeward, Angel* against the backdrop of Asheville's rapid growth, which brought prosperity to Wolfe's hard-charging, fast-trading mother but left him assailing the New South definition of "Progress" as "more Ford automobiles [and] more Rotary Clubs." Wolfe admonished his mother that "we are not necessarily four times as civilized as our grandfathers because we go four times as fast in our automobiles," or "because our buildings are four times as tall." Elsewhere, although Alabama remained overwhelmingly rural and agricultural in 1930, Clarence Cason expressed concern "with the changes which the inevitable industrial development is making on the social and economic landscape of Alabama." Finally, writing in 1933 from a once sleepy Oxford, Mississippi, William Faulkner bemoaned the passing of the traditional, communal South that he pronounced "old since dead" at the hands of "a thing known whimsically as the New South." This, he was quite certain, was "not the South" but "a land of immigrants" intent on rebuilding Dixie in the image of "the towns and cities in Kansas and Iowa and Illinois."

Wolfe, Cason, Faulkner, and a great many other Southern writers of the post-World War I era seemed much like their counterparts who lived in modernizing societies in the nineteenth century and, according to Robert A. Nisbet, "exhibit the same burning sense of society's sudden convulsive turn from a path it had followed for millennia." Steeped in the New South's mythology of a glorious past, but confronted everywhere with overwhelming contemporary evidence of their region's backwardness, Southern intellectuals of the Renaissance era did in fact have much in common with their counterparts in other "developing" societies. Certainly, in the 1920s the South appeared to reach a point where as Dewey Grantham put it, "the earlier equilibrium between the forces of modernization and those of cultural tradition could no longer be sustained."

A case in point was the Scopes trial, described by Fred Hobson as "the event that most forcefully dramatized the struggle between Southern provincialism and the modern, secular world . . . the event that caused Southerners to face squarely the matter of the South and their own place in it." Prior to the spectacle at Dayton, John Crowe Ransom, Donald Davidson, and Allen Tate had shown no particular inclination to challenge either the New South ideal of progress or the steady stream of criticism leveled by Mencken and his disciples. Shocked by the abuse heaped on their region in the wake of the Scopes fiasco, however, the Nashville "Agrarians" began to sense that their real enemies were not the South's literary romanticizers but its would-be economic and cultural modernizers. In 1927 Tate announced to Davidson that he would no longer attack the South in any fashion "except in so far as it may be necessary to point out that the chief defect the Old South had was that it produced, through whatever cause, the New South." An enthusiastic Davidson replied, "You know that I'm with you on the anti-New South stuff...I feel so strongly on these points that I can hardly trust myself to write." In 1930 Ransom, Davidson, and Tate joined forces to pull together a volume of essays published as *I'll Take My Stand: The South and the Agrarian Tradition*. Identifying themselves collectively as "Twelve Southerners," the authors produced essays that varied widely in subject matter, emphasis, and quality, but generally featured consistently vague tributes to the virtues of "agrarian" life and consistently severe condemnations of "industrialism."

In reality, however, the contributors to *I'll Take My Stand* were less intent on defining agrarianism or even deriding industrialism than rallying their fellow white Southerners to rise in revolt against what they saw as the ongoing New South effort to northernize their society. As New South advocates sought to beat the North at its own game by emulating and even surpassing the North's economic achievement, the Agrarians insisted that the South's way of life was already superior to that of the North, and, therefore, the effort to northernize the South's economy was more likely to pull the region down than to lift it up.

In essence, the Agrarians sought in their erudite but diffuse treatises to discredit the dynamic, appealing, economically and politically pragmatic New South doctrine by emphasizing the threat that it posed to Southern cultural autonomy. Twenty years after the appearance of *I'll Take My Stand*, Agrarian Frank L. Owsley explained "much of the bitter resentment of backward peoples in the Orient against, what they term 'Yankee imperialism' is similar to that felt by the contributors to *I'll Take My Stand* in 1930." Expanding on Owsley's comment some thirty years later, John Shelton Reed insisted: "If we ask what else the Agrarians had in common with those backward but anticolonial peoples in the Orient, if we examine *I'll Take My Stand* in the light of nationalist manifestos from around the world, the similarities are obvious."

Reed explained that "when nationalists come from a nation that is economically 'peripheral' in the world economy, one like the South of the 1920s that produced raw materials and supplied unskilled labor for a more 'advanced' economy, they often adopt the same stance the Agrarians did, rejecting the Western science and technology that, in any case, they do not have, and insisting that their very backwardness in 'Western' terms has preserved a spiritual and cultural superiority." Reed's analysis suggested the words of Mohandas Gandhi, who, as he lamented the incursions of Western culture and technology into India, insisted "we consider our civilization to be far superior to yours."

Ironically, the effort by the "Twelve Southerners" to invent an anti-New South agrarian tradition was, at least in part, a by-product of the very modernization effort they sought to discredit. Citing the Westernizers and Slavophils of Tsarist Russia as examples, Bendix described the schism that is likely to occur "between those who would see their country progress by imitating the more advanced countries and those who denounce that advance as alien and evil and emphasize instead the wellsprings of strength existing among their own people and in their native culture." Educated and well traveled (as the Agrarians obviously were), these latter intellectuals may actually

feel somewhat alienated from the masses of their contemporaries, but as the beneficiaries of modernization, they also possess "the ideological vocabulary to interpret
their alienation and to defend their culture" and, ironically enough, as Reed notes,
"modernization itself is what they protest."

As Southern cultural supremacists, the Agrarians had no patience with Southerners
who seemed to occupy themselves with documenting and publicizing the South's
defects and working tirelessly to help the region "catch up" with the rest of the
nation. Thus one of their principal targets (within the South, at least) was University
of North Carolina sociologist Howard W. Odum, who led his "regionalist" disciples
in unloosing an avalanche of statistics and social research data pointing to the need to
modernize the South's economy and institutions through a scientific, planned effort to
promote both industrial development and agricultural revitalization. Odum's insistence on a realistic, candid appraisal of Southern problems led him to reject the
Agrarians' treatises as fanciful and vague, but it likewise set him squarely at odds
with "the gross spirit of materialism" and the self-serving optimism that characterized
the New South Creed. Established in 1922, Odum's *Journal of Social Forces* became the
principal outlet for discussions of the South's deficiencies and failures and the inad-
equacies of Southern leadership and institutions. Odum boldly proclaimed that the
South needed "criticism and severe criticism," and H. L. Mencken, who had certainly
done his share of criticizing, cited Odum as the key figure in getting the Southern
Renaissance "in motion."

As historian Mary Matossian has pointed out, intellectuals in non-Western societies
facing the challenge of "Westernization" often adopt a position that is "ambiguous,
embracing the polar extremes of Xenophobia and Xenophilia." Like a host of other
key figures in the Southern Renaissance, Odum struggled on a personal level with the
intense emotional divisions and anxieties that could also be wrought by the prospect
of wholesale changes in an intellectual's society and culture. Bendix observed that as
intellectuals search for a means of overcoming their country's backwardness, "a typical
part of this search consists in the ambivalent job of preserving or strengthening the
indigenous character of the native culture while attempting to close the gap created
by the advanced development of the 'reference society or societies.'" Bendix's observation could hardly have described Howard Odum better.

While Mencken saw the Scopes trial as nothing short of a laugh riot, at Dayton
Odum saw "more pathos than joke, more futility than fighting, more tragedy than
comedy." Odum's ambivalence toward his own region permeated his *American Epoch*,
which appeared a month before *I'll Take My Stand*. He explained, somewhat oxymor-
onically, that his approach in *American Epoch* represented a "new romantic realism,"
and he described the book itself as a "critical analysis based upon sympathetic
understanding of facts." In successive chapters, "The Glory That Was the South"
and "The Grandeur That Was Not," Odum offered a contrasting and thoroughly
confusing portrait of erudite, genteel, and benevolent planters and loyal slaves on the
one hand and the "extreme snobbishness" of an "imitation-aristocracy," as well as
violence, and racial and social injustice on the other.

As Wayne D. Brazil explained, although Odum "intended his exploration of the region's past to help explain its current condition," he failed generally to "define the specific lines of influence" or evaluate the relative importance of key historical factors. Still, as a partly fictionalized history of Odum's own family over four generations (the two principal characters, "the old Major" and "Uncle John," were Odum's own grandfathers), *American Epoch* also amounted to a social, economic, political, and cultural history of the nineteenth-century South. Despite its ambivalence and imprecision, Odum's book anticipated the efforts of later writers who proved more effective in exploring the ties between the South's past and present. In fact, Odum's approach in *American Epoch* suggested the direction of some of the best writing of the Southern Renaissance, including that of Odum protégés C. Vann Woodward and W. J. Cash, as well as that of William Faulkner, whom Odum admired for daring to ask whether the South might well have both a "barbaric past" and "a flawed and cherished past."

Unlike Odum, many of the critical commentators on the South in the 1920s seemed too astonished by the ongoing panorama of ignorance and depravity that it presented to reflect seriously on the historical context from which this sorry state of affairs had evolved. With the onset of the Great Depression, however, so many thoughtful Southerners began to seek out the historical origins of the contemporary South's distress that, as Donald Davidson observed in 1937, "The historian's question – What the South was? – and the related question – What the South is? – underlie every important literary work or social investigation of the past fifteen years." Owing to the stifling influence of the New South Creed on any impulse toward historical objectivity or candor, however, as the 1930s began the Southerners least likely to be asking what Davidson called "the historian's question" were the region's historians themselves. This meant that as the 1930s unfolded, many Southern intellectuals were simply practicing history without a license, including not only Davidson's Agrarian colleagues in Nashville, but also their Regionalist adversaries Howard Odum and Rupert Vance in Chapel Hill.

Although he, like Odum, was trained as a sociologist, Vance's contributions to the study of Southern history were particularly significant. Heavily influenced by historian U. B. Phillips's treatments of the antebellum South, Vance shared Phillips's respect for the influence of the frontier on Southern history, but he broke with Phillips on the interaction between plantation and frontier. Where Phillips saw the planters' gentility imposing a countervailing influence against the rugged individualism and rough-and-tumble folk culture spawned by the frontier, Vance saw the plantation reinforcing, perpetuating, and passing on the problematic legacy of the frontier. "While they were formative," Vance insisted, "the folkways of the South got the stamp of the frontier. From the frontier, part of the area passed to the plantation, but the plantation area retained many of the frontier traits." As Singal observed, "Almost everywhere he turned in surveying the modern South, Vance discovered that the basic patterns of the frontier still prevailed. The region continued to make its living by exploiting its natural resources heedlessly, applying little capital, skill or technology, with dramatically low levels of income and living standards the result."

While Phillips had stressed the importance of environmental influences in shaping the Southern (white) character, Vance insisted "History, not geography, made the solid South." Like Odum's, Vance's work was cited and quoted again and again by Southern historians. He frequently reviewed books for the *Journal of Southern History*, and the editors of the Louisiana State University Press's History of the South series had even invited him to write the volume in that series that was to follow C. Vann Woodward's *Origins of the New South, 1877–1913*. Vance eventually abandoned that project, but he nonetheless exerted a profound influence on Woodward, encouraging and challenging him as a graduate student at Chapel Hill and continuing to read and critique his work well into the 1950s.

One of the first professional historians to attack the historical foundations of the New South identity, Woodward joined Vance and the other Southern intellectuals of the 1930s who were intent on making the past more accountable to the present. When he arrived at the University of North Carolina in 1934, Woodward expected to be caught up in the same "surge of innovation and creativity" that was sweeping the Southern literary scene, but the zealous young graduate student was sorely disappointed as he surveyed his own chosen field, where he found "no renaissance . . . no rebirth of energy, no compelling new vision." Far from "making waves," the masters of Southern history were "united not so much in their view of the past as in their dedication to the present order, the system founded on the ruins of Reconstruction called the New South."

Already inclined to liberal activism, the young historian plunged into a career that, over the next two decades, would help to revolutionize the study of Southern history. Woodward's first step in this direction came in *Tom Watson: Agrarian Rebel*, a biography of the charismatic Georgia Populist who seemed to degenerate into a malicious racial and religious bigot of the worst sort in the wake of the Populists' demise. As Woodward explained, "Not only was it a fascinating story in itself, but it plunged the historian into all the dark, neglected, and forbidden corners of Southern life shunned by the New South school." Because Populism had been an "embarrassment" to New South doctrines and contradicted historians' "pet themes of white unity and black satisfaction, it was generally shunted aside, minimized, or silently passed over." The Populists had dared to challenge not only the hallowed Redeemers who had overthrown Reconstruction, but also Henry Grady and other New South icons, as well as "the New South double-think of worshipping the symbols and myths of the Lost Cause and simultaneously serving the masters of the new plutocracy."

Woodward sharpened his attack on both the Redeemers and the New South version of Southern history in his *Origins of the New South*, a book that he actually began at the end of the 1930s but with the interruptions brought on by World War II did not complete until 1951. In *Origins* Woodward took a more straightforward approach, celebrating "a sort of historical black mass in the eyes of the believers," by disputing the Redeemers' ties to the old planter regime, thus undermining their claims – and those of their New South descendants as well – to ancestral legitimacy through their roots in the old mythical cavalier order. Having challenged their pedigrees, Woodward proceeded to impugn their character as well, exposing their thievery and corruption and their willingness to serve up the South's people and its natural resources to the highest bidders among a group of greedy, exploitive Yankee capitalists.

A few years later, as the Supreme Court mulled over the Brown decision, Woodward set out in his *Strange Career of Jim Crow* to show that contrary to New South mythology, segregation (in his words) "did not appear with the end of slavery but toward the end of the century and later" after a period "of experiment and variety" in race relations "in which segregation was not the invariable rule." By attempting to expose segregation and disfranchisement as two of the New South's invented trad-itions, Woodward sought, as King explained, "to demythologize the existing social and legal institutions that regulated race relations."

In his career retrospective that appeared in 1986, Woodward recalled that "the intellectual present in which I came of age was the peak and crest of the Southern Literary Renaissance. No Southern youth of any sensitivity could help being excited by the explosion of creativity taking place during the early 1930s – in fiction, in poetry and drama." The writers to whom Woodward referred were indeed turning out impressive works of fiction, but as they too struggled to sort out the myths and inconsistencies of the New South doctrine, the major literary figures of the Southern Renaissance also had little choice but to grapple with what Louis Rubin called "the impossible load of the past." Coming to maturity in an age of such rapid change where old and new collided so frequently and often so violently, they acquired an almost unique "two way vision," that, as Rubin explained, "translated what they saw in terms of what *had been* as well as what was now."

A major figure in the Southern Renaissance in her own right, Ellen Glasgow cited this move to the middle ground between sentiment and skepticism as the key to the emergence of a new breed of Southern writer. What distinguished the new generation of writers from their predecessors, Glasgow believed, was "a detached and steadfast point of view." For Glasgow, however, detachment from the myth of the Old South was no more crucial than detachment from that of the New. She had begun to exhibit this detachment herself well in advance of some of her Renaissance era contemporar-ies. In the first decades of the twentieth century, Glasgow, whose father had been the manager of Richmond's Tredegar Iron Works, began in her novels to criticize both the intellectual stagnation bred by the Old South and the rampant materialism unloosed by the New South crusade. Much of her writing seemed to anticipate the extent to which the key figures of the Southern Renaissance would be forced to confront simultaneously both the Old South legend and the New South reality.

Glasgow's 1913 novel, *Virginia*, was set in the Virginia of the 1880s, where "the smoke of factories was already succeeding the smoke of the battlefields and from the ashes of a vanquished idealism the spirit of commercial materialism was born." This New South materialist ethos was personified by tobacco manufacturer and railroad builder Cyrus Treadwell, who was "at once the destroyer and the builder – the inexorable foe of the old feudal order and the beneficent source of the new industrialism." Meanwhile, the Old South found its embodiment in Miss Priscilla Batte, headmistress of a female academy and the daughter of a fallen Confederate general who stood firmly rooted in "all that was static, in all that was obsolete and outgrown, in the Virginia of the eighties." The ultimate provincial, Priscilla is also the ultimate New South booster. Actually, much as W. J. Cash would later suggest, Priscilla and Cyrus – Old South and New—shared a common suspicion of art and ideas and ignored the racial and other problems their society faced, choosing instead to worship "the illusion of success."

In 1928 Glasgow warned that the New South's crusade for modernization threatened to reduce Southern life to "a comfortable level of mediocrity" and had therefore driven into revolt "an impressive group of Southern writers" who had broken away "from a petrified past overgrown by a funereal tradition" but had also recoiled from "the uniform concrete surface of an industrialized South." Glasgow's description clearly foreshadowed the work of both William Faulkner and Thomas Wolfe. In *Sartoris* Faulkner drew heavily on both personal feelings and family experiences, presenting the ineffectual struggle of a venerable Southern family confronted with the unfamiliar realities of life in a rapidly changing post-World War I South. He went on to explore in grimmer and more complex detail the decline of a family, society, and a tradition in *The Sound and the Fury*. In Faulkner's story, the once patrician Compsons have reached the point of seemingly irreversible degeneration and decay and the entire clan is dwarfed in courage, wisdom, and integrity by their black servant Dilsey. The promiscuous daughter Caddy is the ultimate lost soul, and the obsessive son Quentin outdoes even the self-destructive Bayard Sartoris on his way to his suicidal demise. Ultimately, the only sane surviving Compson is the cold-blooded, mercenary Jason. Insisting, "I haven't got much pride, I can't afford it," Jason embodies the most sinister aspects of the materialistic and soulless New South and bears no small resemblance to the Snopeses, whose sinister ascent Faulkner would soon begin to trace.

A few years later in *Absalom! Absalom!* Faulkner explored the antebellum adolescence of the South's aristocratic tradition and in the process exposed the fundamental weaknesses that would make this tradition so susceptible to postbellum decay. This is the chilling story of the rise and fall of the relentless single-minded parvenu Thomas Sutpen, who, as Irving Howe saw him, "is a latecomer, an interloper who, in order to compress into his lifetime the social rise which in other families had taken generations, must act with an impersonal ruthlessness . . . which the Sartorises have learned to disguise or modulate."

If he was ambivalent about the underpinnings and the unexplored inner reality of the South's aristocratic tradition, Faulkner was repulsed outright by what he saw replacing it. In *The Hamlet* he began to trace the rise of the odious Flem Snopes and his soon-to-be ubiquitous clan. "It is the historical perspective that renders this the more tragic," wrote Louis Rubin, who underscored the essential contradiction confronting Faulkner and his literary contemporaries when he pointed out: "The South has not always been this way; it has become this way. The image of the heroic past renders the distraught present so distasteful, just as it is this very same heroic past that has caused the present."

The paradox of social and cultural decline intertwined with economic and material advancement was also a dominant concern for Thomas Wolfe, whose autobiographical 1929 novel, *Look Homeward, Angel*, anticipated Faulkner's focus on the paradox of family and community decline in the midst of New South progress. Actually, Wolfe's characters seemed more contemptuous of the South's sordid and materialistic present than of its mythically glorious past. In *Look Homeward, Angel* Eugene Gant dismissed the South as a "barren spiritual wilderness" dominated by a "cheap mythology," while in *The Web and the Rock* George Webber identified "the curse of South Carolina and its Southernness – of always pretending you used to be even though you are not now."

When Ellen Glasgow updated her list of Southern literary rebels in 1943, it included not only Wolfe and Faulkner but also, surprisingly to some, Margaret Mitchell. Despite its dismissive treatment at the hands of historians and literary critics alike, Mitchell's *Gone With the Wind* did raise a challenge to the aristocratic Old South myth, principally in the person of upwardly mobile but untutored and often uncouth master of Tara, Gerald O'Hara. Likewise, Mitchell's literary portrayal of a war-hardened Scarlett O'Hara's metamorphosis from flighty Old South coquette to ruthless New South lumber baroness offered readers a healthy dose of the same greed, materialism, brutality, and forsaken tradition that would eventually pervade Woodward's *Origins of the New South*. Willie Lee Rose noted *Gone With the Wind*'s unflinching economic realism and observed, as Mitchell herself acknowledged, that Scarlett's "sheer greed" and "shabby business dealings" were "meant as a personal characterization of the city of Atlanta itself, and by extension, the New South." For Mitchell, the story of the New South lay not so much in Atlanta's rising from the ashes, as in Scarlett's rising from the garden at Tara and heading off to Atlanta to make good on her vow never to be hungry again.

If Mitchell's subtle challenge to the New South Creed was largely lost in the rush to romanticize her novel into a blockbuster movie, there was no mistaking the message of W. J. Cash's 1941 classic, *The Mind of the South*. Cash began by emphasizing the South's "peculiar history" as the source of the "fairly definite mental pattern" that characterized white Southerners in general. He suggested at the outset that in order to understand how its history had transformed the South into almost "a nation within a nation" it was necessary to disabuse oneself of "two correlated legends – those of the Old and the New Souths."

Accordingly, Cash went to great lengths to ridicule the Old South myth of aristocracy and grandeur as a "sort of stage piece out of the eighteenth century." Rather than descendants of "the old gentlefolk who for many generations had made up the ruling classes of Europe," Cash insisted, the Old South's planters were little more than "superior farmers" scarcely distinguishable from – and actually, in many cases, risen from – the frontiersmen who inhabited "the vast backcountry of the seaboard states."

To support this contention, Cash afforded "a concrete case," the story of "the stout young Irishman," a character based loosely on Cash's great grandfather and one who was also strikingly similar not only to Odum's "the Major" but to Margaret Mitchell's Gerald O'Hara. Cash's Irishman had arrived with his bride in the Carolina upcountry in 1800, and used his life savings of $20 to buy 40 acres of land, toiling round the clock with his wife's help to clear and plant cotton on it. At his death in 1854, the Irishman's estate included 2,000 acres of land, more than a hundred slaves and four cotton gins and, of course, the fledgling county-seat newspaper eulogized the former backwoods yeoman as "a gentleman of the old school" and "a noble specimen of the chivalry at its best."

If the Irishman's ascent seemed miraculously rapid, Cash insisted that in areas like Mississippi "because of the almost unparalleled productivity of the soil" the same thing happened "in accelerated tempo." Such an observation underscored the similarities between Cash's Irishman and Faulkner's Thomas Sutpen, although the latter met with a considerably less glorious fate.

Scoffing at the notion of antebellum Southern cultural superiority, Cash sounded much like Walter Hines Page when he asked of the Old South: "What ideas did it generate? Who were its philosophers and artists?" Cash attributed this Old South's barrenness to a host of factors, including the generally modest social origins of white Southerners at large, as well as a simple, uncomplex, unvarying human and natural environment replete with "wide fields and blue woods and flooding yellow sunlight...a world in which horses, guns, not books and ideas and art were his [the planter's] normal and absorbing interests." Here Cash seemed to echo Ellen Glasgow, who had insisted more than a decade earlier that because its "Soil, scenery, all the color and animation of the external world, tempted a convivial race to an endless festival of the seasons"; in the Old South "philosophy, like heresy, was either suspected or prohibited."

Not only did Cash's book thoroughly debunk the myth of an aristocratic and cultured Old South, it also challenged soothing New South myths of hospitality and charm with the shocking realities of emotional schizophrenia and appalling violence. His dismissive treatment of the Populists notwithstanding, unlike New South apologists who insisted on the fundamental unity of spirit and purpose among white Southerners, Cash understood that Southern white society seemed unified only because the Southern color line was so rigid and inviolable. As he explained it, a "Proto-Dorian convention" assured common whites that, whatever their circumstances might otherwise lack, their skin color guaranteed them that they would never be at the bottom of the social pyramid so long as they remained supportive of their more prosperous but pragmatically folksy and cunningly manipulative white superiors.

If Cash blamed Radical Reconstruction for turning the white South into a quasi-nation and engendering the intolerance, conformity, and often violent resistance to change that formed the basis of the "savage ideal," he likewise argued (as did C. Vann Woodward a decade later) that for all their supposed benevolence and foresight, the Redeemers and their New South descendants had done little to make things better.

In the final analysis, *The Mind of the South* was a book with the potential to offend practically everyone. Not only did the downtrodden but ambitious New South not have the grand aristocratic past that was always invoked when the region's critics or its self-evident ills became too unpleasant to bear or contemplate, but if the past looked far less rosy than many white Southerners wanted desperately to believe, the myths of the present-day progress and future prosperity were largely hollow and false as well. As Singal noted, Cash's book "represented a complete reversal of the region's history once offered by the New South writers – it read like a compendium of those aspects of the South they had deliberately screened out."

Despite its potential to offend, however, the response to *The Mind of the South* in the Southern press was overwhelmingly positive. The favorable reception accorded Cash's book seems less remarkable in light of the fact that much of what he said about the South had actually been said before, and, in many cases, more than once by a number of Southern writers stretching from Page and Cable through Glasgow, Odum, Wolfe, and Faulkner, to name but a few. It was not only the keenness of Cash's own insights or the boldness with which he presented them, but also his skill in synthesizing and summarizing the views of other thoughtful Southern whites of his and previous generations that established *The Mind of the South* as the "quintessential expression" of the spirit of the Southern Renaissance and the culmination of a revolt against a New South identity that had held sway in the region for half a century.

By exposing the roots of an imperfect present in an imperfect past, the key figures of the Southern Renaissance played a major role in toppling one New South identity and clearing the way for the emergence of another. Many observers agree, in general terms, however, that the Southern Renaissance had largely run its course within a decade after *The Mind of the South* appeared. The New South Creed's inaccuracies and distortions had been laid bare by the Great Depression, and they seemed all the more egregious in the context of World War II, which focused particularly critical attention on the region's undemocratic and repressive racial practices. The 1940s also saw a number of black writers make major contributions to exposing the ugly realities of Jim Crow's New South. Ralph Ellison produced several noteworthy short stories suffused with the irony of black soldiers ostensibly fighting for democracy but unsure whether their worst enemies were abroad or at home. The most influential contribution to this literature of protest came from Richard Wright, whose *Black Boy* received a five-page, illustrated spread in *Life Magazine* which described it in June 1945 as "not only a brilliant autobiography but a powerful indictment of a caste system that is one of America's biggest problems." American aspirations to free world leadership at the onset of the Cold War only made the Southern racial situation seem even more intolerable, and as the long-awaited assault on the Jim Crow system finally began, it was fair to say that by the middle of the twentieth century Grady's South of progress and harmony had largely dissolved into Cash's South of backwardness and conflict.

Instead of disappearing, however, the term "New South" quickly resurfaced, albeit in much transfigured form, as the cliché of choice among would-be reformers pursuing an agenda of dramatic change, especially along racial lines. As Cash's South supplanted Grady's, the "Southern way of life" became, to defenders and detractors alike, largely synonymous with white supremacy and segregation. (Walker Percy actually came to dread the phrase because he knew that "in New Orleans, which has a delightful way of life, the 'Southern Way of Life'" usually means "let's keep McDonough No. 6 segregated.") Consequently, the Renaissance era's sensitive, tentative probings of the relationship between past and present and its almost palpable anxiety about the changes that seemed to lie just ahead quickly gave way to the moral absolutism and scorched earth rhetoric of what Fred Hobson called the Southern school of "shame and guilt." Personified by Lillian Smith, who proved both unyielding in her opposition to segregation and contemptuous not only of its defenders but also of those who urged moderation in the fight against it, the writers of the shame and guilt school saw little worth saving in "a way of life so wounding, so hideous in its effect upon the spirit of both black and white."

The post-Renaissance "shame and guilt" writers were not entirely free of ambivalence about the wholesale transformation they advocated, but former Mississippi congressman Frank E. Smith spoke for many of his colleagues when, all but echoing George Washington Cable, he insisted in 1965 that "what is needed is not a New South but a South that is inextricably and indefinably a part of the United States." The loss of "Southern identity," Smith believed, was a relatively minor price "to be paid for removal of the racial scar which has been the mark of things Southern, both the South and the country will have gained thereby."

As the twenty-first century begins, many would argue that Smith's wish has finally come true, although in a manner almost precisely opposite from what he and Cable had envisioned. As the civil rights movement spilled over the Mason Dixon line, the racial animosities that had long simmered just below the surface elsewhere in the nation finally began to boil over. The Republican Party's "Southern strategy" had sought initially to woo Southern whites disenchanted with the Democratic Party's vigorous support of civil rights, but it also proved effective in winning the allegiance of formerly Democratic working-class whites in other areas as well. As early as 1974 John Egerton was writing of the rightward shift he called the "Southernization of America," and by 1996 Peter Applebome saw Southern white conservatism shaping the "values, politics and culture" of the entire nation. Whether the American mainstream has captured the South or vice versa, the region's differences with the remainder of the United States now seem minimal at best to a number of observers.

Although its defenders once insisted that *de jure* racial segregation was the fundamental element of "the Southern Way of Life," in the wake of the civil rights movement many Southern whites have refused to concede that the New South is now the "No South." Instead, they have mounted an almost frantic effort to reassemble a new but still distinctive post-Jim Crow identity for themselves and their region, embracing a slickly marketed version of their regional identity as presented in upscale magazines such as *Southern Living* or devouring the books and tapes of good-ol'-boy humorists like Lewis Grizzard and Jeff Foxworthy.

Ironically, while many Southern whites immersed themselves in a cleverly caricatured and commodified version of their cultural identity, a number of African
Americans simply and matter-of-factly stepped forward to claim the South as their
homeland and to acknowledge and even celebrate their Southern roots. Reversing a
longstanding demographic pattern, they also responded to the region's racial and
economic progress by returning to the South in large numbers. In dozens of memoirs
and reminiscences black Southerners have affirmed Thadious M. Davis's contention
that they were embracing "a region and a culture that, though fraught with pain and
difficulty, provides a major grounding for identity." At the same time, determined to
have their say about the way their regional identity is represented, Southern blacks
have enjoyed considerable success in attacking the state-sanctioned display of the
Confederate flag and moved to establish monuments and memorials to their own
crusade to overturn the racial system that they feel this flag represents.

The civil rights revolution and the subsequent "Sunbelt" economic boom also
brought major changes in the South's literature. Many white novelists followed the
lead of Walker Percy by spurning identification as "Southern" writers and shunning
specifically regional themes and settings in favor of more generic universalist treatments of contemporary life. On the other hand, black writers like Alice Walker,
Ernest J. Gaines, and Dori Sanders actually emphasized the Southernness of
the characters and contexts they created. In fact, as Fred Hobson observed in 1991,
in their focus on place, family, and community, and especially the past, African-
American writers have become "the truest contemporary heirs to the Southern literary
tradition."

Anthropologist Anthony P. Cohen has suggested that cultures whose distinctions
seem to be fading tend to "write large" the traits and symbols that "express contrast
and distinction" with other cultures. Certainly, resistance by both black and white
Southerners to what Egerton called "the Americanization of Dixie" is far from unique.
It simply parallels the efforts of other societies around the world to preserve their
identities in the face of a rapidly evolving global econoculture in which the significance of regional or even national distinctions seems to be diminishing by the day. As
Richard King observed, "Left-wing French intellectuals bellyaching about the American cultural invasion sound like nothing so much as conservative Agrarians taking
their stand."

Regardless of the setting, be it France, Italy, Ireland, the Balkans, or the American
South, conflicts over national or regional identity affirm Eric Hobsbawm's observation that history is the essential "raw material" from which all group identities are
manufactured. Certainly, the original New South identity rested on a carefully crafted,
meticulously sanitized and rigidly exclusionary (as to both race and class) version of
the region's past. Whether the dramatically reconfigured New South that emerged in
the wake of World War II simply fades into a bland, anonymous, and indistinguishable "No South" remains to be seen. More than anything else, its fate may well depend
on the willingness of Southerners, black and white, to look beyond symbols and
monuments and embrace a more candid and democratized construction of their

history, one that can remind them of who they are without obscuring their vision of what, together, they might still become.

REFERENCES AND FURTHER READING

Bendix, Reinhard (1967) "Tradition and Modernity Reconsidered," *Comparative Studies in Society and History*, 9: 292–346.

Cash, W. J. (1941) *The Mind of the South*. New York: Alfred A. Knopf.

Clayton, Bruce (1972) *The Savage Ideal: Intolerance and Intellectual Leadership in the South, 1890–1914*. Baltimore, MD: Johns Hopkins University Press.

Cobb, James C. (1999) *Redefining Southern Culture: Mind and Identity in the Modern South*. Atlanta: University of Georgia Press.

Egerton, John (1974) *The Americanization of Dixie: The Southernization of America*. New York: Harper's Magazine Press.

Gaston, Paul M. (1971) *The New South Creed: A Study in Southern Mythmaking*. Baton Rouge: Louisiana State University Press.

Harvard, William C. and Sullivan, Walter (eds.) (1982) *A Band of Prophets: The Vanderbilt Agrarians after Fifty Years*. Baton Rouge: Louisiana State University Press.

Hobson, Fred C. (1991) *The Southern Writer in the Postmodern World*. Athens, GA: University of Georgia Press.

Jones, Anne Goodwyn (1981) *Tomorrow is Another Day: The Woman Writer in the South, 1859–1936*. Baton Rouge: Louisiana State University Press.

King, Richard H. (1980) *A Southern Renaissance: The Cultural Awakening of the American South, 1930–1955*. New York: Oxford University Press.

Matossian, Mary (1958) "Ideologies of Delayed Industrialization: Some Tensions and Ambiguities," *Economic Development and Cultural Change*, 6: 217–28.

Mixon, Wayne (1980) *Southern Writers and the New South Movement, 1865–1913*. Chapel Hill: University of North Carolina Press.

O'Brien, Michael (1979) *The Idea of the American South*. Baltimore, MD: Johns Hopkins University Press.

Reed, John Shelton (1983) *Southerners: The Social Psychology of Sectionalism*. Chapel Hill: University of North Carolina Press.

Rubin, Louis D., Jr. (1956) "The Historical Image of Modern Southern Writing," *Journal of Southern History*, 22: 147–66.

Singal, Daniel J. (1982) *The War Within: From Vietnam to Modernist Thought in the South*. Chapel Hill: University of North Carolina Press.

Tate, Allen (1935) "The Profession of Letters in the South," *Virginia Quarterly Review*, 11 (April): 161–76.

Woodward, C. Vann (1938) *Tom Watson: Agrarian Rebel*. New York: Macmillan.

Woodward, C. Vann (1951) *Origins of the New South, 1877–1913*. Baton Rouge: Louisiana State University Press.

Index

LaVergne, TN USA
22 December 2009
167797LV00001B/10/P